# ACKNOWLEDGMENTS AND REFERENCES

Several legal instructors throughout the state of Michigan contributed to the development of this and previous editions of this manual in hopes that it will help police officers and police recruits comprehend the legal parameters that they operate within on a day-to-day basis. Their assistance is greatly appreciated, as any success this book has is a result of their insight and dedication.

The content of this edition was revised and edited by:

Steven G. Beatty, J.D.
Matt W. Bolger, J.D.
Thomas M. Deasy, J.D.
Christopher J. Hawkins, J.D.
Aimee L. Maike, J.D.
Gregory J. Zarotney, J.D.

The content editors acknowledge and thank Alexander S. Gualdoni, J.D., Sierra K. Medrano, and Robert M. Miller for their countless hours of assistance with editing and revising this edition of the manual. Their assistance was invaluable! The content editors also thank Julie Ellsworth for designing the cover. Her creativity is greatly appreciated.

This manual should be used for guidance only. Officers are encouraged to review issues with their local prosecutors for their interpretations. Many of the statutes in this book are broken down into basic elements or edited for clarity. For the complete text of any statute, officers should review the Michigan Complied Laws which can be accessed at the Michigan Legislature's website (www.michiganlegislature.org).

The Michigan State Police Legal Resource and Education webpage (www.michigan .gov/msp-legal) contains a variety of legal research tools and other materials that supplement this manual. Additionally, the Legal Resource and Education Unit publishes a legal update newsletter that describes changes to statutes and new court cases that impact the daily activities of police officers. To view current and past editions of the newsletter, or to subscribe to receive it via email, visit the Legal Resource and Education webpage.

# MICHIGAN CRIMINAL LAW & PROCEDURE

## A Manual for Michigan Police Officers

Third Edition

**Kendall Hunt**
publishing company

**Kendall Hunt**
publishing company

www.kendallhunt.com
*Send all inquiries to:*
4050 Westmark Drive
Dubuque, IA 52004-1840

# CONTENTS

## Chapter 5  Domestic Violence

## Chapter 6  Sex Offenses

## Chapter 7  Homicide and Kidnapping

## Chapter 8  Robbery

## Chapter 9  Crimes Against Persons: Selected Statutes

# Chapter 10 Destruction of Property

# Chapter 11 Burglary

# Chapter 12 Theft Crimes

# Chapter 13 Financial Crimes

# Chapter 14 Crimes Against Property: Selected Statutes

# Chapter 15 Controlled Substances

## Chapter 16  Explosives and Weapons

## Chapter 17  Impersonation and Obstruction of Justice

## Chapter 18  Public Interest Crimes: Selected Statutes

## Chapter 19  Laws of Arrest

## Chapter 20  Admissions and Confessions

## Chapter 21  Laws on Suspect Identification

## Chapter 22  Search and Seizure

## Chapter 23  Warrantless Searches

## Chapter 24  Laws of Evidence

## Chapter 25  O.W.I. Law

# Chapter 26  Juvenile Law

# Chapter 27  Laws on Use of Force

# Chapter 28  Civil Law and Liability

# CONSTITUTIONAL LAW

## DECLARATION OF INDEPENDENCE

Under English rule, the American colonists experienced great unfairness:

- There were no trials.
- Fictitious charges were brought against people.
- The army was sent to compel compliance with the King's wishes.
- The army forced its way into homes.

With these concerns in mind, the Declaration of Independence was written.

*We hold these truths to be self-evident, that all men are created equal, that they are endowed by their Creator with certain unalienable Rights, that among these are Life, Liberty and the pursuit of Happiness.—That to secure these rights, Governments are instituted among Men, deriving their just powers from the consent of the governed, That whenever any Form of Government becomes destructive of these ends, it is the Right of the People to alter or to abolish it, and to institute new Government, laying its foundation on such principles and organizing its powers in such form, as to them shall seem most likely to effect their Safety and Happiness. Prudence, indeed, will dictate that Governments long established should not be changed for light and transient causes; and accordingly all experience hath shown, that mankind are more disposed to suffer, while evils are sufferable, than to right themselves by abolishing the forms to which they are accustomed. But when*

*a long train of abuses and usurpations, pursuing invariably the same Object evinces a design to reduce them under absolute Despotism, it is their right, it is their duty, to throw off such Government, and to provide new Guards for their future security.*

## U.S. CONSTITUTION

Three main provisions:

1. Establish the framework of government to ensure proper checks and balances.
2. Delegate and assign power to the government.
3. Restrain powers of governmental agents in order to protect individual rights.

### Bill of Rights

The founding delegates would not ratify the Constitution until a bill of rights was written.

### The Preamble to the Bill of Rights

*Congress of the United States begun and held at the City of New York, on Wednesday the fourth of March, one thousand seven hundred and eighty nine. The Conventions of a number of the States, having at the time of their adopting the Constitution, expressed a desire, in order to prevent misconstruction or abuse of its powers, that further declaratory and restrictive clauses should be added: And as extending the ground of public confidence in the Government, will best ensure the beneficent ends of its institution.*

### The First Ten Amendments to the Constitution as Ratified by the States

Note: The following text is a transcription of the first ten amendments to the Constitution in their original form. These amendments were ratified December 15, 1791, and form what is known as the Bill of Rights.

*Amendment I:* Congress shall make no law respecting an establishment of religion, or prohibiting the free exercise thereof; or abridging the freedom of speech, or of the press; or the right of the people peaceably to assemble, and to petition the Government for a redress of grievances.

*Amendment II:* A well regulated Militia, being necessary to the security of a free State, the right of the people to keep and bear Arms, shall not be infringed.

*Amendment III:* No Soldier shall, in time of peace be quartered in any house, without the consent of the Owner, nor in time of war, but in a manner to be prescribed by law.

*Amendment IV:* The right of the people to be secure in their persons, houses, papers, and effects, against unreasonable searches and seizures, shall not be violated, and no Warrants shall issue, but upon probable cause, supported by Oath or affirmation, and particularly describing the place to be searched, and the persons or things to be seized.

*Amendment V:* No person shall be held to answer for a capital, or otherwise infamous crime, unless on a presentment or indictment of a Grand Jury, except in cases arising in the land or naval forces, or in the Militia, when in actual service in time of War or public danger; nor shall any person be subject for the same offence to be twice put in jeopardy of life or limb; nor shall be compelled in any criminal case to be a witness against himself, nor be deprived of life, liberty, or property, without due process of law; nor shall private property be taken for public use, without just compensation.

*Amendment VI:* In all criminal prosecutions, the accused shall enjoy the right to a speedy and public trial, by an impartial jury of the State and district wherein the crime shall have been committed, which district shall have been previously ascertained by law, and to be informed of the nature and cause of the accusation; to be confronted with the witnesses against him; to have compulsory process for obtaining witnesses in his favor, and to have the Assistance of Counsel for his defense.

*Amendment VII:* In Suits at common law, where the value in controversy shall exceed twenty dollars, the right of trial by jury shall be preserved, and no fact tried by a jury, shall be otherwise reexamined in any court of the United States, than according to the rules of the common law.

*Amendment VIII:* Excessive bail shall not be required, nor excessive fines imposed, nor cruel and unusual punishments inflicted.

*Amendment IX:* The enumeration in the Constitution, of certain rights, shall not be construed to deny or disparage others retained by the people.

*Amendment X:* The powers not delegated to the United States by the Constitution, nor prohibited by it to the States, are reserved to the States respectively, or to the people.

### The Fourteenth Amendment

The Fourteenth Amendment establishes that persons in the United States have dual citizenship. They are citizens of both the United States and their individual states. The Bill of Rights establishes the basic rights that all citizens in the United States possess. The individual states may give more rights, but they cannot give fewer.

*Amendment XIV* (Passed by Congress June 13, 1866. Ratified July 9, 1868): All persons born or naturalized in the United States, and subject to the jurisdiction thereof, are citizens of the United States and of the State wherein they reside. No State shall make or enforce any law which shall abridge the privileges or immunities of citizens of the United States; nor shall any State deprive any person of life, liberty, or property, without due process of law; nor deny to any person within its jurisdiction the equal protection of the laws.

## THREE BRANCHES OF THE FEDERAL GOVERNMENT

### Legislative Branch (Article I) (lawmakers)

The **legislative branch** is bicameral, meaning it has two chambers, which are together called the Congress:

- The Senate: Two members from each state.
- The House of Representatives: 435 members apportioned based on population. No fewer than one per state.

Congress is responsible for passing laws. The following types of laws cannot be passed:

- No Bills of Attainder: Laws enacted naming individuals or an ascertainable group designed to punish them without a trial.
- No *Ex Post Facto* laws: Laws passed designed to punish conduct that occurred before the law was passed.

### Executive Branch (Article II) (enforcement)

The **executive branch** is responsible for the following:

- Making treaties.
- Appointing federal judges.
- Enforcing laws (e.g., FBI, DEA, and Secret Service).

### Judicial Branch (Article III) (interprets laws and treaties)

The **judicial branch** has **jurisdiction** in the following areas:

- Reviews constitutional questions and treaties.
- Interprets the laws of the United States.
- Resolves controversies between states.

> The Supreme Court held that it has the power to review the constitutional validity of actions taken by the other two branches of government as long as there is a case or controversy. The Supreme Court also has the power to declare acts of Congress as unconstitutional. This authority stems from *Marbury v. Madison*, 5 U.S. 137 (1803).

# DUE PROCESS

Both the Fifth and Fourteenth Amendments guarantee that no person shall be deprived of life, liberty, or property without due process of law. The Fifth Amendment's Due Process Clause is applicable to the federal government, and the Fourteenth Amendment's Due Process Clause is applicable to the states. The Due Process clauses prohibit the government from arbitrarily or unreasonably depriving a person of life, liberty, or property. The essential purpose of due process is to ensure fundamental fairness. There are two types of due process: procedural due process and substantive due process.

### Procedural Due Process

Procedural due process examines the procedure required by the government when the government seeks to deprive people of life, liberty, or property.

In general, the more important the person's interest that will be affected, the more process the government must afford. The basic requirements of procedural due process are notice and an opportunity to be heard by an impartial decision maker.

Examples of procedural due process protections that may be required include:

- Right to counsel.
- Right to a jury trial.
- Right to confrontation.
- Right against compelled self-incrimination.

### Substantive Due Process

Substantive due process examines the government's power to deprive a person of life, liberty, or property regardless of the procedures followed by the government. In general, the more important the person's interest that will be affected, the more compelling the government's reason for the law must be, and there must be a greater necessity for the chosen means. For example, if a state statute is enacted that makes it a misdemeanor for a person to speak in public, this statute will violate substantive due process no matter how fair the process of enactment and enforcement are.

In procedural due process claims, the deprivation by State action of a constitutionally protected interest in life, liberty, or property is not in itself unconstitutional; what is unconstitutional is the deprivation of such an interest *without due process of law*. Procedural due process rules are meant to protect persons not from the deprivation, but from the mistaken or unjustified deprivation of life, liberty, or property. A procedural due process violation occurs when the government unlawfully interferes with a protected property or liberty interest without providing adequate procedural safeguards.

Substantive due process protects individual liberty and property interests from arbitrary government actions regardless of the fairness of any implementing procedures. The right to substantive due process is violated when legislation is unreasonable and clearly arbitrary, having no substantial relationship to the health, safety, morals, and general welfare of the public.

> Procedural due process differs from substantive due process in that procedural due process principles protect persons from deficient procedures that lead to the deprivation of cognizable [property] interests. A substantive due process

claim is, fundamentally, not a claim of procedural deficiency, but, rather, a claim that the state's conduct is inherently impermissible. *Bonner v. City of Brighton*, 298 Mich. App. 693 (2012).

# EQUAL PROTECTION

Under the Fourteenth Amendment, "No State shall . . . deny to any person within its jurisdiction the equal protection of the laws." This means that no person or class of persons shall be denied the same protection of the laws that is enjoyed by other persons or other classes in like circumstances in their lives, liberty, property, and in their pursuit of happiness. *Black's Law Dictionary* 616 (9th ed. 2009).

# MICHIGAN CONSTITUTION AND UNITED STATES CONSTITUTION

Generally, the Michigan Constitution closely follows the United States Constitution. Although there are textual differences between the two, Michigan courts usually interpret provisions in the Michigan Constitution the same as the United States Supreme Court interprets similar provisions in the United States Constitution.

The Bill of Rights provides basic protections to all people in the United States. As a practical matter, states can provide more protections to their citizens than what is provided in the United States Constitution, but states cannot deprive a citizen of a basic right guaranteed by the United States Constitution. The following are examples of these principles:

Although sobriety checkpoints aimed at reducing drunk driving within the state of Michigan do not violate the search and seizure provisions of the Fourth Amendment, the Michigan Supreme Court has held that sobriety checkpoints violate the search and seizure provisions of the Michigan Constitution. *Sitz v. Department of State Police*, 443 Mich. 744 (1993).

The Michigan Constitution, Article I, Section 11, prohibits unreasonable searches and seizures; however, there is a clause in the section that states the provisions do not bar narcotics and certain dangerous weapons seized by a peace officer outside the curtilage of any dwelling house from being admissible at trial. The United States Supreme Court has held that evidence seized as a result of unreasonable searches and seizures in violation of the Fourth Amendment are inadmissible in a state court. For example, a gun found illegally during a traffic stop would be inadmissible at trial under the United States Constitution, but would be admissible at trial under the Michigan Constitution. The Michigan Supreme Court held that this clause is in conflict with the United States Constitution and a federal Supreme Court decision, and the provision could not stand. *People v. Pennington*, 383 Mich. 611 (1970).

The Michigan Constitution, Article I, Section 17, prohibits a person from being compelled in any criminal case to be a witness against himself and deprivation of life, liberty, or property without due process of the law. The self-incrimination provision of the Michigan Constitution is nearly identical to self-incrimination provision of the United States Constitution. The Michigan Supreme Court, like the United States Supreme Court, applies *Miranda* only to custodial interrogations. *People v. Hill*, 429 Mich. 382 (1987).

# FOOT SOLDIERS OF THE CONSTITUTION

Police officers are the foot soldiers of the Constitution due to their role in preserving society's norms and values. It is the sense of "constitution" that prevents ethical breakdowns and strengthens a police officer's resolve to do right. As General Colin Powell once said:

*I took an oath to support and defend the Constitution of the United States. . . . Our Constitution and our national conscience demand that every American be accorded dignity and respect, and receive the same treatment under the law.*

# COURT FUNCTIONS AND BASIC LEGAL TERMINOLOGY

## ORGANIZATION AND FUNCTION OF STATE AND FEDERAL COURTS

### Federal Court System

*United States District Courts:* United States district courts are the trial courts for the federal court system. The district courts hear both civil and criminal matters. There are 94 federal judicial district courts, including at least one district in each state, the District of Columbia, and Puerto Rico.

- The United States District Court for the Eastern District of Michigan is the federal district court with jurisdiction over the eastern portion of Michigan.
- The United States District Court for the Western District of Michigan is the federal district court with jurisdiction over the western portion of Michigan.

*United States Courts of Appeals:* The United States district courts are organized into 12 regional circuits, each of which has a United States court of appeals. A court of appeals hears appeals from the district courts located within its circuit.

- The United States Court of Appeals for the Sixth Circuit reviews appeals from the federal district courts in Michigan, Kentucky, Ohio, and Tennessee.

*The United States Supreme Court:* The United States Supreme Court has appellate jurisdiction from the United States courts of appeals and may review constitutional issues from state supreme courts. The Court also has original jurisdiction in suits between states.

### Appeal Process in Federal Court

Decisions from United States district courts are appealed to the United States courts of appeals. In criminal cases, convictions following trials in the United States district courts are appealed to the United States courts of appeals by right. Appeals to the United States Supreme Court are by petition for a writ of certiorari. A petition for a writ of certiorari is a legal document asking the court to review the case. The United States Supreme Court, however, does not have to agree to review the case. In general, the United States Supreme Court will only agree to hear cases involving important legal issues or when there is a conflict of law in the United States courts of appeals or state supreme courts. If the United States Supreme Court agrees to review the case, it grants certiorari and issues a writ of certiorari. A writ of certiorari is an order to a lower court to deliver its record in a case so that the higher court may review it. If the United States Supreme Court decides not to review the case, it denies certiorari.

## State Court System

**District Courts** are responsible for the following:

- Small claims up to $5,000. Note: As detailed in MCL 600.8401, this dollar amount will increase in 2015 and subsequent years.
- Civil suits of $25,000 or less.
- Criminal trials for l-year misdemeanors and all lesser offenses.
- Arraignments.
- Setting bail.
- Preliminary examinations for felonies and circuit court misdemeanors.
- Issuing search and arrest warrants.
- District Court magistrate (see below).

**Circuit Courts** are responsible for the following:

- Civil suits in excess of $25,000.
- Criminal felony and circuit court misdemeanor trials.
- Personal Protection Orders.
- Supervisory control over District Courts.
- The Family Law Division of the Circuit Court hears all matters concerning juveniles, excluding civil infractions.

The Court of Appeals hears appeals from the lower courts.

The Supreme Court hears appeals from Court of Appeals.

## Appeal Process in State Court

Decisions from the district court are appealed to the circuit court. Convictions following trial in the district court are appealed to the circuit court as of right or automatic. Circuit court decisions are appealed to the court of appeals. Convictions for felonies and circuit court misdemeanors following trial in the circuit court are appealed as of right or automatic. All appeals based on pleas of guilty or no contest/*nolo contendere* are by application for leave to appeal. Appeals to the Supreme Court are by application for leave to appeal. Cases involving constitutional issues may be appealed from the Michigan Supreme Court to the United States Supreme Court by petition of certiorari.

# ROLES WITHIN THE JUDICIAL SYSTEM

## Judges

Judges perform the following functions:

- Issue arrest warrants.
- Issue search warrants.

- Make legal rulings.
- Act as fact finders in bench trials only.
- Preside over all trials.

## The Jury

- An accused has the right to trial by jury.
- The jury is the finder of fact.

## Prosecuting Attorney

The prosecuting attorney is the chief law enforcement officer of a county, who:

- Authorizes complaints.
- Represents the county in all civil matters in those counties without corporation counsel.
- Represents the people in all criminal matters.

## Defense Attorney

The defense attorney safeguards the guaranteed rights of the accused.

## District Court Magistrate

- Hears informal civil infraction hearings.
- May issue search warrants.
- Sets bail and accepts bond in all cases.
- Issues warrants for arrest.
- Arraigns and sentences for limited violations upon pleas of guilty and *nolo contendere*.

MCL 600.8511.

# LEGAL TERMINOLOGY

*Jurisdiction:* The types of cases a court has the power to hear.

*Venue:* The geographic areas a court may preside over (e.g., Wayne County Circuit Court).

## In-state prosecution for criminal offense— MCL 762.2

(1) *A person may be prosecuted for a criminal offense he or she commits while he or she is physically located within this state or outside of this state if any of the following circumstances exist:*

   (a) *He or she commits a criminal offense wholly or partly within this state.*

   (b) *His or her conduct constitutes an attempt to commit a criminal offense within this state.*

   (c) *His or her conduct constitutes a conspiracy to commit a criminal offense within this state and an act in furtherance of the conspiracy is committed within this state by the offender, or at his or her instigation, or by another member of the conspiracy.*

(d) *A victim of the offense or an employee or agent of a governmental unit posing as a victim resides in this state or is located in this state at the time the criminal offense is committed.*

(e) *The criminal offense produces substantial and detrimental effects within this state.*

(2) *A criminal offense is considered under subsection (1) to be committed partly within this state if any of the following apply:*

(a) *An act constituting an element of the criminal offense is committed within this state.*

(b) *The result or consequences of an act constituting an element of the criminal offense occur within this state.*

(c) *The criminal offense produces consequences that have a materially harmful impact upon the system of government or the community welfare of this state, or results in persons within this state being defrauded or otherwise harmed.*

A defendant could be charged in Michigan for a murder that occurred in Indiana where the evidence showed that he made essential preparations for the crime while present in this state, such as acquiring the murder weapon and planning to take the victim across the state line into Indiana. Also, he began the felony of kidnapping in this state, which gave the state jurisdiction for felony murder. *People v. Gayheart,* 285 Mich. App. 202 (2009).

**Information and belief:**   The belief something is true but it is not based on firsthand knowledge.

**Complaint and warrant for arrest:**   The complaint consists of the essential facts constituting the offense charged; the warrant for arrest is issued upon reasonable grounds to believe an offense has occurred.

**Indictment:**   A formal written accusation issued by a grand jury or similar entity charging one or more people with a crime.

**Arraignment:**   The first appearance of the defendant before a judge or magistrate following an arrest. The arraignment process consists of the following actions: The defendant is formally advised

of charges. An attorney may be appointed. Bond is set.

**Preliminary examination:**   A preliminary examination is held for felonies and circuit court misdemeanors. The purpose is to determine if probable cause exists to believe a crime has been committed and to determine if probable cause exists that the defendant committed the offense. The prosecutor has the burden of proof.

**Arraignment on the information:**   Occurs after bindover in a felony or circuit court misdemeanor.

**Pretrial motions:**   Pretrial motions are presented to the judge in an attempt to exclude evidence. For example, during a *Walker* hearing, arguments are made to exclude confessions. Pretrial motions are also brought to exclude the admission of other types of evidence or to raise issues such as entrapment. The burden of proof in pretrial motions depends on the type of motion and who is bringing it. In a *Walker* hearing, the prosecutor has the burden, whereas in entrapment, the burden is on the defendant. The standard of proof is preponderance of the evidence.

**Motion in limine:**   A written motion to a judge requesting that the judge rule that certain evidence is admissible or inadmissible at trial.

**Voir dire examination:**   *Voir dire* is the questioning of prospective jurors to determine their suitability to sit as jurors. A person has the right to an impartial jury of his or her peers. There are two times a juror may be disqualified from jury duty: (1) **Challenge for cause** is the exclusion of a prospective juror based on some prejudice or interest. For example, the juror may be a relative of the defendant. There is no limit to this type of challenge. (2) **Peremptory challenge** is the exclusion of a juror for no stated reason. The court rules have placed limits on this type of challenge. MCR 6.412, MCR 2.510, and MCR 2.511.

**Double jeopardy:**   The Fifth Amendment states, "Nor shall any person be subject for the same offense to be twice put in jeopardy of life or limb." Double jeopardy is being tried twice for the same crime. Double jeopardy does not preclude trial by state and federal courts because they are separate sovereigns.

If there is a clear legislative intent to allow multiple punishments for a single wrong act, double jeopardy is not violated. *People v. Sturgis,* 427 Mich. 392 (1986).

In determining whether the same act constitutes a violation of two different statutes, the test to be applied is whether each statute requires proof of an additional fact that the other does not. A defendant may be charged with home invasion in one county and possession of the property stolen from the home invasion in another county. The same "element test" for double jeopardy purposes replaced the same "criminal transaction" test. *People v. Nutt*, 469 Mich. 565 (2004). *See also Blockburger v. United States*, 284 U.S. 299 (1932).

Double jeopardy rights attach during different times in the judicial process. If the defendant is facing a jury trial, jeopardy attaches when the jury is impaneled and sworn. In a bench trial, jeopardy attaches when the first witness is sworn. If the defendant pleads guilty, jeopardy attaches when he or she is sentenced.

*14-Day Rule (MCL 766.4):* A preliminary examination must be held within 14 days of an arraignment. MCL 766.7 states that a preliminary exam may be adjourned for good cause only.

*180-Day Rule (MCL 780.131):* Inmates of the Department of Corrections must be brought before the court for trial within 180 days. This allows a prisoner to serve his or her time concurrently if additional charges are brought against him or her. A good faith effort must be accomplished in bringing the inmate to trial within the time period.

*Plea bargaining:* The process where the accused and the prosecutor negotiate an agreement as to the disposition of a case. The defendant usually pleads guilty to a lesser charge or to one of a number of charges.

*Presentence investigation:* Prior to sentencing, the probation department will review the defendant's criminal record, investigating officers' comments, and other factors to make a recommendation to the judge for sentencing.

*Sentencing requirements:* Some sentences are set by statute—for example, first-degree murder, which is mandatory life in prison. Others are left more to the discretion of the judge who must sentence within guidelines.

*Bond requirements:* Under the Eighth Amendment, bail cannot be excessive. The judge sets bond by looking at such factors as the nature of the offense, community ties, prior record, and flight risk. MCR 6.106. Under MCL 766.7, there is no bond for murder or treason.

*Probable cause:* Facts and circumstances sufficient to cause a person of reasonable caution to suspect the person to be arrested is committing or has committed a crime or that the place to be searched contains the evidence sought. It has been described as a "fair probability." Probable cause is also known as **reasonable cause**, sufficient cause, or reasonable grounds. For a more detailed discussion, see Chapter 19 on arrests.

*Reasonable suspicion:* An objective basis—supported by specific and articulable facts—for suspecting a person of committing a crime. This is a standard most commonly applied in the context of searches. For more information, see Chapter 23.

*Beyond a reasonable doubt:* A reasonable doubt is a fair, honest doubt growing out of the evidence or lack of evidence. It is not merely an imaginary or possible doubt, but a doubt based on reason and common sense. A reasonable doubt is just a doubt that is reasonable, after a careful and considered examination of the facts and circumstances of this case. CJI2d 1.9(3).

*Clear and convincing evidence:* Evidence indicating that something is substantially more likely true than not true.

*Preponderance of the evidence:* Evidence sufficient to convince an impartial person to decide an issue one way rather than the other. This is often characterized as 51 percent. This is the burden of proof in civil trials and some evidentiary hearings.

*Entrapment:* Entrapment occurs if (1) the police engage in impermissible conduct that would induce an otherwise law-abiding person to commit a crime in similar circumstances or (2) the police engage in conduct so reprehensible that it cannot be tolerated by the court.

When examining whether governmental activity would impermissibly induce criminal conduct, several factors are considered: (1) whether there existed appeals to the defendant's sympathy as a friend, (2) whether the defendant had been known to commit the crime with which he or she was charged, (3) whether there were any long time lapses between the investigation and the arrest, (4) whether there existed any inducements that would make the commission of a crime unusually attractive to a hypothetical law-abiding citizen, (5) whether there were offers of excessive consideration or other enticement, (6) whether there was a guarantee that the acts alleged as crimes were not illegal, (7) whether, and to what extent, any government pressure existed, (8) whether there existed sexual favors, (9) whether there were any threats of arrest, (10) whether there existed any government procedures that tended to escalate the criminal culpability of the defendant, (11) whether there was police control over any informant, and (12) whether the investigation was targeted. *People v. Johnson*, 466 Mich. 491 (2002).

An undercover officer's willingness to negotiate a contract price for a hit did not amount to an attractive inducement for an otherwise law-abiding citizen to commit a crime. Police actions were insufficient to induce or instigate the commission of a crime by the average person, similarly situated to defendant, who was not ready and willing to commit it. The record shows that the police did nothing more than present the defendant with the opportunity to commit the crime of which he was convicted. *People v. Fyda*, 288 Mich. App. 446 (2010).

*The outcome of court cases:* There are essentially four terms that describe the end result of decisions made by the courts. They are often, but incorrectly, used interchangeably. Note that each has a distinct meaning:

- *Ruling:* The outcome of a court's decision on a specific point or a case as a whole.
- *Holding:* A court's determination of a matter of law, a specific legal principle contained in an opinion, or a court's ruling concerning a specific question.
- *Opinion:* A court's written statement explaining its decision in a case.
- *Finding:* A determination by a judge or jury of a fact.

# BASIC CONCEPTS OF CRIMINAL LAW

## Mens Rea

This is translated from the Latin to mean the "guilty mind." To be guilty of most crimes, the defendant must have committed the act in a certain mental state. This is the *mens rea* and there are two types:

## Specific Intent

- For specific intent, the prosecution must prove not only that the defendant did certain acts, but also that he or she did the acts with the intent to cause a particular result. For example, larceny requires the prosecutor to prove that the defendant had the specific intent to permanently deprive the owner of the property.
- The defendant's intent may be proved by what he or she said, what he or she did, how he or she did it, or by any other acts and circumstances in evidence.

CJI2d 3.9.

## General Intent

This is defined as the intent to do an act that the law prohibits. It is not necessary for the prosecution to prove that the defendant intended the precise harm or the precise result that occurred. *Black's Law Dictionary* 882 (9th ed. 2009).

## Actus Reus

This term is translated as the "guilty act." This is the wrongful deed that renders the actor criminally liable if combined with the *mens rea*. For example, the *actus reus* for larceny would be the taking of the property.

## Corpus Delicti

This is another term translated from the Latin and means the "body of the crime" or the substance of the crime. It includes each element of the crime.

## Definition of a Crime—MCL 750.5

"*Crime*" means an act or omission forbidden by law that is not designated as a civil infraction and that is punishable upon conviction by any one or more of the following:

- Imprisonment.
- Fine not designated a civil fine.
- Removal from office.
- Disqualification to hold an office of trust, honor, or profit under the state.
- Other penal discipline.

## Lesser Included Crimes—MCL 768.32

If a crime consists of different degrees, the fact finder may find the accused not guilty of the offense in the degree charged, but may find the accused person guilty of a lesser included offense or of an attempt to commit that offense. For example, CSC third is a lesser included crime of CSC first.

## Felony—MCL 761.1

"*Felony*" means a violation of a penal law of this state for which the offender may be punished by death or by imprisonment for more than one year or an offense expressly designated by law to be a felony.

---

*The term "felony" means an offense for which the offender may be punished by death, or by imprisonment in state prison. MCL 750.7.*

---

Unless specifically stated otherwise, a felony is punishable by imprisonment for not more than four years. MCL 750.503.

## Misdemeanor—MCL 761.1

"*Misdemeanor*" means a violation of a penal law of this state that is not a felony or a violation of an order, rule, or regulation of a state agency that is punishable by imprisonment or a fine that is not a civil fine.

Unless specifically stated otherwise, a misdemeanor is punishable by imprisonment for not more than 90 days. MCL 750.504.

## Statute of Limitations—MCL 767.24

---

(1) *An indictment for murder, conspiracy to commit murder, solicitation to commit murder, criminal sexual conduct in the first degree, or a violation of the Michigan anti-terrorism act, chapter LXXXIII-A of the Michigan penal code, 1931 PA 328, MCL 750.543a to 750.543z, or a violation of chapter XXXIII of the Michigan penal code, 1931 PA 328, MCL 750.200 to 750.212a, that is punishable by life imprisonment may be found and filed at any time.*

(2) *An indictment for a violation or attempted violation of section 145c, 520c, 520d, 520e, or 520g of the Michigan penal code, 1931 PA 328, MCL 750.145c, 750.520c, 750.520d, 750.520e, and 750.520g, may be found and filed as follows:*

   (a) *Except as otherwise provided in subdivision (b), an indictment may be found and filed within 10 years after the*

*offense is committed or by the alleged victim's twenty-first birthday, whichever is later.*

   (b) *If evidence of the offense is obtained and that evidence contains DNA that is determined to be from an unidentified individual, an indictment against that individual for the offense may be found and filed at any time after the offense is committed. However, after the individual is identified, the indictment may be found and filed within 10 years after the individual is identified or by the alleged victim's twenty-first birthday, whichever is later.*

   (c) *As used in this subsection:*

      (i) *"DNA" means human deoxyribonucleic acid.*

      (ii) *"Identified" means the individual's legal name is known and he or she has been determined to be the source of the DNA.*

(3) *An indictment for kidnapping, extortion, assault with intent to commit murder, attempted murder, manslaughter, or first-degree home invasion may be found and filed as follows:*

   (a) *Except as otherwise provided in subdivision (b), an indictment may be found and filed within 10 years after the offense is committed.*

   (b) *If the offense is reported to a police agency within 1 year after the offense is committed and the individual who committed the offense is unknown, and indictment for that offense may be found and filed within 10 years after the individual is identified. This subsection shall be known and me be cited as Brandon D'Annunzio's Law. As used in this subsection, "identified" means the individual's legal name is known.*

(4) *An indictment for identity theft or attempted identity theft may be found and filed as follows:*

   (a) *Except as otherwise provided in subdivision (b), an indictment may be found and filed within 6 years after the offense is committed.*

   (b) *If evidence of the offense is obtained and the individual who committed the offense has not been identified, an indictment may be found and filed at any time after the offense is committed, but not more than 6 years after the individual is identified.*

(c) *As used in this subsection:*

   (i) *"Identified" means the individual's legal name is known.*

   (ii) *"Identity theft" means 1 or more of the following:*

      (A) *Conduct prohibited in section 5 or 7 of the identity theft protection act, 2004 PA 452, MCL 445.65 and 445.67.*

      (B) *Conduct prohibited under former section 285 of the Michigan penal code, 1931 PA 328.*

(5) *An indictment for false pretenses involving real property, forgery or uttering and publishing of an instrument affecting an interest in real property, or mortgage fraud may be found and filed within 10 years after the offense was committed or within 10 years after the instrument affecting real property was recorded, whichever occurs later.*

(6) *All other indictments may be found and filed within 6 years after the offense is committed.*

(7) *Any period during which the party charged did not usually and publicly reside within this state is not part of the time within which the respective indictments may be found and filed.*

(8) *The extension or tolling, as applicable, of the limitations period provided in this section applies to any of those violations for which the limitations period has not expired at the time the extension or tolling takes effect.*

# SOURCES OF MICHIGAN LAW

Michigan law is primarily gleaned from five sources:

1. Statutes.
2. Court opinions (case law).
3. Administrative rules.
4. Executive orders.
5. Attorney General opinions.

## Statutes

Statutes are laws enacted by the Legislature and governor or directly by the people. When the Legislature enacts (passes) a law, both houses must approve it by majority vote; the Legislature votes on items called bills. Once passed by both houses, a bill will become a public act only if approved by the governor. Public acts are then recorded as statutes in the Michigan Compiled Laws, which is a publication maintained by the Legislature.

The statutes most commonly used by police officers typically do one of two things: They govern the conduct of the public, or they control the conduct of the government (i.e., police officers). Police officers enforce the statutes that govern the public within the rules established by the statutes that control the government.

The Michigan Compiled Laws (MCL) is divided into chapters that are loosely organized by related subject matter. Many chapters contain statutes that can be enforced by law enforcement officers. The most common are Chapter 750 (Penal Code), Chapter 257 (Vehicle Code), Chapter 333 (Public Health Code), and Chapter 324 (Natural Resources).

Generally, statutes enforced by police officers tell the public what they must not do or how to do something they are allowed to do, and they provide penalties for doing something that is prohibited or doing something incorrectly. Unless exceptions are listed in a statute, they almost never tell people what they are allowed to do. As a rule, if something is not expressly made illegal, it is legal. Police officers must never take action (e.g., arrest or citation) for something that is not illegal. Thus, knowing what is illegal (i.e., an act prohibited by law or a legal act done illegally) is paramount for all police officers.

## Citations

Michigan statutes are identified by citations that begin with the designation "MCL" and identify the chapter and section in the MCL where the statute can be found. When appropriate, the subsection can also be included.

Example: Subsection 2 of section 227 of the Penal Code (chapter 750) makes it illegal for a person to possess a pistol in a vehicle without a license. That statute is properly cited as: MCL 750.227(2).

## Court Opinions

Court opinions are written statements by a court explaining the decision in a particular case. Courts interpret and apply statutes, decide the constitutionality of statutes, and in some cases, make law. When an opinion contains a rule of law, police may be required to follow the rule if the opinion is binding. Whether an opinion is binding depends on which court issued the opinion and whether the opinion is published or unpublished.

Generally, court opinions are binding as follows:

| Court | Effect of Opinion |
|---|---|
| United States Supreme Court | Binding on all lower courts—police must follow |
| Michigan Supreme Court | Binding on all lower Michigan state courts—police in Michigan must follow |
| Michigan Court of Appeals | Published opinions are binding, unpublished opinions are not binding—police must follow published opinions |
| 6th Circuit Court of Appeals | Binding on federal courts within the circuit and on Michigan in some circumstances |
| Trial Courts | Binding only on that court for that case |

## Citations

Court cases are cited by their name (which includes two parties separated by a "v" for versus) and reference to where they can be found (volume and page) in books in which the cases are published, followed by the year the decision was rendered and other clarifying information when needed (such as the name of the court when it is not obvious from the citation which court rendered the opinion). Those books are called "reporters."

For example, the United States Supreme Court case of *Terry versus Ohio*, decided in 1968, was published in volume 392 of the United States Reports beginning on page 1 of that volume. The citation looks like this: *Terry v. Ohio*, 392 U.S. 1 (1968).

There are a variety of other ways in which court opinions may be properly cited (e.g., by docket number or by listing multiple cites). In this book, you will generally find court cases cited to the official reporter. From time to time, you may also see various citation formats, such as underlined case names instead of italicized, string cites (listing multiple reporters after the case name), and pinpoint cites (listing a second page number that points to a specific page within an opinion). In this book, we do not generally string cite or pinpoint cite.

| Court | Official Reporter | Other Common Reporters | Clarifying Information |
|---|---|---|---|
| United States Supreme Court | United States Reports (U.S.) | Supreme Court Reporter (S. Ct.) | None |
| United States Courts of Appeals | Federal Reporter (F., F.2d, or F.3d) | Federal Appendix (F.App'x) | The circuit will be identified by number at the end of the citation (e.g., 6th Cir.) |
| Michigan Supreme Court | Michigan Reports (Mich.) | North Western Reporter (N.W. or N.W.2d) | "Mich." will appear with the date when cited to N.W. |
| Michigan Court of Appeals | Michigan Appeals Reports (Mich. App.) | North Western Reporter (N.W. or N.W.2d) | "Mich. App." will appear with the date when cited to N.W. |

## Administrative Rules

Administrative rules are rules written and passed (promulgated) by executive branch agencies under authority of a statute. They have the same force and effect as a statute and can be found in the Michigan Administrative Code. Citations to rules appear much like statutes, with an "R" appearing where MCL would appear.

## Executive Orders

Executive Orders are orders issued by the governor under authority granted by the Michigan Constitution. Executive Orders may (1) reorganize or rename departments or agencies within the executive branch, (2) reassign functions within the executive branch, (3) create or dissolve an executive body, or (4) proclaim or end a state of emergency.

Executive Orders will eventually be codified as part of the MCL.

## Citations

Executive Orders may be cited by their MCL section, by the designation E.O. (e.g., E.O. No. 2008-17), or by the designation E.R.O., which stands for Executive Reorganization Order (e.g., E.R.O. No. 2009-5). When cited as an E.O. or E.R.O., the citation includes the year issued and the sequential number of the order. An E.R.O. always starts as an E.O., but the sequential numbers may be different.

## Attorney General Opinions

Attorney General opinions are documents issued by the Michigan Attorney General that answer a specific question posed by a member of the executive branch or the Legislature. AG opinions may be formal or informal. Informal opinions only provide legal guidance and are not binding. Formal opinions are published as a matter of public record and are binding on the executive branch of state government. Formal opinions are given deference by the courts, but they are not binding on the courts.

Formal AG opinions are only binding as to the specific question answered.

## Other Sources of Law

There are a number of other legal documents that affect law enforcement, although they may not require police officers to do anything during their day-to-day work. For example, the Michigan Supreme Court has created a number of rules that control the function of Michigan's courts, most notably the Michigan Rules of Evidence (cited as "MRE") and the Michigan Court Rules (cited as "MCR"). While these rules do not bind law enforcement, they impact police officers because they control how courts operate and what may be properly admitted as evidence in court proceedings.

Also worth noting are the Criminal Jury Instructions (cited as "CJI" or "CJI2d"). The CJI are used by judges to tell jurors what they must determine in order to find a defendant guilty. Although not binding law, they were created using statutes and case law and generally provide a concise description of the elements of a crime or defense.

# INCHOATE OFFENSES

## INCHOATE OFFENSES

Inchoate offenses are incomplete crimes or a step toward another crime where the step itself is punishable as a crime. *Black's Law Dictionary* 885 (Abridged 7th ed. 2000).

Attempt, conspiracy, and solicitation are the crimes typically considered inchoate offenses. In this chapter, we discuss those offenses and several others that are incident to, or part of, another offense. These acts are typically punished as if a the defendant committed the offense and is responsible for the natural and probable results.We have left some offenses for other chapters that might fit here, but are closely related to the subject of another chapter (e.g., assault with intent to maim appears in Chapter 4 covering assaults).

### Aiding and Abetting—MCL 767.39

Anyone who intentionally assists someone else in committing a crime is as guilty as the person who directly commits it and can be convicted of that crime as an aider and abettor. Aiding and abetting occurs before or while an offense is committed.

### Elements

1. The alleged crime was actually committed, either by the defendant or someone else. It does not matter whether anyone else has been convicted of the crime.
2. Before or during the crime, the defendant did something to assist in the commission of the crime.
3. The defendant must have intended the commission of the crime alleged or must have known that the other person intended its commission or that the crime alleged was a natural and probable consequence of the commission of the crime intended.

CJI2d 8.3.

The defendant agreed to assist Pannell in committing an aggravated assault. The assault was intended as an act of revenge after the victim threatened Pannell's family. After repeatedly punching and kicking the victim, the defendant told Pannell, "That's enough" and left the scene. After the defendant left, Pannell shot and killed the victim. The court held that when a person aids another in the commission of one crime, he or she can be criminally liable for any other crime that is the "natural and probable" result of the original crime. Therefore, the defendant could properly be convicted of murder. *People v. Robinson*, 475 Mich. 1 (2006).

### Inducement

It does not matter how much aid, advice, or encouragement the defendant gave. However, the defendant must have intended to assist another in committing the crime, and the help, advice, or encouragement actually did help, advise, or encourage the crime. CJI2d 8.4.

## Mere Presence Insufficient

Even if the defendant knew that the alleged crime was planned or was being committed, the mere fact that the defendant was present when it was committed is not enough to prove that he or she assisted in committing it. CJI2d 8.5.

> Aiding and abetting describes all forms of assistance rendered to the perpetrator of a crime and comprehends all words or deeds that might support, encourage, or incite the commission of a crime. *People v. Bulls*, 262 Mich. App. 618 (2004).

## Accessory after the Fact—MCL 750.505 (felony)

An accessory after the fact is someone who knowingly helps a felon avoid discovery, arrest, trial, or punishment after the principal offense has occurred. This is one of a handful of common law offenses punishable under MCL 750.505, but not otherwise specifically addressed in a statute.

### Elements

1. Someone else committed an offense. The prosecutor does not have to prove that the other person has been charged with or convicted of the underlying offense; he or she just has to prove that the underlying offense was committed.
2. The defendant helped the other person in an effort to avoid discovery, arrest, trial, or punishment.
3. When the defendant gave help, he or she knew the other person had committed a felony.
4. The defendant intended to help the other person avoid discovery, arrest, trial, or punishment. CJI2d 8.6.

> The principal offender does not need to be convicted in order to convict an accessory as an accessory, but the prosecutor must prove that the original crime did occur. *People v. Williams*, 117 Mich. App. 505 (1982).

## Difference Between Aider and Abettor and Accessory After the Fact

If the prosecutor has proved beyond a reasonable doubt that before or during the offense, the defendant gave encouragement or assistance intending to help another commit that crime, then the defendant may be found guilty of aiding and abetting the crime.

If the prosecutor has proved beyond a reasonable doubt that the defendant knew about the offense and helped the person who committed it avoid discovery, arrest, trial, or punishment after the crime ended, then the defendant may be found guilty of being an accessory after the fact. CJI2d 8.7.

> A person cannot be an aider and abettor and an accessory after the fact on the same crime. *People v. Lucas*, 402 Mich. 302 (1978).

## Attempts—MCL 750.92

### Elements

1. The defendant intended to commit an offense.
2. The defendant took some action toward committing the alleged crime, but failed to complete the crime. It is not enough to prove that the defendant made preparations for committing the crime. Things like planning the crime or arranging how it will be committed are just preparations; they do not qualify as an attempt. In order to qualify as an attempt, the action must go beyond mere preparation, to the point where the crime would have been completed if it had not been interrupted by outside circumstances. To qualify as an attempt, the act must clearly and directly be related to the crime that the defendant is charged with attempting and not some other objective. CJI2d 9.1.

> A defendant who commits any act toward the commission of a criminal offense, but who fails in the perpetration, or is intercepted or prevented in the execution of the offense, may be found to have attempted the offense. *People v. Davenport*, 165 Mich. App. 256 (1987).

An accused can be convicted of attempt even if the evidence establishes the completed crime. *People v. Bradovich,* 305 Mich. 329 (1943).

Penalties:

| Attempted crime punishable by life or more than 5 years | 5-year felony, but punishment cannot exceed ½ the greatest penalty for the actual crime |
|---|---|
| Attempted crime punishable by less than 5 years | 2-year misdemeanor, but punishment cannot exceed ½ the greatest penalty for the actual crime |

The general attempt statute applies only if there is no express provision for attempt in the statute for the underlying offense. *People v. Denmark,* 74 Mich. App. 402 (1977)

## Impossibility Is Not a Defense

A person can be found guilty of attempting to commit a crime even if he or she could not finish the crime because circumstances turned out to be different than he or she expected or he or she was stopped before he or she could finish. CJI2d 9.3.

## Conspiracy—MCL 750.157a

Anyone who knowingly agrees with someone else to commit a crime is guilty of conspiracy.

### Elements

1. The defendant and one or more persons knowingly agreed to commit a crime.
2. The defendant specifically intended to commit or help commit that crime.
CJI2d 10.2.

## Agreement for Conspiracy

The agreement for conspiracy includes the following:

- An agreement is the coming together or meeting of the minds of two or more people, with each person intending and expressing the same purpose.
- It is not necessary for the people involved to have made a formal agreement to commit the crime or to write down how they were going to do it.
- In deciding whether there was an agreement to commit a crime, think about how all the members of the alleged conspiracy acted and what they said as well as all the other evidence.
- To find the defendant guilty of conspiracy, the judge or jury must be satisfied beyond a reasonable doubt that there was an agreement to commit a crime. However, it can be inferred that there was an agreement from the circumstances, such as how the members of the alleged conspiracy acted, but only if there is no other reasonable explanation for those circumstances.
CJI2d 10.2.

Michigan is a "no one-man conspiracy" state. If two people are charged with a crime and one is acquitted and one is convicted, the conspiracy charges must be dropped. The charges do not have to be dropped if the indictment refers to unknown or unnamed conspirators and there is sufficient evidence to show the existence of a conspiracy between the convicted defendant and these other conspirators. *People v. Williams,* 240 Mich. App. 316 (2000).

However, when alleged conspirators are tried separately or jointly with separate finders of fact, the "no one-man conspiracy" rule does not apply. *See People v. Anderson,* 418 Mich. 31 (1983) (holding that co-conspirator could be found guilty at trial even where his alleged co-conspirator was acquitted in a separate trial); *People v. Cummings,* 139 Mich. App. 286 (1984) (holding that even though the defendant was tried jointly with three alleged co-conspirators who were acquitted by the judge, his conviction by jury was proper).

Where police have frustrated a conspiracy's specific objective, but conspirators, unaware of that fact, have neither abandoned the conspiracy nor withdrawn, the special conspiracy-related dangers remain, as does the conspiracy's essence—the agreement to commit the crime. *United States v. Recio,* 537 U.S. 270 (2003).

Penalties:

| Conspiracy to commit a crime punishable by 1 year or more of imprisonment | Imprisonment for up to the maximum term of the underlying crime |
|---|---|
| Conspiracy related to illegal gambling | 5-year felony |
| Conspiracy to commit an act punishably by less than 1 year of imprisonment | Up to 1 year of imprisonment |
| Conspiracy to commit a legal act in an illegal manner | 5-year felony |

## Solicitation to Commit a Felony—MCL 750.157b

### Elements

1. The defendant, through words or actions, offered, promised, or gave money, services, or anything of value, or forgave or promised to forgive a debt or obligation owed to another person.
2. The defendant intended that what he or she said or did would cause the felony to be committed.
3. The prosecutor does not have to prove that the person the defendant solicited actually committed, attempted to commit, or intended to commit the crime.

CJI2d 10.6.

# ASSAULT AND CHILD ABUSE

## ASSAULTS

### Assault and Battery—MCL 750.81 (93-day misdemeanor)

(1) Except as otherwise provided in this section, a person who assaults or assaults and batters an individual, if no other punishment is prescribed by law, is guilty of a misdemeanor punishable by imprisonment for not more than 93 days or a fine of not more than $500.00, or both.

(2) Except as provided in subsection (3) or (4), an individual who assaults or assaults and batters his or her spouse or former spouse, an individual with whom he or she has or has had a dating relationship, an individual with whom he or she has had a child in common, or a resident or former resident of his or her household, is guilty of a misdemeanor punishable by imprisonment for not more than 93 days or a fine of not more than $500.00, or both.

(3) An individual who commits an assault or an assault and battery in violation of subsection (2), and who has previously been convicted of assaulting or assaulting and battering his or her spouse or former spouse, an individual with whom he or she has or has had a dating relationship, an individual with whom he or she has had a child in common, or a resident or former resident of his or her household, under any of the following, may be punished by imprisonment for not more than 1 year or a fine of not more than $1,000.00, or both:

   (a) This section or an ordinance of a political subdivision of this state substantially corresponding to this section.
   (b) Section 81a, 82, 83, 84, or 86.
   (c) A law of another state or an ordinance of a political subdivision of another state substantially corresponding to this section or section 81a, 82, 83, 84, or 86.

(4) An individual who commits an assault or an assault and battery in violation of subsection (2), and who has 2 or more previous convictions for assaulting or assaulting and battering his or her spouse or former spouse, an individual with whom he or she has or has had a dating relationship, an individual with whom he or she has had a child in common, or a resident or former resident of his or her household, under any of the following, is guilty of a felony punishable by imprisonment for not more than 5 years or a fine of not more than $5,000.00, or both:

   (a) This section or an ordinance of a political subdivision of this state substantially corresponding to this section.
   (b) Section 81a, 82, 83, 84, or 86.

(c) *A law of another state or an ordinance of a political subdivision of another state substantially corresponding to this section or section 81a, 82, 83, 84, or 86.*

(5) *This section does not apply to an individual using necessary reasonable physical force in compliance with section 1312 of the revised school code, 1976 PA 451, MCL 380.1312.*

(6) *As used in this section, "dating relationship" means frequent, intimate associations primarily characterized by the expectation of affectional involvement. This term does not include a casual relationship or an ordinary fraternization between 2 individuals in a business or social context.*

## Assault—MCL 750.81 (93-day misdemeanor)

### Elements

1. The defendant either attempted to commit a battery or did an act that would cause a reasonable person to fear or apprehend an immediate battery. A battery is a forceful, violent, or offensive touching of the person or something closely connected with the person of another.
2. The defendant intended either to commit a battery on the victim or to make the victim reasonably fear an immediate battery.
3. The defendant, at the time, had the ability to commit a battery, appeared to have the ability, or thought he or she had the ability.
CJI2d 17.1.

Placing a hand in a diaper bag and pointing at the victim in a threatening manner constituted an assault even though no weapon was located. The assault element is satisfied where circumstances indicate that an assailant, by overt conduct, causes the victim to reasonably believe that he will do what is threatened. *People v. Reeves*, 458 Mich. 236 (1998).

A victim's subjective experience of the emotion of fear is not an element of assault, even in "apprehension" types of criminal assault cases. A particular victim's subjective experience of fear was not as important as the defendant's intent to scare or intimidate the victim and whether an ordinary person facing the same conduct would reasonably perceive a legitimate threat of harmful contact. *People v. Davis*, 277 Mich. App. 676 (2008).

## Assault and Battery—MCL 750.81 (93-day misdemeanor)

### Elements

1. The defendant committed a battery on the victim. A battery is a forceful, violent, or offensive touching of the person or something closely connected with the person of another. The touching must have been intended by the defendant, that is, not accidental, and it must have been against the victim's will. It does not matter whether the touching caused an injury.
2. The defendant intended either to commit a battery upon the victim or to make the victim reasonably fear an immediate battery.
CJI2d 17.2.

An officer testified that a suspect hit him with a closed fist. His partner testified that the officer was pushed with an open hand. The court held that the testimony was sufficient evidence for a guilty verdict on assault charges regardless of whether the strike was with a closed fist or open hand. *People v. Solak*, 146 Mich. App. 659 (1985).

## Domestic Assault and Battery—MCL 750.81(2)

### Elements

1. The defendant assaulted or assaulted and battered the victim. The touching must have been intended by the defendant, that is, not accidental, and it must have been against the victim's will. An assault is an attempt to commit a battery or an act that would cause a reasonable person to fear or apprehend an immediate battery. At the time of an assault, the defendant must have had the ability to commit a battery, must have appeared to have the ability, or must have thought he had the ability.
2. At the time, the victim was any of the following:

   a. The defendant's spouse.
   b. The defendant's former spouse.
   c. Had a child in common with the defendant.
   d. A resident or former resident of the same household as the defendant.
   e. A person with whom the defendant had or previously had a dating relationship. A "dating relationship" means frequent, intimate association primarily characterized by the expectation of affectional involvement. It does not include a casual relationship or an ordinary fraternization between two individuals in a business or social context.
CJI2d 17.2a.

Penalties:

| First offense | 93-day misdemeanor |
| --- | --- |
| Second offense | 1-year misdemeanor |
| Third offense | 5-year felony |

## Aggravated Assault—MCL 750.81a (1-year misdemeanor)

(1) *Except as otherwise provided in this section, a person who assaults an individual without a weapon and inflicts serious or aggravated injury upon that individual without intending to commit murder or to inflict great bodily harm less than murder is guilty of a misdemeanor punishable by imprisonment for not more than 1 year or a fine of not more than $1,000.00, or both.*

(2) *Except as provided in subsection (3), an individual who assaults his or her spouse or former spouse, an individual with whom he or she has or has had a dating relationship, an individual with whom he or she has had a child in common, or a resident or former resident of the same household without a weapon and inflicts serious or aggravated injury upon that individual without intending to commit murder or to inflict great bodily harm less than murder is guilty of a misdemeanor punishable by imprisonment for not more than 1 year or a fine of not more than $1,000.00, or both.*

(3) *An individual who commits an assault and battery in violation of subsection (2), and who has 1 or more previous convictions for assaulting or assaulting and battering his or her spouse or former spouse, an individual with whom he or she has or has had a dating relationship, an individual with whom he or she has had a child in common, or a resident or former resident of the same household, in violation of any of the following, is guilty of a felony punishable by imprisonment for not more than 5 years or a fine of not more than $5,000.00, or both:*

  (a) *This section or an ordinance of a political subdivision of this state substantially corresponding to this section.*

  (b) *Section 81, 82, 83, 84, or 86.*

  (c) *A law of another state or an ordinance of a political subdivision of another state substantially corresponding to this section or section 81, 82, 83, 84, or 86.*

(4) *As used in this section, "dating relationship" means frequent, intimate associations primarily characterized by the expectation of affectional involvement. This term does not include a casual relationship or an ordinary fraternization between 2 individuals in a business or social context.*

## Elements

1. The defendant tried to physically injure another person (without a weapon).
2. The defendant intended to injure the victim or make the victim reasonably fear an immediate battery.
3. The defendant caused a serious or aggravated injury. A serious or aggravated injury is a physical injury that requires immediate medical treatment or that causes disfigurement, impairment of health, or impairment of a part of the body.

CJI2d 17.6.

A number of witnesses testified that the victim was rendered unconscious by a blow to the head and suffered injuries to his face, eye, and neck during a fight with the defendant. The court held that this evidence was sufficient to justify a reasonable person in concluding that the defendant inflicted a serious or aggravated injury on the victim, thus the defendant's conviction of aggravated assault was proper. Further, the fact that the victim did not seek medical attention until the evening following the attack is only one factor used in determining whether there was a serious or aggravated injury. The element of "serious or aggravated injury" is satisfied by the introduction of testimony showing that the victim's injuries constituted a substantial bodily injury that necessitated immediate medical treatment or caused disfigurement, impairment of health, or impairment of any bodily part. No expert testimony is required on this element. *People v. Brown*, 97 Mich. App. 606 (1980).

Penalties:

| First offense | 1-year misdemeanor |
| --- | --- |
| Previous conviction for domestic assault | 5-year felony |

## Assault Upon an FIA Worker—MCL 750.81c

### Elements

1. A person who communicates to any person a threat that he or she will physically harm an employee of the Family Independence Agency and does so because of the employee's status with the agency commits a 1-year misdemeanor.
2. A person assaults or assaults and batters an employee of the Family Independence Agency because of the employee's status with the agency.

Penalties:

| Causes physical injury | 2-year felony |
|---|---|
| Causes serious impairment of bodily function | 5-year felony |

## Assaulting a Peace Officer, EMT, Firefighter, or Search and Rescue Team Performing Duties—MCL 750.81d (felony)

It is unlawful to assault, batter, wound, resist, obstruct, oppose, or endanger any of the following:

- Police officers, motor carrier officers, or capitol security officers.
- State and Federal conservation officers.
- Federal peace officers.
- Firefighters.
- Emergency medical service personnel.
- Search and rescue teams.

This section applies when the individual knows, or has reason to know, that any of the above persons are performing their duties.

### Elements

1. The defendant assaulted, battered, wounded, resisted, obstructed, opposed, or endangered a police officer or other authorized person. "Obstruct" includes the use or threatened use of physical interference or force or a knowing failure to comply with a lawful command. The defendant must have actually resisted by what he or she said or did, but physical violence is not necessary.
2. The defendant knew or had reason to know that the person was a police officer or other authorized person performing his or her duties at the time.
CJI2d 13.1.

Penalties:

| Without injury | 2-year felony |
|---|---|
| Causes bodily injury requiring medical attention | 4-year felony |
| Causes serious impairment of bodily function | 15-year felony |
| Causes death | 20-year felony |

"Serious impairment of a body function" includes, but is not limited to, one or more of the following:

- Loss of a limb or loss of use of a limb.
- Loss of a foot, hand, finger, or thumb or loss of use of a foot, hand, finger, or thumb.
- Loss of an eye or ear or loss of use of an eye or ear.
- Loss or substantial impairment of a bodily function.

- Serious visible disfigurement.
- A comatose state that lasts for more than three days.
- Measurable brain or mental impairment.
- A skull fracture or other serious bone fracture.
- Subdural hemorrhage or subdural hematoma.
- Loss of an organ.

Physical resistance, threats, and abusive speech can be relevant facts in a prosecution under this statute, but none is a necessary element. The classic example of resisting or obstructing involves a defendant who physically interferes with the officer; actual physical interference is not necessary. The court held that an expressed threat is sufficient to support a charge under these statutes; however, here the defendant's mere polite refusal to submit to a search warrant for his blood following a DUI arrest was sufficient to support a resisting and obstructing charge. *People v. Philabaun*, 461 Mich. 255 (1999).

Under MCL 750.479, an officer's efforts to keep the peace are not limited to arrest; rather keeping the peace includes all duties legally performed by an officer. Lying about one's age and name is not sufficient to support a charge of resisting and obstructing. *People v. Vasquez*, 465 Mich. 83 (2001).

Lying about age or identity, however, may be sufficient to support charges of knowingly providing false or misleading statements regarding a material fact to a police officer conducting a criminal investigation under MCL 750.479c. Case law is underdeveloped for this statute passed in mid-2012.

Whether the violation of a resisting and obstructing statute is a crime of violence is based on the totality of circumstances. Absent use of force or threat of force by a defendant, a violation of resisting and obstructing statutes is probably not a crime of violence. *United States v. Mosley*, 575 F.3d 603 (6th Cir. 2009).

Officers were questioning occupants of a house through their front door about the whereabouts of their neighbor. During the questioning, officers smelled burnt marijuana and observed through a basement window liquor bottles and people hiding. The officers informed the occupant with whom they were speaking that they were going to enter the house to verify the identities of those inside and to secure it while they waited for a search warrant. The defendant told the officers they may not enter without a warrant and attempted to shut the door. One officer attempted to push the door open while the defendant tried to close it. The officer tore his hamstring and bruised his elbow but ultimately subdued and arrested the defendant for assaulting, obstructing, or resisting police officers in the performance of their duties and assaulting, obstructing, or resisting police officers in the performance of their duties causing injury. In overturning the defendant's conviction, the court held that in order to set aside common law rights, the Legislature must do so in no uncertain terms. Because MCL 750.81d said nothing about the common law right to resist unlawful police conduct, the court held that MCL 750.81d did not abrogate the common-law right to resist illegal police conduct, including unlawful arrests and unlawful entries into constitutionally protected areas. *People v. Moreno*, 491 Mich. 38 (2012).

A lesser injury may be considered a serious injury when the lesser injury lasts for a much greater time than the statutory listed time for a serious injury. Here, the officer lost the use of his leg for several weeks. Though completely healed at trial, his loss of leg use was much greater than the three days of comatose state described in MCL 257.58c. Also, a hemorrhage or hematoma affecting the brain or spine is a serious injury per se; therefore, so is a fracture to the spine or skull. *People v. Thomas*, 263 Mich. App. 70 (2004).

Obstruction charges were proper where an intoxicated passenger assaulted officers after they had arrested the driver for OWI. Even though it was evident that the criminal investigation had likely been completed by the time the defendant exited the vehicle and assaulted the officers, they were still performing duties at the scene, including maintaining the peace and controlling the scene, locating a sober driver to move the vehicle from the roadway, and protecting the safety of the defendant, especially considering her intoxicated state and the inclement weather conditions. Such non-investigatory duties have been recognized by our courts as official duties of the police. *People v. Corr*, 287 Mich. App. 499 (2010).

## Resisting or Obstructing Officers in Discharge of Duty—MCL 750.479 (felony)

It is unlawful to knowingly and willfully assault, batter, wound, obstruct, or endanger any of the following:

- Medical examiner.
- Township treasurer.

- Judge, magistrate, court employee, or court officer.
- Probation or parole officer.
- Prosecutor or city attorney.
- Officers or duly authorized persons serving or attempting to serve process.
- Officers enforcing ordinance, law, rule, order, or resolution of local government.

This section applies when the individual knows, or has reason to know, that any of the above persons are performing their duties.

### Elements

1. The defendant assaulted, battered, wounded, obstructed, or endangered an officer or other authorized person who was performing his or her duties. "Obstruct" includes the use or threatened use of physical interference or force or a knowing failure to comply with a lawful command.
2. The defendant knew the person was then an officer [or other authorized person] performing his or her duties.
3. The defendant's actions were intended by the defendant, that is, not accidental.

CJI2d 13.2.

Penalties:

| Without injury | 2-year felony |
|---|---|
| Causes bodily injury requiring medical attention | 4-year felony |
| Causes serious impairment of bodily function | 10-year felony |
| Causes death | 20-year felony |

## Assault Upon A Public Utility Worker—MCL 750.81e

- A person who assaults, batters, or assaults and batters an individual while the individual is performing his or her duties as an employee or contractor of a public utility or because of the individual's status as an employee or contractor of a public utility is guilty of a one-year misdemeanor.
- "Public utility" means a utility that provides steam, gas, heat, electricity, water, cable television, telecommunications services, or pipeline services whether privately, municipally, or cooperatively owned.

Penalties:

| Causes physical injury | 2-year felony |
|---|---|
| Causes serious impairment of bodily function | 5-year felony |

## Assault with a Dangerous Weapon (Felonious Assault)—MCL 750.82 (felony)

*A person who assaults another person with a gun, revolver, pistol, knife, iron bar, club, brass knuckles, or other dangerous weapon without intending to commit murder or to inflict great bodily harm less than murder is guilty of a felony punishable by imprisonment for not more than 4 years or a fine of not more than $2,000.00, or both.*

### Elements

1. The defendant either attempted to commit a battery or committed an act that would cause a reasonable person to fear or apprehend an immediate battery.
2. The defendant intended to injure or make the victim reasonably fear an immediate battery.
3. The defendant had the ability, appeared to have the ability, or thought he or she had the ability to commit a battery.
4. The defendant committed the assault with a dangerous weapon.

CJI2d 17.9.

A dangerous weapon is any object that is used in a way that is likely to cause serious physical injury or death.

Some objects, such as guns or bombs, are dangerous because they are specifically designed to be dangerous. Other objects are designed for peaceful purposes but may be used as dangerous weapons. The way an object is used or intended to be used in an assault determines whether it is a dangerous weapon. If an object is used in a way that is likely to cause serious physical injury or death, it is a dangerous weapon. CJI2d 17.10.

- A gun, revolver, or pistol is a firearm. A firearm includes any weapon from which a dangerous object can be shot or propelled by the use of explosives, gas, or air. A firearm does not include smooth bore rifles or handguns designed and manufactured exclusively for shooting BBs no larger than .177 caliber by means of spring, gas, or air.
- It does not matter whether or not the gun was loaded. CJI2d 17.11.
- A gun that is totally unusable as a firearm and cannot easily be made operable is not included here.

CJI2d 17.13.

### Examples of Dangerous Weapons:

The statute is not restricted to weapons of the same type and kind enumerated in the statute. "Some weapons carry their dangerous character because so designed and are, when employed, per se, deadly, while other instrumentalities are not dangerous weapons unless turned to such purpose. The test as to the latter is whether the instrumentality was used as a weapon and, when so employed in an assault, dangerous. The character of a dangerous weapon attaches by adoption when the instrumentality is applied to use against another in furtherance of an assault." *People v. Goolsby*, 284 Mich. 375 (1938).

- A pellet gun. *People v. Jones*, 150 Mich. App. 440 (1986).
- A dog. *People v. Kay*, 121 Mich. App. 438 (1982).
- A broomstick thrown at head level or just below. *People v. Knapp*, 34 Mich. App. 325 (1971).
- An automobile. *People v. Sheets*, 138 Mich. App. 794 (1984).
- An unloaded gun. *People v. Smith*, 231 Mich. App. 50 (1998).
- A starter pistol that could not fire was not a dangerous weapon for felonious assault. *People v. Stevens*, 409 Mich. 564 (1980).
- Bare hands are not weapons under the statute. *People v. Van Diver*, 80 Mich. App. 352 (1977).
- Kicking of victim with boot. *People v. Buford*, 69 Mich. App. 27 (1976).

Lighter fluid when used to set fire to victims.

Evidence of wounds inflicted by the use of an implement that is not dangerous per se is properly admitted to show the instrument's character as a dangerous weapon. Since lighter fluid is not an obviously dangerous weapon, photographs of the burned back of one of the complainants were properly admitted. *People v. Morgan*, 50 Mich. App. 288 (1973).

## Assault with the Intent to Murder—MCL 750.83 (felony)

Any person who shall assault another with intent to commit the crime of murder, shall be guilty of a felony, punishable by imprisonment in the state prison for life or any number of years.

### Elements

1. The defendant tried to physically injure another person.

2. When defendant committed the assault, he or she had the ability or at least believed he or she had the ability to cause an injury.
3. The defendant intended to kill the person assaulted.
CJI2d 17.3.

Assault with intent to murder is an assault where the suspect intended to kill the victim without justification.

> The elements of the crime of assault with intent to commit murder are:
>
> 1. An assault;
> 2. With specific intent to murder;
> 3. Which, if successful, would make the killing murder.
>
> *People v. Branner*, 53 Mich. App. 541 (1974).
>
> Specific intent to kill is the only form of malice which supports the conviction of assault with intent to commit murder. *People v. Gjidoda*, 140 Mich. App. 294 (1985).
>
> Intent to inflict great bodily harm or wanton and wilful disregard of the recklessness of one's conduct is insufficient to support a conviction for assault with intent to commit murder. *People v. Taylor*, 422 Mich. 554 (1985).
>
> This includes a choking where had the choking continued the victim would have died. *People v. Anderson*, 112 Mich. App. 640 (1981).

## Assault with the Intent to Do Great Bodily Harm Less than Murder—MCL 750.84(a) (felony)

*Any person who shall assault another with intent to do great bodily harm, less than the crime of murder, shall be guilty of a felony punishable by imprisonment in the state prison not more than 10 years or by fine of not more than $5,000.00.*

### Elements

1. The defendant tried to physically injure another person.
2. At the time of the assault, the defendant had the ability to cause an injury or at least believed that he had the ability.
3. The defendant intended to cause great bodily harm. Actual injury is not necessary, but if there was an injury, it may be considered as evidence in deciding whether the defendant intended

to cause great bodily harm. Great bodily harm means any physical injury that could seriously harm the health or function of the body. CJI2d 17.7.

> The defendant's intent to cause great bodily harm was established by beating and kicking the victim in her arms, face, head, and chest. *People v. Pena*, 224 Mich. App. 650 (1997).

## Assault by Strangulation or Suffocation—MCL 750.84(b) (felony)

Any person who shall assault another by strangulation or suffocation, shall be guilty of a felony punishable by imprisonment in the state prison not more than 10 years or by fine of not more than $5,000.00.

"*Strangulation or suffocation*" means intentionally impeding normal breathing or circulation of the blood by applying pressure on the throat or neck or by blocking the nose or mouth of another person.

## Assault with the Intent to Maim—MCL 750.86 (felony)

*Any person who shall assault another with intent to maim or disfigure his or her person by cutting out or maiming the tongue, putting out or destroying an eye, cutting or tearing off an ear, cutting or slitting or mutilating the nose or lips, or cutting off or disabling a limb, organ, or member, shall be guilty of a felony, punishable by imprisonment in the state prison not more than 10 years or by fine of not more than $5,000.00.*

> Assault with intent to maim includes actual and attempted maiming. Placing thumbs against the victim's eyes and stating that her eyes were going to be poked out was sufficient to support a conviction for violation of MCL 750.82 without the actual destruction of an eye. *People v. Ward*, 211 Mich. App. 489 (1995).

## Assault with Intent to Commit a Felony—MCL 750.87 (felony)

*Any person who shall assault another, with intent to commit any burglary, or any other felony, the punishment of which assault is not otherwise in this act prescribed, shall be guilty of a felony, punishable by imprisonment in the state prison not more than 10 years, or by fine of not more than $5,000.*

## Elements

1. The defendant either attempted to commit a battery on the victim or did an act that would cause a reasonable person to fear or apprehend an immediate battery.
2. The defendant intended either to injure the victim or to make the victim reasonably fear an immediate battery.
3. At the time, the defendant had the ability to commit a battery, appeared to have the ability, or thought he had the ability.
4. When he assaulted the victim, the defendant intended to commit a felony. It does not matter whether the felony was actually committed.

CJI2d 17.5.

## Assault with the Intent to Rob; Unarmed—MCL 750.88 (felony)

*Any person, not being armed with a dangerous weapon, who shall assault another with force and violence, and with intent to rob and steal, shall be guilty of a felony, punishable by imprisonment in the state prison not more than 15 years.*

## Elements

1. The defendant assaulted the victim with force or violence. The defendant must have attempted or threatened to do immediate injury to the victim and was able to do so, or the defendant must have committed an act that would cause a reasonable person to fear or apprehend an immediate battery.
2. At the time of the assault, the defendant intended to commit robbery. Robbery occurs when a person assaults someone else and takes money or property from the victim or in the victim's presence, intending to take it from the victim permanently. It is not necessary that the crime be completed or that the defendant actually took any money or property.

CJI2d 18.4.

The assault element was satisfied where the defendant caused the victim to reasonably apprehend an immediate battery by placing a hand in a bag and pointing it at the victim in a menacing manner while saying, "What's more important, your job or your life?" *People v. Reeves*, 458 Mich 236 (1998).

## Assault with the Intent to Rob; Armed—MCL 750.89 (felony)

*Any person, being armed with a dangerous weapon, or any article used or fashioned in a manner to lead a person so assaulted reasonably to believe it to be a dangerous weapon, who shall assault another with intent to rob and steal shall be guilty of a felony, punishable by imprisonment in the state prison for life, or for any term of years.*

## Elements

1. The defendant assaulted the victim. The defendant must have attempted or threatened to do immediate injury to the victim and was able to do so, or the defendant must have committed an act that would cause a reasonable person to fear or apprehend an immediate injury.
2. At the time of the assault, the defendant was armed with one or more of the following:

   a. A weapon designed to be dangerous and capable of causing death or serious injury.
   b. Any other object capable of causing death or serious injury that the defendant used as a weapon.
   c. Any other object used or fashioned in a manner to lead the person who was assaulted to reasonably believe that it was a dangerous weapon.

3. At the time of the assault, the defendant intended to commit robbery. Robbery occurs when a person assaults someone else and takes money or property from the victim or in the victim's presence, intending to take it from the victim permanently. It is not necessary that the crime be completed or that the defendant actually took any money or property.

CJI2d 18.3.

## Assault on a Third Person

If the defendant intended to assault one person, but by mistake or accident assaulted another, the crime is the same as if the first person had been assaulted. CJI2d 17.17.

## Torture—MCL 750.85 (felony)

*A person who, with the intent to cause cruel or extreme physical or mental pain and suffering, inflicts great bodily injury or severe mental pain or suffering upon another person within his or her custody or physical control commits torture and is guilty of a felony punishable by imprisonment for life or any term of years.*

*"Cruel" means brutal, inhuman, sadistic or that which torments.*

*"Custody or physical control" means the forcible restriction of a person's movements or forcible confinement of the person so as to interfere with that person's liberty, without that person's consent or without lawful authority.*

*"Great bodily injury" means either of the following:*

(i) *Serious impairment of a body function as that term is defined in section 58c of the Michigan vehicle code, 1949 PA 300, MCL 257.58c, or*

(ii) *One or more of the following conditions: internal injury, poisoning, serious burns or scalding, severe cuts, or multiple puncture wounds.*

*"Severe mental pain or suffering" means a mental injury that results in a substantial alteration of mental functioning that is manifested in a visibly demonstrable manner caused by or resulting from any of the following:*

(i) *The intentional infliction or threatened infliction of great bodily injury,*

(ii) *The administration or application, or threatened administration or application, of mind-altering substances or other procedures calculated to disrupt the senses or the personality,*

(iii) *The threat of imminent death,*

(iv) *The threat that another person will imminently be subjected to death, great bodily injury, or the administration or application of mind-altering substances or other procedures calculated to disrupt the senses or personality.*

*Proof that a victim suffered pain is not an element of the crime under this section.*

Severe mental pain and suffering occurred under the torture statute where the victim started to hallucinate after the incident because it put her in a state that she could not control. The incident scarred her and affected her substantially. She had a previous mental illness, and the incident caused her to relapse. That the victim experienced hallucinations and had to resume her medication after the attack was evidence of a substantial altering of mental functioning and evidence of a visibly demonstrable mental injury. *People v. Schaw*, 288 Mich. App. 231 (2010).

# INJURY TO FETUS OR EMBRYO

An embryo is an unborn human from conception until the development of organs, approximately the eighth week of pregnancy. This includes both viable and nonviable fetuses. *People v. Kurr*, 253 Mich. App. 317 (2002).

## Injury to a Fetus or Embryo—MCL 750.90a (felony)

The suspect either intentionally caused a miscarriage or stillbirth or committed an act in wanton or willful disregard which caused a miscarriage or stillbirth.

## Intentionally Commits any Assault—MCL 750.81 to MCL 750.89 Upon a Pregnant Individual—MCL 750.90b

Penalties:

| | |
|---|---|
| Results in physical injury to embryo or fetus | 93-day misdemeanor |
| Results in serious or aggravated injury to embryo or fetus | 1-year misdemeanor |
| Results in great bodily harm to embryo or fetus | 10-year felony |
| Results in miscarriage or stillbirth or death to embryo or fetus | 15-year felony |

## Commits Gross Negligence to a Pregnant Individual—MCL 750.90c

Penalties:

| | |
|---|---|
| Results in physical injury to embryo or fetus | 93-day misdemeanour |
| Results in serious or aggravated injury to embryo or fetus | 6-month misdemeanour |
| Results in great bodily harm to embryo or fetus | 5-year felony |
| Results in miscarriage or stillbirth or death to embryo or fetus | 15-year felony |

## Operating While Intoxicated (O.W.I.)—MCL 750.90d

Penalties:

| Results in great bodily harm to embryo or fetus | 5-year felony |
|---|---|
| Results in miscarriage or still-birth or death to embryo or fetus | 15-year felony |

## Operating a Vehicle in Careless or Reckless Manner—MCL 750. 90e

Penalties:

| Results in miscarriage or still-birth or death to embryo or fetus | 2-year misdemeanor |
|---|---|

NOTE: Above sections do not apply to acts committed by the pregnant individual or lawful medical procedures.

# CHILD ABUSE

## Definitions—MCL 750.136b

The suspect must be one of the following:

- A parent or guardian of a child.
- A person who had care, custody, or authority over the child.

*Child:* A person younger than 18 years old.

*Serious physical harm to a child*: Any physical injury to a child that seriously impairs the child's health or physical well-being, including, but not limited to, brain damage, a skull or bone fracture, subdural hemorrhage or hematoma, dislocation, sprain, internal injury, poisoning, burn or scald, or severe cut.

*Physical harm*: Any injury to a child's physical condition.

*Serious mental harm to a child*: Injury to mental condition that results in visible signs of impairment in child's judgment, behavior, ability to recognize reality, or ability to cope with ordinary demands of life.

*Omission*: Willfully fail to provide food, clothing, or shelter necessary for the welfare of the child, or to abandon the child.

*Cruel*: Brutal, inhuman, sadistic, or that which torments.

## First Degree—MCL 750.136b(2) (felony)

The suspect knowingly or intentionally caused serious physical or mental harm to a child.

## Elements

1. The defendant is the parent or guardian of the child or any other person who cares for, has custody of, or has authority over a child regardless of the length of time that a child is cared for, in the custody of, or subject to the authority of that person.
2. The defendant knowingly or intentionally caused serious physical harm or serious mental harm to the child.
3. The child was at the time under the age of 18. CJI2d 17.18

First-degree child abuse requires the prosecution to establish not only that the defendant intended to commit the act, but also that the defendant intended to cause serious physical harm or knew that serious physical harm would be caused by his or her act. *People v. Maynor*, 470 Mich. 289 (2004).

## Second Degree—MCL 750.136b(3) (felony)

## Elements

1. The defendant is the parent or guardian of the child or any other person who cares for, has custody of, or has authority over a child regardless of the length of time that a child is cared for, in the custody of, or subject to the authority of that person.
2. The defendant did one or more of the following:
   a. Willfully failed to provide food, clothing, or shelter necessary for the welfare of the child or abandoned the child resulting in serious physical or mental harm to the child. CJI2d 17.19.
   b. Did some reckless act and, as a result, the child suffered serious physical harm. CJI2d 17.20.
   c. Knowingly or intentionally did an act likely to cause serious physical or mental harm to a child regardless of whether such harm resulted. CJI2d 17.20a.
   d. Knowingly or intentionally did an act that was cruel to the child. "Cruel" means brutal, inhuman, sadistic, or that which torments, regardless of whether harm results. CJI2d 17.20b.
3. The child was at the time under the age of 18.

The defendant was in a high-speed chase with several deputies instigated by the defendant's flight. The defendant's infant son and 4-year-old stepson were in the vehicle at the time and were not restrained by either seatbelts or legally mandated child safety seats. The defendant raced through a maze of streets, taking many twists and turns, with several patrol cars joining the pursuit. During the 24-mile chase, the defendant reached speeds of up to 100 miles an hour, crossed the centerline, and flew past traffic signals and signs. Ultimately, the defendant traveled into Benzie County and entered Crystal Mountain Resort. The defendant drove his vehicle up a hill and crashed into the resort's large "Alpine Slide." The defendant escaped on foot and was not captured that night. The deputies searched the vehicle and found no child safety seats for the two small children. One week later, an Arkansas state trooper arrested the defendant while he attempted to escape to Mexico with his wife and their children.

The defendant argued that the prosecution presented insufficient evidence that his actions were likely to cause serious harm to his child passengers in support of the second-degree child abuse charges. Further, the defendant contended that his act of engaging in a high-speed chase with police with his young children unrestrained in his vehicle was not "likely" to cause harm to the children as required to establish a violation of MCL 750.136b(3)(b). The Court of Appeals disagreed.

The court held that the "Prosecution presented sufficient evidence from which a jury could determine beyond a reasonable doubt that defendant's acts could probably have resulted in serious harm to his young children. The defendant fled from law enforcement with two small children unrestrained in his car. The defendant led the police on a 24-mile chase, reaching speeds of 100 miles an hour." *People v. Nix*, 301 Mich. App. 195 (2013).

## Third Degree—MCL 750.136b(5) (felony)

### Elements

1. The defendant is the parent or guardian of the child or had care or custody of, or authority over a child when the abuse happened.
2. The defendant did either of the following:
   a. Knowingly or intentionally caused physical harm to the child.
   b. Knowingly or intentionally committed an act that under the circumstances posed an unreasonable risk of harm or injury to the child and the act resulted in physical harm.
3. The child was at the time under the age of 18. CJI2d 17.21.

Third-degree child abuse occurred where the mother knew the child's susceptibility to bruising and still spanked her with enough force to dislodge a blood clot in her nose and cause substantial bruising. *People v. Sherman-Huffman*, 466 Mich. 39 (2002).

## Fourth Degree—MCL 750.136b(7) (misdemeanor)

### Elements

1. The defendant is the parent or guardian of the child or had care or custody of, or authority over a child when the abuse happened.
2. The defendant did either of the following:
   a. Willfully failed to provide food, clothing, or shelter necessary for the welfare of the child or abandoned the child resulting in physical harm to the child. CJI2d 17.22.
   b. Knowingly or intentionally committed an act that under the circumstances posed an unreasonable risk of harm or injury to the child. Actual injury is not necessary. CJI2d 17.23.
   c. The defendant's omission or reckless act caused physical harm to the child. CJI2d 17.23.
3. The child was at the time under the age of 18.

## Child Abuse in the Presence of Another Child—MCL 750.136d (felony)

The suspect did the following:

- Committed first-, second-, or third-degree child abuse.
- The violation occurred in the presence of a child other than the victim.

## Parental Discipline—MCL 750.136b(9)

Reasonable parental discipline is not against the law, including reasonable force.

Blood blisters, bruises, and a hand-shaped welt on the side of a child's face that was still visible a week after the incident was not reasonable discipline. *People v. Gregg*, 206 Mich. App. 208 (1994).

## Child Abandonment—MCL 750.135 (felony)

Any father or mother of a child under the age of 6 years, or any other person who shall expose such child in any street, field, house, or other place, with intent to injure or wholly to abandon, shall be guilty of felony.

Except for a situation involving actual or suspected child abuse or child neglect, it is an affirmative defense to a prosecution that the child was not more than 72 hours old and was surrendered to an emergency service provider. A criminal investigation shall not be initiated solely on the basis of a newborn being surrendered to an emergency service provider.

As used in this section, an "emergency service provider" means a uniformed employee or contractor of a fire department, hospital, or police station when that individual is inside the premises and on duty.

## Leaving Child Unattended in Vehicle—MCL 750.135a

A person who is responsible for the care or welfare of a child shall not leave that child unattended in a vehicle for a period of time that poses an unreasonable risk of harm or injury to the child or under circumstances that pose an unreasonable risk of harm or injury to the child. For the purposes of this statute, a "child" is a person under the age of 6 years old, and "unattended" means without supervision by a person 13 years old or older.

Penalties:

| | |
|---|---|
| Results in no harm to the child | 93-day misdemeanor |
| Results in physical harm other than serious physical harm | 1-year misdemeanor |
| Results in serious physical harm to the child | 10-year felony |
| Results in death of the child | 15-year felony |

## Sale of Children—MCL 750.136c (felony)

(1) *A person shall not transfer or attempt to transfer the legal or physical custody of an individual to another person for money or other valuable consideration, except as otherwise permitted by law.*

(2) *A person shall not acquire or attempt to acquire the legal or physical custody of an individual for payment of money or other valuable consideration to another person, except as otherwise permitted by law.*

(3) *A person who violates this section is guilty of a felony punishable by imprisonment for not more than 20 years or a fine of not more than $100,000.00, or both.*

## Requirements to Report Child Abuse or Neglect— MCL 722.623(1)

(1) *An individual is required to report under this act as follows:*

(a) *A physician, dentist, physician's assistant, registered dental hygienist, medical examiner, nurse, person licensed to provide emergency medical care, audiologist, psychologist, marriage and family therapist, licensed professional counselor, social worker, licensed master's social worker, licensed bachelor's social worker, registered social service technician, social service technician, a person employed in a professional capacity in any office of the friend of the court, school administrator, school counselor or teacher, law enforcement officer, member of the clergy, or regulated child care provider who has reasonable cause to suspect child abuse or neglect shall make immediately, by telephone or otherwise, an oral report, or cause an oral report to be made, of the suspected child abuse or neglect to the department. Within 72 hours after making the oral report, the reporting person shall file a written report as required in this act. If the reporting person is a member of the staff of a hospital, agency, or school, the reporting person shall notify the person in charge of the hospital, agency, or school of his or her finding and that the report has been made, and shall make a copy of the written report available to the person in charge. A notification to the person in charge of a hospital, agency, or school does not relieve the member of the staff of the hospital, agency, or school of the obligation of reporting to the department as required by this section. One report from a hospital, agency, or school is adequate to meet the reporting requirement. A member of the staff of a hospital, agency, or school shall not be dismissed or otherwise penalized for making a report required by this act or for cooperating in an investigation.*

## Failure to Report Child Abuse/False Report of Child Abuse—MCL 722.633 (93-day misdemeanour)

(1) *A person who is required by this act to report an instance of suspected child abuse or neglect*

*and who fails to do so is civilly liable for the damages proximately caused by the failure.*

(2) *A person who is required by this act to report an instance of suspected child abuse or neglect and who knowingly fails to do so is guilty of a misdemeanor punishable by imprisonment for not more than 93 days or a fine of not more than $500.00, or both.*

(3) *Except as provided in section 7, a person who disseminates, or who permits or encourages the dissemination of, information contained in the central registry and in reports and records made as provided in this act is guilty of a misdemeanor punishable by imprisonment for not more than 93 days or a fine of not more than $100.00, or both, and is civilly liable for the damages proximately caused by the dissemination.*

(4) *A person who willfully maintains a report or record required to be expunged under section 7 is guilty of a misdemeanor punishable by imprisonment for not more than 93 days or a fine of not more than $100.00, or both.*

(5) *A person who intentionally makes a false report of child abuse or neglect under this act knowing that the report is false is guilty of a crime as follows:*

(a) *If the child abuse or neglect reported would not constitute a crime or would constitute a misdemeanor if the report were true, the person is guilty of a misdemeanor punishable by imprisonment for not more than 93 days or a fine of not more than $100.00, or both.*

(b) *If the child abuse or neglect reported would constitute a felony if the report were true, the person is guilty of a felony punishable by the lesser of the following:*

(i) *The penalty for the child abuse or neglect falsely reported.*

(ii) *Imprisonment for not more than 4 years or a fine of not more than $2,000.00, or both.*

# VIOLATIONS INVOLVING MINORS

## Allowing Minor to Stay in Bar—MCL 750.141 (90-day misdemeanor)

*A child under 17 years of age shall not be permitted to remain in any place where spirituous or alcoholic liquor, wine or beer is sold, given away or furnished for a beverage, unless the minor is accompanied by parent or guardian. A proprietor, keeper or manager who permits a minor child to remain, and a person who encourages or induces, in any way the minor child to enter the place or to remain therein, shall be deemed guilty of a misdemeanor.*

## Allowing Minor to Consume or Possess Alcoholic Liquor or a Controlled Substance at a Social Gathering—MCL 750.141a

*An owner, tenant, or other person having control over any premises, residence, or other real property shall not do either of the following:*

(a) *Knowingly allow a minor to consume or possess an alcoholic beverage at a social gathering on or within that premises, residence, or other real property.*

(b) *Knowingly allow any individual to consume or possess a controlled substance at a social gathering on or within that premises, residence, or other real property.*

*. . . .*

*Evidence of all of the following gives rise to a rebuttable presumption that the defendant allowed the consumption or possession of an alcoholic beverage or a controlled substance on or within a premises, residence, or other real property, in violation of this section:*

(a) *The defendant had control over the premises, residence, or other real property.*

(b) *The defendant knew that a minor was consuming or in possession of an alcoholic beverage or knew that an individual was consuming or in possession of a controlled substance at a social gathering on or within that premises, residence, or other real property.*

(c) *The defendant failed to take corrective action.*

*Allow:* To give permission for, or approval of, possession or consumption of an alcoholic beverage or a controlled substance, by any of the following means:

- In writing.
- By one or more oral statements.
- By any form of conduct, including a failure to take corrective action, that would cause a reasonable person to believe that permission or approval has been given.

*Control over any premises, residence, or other real property:* The authority to regulate, direct, restrain, superintend, control, or govern the conduct of other individuals on or within that premises, residence, or other real property, and includes, but is not limited to, a possessory right.

*Corrective action:* Any of the following:

- Making a prompt demand that the minor or other individual depart from the premises, residence, or other real property, or refrain from the unlawful possession or consumption of the alcoholic beverage or controlled substance on or within that premises, residence, or other real property, and taking additional action described in subparagraph (ii) or (iii) if the minor or other individual does not comply with the request.
- Making a prompt report of the unlawful possession or consumption of alcoholic liquor or a controlled substance to a law enforcement agency having jurisdiction over the violation.
- Making a prompt report of the unlawful possession or consumption of alcoholic liquor or a controlled substance to another person having a greater degree of authority or control over the conduct of persons on or within the premises, residence, or other real property.

*Social gathering:* An assembly of two or more individuals for any purpose, unless all of the individuals attending the assembly are members of the same household or immediate family.

This statute does not apply to the use, consumption, or possession of a controlled substance by an individual pursuant to a lawful prescription, or to the use, consumption, or possession of an alcoholic beverage by a minor for religious purposes.

Penalties:

| First offense | 30-day misdemeanor |
|---|---|
| Second or subsequent offense | 90-day misdemeanor |

## Tobacco Violations

### Furnishing Tobacco to a Person Under 18—MCL 722.641 (90-day misdemeanor)

*A person shall not sell, give, or furnish a tobacco product to a minor. A person who violates this subsection is guilty of a misdemeanor punishable by a fine of not more than $50.00 for each violation.*

### Possession by a Person Under 18—MCL 722.642 (90-day misdemeanor)

*A minor shall not do any of the following:*

*(a) Purchase or attempt to purchase a tobacco product.*

*(b) Possess or attempt to possess a tobacco product.*

*(c) Use a tobacco product in a public place.*

*(d) Present or offer to an individual a purported proof of age that is false, fraudulent, or not actually his or her own proof of age for the purpose of purchasing, attempting to purchase, possessing, or attempting to possess a tobacco product.*

### Contributing to the Delinquency of a Minor—MCL 750.145 (90-day misdemeanor)

*Any person who shall by any act, or by any word, encourage, contribute toward, cause or tend to cause any minor child under the age of 17 years to become neglected or delinquent so as to come or tend to come under the jurisdiction of the family division of the circuit court whether or not such child shall in fact be adjudicated a ward of the court, shall be guilty of a misdemeanor.*

A defendant was convicted under this statute for inducing a minor to run away from home through promises of a place to stay and aiding and abetting her in the process. *People v. Owens,* 13 Mich. App. 469 (1968).

### Soliciting Child for Immoral Purposes—MCL 750.145a (felony)

*A person who accosts, entices, or solicits a child less than 16 years of age, regardless of whether the person knows the individual is a child or knows the actual age of the child, or an individual whom he or she believes is a child less than 16 years of age with the intent to induce or force that child or individual to commit an immoral act, to submit to an act of sexual intercourse or an act of gross indecency, or to any other act of depravity or delinquency, or who encourages a child less than 16 years of age, regardless of whether the person knows the individual is a child or knows the actual age of the child, or an individual whom he or she believes is a child less than 16 years of age to engage in any of those acts is guilty of a felony punishable by imprisonment for not more than 4 years or a fine of not more than $4,000.00, or both.*

The defendant thought that he was talking to a 15-year-old girl on the computer who was actually a police officer. At the outset, the defendant invited her to engage in role playing or cybersex.

After learning her age, the defendant continued to guide the course of the conversation in a manner intended to heighten the sexualized nature of the chats. He was eventually charged but argued that he was merely talking to her and did not actually set up any meeting with her. "Defendant engaged in highly sexualized online chats with a person whom he believed to be a 15-year-old girl. In doing so, he accosted, enticed, solicited, or encouraged a child to commit an immoral, grossly indecent, delinquent, or depraved act within the meaning of those terms in MCL 750.145a." *People v. Kowalski*, 489 Mich. 488 (2011).

## Soliciting a Minor to Commit a Felony—MCL 750.157c

*A person 17 years of age or older who recruits, induces, solicits, or coerces a minor less than 17 years of age to commit or attempt to commit an act that would be a felony if committed by an adult is guilty of a felony and shall be punished by imprisonment for not more than the maximum term of imprisonment authorized by law for that act. The person may also be punished by a fine of not more than 3 times the amount of the fine authorized by law for that act.*

The defendant recruited a 15-year-old boy to help him kill and rape young children by offering the boy alcohol and cigarettes. This section applied even though the minor never planned to actually commit the act. *People v. Pfaffle*, 246 Mich. App. 282 (2001).

## Child Sexually Abusive Material—MCL 750.145c
## DEFINITIONS

*Access:* Intentionally cause to be viewed by or transmitted to a person.

*Appears to include a child:* The depiction appears to include, or conveys the impression that it includes, a person who is less than 18 years of age, and the depiction meets either of the following conditions:

- It was created using a depiction of any part of an actual person under the age of 18.
- It was not created using a depiction of any part of an actual person under the age of 18, but all of the following apply to that depiction:
- The average individual, applying contemporary community standards, would find the depiction, taken as a whole, appeals to the prurient interest.
- The reasonable person would find the depiction, taken as a whole, lacks serious literary, artistic, political, or scientific value.
- The depiction depicts or describes a listed sexual act in a patently offensive way.

*Child:* A person less than 18 years old who is not emancipated.

*Child sexually abusive material:* Any depiction, whether made or produced by electronic, mechanical, or other means, including a developed or undeveloped photograph, picture, film, slide, video, electronic visual image, computer diskette, computer or computer-generated image, or picture, or sound recording which is of a child or appears to include a child engaging in a listed sexual act; a book, magazine, computer, computer storage device, or other visual or print or printable medium containing such a photograph, picture, film, slide, video, electronic visual image, computer, or computer-generated image, or picture, or sound recording; or any reproduction, copy, or print of such a photograph, picture, film, slide, video, electronic visual image, book, magazine, computer, or computer-generated image, or picture, other visual or print or printable medium, or sound recording.

*Child sexually abusive activity:* Child engaged in a listed sexual act.

*Commercial film or photographic print processor:* A person or his or her employee who, for compensation, develops exposed photographic film into movie films, negatives, slides, or prints; makes prints from negatives or slides; or duplicates movie films or videotapes.

*Contemporary community standards:* The customary limits of candor and decency in this state at or near the time of the alleged violation of this section.

*Erotic fondling:* Touching a person's clothed or unclothed genitals, pubic area, buttocks, or, if the person is female, breasts, or if the person is a child, the developing or undeveloped breast area, for the purpose of real or simulated overt sexual gratification or stimulation of one or more of the persons involved. Erotic fondling does not include physical contact, even if affectionate, that is not for the purpose of real or simulated overt sexual gratification or stimulation of one or more of the persons involved.

*Erotic nudity:* The lascivious exhibition of the genital, pubic, or rectal area of any person. As used in this subdivision, "lascivious" means wanton, lewd, and lustful and tending to produce voluptuous or lewd emotions.

***Listed sexual act:*** Sexual intercourse, erotic fondling, sadomasochistic abuse, masturbation, passive sexual involvement, sexual excitement, or erotic nudity.

***Make:*** To bring into existence by copying, shaping, changing, or combining material, and specifically includes, but is not limited to, intentionally creating a reproduction, copy, or print of child sexually abusive material, in whole or part. Make does not include the creation of an identical reproduction or copy of child sexually abusive material within the same digital storage device or the same piece of digital storage media.

***Masturbation:*** The real or simulated touching, rubbing, or otherwise stimulating of a person's own clothed or unclothed genitals, pubic area, buttocks, or, if the person is female, breasts, or if the person is a child, the developing or undeveloped breast area, either by manual manipulation or self-induced or with an artificial instrument, for the purpose of real or simulated overt sexual gratification or arousal of the person.

***Passive sexual involvement:*** An act, real or simulated, that exposes another person to or draws another person's attention to an act of sexual intercourse, erotic fondling, sadomasochistic abuse, masturbation, sexual excitement, or erotic nudity because of viewing any of these acts or because of the proximity of the act to that person, for the purpose of real or simulated overt sexual gratification or stimulation of one or more of the persons involved.

***Prurient interest:*** A shameful or morbid interest in nudity, sex, or excretion.

***Sadomasochistic abuse:*** Abuse that is either of the following:

- Flagellation or torture, real or simulated, for the purpose of real or simulated sexual stimulation or gratification, by or upon a person.
- The condition, real or simulated, of being fettered, bound, or otherwise physically restrained for sexual stimulation or gratification of a person.

***Sexual excitement:*** The condition, real or simulated, of human male or female genitals in a state of real or simulated overt sexual stimulation or arousal.

***Sexual intercourse:*** Intercourse, real or simulated, whether genital-genital, oral-genital, anal-genital, or oral-anal, whether between persons of the same or opposite sex or between a human and an animal, or with an artificial genital.

## Producing Child Sexually Abusive Material—MCL 750.145c(2) (felony)

*The suspect does one of the following:*

- *Persuades, induces, entices, coerces, causes, or knowingly allows a child to engage in activity to produce child sexually abusive material.*
- *Arranges for, produces, makes, copies, reproduces or finances child sexually abusive material.*
- *Attempts, prepares, or conspires to arrange for, produce, make, copy, reproduce, or finance child sexually abusive material.*

The defendant advertised in a newspaper for models. The 17-year-old victim responded to the advertisement, and she and her father met with the defendant. The defendant requested, and the victim's father signed, a release stating, "I understand my daughter is under . . . 18 years of age and that my daughter will be performing nudity in an R- and X-rated capacity." The release also provided, "I also understand that my daughter has full permission to make her own decisions and will have our full support." The defendant subsequently began taking photographs of her—first clothed and then unclothed. The defendant also filmed the victim performing different sexual acts. The defendant was convicted of manufacturing child sexually abusive materials. He argued that the law was unconstitutional because it infringes on the right of consenting individuals to engage in recreational or expressive sexual intercourse. Also, since the father signed the form, the victim should be considered an emancipated adult. In its holding, the court stated, "We reject Defendant's argument that he could present enough evidence to convince a court that the child has been emancipated because the parents signed a release permitting her to engage in adult activities. In addition, we conclude that MCL 750.145c(2) is not unconstitutionally overbroad. MCL 750.145c does not impinge on any privacy interest because the statute does not criminalize consensual sexual activity engaged in by persons between 16 and 18 years of age, but only criminalizes the recording and photographing of such activity." *People v. Roberts*, 292 Mich. App. 492 (2011).

For the purposes of MCL 750.145c(2), copying child pornography from the Internet onto a CD is not producing child sexually abusive material if the copies are "for personal use only." It is, however, possession of child sexually abusive material as prohibited by MCL 750.145c(4). *People v. Hill*, 486 Mich. 658 (2010).

The defendant was convicted of producing child sexually abusive material for videotaping a 3-year-old girl performing fellatio on a 1-year-old boy. The court held that an intent to distribute is not required by the statute. *People v. Hack*, 219 Mich. App. 299 (1996).

A person may be convicted of producing child sexually abusive material when a recording of otherwise ordinary nudity is edited to focus on, slow down, and replay a child's innocent exposure of the genitals. This turns the innocent nudity not done at the request of the defendant into erotic nudity prohibited by the statute. *People v. Riggs*, 237 Mich. App. 584 (1999).

A defendant may be found guilty under this section for attempted arrangement of sexually abusive activities with a child for engaging a perceived child in sexually explicit conversations on the Internet and attempting to set up a meeting for sexual activities even though the perceived child was in actuality an adult. The court did not believe that it is legally significant that "Bekka" was an adult rather than a child in determining whether the defendant made preparations to engage in child sexually abusive activity. It does not change the fact that the defendant was endeavoring to find a child, to entice a child to engage in sexual activity, or to arrange to meet a child for sexual activity. *People v. Thousand*, 241 Mich. App. 102 (2000).

A defendant may be arrested and tried in Michigan for attempted arrangement of sexually abusive activities with a child for meeting or attempting to meet a child for a sexually abusive activity in Michigan even though the communication and arrangements for the meeting took place wholly outside of the state. MCL 762.2(2)(a) provides that Michigan has jurisdiction over any crime in which any act constituting an element of the crime is committed within Michigan. *People v. Aspy*, 292 Mich. App. 36 (2011).

Counts of sexually abusive material may be based on each picture taken. *People v. Harmon*, 248 Mich. App. 522 (2001).

Although the age of consent in Michigan is 16 years old, under MCL 750.145c(2) no person under 18 years old may consent to the production of child sexually abusive material. Therefore, consent by the child is not a valid defense to producing sexually abusive material. *People v. Wilkens*, 267 Mich. App. 728 (2005).

## Distribute or Promote Child Sexually Abusive Material—MCL 750.145c(3) (felony)

The suspect does one of the following:

- Distributes, promotes, or finances the distribution or promotion of child sexually abusive material or activity.
- Receives for the purpose of distributing or promoting child sexually abusive material.
- Conspires, attempts, or prepares to distribute, receive, finance, or promote child sexually abusive material or activity.

To "distribute" requires criminal intent to disseminate child sexually abusive material to others. *People v. Tombs*, 472 Mich. 446 (2005).

This section does not apply to parents or guardians who distribute explicit material to their child or ward unless the dissemination was for the sexual gratification of the parent or guardian.

## Possession of Child Sexually Abusive Material—MCL 750.145c(4) (felony)

The suspect knowingly possessed or sought and accessed child sexually abusive material. This applies to a person who knows, has reason to know, or should reasonably be expected to know the child is a child, or that person has not taken reasonable precautions to determine the age of the child.

This section does not apply to:

- A police officer acting within the scope of his or her duties.
- An employee or contract agent of the department of social services acting within the scope of his or her duties.
- A judicial officer or judicial employee acting within the scope of his or her duties.
- A party or witness in a criminal or civil proceeding acting within the scope of that criminal or civil proceeding.
- A physician, psychologist, limited license psychologist, professional counselor, or registered nurse licensed under the public health code, acting within the scope of practice for which he or she is licensed.
- A social worker registered in this state acting within the scope of practice for which he or she is registered.
- A commercial film or photographic print processor or computer technician acting within the scope of his or her professional capacity or employment.

The defendant intentionally accessed and purposely viewed depictions of child sexually abusive material on the Internet. The only child sexually abusive material later found on his computers, however, had been automatically stored in temporary Internet files. The defendant contended that based on this location, he did not knowingly "possess" child sexually abusive material. The court held that the term "possess" under MCL 750.145c(4) includes both actual and constructive possession. The evidence presented at the preliminary examinations established that the defendant did more than passively view child sexually abusive material on the Internet. When any depiction of child sexually abusive material was displayed on the defendant's computer screen, he knowingly had the power and the intention to exercise dominion or control over that depiction. As a result, he constructively possessed those images, which amounts to possession of child sexually abusive material. *People v. Flick*, 487 Mich. 1 (2010).

## Film Developers/Computer Technicians

If a commercial film or photographic print processor or computer technician reports to the local prosecuting attorney his or her knowledge or observation, within the scope of his or her professional capacity or employment, of a film, photograph, movie film, videotape, negative, or slide depicting a person that the processor has reason to know or reason to believe is a child engaged in a listed sexual act; furnishes a copy of the film, photograph, movie film, videotape, negative, or slide to the prosecuting attorney; or keeps the film, photograph, movie film, videotape, negative, or slide according to the prosecuting attorney's instructions, both of the following shall apply:

- The identity of the processor shall be confidential, subject to disclosure only with his or her consent or by judicial process.
- If the processor acted in good faith, he or she shall be immune from civil liability that might otherwise be incurred by his or her actions. This immunity extends only to acts described in this subsection.

The prosecutor must prove that the defendant knew or should have known the pictures were those of children under 18 years old. Expert testimony may be used but is not required if other evidence exists. *People v. Girard*, 269 Mich. App. 15 (2005).

# DOMESTIC VIOLENCE

## ARREST POWERS

### General Arrest Powers: Non-Domestic Relationship Incident

In non-domestic cases, a police officer's authority to make an arrest is governed by the general laws of arrest. Typically, that authority is limited to the following circumstances:

- Pursuant to a warrant.
- Violation of parole or probation.
- For a felony or misdemeanor punishable in excess of 92 days, officers may arrest either on probable cause or if the offense is witnessed by an officer.
- For other misdemeanors, the offense generally must be committed in the officer's presence.

For more information about an officer's general arrest authority, see Chapter 19.

### Domestic Violence Arrest Powers—MCL 764.15a

MCL 764.15a authorizes a peace officer to make an arrest if he or she has reasonable cause to believe, or receives positive information that another officer has reasonable cause to believe, both of the following:

1. An assault, assault and battery, or aggravated assault has taken place or is taking place.

2. The individual being arrested:
   a. Is a spouse or former spouse of the victim,
   b. Resides or has resided in the same household as the victim,
   c. Has a child in common with the victim, or
   d. Has or has had a dating relationship with the victim.

A "*dating relationship*" means frequent, intimate association primarily characterized by the expectation of affectional involvement. It does not include a casual relationship or an ordinary fraternization between two individuals in a business or social context.

The officer may make this arrest *without a warrant*, regardless of whether the offense was committed in the officer's presence. Officers should not arrest an individual if the officer has reasonable cause to believe the individual was acting in *lawful self-defense* or in the defense of another.

If an arrest is made, the officer may become the complainant under MCL 764.1a, which allows a magistrate to accept complaints of assault, assault and battery, or aggravated assault on a domestic victim where the complaint is signed based on information and belief by individuals other than the victim. The magistrate shall not refuse to accept a complaint on the grounds that the complaint is signed upon information and belief by an individual other than the victim.

A peace officer may make a warrantless arrest for a misdemeanor of assault or assault and battery committed outside of the officer's presence, *in the absence of physical evidence of domestic abuse,* when there is other corroborating evidence sufficient to constitute probable cause to believe that the person to be arrested committed the offense. OAG 1993–1994, No. 6,822, p. 201 (November 23, 1994).

## Domestic Violence Can Be Accomplished With Words Alone.

The Legislature has clearly defined "domestic violence" to include several enumerated acts that can be readily accomplished by words alone. These acts include causing or attempting to cause "mental harm" to a family or household member, placing such person in "fear of mental harm," or engaging in any act toward such person that would cause a reasonable person to feel frightened, intimidated, or threatened. Causing a family or household member to fear harm or to feel frightened, intimidated, or threatened may be accomplished by words alone. OAG, 2002, No. 7,114 (July 26, 2002).

# INTERIM BOND—MCL 780.582a

A person arrested for domestic violence shall not be released on an interim bond or on his or her own recognizance until he or she can be arraigned or have interim bond set by a judge or district court magistrate.

# SUBSTANTIVE CRIMES ASSOCIATED WITH DOMESTIC VIOLENCE

## Stalking

There have been a number of studies done on the relationship between stalking and domestic violence which tend to indicate the following:

- The largest category of stalking cases involves current or former intimate partners.
- There is often a history of physical violence, sexual violence, and controlling behavior in cases of intimate partner stalking.
- The majority of intimate partner stalking victims report that the stalking began during the relationship and increased during periods of separation.

See Chapter 9 for a more detailed discussion of the following stalking offenses:

## Misdemeanor Stalking—MCL 750.411h (1–year misdemeanor)

Penalties:

| First offense | 1-year misdemeanor |
|---|---|
| Victim less than 18, defendant 5 or more years older than victim | 5-year felony |

## Aggravated Stalking—MCL 750.411i (felony)

| First offense | 5-year felony |
|---|---|
| Victim less than 18, defendant 5 or more years older than victim | 10-year felony |

## Assault and Battery—MCL 750.81 (domestic relationship victim)

The suspect assaults or assaults and batters an individual who:

- Is a spouse or former spouse,
- Resides or has resided in the same household as the suspect,
- Has a child in common with the suspect, or
- Has or has had a dating relationship with the suspect.

Penalties:

| First offense | 93-day misdemeanor |
|---|---|
| One prior conviction | 1-year misdemeanor |
| Two or more prior convictions | 5-year felony |

## Aggravated Assault—MCL 750.81a (domestic relationship victim)

Assault or assault and battery of an individual, without a weapon, which inflicts a serious or aggravated injury without intending to commit murder or inflict great bodily harm less than murder, when the victim:

- Is a spouse or former spouse,
- Resides or has resided in the same household as the suspect,
- Has a child in common with the suspect, or
- Has or has had a dating relationship with the suspect.

Penalties:

| First offense | 1-year misdemeanor |
|---|---|
| Previous conviction of domestic violence | 5-year felony |

The following laws are also commonly associated with domestic violence cases. See the appropriate chapter for a more detailed discussion of these laws.

**Felonious Assault (MCL 750.82). Chapter 4.**

**Assault with Intent to Do Great Bodily Harm Less than Murder (MCL 750.84). Chapter 4.**

**Assault with Intent to Commit Murder (MCL 750.83). Chapter 4.**

**Child Abuse (MCL 750.136b). Chapter 4.**

**Criminal Sexual Conduct (MCL 750.520b-g). Chapter 6.**

**Kidnapping (MCL 750.349). Chapter 7.**

**Parental Kidnapping (MCL 750.350a). Chapter 7.**

**Malicious Destruction of Property (MCL 750.377a). Chapter 10.**

**Breaking & Entering, Home Invasion (MCL 750.110a). Chapter 11.**

**Entering without Permission (MCL 750.115). Chapter 11.**

**Cruelty to Animals (MCL 750.50). Chapter 18.**

**Local Ordinances**

# MICHIGAN PERSONAL PROTECTION ORDERS (PPO)—MCL 600.2950 AND 764.15b

A PPO is an injunctive order issued by the Circuit Court or the Family Division of Circuit Court restraining or enjoining activity and individuals from certain conduct. The two types of PPOs issued by circuit courts are:

- Domestic Relationship PPO.
- Non-domestic Stalking PPO.

While at a hockey game, the victim was physically assaulted by another man who also threatened to kill him. The victim sought and obtained a stalking PPO against his attacker based on this one incident. The Court of Appeals terminated the PPO because for stalking the pattern of conduct must consist of two or more separate, noncontinuous acts evincing a continuity of purpose. *Pobursky v. Gee,* 249 Mich. App. 44 (2001).

A person may seek to obtain a Domestic Relations PPO for the following relationships:

- A spouse or former spouse.
- An individual with whom he or she has had a child in common.
- An individual residing or having resided in the same household.
- An individual with whom he or she has or has had a dating relationship.

A "*dating relationship*" means frequent, intimate associations primarily characterized by the expectation of affectional involvement. This term does not include a casual relationship or an ordinary fraternization between two individuals in a business or social context.

### Enforcement of PPO

A PPO is immediately enforceable anywhere in Michigan by any law enforcement agency or officer if the officer:

- Has received a true copy of the order,
- Is shown a true copy of the order (the victim may have a copy), or
- Has verified its existence in LEIN.

If an officer arrives at the scene of a call and the individual restrained or enjoined has been served the PPO prior to the officer's arrival and the individual is currently violating the PPO in the presence of the officer, the officer shall verify that the PPO is still valid. If the PPO is valid and LEIN verifies that the individual has received notice of the PPO, the officer may immediately arrest the individual who has been enjoined or restrained.

To show actual knowledge of PPO by the defendant, the prosecutor need not show actual service, but may show it by the defendant's statements concerning evasion of service and conversations with the victim. *People v. Threatt,* 254 Mich. App. 504 (2002).

## Serving a PPO

A law enforcement officer or court clerk may serve a PPO at any time (e.g., traffic stops). The officer does need to file proof of oral service with the court issuing the order.

If an officer arrives at the scene of a call and the individual restrained or enjoined *has not been served the* PPO, the law enforcement agency or officer responding to a call alleging a violation of a PPO shall:

- Serve the individual restrained or enjoined with a true copy of the PPO; or advise the individual restrained or enjoined about the existence of the PPO, *the specific conduct enjoined*, the penalties for violating the PPO, and where the individual restrained or enjoined may obtain a copy of the order.
- If the individual has not received prior notice of the PPO, the individual shall be given a reasonable opportunity to comply with the PPO before the law enforcement officer makes a custodial arrest for a violation of the PPO. Failure to immediately comply is grounds for custodial arrest.
- Immediately enter or cause to be entered into LEIN that the individual restrained or enjoined has actual notice of the PPO.
- File proof of service or proof of oral notice with the clerk of court issuing the PPO.

## Arrest

For an arrest, the PPO must state on its face that a violation subjects the individual to immediate arrest and criminal contempt of court and, if found guilty, imprisonment for not more than 93 days or a fine of not more than $500. A police officer may arrest and take a person into custody when the officer has reasonable cause to believe that a valid PPO has been violated. A juvenile may be taken into custody without a court order upon reasonable cause to believe the minor is violating or has violated a PPO. An arrest can be made when:

- The PPO has been issued by a circuit court.
- The individual named in the PPO is violating or has violated the order. An individual is violating or has violated the order if that individual commits one or more of the following acts *and* the order specifically restrains or enjoins the individual from:
    - Entering onto premises.
    - Assaulting, attacking, beating, molesting, or wounding a named individual.
    - Threatening to kill or physically injure a named individual.
    - Removing minor children from the individual having legal custody of the children,

except as otherwise authorized by a custody order or parenting time order issued by a court of competent jurisdiction.
    - Purchasing or possessing a firearm.
    - Interfering with the petitioner's efforts to remove the petitioner's children or personal property from premises that are solely owned or leased by the individual to be restrained or enjoined.
    - Interfering with the petitioner at the petitioner's place of employment or education or engaging in conduct that impairs the petitioner's employment or educational relationship or environment.
    - Having access to information in records concerning a minor child of both the petitioner and the respondent that will inform the respondent about the address or telephone number of the petitioner and the petitioner's minor child or about the petitioner's employment address.
    - Engaging in conduct that is prohibited under the stalking statutes, MCL 750.411h and 750.411i.

- Any other specific act or conduct that imposes upon or interferes with personal liberty or that causes a reasonable apprehension of violence.

## Bond/Court Appearance

A person arrested for violation of a PPO *shall not* be released on interim bond. The person must be brought before the circuit court within 24 hours of arrest. The circuit court where the violation occurred has primary jurisdiction. If the circuit court is not available, the person arrested shall be brought before the district court.

# FOREIGN PROTECTION ORDER (FPO)—MCL 600.2950h–m

An FPO is an injunction or other court order issued by a court of another state, Indian tribe, or United States Territory; it does not include foreign countries.

The order's purpose must be to prevent a person's violent or threatening acts against, harassment of, contact with, communication with, or physical proximity to another person.

The order must be issued against a spouse or intimate partner. A spouse or intimate partner includes:

- A spouse.
- A former spouse.
- A person with whom the petitioner has had a child in common.

- A person residing or having resided in the same household as the petitioner.
- A person with whom the petitioner has or has had a dating relationship.

The order may be a temporary or final order, and the order may be issued by a civil or criminal court.

- A civil FPO must be issued in response to a pleading filed or on behalf of the person seeking protection; mutual orders are not permitted.
- A criminal FPO may be either a conditional release order or a probation order.

A support or child custody order issued under divorce or custody laws is not an FPO.

## Enforcement of FPO

### Mutual Orders—MCL 600.2950k

An FPO that includes language restraining both the petitioner and the respondent is:

- Enforceable against the respondent.
- Enforceable against the petitioner *only* if all of the following are present:
  - The respondent filed a cross or counter petition.
  - The court made specific findings against the respondent.
  - The court determined that the respondent was entitled to relief.

### Enforce All Provisions—MCL 600.2950j

The provisions of an FPO are enforceable even if they would not be available under Michigan law. This includes child custody or support provisions that are part of an FPO.

### Copy of Order Available—MCL 600.2950l

An officer may rely upon a copy of an FPO received from any source if the FPO appears to contain all of the following:

- The names of the parties.
- The date the protection order was issued, which is prior to the date when enforcement is sought.
- The terms and conditions against respondent.
- The name of the issuing court.
- The signature of or on behalf of a judicial officer.
- No obvious indication that the order is invalid, such as an expiration date that is before the date enforcement is sought.

If a copy of an FPO cannot be verified on LEIN or the NCIC national protection order file, lack of verification is not grounds for an officer to refuse to enforce the terms of the order. An officer may rely on the statement of the petitioner that the FPO remains in effect and may rely on the statement of the petitioner or respondent that the respondent has received notice of the order.

### Copy of Order Not Available; Attempt to Verify—MCL 600.2950l

If a copy of an FPO is not available, the officer must attempt to verify the order through LEIN, the NCIC protection order file, administrative messaging, by contacting the court that issued the FPO, by contacting the law enforcement agency in the issuing jurisdiction, by contacting the issuing jurisdiction's protection order registry, or by any other method the officer believes to be reliable. The officer must verify the existence of the order and:

- The names of the parties.
- The date the foreign protection order was issued, which is prior to the date when enforcement is sought.
- Terms and conditions against the respondent.
- The name of the issuing court.
- No obvious indication that the foreign protection order is invalid, such as an expiration date that is before the date enforcement is sought.

If an officer verifies an FPO through this procedure, the FPO is enforceable.

### No Copy of the Order and No Verification—MCL 600.2950l

If the officer is not shown a copy of the order and cannot verify the order through other means, the officer shall maintain the peace and take appropriate action with regard to any violation of criminal law.

### No Notice of Order—MCL 600.2950l

If there is no evidence that the respondent has been served with or received notice of the FPO, the law enforcement officer shall:

- Serve the respondent with a copy of the FPO if a copy is available.
- If a copy is not available, advise the respondent of the following:
  - The existence of the FPO.
  - The name of the issuing court.
  - The specific conduct enjoined.
  - The penalties for violating the order in Michigan.
  - The penalties for violating the order in the issuing jurisdiction if the officer is aware of those penalties.

If there is no evidence that the respondent has received notice of the FPO:

- The respondent shall be given an opportunity to comply before the officer makes a custodial arrest for violation of the order.
- Failure to comply immediately with the FPO is grounds for an immediate custodial arrest.

### Proof of Service or Oral Notice—MCL 600.2950l

If the officer serves or provides oral notice of an FPO, the officer shall:

- Provide the petitioner with proof of service or proof of oral notice.
- Provide the issuing court with a proof of service or proof of oral notice, if the address of the issuing court is apparent on the face of the FPO or otherwise is readily available to the officer.
- If the FPO is entered into LEIN or the NCIC protection order file, provide that entity or the entering agency with a proof of service or proof of oral notice.

### Other Enforcement Procedures; Civil FPO—MCL 600.2950l

A violation of a civil FPO is criminal contempt of court and the other enforcement procedures related to arrest, bond, court appearances, domestic violence reports, and fingerprinting are the same as for a Michigan PPO.

### Other Enforcement Procedures, Criminal FPO—MCL 600.2950m; MCL 764.15

A violation of a criminal FPO (conditional release order or probation order) is a 93-day misdemeanor and may be enforced by:

- Warrantless arrest and a criminal prosecution, or
- Warrantless arrest and extradition.

Officers must complete a domestic violence report for a violation of a criminal FPO. (See section on report requirements.)

### Good Faith Immunity for Enforcement of FPO—MCL 600.2950l(10)

A law enforcement officer, prosecutor, or court personnel who acts in good faith while enforcing an FPO is immune from civil and criminal liability in any action arising from the enforcement of the FPO.

# AUTHORITY OF LAW ENFORCEMENT TO ENTER SCENE OF DOMESTIC VIOLENCE
## Consent

Consent must be freely and intelligently given without any duress or coercion on the part of the police. *People v. Malone,* 180 Mich. App. 347 (1989).

Consent to search may be revoked at any time; however, revocation of consent to search does not invalidate search conducted before the revocation. *People v. Powell,* 199 Mich. App. 492 (1993).

A person must have actual or apparent authority over premises to give consent. With apparent authority, police may rely in good faith on the apparent capability of an individual to consent to a search. *Illinois v. Rodriguez,* 497 U.S. 177 (1990).

Consent by a third person is allowed where there is equal right to possession or control over the premises. *People v. Barbat,* 49 Mich. App. 519 (1973).

When the prosecution relies on consent to justify a search, it has the burden of proving that the person who gave the consent was authorized to do so and did so freely and voluntarily. *People v. Wagner,* 104 Mich. App. 169, (1981).

## Emergency Circumstances

Police may enter a dwelling without a warrant when they reasonably believe that a person within is in need of immediate aid. The police must possess specific and articulable facts that lead to this conclusion and limit their entry to the reason for justification. Police must do only that which is reasonably necessary to determine if a person is in need of assistance and render that assistance. *People v. Davis,* 442 Mich. 1 (1993).

A police officer may enter a dwelling without a warrant where it is reasonably believed that a person inside is in need of medical assistance. The entry must be limited to the reason for its justification. The officer must be motivated primarily by a perceived need to render assistance and may do no more than is reasonably necessary to determine whether assistance is required and render it. Once lawfully inside the residence, the officer may make an arrest without a warrant that is authorized by law, and, absent a reason for exclusion, evidence obtained is admissible. *City of Troy v. Ohlinger,* 438 Mich. 477 (1991).

# VICTIM'S RIGHTS—MCL 764.15c

After intervening in a domestic violence dispute, the peace officer shall provide the following written information to the victim:

- The name and telephone number of the responding police agency.
- The name and badge number of the responding officer.
- The following statement:
  "You may obtain a copy of the police incident report for your case by contacting this law enforcement agency at the telephone number provided.

  The domestic violence shelter program and other resources in your area are (include local information).

  Information about emergency shelter, counseling services, and the legal rights of domestic violence victims is available from these resources.

  Your legal rights include the right to go to court and file a petition requesting a personal protection order to protect you or other members of your household from domestic abuse, which could include restraining or enjoining the abuser from doing the following:

  (a) Entering onto premises.
  (b) Assaulting, attacking, beating, molesting, or wounding you.
  (c) Threatening to kill or physically injure you or another person.
  (d) Removing minor children from you, except as otherwise authorized by a custody or parenting time order issued by a court of competent jurisdiction.
  (e) Engaging in stalking behavior.
  (f) Purchasing or possessing a firearm.
  (g) Interfering with your efforts to remove your children or personal property from premises that are solely owned or leased by the abuser.
  (h) Interfering with you at your place of employment or education or engaging in conduct that impairs your employment relationship or your employment or educational environment.
  (i) Engaging in any other specific act or conduct that imposes upon or interferes with your personal liberty or that causes a reasonable apprehension of violence.
  (j) Having access to information in records concerning any minor child you have with the abuser that would inform the abuser about your address or telephone number, the child's address or telephone number, or your employment address.

  Your legal rights also include the right to go to court and file a motion for an order to show cause and a hearing if the abuser is violating or has violated a personal protection order and has not been arrested."

# PREPARING A DOMESTIC VIOLENCE REPORT

## Report Requirements—MCL 764.15c

- Officers shall prepare a domestic violence report after investigating or intervening at a domestic violence scene. The intervention or investigation is the trigger for the report, and it does not require an arrest.
- Officers shall use the standard domestic violence incident form or a form substantially similar to that standard form to report a domestic violence incident.
- The report must be filed with the prosecuting attorney within 48 hours after the incident is reported to police.
- The report shall contain the following:

  - Address, date, and time of incident.
  - VICTIM'S name, address, home and work telephone numbers, race, sex, and date of birth.
  - SUSPECT'S name, address, home and work telephone numbers, race, sex, date of birth, and whether a PPO covering the suspect exists.
  - WITNESS'S name, address, home and work telephone numbers, race, sex, date of birth, and relationship to victim and/or suspect.
  - The name of the person WHO CALLED THE POLICE.
  - The RELATIONSHIP of the victim and suspect.
  - Whether ALCOHOL or CONTROLLED SUBSTANCE use was involved and by whom.
  - A NARRATIVE describing the incident and the circumstances that led to it.
  - Whether and how many times the suspect PHYSICALLY ASSAULTED the victim.
  - A description of any WEAPON or object used.

- A description of all INJURIES sustained by the victim and how they were sustained.
- Information concerning MEDICAL ATTENTION, if sought by the victim, including where and how transported, admission to a hospital or clinic and name and address of the attending physician.
- A description of any PROPERTY DAMAGE reported or evident at the scene.
- PREVIOUS DOMESTIC VIOLENCE between the victim and the suspect.
- The date and time of report, name, badge number, and signature of the officer completing the report.

## Liability

### 42 U.S.C. § 1983

For government officials to be liable for discretionary actions under section 1983, they must violate clearly established statutory or constitutional rights of which a reasonable person would have known. *Buckley v. Fitzsimmons*, 509 U.S. 259 (1993).

## State Tort Actions

Michigan has a public-duty doctrine. This doctrine gives police officers protection from public suit for duties owed to the public in general that are performed incompetently, negligently, or inadequately. Officers may still be criminally liable for improper performance of their duties. If a special relationship existed between the officer and the victim, the officer may be sued for damages in a tort action. A special relationship exists if:

- The police officer made assurances of protection or assumed, by his or her actions, the protection of the individual,
- The police officer knew that without his or her action, harm could come to the victim,
- The police officer was in direct contact with the victim, and
- The victim relied on the officer's assurances of protection.

*White v. Beasley*, 453 Mich. 308 (1996).

Public-duty doctrine protects only police officers. It does not extend to dispatchers or other government agents. *Beaudrie v. Henderson*, 465 Mich. 124 (2001).

© 2014, Shutterstock, Inc.

# SEX OFFENSES

## CRIMINAL SEXUAL CONDUCT

### Definitions—MCL 750.520a

***Sexual penetration:*** Sexual intercourse, cunnilingus, fellatio, anal intercourse, or any other intrusion, however slight, of any part of a person's body or of any object into the genital or anal opening of another person's body, but emission of semen is not required.

Penetration occurred where the defendant forced his finger into the vagina of his nine-year-old daughter through her underwear. *People v. Hammons*, 210 Mich. App. 554 (1995).

Each separate act of sexual penetration constitutes a separate act of CSC. *People v. Dowdy*, 148 Mich. App. 517 (1986).

According to the law, "penetration" is any intrusion, however slight, into the vagina or the labia majora. The victim testified that she and the defendant were attempting to have sexual intercourse and that the defendant's "private" was touching her "private." She testified that the defendant's "private" was touching where she would use tissue while wiping after urination and that she experienced pain going into her "private parts." When viewing the victim's testimony in the light most favorable to the prosecution,

the jury could have reasonably inferred that the defendant's penis intruded, however slightly, into the victim's vagina or labia majora. *People v. Lockett*, 295 Mich. App. 165 (2012).

***Sexual contact:*** Includes the intentional touching of the victim's or actor's intimate parts or the intentional touching of the clothing covering the immediate area of the victim's or actor's intimate parts, if that intentional touching can reasonably be construed as being for the purpose of sexual arousal or gratification, done for a sexual purpose, or in a sexual manner for: (i) revenge, (ii) to inflict humiliation, or (iii) out of anger.

***Intimate part:*** The primary genital area, groin, inner thigh, buttock, or breast of a human being.

***Personal injury:*** Bodily injury, disfigurement, mental anguish, chronic pain, pregnancy, disease, or loss or impairment of a sexual or reproductive organ.

Pregnancy and subsequent abortion are considered bodily injuries. *People v. Woods*, 204 Mich. App. 472 (1994).

Bodily injury includes a neck injury where a doctor testified that the neck was still tender several hours after the attack. *People v. Perry*, 172 Mich. App. 609 (1988).

*Mental anguish:* Extreme or excruciating pain, distress, or suffering of the mind that occurs either at the time of the incident or later as a result of the incident.

Mental anguish under the CSC statute may include threats of future harm and being forced to beg. *People v. Mackle*, 241 Mich. App. 583 (2000).

*Mentally incapable:* Person suffers from a mental disease or defect that renders that person temporarily or permanently incapable of appraising the nature of his or her conduct.

*Mentally incapacitated:* A person is temporarily incapable of appraising or controlling his or her conduct due to the influence of a narcotic anesthetic, or other substance administered to that person without his or her consent, or due to any other act committed upon that person without his or her consent.

*Mentally disabled:* Person who has mental illness, is mentally retarded, or has a developmental disability.

*Physically helpless:* Person was unconscious, asleep, or for any other reason was physically unable to communicate an unwillingness to act.

*Force or coercion:* The defendant either used physical force or did something to make the victim reasonably afraid of present or future danger, including, but not limited to, any of the following circumstances:

- When the actor overcomes the victim through the actual application of physical force or physical violence.
- When the actor coerces the victim to submit by threatening to use force or violence on the victim and the victim believes that the actor has the present ability to execute these threats.
- When the actor coerces the victim to submit by threatening to retaliate in the future against the victim, or any other person, and the victim believes that the actor has the ability to execute this threat. As used in this subdivision, "to retaliate" includes threats of physical punishment, kidnapping, or extortion.
- When the actor engages in the medical treatment or examination of the victim in a manner or for purposes which are medically recognized as unethical or unacceptable.
- When the actor, through concealment or by the element of surprise, is able to overcome the victim.

Coercion may be inferred from the totality of the circumstances even though the actions did not specifically match any statutory definition. Here, the defendant's repeated unconsented

touching of a 13-year-old girl in an isolated area 45 minutes from her home in an area where she knew no one, created in the victim a reasonable fear of dangerous consequences absent physical violence or verbal threat. *People v. McGill*, 131 Mich. App. 465 (1984).

Pinching the victim's buttocks satisfied the force element. *People v. Premo*, 213 Mich. App. 406 (1995).

Force or coercion under the CSC statute may occur where the suspect is disguised. *People v. Crippen*, 242 Mich. App. 278 (2000).

The prohibited "force" for CSC encompasses the use of force against a victim to either induce the victim to submit to sexual penetration or to seize control of the victim in a manner to facilitate the accomplishment of sexual penetration without regard to the victim's wishes. *People v. Carlson*, 466 Mich. 130 (2002).

The minor victim asked for soda. The defendant required the victim to perform oral sex on him and to allow him to anally penetrate her before she could have the soda. The victim testified that she believed sexual conduct would "happen whether I wanted it or not," which was reasonable in light of long history of the defendant's sexually abusing the victim and making her comply with his demands. The victim's testimony was sufficient to show that sexual penetration was by force or coercion, as required to support conviction for third-degree criminal sexual conduct. *People v. Eisen*, 296 Mich. App. 326 (2012).

Force or coercion may occur through the element of "surprise." In this case, the victim consented to digital penetration but said "no" to sexual intercourse. She was unaware that the defendant had removed his pants and was surprised when he penetrated her vagina with his penis. *People v. Phelps*, 288 Mich. App. 123 (2010).

Degrees of affinity:

| First degree | Parents and children |
|---|---|
| Second degree | Grandparents, brothers, sisters, grandchildren |
| Third degree | Great-grandparents, uncles, aunts, nephews, nieces, great-grandchildren |
| Fourth degree | Great-great-grandparents, Great-uncles, great-aunts, first cousins, grand-nephews, grand-nieces, great-great-grandchildren |

## First Degree—MCL 750.520b (felony)
### Elements
#### CSC First Degree—Person Under 13

1. The defendant engaged in sexual penetration, and
2. The victim is under age 13.

#### CSC First Degree—Relationship

1. The defendant engaged in sexual penetration, and
2. The victim was at least 13 but less than 16 years of age, and
3. One or more of the following:

   a. The defendant and victim were related by blood or affinity to the fourth degree.
   b. The defendant coerced the victim to submit by exerting his or her authoritative position.
   c. The defendant and victim were members of the same household.
   d. The defendant was a teacher, substitute teacher, or administrator of the school, school district, or intermediate school district where the victim was enrolled.
   e. The defendant was an employee, contractual service provider, non-student volunteer of, or an employee of the United States, the state, or a local unit of government who is assigned to provide services to the school, school district, or intermediate school district where the victim was enrolled and used his or her status to gain access to or establish a relationship with the victim.
   f. The defendant was an employee, a contractual service provider, or a volunteer of a child care organization or was a person licensed to operate a foster family home or foster family group home in which the victim was a resident and the sexual penetration occurred during the period of the victim's residency.

The suspect and victim were members of the same household where the victim lived with the suspect for four months, and the suspect was attempting to adopt the victim. *People v. Phillips*, 251 Mich. App. 100 (2002).

The defendant pled guilty to first-degree criminal sexual conduct under MCL 750.520b(1)(b)(ii) (victim and defendant related by blood or affinity to the fourth degree). The plea was conditioned on him being permitted to appeal that he was not related by blood or affinity and committed only third-degree criminal sexual conduct, MCL 750.520d(1)(a) (penetration with person at least 13 but less than 16 years of age). The defendant was born in 1977 during the marriage of Walter and Karen Zajaczkowski. Walter and Karen

divorced in 1979. The divorce judgment referred to the defendant as the minor child of the parties. In 1992, Walter had a child with another woman; that child was the victim in this case. In 2007, when the defendant was approximately 30 years old and the victim was 14 years old, the criminal sexual conduct occurred. Subsequent genetic testing indicated that Walter was not the defendant's biological father.

The elements of first-degree criminal sexual conduct under MCL 750.520b(1)(b)(ii) are (1) a sexual penetration, (2) a victim who is at least 13 but less than 16 years of age, and (3) a relationship by blood or affinity to the fourth degree between the victim and the defendant. In this case, the defendant did not dispute that the first two elements were met, and the prosecution conceded in the Court of Appeals that there was no evidence of a relationship by affinity between the victim and the defendant. A relationship by blood means a relationship between persons arising by descent from a common ancestor or a relationship by birth rather than marriage. The DNA evidence established that the victim's father was not the defendant's biological father. Accordingly, the defendant was not related to the victim by blood to the fourth degree and the prosecution could not establish the relationship element of the crime. *People v. Zajaczkowski*, 493 Mich. 6 (2012).

#### CSC First Degree—During a Felony

1. The defendant engaged in sexual penetration, and
2. The circumstances involved the commission of any other felony.

Production of sexually abusive material of persons under the age of 18 is a felony. Even though the victim could consent to sex acts as a 16-year-old, she could not consent to the underlying felony. Therefore, her consent to the sex acts was invalid, thus supporting the CSC I charges against the defendant. *People v. Wilkins*, 267 Mich. App. 728 (2005).

#### CSC First Degree—Accomplices

1. The defendant engaged in sexual penetration,
2. While aided or abetted by one or more other persons, and
3. Either of the following:

   a. Knows or had reason to know that the victim is mentally incapable, mentally incapacitated, or physically helpless.

b. Used force or coercion to accomplish the sexual penetration.

### CSC First Degree—Weapon Used

1. The defendant engaged in sexual penetration, and
2. Was armed with a weapon or any object used or fashioned in a manner to lead the victim to reasonably believe it to be a weapon.

### CSC First Degree—Personal Injury

1. The defendant engaged in sexual penetration,
2. While using force or coercion to accomplish sexual penetration, and
3. Caused personal injury to the victim.

A beating to the victim that causes personal injury prior to a series of sexual penetrations is sufficient to provide the force and personal injury to support CSC I charges for each penetration. *People v. Hunt*, 170 Mich. App. 1 (1988).

### CSC First Degree—Injury to Incapacitated Victim

1. The defendant engaged in sexual penetration,
2. While knowing or having reason to know that the victim is mentally incapable, mentally incapacitated, or physically helpless, and
3. Caused personal injury to the victim.

### CSC First Degree—Mentally Disabled+Relationship

1. The defendant engaged in sexual penetration,
2. When the victim is mentally incapable, mentally incapacitated, or physically helpless, and
3. Either of the following:

   a. The defendant and the victim were related by blood or affinity to the fourth degree.
   b. The defendant was in a position of authority over the victim and used this authority to coerce the victim to submit.

## Second Degree—MCL 750.520c (felony)

### Elements

### CSC Second Degree—Person Under 13

1. The defendant engaged in sexual contact, and
2. The victim is under age 13.

### CSC Second Degree—Relationship

1. The defendant engaged in sexual contact,
2. The victim was at least 13 but less than 16 years of age, and
3. One or more of the following:

   a. The defendant and victim were related by blood or affinity to the fourth degree.

b. The defendant coerced the victim to submit by exerting his or her authoritative position.
c. The defendant and victim were members of the same household.
d. The defendant was a teacher, substitute teacher, or administrator of the school, school district, or intermediate school district where the victim was enrolled.
e. The defendant was an employee, contractual service provider, non-student volunteer of, or an employee of the United States, the state, or a local unit of government who is assigned to provide services to the school, school district, or intermediate school district where the victim was enrolled and used his or her status to gain access to or establish a relationship with the victim.
f. The defendant was an employee, a contractual service provider, or a volunteer of a child care organization or was a person licensed to operate a foster family home or foster family group home in which the victim was a resident and the sexual penetration occurred during the period of the victim's residency.

A spiritual therapist who taught classes on spiritual healing in the home of another therapist was, for purposes of the statute, the teacher of the 14-year-old victim who attended the classes. This placed the defendant in a position of authority over the victim. A person need not teach in a traditional classroom setting for purposes of this statute. *People v. Knapp*, 244 Mich. App. 361 (2001).

### CSC Second Degree—During a Felony

1. The defendant engaged in sexual contact, and
2. The circumstances involved the commission of any other felony.

### CSC Second Degree—Accomplices

1. The defendant engaged in sexual contact,
2. While aided or abetted by one or more other persons, and
3. Either of the following:

   a. Knows or had reason to know that the victim is mentally incapable, mentally incapacitated, or physically helpless.
   b. Used force or coercion to accomplish the sexual contact.

### CSC Second Degree—Weapon Used

1. The defendant engaged in sexual contact, and
2. Was armed with a weapon or any object used or fashioned in a manner to lead the victim to reasonably believe it to be a weapon.

## CSC Second Degree—Personal Injury

1. The defendant engaged in contact,
2. While using force or coercion to accomplish sexual contact, and
3. Caused personal injury to the victim.

## CSC Second Degree—Injury to Incapacitated Victim

1. The defendant engaged in sexual contact,
2. While knowing or having reason to know that the victim is mentally incapable, mentally incapacitated, or physically helpless, and
3. Caused personal injury to the victim.

## CSC Second Degree—Mentally Disabled–Relationship

1. The defendant engaged in sexual contact,
2. When the victim is mentally incapable, mentally incapacitated, or physically helpless, and
3. Either of the following:

   a. The defendant and the victim were related by blood or affinity to the fourth degree.

   b. The defendant was in a position of authority over the victim and used this authority to coerce the victim to submit.

## CSC Second Degree—State Prisoner

1. The defendant engaged in sexual contact,
2. When the victim is under the jurisdiction of the department of corrections, and
3. The defendant is an employee, contractual employee, or a volunteer with the department of corrections who knows that the victim is under the jurisdiction of the department of corrections.

## CSC Second Degree—State Prisoner in Private Youth Facility

1. The defendant engaged in sexual contact,
2. When the victim is under the jurisdiction of the department of corrections, and
3. The defendant is an employee, contractual employee, or a volunteer with a private vendor that operates a youth correctional facility who knows that the victim is under the jurisdiction of the department of corrections.

## CSC Second Degree—County Prisoner

1. The defendant engaged in sexual contact,
2. When the victim is a prisoner or probationer under the jurisdiction of a county for purposes of imprisonment or a work program or other probationary program, and
3. The defendant is an employee, contractual employee, or a volunteer with the county or department of corrections who knows that the victim is under the county's jurisdiction.

## CSC Second Degree—Detained Juvenile

1. The defendant engaged in sexual contact,
2. When the defendant knows or has reason to know that a court has detained the victim in a facility while the victim is awaiting a trial or hearing or committed the victim to a facility as a result of the victim having been found responsible for committing an act that would be a crime if committed by an adult, and
3. The defendant is an employee, contractual employee, or a volunteer with the facility in which the victim is detained or to which the victim was committed.

## CSC Second Degree—Person under 13, Defendant 17 years of age or older

1. The defendant engaged in sexual contact,
2. When the victim is under age 13, and
3. The defendant is 17 years of age or older.

# Third Degree—MCL 750.520d (felony)

## Elements

### CSC Third Degree—Person 13 through 15

1. The defendant engaged in sexual penetration, and
2. The victim was at least 13 years of age and under 16 years of age.

### CSC Third Degree—Force or Coercion

1. The defendant engaged in sexual penetration, and
2. Was using force or coercion to accomplish the sexual penetration.

### CSC Third Degree—Incapacitated Victim

1. The defendant engaged in sexual penetration, and
2. Knew or had reason to know that the victim is mentally incapable, mentally incapacitated, or physically helpless.

### CSC Third Degree—Incest

1. The defendant engaged in sexual penetration, and
2. The defendant and victim were related by blood or affinity to the third degree. This subdivision does not apply if both persons are lawfully married to each other at the time of the alleged violation.

The term "affinity" includes the relationship between a stepbrother and stepsister. *People v. Armstrong*, 212 Mich. App. 121 (1995).

The term "affinity" includes the relationship between a stepfather and stepdaughter. *People v. Goold*, 241 Mich. App. 333 (2000).

## CSC Third Degree—Student

1. The defendant engaged in sexual penetration,
2. The victim was at least 16 years of age but less than 18 years of age,
3. The victim was a student at a public or non-public school, and
4. Either of the following:

   a. The defendant was a teacher, substitute teacher, or administrator of that public school, nonpublic school, school district, or intermediate school district. This subdivision does not apply if the victim is emancipated or if both persons are lawfully married to each other at the time of the alleged violation.

   b. The defendant was an employee or a contractual service provider of the public school, nonpublic school, school district, or intermediate school district in which the victim is enrolled, is a volunteer who is not a student in any public school or nonpublic school, or is an employee of this state or of a local unit of government of this state or of the United States assigned to provide any service to that public school, nonpublic school, school district, or intermediate school district, and the defendant uses his or her employee, contractual, or volunteer status to gain access to or to establish a relationship with the victim.

In the summer of 2010, the complainants alleged that they engaged in sexual acts with the defendant, an alleged substitute teacher in their school district. The trial judge dismissed the charges because the acts did not occur during the school year. The Court of Appeals reversed, holding "Based on the record presented, there may be evidence that defendant acted as a substitute teacher in the public school district in which the complainants were students between the ages of 16 and 18 during the previous school year. The testimony reflected that defendant served as a 'long term' substitute for the students' British Literature class. . . . Although we conclude that the plain language of the statute includes prosecution of a substitute teacher for acts that occur during the summer, we also note that a construction to the contrary, i.e. one that allows for sexual penetration to occur between relevant-age students and substitute teachers after hours, on weekends, or during the summer, leads to absurd results. . . . Accordingly, the trial court erred by dismissing the charges against defendant." *People v. Lewis*, 302 Mich. App. 338 (2013).

## CSC Third Degree—Special Education Student

1. The defendant engaged in sexual penetration,
2. The victim was at least 16 years of age but less than 26 years of age, and
3. The victim is receiving special education services, and
4. Either of the following:

   a. The defendant was a teacher, substitute teacher, or administrator of that public school, nonpublic school, school district, or intermediate school district. This subdivision does not apply if the victim is emancipated or if both persons are lawfully married to each other at the time of the alleged violation.

   b. The defendant was an employee or a contractual service provider of the public school, nonpublic school, school district, or intermediate school district in which the victim is enrolled, or is a volunteer who is not a student in any public school or nonpublic school, or is an employee of this state or of a local unit of government of this state or of the United States assigned to provide any service to that public school, nonpublic school, school district, or intermediate school district, and the defendant uses his or her employee, contractual, or volunteer status to gain access to or to establish a relationship with the victim.

## CSC Third Degree—Foster Care

1. The defendant engaged in sexual penetration,
2. The victim was at least 16 years of age, and
3. The defendant was an employee, a contractual service provider, or a volunteer of a child care organization or was a person licensed to operate a foster family home or foster family group home in which the victim was a resident and the sexual penetration occurred during the period of the victim's residency.

# Fourth Degree—MCL 750.520e (2-year misdemeanor)

## Elements

### CSC Fourth Degree—Person 13 through 15, Defendant 5 or more years older

1. The defendant engaged in sexual contact,
2. The victim was at least 13 years of age and under 16 years of age, and
3. The defendant was five or more years older than the victim.

### CSC Fourth Degree—Force or Coercion

1. The defendant engaged in sexual contact, and
2. Was using force or coercion to accomplish the sexual contact.

### CSC Fourth Degree—Incapacitated Victim

1. Defendant engaged in sexual contact, and
2. Knew or had reason to know that the victim is mentally incapable, mentally incapacitated, or physically helpless.

### CSC Fourth Degree—Incest

1. Defendant engaged in sexual contact, and
2. The defendant and victim were related by blood or affinity to the third degree.

### CSC Fourth Degree—Student

1. Defendant engaged in sexual contact,
2. The victim was at least 16 years of age but less than 18 years of age,
3. The victim was a student at a public or nonpublic school, and
4. Either of the following:

   a. Defendant was a teacher, substitute teacher, or administrator of that public school, nonpublic school, school district, or intermediate school district. This subdivision does not apply if the victim is emancipated or if both persons are lawfully married to each other at the time of the alleged violation.

   b. Defendant was an employee or a contractual service provider of the public school, nonpublic school, school district, or intermediate school district in which the victim is enrolled, or is a volunteer who is not a student in any public school or nonpublic school, or is an employee of this state or of a local unit of government of this state or of the United States assigned to provide any service to that public school, nonpublic school, school district, or intermediate school district, and the defendant uses his or her employee, contractual, or volunteer status to gain access to or to establish a relationship with the victim.

### CSC Fourth Degree—Special Education Student

1. Defendant engaged in sexual contact,
2. The victim was at least 16 years of age but less than 26 years of age,
3. The victim is receiving special education services, and
4. Either of the following:

   a. Defendant was a teacher, substitute teacher, or administrator of that public school, nonpublic school, school district, or intermediate school district. This subdivision does not apply if the victim is emancipated or if both persons are lawfully married to each other at the time of the alleged violation.

   b. Defendant was an employee or a contractual service provider of the public school, non-

public school, school district, or intermediate school district in which the victim is enrolled, or is a volunteer who is not a student in any public school or nonpublic school, or is an employee of this state or of a local unit of government of this state or of the United States assigned to provide any service to that public school, nonpublic school, school district, or intermediate school district, and the defendant uses his or her employee, contractual, or volunteer status to gain access to or to establish a relationship with the victim.

### CSC Fourth Degree—Foster Care

1. Defendant engaged in sexual contact,
2. The victim was at least 16 years of age, and
3. Defendant was an employee, a contractual service provider, or a volunteer of a child care organization or was a person licensed to operate a foster family home or foster family group home in which the victim was a resident and the sexual contact occurred during the period of the victim's residency.

### CSC Fourth Degree—Mental Health Professional

1. Defendant engaged in sexual contact, and
2. Defendant was a mental health professional, and the sexual contact occurred while the victim was the defendant's client or patient, or occurred within two years after the period in which the victim was the defendant's client or patient.

The consent of the victim is not a defense and a prosecution under this subsection shall not be used as evidence that the victim is mentally incompetent.

## Assault with Intent to Commit CSC With Penetration—MCL 750.520g

*Assault with intent to commit criminal sexual conduct involving sexual penetration shall be a felony punishable by imprisonment for not more than 10 years.*

### Elements

1. The defendant either attempted to commit a battery on the victim or did an act that would cause a reasonable person to fear or apprehend an immediate battery. A battery is a forceful or violent touching of the person or something closely connected with the person of another.
2. The defendant intended either to injure the victim or intended to make the victim reasonably fear an immediate battery.
3. At the time, the defendant had the ability to commit a battery, appeared to have the ability, or thought he had the ability.

4. When the defendant assaulted the victim, the defendant intended to commit a sexual act involving criminal sexual penetration. This means that the defendant must have intended some actual entry into one person's genital opening, anal opening, mouth with another person's penis, finger, tongue, or other object. CJI2d 20.17.

It is not required that the defendant actually began to commit the sexual act, just that the defendant made an attempt or a threat while intending to commit the act. An actual touching or penetration is not required, just that the defendant committed the assault and intended to commit criminal sexual penetration. CJI2d 20.17.

## Assault with Intent to Commit CSC Without Penetration—MCL 750.520g

*Assault with intent to commit criminal sexual conduct in the second degree is a felony punishable by imprisonment for not more than 5 years.*

### Elements

1. The defendant either attempted to commit a battery on the victim or did an act that would cause a reasonable person to fear or apprehend an immediate battery.
2. The defendant intended to either injure the victim or make the victim reasonably fear an immediate battery.
3. At the time, the defendant had the ability to commit a battery, appeared to have the ability, or thought he had the ability.
4. When the defendant assaulted the victim, the defendant intended to commit a sexual act involving criminal sexual contact. This means that the defendant must have specifically intended to touch the victim's genital area, groin, inner thigh, buttock, breast, or the clothing covering those areas or have the victim touch his genital area, groin, inner thigh, buttock, breast, or the clothing covering those areas. Actual touching is not required.
5. When the defendant assaulted the victim, the defendant must have specifically intended to do the act involving criminal sexual contact for the purpose of sexual arousal or gratification.
6. If completed, the act occurred under circumstances such that the act would have been a violation of MCL 750.520c. CJI2d 20.18.

## Resistance—MCL 750.520i

A victim need not resist the actor for prosecution of CSC.

## Married Persons—MCL 750.520l

A person can be convicted of CSC even though the victim is his or her legal spouse.

## Rape Kits and Sexual Assault Forensic Medical Examinations

### Sexual Assault Evidence Kit—MCL 333.21527

- If an individual alleges to a physician or other member of the attending or admitting staff of a hospital that within the preceding 24 hours, the individual has been the victim of criminal sexual conduct, the attending health care personnel responsible for examining or treating the individual immediately shall inform the individual of the availability of a sexual assault evidence kit and, with the consent of the individual, shall perform or have performed on the individual the procedures required by the sexual assault evidence kit.
- For the purposes of this section, the administration of a sexual assault evidence kit is not a medical procedure.
- *Sexual Assault Evidence Kit:* A standardized set of equipment and written procedures approved by the department of state police which have been designed to be administered to an individual principally for the purpose of gathering evidence of sexual conduct, which evidence is of the type offered in court by the forensic science division of the department of state police for prosecuting a case of criminal sexual conduct.

### Sexual Assault Medical Forensic Examination—MCL 18.355a

Sexual Assault Medical Forensic Examination is an examination that includes the following:

- The collection of a medical history.
- A general medical examination, including, but not limited to, the use of laboratory services and the dispensing of prescribed pharmaceutical items.
- One or more of the following:
  - A detailed oral examination.
  - A detailed anal examination.
  - A detailed genital examination.
- Administration of a sexual assault evidence kit and related medical procedures and laboratory and pharmacological services.

A victim of sexual assault shall not be required to participate in the criminal justice system or cooperate with law enforcement as a condition of being administered a sexual assault medical forensic examination.

# CRIMES OF INDECENCY

## Sodomy—MCL 750.158 (felony)

*Any person who shall commit the abominable and detestable crime against nature either with mankind or with any animal shall be guilty of a felony, punishable by imprisonment in the state prison not more than 15 years, or if such person was at the time of the said offense a sexually delinquent person, may be punishable by imprisonment in the state prison for an indeterminate term, the minimum of which shall be 1 day and the maximum of which shall be life.*

Bestiality, which is a sexual connection between man or woman and an animal, is a crime against nature, thus it falls under this section. *People v. Carrier*, 74 Mich. App. 161 (1977).

## Lewd and Lascivious Behavior—MCL 750.335 (1-year misdemeanor)

*Any man or woman, not being married to each other, who lewdly and lasciviously associates and cohabits together, and any man or woman, married or unmarried, who is guilty of open and gross lewdness and lascivious behavior, is guilty of a misdemeanor punishable by imprisonment for not more than 1 year, or a fine of not more than $1,000.00. No prosecution shall be commenced under this section after 1 year from the time of committing the offense.*

Includes the following:

- Any man or woman, not married, who shall lewdly and lasciviously associate and cohabitate together, or
- Any man or woman who commits open and gross lewdness and lascivious behavior.

During a lap dance at a nightclub, a dancer allowed patrons to kiss and suck her breast. This was held to be lewd and lascivious behavior. *People v. Mell*, 459 Mich. 881 (1998).

## Indecent Exposure—MCL 750.335a(1) (1-year misdemeanor)

*A person shall not knowingly make any open or indecent exposure of his or her person or of the person of another.*

### Elements

1. The defendant exposed a prohibited body part.
2. The defendant knew that the body part was being exposed.
3. The defendant did this in a place under circumstances in which another person might reasonably have been expected to observe it and which created a substantial risk that someone might be offended or in a place where such exposure is likely to be an offense against your community's generally accepted standards of decency and morality.

CJ12d 20.33.

Under this statute, there is no requirement that the defendant's exposure actually be witnessed by another person to constitute "open or indecent exposure" as long as the exposure occurred in a public place under circumstances in which another person might reasonably have been expected to observe it. In this case, the defendant was masturbating in a parked car on a public street during the day. *People v. Vronko*, 228 Mich. App. 649 (1998).

Indecent exposure occurred where the defendant exposed his erect penis to a minor female while they were standing in his bedroom. The statute's focus is not the location of the exposure, but rather on a defendant's conduct, his intent in making the exposure, and the reasonable reaction to the exposure by the viewer. Therefore, the statute does not require that the indecent exposure be made in a public place. *People v. Neal*, 266 Mich. App. 654 (2005).

Indecent exposure has been defined as "the exhibition of those private parts of the person which instinctive modesty, human decency, or natural self-respect requires shall be customarily kept covered in the presence of others." *People v. Kratz*, 230 Mich. 334 (1925).

## Indecent Exposure, Aggravated—MCL 750.335a(2)(b) (2-year misdemeanor)

*A person shall not knowingly make any open or indecent exposure of his or her person or of the person of another while fondling his or her genitals, pubic area, buttocks, or, if the person is female, her breasts.*

## Elements

1. The defendant exposed a prohibited body part.
2. The defendant knew that the body part was being exposed.
3. The defendant did this in a place under circumstances in which another person might reasonably have been expected to observe it and which created a substantial risk that someone might be offended or in a place where such exposure is likely to be an offense against your community's generally accepted standards of decency and morality.
4. The defendant was fondling his or her genital, pubic area, buttocks, or her breasts.

CJ12d 20.33.

## Indecent Exposure, Sexually Delinquent Person—MCL 750.335a(c)

A person who commits an act of indecent exposure while being a sexually delinquent person faces a minimum sentence of one day to a maximum sentence of life.

A *"sexually delinquent person"* is defined in MCL 750.10a as: "any person whose sexual behavior is characterized by repetitive or compulsive acts which indicate a disregard of consequences or the recognized rights of others, or by the use of force upon another person in attempting sex relations of either a heterosexual or homosexual nature, or by the commission of sexual aggressions against children under the age of 16."

## Gross Indecency—MCL 750.338, MCL 750.338a, and 750.338b

### Elements

1. The defendant engaged in a sexual act that involved one or more of the following regardless of whether the sexual act was completed or semen was ejaculated:

   a. Entry into another person's vagina or anus by the defendant's penis, finger, tongue, or other object. Any entry, no matter how slight, is enough.
   b. Entry into another person's mouth by the defendant's penis. Any entry, no matter how slight, is enough.
   c. Touching of another person's genital openings or genital organs with the defendant's mouth or tongue.
   d. Entry by any part of one person's body or some object into the genital or anal opening of another person's body. Any entry, no matter how slight, is enough.

   e. Masturbation of oneself or another.
   f. Masturbation in the presence of a minor, whether in a public place or private place.

2. The sexual act was committed in a public place. A place is public when a member of the public, who is in a place the public is generally invited or allowed to be, could have been exposed to or viewed the act.

CJI2d 20.31.

## Gross Indecency Between Males—MCL 750.338 (5-year felony)

*Any male person who, in public or in private, commits or is a party to the commission of or procures or attempts to procure the commission by any male person of any act of gross indecency with another male person shall be guilty of a felony, punishable by imprisonment in the state prison for not more than 5 years, or by a fine of not more than $2,500.00, or if such person was at the time of the said offense a sexually delinquent person, may be punishable by imprisonment in the state prison for an indeterminate term, the minimum of which shall be 1 day and the maximum of which shall be life.*

A public act of oral sex is grossly indecent. *People v. Lino*, 447 Mich. 567 (1994).

Attempting to procure oral, anal, or other sexual act with a person under the age of consent falls under gross indecency even if the act occurs in private and there is no sexual contact between the minor and the defendant. *People v. Lino*, 447 Mich. 567 (1994).

Gross indecency does not require penetration. Gross indecency includes an ultimate sex act, including masturbation, committed in a public place. In this case, the act occurred between two males in a public restroom. *People v. Bono*, 249 Mich. App. 115 (2002).

## Gross Indecency Between Females—MCL 750.338a (5-year felony)

*Any female person who, in public or in private, commits or is a party to the commission of, or any person who procures or attempts to procure the commission by any female person of any act of gross indecency with another female person shall be guilty of a felony, punishable by imprisonment in the state prison for not more than 5 years, or by a fine of not more than $2,500.00, or if such person* *was at the time of the said offense a sexually delin-quent person, may be punishable by imprisonment in the state prison for an indeterminate term, the minimum of which shall be 1 day and the maximum of which shall be life.*

Oral sex in a closed room in a massage parlor could fall under the gross indecency statute if there was a possibility the unsuspecting public could be exposed to or view the act. *People v. Brown*, 222 Mich. App. 586 (1997).

## Gross Indecency Between Male and Female Persons—MCL 750.338b (5-year felony)

*Any male person who, in public or in private, commits or is a party to the commission of any act of gross indecency with a female person shall be guilty of a felony, punishable as provided in this section. Any female person who, in public or in private, commits or is a party to the commission of any act of gross indecency with a male person shall be guilty of a felony punishable as provided in this section. Any person who procures or attempts to procure the commission of any act of gross indecency by and between any male person and any female person shall be guilty of a felony punishable as provided in this section. Any person convicted of a felony as provided in this section shall be punished by imprisonment in the state prison for not more than 5 years, or by a fine of not more than $2,500.00, or if such person was at the time of the said offense a sexually delinquent person, may be punishable by imprisonment in the state prison for an indeterminate term, the minimum of which shall be 1 day and the maximum of which shall be life.*

Sexual intercourse between a male and female in a visitation room at a prison falls with the statute. *People v. Jones*, 222 Mich. App. 595 (1997).

Gross indecency need not include an overtly sexual act. In one case, the defendant could be charged where he paid teenage females to beat him, spit on him, and provide him with urine and feces because he could reasonably be found to have received sexual gratification from these acts. *People v. Drake*, 246 Mich. App. 637 (2001).

# PROSTITUTION
## Soliciting for Prostitution—MCL 750.448

*A person 16 years of age or older who accosts, solicits, or invites another person in a public place or in or from a building or vehicle, by word, gesture, or any other means, to commit prostitution or to do any other lewd or immoral act, is guilty of a crime punishable as provided in section 451.*

### Elements

Applies to the following:

1. Any person 16 year of age or older, who accosts, solicits, or invites another,
2. By word, gesture or other means, to commit prostitution or other lewd or immoral act, and
3. Did so while in public or from a building or vehicle.

Penalties:

| First offense | 93-day misdemeanor |
| --- | --- |
| Second offense | 1-year misdemeanor |
| Third offense | 2-year felony |

## Permitting a Place of Prostitution—MCL 750.449

*A person 16 years of age or older who receives or admits or offers to receive or admit a person into a place, structure, house, building, or vehicle for the purpose of prostitution, lewdness, or assignation, or who knowingly permits a person to remain in a place, structure, house, building, or vehicle for the purpose of prostitution, lewdness, or assignation, is guilty of a crime punishable as provided in section 451.*

Penalties:

| First offense | 93-day misdemeanor |
| --- | --- |
| Second offense | 1-year misdemeanor |
| Third offense | 2-year felony |

## Solicitor for Prostitution—MCL 750.449a

*Any male person who engages or offers to engage the services of a female person, not his wife, for the purpose of prostitution, lewdness or assignation, by the payment in money or other forms of consideration, is guilty of a misdemeanor. Any person convicted of violating this section shall be subject to the provisions of Act No. 6 of the Public Acts of the Second Extra Session of 1942, being sections 329.201 to 329.208 of the Compiled Laws of 1948.*

Note that this statute entails a MALE person who solicits a FEMALE person.

## Aiding and Abetting Prostitution—MCL 750.450

*Any person 16 years of age or older who aids, assists, or abets another person to commit or offer to commit an act prohibited under section 448 or 449 is guilty of a crime punishable as provided in section 451.*

Penalties:

| First offense | 93-day misdemeanor |
| Second offense | 1-year misdemeanor |
| Third offense | 2-year felony |

## Allowing Minor to Remain in House of Prostitution—MCL 750.462

*A person who, for a purpose other than prostitution, takes or conveys to, or employs, receives, detains, or allows a person 16 years of age or less to remain in, a house of prostitution, house of ill-fame, bawdy-house, house of assignation, or any house or place for the resort of prostitutes or other disorderly persons is guilty of a crime punishable as provided in section 451.*

Penalties:

| First offense | 93-day misdemeanor |
| Second offense | 1-year misdemeanor |
| Third offense | 2-year felony |

## Penalties for Prostitution—MCL 750.451

Previous convictions can be proved by one or more of the following:

- A copy of the judgment of conviction.
- A transcript of the previous trial, plea, or sentencing.
- Information from the presentence report.
- The defendant's own statement.

## Pandering—MCL 750.455 (felony)

*Any person who shall procure a female inmate for a house of prostitution; or who shall induce, persuade, encourage, inveigle or entice a female person to become a prostitute; or who by promises, threats, violence or by any device or scheme, shall cause, induce, persuade, encourage, take, place, harbor, inveigle or entice a female person to become an inmate of a house of prostitution or assignation place, or any place where prostitution is practiced, encouraged or allowed; or any person who shall, by promises, threats, violence or by any device or scheme, cause, induce, persuade, encourage, inveigle or entice an inmate of a house of prostitution or place of assignation to remain therein as such inmate; or any person who by promises, threats, violence, by any device or scheme, by fraud or artifice, or by duress of person or goods, or by abuse of any position of confidence or authority, or having legal charge, shall take, place, harbor, inveigle, entice, persuade, encourage or procure any female person to enter any place within this state in which prostitution is practiced, encouraged or allowed, for the purpose of prostitution; or who shall inveigle, entice, persuade, encourage, or procure any female person to come into this state or to leave this state for the purpose of prostitution; or who upon the pretense of marriage takes or detains a female person for the purpose of sexual intercourse; or who shall receive or give or agree to receive or give any money or thing of value for procuring or attempting to procure any female person to become a prostitute or to come into this state or leave this state for the purpose of prostitution, shall be guilty of a felony, punishable by imprisonment in the state prison for not more than 20 years.*

### Elements

1. The defendant knowingly and intentionally did one or more of the following:

   a. Forced, persuaded, encouraged, or tricked another person to become a prostitute.
   b. Took, agreed to take, gave, or agreed to give money or something of value for making or attempting to make another person become a prostitute.

CJ12d 20.34.

A prostitute is a person who does sexual acts for money. CJ12d 20.34.

This statute applies to a defendant who encourages someone to become a prostitute, but it does not apply to a defendant who encourages a current prostitute to engage in further acts of prostitution. Pandering requires that the defendant must have enticed or induced a woman "to become a prostitute." *People v. Morey*, 461 Mich. 325 (1999).

Applies to any person who commits one of the following:

- Who shall induce, persuade, encourage, or entice a female person to become a prostitute.
- Procures a female inmate for a house of prostitution.
- Promises, threats, or uses violence or a scheme to cause, induce, encourage, take, place, harbor or entice a female to become a prostitute.
- Uses promise, threat, violence, or scheme to keep a female in a place of prostitution.
- For any reason shall induce, persuade, encourage, inveigle, or entice a female to come into this state or leave this state for the purposes of prostitution.
- Takes or detains a female person for the purpose of sexual intercourse, upon the pretense of marriage.
- Who shall give money or anything of value for procuring or attempting to procure to become a prostitute or leave this state for the purpose of prostitution.

## Accepting the Earnings of a Prostitute—MCL 750.457 (felony)

*Any person who shall knowingly accept, receive, levy or appropriate any money or valuable thing without consideration from the proceeds of the earnings of any woman engaged in prostitution, or any person, knowing a female to be a prostitute, shall live or derive support or maintenance, in whole or in part, from the earnings or proceeds of the prostitution of said prostitute, or from moneys loaned or advanced to or charged against her by any keeper or manager or inmate of a house or other place where prostitution is practiced or allowed, shall be guilty of a felony, punishable by imprisonment in the state prison not more than 20 years. And such acceptance, receipt, levy or appropriation of such money or valuable thing, shall, upon any proceeding or trial for violation of this section, be presumptive evidence of lack of consideration.*

## Elements

1. The defendant received or took money or something of value from a prostitute,
2. The defendant knew that the woman was a prostitute,
3. The defendant knew that the money had been earned by prostitution, and
4. The defendant did not give the prostitute anything of value in exchange or made a profit from the exchange.

CJ12d 20.35.

During an undercover investigation involving a massage parlor that the defendant owned, two women were sent to meet an officer. The defendant knew that the second was being sent for the purposes of sex. When they returned, she accepted the money they had received and was arrested and charged with accepting the earnings of a prostitute and pandering. The pandering charges were dismissed because there was no evidence presented that the defendant enticed either woman to become a prostitute. The charge of accepting the earnings of a prostitute was upheld. *People v. Morey*, 461 Mich. 325 (1999).

"Prostitution" does not require actual sexual intercourse: the court found that the defendant had accepted earnings from prostitutes where the prostitutes manually stimulated a customer's genitals at a massage parlor. *People v. Warren*, 449 Mich. 341 (1995).

# REGISTRATION OF SEX OFFENDERS— MCL 28.722–28.732

## Definitions—MCL 28.722

*Convicted:*   One or more of the following:

- Having a judgment of conviction or a probation order entered in any court having jurisdiction over criminal offenses.
- Being assigned to youthful trainee status under MCL 762.11 to 762.15 unless a petition was granted under MCL 28.728 at any time allowing the individual to discontinue registration under this act.
- Having an order of disposition entered under MCL 712A.18 if both of the following apply:
    - The individual was 14 years of age or older at the time of the offense.
    - The order of disposition is for the commission of an offense that would classify the individual as a tier III offender.
- Having an order of disposition or other adjudication in a juvenile matter in another state or country if both of the following apply:
    - The individual is 14 years of age or older at the time of the offense.
    - The order of disposition or other adjudication is for the commission of an offense that would classify the individual as a tier III offender.

*Custodial authority:*    One or more of the following apply:

- The actor was a member of the same household as the victim.
- The actor was related to the victim by blood or affinity to the fourth degree.
- The actor was in a position of authority over the victim and used this authority to coerce the victim to submit.
- The actor was a teacher, substitute teacher, or administrator of the public school, nonpublic school, school district, or intermediate school district in which that other person was enrolled.
- The actor was an employee or a contractual service provider of the public school, nonpublic school, school district, or intermediate school district in which that other person was enrolled, or was a volunteer who was not a student in any public school or nonpublic school, or was an employee of this state or of a local unit of government of this state or of the United States assigned to provide any service to that public school, nonpublic school, school district, or intermediate school district, and the actor used his or her employee, contractual, or volunteer status to gain access to, or to establish a relationship with, that other person.
- That other person was under the jurisdiction of the department of corrections and the actor was an employee or a contractual employee of, or a volunteer with, the department of corrections who knew that the other person was under the jurisdiction of the department of corrections and used his or her position of authority over the victim to gain access to or to coerce or otherwise encourage the victim to engage in sexual contact.
- That other person was under the jurisdiction of the department of corrections and the actor was an employee or a contractual employee of, or a volunteer with, a private vendor that operated a youth correctional facility under section 20g of the corrections code of 1953, 1953 PA 232, MCL 791.220g, who knew that the other person was under the jurisdiction of the department of corrections.
- That other person was a prisoner or probationer under the jurisdiction of a county for purposes of imprisonment or a work program or other probationary program and the actor was an employee or a contractual employee of, or a volunteer with, the county or the department of corrections who knew that the other person was under the county's jurisdiction and used his or her position of authority over the victim to gain

access to or to coerce or otherwise encourage the victim to engage in sexual contact.
- The actor knew or had reason to know that a court had detained the victim in a facility while the victim was awaiting a trial or hearing, or committed the victim to a facility as a result of the victim having been found responsible for committing an act that would be a crime if committed by an adult, and the actor was an employee or contractual employee of, or a volunteer with, the facility in which the victim was detained or to which the victim was committed.

*Department:*    The department of state police.

*Employee:*    An individual who is self-employed or works for any other entity as a full-time or part-time employee, contractual provider, or volunteer, regardless of whether he or she is financially compensated.

*Felony:*    That term as defined in section 1 of chapter I of the code of criminal procedure, 1927 PA 174, MCL 761.1.

*Immediately:*    Within three business days.

*Indigent:*    An individual who has been found by a court to be indigent within the last 6 months, who qualifies for and receives assistance from the department of human services food assistance program, or who demonstrates an annual income below the current federal poverty guidelines.

*Institution of higher education:*    A public or private community college, college, or university or a public or private trade, vocational, or occupational school.

*Local law enforcement agency:*    The police department of a municipality.

*Listed offense:*    A tier I, tier II, or tier III offense.

*Minor:*    A victim of a listed offense who was less than 18 years of age at the time the offense was committed.

*Municipality:*    A city, village, or township of this state.

*Registering authority:*    The local law enforcement agency or sheriff's office having jurisdiction over the individual's residence, place of employment, or institution of higher learning, or the nearest department post designated to receive or enter sex offender registration information within a registration jurisdiction.

*Registration jurisdiction:*    Each of the 50 states, the District of Columbia, the Commonwealth of Puerto Rico, Guam, the Northern Mariana Islands, the United States Virgin Islands, American Samoa, and the Indian tribes within the United States that elect to function as a registration jurisdiction.

*Residence:*   As used in this act, for registration and voting purposes means that place at which a person habitually sleeps, keeps his or her personal effects, and has a regular place of lodging. If a person has more than one residence, or if a wife has a residence separate from that of the husband, that place at which the person resides the greater part of the time shall be his or her official residence for the purposes of this act. If a person is homeless or otherwise lacks a fixed or temporary residence, residence means the village, city, or township where the person spends a majority of his or her time. This section shall not be construed to affect existing judicial interpretation of the term residence for purposes other than the purposes of this act.

*Student:*   An individual enrolled on a full- or part-time basis in a public or private educational institution, including, but not limited to, a secondary school, trade school, professional institution, or institution of higher education.

*Tier I offender:*   An individual convicted of a tier I offense who is not a tier II or tier III offender.

*Tier I offense:*   One or more of the following:

- Possession of child sexually abusive material. MCL 750.145c(4).
- Indecent exposure if the victim is a minor. MCL 750.335a.
- Unlawful imprisonment if the victim is a minor. MCL 750.349b.
- CSC fourth degree if the victim is 18 years or older. MCL 750.520e.
- Assault with intent to commit CSC if the victim is 18 years or older. MCL 750.520g.
- Surveilling or capturing/distributing image of unclothed person if the victim is a minor. MCL 750.539j.
- Any other violation of a law of this state or a local ordinance of a municipality, other than a tier II or tier III offense, that by its nature constitutes a sexual offense against an individual who is a minor.
- An offense committed by a person who was, at the time of the offense, a sexually delinquent person as defined in section 10a of the Michigan penal code, 1931 PA 328, MCL 750.10a.
- An attempt or conspiracy to commit an offense described above.
- An offense substantially similar to an offense described above under a law of the United States that is specifically enumerated in 42 USC 16911, under a law of any state or any country, or under tribal or military law.

*Tier II offender:*   A tier I offender who is subsequently convicted of another offense that is a tier I offense or an individual convicted of a tier II offense who is not a tier III offender.

*Tier II offense:*   One or more of the following:

- Accosting, enticing, or soliciting a child for an immoral purpose. MCL 750.145a.
- Accosting, enticing, or soliciting a child for an immoral purpose with prior convictions. MCL 750.145b.
- Child sexually abusive activity. MCL 750.145c(2).
- Distributing or promoting child sexually abusive activity or material. MCL 750.145c(3).
- Use of Internet or computer to commit certain crimes involving minors. MCL 750.145d(1)(a).
- Sodomy committed against a minor unless either:
  - The victim was at least 13 years of age but less than 16 years of age and consented to the conduct constituting the violation and the defendant was not more than four years older than the victim.
  - The victim was 16 or 17 years of age and consented to the conduct constituting the violation and was not under the custodial authority of the defendant at the time of the violation. MCL 750.158.
- Gross indecency between male persons committed against an individual 13 years of age or older but less than 18 years of age unless either:
  - The victim was at least 13 years of age but less than 16 years of age and consented to the conduct constituting the violation and the defendant was not more than four years older than the victim.
  - The victim was 16 or 17 years of age and consented to the conduct constituting the violation and was not under the custodial authority of the defendant at the time of the violation. MCL 750.338.
- Gross indecency between female persons committed against an individual 13 years of age or older but less than 18 years of age unless either:
  - The victim was at least 13 years of age but less than 16 years of age and consented to the conduct constituting the violation and the defendant was not more than four years older than the victim.
  - The victim was 16 or 17 years of age and consented to the conduct constituting the violation and was not under the custodial authority of the defendant at the time of the violation. MCL 750.338a.

- Gross indecency between male and female persons committed against an individual 13 years of age or older but less than 18 years of age unless either:
    - The victim was at least 13 years of age but less than 16 years of age and consented to the conduct constituting the violation and the defendant was not more than four years older than the victim; or
    - The victim was 16 or 17 years of age and consented to the conduct constituting the violation and was not under the custodial authority of the defendant at the time of the violation. MCL 750.338b.
- Soliciting for prostitution if the victim is a minor. MCL 750.448.
- Pandering. MCL 750.455.
- CSC second degree if the victim is 13 years or older but less than 18 years of age. MCL 750.520c.
- CSC fourth degree if the victim is 13 years or older but less than 18 years of age. MCL 750.520e.
- Assault with intent to commit CSC if the victim is 13 years or older but less than 18 years of age. MCL 750.520g(2).
- CSC second degree if the victim is 18 years of age or older. MCL 750.520c.
- An attempt or conspiracy to commit an offense described above.
- An offense substantially similar to an offense described in subparagraphs (i) to (xi) under a law of the United States that is specifically enumerated in 42 USC 16911, under a law of any state or any country, or under tribal or military law.

*Tier III offender:*   A tier II offender subsequently convicted of a tier I or tier II offense or an individual convicted of a tier III offense.

*Tier III offense:*   One or more of the following:

- Gross indecency between male persons committed against an individual less than 13 years of age. MCL 750.338.
- Gross indecency between female persons committed against an individual less than 13 years of age. MCL 750.338a.
- Gross indecency between male and female persons committed against an individual less than 13 years of age. MCL 750.338b.
- Kidnapping if the victim is a minor. MCL 750.349.
- Leading, taking, carrying away, decoying, or enticing away child under 14 years of age. MCL 750.350.
- CSC first degree. MCL 750.520b.
    - Does not apply if the court determines that the victim consented to the conduct

constituting the violation, the victim was at least 13 years of age but less than 16 years of age at the time of the offense, and the defendant is not more than four years older than the victim.

- CSC third degree. MCL 750.520d.
    - Does not apply if the court determines that the victim consented to the conduct constituting the violation, the victim was at least 13 years of age but less than 16 years of age at the time of the offense, and the defendant is not more than four years older than the victim.
- Assault with intent to commit CSC. MCL 750.520g(1).
    - Does not apply if the court determines that the victim consented to the conduct constituting the violation, the victim was at least 13 years of age but less than 16 years of age at the time of the offense, and the defendant is not more than four years older than the victim.
- CSC second degree if the victim is less than 13 years of age. MCL 750.520c.
- Assault with intent to commit CSC if the victim is less than 13 years of age. MCL 750.520g(2).
- Assault with intent to commit CSC if the defendant is 17 years of age or older and victim is less than 13 years of age. MCL 750.520e.
- An attempt or conspiracy to commit an offense described above.
- An offense substantially similar to an offense described above under a law of the United States that is specifically enumerated in 42 USC 16911, under a law of any state or any country, or under tribal or military law.

*Vehicle:*   That term as defined in section 79 of the Michigan vehicle code, 1949 PA 300, MCL 257.79.

*Vessel:*   That term as defined in section 44501 of the natural resources and environmental protection act, 1994 PA 451, MCL 324.44501.

## Individuals Required to be Registered—MCL 28.723

Individuals convicted of a tier I, tier II, or tier III listed offense after October 1, 1995 are required to be registered under the Sex Offenders Registration Act (SORA) if they:

- Are domiciled or temporarily reside in Michigan, or
- Work with or without compensation or are students in Michigan.

Individuals from another state who are required to register or otherwise be identified as a sex or child offender or predator under a comparable statute of that state must register under the SORA if they meet the criteria listed above. Additionally, MCL 28.723 also addresses registration requirements for individuals convicted of a listed offense on or before October 1, 1995.

### Duration of Required Registration—MCL 28.725(6)

Unless an individual obtains a court order allowing him or her to discontinue registration, an individual registered under the SORA shall comply with the verification and proof of residence procedures as follows:

- Tier I offenders must comply with registration requirements for a period of 15 years. MCL 28.725(10).
- Tier II offenders must comply with registration requirements for a period of 25 years. MCL 28.725(11).
- Tier III offenders must comply with registration requirements for life. MCL 28.725(12).

The registration periods exclude any period of incarceration for committing a crime and any period of civil commitment. MCL 28.725(13).

### Institutes of Higher Learning—MCL 28.724a

Within three business days, an individual required to register as a sex offender who is not a resident of Michigan shall report in person to the registration authority with jurisdiction over an institution of higher education if:

- The individual is or enrolls as a student at the institution, or
- The individual discontinues education at the institution, or
- The individual is present at any location in any state or territory or possession of the United States as a part of their studies with a Michigan institution of higher education or the individual discontinues their education at that location.

Within three business days, a resident of Michigan required to register as a sex offender shall report in person to the registration authority with jurisdiction over his new residence or domicile if:

- The individual is or enrolls as a student at an institution of higher learning, or
- The individual discontinues education at an institution of higher learning, or
- The individual is present at any location in any state or territory or possession of the United

States as a part of their studies with a Michigan institution of higher education or the individual discontinues their education at that location.

The individual shall pay the registration fee and submit written documentation of employment status, contractual relationship, volunteer status, or student status. Documentation includes but is not limited to the following:

- W-2 form, pay stub, or written statement by an employer.
- A contract.
- A student identification card or a student transcript.

Exception: The registration requirements do not apply to individuals whose enrollment and participation at an institution of higher learning is solely through the mail or Internet from a remote location.

### Change of Domicile or Residence, School, Place of Work—MCL 28.725 (felony)

Registered sex offenders must report in person and notify their local law enforcement agency, sheriff's department, or Michigan State Police Post within three business days after he or she does any of the following:

- Changes or vacates his or her residence.
- Changes his or her place of employment.
- Discontinues employment.
- Enrolls at an institution of higher education or discontinues enrolment.
- Changes his or her name.
- Intends to reside at any place other than his or her residence for more than seven days.
- Establishes any method of Internet communication.
- Purchases or begins to regularly operate any vehicle or when ownership or operation is discontinued.
- Makes any change to status at institution of higher education under MCL 28.724a.

Non-residents of Michigan who work within Michigan are required to notify the registering authority having jurisdiction over his or her place of work immediately after changing employment or employment is discontinued.

### Moving Out-of-State—MCL 28.725(6)

An individual who is a resident of Michigan and is required to register as a sex offender reports in person immediately to the registration authority having jurisdiction over his or her current residence before he or she changes his or her residence to another state. The individual shall indicate to the registration authority the new state and, if known, the new address.

## International Travel—MCL 28.725(7)

An individual who is a resident of Michigan and is required to register as a sex offender reports in person to the registering authority having jurisdiction over his or her current residence at least 21 days prior to moving to another country or travelling to another country for more than seven days. The individual shall indicate the country of travel and, if known, the new address or place of stay.

## Penalties for Failure to Comply With Registration Act by Violating MCL 28.723, 28.724, or 28.725—MCL 28.729(1):

| | |
|---|---|
| No prior convictions for a violation of the SORA* | 4-year felony |
| One prior conviction for a violation of the SORA* | 7-year felony |
| Two or more prior convictions for a violation of the SORA* | 10-year felony |

*Prior convictions other than failure to comply with MCL 28.725a.

## Hearing to Determine if Individual Exempt From Registration—MCL 28.723a "Romeo and Juliet" Exception

An individual convicted of a Tier II or Tier III CSC offense may be exempt from registration if:

- The victim was 13–16 years old,
- The offender was not more than four years older than the victim, and
- The conduct was consensual.
  or
- The victim was 16 or 17 years old,
- The victim was not under the custodial authority of the offender, and
- The conduct was consensual.

If the individual alleges that he or she is not required to be registered under the SORA and the prosecutor disputes the individual's eligibility to do so, the court shall conduct a hearing prior to sentencing or disposition to determine whether the individual is required to be registered under the act. At such hearing, the individual has the burden of proving by a preponderance of the evidence that his or her conduct falls within one of the above-mentioned exceptions and that he or she is therefore not required to register under the act.

## Reporting Duties—MCL 28.725a

An individual required to be registered under this act who is not incarcerated shall report in person to the registering authority where he or she is domiciled or resides no earlier than the first day or later than the last day of the month in which the individual is required to report, for verification of domicile or residence as follows:

**Tier I Offenders:** If the individual is a tier I offender, the individual shall report once each year during the individual's month of birth.

**Tier II Offenders:** If the individual is a tier II offender, the individual shall report twice each year according to the following schedule:

| Birth Month | Reporting Months |
|---|---|
| January | January and July |
| February | February and August |
| March | March and September |
| April | April and October |
| May | May and November |
| June | June and December |
| July | January and July |
| August | February and August |
| September | March and September |
| October | April and October |
| November | May and November |
| December | June and December |

**Tier III Offenders:** If the individual is a tier III offender, the individual shall report four times each year according to the following schedule:

| Birth Month | Reporting Months |
|---|---|
| January | January, April, July, and October |
| February | February, May, August, and November |
| March | March, June, September, and December |
| April | April, July, October, and January |
| May | May, August, November, and February |
| June | June, September, December, and March |
| July | July, October, January, and April |
| August | August, November, February, and May |
| September | September, December, March, and June |
| October | October, January, April, and July |
| November | November, February, May, and August |
| December | December, March, June, and September |

When an individual reports as required above, the individual shall review all registration information for accuracy.

## Required Identification—MCL 28.725a(7)

*An individual required to be registered under this act shall maintain either a valid operator's or chauffeur's license issued under the Michigan vehicle code, 1949 PA 300, MCL 257.1 to 257.923, or an official state personal identification card issued under 1972 PA 222, MCL 28.291 to 28.300, with the individual's current address. The license or card may be used as proof of domicile or residence under this section. In addition, the officer or authorized employee may require the individual to produce another document bearing his or her name and address, including, but not limited to, voter registration or a utility or other bill. The department may specify other satisfactory proof of domicile or residence.*

## Incarcerated Individuals—MCL 28.725a(8)

*An individual registered under this act who is incarcerated shall report to the secretary of state under this subsection immediately after he or she is released to have his or her digitalized photograph taken. The individual is not required to report under this subsection if he or she had a digitized photograph taken for an operator's or chauffeur's license or official state personal identification card before January 1, 2000, or within 2 years before he or she is released unless his or her appearance has changed from the date of that photograph. Unless the person is a nonresident, the photograph shall be used on the individual's operator's or chauffeur's license or official state personal identification card. The individual shall have a new photograph taken when he or she renews the license or identification card as provided by law, or as otherwise provided in this act. The secretary of state shall make the digitized photograph available to the department for a registration under this act.*

## Failure to Comply with Reporting Duties—MCL 28.729(2) (2-year misdemeanor)

*An individual who fails to comply with section 5a, other than payment of the fee required under section 5a(6), is guilty of a misdemeanor punishable by imprisonment for not more than 2 years or a fine of not more than $2,000.00 or both.*

## Registration Information—MCL 28.727

The following information shall be obtained or otherwise provided for registration purposes:

- *Names:* The individual's legal name and any aliases, nicknames, ethnic or tribal names, or other names by which the individual is or has been known.
- *Social Security Numbers:* The individual's social security number and any social security numbers or alleged social security numbers previously used by the individual.
- *Dates of Birth:* The individual's date of birth and any alleged dates of birth previously used by the individual.
- *Residential Address:* The address where the individual resides or will reside. If the individual does not have a residential address, information under this subsection shall identify the location or area used or to be used by the individual in lieu of a residence or, if the individual is homeless, the village, city, or township where the person spends or will spend the majority of his or her time.
- *Temporary Lodging:* The name and address of any place of temporary lodging used or to be used by the individual during any period in which the individual is away, or is expected to be away, from his or her residence for more than seven days. Information under this subdivision shall include the dates the lodging is used or to be used.
- *Employers:* The name and address of each of the individual's employers. For purposes of this subdivision, "employer" includes a contractor and any individual who has agreed to hire or contract with the individual for his or her services. Information under this subsection shall include the address or location of employment if different from the address of the employer. If the individual lacks a fixed employment location, the information obtained under this subdivision shall include the general areas where the individual works and the normal travel routes taken by the individual in the course of his or her employment.
- *Schools:* The name and address of any school being attended by the individual and any school that has accepted the individual as a student that he or she plans to attend. For purposes of this subdivision, "school" means a public or private postsecondary school or school of higher education, including a trade school.
- *Telephone Numbers:* All telephone numbers registered to the individual or routinely used by the individual.

- *Email and Instant Messaging Addresses:* All electronic mail addresses and instant message addresses assigned to the individual or routinely used by the individual and all login names or other identifiers used by the individual when using any electronic mail address or instant messaging system.
- *Vehicle Information:* The license plate number, registration number, and description of any motor vehicle, aircraft, or vessel owned or regularly operated by the individual and the location at which the motor vehicle, aircraft, or vessel is habitually stored or kept.
- *Driver's License/State Identification Numbers:* The individual's driver license number or state personal identification card number.
- *Passport and Immigration Documents:* A digital copy of the individual's passport and other immigration documents.
- *Occupational and Professional Licenses:* The individual's occupational and professional licensing information, including any license that authorizes the individual to engage in any occupation, profession, trade, or business.
- *Summary of Listed Offenses:* A brief summary of the individual's convictions for listed offenses regardless of when the conviction occurred, including where the offense occurred and the original charge if the conviction was for a lesser offense.
- *Physical Description:* A complete physical description of the individual.
- *Photograph*: The photograph required under MCL 28.725a.
- *Fingerprints and Palm Prints:* The individual's fingerprints and palm prints if not already on file.

### Refusal or Failure to Pay Registration Fees—MCL 28.729(4) (90-day misdemeanor)

*An individual who willfully refuses or fails to pay the registration fee prescribed in section 5a(6) or section 7(1) within 90 days of the date the individual reports under section 4a or 5a is guilty of a misdemeanor punishable by imprisonment for not more than 90 days.*

An individual required to report under the SORA shall pay a $50.00 registration fee as follows:

- Upon initial registration.
- Annually following the year of initial registration.
- The sum of the amounts required to be paid shall not exceed $550.00.

*Indigent Offenders:* The required registration fees shall be waived for a period of 90 days if the individual reporting can prove the fact of indigence to the satisfaction of the local law enforcement agency, sheriff's department, or Michigan State Police Post where the offender is reporting. MCL 28.725b.

### Failure to Sign Registration and Notice—MCL 28.727(4). (93-day misdemeanor)

*An individual who willfully fails to sign a registration and notice as provided in section 7(4) is guilty of a misdemeanor punishable by imprisonment for not more than 93 days or a fine of not more than $1,000.00, or both.*

### Prosecution—MCL 28.729(8)

Prosecution for an individual's failure to register as required by the SORA or failure to notify of a change in domicile, residence, place of work, or education may be prosecuted in the judicial district of any of the following:

- The individual's last registered address.
- The individual's actual address.
- Where arrest was made.

### Student Safety Zones—MCL 28.733–28.736

#### Definitions—MCL 28.733

*Loiter:* To remain for a period of time and under circumstances that a reasonable person would determine is for the primary purpose of observing or contacting minors.

*Minor:* An individual less than 18 years of age.

*School:* A public, private, denominational, or parochial school offering developmental kindergarten, kindergarten, or any grade from 1 through 12. School does not include a home school.

*School property:* A building, facility, structure, or real property owned, leased, or otherwise controlled by a school, other than a building, facility, structure, or real property that is no longer in use on a permanent or continuous basis, to which either of the following applies:

- It is used to impart educational instruction.
- It is for use by students not more than 19 years of age for sports or other recreational activities.

*Student safety zone:* The area that lies 1,000 feet or less from school property.

## Working in a Student Safety Zone—MCL 28.734 & MCL 28.736

Registered sex offenders are prohibited from working in a student safety zone, unless the following apply:

- The offender was working within a student safety zone on January 1, 2006. However, this exception does not apply to an offender who initiates or maintains contact with a minor within that student safety zone.
- The offender's place of employment is within a student safety zone solely because a school is relocated or initially established 1,000 feet or less from the offender's place of employment. However, this exception does not apply to an offender who initiates or maintains contact with a minor within that student safety zone.
- The offender who only intermittently or sporadically enters a student safety zone for the purpose of work. However, this exception does not apply to an offender who initiates or maintains contact with a minor within that student safety zone.
- The offender was convicted as a juvenile of committing, attempting to commit, or conspiring to commit MCL 750.520b(1)(a), MCL 750.520c(1)(a), or MCL 750.520d(1)(a) and one of the following applies:
  - The offender was under 13 years of age when he or she committed the offense and is not more than five years older than the victim.
  - The offender was 13 years of age or older but less than 17 years of age when he or she committed the offense and is not more than three years older than the victim.
  - This exception does not apply if the offender is convicted of more than one offense described in this section or the below section.
- The offender was charged with committing, attempting to commit, or conspiring to commit MCL 750.520b(1) (a), MCL 750.520c(1) (a), or MCL 750.520d(1) (a) and is convicted as a juvenile of violating, attempting to violate, or conspiring to violate, MCL 750.520e or MCL 750.520g and one of the following applies:
  - The offender was under 13 years of age when he or she committed the offense and is not more than five years older than the victim.
  - The offender was 13 years of age or older but less than 17 years of age when he or she committed the offense and is not more than three years older than the victim.

- This exception does not apply if the offender is convicted of more than one offense described in this section or the above section.
- The offender has successfully completed his or her probation period and has been discharged from youthful trainee status.
- The offender was convicted of committing or attempting to commit MCL 750.520e(1) (a), who at the time of the violation was 17 years of age or older but less than 21 years of age and who is not more than five years older than the victim.

## Loitering in a Student Safety Zone—MCL 28.734, MCL 28.736

Registered sex offenders are prohibited from loitering in a student safety zone, unless the following apply:

- The offender was convicted as a juvenile of committing, attempting to commit, or conspiring to commit MCL 750.520b(1)(a), MCL 750.520c(1)(a), or MCL 750.520d(1)(a) and one of the following applies:
  - The offender was under 13 years of age when he or she committed the offense and is not more than five years older than the victim.
  - The offender was 13 years of age or older but less than 17 years of age when he or she committed the offense and is not more than three years older than the victim.
  - This exception does not apply if the offender is convicted of more than one offense described in this section or the below section.
- The offender was charged with committing, attempting to commit, or conspiring to commit MCL 750.520b(1)(a), MCL 750.520c(1)(a), or MCL 750.520d(1)(a) and is convicted as a juvenile of violating, attempting to violate, or conspiring to violate, MCL 750.520e or MCL 750.520g and one of the following applies:
  - The offender was under 13 years of age when he or she committed the offense and is not more than five years older than the victim.
  - The offender was 13 years of age or older but less than 17 years of age when he or she committed the offense and is not more than three years older than the victim.
  - This exception does not apply if the offender is convicted of more than one offense described in this section or the above section.

- The offender has successfully completed his or her probation period and has been discharged from youthful trainee status.
- The offender was convicted of committing or attempting to commit MCL 750.520e(1)(a), who at the time of the violation was 17 years of age or older but less than 21 years of age and who is not more than five years older that the victim.

## Residing in a Student Safety Zone—MCL 28.734, MCL 28.736

Registered sex offenders are prohibited from residing in a student safety zone, unless the following apply:

- The offender is 18 years of age or younger and attends secondary school or postsecondary school and resides with his or her parent or guardian. This exception does not apply to an offender who initiates or maintains contact with a minor within that student safety zone. The offender may initiate or maintain contact with a minor with whom he or she attends secondary school or postsecondary school in conjunction with that school attendance.
- The offender is 26 years of age or younger and attends a special education program *and* resides with his or her parent or guardian or resides in a group home or assisted living facility. However, an offender described in this subdivision shall not initiate or maintain contact with a minor within that student safety zone. The offender shall be permitted to initiate or maintain contact with a minor with whom he or she attends a special education program in conjunction with that attendance.
- The offender was residing within that student safety zone on January 1, 2006. However, this exception does not apply to an offender who initiates or maintains contact with a minor within that student safety zone.
- The offender is a patient in a hospital or hospice that is located within a student safety zone. However, this exception does not apply to an offender who initiates or maintains contact with a minor within that student safety zone.
- The offender resides within a student safety zone because the offender is an inmate or resident of a prison, jail, juvenile facility, or other correctional facility or is a patient of a mental health facility under an order of commitment. However, this exception does not apply to an offender who initiates or maintains contact with a minor within that student safety zone.
- The offender was convicted as a juvenile of committing, attempting to commit, or conspiring to commit MCL 750.520b(1)(a), MCL 750.520c(1)(a), or MCL 750.520d(1)(a) and one of the following applies:
  - The offender was under 13 years of age when he or she committed the offense and is not more than five years older than the victim.
  - The offender was 13 years of age or older but less than 17 years of age when he or she committed the offense and is not more than three years older than the victim.
  - This exception does not apply if the offender is convicted of more than one offense described in this section or the below section.
- The offender was charged with committing, attempting to commit, or conspiring to commit MCL 750.520b(1)(a), MCL 750.520c(1)(a), or MCL 750.520d(1)(a) and is convicted as a juvenile of violating, attempting to violate, or conspiring to violate, MCL 750.520e or MCL 750.520g and one of the following applies:
  - The offender was under 13 years of age when he or she committed the offense and is not more than five years older than the victim.
  - The offender was 13 years of age or older but less than 17 years of age when he or she committed the offense and is not more than three years older than the victim.
  - This exception does not apply if the offender is convicted of more than one offense described in this section or the above section.
- The offender has successfully completed his or her probation period *and* has been discharged from youthful trainee status.
- The offender was convicted of committing or attempting to commit MCL 750.520e(1)(a), who at the time of the violation was 17 years of age or older but less than 21 years of age and who is not more than five years older than the victim.

An individual who resides within a student safety zone and who is subsequently required to register as a sex offender shall change his or her residence to a location outside the student safety zone not more than 90 days after he or she is sentenced for the conviction that gives rise to the obligation to register under the Sex Offenders Registration Act.

Penalties for Working, Loitering, or Residing in Student Safety Zones—MCL 28.734, MCL 28.735

| First offense | 1-year misdemeanor |
|---|---|
| Second offense | 2-year felony |

© 2014, Shutterstock, Inc.

# HOMICIDE AND KIDNAPPING

## HOMICIDE

### First Degree—MCL 750.316 (felony)

**Elements**

1. Defendant caused the death of the victim.
2. Defendant intended to kill the victim.
3. The intent to kill was premeditated, meaning it was thought out beforehand.
4. The killing was deliberate and premeditated, meaning the killing was not the result of sudden impulse, but rather, the defendant had a chance to think about the intent to kill.
5. The killing was not justified, excused, or done under circumstances that reduce it to a lesser crime.

CJI2d 16.1.

Time for a second look occurred where the victim was dragged to a secluded area and strangled. *People v. Johnson,* 460 Mich. 720 (1999).

### Intervening Causes

The defendant severely beat the victim and left her to die. When the victim was found, she was comatose and then was placed on a ventilator. The Court ruled that removal of life support was not an intervening cause of death; termination of life support merely allowed the victim to die of her injuries. *People v. Bowles,* 461 Mich. 555 (2000).

### Felony Murder—MCL 750.316(1)(b)

*Murder committed in the perpetration of, or attempt to perpetrate, arson, criminal sexual conduct in the first, second, or third degree, child abuse in the first degree, a major controlled substance offense, robbery, carjacking, breaking and entering of a dwelling, home invasion in the first or second degree, larceny of any kind, extortion, kidnapping, vulnerable adult abuse in the first or second degree, torture, or aggravated stalking.*

**Elements**

1. The defendant caused the death of the victim.
2. The defendant intended to kill the victim, intended to do great bodily harm to the victim, or knowingly created a very high risk of death or great bodily harm knowing that death or such harm would be the likely result of his actions.
3. When he or she did the act that caused the death of the victim, the defendant was committing, or helping someone else commit a felony. To help means to perform acts or give encouragement, before or during the commission of the crime, that aids or assists in its commission. At the time of giving aid

or encouragement, the defendant must have intended the commission of the felony.

4. The killing was not justified, excused, or done under circumstances that reduce it to a lesser crime.

5. For felony murder where the underlying felony was not completed, the evidence must show the defendant intended to commit the underlying felony and that he took some action toward committing that crime, but failed to complete it. Things like planning the crime or arranging how it will be committed are just preparations; they do not qualify as an attempt. In order to qualify as an attempt, the action must go beyond mere preparation, to the point where the crime would have been completed if it had not been interrupted by outside circumstances. To qualify as an attempt, the act must be clearly and directly related to the felony and not some other objective.

CJI2d 16.4.

Additional considerations:

- The length of time between the commission of the felony and the murder.
- The distance between the scene of the felony and the scene of the murder.
- Whether there is a causal connection between the murder and the felony.
- Whether there is continuity of action between the felony and the murder.
- Whether the murder was committed during an attempt to escape.

CJI2d 16.4b.

Felony murder occurs where the suspect committed murder while perpetrating or attempting to perpetrate one of the following:

- Arson.
- CSC first, second, or third degrees.
- Child abuse first degree.

Felony murder occurred where underlying felony was child abuse in the first degree. *People v. Magyar*, 250 Mich. App. 408 (2002).

- Major controlled substance offense.
- Robbery.

Assault with intent to rob while armed is a proper underlying felony for supporting a felony-murder conviction. Assault with attempt to rob unarmed is also a proper underlying felony. *People v. Akins*, 259 Mich. App. 545 (2003).

- Breaking and entering of a dwelling.
- Home invasion first or second degrees.

Felony murder may be predicated on home invasion in the first degree. *People v. McCrady*, 244 Mich. App. 27 (2000).

- Larceny of any kind
- Extortion
- Kidnapping
- Aggravated stalking
- Torture
- Carjacking
- Vulnerable adult abuse (first or second degree).

Neither premeditation nor specific intent to kill is required to prove felony murder.

## Murder of a Police Officer or Corrections Employee—MCL 750.316(1)(c) (felony)

### Elements

1. The defendant caused the death of victim.
2. The defendant intended to kill the victim, intended to do great bodily harm to the victim, or knowingly created a very high risk of death or great bodily harm knowing that death or such harm would be the likely result of his actions.
3. The victim was at the time a police officer, conservation officer, or a corrections officer.
4. The victim was at the time lawfully engaged in the performance of his duties as a peace officer or a corrections officer.
5. The defendant knew at the time that the victim was so engaged.

CJI2d 16.04a.

A statute that classified killing a police officer as first-degree murder was upheld as constitutional. *People v. Clark*, 243 Mich. App. 424 (2000).

The statute defines corrections officer as "a prison or jail guard or other prison or jail personnel." This includes the manager of a prison store. *People v. Herndon*, 246 Mich. App. 371 (2001).

### Inferring State of Mind

The defendant's state of mind may be inferred from the kind of weapon used, the type of wounds inflicted, the acts and words of the defendant, and any other circumstances surrounding the alleged killing.

Intent to kill may be inferred if the defendant used a dangerous weapon in a way that was likely to cause death. Likewise, it may be inferred that the defendant intended the usual results that follow from the use of a dangerous weapon.

A dangerous weapon is any instrument that is used in a way that is likely to cause serious physical injury or death. A gun is a dangerous weapon.

Premeditation and deliberation may be inferred from any actions of the defendant that show planning or from any other circumstances surrounding the killing. Motive by itself does not prove premeditation and deliberation. CJI2d 16.21.

## Transferred intent

If the defendant intended to kill one person, but by mistake or accident killed another person, the crime is the same as if the first person had actually been killed. CJI2d 16.22.

## Second-Degree Murder—MCL 750.317 (felony)

### Elements

1. The defendant caused the death of the victim.
2. The defendant intended to kill, or intended to do great bodily harm to the victim, or the defendant knowingly created a very high risk of death or great bodily harm knowing that death or such harm would likely be the result of their actions.
3. The killing was not justified, excused, or done under circumstances that reduce it to a lesser crime.

CJI2d 16.5.

The defendant's brother was in an altercation with the victim. The defendant attempted to break up the fight and drew his pistol when the victim knocked down the defendant's brother. The victim retreated and the defendant shot him in the back. The court held that the one second to one minute that elapsed before the shooting was sufficient time to give the defendant the opportunity to consider his actions supporting premeditation for first-degree murder purposes. However, the court also held that the defendant was incapable of cool orderly reasoning before he shot the victim; the defendant likely believed his brother was seriously injured when he fell to the ground after being punched twice in the face by the victim and the defendant had a

BAC of 0.10 when he shot the victim. The court reasoned that, due to the heated situation and the defendant's intoxication, it was unlikely the defendant was able to or did subject his actions to any analysis that could support a premeditation under first-degree murder, thus he could only be convicted of second-degree murder. *People v. Plummer*, 229 Mich. App. 293 (1998).

Wanton misconduct can be a substitute for malice to support a second-degree murder charge under the depraved heart theory. Based on the totality of the circumstances surrounding a drunk driving accident causing death, a second-degree murder charge could be sustained rather than an OUIL resulting in death charge. *People v. Goecke*, 457 Mich. 442 (1998).

## Delivery of a Controlled Substance Resulting in Death—MCL 750.317a (felony)

*A person who delivers a schedule 1 or 2 controlled substance, other than marihuana, to another person in violation of section 7401 of the public health code, 1978 PA 368, MCL 333.7401, that is consumed by that person or any other person and that causes the death of that person or other person is guilty of a felony punishable by imprisonment for life or any term of years.*

## Manslaughter—MCL 750.321 (felony)

*Any person who shall commit the crime of manslaughter shall be guilty of a felony punishable by imprisonment in the state prison, not more than 15 years or by fine of not more than 7,500 dollars, or both, at the discretion of the court.*

## Voluntary manslaughter—heat of passion

### Elements

1. The defendant caused the death of the victim.
2. The defendant intended to kill the victim, intended to do great bodily harm to the victim, or knowingly created a very high risk of death or great bodily harm knowing that death or such harm would be the likely result of his or her actions.
3. The defendant caused the death without lawful excuse or justification.

CJI2d 16.8.

For the crime of murder to be reduced to voluntary manslaughter, the following two things must be present:

- When the defendant acted, his or her thinking was disturbed by emotional excitement to the point that a reasonable person might have acted on impulse, without thinking twice, from passion instead of judgment. The emotional excitement must have been something that would cause a reasonable person to act rashly or on impulse.
- The killing itself must result from this emotional excitement. The defendant must have acted before a reasonable time had passed to calm down and return to reason.

CJI2d 16.9.

A reasonable cooling time is a reasonable time for the sudden inciting passion to naturally and rationally fade away. "But if the act of killing, though intentional, be committed under the influence of passion or in heat of blood, produced by an adequate or reasonable provocation, and before a reasonable time has elapsed for the blood to cool and reason to resume its habitual control, and is the result of the temporary excitement, by which the control of reason was disturbed, rather than of any wickedness of heart or cruelty or recklessness of disposition; then the law, out of indulgence to the frailty of human nature, or rather, in recognition of the laws upon which human nature is constituted, very properly regards the offense as of a less heinous character than murder, and gives it the designation of manslaughter." *Maher v. People*, 10 Mich. 212 (1862).

The defendant was convicted of voluntary manslaughter. On appeal, the court decided that the "cooling off" period, a time that would enable the defendant to recover from the passion and provocation that inflamed him, was unreasonable in this case. The defendant returned to the victim's house 24 hours after the initial incident, confronted the victim, then returned to his car, got his gun, and then shot the victim three times. The court found that the defendant was not compelled by the previous provocation to return to the victim's house and shoot him. Rather, the defendant chose to confront the victim and kill him, thus the cooling-off period was sufficient to allow the defendant to control his passion. The Court of Appeals held that the defendant should have been convicted of second-degree murder, but the trial court's error was not appealable by the prosecutor. *People v. Wofford*, 196 Mich. App. 275 (1992).

### Involuntary manslaughter—gross negligence

The suspect did one of the following that resulted in death of another person:

1. Acted in a grossly negligent manner.
2. At the time of the act, the defendant had the intent to hurt or injure the deceased (e.g., assault and battery).

CJI2d 16.10.

*Gross negligence* means more than carelessness. It means willfully disregarding the results to others that might reasonably follow from an act or failure to act. In order to find that the defendant was grossly negligent, each of the following three things must exist beyond a reasonable doubt:

1. The defendant knew of the danger to another, that is, he knew that there was a situation that required him to take ordinary care to avoid injuring another.
2. The defendant could have avoided injuring another by using ordinary care.
3. The defendant failed to use ordinary care to prevent injuring another when, to a reasonable person, it must have been apparent that the result was likely to be serious injury.

CJI2d 16.18.

The defendant's conduct was grossly negligent when she ran four red lights causing an accident, which resulted in the death of the victim. *People v. Moseler*, 202 Mich. App. 296 (1993).

### Involuntary manslaughter—discharge of a firearm intentionally aimed

#### Elements

1. The defendant caused the death of the victim.
2. Death resulted from the discharge of a firearm. A firearm is an instrument from which a projectile is propelled by the explosion of gunpowder.
3. At the time the firearm went off, the defendant was pointing it at the victim.

4. At that time, the defendant intended to point the firearm at the victim.
5. The defendant caused the death without lawful excuse or justification.

CJI2d 16.11.

## Moving Violation Causing Death—MCL 257.601d(1) (1-year misdemeanor)

**Elements**

1. The defendant committed a moving violation. "Moving violation" means an act or omission prohibited under this act or a local ordinance substantially corresponding to this act that involves the operation of a motor vehicle, and for which a fine may be assessed.
2. The moving violation was a cause of the death of the victim. To "cause" the victim's death, the defendant's operation of the vehicle must have been a factual cause of the death, that is, but for the defendant's operation of the vehicle, the death would not have occurred. In addition, operation of the vehicle must have been a proximate cause of death, that is, death or serious injury must have been a direct and natural result of operating the vehicle.

CJI2d 15.18.

If the moving violation causing death occurred in a work zone, emergency scene, school zone, or school bus zone, the penalty increases to a 15-year felony. MCL 257.601b(3).

If the moving violation causing death occurred to a person operating an implement of husbandry on the highway, the penalty increases to a 15-year felony. MCL 257.601c(2).

## Moving Violation Causing Serious Impairment of a Body Function—MCL 257.601d(2) (93-day misdemeanor)

**Elements**

1. The defendant committed a moving violation. "Moving violation" means an act or omission prohibited under this act or a local ordinance substantially corresponding to this act that involves the operation of a motor vehicle, and for which a fine may be assessed.
2. The defendant's operation of the vehicle caused a serious impairment of a body function to the victim. To "cause" such injury, the defendant's operation of the vehicle must have been a factual cause of the injury, that is, but for the

defendant's operation of the vehicle the injury would not have occurred. In addition, operation of the vehicle must have been a proximate cause of the injury, that is, the injury must have been a direct and natural result of operating the vehicle.

CJI2d 15.19.

If the moving violation causing injury occurred in a work zone, emergency scene, school zone, or school bus zone, the penalty increases to a 1-year misdemeanor. MCL 257.601b(2).

If the moving violation causing injury occurred to a person operating an implement of husbandry on the highway, the penalty increases to a 1-year misdemeanor. MCL 257.601c(1).

## Reckless Driving Causing Death—MCL 257.626(4) (felony)

**Elements**

1. The defendant drove a motor vehicle on a highway or other place open to the public or generally accessible to motor vehicles, including a designated parking area.
2. The defendant drove the motor vehicle in willful or wanton disregard for the safety of persons or property. "Willful or wanton disregard" means more than simple carelessness but does not require proof of an intent to cause harm. It means knowingly disregarding the possible risks to the safety of people or property.
3. The defendant's operation of the vehicle caused the victim's death. To "cause" the victim's death, the defendant's operation of the vehicle must have been a factual cause of the death, that is, but for the defendant's operation of the vehicle the death would not have occurred. In addition, operation of the vehicle must have been a proximate cause of death, that is, death or serious injury must have been a direct and natural result of operating the vehicle.

CJI2d 16.18.

## Reckless Driving Causing Serious Impairment of a Body Function—MCL 257.626(3) (felony)

**Elements**

1. The defendant drove a motor vehicle on a highway or other place open to the public or generally accessible to motor vehicles, including a designated parking area.

2. The defendant drove the motor vehicle in willful or wanton disregard for the safety of persons or property. "Willful or wanton disregard" means more than simple carelessness but does not require proof of an intent to cause harm. It means knowingly disregarding the possible risks to the safety of people or property.
3. Third, that the defendant's operation of the vehicle caused a serious impairment of a body function to the victim. To "cause" such injury, the defendant's operation of the vehicle must have been a factual cause of the injury, that is, but for the defendant's operation of the vehicle the injury would not have occurred. In addition, operation of the vehicle must have been a proximate cause of the injury, that is, the injury must have been a direct and natural result of operating the vehicle.

CJI2d 16.19.

## Kidnapping—MCL 750.349 (felony)

### Elements

1. The defendant knowingly restrained another person. "Restrain" means to restrict a person's movements or to confine the person so as to interfere with that person's liberty without that person's consent or without legal authority. The restraint does not have to exist for any particular length of time and may be related or incidental to the commission of other criminal acts.
2. By doing so the defendant must have intended to do one or more of the following:

   a. Hold that person for ransom or reward.
   b. Use that person as a shield or hostage.
   c. Engage in criminal sexual penetration or criminal sexual contact with that person.
   d. Take that person outside of this state.
   e. Hold that person in involuntary servitude.

CJI2d 19.1.

## Unlawful Imprisonment—MCL 750.349b (felony)

### Elements

1. The defendant knowingly restrained another person. "Restrain" means to forcibly restrict a person's movements or to forcibly confine the person so as to interfere with that person's liberty without that person's consent or without lawful authority. The restraint does not have to exist for any particular length of time and may be related or incidental to the commission of other criminal acts.

2. The defendant did so under one or more of the following circumstances:

   a. The person is restrained by means of a weapon or dangerous instrument.
   b. The restrained person was secretly confined, which means to keep the confinement or location of the restrained person a secret.
   c. The person was restrained to facilitate the commission of another felony or to facilitate flight after commission of another felony.

CJI2d 19.8.

Unlawful confinement occurred where the victim was forcibly confined against her will and dragged by her hair into a car. Even though the car was parked, she dared not leave because of previous assaults. Also, when a family member called, the victim was instructed to say she was fine. *People v. Railer*, 288 Mich. App. 213 (2010).

## Child Kidnapping—MCL 750.350 (felony)

*(1) A person shall not maliciously, forcibly, or fraudulently lead, take, carry away, decoy, or entice away, any child under the age of 14 years, with the intent to detain or conceal the child from the child's parent or legal guardian, or from the person or persons who have adopted the child, or from any other person having the lawful charge of the child. A person who violates this section is guilty of a felony, punishable by imprisonment for life or any term of years.*

*(2) An adoptive or natural parent of the child shall not be charged with and convicted for a violation of this section.*

The suspect maliciously, forcibly, or fraudulently took or enticed away a child younger than 14 years of age with the intent to detain or conceal the child.

## Parental Kidnapping—MCL 750.350a (felony)

### Elements

1. The adoptive or natural parent of a child took the child or kept the child for more than 24 hours.
2. The defendant intended to keep or conceal the child from:

   a. The parent or legal guardian who had legal custody or visitation rights at the time;
   b. The person who had adopted the child; or
   c. The person who had lawful charge of the child at the time.

CJI2d 19.6.

If the defendant took or kept the child to protect the child from an immediate and actual threat of physical or mental harm, abuse, or neglect, it is a defense to this charge. CJI2d 19.7.

## Human Trafficking

### Definitions—MCL 750.462a

*Child sexually abusive activity:* A child engaged in sexual intercourse, erotic fondling, sadomasochistic abuse, masturbation, passive sexual involvement, sexual excitement, or erotic nudity.

*Commercial sexual activity:* An act of sexual penetration or sexual contact for which anything of value is given or received by any person; or the production, distribution, or promotion of child sexually abusive material.

*Extortion:* Conduct prohibited by MCL 750.213, including, but not limited to, a threat to expose any secret tending to subject a person to hatred, contempt, or ridicule.

*Financial harm:* Includes any of the following:

- Criminal usury. MCL 438.41.
- Extortion. MCL 750.213.
- Employment contracts that violate statutes regarding payment of wages and fringe benefits. MCL 408.471 through MCL 408.490.
- Any other adverse financial consequence.

*Forced labor or services:* Labor or services that are obtained or maintained through one or more of the following:

- Causing or threatening to cause serious physical harm to another person.
- Physically restraining or threatening to physically restrain another person.
- Abusing or threatening to abuse the law or legal process.
- Knowingly destroying, concealing, removing, confiscating, or possessing any actual or purported passport or other immigration document, or any other actual or purported government identification document, of another person.
- Blackmail.
- Causing or threatening to cause financial harm to any person.

*Labor:* Work of economic or financial value.

*Maintain:* To secure continued performance of labor or services, regardless of any initial agreement on the part of the victim to perform the labor or services.

*Minor:* A person under 18 years of age.

*Obtain:* To secure performance of labor or services.

*Services:* An ongoing relationship between a person and another person in which the other person performs activities under the supervision of or for the benefit of the person, including, but not limited to, commercial sexual activity and sexually explicit performances.

### Human Trafficking—MCL 750.462a-j (felony)

It is unlawful to facilitate human trafficking, benefit financially from human trafficking, or receive anything of value from a venture engaged in human trafficking or to knowingly subject or attempt to subject another person to forced labor or services by:

- Causing or threatening physical harm to another. MCL 750.462b.
- Physically restraining or threatening to physically restrain another person. MCL 750.462c.
- Abusing or threatening to abuse the law or legal process. MCL 750.462d.
- Destroying, concealing, removing, confiscating, or possessing an actual or purported passport or other government identification. MCL 750.462e.
- Using blackmail, threatening or causing financial harm, or exerting or threatening to exert financial control. MCL 750.462f.
- Using a minor for child sexually abusive activity. MCL 750.462g.
- Providing or obtaining labor or services by force fraud, or coercion. MCL 750.462j(1).
- Recruiting, harboring, transporting, providing, or obtaining person for involuntary servitude or debt bondage. MCL 750.462j(2).

### Elements

1. The defendant forcibly confined or imprisoned the victim against his will.
2. The defendant did not have legal authority to confine victim.
3. The defendant acted willfully and maliciously. This means that the defendant knew that it was wrong to confine the victim and knew that he did not have the legal authority to do so.
4. The defendant intended to force or coerce the victim to perform labor or services. This may be done through the wrongful use or threatened use of physical force or any other means.

CJI2d 19.5.

Penalties:

| | |
|---|---|
| No injury | 10-year felony |
| Injury to victim | 15-year felony |
| Victim is a minor | 20-year felony |
| Violation involves a commercial sex act. MCL 750.462j only | 20-year felony |
| Violation involves serious physical harm. MCL 750.462j only | 20-year felony |
| Violation involves kidnapping or attempt, CSC or attempt, or attempted murder | Life felony |
| Death of victim | Life felony |

# ROBBERY

## ROBBERY

### Larceny from the Person—MCL 750.357 (felony)

*Any person who shall commit the offense of larceny by stealing from the person of another shall be guilty of a felony, punishable by imprisonment in the state prison not more than 10 years.*

### Elements

1. Defendant took someone else's property.
2. The property was taken without consent.
3. There was some movement of the property. It does not matter whether the defendant actually kept the property.
4. The property was taken from the victim's person or from the victim's immediate area of control or immediate presence.
5. At the time the property was taken, the defendant intended to permanently deprive the victim of the property.

CJI2d 23.3.

### Unarmed Robbery—MCL 750.530 (felony)

*(1) A person who, in the course of committing a larceny of any money or other property that may be the subject of larceny, uses force or violence against any person who is present, or who assaults or puts the person in fear, is guilty of a felony punishable by imprisonment for not more than 15 years.*

*(2) As used in this section, "in the course of committing a larceny" includes acts that occur in an attempt to commit the larceny, or during commission of the larceny, or in flight or attempted flight after the commission of the larceny, or in an attempt to retain possession of the property.*

### Elements

1. Defendant used force or violence or assaulted victim or put the victim in fear.
2. Defendant did so while in the course of committing a larceny.
3. The victim was present while defendant was in the course of committing the larceny.

CJI2d 18.2.

When four men surrounded the victim, demanded money, and then assaulted him there was sufficient evidence to support the conclusion that the victim parted with his money from the force or fear of additional force. This supported the robbery charges. *People v. Richardson*, 25 Mich. App. 117 (1970).

Unarmed robbery requires that the defendant took property by force or violence, by assault, or by putting the victim in fear. In this case, the court held that the defendant used force both when he tugged on the victim's purse and when he pulled the purse away from the victim. *People v. Hicks*, 259 Mich. App. 518 (2003).

## Armed Robbery—MCL 750.529 (felony)

*A person who engages in conduct proscribed under section 530 and who in the course of engaging in that conduct, possesses a dangerous weapon or an article used or fashioned in a manner to lead any person present to reasonably believe the article is a dangerous weapon, or who represents orally or otherwise that he or she is in possession of a dangerous weapon, is guilty of a felony punishable by imprisonment for life or for any term of years. If an aggravated assault or serious injury is inflicted by any person while violating this section, the person shall be sentenced to a minimum term of imprisonment of not less than 2 years.*

### Elements

1. The defendant used force or violence or assaulted the victim or put the victim in fear.
2. The defendant did so while in the course of committing a larceny.
3. The victim was present while the defendant was in the course of committing the larceny.
4. While in the course of committing the larceny, the defendant did any of the following:

   a. Possessed a dangerous weapon.
   b. Possessed any other object capable of causing death or serious injury.
   c. Possessed an object used or fashioned in a manner to lead a person to believe it was a weapon.
   d. Represented orally or otherwise that they were in possession of a weapon.
5. "In the course of committing a larceny" includes acts that occur:

   a. In an attempt to commit the larceny, or
   b. During commission of the larceny, or
   c. In flight or attempted flight after the commission of the larceny, or
   d. In an attempt to retain possession of the property.
   CJI2d 18.1.

The complainant need not be the rightful owner of the property; he or she may be any person present while the defendant was in the course of the larceny.

A bulge in the defendant's vest combined with threats to the victim of being shot justified charges of armed robbery. *People v. Jolly*, 442 Mich. 458 (1993).

The defendant's showing of a knife handle to the victim with threats to cut her throat are evidence of a dangerous weapon sufficient to support an armed robbery charge. *People v. Rutherford*, 140 Mich. App. 272 (1985).

The victim may reasonably infer the defendant had a dangerous weapon when the defendant had his hand in a paper bag and indicated he was armed. *People v. Kimble*, 109 Mich. App. 659 (1981).

Armed robbery occurred where the defendant placed his hand under his clothing, the victim observed a bulge under the clothing and defendant announced, "This is a stick up." *People v. Taylor*, 245 Mich. App. 293 (2001).

Each employee of an establishment may be a victim of an armed robbery even though he or she does not have access to the cash register since each employee has a superior right to the property than the suspect. *People v. Rodgers*, 248 Mich. App. 702 (2001).

A defendant need not complete a larceny to sustain armed robbery charges, merely attempt to commit the larceny while armed or indicating he is armed. *People v. Williams*, 491 Mich. 164 (2012).

## CARJACKING—MCL 750.529a (felony)

*(1) A person who in the course of committing a larceny of a motor vehicle uses force or violence or the threat of force or violence, or who puts in fear any operator, passenger, or person in lawful possession of the motor vehicle, or any person lawfully attempting to recover the motor vehicle, is guilty of carjacking, a felony punishable by imprisonment for life or for any term of years.*

*(2) As used in this section, "in the course of committing a larceny of a motor vehicle" includes acts that occur in an attempt to commit the larceny, or during commission of the larceny, or in flight or attempted flight after the commission of the larceny, or in an attempt to retain possession of the motor vehicle.*

## Elements

1. The defendant used force or violence, threatened force or violence, assaulted, or put in fear the victim.
2. The defendant did so while in the course of committing a larceny of a motor vehicle.
3. The victim was the operator, passenger, person in lawful possession, or person attempting to recover possession of the vehicle.

CJI2d 18.4a.

Use of force includes jumping into the passenger side of a stopped automobile and aggressively moving over to the driver's side such that the driver exited. The statute has no requirement that the defendant intend to permanently deprive the owner of the vehicle. *People v. Terry*, 224 Mich. App. 447 (1997).

Taking a motor vehicle by force does not require removal of the occupants. The defendant committed carjacking when he made the driver take him to an ATM by sticking a pistol in her mouth. *People v. Green*, 228 Mich. App. 684 (1998).

The defendant could only be charged with one count of carjacking, even though the vehicle had multiple occupants. *People v. Davis*, 468 Mich. 77 (2003).

The Legislature did not intend to require "legal possession" as a prerequisite to all carjacking convictions. *People v. Small*, 467 Mich. 259 (2002).

# EXTORTION—MCL 750.213 (felony)

*Any person who shall, either orally or by a written or printed communication, maliciously threaten to accuse another of any crime or offense, or shall orally or by any written or printed communication maliciously threaten any injury to the person or property or mother, father, husband, wife or child of another with intent thereby to extort money or any pecuniary advantage whatever, or with intent to compel the person so threatened to do or refrain from doing any act against his will, shall be guilty of a felony, punishable by imprisonment in the state prison not more than 20 years or by a fine of not more than 10,000 dollars.*

## Elements

1. The defendant threatened to injure the victim, victim's property, or someone in the victim's immediate family or threatened to accuse the victim of a crime.
2. The defendant made this threat by saying it or by writing it down. A gesture alone is not enough.
3. The defendant made the threat willfully, without just cause or excuse, and with the intent to gain money, make the person threatened do or not do something against the person's will, or accomplish some other goal.

CJI2d 21.1-21.2.

All elements of the extortion statute were satisfied when, after assaulting the victim, the defendant told her, "You better not tell the cops." *People v. Pena*, 224 Mich. App. 650 (1997).

The defendant hired the victim to fix the transmission on his truck. The victim began work, but stopped when it began to rain. The defendant went into his house and returned with a gun. He told the victim he would "silence him" unless he finished the work or returned some of the money. The police arrived and arrested the defendant who was later convicted of extortion.

Extortion requires (1) either orally or by a written or printed communication, maliciously threatens (2) to accuse another of any crime or offense, or to injure the person or property or mother, father, spouse or child of another (3) with the intent to extort money or any pecuniary advantage whatever, or with the intent to compel the person threatened to do or refrain from doing any act against his or her will. The court held the third section encompasses any act, not just those involving serious consequences to the victim. The defendant orally communicated a malicious threat to injure the victim, thereby satisfying the first two elements of statutory extortion, when he threatened to "silence" the victim while waving a gun. The defendant made the threat with the intent to compel the victim to undertake an act against his will, i.e. work on the truck in the rain, thereby satisfying the third element of statutory extortion. His conviction was affirmed. *People v. Harris*, 495 Mich. 120 (2014)

## Threat for Extortion

A threat for the purpose of extortion is a written or spoken statement of an intent to injure another person or that person's property or family. A threat does not have to be said in certain words, but it can be made in general or vague terms without exactly stating what kind of injury is being threatened. It can be made by suggestion, but a threat must be definite enough to be understood by a person of ordinary intelligence as a threat of injury. CJI2d 21.3.

## Completion of Extortion

It does not matter whether the threat was successful or whether the person threatened was afraid. It does not matter whether the victim actually did what the defendant wanted. The crime is complete when the threat is made, and it is not a defense that the defendant later abandoned his intent to injure the victim. No act other than the threat is necessary. CJI2d 21.5.

# CRIMES AGAINST PERSONS: SELECTED STATUTES

## VULNERABLE ADULT ABUSE

### Definitions—MCL 750.145m

*Caregiver:* An individual who directly cares for or has physical custody of a vulnerable adult.

*Vulnerable adult:* An individual age 18 or over who, because of age, developmental disability, mental illness, or physical disability requires supervision or personal care or lacks the personal and social skills required to live independently; or a person who is placed in an adult foster care family home or an adult foster care small group home pursuant to section 5(6) or (8) of 1973 PA 116, MCL 722.115; or is in a condition in which an adult is unable to protect himself or herself from abuse, neglect, or exploitation because of a mental or physical impairment or because of advanced age.

*Serious physical harm:* A physical injury that threatens the life of a vulnerable adult, causes substantial bodily disfigurement, or seriously impairs the functioning or well-being of the vulnerable adult.

*Serious mental harm:* A mental injury that results in substantial alteration of mental functioning that is manifested in a visibly demonstrable manner.

*Physical harm:* Any injury to a vulnerable adult's physical condition.

*Reckless act or reckless failure to act:* Conduct that demonstrates a deliberate disregard of the likelihood that the natural tendency of the act or failure to act is to cause physical harm, serious physical harm, or serious mental harm.

This statute "does not prohibit a caregiver or other person with authority over a vulnerable adult from taking reasonable action to prevent a vulnerable adult from being harmed or from harming others." MCL 750.145n(5).

This statute "does not apply to an act or failure to act that is carried out as directed by a patient advocate under a patient advocate designation executed in accordance with sections 5506 to 5515 of the estates and protected individuals code, 1998 PA 386, MCL 700.5506 to 700.5515. MCL 750.145n(6).

A foster care patient jumped or fell from the roof of a facility and subsequently complained of pain and paralysis, but the primary case manager failed to summon medical attention until the following day. This was sufficient evidence to establish the "reckless act or reckless failure to act" element of second-degree vulnerable adult abuse. *People v. DeKorte*, 233 Mich. App. 564 (1999).

## First Degree—MCL 750.145n(1) (felony)

A caregiver intentionally causes serious physical harm or serious mental harm to a vulnerable adult.

### Elements

1. The defendant was a caregiver of the victim.
2. The defendant intentionally caused serious physical harm or serious mental harm to the victim. "Serious physical harm" means an injury that threatens the life of a vulnerable adult, causes substantial bodily disfigurement, or seriously impairs the functioning or well-being of the vulnerable adult. "Serious mental harm" means an injury that results in a substantial alteration of mental functioning that is manifested in a visibly demonstrable manner.
3. The victim was at the time a "vulnerable adult." The term "vulnerable adult" means one or more of the following:

   a. An individual age 18 or over who, because of age, developmental disability, mental illness, or physical handicap requires supervision or personal care or lacks the personal and social skills required to live independently.
   b. A person 18 years of age or older who is placed in an adult foster care family home or an adult foster care small group home.
   c. A person not less than 18 years of age who is suspected of being or believed to be abused, neglected, or exploited.

CJI2d 17.30.

## Second Degree—MCL 750.145n(2) (felony)

The reckless act or reckless failure to act of a caregiver or other person with authority over a vulnerable adult causes serious physical or mental harm to a vulnerable adult.

### Elements

1. The defendant was a caregiver of the victim.
2. The defendant by his reckless act or reckless failure to act caused serious physical harm, or serious mental harm to the victim. "Reckless act or reckless failure to act" means that the defendant's conduct demonstrates a deliberate disregard of the likelihood that the natural tendency

of the act or failure to act is to cause serious physical harm or serious mental harm.
3. The victim was at the time a "vulnerable adult." CJI2d 17.31.

To prove this charge, the prosecutor must introduce evidence that the defendant engaged in a reckless act or reckless failure to act causing the injuries to the victim. *People v. Hudson*, 241 Mich. App. 268 (2000).

## Third Degree—MCL 750.145n(3) (2-year misdemeanor)

A caregiver intentionally causes physical harm to a vulnerable adult.

### Elements

1. The defendant was a caregiver or other person with authority over the victim.
2. The defendant intentionally caused physical harm to the victim. "Physical harm" means any injury to a vulnerable adult's physical condition.
3. The victim was at the time a "vulnerable adult." CJI2d 17.32.

## Fourth Degree—MCL 750.145n(4) (1-year misdemeanor)

The reckless act or reckless failure to act of a caregiver or other person with authority over a vulnerable adult causes physical harm to a vulnerable adult.

### Elements

1. The defendant was a caregiver or other person with authority over the victim.
2. The defendant by his reckless act or reckless failure to act caused physical harm to the victim. "Physical harm" means any injury to a vulnerable adult's physical condition.
3. The victim was at the time a "vulnerable adult." CJI2d 17.33.

## Vulnerable Adult Fraud—MCL 750.174a

*A person shall not through fraud, deceit, misrepresentation, coercion, or unjust enrichment obtain or use or attempt to obtain or use a vulnerable adult's money or property to directly or indirectly benefit that person knowing or having reason to know the vulnerable adult is a vulnerable adult.*

- The value of property fraudulently obtained, used, or attempted to be used or obtained in separate incidents pursuant to a scheme or course of conduct within a 12-month period may be aggregated to determine the total value. If the scheme or course of conduct is directed at one person, there is no aggregation time limit.
- A financial institution or a broker or a director, officer, employee, or agent of a financial institution or broker is not in violation of this section while performing duties in the normal course of business of a financial institution or broker or a director, officer, employee, or agent of a financial institution or broker.

Penalties:

| Less than $200 | 93-day misdemeanor |
| --- | --- |
| At least $200, but less than $1,000; or less than $200 if previously convicted | 1-year misdemeanor |
| At least $1,000, but less than $20,000; or at least $200, but less than $1,000 if previously convicted | 5-year felony |
| At least $20,000, but less than $50,000; or at least $1,000, but less than $1,000 if previously convicted twice | 10-year felony |
| At least $50,000, but less than $100,000; or at least $20,000, but less than $50,000 if previously convicted twice | 15-year felony |
| More than $100,000; or at least $50,000, but less than $100,000 if previously convicted twice | 20-year felony |

## Fraudulently Obtaining Signature—MCL 750.273 (felony)

*A person who fraudulently obtains the signature of any person with the intent to cheat and defraud that person is guilty of a felony punishable by imprisonment for not more than 10 years or a fine of not more than $5,000.00, or both.*

## Mozelle Senior or Vulnerable Adult Medical Alert Act

### Definitions—MCL 28.712

*Missing senior or vulnerable adult:* A resident of this state who is one of the following:

- At least 60 years of age and is believed to be incapable of returning to his or her residence without assistance and is reported missing by a person familiar with that individual.
- A vulnerable adult, as that term is defined in MCL 750.145m, who is reported missing by a person familiar with that individual.
- A person who is missing and suffering from senility or a physical or mental condition that subjects the person or others to personal and immediate danger.

*Person familiar with the missing senior or vulnerable adult:* A missing senior's or vulnerable adult's guardian, custodian, or guardian ad litem or an individual who provides the missing senior or vulnerable adult with home health aid services, possesses a health care power of attorney for the missing senior or vulnerable adult, has proof that the missing senior or vulnerable adult has a medical condition, or otherwise has information regarding the missing senior or vulnerable adult.

### Missing Senior or Vulnerable Adult Report—MCL 28.713

A law enforcement agency that receives notice of a missing senior or vulnerable adult from a person familiar with the missing senior or vulnerable adult shall prepare a report on the missing senior or vulnerable adult. The report shall include the following:

- Relevant information obtained from the notification concerning the missing senior or vulnerable adult, including the following:
  - A physical description of the missing senior or vulnerable adult.
  - The date, time, and place that the missing senior or vulnerable adult was last seen.
  - The missing senior's or vulnerable adult's address.
- Information gathered by a preliminary investigation, if one was made.
- A statement by the law enforcement officer in charge setting forth that officer's assessment of the case based upon the evidence and information received.

## Preparation of Report—MCL 28.714

The law enforcement agency shall prepare the report required by MCL 28.713 as soon as practicable after the law enforcement agency receives notification of a missing senior or vulnerable adult.

## Forwarding Information—MCL 28.715

After obtaining the information identified in MCL 28.713, the law enforcement agency shall as soon as practicable forward that information to all of the following:

- All law enforcement agencies that have jurisdiction in the location where the missing senior or vulnerable adult resides and all law enforcement agencies that have jurisdiction in the location where the missing senior or vulnerable adult was last seen.
- All law enforcement agencies to which the person who made the notification concerning the missing senior or vulnerable adult requests the report be sent, if the law enforcement agency determines that the request is reasonable in light of the information received.
- All law enforcement agencies that request a copy of the report.
- One or more broadcasters that broadcast in an area where the missing senior or vulnerable adult may be located.

Upon completion of the report required by MCL 28.713, a law enforcement agency may forward a copy of the contents of the report to one or more newspapers distributed in an area where the missing senior or vulnerable adult may be located.

After forwarding the contents of the report to a broadcaster or newspaper under this section, the law enforcement agency shall request that the broadcaster or newspaper do the following:

- Notify the public that there is a missing senior or vulnerable adult medical alert.
- Broadcast or publish a description of the missing senior or vulnerable adult and any other relevant information that would assist in locating the missing senior or vulnerable adult.

## Investigation—MCL 28.716

A law enforcement agency shall begin an investigation concerning the missing senior or vulnerable adult as soon as possible after receiving notification of a missing senior or vulnerable adult.

## Notification that Missing Senior or Vulnerable Adult is Found—MCL 28.717

A person familiar with the missing senior or vulnerable adult who notifies a law enforcement agency concerning a missing senior or vulnerable adult shall notify the law enforcement agency when he or she becomes aware that the missing senior or vulnerable adult has been found.

## Immunity from Civil Liability—MCL 28.718

A broadcaster or newspaper that notifies the public that there is a missing senior or vulnerable adult medical alert and broadcasts or publishes to the public information contained in the report forwarded to the broadcaster or newspaper by a law enforcement agency, including a description of the missing senior or vulnerable adult and any other relevant information that would assist in locating the missing senior or vulnerable adult, is immune from civil liability for an act or omission related to the broadcast or the publication of the newspaper.

The civil immunity described above does not apply to an act or omission that constitutes gross negligence or willful, wanton, or intentional misconduct.

# ETHNIC INTIMIDATION—MCL 750.147b (felony)

(1) *A person is guilty of ethnic intimidation if that person maliciously, and with specific intent to intimidate or harass another person because of that person's race, color, religion, gender, or national origin, does any of the following:*

(a) *Causes physical contact with another person.*

(b) *Damages, destroys, or defaces any real or personal property of another person.*

(c) *Threatens, by word or act, to do an act described in subdivision (a) or (b), if there is reasonable cause to believe that an act described in subdivision (a) or (b) will occur.*

(2) *Ethnic intimidation is a felony punishable by imprisonment for not more than 2 years, or by a fine of not more than $5,000.00, or both.*

*(3) Regardless of the existence or outcome of any criminal prosecution, a person who suffers injury to his or her person or damage to his or her property as a result of ethnic intimidation may bring a civil cause of action against the person who commits the offense to secure an injunction, actual damages, including damages for emotional distress, or other appropriate relief. A plaintiff who prevails in a civil action brought pursuant to this section may recover both of the following:*

*(a) Damages in the amount of 3 times the actual damages described in this subsection or $2,000.00, whichever is greater.*

*(b) Reasonable attorney fees and costs.*

## Elements

1. The defendant did one or more of the following:

   a. Caused physical contact with the victim.
   b. Threatened, by what he said or did, to cause physical contact with the victim and that there was reasonable cause to believe that such an act would occur.
   c. Damaged, destroyed, or defaced property of the victim.
   d. Threatened, by what he said or did, to damage, destroy, or deface property of the victim and that there was reasonable cause to believe that such an act would occur.

2. The defendant did this without just cause or excuse.

3. The defendant did so because of the race, color, religion, gender, or national origin of the victim.
CJI2d 17.34.

---

The defendant started a heated argument over a trivial matter at a restaurant. He called the victim a "nigger" and said, "You people should not be allowed in here." He threatened to "whip your fat ass" and threw a punch at the victim. The defendant's threat and act of throwing a punch at the complainant provided reasonable cause to believe that physical contact would occur, thus violating the statute. *People v. Stevens*, 230 Mich. App. 502 (1998).

Ethnic intimidation occurred where the defendant and the victim were involved in a road-rage incident, and, prior to an assault, the defendant shouted racial slurs at the victim. Racial intent need not be the sole motivation for the crime. *People v. Schutter*, 265 Mich. App. 423 (2005).

# STALKING

## Definitions—MCL 750.411h(1)

***Course of conduct:*** A pattern of conduct composed of a series of two or more separate noncontinuous acts evidencing a continuity of purpose.

***Credible threat:*** A threat to kill another individual or a threat to inflict physical injury upon another individual that is made in any manner or in any context that causes the individual hearing or receiving the threat to reasonably fear for his or her safety or the safety of another individual.

***Emotional distress:*** Significant mental suffering or distress that may, but does not necessarily, require medical or other professional treatment or counseling.

***Harassment:*** Conduct directed toward a victim that includes, but is not limited to, repeated or continuing unconsented contact that would cause a reasonable individual to suffer emotional distress and that actually causes the victim to suffer emotional distress. Harassment does not include constitutionally protected activity or conduct that serves a legitimate purpose.

***Stalking:*** A willful course of conduct involving repeated or continuing harassment of another individual that would cause a reasonable person to feel terrorized, frightened, intimidated, threatened, harassed, or molested and that actually causes the victim to feel terrorized, frightened, intimidated, threatened, harassed, or molested.

***Unconsented contact:*** Any contact with another individual that is initiated or continued without that individual's consent or in disregard of that individual's expressed desire that the contact be avoided or discontinued. Unconsented contact includes, but is not limited to, any of the following:

- Following or appearing within the sight of that individual.
- Approaching or confronting that individual in a public place or on private property.
- Appearing at that individual's workplace or residence.
- Entering onto or remaining on property owned, leased, or occupied by that individual.
- Contacting that individual by telephone.
- Sending mail or electronic communications to that individual.
- Placing an object on, or delivering an object to, property owned, leased, or occupied by that individual.

*Victim:* An individual who is the target of a willful course of conduct involving repeated or continuing harassment.

## Misdemeanor Stalking—MCL 750.411h(2) (1-year misdemeanor)

### Elements

1. The defendant committed two or more willful, separate, and noncontinuous acts of unconsented contact with the victim.
2. The contact would cause a reasonable individual to suffer emotional distress.
3. The contact caused the victim to suffer emotional distress.
4. The contact would cause a reasonable individual to feel terrorized, frightened, intimidated, threatened, harassed, or molested.
5. The contact caused the victim to feel terrorized, frightened, intimidated, threatened, harassed, or molested.

   CJI2d 17.25.

If the victim was less than 18 years of age at any time during the individual's course of conduct and the individual is five or more years older than the victim, the stalker is guilty of a felony punishable by not more than five years.

## Aggravated Stalking—MCL 750.411i (felony)

### Elements

1. The defendant committed two or more willful, separate, and noncontinuous acts of unconsented contact with the victim.
2. The contact would cause a reasonable individual to suffer emotional distress.
3. The contact caused the victim to suffer emotional distress.
4. The contact would cause a reasonable individual to feel terrorized, frightened, intimidated, threatened, harassed, or molested.
5. The contact caused the victim to feel terrorized, frightened, intimidated, threatened, harassed, or molested.
6. One or more of the following:

   a. Was committed in violation of a court order.
   b. Was committed in violation of a restraining order of which the defendant had actual notice.
   c. Included the defendant making one or more credible threats against the complainant, a member of his or her family, or someone living in his or her household or
   d. The defendant was previously convicted of a stalking offense.

   CJI2d 17.25.

If the victim was less than 18 years of age at any time during the individual's course of conduct and the individual is five or more years older than the victim, the aggravated stalker is guilty of a felony punishable by not more than 10 years in prison.

## Posting a Message—MCL 750.411s (felony)

A person shall not post a message through the use of any medium of communication, including the Internet or a computer, computer program, computer system or computer network, or other electronic medium of communication, without the victim's consent, if all the following apply:

- The person knows or has reason to know that the posting could cause two or more separate noncontinuous acts of unconsented contact with the victim.
- Posting the message is intended to cause conduct that would make the victim feel terrorized, frightened, intimidated, threatened, harassed, or molested.
- Conduct arising from the posting would cause a reasonable person to suffer emotional distress and to feel terrorized, frightened, intimidated, threatened, harassed, or molested.
- Conduct arising from the posting actually causes the victim to suffer emotional distress and to feel terrorized, frightened, intimidated, threatened, harassed, or molested.

Except as provided below, posting a message is a two-year felony.

Posting a message is a five-year felony if the act includes any of the following:

- Posting the message violates a restraining order and the person has received notice.
- Posting the message violates a condition of probation, parole or conditional release.
- The message results in a credible threat communicated to the victim or member of the victim's family or another individual living in the same household as the victim.
- The person has been previously convicted of stalking, MCL 750.145d, or MCL 752.796 or a law substantially similar from another state.
- The victim is less than 18 years of age and the person is five or more years older.

Prosecution may be sought if one of the following apply:

- The person posts the message while in this state.
- Conduct arising from posting the message occurs in this state.

- The victim is present in this state at the time the offense or any element of the offense occurs.
- The person posting the message knows that the victim resides in this state.

# HAZING—MCL 750.411t

*A person who attends, is employed by, or is a volunteer of an educational institution shall not engage in or participate in the hazing of an individual.*

- A criminal penalty provided for under this section may be imposed in addition to any penalty that may be imposed for any other criminal offense arising from the same conduct.
- This section does not apply to an individual who is the subject of the hazing, regardless of whether the individual voluntarily allowed himself or herself to be hazed.
- This section does not apply to an activity that is normal and customary in an athletic, physical education, military training, or similar program sanctioned by the educational institution.
- It is not a defense to a prosecution for a crime under this section that the individual against whom the hazing was directed consented to or acquiesced in the hazing.

## Definitions

*Educational Institution:* A public or private school that is a middle school, junior high school, high school, vocational school, college, or university located in this state.

*Hazing:* An intentional, knowing, or reckless act by a person acting alone or acting with others that is directed against an individual and that the person knew or should have known endangers the physical health or safety of the individual and that is done for the purpose of pledging, being initiated into, affiliating with, participating in, holding office in, or maintaining membership in any organization. Hazing includes any of the following that is done for such a purpose:

- Physical brutality, such as whipping, beating, striking, branding, electronic shocking, placing of a harmful substance on the body, or similar activity.
- Physical activity, such as sleep deprivation, exposure to the elements, confinement in a small space, or calisthenics that subjects the other person to an unreasonable risk of harm or that adversely affects the physical health or safety of the individual.

- Activity involving consumption of a food, liquid, alcoholic beverage, liquor, drug, or other substance that subjects the individual to an unreasonable risk of harm or that adversely affects the physical health or safety of the individual.
- Activity that induces, causes, or requires an individual to perform a duty or task that involves the commission of a crime or an act of hazing.

*Organization:* A fraternity, sorority, association, corporation, order, society, corps, cooperative, club, service group, social group, athletic team, or similar group whose members are primarily students at an educational institution.

*Pledge:* An individual who has been accepted by, is considering an offer of membership from, or is in the process of qualifying for membership in any organization.

*Pledging:* Any action or activity related to becoming a member of an organization.

*Serious impairment of a body function:* Includes, but is not limited to, one or more of the following:

- Loss of a limb or loss of use of a limb.
- Loss of a foot, hand, finger, or thumb or loss of use of a foot, hand, finger, or thumb.
- Loss of an eye or ear or loss of use of an eye or ear.
- Loss or substantial impairment of a bodily function.
- Serious visible disfigurement.
- A comatose state that lasts for more than three days.
- Measurable brain or mental impairment.
- A skull fracture or other serious bone fracture.
- Subdural hemorrhage or subdural hematoma.
- Loss of an organ.

Penalties:

| Results in physical injury | 93-day misdemeanor |
|---|---|
| Results in serious impairment of a body function | 5-year felony |
| Results in death | 15-year felony |

# EAVESDROPPING

## Definitions—MCL 750.539a

*Private place:* A place where one may reasonably expect to be safe from casual or hostile intrusion or surveillance but does not include a place to which the public or substantial group of the public has access.

*Eavesdrop or eavesdropping:* To overhear, record, amplify, or transmit any part of the private discourse of others without the permission of all persons engaged in the discourse. Neither this definition nor any other provision of this act shall modify or affect any law or regulation concerning interception, divulgence, or recording of messages transmitted by communications common carriers.

*Surveillance:* To secretly observe the activities of another person for the purpose of spying upon and invading the privacy of the person observed.

*Person:* Any individual, partnership, corporation, or association.

## Trespassing for Purpose of Eavesdropping—MCL 750.539b (90-day misdemeanor)

*A person who trespasses on property owned or under the control of any other person, to subject that person to eavesdropping or surveillance is guilty of a misdemeanor.*

## Eavesdropping Upon Private Conversation—MCL 750.539c (felony)

*Any person who is present or who is not present during a private conversation and who willfully uses any device to eavesdrop upon the conversation without the consent of all parties thereto, or who knowingly aids, employs or procures another person to do the same in violation of this section, is guilty of a felony punishable by imprisonment in a state prison for not more than 2 years or by a fine of not more than $2,000.00, or both.*

The statute does not prohibit a party to a telephone conversation from tape recording the conversation and such recording does not require consent of all other participants. *Sullivan v Gray*, 117 Mich. App. 476 (1982).

Eavesdropping includes a person listening in on cordless phone conversations by means of a police scanner. *People v. Stone*, 463 Mich. 558 (2001).

It did not violate the defendant's Fourth Amendment rights for the admission into evidence of a phone conversation between the defendant and his brother, that the brother allowed police to listen in on. *People v. Rappuhn*, 55 Mich. App. 52 (1974).

The defendant was on trial for violating the Taft-Hartley Act. During trial, he had a hotel suite and frequently met with advisors and union officials. One of the union officials reported his conversations with the defendant to the FBI, describing the defendant's efforts to bribe the jury. The defendant argued admission of the FBI reports and the union official's testimony into evidence at trial violated his Fourth Amendment rights. The court held, "Neither this Court nor any member of it has ever expressed the view that the Fourth Amendment protects a wrongdoer's misplaced belief that a person to whom he voluntarily confides his wrongdoing will not reveal it." Further, the court held the risk of being overheard or having the contents of a conversation revealed to police is a risk inherent in human society; such actions, where there is no unlawful intrusion on the conversation, do not violate the Fourth Amendment. *Hoffa v. United States*, 385 U.S. 293 (1966).

Detroit police officers and officials met with concert promoters prior to a concert at Joe Louis Arena to halt the display of a video allegedly showing sexually explicit activities. The "private conversation" was carried on in the presence of many third parties and video crews, including one cameraman obviously recording the entire discourse. The conversation was released as a bonus feature on a tour DVD. The officers and officials brought suit against the concert promoters for using the video camera to eavesdrop on a private conversation. The court dismissed the complaint, holding that the complainants had no reasonable expectation of privacy in the conversation as the defendants controlled access to the room, multiple third parties came and went during the conversation, and the conversation was openly videotaped by the defendant's camera crew. *Bowens v. Ary, Inc.*, 489 Mich. 851 (2011).

## Installation of Device for Observing, Photographing, or Eavesdropping in Private Place—MCL 750.539d (felony)

*A person shall not install, place, or use in any private place, without the consent of the person or persons entitled to privacy in that place, any device for observing, recording, transmitting, photographing, or eavesdropping upon the sounds or events in that place.*

Penalties:

| First offense or attempted first offense | 2-year felony |
|---|---|
| Second offense or attempted second offense | 5-year felony |

*A person shall not distribute, disseminate, or transmit for access by any other person a recording, photograph, or visual image the person knows or has reason to know was obtained in violation of this section.*

Penalty:

| First offense or attempted first offense | 5-year felony |
|---|---|

This section does not prohibit security monitoring in a residence if conducted by or at the direction of the owner or principal occupant of that residence unless conducted for a lewd or lascivious purpose. MCL 750.539d(2).

Eavesdropping could apply to a subject who hides a video camera in his bedroom to secretly videotape consensual sexual activity between himself and his girlfriends. *Lewis v. Legrow*, 258 Mich. App. 175 (2003).

## Use or Divulgence of Information Unlawfully Obtained—MCL 750.539e (felony)

*Any person who uses or divulges any information which he knows or reasonably should know was obtained in violation of sections 539b, 539c or 539d is guilty of a felony, punishable by imprisonment in a state prison not more than 2 years, or by a fine of not more than $2,000.00.*

## Surveillance of Individual Having Reasonable Expectation of Privacy— MCL 750.539j (felony)

*A person shall not surveil another individual who is clad only in his or her undergarments, the unclad genitalia or buttocks of another individual, or the unclad breasts of a female individual under circumstances in which the individual would have a reasonable expectation of privacy.*

***Surveil:*** To subject an individual to surveillance.

Penalties:

| First offense or attempted first offense | 2-year felony |
|---|---|
| Second offense or attempted second offense | 5-year felony |

*A person shall not photograph, or otherwise capture or record, the visual image of the undergarments worn by another individual, the unclad genitalia or buttocks of another individual, or the unclad breasts of a female individual under circumstances in which the individual would have a reasonable expectation of privacy.*

Penalty:

| First offense or attempted first offense | 5-year felony |
|---|---|

*A person shall not distribute, disseminate, or transmit for access by any other person a recording, photograph, or visual image the person knows or has reason to know was obtained in violation of this section.*

Penalty:

| First offense or attempted first offense | 5-year felony |
|---|---|

This section does not prohibit security monitoring in a residence if conducted by or at the direction of the owner or principal occupant of that residence unless conducted for a lewd or lascivious purpose.

This section does not apply to a peace officer of this state or the federal government, or the officer's agent, while in the performance of the officer's duties.

## Install a GPS-Tracking Device on the Vehicle of Another—MCL 750.539l (1-year misdemeanor)

A person who does any of the following is guilty of a misdemeanor punishable by imprisonment for not more than one year or a fine of not more than $1,000.00, or both:

- Installs or places a tracking device, or causes a tracking device to be installed or placed, in or on a motor vehicle without the knowledge and consent of the owner of that motor vehicle or, if the motor vehicle is leased, the lessee of that motor vehicle.
- Tracks the location of a motor vehicle with a tracking device without the knowledge and consent of either the owner or the authorized operator of that motor vehicle or, if the motor

vehicle is leased, either the lessee or the authorized operator of that motor vehicle.

- While being the restrained party under a protective order, tracks the location of a motor vehicle operated or occupied by an individual protected under that order with a tracking device.
- While on probation or parole for an assaultive crime or a violation of section 81(3) or (4) [domestic violence second or third offense] or section 81a(2) or (3) [aggravated domestic violence first or second offense], tracks the location of a motor vehicle operated or occupied by a victim of that crime or by a family member of the victim of that crime without the knowledge and consent of that victim or family member.

### Definitions

*Assaultive crime:*   That term as defined in MCL 770.9a.

*Minor:*   An individual less than 18 years of age.

*Motor vehicle:*   All vehicles impelled on the public highways of this state by mechanical power, except traction engines, road rollers, and such vehicles as run only upon rails or tracks.

*Professional investigator:*   A person licensed under the professional investigator licensure act, MCL 338.821 to 338.851.

*Protective order:*   The following:

- A personal protection order or foreign protection order entered under MCL 600.2950, 600.2950a, and 600.2950h.
- Conditions reasonably necessary for the protection of one or more named persons as part of an order for pretrial release under MCL 765.6b.
- Conditions reasonably necessary for the protection of one or more named persons as part of an order of probation under MCL 771.3.
- Orders removing abusive persons from a juveniles home under MCL 712A.13a.
- Conditions intended for the protection of one or more named persons as part of a parole order under MCL 791.236.
- A foreign protection order as defined in MCL 600.2950h.

*Tracking device:*   Any electronic device that is designed or intended to be used to track the location of a motor vehicle regardless of whether that information is recorded.

### Exceptions

This statute does not apply to any of the following:

- The installation or use of any device that provides vehicle tracking for purposes of providing mechanical, operational, directional, navigation, weather, or traffic information to the operator of the vehicle.
- The installation or use of any device for providing emergency assistance to the operator or passengers of the vehicle under the terms and conditions of a subscription service, including any trial period of that subscription service.
- The installation or use of any device for providing missing vehicle assistance for the benefit of the owner or operator of the vehicle.
- The installation or use of any device to provide diagnostic services regarding the mechanical operation of a vehicle under the terms and conditions of a subscription service, including any trial period of the subscription service.
- The installation or use of any device or service that provides the lessee of the vehicle with clear notice that the vehicle may be tracked. For a lessor who installs a tracking device subsequent to the original vehicle manufacture, the notice shall be provided in writing with an acknowledgment signed by the lessee, regardless of whether the tracking device is original equipment, a retrofit, or an aftermarket product. The requirement for written acknowledgment placed upon the lessor is not imposed upon the manufacturer of the tracking device or the manufacturer of the vehicle.
- The installation or use of any tracking device by the parent or guardian of a minor on any vehicle owned or leased by that parent or guardian or the minor and operated by the minor.
- The installation or use of a tracking device by a police officer while lawfully performing his or her duties as a police officer.
- The installation or use of a tracking device by a court officer appointed under section 8321 of the revised judicature act of 1961, 1961 PA 236, MCL 600.8321, while lawfully performing his or her duties as a court officer.
- The installation or use of a tracking device by a person lawfully performing his or her duties as a bail agent as authorized under section 167b or as an employee or contractor of that bail agent lawfully performing his or her duties as an employee or contractor of a bail agent.
- The installation or use of a tracking device by a professional investigator or an employee of a professional investigator lawfully performing his or her duties as a professional investigator or employee of a professional investigator for the purpose of obtaining information with reference to any of the following:
  - Securing evidence to be used before a court, board, officer, or investigating committee.

♦ Crimes or wrongs done, threatened, or suspected against the United States or a state or territory of the United States or any other person or legal entity.

♦ Locating an individual known to be a fugitive from justice.

♦ Locating lost or stolen property or other assets that have been awarded by the court.

The "professional investigator" exemption does not apply if either of the following applies:

• The professional investigator or the employee of the professional investigator is working on behalf of a client who is the restrained party under a protective order.

• The professional investigator or the employee of the professional investigator knows or has reason to know that the person seeking his or her investigative services, including the installation or use of a tracking device, is doing so to aid in the commission of a crime or wrong.

A person who illegally installs or uses a tracking device or a bail agent of professional investigator who installs or uses a tracking device is liable for all damages incurred by the owner or lessee of the motor vehicle caused by the installation or use of the tracking device.

## Operating an Audiovisual Device in a Movie Theaters—MCL 750.465a

### Definitions

*Audiovisual recording function:*   The capability of a device to record or transmit a motion picture or any part of a motion picture by technological means.

*Theatrical facility:*   A facility being used to exhibit a motion picture to the public, but does not include an individual's residence or a retail establishment.

A person who knowingly operates an audiovisual recording function of a device in a theatrical facility where a motion picture is being exhibited without the consent of the owner or lessee of that theatrical facility and of the licensor of the motion picture being exhibited is guilty of a crime as follows:

Penalties:

| First offense | 1-year misdemeanor |
| Second offense | 2-year felony |
| Third offense | 4-year felony |

This section does not prevent any lawfully authorized investigative, law enforcement, protective, or intelligence—gathering employee or agent, of this state or the United States, from operating the audiovisual recording function of a device in a theatrical facility where a motion picture is being exhibited as part of an investigative, protective, law enforcement, or intelligence-gathering activity.

## Tampering with Electronic Communication— MCL 750.540 (felony)

### Definitions

*Computer:*   Any connected, directly interoperable or interactive device, equipment, or facility that uses a computer program or other instructions to perform specific operations including logical, arithmetic, or memory functions with or on computer data or a computer program and that can store, retrieve, alter, or communicate the results of the operations to a person, computer program, computer, computer system, or computer network.

*Computer network:*   The interconnection of hardwire or wireless communication lines with a computer through remote terminals, or a complex consisting of two or more interconnected computers.

*Computer program:*   A series of internal or external instructions communicated in a form acceptable to a computer that directs the functioning of a computer, computer system, or computer network in a manner designed to provide or produce products or results from the computer, computer system, or computer network.

*Computer system:*   A set of related, connected or unconnected, computer equipment, devices, software, or hardware.

*Internet:*   That term as defined in section 230 of title II of the Communications Act of 1934, 47 U.S.C. § 230, and includes voice over Internet protocol services.

A person shall not willfully and maliciously do any of the following:

• Cut, break, disconnect, interrupt, tap, or make any unauthorized connection with any electronic medium of communication, including the Internet or a computer, computer program, computer system, or computer network, or a telephone.

• Read or copy any message from any telegraph, telephone line, wire, cable, computer network, computer program, or computer system, or telephone or other electronic medium of communication that the person accessed without authorization.

• Make unauthorized use of any electronic medium of communication, including the

Internet or a computer, computer program, computer system, or computer network, or telephone.

- Prevent, obstruct, or delay by any means the sending, conveyance, or delivery of any authorized communication, by or through any telegraph or telephone line, cable, wire, or any electronic medium of communication, including the Internet or a computer, computer program, computer system, or computer network.

Penalties:

| If causes no injury | 2-year felony |
|---|---|
| If results in injury or death of any person | 4-year felony |

# OBSCENE, HARASSING, OR THREATENING PHONE CALLS

## Malicious Use of Phones—MCL 750.540e (6-month misdemeanor)

A person is guilty of a misdemeanor who maliciously uses any service provided by a telecommunications service provider with intent to terrorize, frighten, intimidate, threaten, harass, molest, or annoy any other person, or to disturb the peace and quiet of any other person by any of the following:

- Threatening physical harm or damage to any person or property.
- Falsely and deliberately reporting by telephone or telegraph message that any person has been injured, has suddenly taken ill, has suffered death, or has been the victim of a crime or accident.
- Deliberately refusing or failing to disengage a connection.
- Using any vulgar, indecent, obscene, or offensive language or suggesting any lewd or lascivious act in the course of a telephone conversation.
- Repeatedly initiating a telephone call and, without speaking, deliberately hanging up or breaking the telephone connection as or after the telephone call is answered.
- Making an unsolicited commercial telephone call that is received between the hours of 9 p.m. and 9 a.m.
- Deliberately engaging or causing to engage the use of a telecommunications service or device of another person in a repetitive manner that causes interruption in telecommunications service or prevents the person from utilizing his or her telecommunications service or device.

An offense is committed under this section if the communication either originates or terminates or both originates and terminates in this state and may be prosecuted at the place of origination or termination.

# IDENTITY THEFT

## Identity Protection Act—MCL 445.63

### Definitions

*Agency:* A department, board, commission, office, agency, authority, or other unit of state government of this state. The term includes an institution of higher education of this state. The term does not include a circuit, probate, district, or municipal court.

*Breach of the security of a database or security breach:* The unauthorized access and acquisition of data that compromises the security or confidentiality of personal information maintained by a person or agency as part of a database of personal information regarding multiple individuals. These terms do not include unauthorized access to data by an employee or other individual if the access meets all of the following:

- The employee or other individual acted in good faith in accessing the data.
- The access was related to the activities of the agency or person.
- The employee or other individual did not misuse any personal information or disclose any personal information to an unauthorized person.

*Child or spousal support:* Support for a child or spouse, paid or provided pursuant to state or federal law under a court order or judgment. Support includes, but is not limited to, any of the following:

- Expenses for day-to-day care.
- Medical, dental, or other health care.
- Child care expenses.
- Educational expenses.
- Expenses in connection with pregnancy or confinement under the paternity act, MCL 722.711 to 722.730.
- Repayment of genetic testing expenses, under the paternity act, MCL 722.711 to 722.730.
- A surcharge as provided by section 3a of the support and parenting time enforcement act, MCL 552.603a.

*Credit card:* That term as defined in section 157m of the Michigan penal code, MCL 750.157m.

*Data:* Computerized personal information.

*Depository institution:* A state or nationally chartered bank or a state or federally chartered savings and loan association, savings bank, or credit union.

*Encrypted:* Transformation of data through the use of an algorithmic process into a form in which there is a low probability of assigning meaning without use of a confidential process or key, or securing information by another method that renders the data elements unreadable or unusable.

*False pretenses:* Includes, but is not limited to, a false, misleading, or fraudulent representation, writing, communication, statement, or message, communicated by any means to another person, that the maker of the representation, writing, communication, statement, or message knows or should have known is false or fraudulent. The false pretense may be a representation regarding a past or existing fact or circumstance or a representation regarding the intention to perform a future event or to have a future event performed.

*Financial institution:* A depository institution, an affiliate of a depository institution, a licensee under the consumer financial services act, 1988 PA 161, MCL 487.2051 to 487.2072, 1984 PA 379, MCL 493.101 to 493.114, the motor vehicle sales finance act, 1950 (Ex Sess) PA 27, MCL 492.101 to 492.141, the secondary mortgage loan act, 1981 PA 125, MCL 493.51 to 493.81, the mortgage brokers, lenders, and servicers licensing act, 1987 PA 173, MCL 445.1651 to 445.1684, or the regulatory loan act, 1939 PA 21, MCL 493.1 to 493.24, a seller under the home improvement finance act, 1965 PA 332, MCL 445.1101 to 445.1431, or the retail installment sales act, 1966 PA 224, MCL 445.851 to 445.873, or a person subject to subtitle A of title V of the Gramm-Leach-Bliley act, 15 USC 6801 to 6809.

*Financial transaction device:* That term as defined in section 157m of the Michigan penal code, 1931 PA 328, MCL 750.157m.

*Identity theft:* Engaging in an act or conduct prohibited in section 5(1).

*Interactive computer service:* An information service or system that enables computer access by multiple users to a computer server, including, but not limited to, a service or system that provides access to the internet or to software services available on a server.

*Law enforcement agency:* That term as defined in section 2804 of the public health code, 1978 PA 368, MCL 333.2804.

*Local registrar:* That term as defined in section 2804 of the public health code, 1978 PA 368, MCL 333.2804.

*Medical records or information:* Includes, but is not limited to, medical and mental health histories, reports, summaries, diagnoses and prognoses, treatment and medication information, notes, entries, and X-rays and other imaging records.

*Person:* An individual, partnership, corporation, limited liability company, association, or other legal entity.

*Personal identifying information:* A name, number, or other information that is used for the purpose of identifying a specific person or providing access to a person's financial accounts, including, but not limited to, a person's name, address, telephone number, driver license or state personal identification card number, social security number, place of employment, employee identification number, employer or taxpayer identification number, government passport number, health insurance identification number, mother's maiden name, demand deposit account number, savings account number, financial transaction device account number or the person's account password, any other account password in combination with sufficient information to identify and access the account, automated or electronic signature, biometrics, stock or other security certificate or account number, credit card number, vital record, or medical records or information.

*Personal information:* The first name or first initial and last name linked to one or more of the following data elements of a resident of this state:

- Social security number.
- Driver license number or state personal identification card number.
- Demand deposit or other financial account number, or credit card or debit card number, in combination with any required security code, access code, or password that would permit access to any of the resident's financial accounts.

*Public utility:* That term as defined in section 1 of 1972 PA 299, MCL 460.111.

*Redact:* To alter or truncate data so that no more than four sequential digits of a driver license number, state personal identification card number, or account number, or no more than five sequential digits of a social security number, are accessible as part of personal information.

*State registrar:* That term as defined in section 2805 of the public health code, 1978 PA 368, MCL 333.2805.

*Trade or commerce:* That term as defined in section 2 of the Michigan consumer protection act, 1971 PA 331, MCL 445.902.

*Vital record:* That term as defined in section 2805 of the public health code, 1978 PA 368, MCL 333.2805.

*Webpage:* A location that has a uniform resource locator or URL with respect to the World Wide Web or another location that can be accessed on the Internet.

## Using/Attempting to Use Personally Identifiable Information of Another Person—MCL 445.65(1)(a)(i) (felony)

### Elements

1. The defendant used or attempted to use the personal identifying information of the victim.
2. The defendant did this with the intent to obtain credit, goods, services, money, property, a vital record, a confidential telephone record, medical records or information, or employment.
3. The defendant did this with the intent to defraud.
CJI2d 30.14.

## Use of Victim's Information to Commit and Illegal Act—MCL 445.65(1)(a)(ii) (felony)

### Elements

1. The defendant used or attempted to use the personal identifying information of the victim.
2. The defendant did this with the intent to commit the illegal act.
CJI2d 30.15.

## Misrepresenting/Withholding/Concealing Identity to Use the Victim's Information to Obtain Credit, Goods, Services, Money, Property, Information, or Employment—MCL 445.65(1)(b)(i) (felony)

### Elements

1. The defendant concealed, withheld, or misrepresented his identity.
2. The defendant used or attempted to use the personal identifying information of the victim.
3. The defendant did this with the intent to obtain credit, goods, services, money, property, a vital record, a confidential telephone record, medical records or information, or employment.
CJI2d 30.16.

## Misrepresenting/Withholding/Concealing Identity to Use the Victim's Information to Commit an Illegal Act—MCL 445.65(1)(b)(ii) (felony)

### Elements

1. The defendant concealed, withheld, or misrepresented his identity.
2. The defendant used or attempted to use the personal identifying information of the victim.

3. The defendant did this with the intent to commit the illegal act.
CJI2d 30.17.

## Additional Prohibited Acts—MCL 445.67 (felony)

A person shall not do any of the following:

- Make any electronic mail or other communication under false pretenses purporting to be by or on behalf of a business, without the authority or approval of the business, and use that electronic mail or other communication to induce, request, or solicit any individual to provide personal identifying information with the intent to use that information to commit identity theft or another crime.
- Create or operate a webpage that represents itself as belonging to or being associated with a business, without the authority or approval of that business, and induces, requests, or solicits any user of the Internet to provide personal identifying information with the intent to use that information to commit identity theft or another crime.
- Alter a setting on a user's computer or similar device or software program through which the user may access the Internet and cause any user of the Internet to view a communication that represents itself as belonging to or being associated with a business, which message has been created or is operated without the authority or approval of that business, and induces, requests, or solicits any user of the Internet to provide personal identifying information with the intent to use that information to commit identity theft or another crime.
- Obtain or possess, or attempt to obtain or possess, personal identifying information of another person with the intent to use that information to commit identity theft or another crime.
- Sell or transfer, or attempt to sell or transfer, personal identifying information of another person if the person knows or has reason to know that the specific intended recipient will use, attempt to use, or further transfer the information to another person for the purpose of committing identity theft or another crime.
- Falsify a police report of identity theft, or knowingly create, possess, or use a false police report of identity theft.

**Penalties—MCL 445.69**

Penalties:

| First offense | 5-year felony |
|---|---|
| Second offense | 10-year felony |
| Third offense | 15-year felony |

MCL 445.65 and MCL 445.67 apply whether an individual who is a victim or intended victim of a violation of one of those sections is alive or deceased at the time of the violation.

The court may order that a term of imprisonment imposed under this section be served consecutively to any term of imprisonment imposed for a conviction of any other violation of law committed by that person using the information obtained in violation of this section or any other violation of law committed by that person while violating or attempting to violate this section.

A person may assert as a defense in a civil action or as an affirmative defense in a criminal prosecution for a violation of MCL 445.65 and MCL 445.67 and has the burden of proof on that defense by a preponderance of the evidence, that the person lawfully transferred, obtained, or attempted to obtain personal identifying information of another person for the purpose of detecting, preventing, or deterring identity theft or another crime or the funding of a criminal activity.

This statute does not apply to a violation of a statute or rule administered by a regulatory board, commission, or officer acting under authority of this state or the United States that confers primary jurisdiction on that regulatory board, commission, or officer to authorize, prohibit, or regulate the transactions and conduct of that person, including, but not limited to, a state or federal statute or rule governing a financial institution and the insurance code of 1956, MCL 500.100 to 500.8302, if the act is committed by a person subject to and regulated by that statute or rule, or by another person who has contracted with that person to use personal identifying information.

### Venue for Prosecution of Identity Theft— MCL 762.10c

(1) *Except as otherwise provided in subsection (3), conduct prohibited by law, or former law, and listed in subsection (2) may be prosecuted in 1 of the following jurisdictions:*

   (a) *The jurisdiction in which the offense occurred.*

   (b) *The jurisdiction in which the information used to commit the violation was illegally used.*

   (c) *The jurisdiction in which the victim resides.*

(2) *Jurisdiction described under subsection (1) applies to conduct prohibited under 1 or more of the following laws and to conduct that is done in furtherance of or arising from the same transaction as conduct prohibited under 1 or more of the following laws:*

   (a) *The identity theft protection act, 2004 PA 452, MCL 445.61 to 445.77.*

   (b) *Former section 285 of the Michigan penal code, 1931 PA 328.*

   (c) *Section 5 of 1972 PA 222, MCL 28.295.*

   (d) *Section 310(7) or 903 of the Michigan vehicle code, 1949 PA 300, MCL 257.310 and 257.903.*

   (e) *Section 157n, 157p, 157q, 157r, 157v, 157w, 218, 219a, 219e, 248, 248a, 249, 362, 363, or 539k of the Michigan penal code, 1931 PA 328, MCL 750.157n, 750.157p, 750.157q, 750.157r, 750.157v, 750.157w, 750.218, 750.219a, 750.219e, 750.248, 750.248a, 750.249, 750.362, 750.363, and 750.539k.*

(3) *If a person is charged with more than 1 violation of the identity theft protection act, 2004 PA 452, MCL 445.61 to 445.77, and those violations may be prosecuted in more than 1 jurisdiction, any of those jurisdictions is a proper jurisdiction for all of the violations.*

### Secretly Capturing Someone's ID—MCL 750.539k (felony)

*A person who is not a party to a transaction that involves the use of a financial transaction device shall not secretly or surreptitiously photograph, or otherwise capture or record, electronically or by any other means, or distribute, disseminate, or transmit, electronically or by any other means, personal identifying information from the transaction without the consent of the individual.*

Penalties:

| First offense | 5-year felony |
|---|---|
| Second offense | 10-year felony |
| Third offense | 15-year felony |

This section does not prohibit the capture or transmission of personal identifying information in the ordinary and lawful course of business.

This section does not apply to a peace officer of this state, or of the federal government, or the officer's agent, while in the lawful performance of the officer's duties.

## Denial of Credit or Public Utility Service to a Victim of Identity Theft—MCL 445.71(1)(a) (93-day misdemeanor)

*A person shall not deny credit or public utility service to or reduce the credit limit of a consumer solely because the consumer was a victim of identity theft, if the person had prior knowledge that the consumer was a victim of identity theft. A consumer is presumed to be a victim of identity theft for the purposes of this subdivision if he or she provides both of the following to the person:*

*(i) A copy of a police report evidencing the claim of the victim of identity theft.*

*(ii) Either a properly completed copy of a standardized affidavit of identity theft developed and made available by the federal trade commission under 15 USC 1681g or an affidavit of fact that is acceptable to the person for that purpose.*

## Failure to Verify Identity of Persons Applying for Credit—MCL 445.71(1)(d) (93-day misdemeanor)

*A person shall not extend credit to a consumer without exercising reasonable procedures to verify the identity of that consumer. Compliance with regulations issued for depository institutions, and to be issued for other financial institutions, by the United States department of treasury under section 326 of the USA patriot act of 2001, 31 USC 5318, is considered compliance with this subdivision. This subdivision does not apply to a purchase of a credit obligation in an acquisition, merger, purchase of assets, or assumption of liabilities or any change to or review of an existing credit account.*

# COMPUTER CRIMES

## Use of Computers to Commit Certain Crimes— MCL 750.145d (felony)

### Definitions

*Computer:* Any connected, directly interoperable or interactive device, equipment, or facility that uses a computer program or other instructions to perform specific operations including logical, arithmetic, or memory functions with or on computer data or a computer program and that can store, retrieve, alter, or communicate the results of the operations to a person, computer program, computer, computer system, or computer network. Computer includes a computer game device or a cellular telephone, personal digital assistant (PDA), or other handheld device.

*Computer network:* The interconnection of hardwire or wireless communication lines with a computer through remote terminals, or a complex consisting of two or more interconnected computers.

*Computer program:* A series of internal or external instructions communicated in a form acceptable to a computer that directs the functioning of a computer, computer system, or computer network in a manner designed to provide or produce products or results from the computer, computer system, or computer network.

*Computer system:* A set of related, connected or unconnected, computer equipment, devices, software, or hardware.

*Device:* Includes, but is not limited to, an electronic, magnetic, electrochemical, biochemical, hydraulic, optical, or organic object that performs input, output, or storage functions by the manipulation of electronic, magnetic, or other impulses.

*Internet:* That term as defined in section 230 of the communications act of 1934, 47 USC 230.

*Minor:* An individual who is less than 18 years of age.

### Elements

1. The defendant used the Internet, a computer, a computer program, a computer network, or a computer system to communicate with any person.
2. The communication was done for the purpose of committing, attempting to commit, conspiring to commit, soliciting another to commit one of the following offenses from either Part A or Part B below:

Part A—if the victim or intended victim was a minor or the defendant believed the victim or intended victim was a minor.

- Accosting a child for immoral purposes. MCL 750.145.
- Child sexually abusive activity. MCL 750.145c.
- Kidnapping. MCL 750.349.
- Enticing away child under 14. MCL 750.350.
- Criminal sexual conduct in the first degree. MCL 750.520b.
- Criminal sexual conduct in the second degree. MCL 750.520c.
- Criminal sexual conduct in the third degree. MCL 750.520d.
- Criminal sexual conduct in the fourth degree. MCL 750.520e.
- Assault with intent to commit criminal sexual conduct. MCL 750.520g.
- Disseminating sexually explicit material to a minor. MCL 722.675(5).

- Sale of explosives to minors. MCL 750.327a.
- Inducing minor to commit felony. MCL 750.157c.

Part B—age is irrelevant.

- Stalking. MCL 750.411h.
- Aggravated stalking. MCL 750.411i.
- Causing death with explosives in vehicle. MCL 750.327.
- Causing death with explosives placed to destroy building. MCL 750.328.
- False report of explosives crime or threatening to commit such a crime. MCL 750.411a(2).

3. It does not matter whether the defendant or anyone else has been convicted of underlying offense. CJI2d 20.37.

Penalties:

| | |
|---|---|
| Underlying crime is a misdemeanor or felony with maximum imprisonment of less than 1 year | 1-year misdemeanor |
| Underlying crime is a misdemeanor or felony with maximum imprisonment of 1 year or more but less than 2 years | 2-year felony |
| Underlying crime is a misdemeanor or felony with maximum imprisonment of 2 years or more but less than 4 years | 4-year felony |
| Underlying crime is a felony with maximum imprisonment of 4 years or more but less than 10 years | 10-year felony |
| Underlying crime is a felony with maximum imprisonment of 10 years or more but less than 15 years | 15-year felony |
| Underlying crime is a felony with maximum imprisonment of 15 years or more or for life | 20-year felony |

- The court may order that a term of imprisonment imposed under this section be served consecutively to any term of imprisonment imposed for conviction of the underlying offense.
- This section applies regardless of whether the person is convicted of committing, attempting to commit, conspiring to commit, or soliciting another person to commit the underlying offense.
- A violation or attempted violation of this section occurs if the communication originates in this state, is intended to terminate in this state, or is intended to terminate with a person who is in this state.
- A violation or attempted violation of this section may be prosecuted in any jurisdiction in which the communication originated or terminated.

The defendant lived in Indiana and used a website chat room to talk to a woman from Ohio who belonged to a group dedicated to identifying Internet "predators." The defendant asked her "asl" (age, sex, and location), the woman responded, "lol im [sic] 14 f [female] mi [Michigan]." The defendant soon steered the discussion toward sexual activity, and for over a one-month period, defendant on a daily basis broached topics including engagement in oral sex, group sex, and bestiality and discussed plans to meet in person. He also discussed the interest in photographing any sexual activity. They eventually agreed to a camping trip, and defendant made online reservations for a campsite near Grand Rapids. He was than given an address in Michigan to pick the girl up where he was arrested. The defendant argued that the court in Michigan did not have jurisdiction to hear his case.

Under MCL 762.2, "Michigan now has statutory territorial jurisdiction over any crime where any act constituting an element of the crime is committed within Michigan even if there is no indication that the accused actually intended the detrimental effects of the offense to be felt in this state." The court found that the "facts offered by the prosecution and proved to the jury were clearly adequate to confer jurisdiction" and that "the prosecution presented more than sufficient evidence to allow a rational jury to conclude that defendant prepared and attempted to commit child sexually abusive activity and that defendant used a computer and the Internet to commit this crime." While Defendant's Internet communication originated in Indiana, not Michigan, the communication was intended to terminate in Michigan. The defendant reserved a campground in Michigan. The defendant stocked his truck with alcohol and drove to Michigan where he then went to a house for the purpose of picking her up to engage in prohibited acts in Michigan. The record evidence supports the fact that although the Internet communication originated elsewhere, defendant clearly intended them to terminate in Michigan. *People v. Aspy*, 292 Mich. App. 36 (2011).

The defendant's receipt of child sexually abusive material through the computer indicates that he communicated his desire to receive such material through the computer. *People v. Tombs*, 260 Mich. App. 201 (2003).

# FRAUDULENT ACCESS TO COMPUTERS, COMPUTER SYSTEMS, AND COMPUTER NETWORKS

## Definitions—MCL 752.794–752.793, 752.797(8)

*Access:* To instruct, communicate with, store data in, retrieve or intercept data from, or otherwise use the resources of a computer program, computer, computer system, or computer network.

*Aggregate amount:* Any direct or indirect loss incurred by a victim or group of victims including, but not limited to, the value of any money, property or service lost, stolen, or rendered unrecoverable by the offense, or any actual expenditure incurred by the victim or group of victims to verify that a computer program, computer, computer system, or computer network was not altered, acquired, damaged, deleted, disrupted, or destroyed by the access. The direct or indirect losses incurred in separate incidents pursuant to a scheme or course of conduct within any 12-month period may be aggregated to determine the total value of the loss involved in the violation of this act.

*Computer:* Any connected, directly interoperable or interactive device, equipment, or facility that uses a computer program or other instructions to perform specific operations including logical, arithmetic, or memory functions with or on computer data or a computer program and that can store, retrieve, alter, or communicate the results of the operations to a person, computer program, computer, computer system, or computer network.

*Computer network:* The interconnection of hardwire or wireless communication lines with a computer through remote terminals, or a complex consisting of two or more interconnected computers.

*Computer program:* A series of internal or external instructions communicated in a form acceptable to a computer that directs the functioning of a computer, computer system, or computer network in a manner designed to provide or produce products or results from the computer, computer system, or computer network.

*Computer system:* A set of related, connected or unconnected, computer equipment, devices, software, or hardware.

*Device:* Includes, but is not limited to, an electronic, magnetic, electrochemical, biochemical, hydraulic, optical, or organic object that performs input, output, or storage functions by the manipulation of electronic, magnetic, or other impulses.

*Prior conviction:* A violation or attempted violation of MCL 750.145d, or this act or a substantially similar law of the United States, another state, or a political subdivision of another state.

*Property:* Includes, but is not limited to, intellectual property, computer data, instructions, or programs in either machine or human readable form, financial instruments or information, medical information, restricted personal information, or any other tangible or intangible item of value.

*Services:* Includes, but is not limited to, computer time, data processing, storage functions, computer memory, or the unauthorized use of a computer program, computer, computer system, or computer network, or communication facilities connected or related to a computer, computer system, or computer network.

## Access to Computer with Attempt to Defraud—MCL 752.794

*A person shall not intentionally access or cause access to be made to a computer program, computer, computer system, or computer network to devise or execute a scheme or artifice with the intent to defraud or to obtain money, property, or a service by a false or fraudulent pretense, representation, or promise.*

### Elements

1. The defendant accessed a computer, computer program, computer system, or computer network.
2. The defendant did so intentionally.
3. The defendant did so for the purpose of devising or executing a scheme or plan to obtain money, property, or a service by a false or fraudulent pretense, representation, or promise.
4. The defendant's acts directly or indirectly caused an aggregate loss of:
   a. $20,000 or more.
      $1,000 or more, but less than $20,000.
      $200 or more, but less than $1,000.
   b. Some amount less than $200.

CJI2d 35.7.

Penalties:

| Less than $200 | 93-day misdemeanor |
|---|---|
| $200 or more, but less than $1,000; or a prior conviction | 1-year misdemeanor |
| $1,000 or more, but less than $20,000; or 2 prior convictions | 5-year felony |
| $20,000 or more; or 3 prior convictions | 10-year felony |

## Unlawful Use of a Computer System—MCL 752.795(a) (felony)

### Elements

1. The defendant accessed a computer, computer program, computer system, or computer network.
2. The defendant did so intentionally.
3. The defendant did so without or by exceeding valid authorization.
4. The defendant did so to acquire, alter, damage, delete, destroy property, or use the services of the computer, computer program, computer system, or computer network.

CJI2d 35.8.

Penalties:

| First offense | 5-year felony |
|---|---|
| Second or subsequent offense | 10-year felony |

- It is a rebuttable presumption in a prosecution for a violation of this section that the person did not have authorization from the owner, system operator, or other person who has authority from the owner or system operator to grant permission to access the computer program, computer, computer system, or computer network or has exceeded authorization unless one or more of the following circumstances existed at the time of access:
  - ◆ Written or oral permission was granted by the owner, system operator, or other person who has authority from the owner or system operator to grant permission of the accessed computer program, computer, computer system, or computer network.
  - ◆ The accessed computer program, computer, computer system, or computer network had a pre-programmed access procedure that would display a bulletin,

command, or other message before access was achieved that a reasonable person would believe identified the computer program, computer, computer system, or computer network as within the public domain.
- ◆ Access was achieved without the use of a set of instructions, code, or computer program that bypasses, defrauds, or otherwise circumvents the pre-programmed access procedure for the computer program, computer, computer system, or computer network.

## Unlawfully Inserting Instructions into Computer—MCL 752.795(b) (felony)

### Elements—Violation of MCL 752.795(b)

1. The defendant inserted, attached, or knowingly created the opportunity for an unknowing and unwanted insertion or attachment of a set of instructions or a computer program into a computer, computer program, computer system, or computer network.
2. The instructions or program was intended to acquire, alter, damage, delete, disrupt, destroy property, or use the services of the computer, computer program, computer system, or computer network.

CJI2d 35.9.

Penalties:

| First offense | 5-year felony |
|---|---|
| Second or subsequent offense | 10-year felony |

- It is a rebuttable presumption in a prosecution for a violation of this section that the person did not have authorization from the owner, system operator, or other person who has authority from the owner or system operator to grant permission to access the computer program, computer, computer system, or computer network or has exceeded authorization unless one or more of the following circumstances existed at the time of access:
  - ◆ Written or oral permission was granted by the owner, system operator, or other person who has authority from the owner or system operator to grant permission of the accessed computer program, computer, computer system, or computer network.
  - ◆ The accessed computer program, computer, computer system, or computer network had a pre-programmed access

procedure that would display a bulletin, command, or other message before access was achieved that a reasonable person would believe identified the computer program, computer, computer system, or computer network as within the public domain.

♦ Access was achieved without the use of a set of instructions, code, or computer program that bypasses, defrauds, or otherwise circumvents the pre-programmed access procedure for the computer program, computer, computer system, or computer network.

## Committing Crime Using Computer—MCL 752.796

*A person shall not use a computer program, computer, computer system, or computer network to commit, attempt to commit, conspire to commit, or solicit another person to commit a crime.*

Penalties:

| | |
|---|---|
| Underlying crime is a misdemeanor or felony with maximum imprisonment of 1 year or less | 1-year misdemeanor |
| Underlying crime is a misdemeanor or felony with maximum imprisonment of more than 1 year but less than 2 years | 2-year felony |
| Underlying crime is a misdemeanor or felony with maximum imprisonment of 2 years or more but less than 4 years | 4-year felony |
| Underlying crime is a felony with maximum imprisonment of 4 years or more but less than 10 years | 7-year felony |
| Underlying crime is a felony with maximum imprisonment of 10 years or more but less than 20 years | 10-year felony |
| Underlying crime is a felony with maximum imprisonment of 20 years or more or for life | 20-year felony |

• This section does not prohibit a person from being charged with, convicted of, or punished for any other violation of law committed by that person while violating or attempting to violate this section, including the underlying offense.

• This section applies regardless of whether the person is convicted of committing, attempting to commit, conspiring to commit, or soliciting another person to commit the underlying offense.

• The court may order that a term of imprisonment imposed under this section be served consecutively to any term of imprisonment imposed for conviction of the underlying offense.

## ADULTERATED FOOD—MCL 750.397a (felony)

*A person who places pins, needles, razor blades, glass, or other harmful objects in any food, or a person who places a harmful substance in any food, with intent to harm the consumer of the food, or who knowingly furnishes any food containing a harmful object or substance to another person, is guilty of a felony and shall be imprisoned for not more than 10 years, or fined not more than $10,000.00, or both.*

### Elements

1. The defendant intended to cause harm, and
2. Knowingly placed pins, needles, razor blades, glass, or any other harmful substance in food.

or

1. The defendant intended to cause harm, and
2. Knowingly furnished food containing harmful substances to another.

Stale urine may be a harmful substance under MCL 750.397a because expert testimony established that it can transmit disease through viruses or bacteria. *People v. Guthrie*, 262 Mich. App. 416 (2004).

## POISONING

### Poison Food/Drink/Medicine/Water Supply— MCL 750.436(a) (felony)

*A person shall not willfully mingle a poison or harmful substance with a food, drink, nonprescription medicine, or pharmaceutical product, or willfully place a poison or harmful substance in a spring, well, reservoir, or public water supply, knowing or having reason to know that the food, drink, nonprescription medicine, pharmaceutical product, or water may be ingested or used by a person to his or her injury.*

### Elements

1. Willfully placed poison or a harmful substance into food, medicine, or a water supply, and
2. Knowing or having reason to know that someone will ingest that item.

Penalties:

| If causes no injury | 15-year felony |
|---|---|
| If results in damage to property of another | 20-year felony |
| If causes physical injury to another | 25-year felony |
| If causes serious impairment | Life or any term of years |

The defendants were convicted under this statute for placing a date rape drug into the victim's drink at a party. *People v. Holtschlag*, 471 Mich. 1 (2004).

The defendant was convicted after she repeatedly placed ant poison in the victims' coffee. *People v. Belknap*, 146 Mich. App. 239 (1985).

## Malicious False Statement of Poisoning— MCL 750.436(b) (felony)

*A person shall not maliciously inform another person that a poison or harmful substance has been or will be placed in a food, drink, nonprescription medicine, pharmaceutical product, spring, well,* reservoir, or public water supply, knowing that the information is false and that it is likely that the information will be disseminated to the public.

### Elements

1. Maliciously informed another person,
2. That poison or a harmful substance had been placed into food, medicine, or a water supply,
3. Knowing that this information is false, and
4. Knowing that this information is likely to be disseminated to the public.

Penalties:

| First offense | 4-year felony |
|---|---|
| Second offense | 10-year felony |

The defendant was convicted for making a false police report when he falsely told police that he had placed poison in his own milk to "get" the person who had been stealing his milk. *People v. Lay*, 336 Mich. 77 (1953).

## Murder by Poison—MCL 750.316(b) (felony)

### Elements

1. Poisoning means that a substance was deliberately introduced into the victim's body, causing death.
2. When the defendant administered the poison, the defendant must have intended to kill the victim.
3. The circumstances of the poisoning must convince you beyond a reasonable doubt that the killing was done willfully, with premeditation and deliberation.

CJI2d 16.3.

# 10

# DESTRUCTION OF PROPERTY

## ARSON

### Definitions

**Burn:**   Setting fire to or doing any act that results in the starting of a fire, or aiding, counseling, inducing, persuading, or procuring another to do such an act. CJI2d 31.2.

**Damage:**   In addition to its ordinary meaning, includes, but is not limited to, charring, melting, scorching, burning, or breaking. CJI2d 31.2.

**Building:**   Includes any structure regardless of class or character and any building or structure that is within the curtilage of that building or structure or that is appurtenant to or connected to that building or structure. CJI2d 31.2.

**Dwelling:**   Includes, but is not limited to, any building, structure, vehicle, watercraft, or trailer adapted for human habitation that was actually lived in or reasonably could have been lived in at the time of the fire or explosion and any building or structure that is within the curtilage of that dwelling or that is appurtenant to or connected to that dwelling. CJI2d 31.2.

A dilapidated abandoned building that had no utilities or running water was not a dwelling house under the arson statute where there was no evidence that it was going to be restored in the near future. *People v. Reeves*, 448 Mich. 1 (1995).

A highway passing between a barn and a house was sufficient to separate the barn from the curtilage of the house. *Carkendall v. People*, 36 Mich. 309 (1877).

A barn 80 feet from a dwelling house and in the back yard is within the curtilage. *People v. Taylor*, 2 Mich. 250 (1851).

A business that is located very close to and used in connection with a dwelling may be considered to be a dwelling. CJI2d 31.4.

**Individual:**   Any person and includes, but is not limited to, a firefighter, a law enforcement officer, or other emergency responder, whether paid or volunteer, performing his or her duties in relation to a violation of this chapter or performing an investigation. CJI2d 31.3.

**Physical injury:**   An injury that includes, but is not limited to, the loss of a limb or use of a limb; loss of a foot, hand, finger, or thumb or loss of use of a foot, hand, finger, or thumb; loss of an eye or ear or loss of use of an eye or ear; loss or substantial impairment of a bodily function; serious, visible disfigurement; a comatose state that lasts for more than three days; measurable brain or mental impairment; a skull fracture or other serious bone fracture; subdural hemorrhage or subdural hematoma; loss of an organ; heart attack; heat stroke; heat exhaustion; smoke inhalation; a burn including a chemical burn; or poisoning. CJI2d 31.3.

*Personal property:* Any personally owned property regardless of class or character. CJI2d 31.6.

## Intent

The only intent required is that the suspect "intended to burn the dwelling or contents or intentionally committed an act that created a very high risk of burning the dwelling or contents and that, while committing the act, the defendant knew of that risk and disregarded it." CJ12d 31.2(4).

> The careless throwing of matches on the floor is not sufficient to support a conviction for willfully burning insured personal property with intent to defraud the insurer. *People v. McCarty*, 303 Mich. 629 (1942).
>
> Arson is not a specific intent crime under Michigan common law. *People v. Nowack*, 462 Mich. 392 (2000).

## First-Degree Arson—MCL 750.72 (felony)

*(1) A person who willfully or maliciously burns, damages, or destroys by fire or explosive any of the following or its contents is guilty of first-degree arson:*

*(a) A multiunit building or structure in which 1 or more units of the building are a dwelling, regardless of whether any of the units are occupied, unoccupied, or vacant at the time of the fire or explosion.*

*(b) Any building or structure or other real property if the fire or explosion results in physical injury to any individual.*

*(c) A mine.*

*(2) Subsection (1) applies regardless of whether the person owns the dwelling, building, structure, or mine or its contents.*

*(3) First-degree arson is a felony punishable by imprisonment for life or any term of years or a fine of not more than $20,000.00 or 3 times the value of the property damaged or destroyed, whichever is greater, or both imprisonment and a fine.*

## First-Degree Arson—Multiunit Building or Mine

### Elements

1. The defendant burned, damaged, or destroyed by fire or explosive property. If any part of the property is burned, no matter how small, that is all that is necessary to count as a burning; the property does not have to be completely destroyed. The property is not burned if it is merely blackened by smoke, but it is burned if it is charred so that any part of it is destroyed.

2. The property that was burned, damaged, or destroyed was a multiunit building or structure in which one or more units of the building were dwellings or a mine. It does not matter whether any of the units were occupied, unoccupied, or vacant at the time of the fire or explosion. It does not matter whether the defendant owned the property or its contents.

3. When the defendant burned, damaged, or destroyed the property or any of its contents, he intended to burn, damage, or destroy the property or its contents or intentionally committed an act that created a very high risk of burning the property or its contents and that, while committing the act, the defendant knew of that risk and disregarded it.

CJI2d 31.2.

## First-Degree Arson—Fire Causing Injury

### Elements

1. The defendant burned, damaged, or destroyed by fire or explosive a real property. If any part of the property is burned, no matter how small, that is all that is necessary to count as a burning; the property does not have to be completely destroyed. The property is not burned if it is merely blackened by smoke, but it is burned if it is charred so that any part of it is destroyed.

2. The property that was burned, damaged, or destroyed was a building, structure, or other real property or any of its contents.

3. The defendant burned, damaged, or destroyed the property or any of its contents, he intended to burn, damage, or destroy the property or its contents or intentionally committed an act that created a very high risk of burning the property or its contents and that, while committing the act, the defendant knew of that risk and disregarded it.

4. As a result of the fire or explosion, an individual was physically injured.

CJI2d 31.3.

An arsonist is liable for the injuries of person who enter a fire to salvage property and any other person injured as a result of the fire even though the injured person was not present when the fire was started. *People v. Jackson*, 211 Mich. App. 414 (1995).

## Second-Degree Arson—MCL 750.73 (felony)

*(1) Except as provided in section 72, a person who willfully or maliciously burns, damages, or destroys by fire or explosive a dwelling, regardless of whether it is occupied, unoccupied, or vacant at the time of the fire or explosion, or its contents, is guilty of second-degree arson.*

*(2) Subsection (1) applies regardless of whether the person owns the dwelling or its contents.*

*(3) Second-degree arson is a felony punishable by imprisonment for not more than 20 years or a fine of not more than $20,000.00 or 3 times the value of the property damaged or destroyed, whichever is greater, or both imprisonment and a fine.*

### Elements

1. The defendant burned, damaged, or destroyed by fire or explosive the property. If any part of the property is burned, no matter how small, that is all that is necessary to count as a burning; the property does not have to be completely destroyed. The property is not burned if it is merely blackened by smoke, but it is burned if it is charred so that any part of it is destroyed.
2. At the time of the burning, the property that was damaged was a dwelling or any of its contents. It does not matter whether the defendant owned or used the dwelling.
3. When the defendant burned the dwelling or any of its contents, he intended to burn the dwelling or its contents or intentionally committed an act that created a very high risk of burning the dwelling or its contents and that, while committing the act, the defendant knew of that risk and disregarded it.

CJI2d 31.4.

## Third-Degree Arson—MCL 750.73 (felony)

*(1) Except as provided in sections 72 and 73, a person who does any of the following is guilty of third-degree arson:*

*(a) Willfully or maliciously burns, damages, or destroys by fire or explosive any building or structure, or its contents, regardless of*

*whether it is occupied, unoccupied, or vacant at the time of the fire or explosion.*

*(b) Willfully and maliciously burns, damages, or destroys by fire or explosive any of the following or its contents:*

*(i) Any personal property having a value of $20,000.00 or more.*

*(ii) Any personal property having a value of $1,000.00 or more if the person has 1 or more prior convictions.*

*(1) Subsection (1) applies regardless of whether the person owns the building, structure, other real property or its contents, or the personal property.*

*(2) Third-degree arson is a felony punishable by imprisonment for not more than 10 years or a fine of not more than $20,000.00 or 3 times the value of the property damaged or destroyed, whichever is greater, or both imprisonment and a fine.*

A school construction site is real property under this statute. *People v. Smock*, 399 Mich. 282 (1976).

### Elements

1. The defendant burned, damaged, or destroyed by fire or explosive the property. If any part of the property is burned, no matter how small, that is all that is necessary to count as a burning; the property does not have to be completely destroyed. The property is not burned if it is merely blackened by smoke, but it is burned if it is charred so that any part of it is destroyed.
2. At the time of the burning, the property was a building, structure, or other real property or its contents. It does not matter whether the building was occupied, unoccupied, or vacant at the time of the fire or explosion. It does not matter whether the defendant owned or used the building.
3. When the defendant burned the building or any of its contents, he intended to burn the building or contents or intentionally committed an act that created a very high risk of burning the building or contents and that, while committing the act, the defendant knew of that risk and disregarded it.

CJI2d 31.5.

## Third-Degree Arson—Personal Property

### Elements

1. The defendant burned, damaged, or destroyed by fire or explosive the property. If any part of the property is burned, no matter how small,

that is all that is necessary to count as a burning; the property does not have to be completely destroyed. The property is not burned if it is merely blackened by smoke, but it is burned if it is charred so that any part of it is destroyed.

2. At the time of the burning, the property that was damaged was any personal property. It does not matter whether the defendant owned the property.

3. When the defendant burned it, the property had a fair market value of:

   a. $20,000 or more.
   b. $1,000 or more if the defendant has a prior conviction.

4. When the defendant burned the property, he intended to burn or intentionally committed an act that created a very high risk of burning the building or contents and that, while committing the act, the defendant knew of that risk and disregarded it.

CJI2d 31.6.

## Fourth-Degree Arson—MCL 750.75 (felony)

(1) *Except as provided in sections 72, 73, and 74, a person who does any of the following is guilty of fourth-degree arson*

   (a) *Willfully and maliciously burns, damages, or destroys by fire or explosive any of the following or its contents:*

      (i) *Any personal property having a value of $1,000.00 or more, but less than $20,000.00.*

      (ii) *Any personal property having a value of $200.00 or more if the person has 1 or more prior convictions.*

   (b) *Willfully or negligently sets fire to a woods, prairie, or grounds of another person or permits fire to pass from his or her own woods, prairie, or grounds to another person's property causing damage or destruction to that other property.*

(2) *Subsection (1)(a) applies regardless of whether the person owns the personal property.*

(3) *Fourth-degree arson is a felony punishable by imprisonment for not more than 5 years or a fine of not more than $10,000.00 or 3 times the value of the property damaged or destroyed, whichever is greater, or both imprisonment and a fine.*

### Elements—Personal Property

1. The defendant burned, damaged, or destroyed by fire or explosive a real property. If any part of the property is burned, no matter how small,

that is all that is necessary to count as a burning; the property does not have to be completely destroyed. The property is not burned if it is merely blackened by smoke, but it is burned if it is charred so that any part of it is destroyed.

2. At the time of the burning, the property was personal property. It does not matter whether the defendant owned the property.

3. When the defendant burned it, the property had a fair market value of:

   a. $1,000 or more but less than $20,000.
   b. $200 or more if the defendant has a prior conviction.

4. When the defendant burned the property, he intended to burn or intentionally committed an act that created a very high risk of burning the building or contents and that, while committing the act, the defendant knew of that risk and disregarded it.

CJI2d 31.7.

## Fifth-Degree Arson—MCL 750.77 (misdemeanor)

(1) *Except as provided in sections 72 to 76, a person who intentionally damages or destroys by fire or explosive any personal property having a value of $1,000.00 or less and who has 1 or more prior convictions is guilty of fifth-degree arson.*

(2) *Subsection (1) applies regardless of whether the person owns the personal property.*

(3) *Fifth-degree arson is a misdemeanor punishable by imprisonment for not more than 1 year or a fine of not more than $2,000.00 or 3 times the value of the property damaged or destroyed, whichever is greater, or both imprisonment and a fine.*

(4) *As used in this section:*

   (a) *"Personal property" includes an automobile, van, truck, motorcycle, trailer, and other personally owned property.*

   (b) *"Prior conviction" means a prior conviction for a violation of this chapter that arises out of a separate transaction from the violation of this section.*

### Elements

1. The defendant intentionally damaged, or destroyed by fire or explosive any personal property,

2. The property had a fair market value of $1,000 or less, and

3. The defendant has one or more prior convictions.

## Prohibited Intentional Acts—MCL 750.78 (misdemeanor)

(1) *Except as provided in sections 72 to 77, a person shall not do any of the following:*

  (a) *Willfully and maliciously burn, damage, or destroy by fire or explosive any of the following or its contents:*

    (i) *Any personal property having a value of $200.00 or more but less than $1,000.00.*

    (ii) *Any personal property having a value of less than $200.00, if the person has 1 or more prior convictions.*

    (iii) *Any personal property having a value of less than $200.00.*

  (b) *Negligently, carelessly, or recklessly set fire to a hotel or motel or its contents, and, by setting that fire, endanger the life or property of another person.*

(2) *Subsection (1) applies regardless of whether the person owns the building, structure, hotel, motel, or its contents, or the personal property.*

(3) *A violation of this section is a misdemeanor punishable as follows:*

  (a) *If the person violates subsection (1)(a)(i) or (ii), imprisonment for not more than 1 year and a fine of not more than $2,000.00 or 3 times the value of the property damaged or destroyed, whichever is greater.*

  (b) *If the person violates subsection (1)(a)(iii) or (b), imprisonment for not more than 93 days and a fine of not more than $500.00 or 3 times the value of the property damaged or destroyed, whichever is greater.*

### Elements (1-year misdemeanor)

1. The defendant willfully and maliciously, burned, damaged, or destroyed any personal property by fire or explosive, and
2. The property had either of the following values:
   a. $200 or more but less than $1,000.
   b. Less than $200 if defendant has a prior conviction.

### Elements (93-day misdemeanor)

1. The defendant willfully and maliciously, burned, damaged, or destroyed any personal property by fire or explosive, and
2. The property had a value of less than $200.

or

1. The defendant negligently, carelessly, or recklessly set fire to a hotel or motel or its contents, and
2. The fire endangered the life or property of another person.

## Fair Market Value Test

The test for the value of property is the reasonable and fair market value of the property at the time and in the area when the crime was committed.

Fair market value is defined as the price the property would have sold for in the open market at that time and in that place if the following things were true: the owner wanted to sell but did not have to, the buyer wanted to buy but did not have to, the owner had a reasonable time to find a buyer, and the buyer knew what the property was worth and what it could be used for. CJI2d 22.01.

## Arson of Insured Property—MCL 750.76 (felony)

(1) *A person who willfully or maliciously burns, damages, or destroys by fire or explosive any of the following or the contents of any of the following is guilty of arson of insured property:*

  (a) *Any dwelling that is insured against loss from fire or explosion if the person caused the fire or explosion with the intent to defraud the insurer.*

  (b) *Except as provided in subdivision (a), any building, structure, or other real property that is insured against loss from fire or explosion if the person caused the fire or explosion with the intent to defraud the insurer.*

  (c) *Any personal property that is insured against loss by fire or explosion if the person caused the fire or explosion with the intent to defraud the insurer.*

(2) *Subsection (1) applies regardless of whether the person owns the dwelling, building, structure, other real property, or personal property.*

(3) *Arson of insured property is a felony punishable as follows:*

  (a) *If the person violates subsection (1)(a), imprisonment for life or any term of years or a fine of not more than $20,000.00 or 3 times the value of the property damaged or destroyed, whichever is greater, or both imprisonment and a fine.*

  (b) *If the person violates subsection (1)(b), imprisonment for not more than 20 years or a fine of not more than $20,000.00 or 3 times the value of the property damaged or destroyed, whichever is greater, or both imprisonment and a fine.*

  (c) *If the person violates subsection (1)(c), imprisonment for not more than 10 years or a fine of not more than $20,000.00 or 3 times the value of the property damaged or destroyed, whichever is greater, or both imprisonment and a fine.*

## Elements

1. The defendant burned, damaged, or destroyed by fire or explosive property. If any part of the property is burned, no matter how small, that is all that is necessary to count as a burning; the property does not have to be completely destroyed. The property is not burned if it is merely blackened by smoke, but it is burned if it is charred so that any part of it is destroyed.

2. The property burned, damaged, or destroyed by fire or explosive was a dwelling, structure, building, other real property, or any of its contents, or personal property. It does not matter whether the defendant owned or used the property.

3. At the time of the burning, the property was insured against loss or damage by fire or explosion. It does not matter whether this was the defendant's property or someone else's.

4. At the time of the burning, the defendant knew that the property was insured against loss or damage by fire or explosion.

5. When the defendant burned the property, he intended to set a fire or explosion, knowing that this would cause injury or damage to another person or property and that the defendant did it without just cause or excuse.

6. When the defendant burned the property, he intended to defraud or cheat the insurer.

CJI2d 31.8-31.10.

> Intent to defraud may exist even if the defendant did not profit from the insurance claim and even if the defendant accepted an insurance payment that did not cover the entire loss. *People v. Rabin*, 317 Mich. 654 (1947).
>
> Convictions for burning a dwelling house (MCL 750.72) and burning insured property (MCL 750.75) during the course of the same fire do not violate the Double Jeopardy Clause. *People v. Ayers*, 213 Mich. App. 708 (1995).

## Preparation to Burn—MCL 750.79

*(1) A person who uses, arranges, places, devises, or distributes an inflammable, combustible, or explosive material, liquid, or substance or any device in or near a building, structure, other real property, or personal property with the intent to commit arson in any degree or who aids, counsels, induces, persuades, or procures another to do so is guilty of a crime as follows:*

*(a) If the property has a combined value of less than $200.00, the person is guilty of a misdemeanor punishable by imprisonment for not more than 93 days or a fine of not more than $500.00 or 3 times the combined value of the property damaged or destroyed, whichever is greater, or both imprisonment and a fine.*

*(b) If any of the following apply, the person is guilty of a misdemeanor punishable by imprisonment for not more than 1 year or a fine of not more than $2,000.00 or 3 times the combined value of the property damaged or destroyed, whichever is greater, or both imprisonment and a fine:*

*(i) The property has a combined value of $200.00 or more but less than $1,000.00.*

*(ii) The person violates subdivision (a) and has 1 or more prior convictions for committing or attempting to commit an offense under this section or a local ordinance substantially corresponding to this section.*

*(c) If any of the following apply, the person is guilty of a felony punishable by imprisonment for not more than 5 years or a fine of not more than $10,000.00 or 3 times the combined value of the property damaged or destroyed, whichever is greater, or both imprisonment and a fine:*

*(i) The property has a combined value of $1,000.00 or more but less than $20,000.00.*

*(ii) The person violates subdivision (b)(i) and has 1 or more prior convictions for violating or attempting to violate this section. For purposes of this subparagraph, however, a prior conviction does not include a conviction for a violation or attempted violation of subdivision (a) or (b)(ii).*

*(iii) Except as provided in subdivisions (d) and (e), the property is a building, structure, or real property. This subparagraph applies regardless of whether the person owns the building, structure, or other real property.*

*(d) If any of the following apply, the person is guilty of a felony punishable by imprisonment for not more than 10 years or a fine of not more than $15,000.00 or 3 times the combined value of the property damaged or destroyed, whichever is greater, or both imprisonment and a fine:*

*(i) The property has a combined value of $20,000.00 or more.*

*(ii) The person violates subdivision (c)(i) and has 2 or more prior convictions for committing or attempting to*

commit an offense under this section. For purposes of this subparagraph, however, a prior conviction does not include a conviction for committing or attempting to commit an offense for a violation or attempted violation of subdivision (a) or (b)(ii).

(iii) The property has a value of more than $2,000.00 and is insured against loss by fire or explosion and the person intended to defraud the insurer.

(iv) Except as provided in subdivisions (c)(iii) and (e) and subparagraphs (v) and (vi), the property is a building, structure, or other real property, and the fire or explosion results in injury to any individual. This subparagraph applies regardless of whether the person owns the building, structure, or other real property.

(v) Except as provided in subdivisions (c)(iii) and (e) and subparagraph (vi), the property is a building, structure, or other real property and insured against loss from fire or explosion, and the person intended to defraud the insurer. This subparagraph applies regardless of whether the person owns the building, structure, or other real property.

(vi) The property is a dwelling. This subparagraph applies regardless of whether the person owns the dwelling.

(e) If any of the following apply, the person is guilty of a felony punishable by imprisonment for not more than 15 years or a fine of not more than $20,000.00 or 3 times the combined value of the property intended to be burned or destroyed, whichever is greater, or both imprisonment and a fine:

(i) The property is a dwelling and is insured against loss by fire or explosion if the person intended to defraud the insurer. This subparagraph applies regardless of whether the person owns the property.

(ii) The property is a dwelling and the fire or explosion results in physical injury to any individual.

(2) The combined value of property intended to be burned in separate incidents pursuant to a scheme or course of conduct within any 12-month period may be aggregated to determine the total value of property damaged or destroyed.

(3) If the prosecuting attorney intends to seek an enhanced sentence based upon the defendant having 1 or more prior convictions, the prosecuting attorney shall include on the complaint and information a statement listing the prior conviction or convictions. The existence of the defendant's prior conviction or convictions shall be determined by the court, without a jury, at sentencing or at a separate hearing for that purpose before sentencing. The existence of a prior conviction may be established by any evidence relevant for that purpose, including, but not limited to, 1 or more of the following:

(a) The total value of property damaged or destroyed.
(b) A transcript of a prior trial, plea-taking, or sentencing.
(c) Information contained in a presentence report.
(d) The defendant's statement.

If the sentence for a conviction under this section is enhanced by 1 or more prior convictions, those prior convictions shall not be used to further enhance the sentence for the conviction under section 10, 11, or 12 of chapter IX of the code of criminal procedure, 1927 PA 175, MCL 769.10, 769.11, and 769.12.

## Preparation to Burn Personal Property

### Elements

1. The defendant put some kind of flammable, combustible, or explosive material, liquid, substance, or device in or near the property or aided, counseled, induced, persuaded, or procured another person to do so.
2. When the defendant did this, he intended to burn, damage, or destroy by fire or explosive the property.
3. That the property had a fair market value when the defendant intended to burn or burned it. CJI2d 31.11.

The combined value of property intended to be burned in separate incidents pursuant to a scheme or course of conduct within any 12-month period may be aggregated to determine the total value of property damaged or destroyed. MCL 750.79(2).

Penalties:

| Less than $200 | 93-day misdemeanor |
|---|---|
| $200 to less than $1,000; or less than $200 if previously convicted | 1-year misdemeanor |
| $1,000 to less than $20,000; or $200 to less than $1,000 if previously convicted | 5-year felony |
| Over $20,000; or $1,000 to less than $20,000 if previously convicted twice | 10-year felony |

## Preparation to Burn Dwelling or Building

### Elements

1. The defendant put some kind of flammable, combustible, or explosive material, liquid, substance, or device in or near the property or aided, counseled, induced, persuaded, or procured another person to do so.
2. When the defendant did this, he intended to burn, damage, or destroy by fire or explosive describe property alleged.
3. The property was a dwelling, building, structure, or other real property. CJI2d 31.13-31.14.

The defendant and the victim were dating and lived together in an apartment. During an argument, the victim attempted to remove herself by walking outside onto the balcony where she told witnesses that defendant had turned the apartment stove's gas burners on and was attempting to "blow up" the apartment complex. On appeal, the defendant challenged the sufficiency of the evidence that he possessed the intent "to willfully and maliciously set fire to or burn the building." The court found that a rational trier of fact could infer that defendant possessed the intent to set fire to the apartment building. "[B]ecause it can be difficult to prove a defendant's state of mind on issues such as knowledge and intent, minimal circumstantial evidence will suffice to establish the defendant's state of mind, which can be inferred from all the evidence presented." *People v Chelmicki*, C/A No. 313708 (April 24, 2014)

This statute applies whether the suspect acted alone or persuaded someone else to act: a defendant was guilty under this section where he helped to make Molotov cocktails even though he was not present at the actual burning and the buildings that were burned were not the ones he thought were going to be burned. *People v. Davis*, 24 Mich. App 304 (1970).

Because the severity level of the crime charged changes with the value of property involved, the prosecution must show evidence of the burned property's value in order to support a conviction under this section of law. *People v. Hill*, 257 Mich. App. 126 (2003).

### Penalties

- Preparation to burn a dwelling house and other real property is essentially always a felony due to the value of the real property.

- Preparation to burn personal property can be either a misdemeanor or a felony, depending on the value of the property.

## Obstructing or Disobeying a Firefighter— MCL 750.241

*(1) Any person who, while in the vicinity of any fire, willfully disobeys any reasonable order or rule of the officer commanding any fire department at the fire, when the order or rule is given by the commanding officer or a firefighter there present, is guilty of a misdemeanor.*

*(2) During a riot or other civil disturbance, any person who knowingly and willfully hinders, obstructs, endangers, or interferes with any person who is engaged in the operation, installation, repair, or maintenance of any essential public service facility, including a facility for the transmission of electricity, gas, telephone messages, or water, is guilty of a felony.*

### Elements

1. The defendant willfully disobeyed any reasonable order or rule of the commanding officer of the fire department,
2. While in the vicinity of any fire, and
3. The order or rule was given by the commanding officer or a firefighter.

also, it is a felony if:

1. The defendant knowingly and willingly,
2. Hindered, obstructed, endangered, or interfered with any person,
3. During a riot or other civil disturbance, and
4. The person was operating, installing, or repairing any essential public service facility.

The firefighter must be carrying out lawful duties to convict a defendant for disobeying a lawful order. Merely entering onto the defendant's property to extinguish a fire does not meet this requirement unless there is evidence that the fire was dangerous or that the firefighter has a statutory right to enter onto the property. However, this does not preclude an assault charge against the suspect if he or she assaults the firefighter. *People v. Simpson*, 207 Mich. App. 560 (1994).

# MALICIOUS DESTRUCTION OF PROPERTY

## Fair Market Value

Fair market value includes the reasonable and fair market value of repairing the damage or replacing the damaged property. The value will be considered at the time and in the place where the damage occurred. CJI2d 32.1.

> "Fair Market Value" may be established by expert testimony and is not necessarily the actual cost incurred by the victim. For example, when the victim replaced a broken car window for $45, but several glass installers testified that it would cost $163 to $241 to replace the window, the court held that there was sufficient evidence to find that the damage was over $100. *People v. Hamblin*, 224 Mich. App. 87 (1997).

## MDOP—Personal Property—MCL 750.377a

(1) *A person who willfully and maliciously destroys or injures the personal property of another person is guilty of a crime as follows:*

  (a) *If any of the following apply, the person is guilty of a felony punishable by imprisonment for not more than 10 years or a fine of not more than $15,000.00 or 3 times the amount of the destruction or injury, whichever is greater, or both imprisonment and a fine:*

    (i) *The amount of the destruction or injury is $20,000.00 or more.*

    (ii) *The person violates subdivision (b)(i) and has 2 or more prior convictions for committing or attempting to commit an offense under this section. For purposes of this subparagraph, however, a prior conviction does not include a conviction for a violation or attempted violation of subdivision (c)(ii) or (d).*

  (b) *If any of the following apply, the person is guilty of a felony punishable by imprisonment for not more than 5 years or a fine of not more than $10,000.00 or 3 times the amount of the destruction or injury, whichever is greater, or both imprisonment and a fine:*

    (i) *The amount of the destruction or injury is $1,000.00 or more but less than $20,000.00.*

    (ii) *The person violates subdivision (c)(i) and has 1 or more prior convictions for committing or attempting to commit an offense under this section. For purposes of this subparagraph, however, a prior conviction does not include a conviction for a violation or attempted violation of subdivision (c)(ii) or (d).*

  (c) *If any of the following apply, the person is guilty of a misdemeanor punishable by imprisonment for not more than 1 year or a fine of not more than $2,000.00 or 3 times the amount of the destruction or injury, whichever is greater, or both imprisonment and a fine:*

    (i) *The amount of the destruction or injury is $200.00 or more but less than $1,000.00.*

    (ii) *The person violates subdivision (d) and has 1 or more prior convictions for committing or attempting to commit an offense under this section or a local ordinance substantially corresponding to this section.*

  (d) *If the amount of the destruction or injury is less than $200.00, the person is guilty of a misdemeanor punishable by imprisonment for not more than 93 days or a fine of not more than $500.00 or 3 times the amount of the destruction or injury, whichever is greater, or both imprisonment and a fine.*

(2) *The amounts of destruction or injury in separate incidents pursuant to a scheme or course of conduct within any 12-month period may be aggregated in determining the total amount of the destruction or injury.*

### Elements

1. The property belonged to someone other than the defendant.
2. The defendant destroyed or damaged the property.
3. The defendant did not have just cause or excuse.
4. The defendant intended to cause the damage. CJI2d 32.2.

Generally, personal property is all property other than real estate.

The total amount can be aggregated over a 12-month period where there are separate incidents that are part of common scheme or plan. MCL 750.377(a)(2).

> MDOP is a specific intent crime. There must also be a showing that the defendant intended to damage or destroy the affected property. Also, there must be actual, physical damage to property, not simply diminished utility. MDOP was not supported where an employee removed several CPA certification exams from cellophane in an attempt to sell them. The court found that no exams were damaged nor did the defendant intend to damage them, and proper charges would have been under a theft statute. *People v. Ewing*, 127 Mich. App. 582 (1983).

Penalties:

| Less than $200 | 93-day misdemeanor |
|---|---|
| $200 to less than $1,000; or less than $200 if previously convicted | 1-year misdemeanor |
| $1,000 to less than $20,000; or $200 to less than $1,000 if previously convicted | 5-year felony |
| Over $20,000; or $1,000 to less than $20,000 if previously convicted twice | 10-year felony |

## MDOP—Real Property—MCL 750.380

The property must belong to someone other than the suspect, and this section includes real property such as houses, barns, stores, and other buildings. Otherwise, this statute is essentially the same as MDOP to personal property. With separate incidents that are part of common scheme or plan, the total amount can be aggregated over 12-month period for total.

### Elements

1. The building, structure, or property belonged to someone else.
2. The defendant destroyed or damaged that building or anything permanently attached to it.
3. The defendant did this knowing that it was wrong, without just cause or excuse, and with the intent to damage or destroy the property. CJI2d 32.3.

Penalties:

| Less than $200 | 93-day misdemeanor |
|---|---|
| $200 to less than $1,000; or less than $200 if previously convicted | 1-year misdemeanor |
| $1,000 to less than $20,000; or $200 to less than $1,000 if previously convicted | 5-year felony |
| Over $20,000; or $1,000 to less than $20,000 if previously convicted twice | 10-year felony |

## MDOP—Police or Fire Department Property—MCL 750.377b (felony)

*Any person who shall willfully and maliciously destroy or injure the personal property of any fire or police department, including the Michigan state police, shall be guilty of a felony.*

Property must be the personal property of a police or fire department. The suspect willfully and maliciously, without just cause or excuse, destroyed or damaged the property.

The defendant was improperly convicted of MDOP to police property where he broke out the windows of a jail. This constitutes real property and MCL 750.377b applies only to the personal property of police or fire departments. Proper charges would have been under MCL 750.380, MDOP to real property. *People v. Fox*, 232 Mich. App. 541 (1998).

The specific identity or proof of the identity of the police vehicle damaged and the officer in custody of the car is not necessary to sustain a conviction of MDOP of police property. *People v. Richardson*, 118 Mich. App. 492 (1982).

## MDOP—School Bus—MCL 750.377c (felony)

(1) *If a person intentionally damages, destroys, or alters a school bus without the permission of the entity that owns that school bus and that damage, destruction, or alteration creates a health or safety hazard to any individual occupying that school bus or who may occupy that school bus, the person is guilty of a felony punishable by imprisonment for not more than 5 years, or a fine of not more than $5,000.00, or both.*

(2) *As used in this section, "school bus" means that term as defined in section 57 of the Michigan vehicle code, Act No. 300 of the Public Acts of 1949, being section 257.57 of the Michigan Compiled Laws. School bus includes a school transportation vehicle as that term is defined in section 57c of Act No. 300 of the Public Acts of 1949, being section 257.57c of the Michigan Compiled Laws, if that vehicle is clearly marked as a school transportation vehicle.*

The suspect damaged, destroyed, or altered a school bus without permission.

NOTE: The damage must create a health or safety hazard to an occupant or person who may have occupied the bus.

## MDOP—Utility Property—MCL 750.383a (felony)

*A person, without lawful authority, shall not willfully cut, break, obstruct, injure, destroy, tamper with or manipulate, deface, or steal any machinery, tools, equipment, telephone line or post, telegraph* *line or post, telecommunication line, tower, or post, electric line, post, tower or supporting structures, electric wire, insulator, switch, or signal, natural gas pipeline, water pipeline, steam heat pipeline or the valves or other appliances or equipment appertaining to or used in connection with those lines, or any other appliance or component of the electric, telecommunication, or natural gas infrastructure that is the property of a utility. A person who violates this section is guilty of a felony punishable by imprisonment for not more than 5 years or a fine of not more than $5,000.00, or both. As used in this section, "utility" includes any pipeline, gas, electric, heat, water, oil, sewer, telephone, telegraph, telecommunication, radio, railway, railroad, airplane, transportation, communication or other system, whether or not publicly owned, that is operated for the public use.*

A person intentionally damages or destroys the property of a public utility.

# BURGLARY

## BREAKING AND ENTERING

### Breaking and Entering—MCL 750.110 (felony)

*A person who breaks and enters, with intent to commit a felony or a larceny therein, a tent, hotel, office, store, shop, warehouse, barn, granary, factory or other building, structure, boat, ship, shipping container, or railroad car is guilty of a felony, punishable by imprisonment for not more than 10 years.*

### Elements

1. The defendant broke into a building. It does not matter whether anything was actually broken; however, some force must have been used. Opening a door, raising a window, and taking off a screen are all examples of enough force to count as a breaking. Entering a building through an already open door or window without using any force does not count as a breaking.
2. The defendant entered the building. It does not matter whether the defendant got his entire body inside. If the defendant put any part of his body into the building after the breaking, that is enough to count as an entry.
3. When the defendant broke and entered the building, he intended to commit a larceny or felony.

CJI2d 25.1.

The mere act of committing the "breaking" and the "entering" does not create an assumption that the suspect intended to commit a larceny. There must be some circumstance that reasonably leads to the conclusion larceny was intended. *People v. Noel*, 123 Mich. App. 478 (1983).

Intent may be inferred by the suspect's actions before and during the breaking and entering. *People v. Uhl*, 169 Mich. App. 217 (1988).

Conviction of both breaking and entering and larceny is not barred by double jeopardy; breaking and entering is complete once part of the defendant enters the structure with the intent to commit larceny. Any crime committed once inside the building is a separate act. *People v. Patterson*, 212 Mich. App. 393 (1995).

### Entry without Owner's Permission (Breaking and Entering/Unlawful Entry)—MCL 750.115 (90-day misdemeanor)

*Any person who shall break and enter, or shall enter without breaking, any dwelling, house, tent, hotel, office, store, shop, warehouse, barn, granary, factory or other building, boat, ship, shipping container, railroad car or structure used or kept for public or private use, or any private apartment therein, or any cottage, clubhouse, boat house,* *hunting or fishing lodge, garage or the outbuildings belonging thereto, ice shanty with a value of $100.00 or more, or any other structure, whether occupied or unoccupied, without first obtaining permission to enter from the owner or occupant, agent, or person having immediate control thereof, shall be guilty of a misdemeanor: Provided, That this section shall not apply to entering without breaking, any place which at the time of such entry was open to the public, unless such entry has been expressly denied.*

*This section shall not apply in cases where the breaking and entering or entering without breaking were committed by a peace officer or someone under his direction in the lawful performance of his duties as such peace officer.*

## Elements

1. The defendant entered a building. It does not matter whether the defendant got his entire body inside. If the defendant put any part of his body into the building, that is enough to count as an entry.
2. The defendant did this without first getting permission to enter from someone who had authority to give permission.
   CJI2d 25.4.

This is essentially breaking and entering without the "intent" element required by MCL 750.110. It includes unauthorized entries where the suspect intends to commit a misdemeanor but not a felony or a larceny.

# HOME INVASION—MCL 750.110a

## Definitions

***Dwelling:*** A structure or shelter used permanently or temporarily as a place of abode, including a structure attached to it.

***Dangerous weapons*** include any of the following:

- Loaded or unloaded firearm, whether operable or not.
- A knife, stabbing instrument, brass knuckles, blackjack, club, or other object specifically designed or customarily carried as a weapon.
- An object that is likely to cause death or bodily injury when used and carried as a weapon.
- Any object that is used or fashioned in such a manner as to lead one to believe it is one of the above.

## First Degree—MCL 750.110a(2) (felony)

### Elements

1. The defendant broke into a dwelling or entered without permission. It does not matter whether anything was actually broken; however, some force must have been used. Opening a door, raising a window, and taking off a screen are all examples of enough force to count as a breaking. Entering a dwelling through an already open door or window without using any force does not count as a breaking.
2. The defendant entered the dwelling. It does not matter whether the defendant got his entire body inside. If the defendant put any part of his body into the dwelling after the breaking, that is enough to count as an entry.
3. Either:

   a. When the defendant broke and entered the dwelling, he intended to commit a larceny, felony, or assault.
   b. When the defendant entered, was present in, or was leaving the dwelling, he committed a felony, larceny, or assault.

4. When the defendant entered, was present in, or was leaving the dwelling, either of the following circumstances existed:

   a. He was armed with a dangerous weapon.
   b. Another person was lawfully present in the dwelling.

   CJI2d 25.2a.

> Fourth-degree CSC is an assault for the purposes of home invasion. *People v. Musser*, 259 Mich. App. 215 (2003).

## Second Degree—MCL 750.110a(3) (felony)

### Elements

1. The defendant broke into a dwelling or entered without permission. It does not matter whether anything was actually broken; however, some force must have been used. Opening a door, raising a window, and taking off a screen are all examples of enough force to count as a breaking.
2. The defendant entered the dwelling. It does not matter whether the defendant got his entire body inside. If the defendant put any part of his body into the dwelling after the breaking, that is enough to count as an entry.

3. Either:

   a. When the defendant broke and entered the dwelling, he intended to commit a larceny, felony, or assault.

   b. When the defendant entered, was present in, or was leaving the dwelling, he committed a larceny, felony, or assault.

CJI2d 25.2b.

The defendant was convicted of second-degree home invasion for breaking into his girlfriend's house. He argued that he could not be charged with home invasion because of his relationship with her. The court held that charges were proper, stating, "[T]he fact that a person is in a dating relationship in no way entitles that person to be present in his or her partner's dwelling at will. The fact that defendant spent some nights at the house is immaterial. In any event, even if we were to presume that defendant had some right to be in the house—which he did not—it is possible to 'break and enter' one's own home if one has lost the legal right to be present in that home." Here, "not only did defendant's relationship not confer any rights upon him, his girlfriend had affirmatively refused his repeated requests for a key, a garage door opener, and alarm access codes for the house. The record overwhelmingly shows, and the jury would have properly concluded, that defendant had no right to be in the house at the time of the invasion." *People v. Dunigan*, 299 Mich. App. 579 (2013).

## Third Degree—MCL 750.110a(4) (felony)

### Elements

1. The defendant broke and entered or entered without permission a dwelling. It does not matter whether anything was actually broken; however, some force must have been used. Opening a door, raising a window, and taking off a screen are all examples of enough force to count as a breaking. For an entry, it does not matter whether the defendant got his entire body inside. If the defendant put any part of his body into the dwelling, that is enough to count as an entry.

2. Either:

   a. At the time of the breaking and entering or entering without permission, the defendant intended to commit a misdemeanor;

   b. When the defendant entered, was present in, or was leaving the dwelling, he committed a misdemeanor;

   c. When the defendant entered, was present in, or was leaving the dwelling, he violated a term or condition of probation, parole, a personal protection order, or a bond or pretrial release that was ordered to protect a named person or persons.

CJI2d 25.5e-25.5f.

## Entering Without Breaking—MCL 750.111 (felony)

*Any person who, without breaking, enters any dwelling, house, tent, hotel, office, store, shop, warehouse, barn, granary, factory or other building, boat, ship, shipping container, railroad car or structure used or kept for public or private use, or any private apartment therein, with intent to commit a felony or any larceny therein, is guilty of a felony punishable by imprisonment for not more than 5 years or a fine of not more than $2,500.00.*

This statute is essentially "breaking and entering" without "breaking."

### Elements

1. The defendant entered a building without breaking. It does not matter whether the defendant got his entire body inside. If the defendant put any part of his body into the building, that is enough to count as an entry.

2. When the defendant entered the building, he intended to commit a felony or larceny.

CJI2d 25.3.

# OTHER STATUTES OF INTEREST

## Possession of Burglary Tools—MCL 750.116 (felony)

*Possession of burglar's tools—Any person who shall knowingly have in his possession any nitroglycerine, or other explosive, thermite, engine, machine, tool or implement, device, chemical or substance, adapted and designed for cutting or burning through, forcing or breaking open any building, room, vault, safe or other depository, in order to steal therefrom any money or other property, knowing the same to be adapted and designed for the purpose aforesaid, with intent to use or employ the same for the purpose aforesaid, shall be guilty of a felony, punishable by imprisonment in the state prison not more than 10 years.*

### Elements

1. The instruments involved were burglary tools. A burglary tool is any tool or instrument or chemical, explosive, or other substance adapted and designed for breaking and entering. "Adapted and designed" means that the tools are not only capable of being used for a breaking and entering, but also designed or expressly planned to be used for this purpose.
2. The defendant knowingly possessed burglary tools.
3. When he possessed the tools, he intended to use them to break and enter.

CJI2d 25.5.

Tools normally associated with a legal purpose become burglar tools when they are adapted or designed for an illegal purpose. In this case, a crowbar was a burglar's tool when it was used to pry a coin box off a pool table and smash glass on arcade and vending machines. *People v. Gross*, 118 Mich. App. 161 (1982).

A chisel was also found to be a burglar tool when found in possession of the defendant near the scene of a crime where pry marks were evident on a door and safe. *People v. Ross*, 39 Mich. App. 697 (1972).

A fiberglass antenna used in conjunction with a piece of metal that were used in an attempt to break into a car was found to be burglary tools. *People v. Wilson*, 180 Mich. App. 12 (1989).

Officers investigated a series of thefts involving the breaking and entering of motor vehicles. All of the vehicles had a smashed window and property stolen from inside. A surveillance camera recorded footage of one of the thefts. The footage showed a black man walking toward one of the victims' car from a white van. There was something in the man's hands. Officers located the van and, after securing a search warrant, they found evidence of the larcenies and a window punch. He was convicted of the larceny and possession of burglary tools. The defendant argued that there was insufficient evidence to convict him of possession of burglar's tools because the burglar's tools statute did not include a reference to motor vehicles. The statute limits the list of tools to those tools used to open "a building, room, vault, safe, or other depository." The term "depository" is a catch-all phrase that includes motor vehicles. Because the defendant was burglarizing motor vehicles, there was sufficient evidence to convict the defendant of the possession of burglar's tools. *People v. Osby*, 291 Mich. App. 412 (2011).

### Burglary Using Explosives—MCL 750.112 (felony)

*Any person who enters any building, and for the purpose of committing any crime therein, uses or attempts to use nitro-glycerine, dynamite, gunpowder, or any other high explosive, shall be guilty of a felony, punishable by imprisonment in the state prison not less than 15 years nor more than 30 years.*

### Bank, Safe and Vault Robbery—MCL 750.531 (felony)

*Bank, safe and vault robbery—Any person who, with intent to commit the crime of larceny, or any felony, shall confine, maim, injure or wound, or attempt, or threaten to confine, kill, maim, injure or wound, or shall put in fear any person for the purpose of stealing from any building, bank, safe or other depository of money, bond or other valuables, or shall by intimidation, fear or threats compel, or attempt to compel any person to disclose or surrender the means of opening any building, bank, safe, vault or other depository of money, bonds, or other valuables, or shall attempt to break, burn, blow up or otherwise injure or destroy any safe, vault or other depository of money, bonds or other valuables in any building or place, shall, whether he succeeds or fails in the perpetration of such larceny or felony, be guilty of a felony, punishable by imprisonment in the state prison for life or any term of years.*

### Elements

1. The defendant attempted to break into, damage, or destroy a bank, vault, safe or other money depository, whether he succeeded or not.
2. The defendant intended to commit a larceny or other felony. It is not necessary that the underlying crime be completed.

CJI2d 18.5.

or

1. The defendant confined or wounded; or attempted or threatened to confine, kill, wound; or put in fear someone else.
2. The defendant did so for the purpose of stealing from a bank, vault, safe, or other type of money depository.
3. The defendant intended to commit a larceny or other felony. It is not necessary that the underlying crime be completed.

CJI2d 18.6.

or

1. The defendant made or attempted to make someone else give him the means to open

the bank, vault, safe, or other type of money depository.

2. The defendant did so by using intimidation or threats.

3. The defendant intended to commit a larceny or other felony. It is not necessary that the underlying crime be completed.

CJI2d 18.6.

## Breaking and Entering or Opening a Coin or Depository Box—MCL 750.113 (6-month misdemeanor)

*Any person who maliciously and willfully, by and with the aid and use of any key, instrument, device or explosive, blows or attempts to blow, or forces or attempts to force an entrance into any coin box, depository box or other receptacle established and maintained for the convenience of the public, or of any person or persons, in making payment for any article of merchandise or service, wherein is contained any money or thing of value, or extracts or obtains, or attempts to extract or obtain, there from any such money or thing of value so deposited or contained therein, shall be guilty of a misdemeanor, punishable by imprisonment in the county jail not more than 6 months or by a fine of not more than 250 dollars.*

## Breaking and Entering a Coin-Operated Device— MCL 752.811 (felony)

*A person shall be guilty of a felony punishable upon conviction by confinement in the state prison for a period not to exceed 3 years or by a fine of not more than $1,000.00 or both if he does either of the following:*

(a) *Enters or forces an entrance, alters or inserts any part of an instrument into any parking meter, vending machine dispensing goods or services, money changer or any other device designed to receive currency or coins with the intent to steal.*

(b) *Knowingly possesses a key or device, or a drawing, print or mold thereof, adapted and designed to open or break into any such machine with intent to steal money or other contents from it.*

To be a coin-operated device, a device must provide some service after the coins are deposited. A bus box is not a coin-operated device because it provides no service to the user. Theft from coin boxes is covered under MCL 750.113. *People v. Craig*, 131 Mich. App. 42 (1983).

# THEFT CRIMES

## AUTO THEFT

### Definition of Motor Vehicle—MCL 750.412

*The term "motor vehicle" as used in this chapter shall include all vehicles impelled on the public highways of this state by mechanical power, except traction engines, road rollers and such vehicles as run only upon rails or tracks.*

The term "motor vehicle" includes motorcycles. *People v. Shipp*, 68 Mich. App. 452 (1976).

An old van which had all doors and fenders attached, which had all wheels in place, but with all tires flat, which had old license plates, and which had a complete motor, which the owner had never tried to run was a "motor vehicle." *People v. Matusik*, 63 Mich. App. 347 (1975).

### Unlawfully Driving Away an Automobile (UDAA)—MCL 750.413 (felony)

*Any person who shall, willfully and without authority, take possession of and drive or take away, and any person who shall assist in or be a party to such taking possession, driving or taking away of any motor vehicle, belonging to another, shall be guilty of a felony, punishable by imprisonment in the state prison for not more than 5 years.*

### Elements

1. The vehicle belonged to someone else.
2. The defendant took possession of the vehicle and drove or took it away.
3. The defendant did not have authority or the owner's permission.
4. The defendant intended to take or drive the vehicle away (it does not matter whether the defendant intended to keep the vehicle).
5. Anyone who assists in taking possession of a vehicle or assists in driving or taking away a vehicle knowing that the vehicle was unlawfully possessed is also guilty of this crime if the assistance was given with the intention of helping another commit this crime.

CJI2d 24.1.

### Unauthorized Use of an Automobile ("Joyriding")— MCL 750.414 (2-year misdemeanor)

*Any person who takes or uses without authority any motor vehicle without intent to steal the same,* *or who is a party to such unauthorized taking or using, is guilty of a misdemeanor punishable by imprisonment for not more than 2 years or a fine of not more than $1,500.00. However, in case of a first offense, the court may reduce the punishment to imprisonment for not more than 3 months or a fine of not more than $500.00. However, this section does not apply to any person or persons employed by the owner of said motor vehicle or anyone else, who, by the nature of his or her employment, has the charge of or the authority to drive said motor vehicle if said motor vehicle is driven or used without the owner's knowledge or consent.*

## Elements

1. The vehicle belonged to someone else.
2. The defendant used the vehicle.
3. The defendant did this without authority.
4. The defendant intended to use the vehicle knowing he or she did not have authority to do so.
5. Anyone who assists in using a vehicle is also guilty of this crime if he or she gave the assistance knowing that the person who was taking or using it did not have the authority to do so.
CJI2d 24.1.

This includes cases where the suspect had limited authority to possess the vehicle and knowingly acted beyond the scope of that authority. *People v. Hayward*, 127 Mich. App. 50 (1983).

This is a general intent crime. No intent is required beyond the intent to do the act itself. *People v. Laur*, 128 Mich. App. 453 (1983).

## Difference between UDAA and Unauthorized Use

The difference between these two offenses is this: to be guilty of unlawfully driving away a vehicle, the defendant must have taken possession of the vehicle unlawfully in the first place. Unlawful use of a vehicle, on the other hand, is a lesser offense that applies if the defendant got possession of the vehicle lawfully in the first place, but then used it in a way he or she knew was unauthorized. CJI2d 24.4.

An automobile was stored at the defendant's garage. His possession of the car was lawful so his driving without authority from the owner was not UDAA, but falls under Unauthorized Use of an Automobile. *People v. Smith*, 213 Mich. 351 (1921).

## Motor Vehicle Identification

### Definitions—MCL 750.415(7)

*Antitheft label:* A label containing the vehicle identification number affixed to a motor vehicle by the manufacturer in accordance with subtitle VI of title 49 of the United States Code, 49 U.S.C. §§ 30101 to 33118.

*Federal safety certification label:* A label affixed to a motor vehicle that certifies that the motor vehicle conforms to current safety standards at the time of production and displays the vehicle identification number.

*Motor vehicle:* A device in, upon, or by which a person or property is or may be transported or drawn upon a street, highway, or waterway, whether subject to or exempt from registration, except a device exclusively moved by human power or used exclusively upon stationary rails or tracks.

*Posident die stamps:* Specially designed die stamps used by motor vehicle manufacturers to produce unique letters and numbers when stamping vehicle identification numbers upon vehicle identification plates, tags, and parts affixed to a motor vehicle.

*Rosette rivet:* A special rivet designed to prevent removal or tampering with a vehicle identification number plate affixed by the manufacturer to a motor vehicle and that, when used to affix a vehicle identification number plate, forms five or six petals at the rivet head.

### Altering Identification of a Motor Vehicle With Intent to Mislead—MCL 750.415(2) (felony)

*A person who, with the intent to mislead another as to the identity of a vehicle, conceals or misrepresents the identity of a motor vehicle or of a mechanical device by removing or defacing the manufacturer's serial number or the engine or motor number on the motor vehicle, or by replacing a part of the motor vehicle or mechanical device bearing the serial number or engine or motor number of the vehicle with a new part upon which the proper serial number or engine or motor number has not been stamped, is guilty of a felony, and if the person is a licensed dealer, the dealer's license shall be revoked.*

### Elements

1. The defendant hid or misrepresented the identity of a motor vehicle (or mechanical device).
2. The defendant did so either by removing, damaging, or altering the VIN or by placing

a replacement part on the vehicle that had a nonmatching VIN.

3. The defendant intended to mislead someone else about the identity of the vehicle.

CJ12d 24.8.

> Possession of an altered motor vehicle is prima facie evidence of intent mislead and supports charges under either the felony or misdemeanor. *People v. Venticinque*, 459 Mich. 90 (1998).
>
> Convictions for receiving and concealing stolen property and for altering a VIN on the same piece of property does not violate the Double Jeopardy Clause. *People v. Griffis*, 218 Mich. App. 95 (1996).
>
> The defendant may be charged in any county where the defendant altered the VIN, misrepresented the VIN, or possessed the vehicle with the altered VIN. *People v. Belanger*, 120 Mich. App. 752 (1982).

## Altering Identification of a Motor Vehicle Without Intent to Mislead—MCL 750.415(1) (90-day misdemeanor)

*A person who, without the intent to mislead another as to the identity of the vehicle, conceals or misrepresents the identity of a motor vehicle or of a mechanical device by removing or defacing the manufacturer's serial number or the engine or motor number on the motor vehicle, or by replacing a part of the motor vehicle or mechanical device bearing the serial number or engine or motor number of the vehicle with a new part upon which the proper serial number or engine or motor number has not been stamped, is guilty of a misdemeanor.*

### Elements

1. The defendant hid or misrepresented the identity of a motor vehicle (or mechanical device).
2. The defendant did so either by removing, damaging, or altering the VIN or by placing a replacement part on the vehicle that had a nonmatching VIN.
3. The defendant did not intend to mislead anyone else about the identity of the vehicle.

CJ12d 24.8, CJ12d 24.9.

This is a lesser-included offense of the above-listed felony.

## Possession or Delivery of VIN Plate or Label—MCL 750.415(5) (felony)

*A person shall not knowingly possess, buy, deliver, or offer to buy, sell, exchange, or give away any manufacturer's vehicle identification number plate, federal safety certification label, antitheft label, posident die stamps, secretary of state vehicle identification label, rosette rivet, or any facsimile thereof. This subsection does not apply to a motor vehicle manufacturer, a motor vehicle parts supplier under contract with a motor vehicle manufacturer, or a law enforcement officer in the official performance of his or her duties or to a motor vehicle in which a manufacturer's vehicle identification plate and each of the applicable labels listed in this subsection have been installed as prescribed by law. A person who violates this subsection is guilty of a felony, punishable by imprisonment for not more than 4 years, a fine of not more than $10,000.00, or both. If the person who violates this subsection is a licensed dealer or repair facility, its license shall be revoked.*

## Buying or Receiving Motor Vehicle or Part Knowing Identification Was Removed or Altered—MCL 750.415(6) (felony)

*A person shall not buy, receive, or obtain control of a motor vehicle or motor vehicle part with the intent to sell or otherwise dispose of the motor vehicle or motor vehicle part knowing that an identification number of that motor vehicle or motor vehicle part has been removed, obliterated, tampered with, or altered. This subsection does not apply to a motor vehicle obtained from or at the direction of a law enforcement agency. A person who violates this subsection is guilty of a felony punishable by imprisonment for not more than 10 years, a fine of not more than $20,000.00, or both.*

## Tampering Or Meddling With a Motor Vehicle—MCL 750.416 (90-day misdemeanor)

*Damaging or unauthorized tampering or meddling with motor vehicle—Any person shall be guilty of a misdemeanor, who shall:*

*Intentionally and without authority from the owner, start or cause to be started the motor of any motor vehicle, or maliciously shift or change the starting device or gears of a standing motor vehicle to a position other than that in which it was left by the owner or driver of said motor vehicle; or*

*Intentionally cut, mark, scratch or damage the chassis, running gear, body, sides, top, covering or upholstering of any motor vehicle, the property of another, or intentionally cut, mash, mark, destroy or damage such motor vehicle, or any of the accessories, equipment, appurtenances or attachments thereof, or any spare or extra parts thereon being or thereto attached, without the permission of the owner thereof; or*

*Intentionally release the brake upon any standing motor vehicle, with intent to injure said machine or cause the same to be removed without the consent of the owner: Provided, That this section shall not apply in case of moving or starting of motor vehicles by the police under authority of local ordinance or by members of fire departments in case of emergency in the vicinity of a fire.*

### Elements

The defendant did any of the following without the owner's permission:

1. Intentionally damaged a part of the vehicle.
2. Started the vehicle or caused it to be started or maliciously shifted the gears or the position of the ignition.
3. Released the brake of the vehicle while it was stopped, making it move, or released the brake, intending to damage the vehicle.
   CJI2d 24.5.

NOTE: The statute contains exceptions for police acting under authority of law and for firefighters acting under a fire emergency.

### Chop Shop—MCL 750.535a (felony)

*A person who knowingly owns, operates, or conducts a chop shop or who knowingly aids and abets another person in owning, operating, or conducting a chop shop is guilty of a felony punishable by imprisonment for not more than 10 years or a fine of not more than $250,000.00, or both.*

*Chop shop:* Any of the following:

- Any area, building, storage lot, field, or other premises or place where one or more persons are engaged or have engaged in altering, dismantling, reassembling, or in any way concealing or disguising the identity of a stolen motor vehicle or of any major component part of a stolen motor vehicle.

- Any area, building, storage lot, field, or other premises or place where there are three or more stolen motor vehicles present or where there are major component parts from three or more stolen motor vehicles present.

For additional definitions, read entire statute.

## SCRAP METAL REGULATORY ACT
### Definitions—MCL 445.423

*Ferrous metal:* A metal that contains significant quantities of iron or steel.

*First purchaser:* The first buyer of a manufactured item that contains ferrous or nonferrous metal in a retail or business-to-business transaction. A person that purchases scrap metal, or other property described in section 10, in violation of this act, or an automotive recycler, pawnshop, scrap metal recycler, or scrap processor is not considered a first purchaser.

*Governmental unit:* A subdivision, agency, department, county, parish, municipality, or other unit of the government of the United States, this state, another state, or a foreign country.

*Industrial or commercial customer:* A person that operates from a fixed location and is a seller of scrap metal to a scrap metal dealer under a written agreement that provides for regular or periodic sale, delivery, purchase, or receiving of scrap metal.

*Nonferrous metal:* A metal that does not contain significant quantities of ferrous metal but contains copper, brass, platinum group-based metals, aluminum, bronze, lead, zinc, nickel, or alloys of those metals.

*Person:* An individual, partnership, corporation, limited liability company, joint venture, trust, association, or other legal entity.

*Public fixture:* An item that contains ferrous or nonferrous metal and is owned or under the exclusive control of a governmental unit. The term includes, but is not limited to, a street light pole or fixture, road or bridge guardrail, traffic sign, traffic light signal, or historical marker.

*Purchase transaction:* A purchase of scrap metal, or the purchase of property described in section 10 if the knowing purchase or offer to purchase that property is not prohibited by that section, by a scrap metal dealer. The term does not include any of the following:

- The purchase of one or more used or secondhand, distressed, or salvage vehicles or vehicle parts by a used or secondhand vehicle dealer or used or secondhand vehicle parts dealer that is licensed as a dealer under MCL 257.248 and is acting within the scope of that dealer's license.

- The purchase of one or more used or second-hand, distressed, or salvage vehicles, vehicle parts, or vehicle scrap by a vehicle scrap metal processor, vehicle salvage pool operator, or foreign salvage vehicle dealer that is licensed as a dealer under MCL 257.248 and is acting within the scope of that dealer's license.
- The purchase of one or more used or second-hand, distressed, or salvage vehicles, vehicle parts, or vehicle scrap by an automotive recycler that is licensed as a dealer under MCL 257.248, if the transaction is authorized under MCL 257.217c; MCL 257.1318; or MCL 257.1352.
- The purchase of scrap metal by a mill, foundry, die caster, or other manufacturing facility that purchases scrap metal from an industrial or commercial customer for its own use in the production of metal articles or materials and does not in the ordinary course of its business purchase scrap metal for resale.
- The purchase of scrap metal from a governmental unit.

*Record:* A paper, electronic, or other generally accepted method of storing information in a retrievable form.

*Scale operator:* The employee of a scrap metal dealer who operates or attends a scale that is used to weigh the scrap metal in a purchase transaction.

*Scrap metal:* Ferrous or nonferrous metal, or items that contain ferrous or nonferrous metal, that are sold or offered for sale for the value of the ferrous or nonferrous metal they contain rather than their original intended use; ferrous or nonferrous metal removed from or obtained by cutting, demolishing, or disassembling a building, structure, or manufactured item; or other metal that cannot be used for its original intended purpose, but can be processed for reuse in a mill, foundry, die caster, or other manufacturing facility.

*Scrap metal dealer:* A person or governmental unit that buys scrap metal and is not a first purchaser. The term includes, but is not limited to, a person, whether or not licensed under state law or local ordinance, that operates a business as a scrap metal recycler, scrap processor, secondhand and junk dealer, or other person that purchases any amount of scrap metal on a regular, sporadic, or one-time basis.

*Scrap metal recycler:* A person that purchases ferrous or nonferrous metal that is intended for recycling or reuse, whether regarded as a scrap processor, core buyer, or other similar business operation.

*Scrap processor:* A person, utilizing machinery and equipment and operating from a fixed location, whose principal business is the processing and manufacturing of iron, steel, nonferrous metals, paper, plastic, or glass, into prepared grades of products suitable for consumption by recycling mills, foundries, and other scrap processors.

*Seller:* A person that regularly, sporadically, or on a one-time basis receives consideration from any other person from the purchase by a scrap metal dealer of scrap metal offered by that seller.

## Method of Payment—MCL 445.425

### Purchase Transactions with "Sellers"— MCL 445.425(1)(a)

Except as otherwise provided, a scrap metal dealer shall only pay a seller using one of the following methods of payment in a purchase transaction and shall not pay the seller in cash or using any other method of payment:

- A check or money order. A scrap metal dealer shall make and retain a photograph or digital or electronic image of the delivery of the check or money order to the seller or individual acting on behalf of the seller in the purchase transaction that includes the face of that seller or individual.
- An electronic payment card or encrypted receipt that may only be converted to cash in an automated teller machine that is located on the scrap metal dealer's premises, is used for the sole purpose of dispensing cash in connection with purchase transactions, and provides a digital or electronic image of the dispensing of the cash to the seller or individual acting on behalf of the seller in the purchase transaction that includes the face of that seller or individual. For purposes of this section and MCL 445.426, payment using an electronic payment card or encrypted receipt described in this subparagraph is not considered a payment in cash.

A scrap metal dealer may accept barter or a trade or exchange of scrap metal or other property in a purchase transaction as all or part of the consideration for that transaction.

### Purchase Transactions with "Industrial or Commercial Customers"—MCL 445.425(1)(b)

The scrap metal dealer may pay using any of the following methods of payment, as agreed to by the scrap metal dealer and the industrial or commercial customer, and except for allowable barter, trade, or exchange, shall not pay the seller in cash or using any other method of payment:

- By check, money order, or payment card or receipt described above. If a payment described in this sub-subparagraph is mailed to the industrial or commercial customer, the scrap metal dealer may mail that payment to the street address or post office box of the industrial or commercial customer or to another person or post office box as directed by the industrial or commercial customer.

- By bank wire transfer or other electronic delivery to an account of the industrial or commercial customer.

A scrap metal dealer may accept barter or a trade or exchange of scrap metal or other property in a purchase transaction as all or part of the consideration for that transaction.

### Identification—MCL 445.425(1)(d)

In a purchase transaction, all of the following apply to a seller, if the seller is an individual, or to an individual acting as an agent or representative of a seller:

- He or she must present his or her operator's or chauffeur's license, military identification card, Michigan identification card, passport, or other government-issued identification containing his or her photograph to the scrap metal dealer and allow the scrap metal dealer to make a photocopy or electronic copy of the identification.
- He or she must allow the scrap metal dealer to take his or her thumbprint, to be used only for identification purposes by the scrap metal dealer and for investigation purposes by a law enforcement agency.
- He or she must provide the scrap metal dealer with a signed statement that certifies that he or she is the owner of, or is otherwise authorized to sell, the scrap metal to the scrap metal dealer and is at least 16 years old.
- An individual who has been convicted of a crime involving the theft, the conversion, or the sale of scrap metal may not enter into a purchase transaction. As part of a purchase transaction, the individual shall certify that he or she has not been convicted of a crime described in this subdivision.

A scrap metal dealer in a purchase transaction shall examine the identification presented as required by the seller or individual acting on behalf of the seller, and if the identification presented displays the date of birth of the individual, confirm that the individual is at least 16 years old based on that date of birth.

A scrap metal dealer shall ensure that it trains each scale operator, purchaser, and supervisor employed by the dealer concerning the legal requirements of this act and the responsibilities of the scrap metal dealer under this act.

### Purchase Transactions Involving Specified Items—MCL 445.426(1)

Certain methods of payment are required in a purchase transaction of any of the following items:

- *Catalytic converters*, unless the seller is an automotive recycler as defined in MCL 257.2a; a manufacturer or wholesaler of catalytic converters; or a muffler shop, tire store, or other retail business that sells converters separately or as part of an exhaust system.
- *Air conditioners*, air conditioner evaporator coils or condensers, or parts of air conditioner evaporator coils and condensers.
- *Copper wire*, including copper wire that is burned in whole or in part to remove the insulation, copper pipe, or copper fittings.

The only methods of payment a scrap metal dealer may use to pay a seller for these specified items are as follows:

- A direct deposit or electronic transfer to the seller's account at a financial institution.
- If the purchase price in a purchase transaction is $25.00 or more, or if the purchase price for all of a seller's purchase transactions in a business day is $25.00 or more, the scrap metal dealer must pay the seller by mailing one of the following items to the seller at the address shown on the identification card presented as required by the seller, and shall not deliver that payment in person or using any other form of delivery:
  - A check or money order.
  - An electronic payment card or encrypted receipt.
  - A nontransferable receipt that the seller may redeem at the scrap dealer's premises for a check or money order, electronic payment card, or encrypted receipt.

These payment requirements do not apply to the purchase of any of the specified items by an industrial or commercial customer.

### Electronic Database—MCL 445.426(2)

Representatives of a group of companies in the scrap metal industry, at their expense, may in consultation with the department of state police develop or contract for the development of, and if selected by the department of state police may implement, operate, and maintain, an electronic database that meets all of the following:

- Is available to all scrap metal dealers in this state.
- Is web-based.
- Has the capability to conduct statewide real-time searches by item description or seller.

- Is accessible to law enforcement agencies through a password supported, Internet-based platform.
- Allows a scrap metal dealer to report all of the following information concerning the purchase of one or more catalytic converters, air conditioners, or copper wire by 12 noon of the next business day after the purchase transaction of the item or items:
  - Name and address of the scrap metal dealer and seller.
  - Date and time of the purchase transaction.
  - A description of the item or items purchased.
  - The weight or volume of the item or items purchased.
- Allows a law enforcement agency to flag the name of any seller that appears in the database and who is an individual who has been convicted of a crime involving the theft, conversion, or sale of scrap metal; and, if a law enforcement agency has flagged the name of that convicted seller, to notify the law enforcement agency if he or she is the seller in subsequent purchase transactions and provide the agency all of the information about that convicted seller and his or her purchase transactions that scrap metal dealers have reported to the database.

### Purchase Transaction Records—MCL 445.427(1)

A scrap metal dealer shall prepare and maintain a separate, accurate, and legible record of each purchase transaction. The dealer shall maintain the records described in this section for at least one year; the dealer shall keep the records in a location that is readily accessible to a local, state, or federal law enforcement agency, or to railroad police in investigation of stolen railroad property, for inspection during normal business hours; and the dealer shall make the records, or copies of those records, available on request to any local, state, or federal law enforcement agency.

The record of a purchase transaction must include all of the following:

- The name and address of the seller and the name and address of the individual who is delivering the scrap metal if he or she is not the seller. If an individual is a seller or representative of a seller in more than one purchase transaction, the scrap metal dealer may retain a copy of the individual's information or document described in this subdivision in a separate file and use that information in future purchase transactions.
- The name, address, and identifying number from the identification presented as required.

A legible scan or photocopy of the identification meets the requirement of this subdivision. If an individual is a seller or representative of a seller in more than one purchase transaction, the scrap metal dealer may retain a copy of the information or document described in this subdivision in a separate file and use that information in future purchase transactions.
- If the scrap metal is delivered by licensed vehicle, the license plate number of the vehicle.
- The date and time of the purchase transaction.
- A description of the predominant types of scrap metal purchased, made in accordance with the custom of the trade.
- The weight, quantity, or volume of the scrap metal purchased, described, and calculated in accordance with the custom of the trade; the name of the scale operator who weighs and inspects that property; and the name of the employee of the scrap metal dealer who purchased or authorized the purchase of the scrap metal on the dealer's behalf if the purchaser was not the scale operator.
- A photograph or digital, electronic, or video image of the scrap metal purchased. A photograph or digital, electronic, or video image that meets one of the following is sufficient for purposes of this subdivision even if each item of scrap metal is not shown in the image:
  - If the scrap metal and the vehicle in which it is delivered are weighed, an overhead photograph or image of the vehicle and the scrap metal in the vehicle on the scale.
  - If only the scrap metal is weighed, a photograph or image of the scrap metal on the scale.
- The consideration paid and the method of payment.
- The signed statement.
- A legible thumbprint.
- A digital photograph of the seller, or the individual who is delivering the scrap metal if he or she is not the seller, which includes his or her face and is taken at the time the scrap metal is delivered to the scrap metal dealer.

A scrap metal dealer is not required to obtain the information described above for a purchase transaction with an industrial or commercial customer that meets all of the following:

- Payment is made directly to the industrial or commercial customer.
- The personal and business identifying information of the industrial or commercial customer is on file with the scrap metal dealer and conforms to a written description of the type of scrap metal customarily purchased by the scrap metal dealer from that customer.

- The information on file with the scrap metal dealer is periodically reviewed at least every two years and validated as current or updated by the scrap metal dealer.

A scrap metal dealer may utilize an electronic record-keeping system if that system allows for immediate access to each seller's purchase transaction activities, documents, and images, including, but not limited to, electronic copies of the records described above, the payment information contained in the card or receipt, and the image required in the method of payment.

### 93-Day Misdemeanor—MCL 445.433(1)

If a person fails to comply with the record-keeping requirements of MCL 445.427 and knows or should have known that a violation has occurred.

### Affirmative defense

If a violation is the result of a malfunction of an electronic record-keeping system authorized by the statute, it is an affirmative defense in an action against the scrap metal dealer that utilizes that system that the dealer diligently pursued repair of the electronic record-keeping system after the malfunction occurred and implemented and maintained a manual record-keeping system for purchase transactions that occurred while the electronic record-keeping system was malfunctioning.

### Prohibited Transactions—MCL 445.430

A person shall not knowingly sell or attempt to sell to a scrap metal dealer, and a scrap metal dealer shall not knowingly purchase or offer to purchase, any of the following types of property:

- Public fixtures. This subdivision does not apply if the seller is a governmental unit or the seller has written authorization from the governmental unit that owned the property to sell the property.
- Metal articles or materials that are clearly marked as property belonging to a person other than the seller. This subdivision does not apply if the seller has authorization from that person to sell the property.
- A commemorative, decorative, or other cemetery-related or apparently ceremonial article. This subdivision does not apply if the seller is the owner of the article, if the seller is authorized by the owner of the article to sell the article, or if the seller of a cemetery-related article is the cemetery in which the article was located.
- Metal articles or materials removed from property owned by a railroad company or from a railroad right-of-way. This subdivision does

not apply if the seller is the owner of the metal articles or materials; is the manufacturer of the metal articles or materials; is a contractor engaged in the business of repairing railroad equipment; or is a person that has written authorization from that owner, manufacturer, or contractor to sell those metal articles or materials.
- A silver alloy telecommunication battery with a threaded insert terminal connection. This subdivision does not apply to a battery used in auto or mobile equipment. This subdivision does not apply if the seller is a provider of telecommunication service or if the seller has written authorization from the provider of telecommunication service that owned the property to sell the property.

### 5-Year Felony—MCL 445.433(2)

A scrap metal dealer that purchases scrap metal or an item of property prohibited under MCL 445.430 and knew or should have known that it was stolen.

A person that sells scrap metal or an item of property prohibited under MCL 445.430 and knew or should have known that it was stolen.

# LARCENY

### Larceny—MCL 750.356

A person who commits larceny by stealing any of the following property of another person is guilty of a crime as provided in this section:

- Money, goods, or chattels.
- A bank note, bank bill, bond, promissory note, due bill, bill of exchange or other bill, draft, order, or certificate.
- A book of accounts for or concerning money or goods due, to become due, or to be delivered.
- A deed or writing containing a conveyance of land or other valuable contract in force.
- A receipt, release, or defeasance.
- A writ, process, or public record.
- Scrap metal.

### Elements

1. The defendant took someone else's property.
2. The property was taken without consent.
3. There was some movement of the property. It does not matter whether the defendant actually kept the property or whether the property was taken off the premises.
4. At the time it was taken, the defendant intended to permanently deprive the owner of the property.

CJI2d 23.1.

Any movement is sufficient to meet the "movement" element. For example, the court found that the movement was sufficient where the suspect picked up a tape deck, put it in a bag, then took it back out of the bag, and placed it on a table without ever leaving the premises. *People v. Wilbourne*, 44 Mich. App. 376 (1973).

*Scrap metal*: Ferrous or nonferrous metal, or items that contain ferrous or nonferrous metal, that are sold or offered for sale for the value of the ferrous or nonferrous metal they contain rather than their original intended use; ferrous or nonferrous metal removed from or obtained by cutting, demolishing, or disassembling a building, structure, or manufactured item; or other metal that cannot be used for its original intended purpose but can be processed for reuse in a mill, foundry, die caster, or other manufacturing facility.

If the property stolen is scrap metal, "the value of the property stolen" is determined by the greatest of:

- The replacement cost of the stolen scrap metal.
- The cost of repairing the damage caused by the larceny of the scrap metal.
- A sum of the replacement cost and the repair cost.

When there are separate incidents that are part of common scheme or plan, the total amount can be aggregated over 12-month period for total.

Penalties:

| Less than $200 | 93-day misdemeanor |
|---|---|
| $200 to less than $1,000; or less than $200 if previously convicted | 1-year misdemeanor |
| $1,000 to less than $20,000; or $200 to less than $1,000 if previously convicted | 5-year felony |
| Over $20,000; or $1,000 to less than $20,000 if previously convicted twice | 10-year felony |

## Larceny from the Person—MCL 750.357 (felony)

*Any person who shall commit the offense of larceny by stealing from the person of another shall be guilty of a felony, punishable by imprisonment in the state prison not more than 10 years.*

### Elements

1. The defendant took someone else's property.
2. The property was taken without consent.
3. There was some movement of the property. It does not matter whether the defendant actually kept the property.
4. The property was taken from the victim's person or from the victim's immediate area of control or immediate presence.
5. At the time it was taken, the defendant intended to permanently deprive the owner of the property.

CJI2d 23.3.

A loss-prevention officer stopped the defendant leaving a store after observing the defendant act nervous and place an item into a bag without paying for it. The judge provided jury instructions on larceny from a person. The court held "that Michigan law requires a defendant to take property from the physical person or immediate presence of a victim to commit a larceny from the person. In rare cases, a taking outside of a victim's immediate presence may satisfy the from-the-person element only if a defendant or the defendant's accomplices use force or threats to create distance between a victim and the victim's property. Because defendant in this case did not take property from the person or immediate presence of the victim, or use force or threats to separate a victim from the victim's property, we conclude that she did not commit a larceny from the person." *People v. Smith-Anthony*, 494 Mich. 669 (2013).

## Larceny in a Building—MCL 750.360 (felony)

*Any person who shall commit the crime of larceny by stealing in any dwelling house, house trailer, office, store, gasoline service station, shop, warehouse, mill, factory, hotel, school, barn, granary, ship, boat, vessel, church, house of worship, locker room or any building used by the public shall be guilty of a felony.*

### Elements

1. The defendant took someone else's property.
2. The property was taken without consent.
3. There was some movement of the property. It does not matter whether the defendant actually kept the property.
4. The property was taken in a building.

5. The property was worth something when it was taken.
6. At the time it was taken, the defendant intended to permanently deprive the owner of the property. CJI2d 23.4.

This section applied to a metal shed in which automobile tires were stored. The shed was bolted down to the cement and enclosed with overlapping padlocked doors. *People v. Williams*, 368 Mich. 494 (1962).

The use of the structure determines if it is a building. The defendant's conviction for larceny in a building was upheld where the larceny occurred in a construction trailer that was being used as an office. *People v. Walters*, 186 Mich. App. 452 (1990).

A conviction for larceny in a building was overturned where the defendant broke into a van that had four flat tires and was being used for storage because there was no evidence that the van was mechanically incapable of locomotion. *People v. Matusik*, 63 Mich. App. 347 (1975).

Whether the theft of two chairs and a rug from the porch of a home is larceny in a building was found to be a jury issue. *People v. Thompson*, 114 Mich. App. 302 (1982).

Larceny in building is complete when there is the taking of property with intent to steal. This intent can be inferred from movement of the object by the defendant. The object need not be removed from the premises. Slight movement of the object by the defendant is sufficient to support intent to steal. *People v. Cavanaugh*, 127 Mich. App. 632 (1983).

The difference between larceny in a building and retail fraud: Retail fraud is generally a lesser charge, but retail fraud requires that the item is *offered for sale*. Thus, it is larceny in a building (a felony) when the suspect steals cleaning or office supplies used by the store. Likewise, it is larceny in a building where one customer purchases an item, leaves it in the loading area of the store, and the suspect then steals it from the loading area.

Under the retail fraud statute, a person may not be charged with larceny from a building under circumstances that warrant retail fraud as the proper charge. This does not prohibit charges of unarmed robbery and the subsequent conviction of either retail fraud or larceny from a building as lesser-included offenses. *People v. Ramsey*, 218 Mich. App. 191 (1996).

### Honest taking exception

When someone takes property because he honestly believes that he has the right to take or use it, this is not larceny, even if the person who took it was mistaken. CJI2d 22.3.

### Other Larcenies

#### Larceny at a Fire—MCL 750.358 (felony)

*Any person who shall commit the offense of larceny by stealing in any building that is on fire, or by stealing any property removed in consequence of alarm caused by fire, shall be guilty of a felony, punishable by imprisonment in the state prison not more than 5 years or by a fine of not more than 2,500 dollars.*

#### Larceny of Livestock—MCL 750.357a (felony)

*Any person who shall commit the offense of larceny by stealing the livestock of another shall be guilty of a felony.*

Livestock includes horses, stallions, colts, geldings, mares, sheep, rams, lambs, bulls, bullocks, steers, heifers, cows, calves, mules, jacks, jennets, burros, goats, kids, and swine.

Where two statutes prohibit the same conduct, the defendant should be charged under the more specific statute. Here, the defendant's conviction for larceny over $100 where he stole valuable "show" goats was remanded because the court reasoned that he should have been prosecuted under the more specific larceny of livestock statute. *People v. Patterson*, 212 Mich. App. 393 (1995).

#### Larceny of Firearms—MCL 750.357b (felony)

*A person who commits larceny by stealing the firearm of another person is guilty of a felony, punishable by imprisonment for not more than 5 years or by a fine of not more than $2,500.00, or both.*

#### Larceny from a Vacant Dwelling—MCL 750.359 (1-year misdemeanor)

*Any person or persons who shall steal or unlawfully remove or in any manner damage any fixture,* *attachment, or other property belonging to, connected with, or used in the construction of any vacant structure or building, whether built or in the process of construction or who shall break into any vacant structure or building with the intention of unlawfully removing, taking therefrom, or in any manner damaging any fixture, attachment, or other property belonging to, connected with, or used in the construction of such vacant structure or building whether built or in the process of construction, is guilty of a misdemeanor punishable by imprisonment for not more than 1 year or a fine of not more than $1,000.00.*

### Elements

1. The defendant stole, unlawfully removed, or damaged,
2. Any fixture, attachment, or property, and
3. Such item belonged to, was connected to, or used in the construction of any vacant building, whether built or under construction.

or

1. The defendant broke into a vacant building, and
2. Did so with the intent of committing a larceny from the building.

The defendant was convicted of breaking and entering into an occupied dwelling in Michigan where the homeowner lived in Ohio during the week. The defendant argued that he should have been charged with larceny from a vacant building because the homeowner only stayed in the Michigan home on the weekends while completing its interior construction. The court held that the owner's occupancy of the home was regular and habitual and the owner had only left the home 30 minutes prior to the defendant's entry, thus the breaking and entering conviction was proper. *People v. McClain*, 105 Mich. App. 323 (1981).

### Larceny from a Motor Vehicle—MCL 750.356a(1) (felony)

*A person who commits larceny by stealing or unlawfully removing or taking any wheel, tire, air bag, catalytic converter, radio, stereo, clock, telephone, computer, or other electronic device in or on any motor vehicle, house trailer, trailer, or semitrailer is guilty of a felony punishable by imprisonment for not more*

*than 5 years or a fine of not more than $10,000.00, or both.*

### Elements

1. The defendant took a wheel, tire, air bag, catalytic converter, radio, stereo, clock, telephone, computer, or other electronic device.
2. The property was taken without consent.
3. The property was in or on a motor vehicle, house trailer, trailer, or semi-trailer when it was taken.
4. There was some movement of the property. It does not matter whether the Defendant actually kept the property.
5. At the time it was taken, the defendant intended to permanently deprive the owner of the property.

CJ12d 23.5.

### Breaking and Entering a Motor Vehicle—MCL 750.356a(2)

*A person who enters or breaks into a motor vehicle, house trailer, trailer, or semitrailer to steal or unlawfully remove property from it is guilty of a crime.*

A person who breaks, tears, cuts, or otherwise damages any part of the motor vehicle, house trailer, trailer, or semitrailer while breaking or entering into a motor vehicle to steal is guilty of a 5-year felony, regardless of the value of the property. MCL 750.356a(3).

### Elements

1. The defendant either broke *or* entered a [motor vehicle]. For a breaking, it does not matter whether anything was actually broken; however, some force must have been used. The opening of a closed door or the pushing open of a vent window, for example, is enough force to count as a breaking. For an entry, it does not matter whether the defendant got his or her entire body inside. If the defendant put any part of his or her body into the [motor vehicle] that is enough to count as an entry.
2. That at the time of the breaking or entering, the defendant intended to take some property and permanently deprive the owner of it. It does not matter whether the defendant actually took the property.
3. That in doing so the defendant broke, tore, cut, or otherwise damaged any part of the motor vehicle.

CJI2d 23.6, 23.6a.

Penalties:

| Less than $200 | 93-day misdemeanor |
|---|---|
| $200 to less than $1,000; or less than $200 if previously convicted | 1-year misdemeanor |
| $1,000 to less than $20,000; or $200 to less than $1,000 if previously convicted | 5-year felony |
| Offense involves break, tear, cut, or other damage to vehicle regardless of value | 5-year felony |
| Over $20,000; or $1,000 to less than $20,000 if previously convicted twice | 10-year felony |

If separate incidents, but part of common scheme or plan, the total amount can be aggregated over 12-month period for total. MCL 750.356a(4).

Evidence that the defendant forced one of the ventilator windows open on an automobile, broke the glass, reached in to open the window, and entered with his head and shoulders, was sufficient to support a conviction under the larceny from a motor vehicle statute. *People v. Hadesman*, 304 Mich. 481 (1943).

Convictions for possession of burglary tools and attempted larceny from a motor vehicle arising from the same incident do not violate the Double Jeopardy Rule. *People v. Wilson*, 180 Mich. App. 12 (1989).

A conviction under MCL 750.356a(1) for larceny of an electronic device from a vehicle does not require the device be permanently attached to the vehicle. Theft of a cell phone from a vehicle is sufficient to support a conviction under this section. *People v. Miller*, 288 Mich. App. 207 (2010).

Any part of a trailer as used in MCL 750.356a(3) covers every and all portions of the trailer in whatever degree or whatever separate or distinct piece of the trailer that is broken, torn, cut, or otherwise damaged. Here, the victim purchased his trailer and the padlocks for his trailer on the same day from the same trailer company. The latches on the trailer were compatible with the padlocks the victim purchased. The padlocks were intended to be purchased with the trailer in order to lock the trailer. The victim purchased the trailer for the purpose of storing and transporting his tools and used the locks to secure his tools while in the trailer. The padlocks on the victim's trailer were a distinct piece of the trailer that served the trailer's function of transporting and securing tools. *People v. Kloosterman*, 295 Mich. App. 68 (2011).

### Larceny of Rental Property—MCL 750.362a (same property values as under larceny)

#### Elements

1. The defendant rented or leased a motor vehicle, trailer, or tangible property.
2. There was a written agreement providing for the item's time and place of return.
3. The time for return has expired.
4. The lessor made a demand for the item's return by registered or certified mail.
5. The defendant refuses or willfully neglects to return the item.
6. The defendant intended to defraud the lessor.

This statute applies to a person who refuses or willfully neglects to return a rented motor vehicle, trailer, or other tangible property with the intent to defraud the lessor.

The rental or lease agreement must provide for its return to a particular place at a particular time. A notice in writing must be sent to the person after expiration of the agreement via registered or certified mail to the last known address.

There is no intent to permanently deprive, which separates it from larceny by conversion.

Conviction under this section requires the rental company place the defendant on notice of a definite time when rental property is to be returned. The defendant's conviction was overturned because a certified letter from the rental company that stated that the vehicle was to be returned "as soon as possible" was too vague to place the defendant on notice of the time frame to return the vehicle. *People v. McKim*, 99 Mich. App. 829 (1980).

### Larceny by Conversion—MCL 750.362 (same property values as under larceny)

*Any person to whom any money, goods or other property, which may be the subject of larceny, shall have been delivered, who shall embezzle or fraudulently convert to his own use, or shall secrete with the intent to embezzle, or fraud-ulently use such goods, money or other property, or any part thereof, shall be deemed by so doing to have committed the crime of larceny and shall be punished as provided in the first section of this chapter.*

## Elements

1. The property was voluntarily transferred to the defendant. It does not matter whether the property was transferred legally.
2. The property had a fair market value at the time it was transferred.
3. The defendant either hid the property or wrongfully deprived the owner of the possession of it. Wrongfully depriving means using or keeping someone else's property without that person's permission.
4. The defendant intended to defraud or cheat the owner out of the property permanently.
5. The act was done without the owner's consent.
6. Any of the following is also true:

    a. The property was given to the defendant for some limited, special, or temporary purpose, but the owner had no intention of actually giving the defendant ownership of it, and the defendant then took the property in a way that the defendant knew was not included in that purpose, that may be considered taking the property without the owner's consent.

    b. The property was given to the defendant because the owner had a relationship of trust with the defendant and the owner had no intention of actually giving the defendant ownership of the property, and the defendant then took the property in a way that the owner did not intend, that may be considered as taking the property without the owner's consent. A relationship of trust means any relationship that exists because of the defendant's position as an agent, servant, employee, trustee, bailee, or custodian.

    c. The defendant got the property by using some trick or pretense and the owner would not have consented to the defendant taking the property if the owner had known the true nature of the act or transaction involved.

CJI23.10.

Example: The property was given to the suspect to borrow. After taking the property, the suspect developed the intent to defraud or cheat the owner by converting the property to his or her own use.

The conversion constitutes the "unlawful taking" and the decision not to return the property is the "felonious intent."

Larceny by conversion is closely related to embezzlement. In both, the property is given to the suspect. However, in embezzlement, there is a position of trust between the suspect and the owner. In larceny by conversion, there is no such position of trust.

Larceny by conversion occurred where a salesman placed a deposit into his personal account instead of his business account and without completing the sale. *People v. Mason*, 247 Mich. App. 64 (2001).

Simply refusing to return the property upon demand is not sufficient to meet the elements of this crime. A felonious taking is required to sustain a charge of conversion. For example, the defendant's conviction was overturned because the prosecution could not prove felonious intent where the defendant borrowed a horse buggy and refused to return it. *People v. Taugher*, 102 Mich. 598 (1894).

## Larceny by Trick—MCL 750.356 (same property values as under larceny)

The suspect used some trick to obtain someone else's property.

## Elements

1. The defendant took someone else's property.
2. The property was taken without consent.
3. There was some movement of the property. It does not matter whether the defendant actually kept the property.
4. Under any of the following circumstances:

    a. At the time the property was taken, the defendant intended to permanently deprive the owner of the property.

    b. The property was given to the defendant for some limited, special, or temporary purpose but the owner had no intention of actually giving the defendant ownership of it, and the defendant then took the property in a way that the defendant knew was not included in that purpose, that may be considered as taking the property without the owner's consent.

    c. The defendant got the property by using some trick or pretense, and the owner would not have consented to the defendant taking the property if the owner had known the true nature of the act or transaction involved.

5. The property was worth something at the time it was taken.

CJI2d 23.8.

Larceny by trick is not a separate crime from larceny, but describes the means used by the suspect to obtain the property. The victim relies on some representation by the accused and gives up possession of his or her property but not title or ownership.

The question to be asked is, "Would the owner have given the property to the suspect had he or she known that the suspect was actually going to keep it?"

If, by trick or artifice, the owner of the property is induced to part with the possession, to one who receives the property with felonious intent, the owner still meaning to retain the right of property, the taking will be larceny; but if the owner part with not only the possession, but right of property also, the offense of the party obtaining the thing will not be larceny, but that of obtaining the goods by false pretenses. *People v. Martin*, 116 Mich. 446 (1898).

Reliance is an element of larceny by trick. The defendant posed as a runner for a hotel and tricked military recruits into giving him their money for safekeeping. An undercover officer was present as part of a sting operation when the defendant attempted to run his scheme. The officer turned over his money then arrested the defendant. The defendant's conviction of larceny by trick was overturned because the officer was not tricked by the defendant's claim to hold onto the money for safekeeping. *People v. Wilson*, 122 Mich. App. 270 (1982).

In larceny, the owner of the thing stolen has no intention to part with his property therein. In false pretenses, the owner does intend to part with his property, but this intention is the result of fraudulent by the taker. *People v. Niver*, 7 Mich. App. 652 (1967).

### Larceny by False Pretense—MCL 750.218 (same property values as under larceny)

*A person who, with the intent to defraud or cheat makes or uses a false pretense to do 1 or more of the following is guilty of a crime punishable as provided in this section:*

(a) *Cause a person to grant, convey, assign, demise, lease, or mortgage land or an interest in land.*

(b) *Obtain a person's signature on a forged written instrument.*
(c) *Obtain from a person any money or personal property or the use of any instrument, facility, article, or other valuable thing or service.*
(d) *By means of a false weight or measure obtain a larger amount or quantity of property than was bargained for.*
(e) *By means of a false weight or measure sell or dispose of a smaller amount or quantity of property than was bargained for.*

### Elements

1. The defendant obtains the money or property of another.
2. The property was obtained by the defendant through a representation or communication to the other party.
3. The representation or communication was false.
4. The defendant knew the communication or representation was false when it was made and made it to defraud or cheat the other party.
5. The communication or representation was made to induce the transfer of money or property.

CJI2d 23.11.

### Pretense

1. A pretense is the use of a statement, writing, or any other device that is false and/or that could mislead the person it is presented to.
2. A pretense is to knowingly do one or more of the following:
   - Make someone else believe something that is false.
   - Keep someone else from finding out important information about the property involved.
   - Sell, transfer, or mortgage property while hiding a claim or other legal obstacle against it.
   - Promise to do something or have something done knowing that it is not really going to be done.

CJI2d 23.9.

This crime differs from larceny by trick in that the victim gives up title and ownership.

False pretense occurred where the suspect short-changed two cashiers $10 each by creating confusion and distracting them and asking for various amounts of change thereby inducing them to give him the extra $10. *People v. Long*, 409 Mich. 346 (1980).

> When the victim realized that the defendant was lying during a "quick-change scheme," the proper charge was larceny from a building because the victim never passed title of the 20-dollar bill the defendant held out as his own. *People v. Jones*, 143 Mich. App. 775 (1985).

## Lost Property—MCL 434.22

The Lost Property Act requires any person finding lost property to report the finding or deliver the property to a law enforcement agency in the jurisdiction where the property was found. If the finder converts the property to his or her own use, with the intent to permanently deprive the owner, he or she is guilty of larceny.

# RETAIL FRAUD

## Retail Fraud-First Degree—MCL 750.356c (felony)

A person who does any of the following in a store or in its immediate vicinity is guilty of retail fraud in the first degree, a felony punishable by imprisonment for not more than five years or a fine of not more than $10,000.00 or three times the value of the difference in price, property stolen, or money or property obtained or attempted to be obtained, whichever is greater, or both imprisonment and a fine:

- While the store is open, *steals* property offered for sale at a price of $1,000 or more.
- While the store is open, *switches* or otherwise misrepresents the price of the property if the resulting difference in price is $1,000 or more.
- With intent to defraud, *falsely exchanges* property if the amount of money or value of property obtained is $1,000 or more.
- Commits a retail fraud second degree with the property value of $200 or more but less than $1,000, and has at least one prior conviction for retail fraud first degree, false pretenses, larceny, retail fraud second degree, larceny in a building, or any attempt of such offenses.

A person who commits a retail fraud first degree cannot be prosecuted for larceny in a building under MCL 750.360.

## Retail Fraud-Second Degree—MCL 750.356d(1) (1-year misdemeanor)

A person who does any of the following in a store or in its immediate vicinity is guilty of retail fraud in the second degree, a misdemeanor punishable by imprisonment for not more than one year or a fine of not more than $2,000.00 or three times the value of the difference in price, property stolen, or money or property obtained or attempted to be obtained, whichever is greater, or both imprisonment and a fine:

- While the store is open, *steals* property offered for sale at a price of $200 or more but less than $1,000.
- While the store is open, *switches* or otherwise misrepresents the price of the property if the resulting difference in price is $200 or more but less than $1,000.
- With intent to defraud, *falsely exchanges* property if the amount of money or value of property obtained is $200 or more but less than $1,000.
- Commits a retail fraud third degree and has at least one prior conviction for retail fraud second degree, false pretenses, larceny, retail fraud first degree, larceny in a building, or any attempt of such offenses.

A person who commits a retail fraud second degree cannot be prosecuted for larceny in a building under MCL 750.360.

## Retail Fraud-Third Degree—MCL 750.356d(4) (93-day misdemeanor)

A person who does any of the following in a store or in its immediate vicinity is guilty of retail fraud in the third degree, a misdemeanor punishable by imprisonment for not more than 93 days or a fine of not more than $500.00 or three times the value of the difference in price, property stolen, or money or property obtained or attempted to be obtained, whichever is greater, or both imprisonment and a fine:

- While the store is open, *steals* property offered for sale at a price of less than $200.
- While the store is open, *switches* or otherwise misrepresents the price of the property if the resulting difference in price is less than $200.
- With intent to defraud, *falsely exchanges* property if the amount of money or value of property obtained is less than $200.

A person who commits a retail fraud third degree cannot be prosecuted for larceny in a building under MCL 750.360.

## Elements-Retail Fraud Involving Theft

1. That the defendant took some property that the store offered for sale.
2. The defendant moved the property. Any movement is enough. It does not matter whether the

defendant actually got the property past the cashier or out of the store.

3. That the defendant intended to steal the property. "Intended to steal" means that the defendant intended to permanently take the property from the store without the store's consent.
4. That this happened either inside the store or in the immediate area around the store, while the store was open to the public.
5. That the price of the property was as follows:

   (a) $1,000 or more.
   (b) $200 or more but less than $1,000.
   (c) Some amount less than $200.

CJI2d 23.13.

## Elements-Retail Fraud Involving Price Switching

1. That the defendant altered or switched a price tag or in some other way misrepresented the price of property.
2. That the defendant did this intending either to pay less than the actual price for the property or not to pay for the property at all.
3. That this happened either inside the store or in the immediate area around the store, while the store was open to the public.
4. That the difference between the sale price and the price the defendant intended to pay was:

   (a) $1,000 or more.
   (b) $200 or more but less than $1,000.
   (c) Some amount less than $200.

CJI2d 23.14.

## Elements-Retail Fraud Involving False Exchange

1. That the defendant exchanged or tried to exchange property that had not been paid for and that belonged to the store. It does not matter whether the defendant tried to exchange it for money or other property.
2. That the defendant did this with the intent to defraud or cheat the store.
3. That this happened during store hours, either inside the store or in the immediate area around the store.
4. That the amount of money or value of the property that the defendant obtained or attempted to obtain was:

   (a) $1,000 or more.
   (b) $200 or more but less than $1,000.
   (c) Some amount less than $200.

CJI2d 23.15.

## Possession of Device Used to Shield Merchandise from Detection—MCL 750.360a

*A person shall not do any of the following:*

   (a) *Possess a laminated or coated bag or device that is intended to shield merchandise from detection by an electronic or magnetic theft detection device with the intent to commit or attempt to commit larceny.*
   (b) *Manufacture, sell, offer for sale, or distribute, or attempt to manufacture, sell, offer for sale, or distribute, a laminated or coated bag or device that is intended to shield merchandise from detection by an electronic or magnetic theft detection device knowing or reasonably believing that the bag or device will be used to commit or attempt to commit larceny.*
   (c) *Possess a tool or device designed to allow the deactivation or removal of a theft detection device from any merchandise with the intent to use the tool or device to deactivate a theft detection device on, or to remove a theft detection device from, any merchandise without the permission of the merchant or person owning or lawfully holding that merchandise with the intent to commit or attempt to commit larceny.*
   (d) *Manufacture, sell, offer for sale, or distribute a tool or device designed to allow the deactivation or removal of a theft detection device from any merchandise without the permission of the merchant or person owning or lawfully holding that merchandise knowing or reasonably believing that the tool or device will be used to commit or attempt to commit larceny.*
   (e) *Deactivate a theft detection device or remove a theft detection device from any merchandise in a retail establishment prior to purchasing the merchandise with the intent to commit or attempt to commit a larceny.*

Penalties:

| First offense | 1-year misdemeanor |
|---|---|
| Second offense | 4-year felony |

## Organized Retail Crime—MCL 752.1084 (felony)

*A person is guilty of organized retail crime when that person, alone or in association with another person, does any of the following:*

   (a) *Knowingly commits an organized retail crime.*
   (b) *Organizes, supervises, finances, or otherwise manages or assists another person in committing an organized retail crime.*

(c) *Removes, destroys, deactivates, or knowingly evades any component of an antishoplifting or inventory control device to prevent the activation of that device or to facilitate another person in committing an organized retail crime.*

(d) *Conspires with another person to commit an organized retail crime.*

(e) *Receives, purchases, or possesses retail merchandise for sale or resale knowing or believing the retail merchandise to be stolen from a retail merchant.*

(f) *Uses any artifice, instrument, container, device, or other article to facilitate the commission of an organized retail crime act.*

(g) *Knowingly causes a fire exit alarm to sound or otherwise activate, or deactivates or prevents a fire exit alarm from sounding, in the commission of an organized retail crime or to facilitate the commission of an organized retail crime by another person.*

(h) *Knowingly purchases a wireless telecommunication device using fraudulent credit, knowingly procures a wireless telecommunications service agreement with the intent to defraud another person or to breach that agreement, or uses another person to obtain a wireless telecommunications service agreement with the intent to defraud another person or to breach that agreement.*

***Organized retail crime:*** The theft of retail merchandise from a retail merchant with the intent or purpose of reselling, distributing, or otherwise reentering the retail merchandise in commerce, including the transfer of the stolen retail merchandise to another retail merchant or to any other person personally, through the mail, or through any electronic medium, including the Internet, in exchange for anything of value. MCL 752.1083.

Organized retail crime is a felony punishable by imprisonment for not more than five years or a fine of $5,000.00 or both.

If the true owner of stolen retail merchandise cannot be identified, the retail merchandise, and any proceeds from the sale or resale of that merchandise, is subject to forfeiture to the state for use by the board in the performance of its duties. The court shall order forfeiture of the retail merchandise in the manner and upon terms and conditions as determined by the court to be appropriate.

The court shall order a person who is found guilty of organized retail crime to make restitution to any retail merchant victim in the manner provided in the crime victim's rights act, MCL 780.751 to 780.834,

and to reimburse the governmental entity for its expenses incurred as a result of the violation of this act in the manner provided in MCL 769.1f.

It is not a defense to a charge under this section that the property was not stolen, embezzled, or converted property at the time of the violation if the property was explicitly represented to the accused person as being stolen, embezzled, or converted property.

# EMBEZZLEMENT

## Embezzlement—MCL 750.174

*A person who as the agent, servant, or employee of another person, governmental entity within this state, or other legal entity or who as the trustee, bailee, or custodian of the property of another person, governmental entity within this state, or other legal entity fraudulently disposes of or converts to his or her own use, or takes or secretes with the intent to convert to his or her own use without the consent of his or her principal, any money or other personal property of his or her principal that has come to that person's possession or that is under his or her charge or control by virtue of his or her being an agent, servant, employee, trustee, bailee, or custodian, is guilty of embezzlement.*

### Elements

1. The money or property belongs to the principal.
2. The defendant had a relationship of trust with the principal because the defendant was an agent, servant, employee, trustee, bailee, or custodian.
3. The defendant obtained possession or control of the money or property because of this relationship.
4. The defendant did any of the following:
   a. Dishonestly disposed of the money or property.
   b. Converted the money or property to his or her own use.
   c. Took or hid the money or property with the intent to convert it to his or her own use without consent of the principal.
5. At the time the defendant did this, he or she intended to defraud or cheat the principal of some property.
   CJI2d 27.1.

The value of property or money embezzled in separate incidents may be aggregated if part of a scheme or course of conduct.

The intent to return the property is no defense. Unlawful use of the funds is the key factor. *People v. Butts*, 128 Mich. 208 (1901).

The distinction between embezzlement and larceny is that in embezzlement the taking is an unlawful appropriation of that which has come into one's possession rightfully. *People v. Bergman*, 246 Mich. 68 (1929).

Penalties:

| | |
|---|---|
| Less than $200 | 93-day misdemeanor |
| Less than $200 from charity or nonprofit victim | 1-year misdemeanor |
| $200 to less than $1,000; or less than $200 if previously convicted | 1-year misdemeanor |
| $200 to less than $1,000 from charity or nonprofit victim | 5-year felony |
| $1,000 to less than $20,000; or $200 to less than $1,000 if previously convicted | 5-year felony |
| $1,000 to less than $20,000 from charity or nonprofit victim | 10-year felony |
| $20,000 to less than $50,000; or 2 or more previous convictions | 10-year felony |
| $50,000 to less than $100,000 | 15-year felony |
| More than $100,000 | 20-year felony |

## Embezzlement by a Public Official—MCL 750.175

*Embezzlement by public officer, his agent, etc.— Any person holding any public office in this state, or the agent or servant of any such person, who knowingly and unlawfully appropriates to his own use, or to the use of any other person, the money or property received by him in his official capacity or employment, of the value of 50 dollars or upwards, shall be guilty of a felony, punishable by imprisonment in the state prison not more than 10 years or by fine of not more than 5,000 dollars.*

In any prosecution under this section, the failure, neglect, or refusal of any public officer to pay over and deliver to his successor all moneys and property which should be in his hands as such officer, shall be prima facie evidence of an offense against the provisions of this section.

### Elements

1. The defendant held a public office or worked for a public official.
2. The defendant received money or property in his or her official duties.
3. The defendant knew that the property or money was public property.
4. The defendant used the property or money for an unauthorized purpose.
CJ12d 27.3.

Refusal by the suspect to deliver the money or property to his successor creates prima facie evidence of a violation of this statute. MCL 750.175.

"The intention of the statute was to prevent any public official from using money or property coming to him in his official capacity for any other purpose than the purpose for which it came to him." *People v. Warren*, 122 Mich. 504 (1899).

Demand for repayment and failure to pay on demand are not elements of MCL 750.175. Repayment is also not a defense to charges under that section. *People v. Jones*, 182 Mich. App. 668 (1990).

## Embezzlement by Police Officer—MCL 257.728(5)(c)

*At or before the completion of his or her tour of duty, a police officer taking a certificate or deposit of money shall deliver the certificate or deposit of money either to the magistrate named in the citation together with a report of the facts relating to the arrest, or to the police chief or person authorized by the police chief to receive certificates and deposits. The police chief or person authorized by the police chief shall deposit with the court the certificate or the money deposited and the citation in the same manner as prescribed for citations in [MCL 257.728a]. Failure to make a report and deliver the money deposited is embezzlement of public money.*

# 13

# FINANCIAL CRIMES

## CHECK LAW VIOLATIONS

### Non-Sufficient Funds (NSF)—MCL 750.131

*(1) A person shall not make, draw, utter, or deliver any check, draft, or order for the payment of money, to apply on account or otherwise, upon any bank or other depository with intent to defraud and knowing at the time of the making, drawing, uttering, or delivering that the maker or drawer does not have sufficient funds in or credit with the bank or other depository to pay the check, draft, or order in full upon its presentation.*

*(2) A person shall not make, draw, utter, or deliver any check, draft, or order for the payment of money, to apply on account or otherwise, upon any bank or other depository with intent to defraud if the person does not have sufficient funds for the payment of the check, draft, or order when presentation for payment is made to the drawee. This subsection does not apply if the lack of funds is due to garnishment, attachment, levy, or other lawful cause and that fact was not known to the person when the person made, drew, uttered, or delivered the check, draft, or order.*

### Elements

1. The defendant wrote or delivered a check, draft, or money order payable to the victim.

2. This check was drawn on a bank or depository.
3. The check, draft, or money order was signed or endorsed.
4. Either:
   a. The defendant knew when he wrote or delivered the check, draft, or money order that he did not have enough money or credit with the bank or depository to pay it in full.
   b. When the check, draft, or money order was presented for payment, there were not sufficient funds at the bank or depository to pay it in full and the defendant knew when he wrote the check, draft, money order that there would not be enough money or credit to pay it in full when it was presented.

5. When he wrote or delivered this check, draft, or money order, the defendant intended to defraud or cheat someone. If the defendant reasonably expected that the check, draft, money order would be paid by the bank, then there was no intent to defraud or cheat.

CJI2d 29.9.

To prove that the defendant passed the check, it is necessary that the prosecution present evidence of identification. This can be done if the cashier remembers the person or verified who the person was by comparing a driver's license or any other form of ID. Other ways include if the suspect admits to the crime during an interview or by using handwriting analysis.

The element of intent to defraud is lacking if at the time of the issuance of the check, the defendant has a reasonable expectation that the check will be paid on presentation. *People v. Bradford*, 144 Mich. App. 416 (1985).

It is not possible to perpetrate a fraud if the check is accepted with full knowledge that there is not enough money in the account. *People v. Jacobson*, 248 Mich. 639 (1929).

Penalties:

| Less than $100—First Offense | 93-day misdemeanor |
|---|---|
| Less than $100—Second offense or subsequent offense | 1-year misdemeanor |
| $100 to less than $500—First and second offense | 1-year misdemeanor |
| $100 to less than $500—Third or more offense | 2-year felony |
| $500 or more | 2-year felony |

## No Account Check—MCL 750.131a(1) (felony)

*A person shall not, with intent to defraud, make, draw, utter, or deliver any check, draft, or order for the payment of money, to apply on an account or otherwise, upon any bank or other depository, if at the time of making, drawing, uttering, or delivering the check, draft, or order he or she does not have an account in or credit with the bank or other depository for the payment of the check, draft, or order upon presentation. A person who violates this subsection is guilty of a felony, punishable by imprisonment for not more than 2 years, or by a fine of not more than $500.00, or both.*

### Elements

1. The defendant wrote or delivered a check, draft, or money order in the amount payable to the victim.
2. This check, draft, or money order was drawn on a bank.
3. When he did this, the defendant did not have an account or credit with that bank.
4. When he wrote or delivered this check, draft, or money order, the defendant intended to defraud or cheat someone.
5. This check, draft, or money order was presented for payment.
CJI2d 29.7.

Presentation of an NSF check is prima facie evidence of intent to defraud so long as the suspect does not make good on the check within five days of receiving notice that the check was not honored. MCL 750.132.

It is not necessary that the suspect receive payment on the check, only that he or she presented it for payment. *People v. Henson*, 18 Mich. App. 259 (1969).

## Three NSF Checks within 10 Days—MCL 750.131a(2) (felony)

*A person shall not, with intent to defraud, make, draw, utter, or deliver, within a period of not more than 10 days, 3 or more checks, drafts, or orders for the payment of money, to apply on account or otherwise, upon any bank or other depository, knowing at the time of making, drawing, uttering, or delivering each of the checks, drafts, or orders that the maker or drawer does not have sufficient funds or credit with the bank or other depository for the payment of the check, draft, or order in full upon its presentation. A person who violates this subsection is guilty of a felony, punishable by imprisonment for not more than 2 years, or by a fine of not more than $500.00, or both.*

### Elements

1. The defendant wrote or delivered three checks, drafts, or money orders.
2. When he did this, the defendant did not have enough money or credit with the bank to pay any of the checks, drafts, or money orders in full.
3. When he did this, the defendant knew that he did not have enough money or credit to pay any of them in full.
4. When he wrote or delivered each of these three checks, drafts, or money orders, the defendant intended to defraud or cheat someone.
CJI2d 29.8.

Where a person issued three checks within 10 days in three different counties, that person may be prosecuted in any one of those counties. OAG, 1945–1946, No. 3,038, p 175 (January 15, 1945).

# FORGERY
## Forgery—MCL 750.248 (felony)

*A person who falsely makes, alters, forges, or counterfeits a public record, or a certificate, return, or attestation of a clerk of a court, register of deeds, notary public, township clerk, or any other public officer, in relation to a matter in which the certificate, return, or attestation may be received as legal proof, or a charter, deed, will, testament, bond, writing obligatory, letter of attorney, policy of insurance, bill of lading, bill of exchange, promissory note, or an order, acquittance [sic] of discharge for money or other property, or a waiver, release, claim or demand, or an acceptance of a bill of exchange, or indorsement [sic], or assignment of a bill of exchange or promissory note for the payment of money, or an accountable receipt for money, goods, or other property with intent to injure or defraud another person is guilty of a felony punishable by imprisonment for not more than 14 years.*

### Elements

1. The document in question was falsely made, altered, forged, or counterfeited, in some manner.
2. The defendant falsely made, altered, forged, or counterfeited this document. Forgery includes any act which falsely makes an instrument appear what it is not.
3. When the defendant did this, he intended to defraud or cheat someone.

CJI2d 28.1.

This statute does not apply to a scrivener's error. Prosecution may be sought in the county in which the forgery was performed, where the forged document was uttered and published, or where the rightful property owner resides. The crime is complete upon the making of the false writing.

> The signing of another's name to a document without authority constitutes forgery. *People v. Cook*, 223 Mich. 291 (1923).
>
> There is no requirement that the document be signed. *People v. Susalla*, 392 Mich. 387 (1974).
>
> While the forgery must expose someone to a risk of loss, there is no requirement that an actual loss occur. *People v. Susalla*, 392 Mich. 387 (1974).

### Forgery Affecting Real Property—MCL 750.248b (felony)

*A person who falsely makes, alters, forges, or counterfeits a deed, a discharge of mortgage, or a power or letter of attorney or other document that affects an interest in real property with intent to injure or*

*defraud another person is guilty of a felony punishable by imprisonment for not more than 14 years.*

This statute does not apply to a scrivener's error. Prosecution may be sought in the county in which the forgery was performed, where the forged document was uttered and published, or where the rightful property owner resides. The crime is complete upon the making of the false writing.

### Uttering and Publishing—MCL 750.249 (felony)

*A person who utters and publishes as true a false, forged, altered, or counterfeit record, instrument, or other writing listed in section 248 knowing it to be false, altered, forged, or counterfeit with intent to injure or defraud is guilty of a felony punishable by imprisonment for not more than 14 years.*

### Definitions

***Uttering:*** To put something into circulation. CJI2d 22.22.

***Utter and publish:*** To offer something as if it is real, whether or not anyone accepts it as real. CJI2d 22.22.

### Elements

1. A document named in MCL 750.248(1) was false, altered, forged, or counterfeited in some manner.
2. The defendant represented, by words or actions or both, that the document was genuine or true and exhibited, offered, or presented it.
3. When the defendant did this, he knew that the document was false, altered, forged, or counterfeit.
4. When the defendant did this, he intended to defraud or cheat someone.

CJI2d 28.2.

It does not matter whether the document was actually accepted as genuine by the person the defendant allegedly tried to cheat. It also does not matter whether the person actually suffered a loss or whether the defendant actually gave anyone the document. It is enough if the defendant offered the document, directly or indirectly, by words or actions, as genuine. CJI2d 28.3.

> Valid gifts certificates purchased with a stolen credit card have been found to be false instruments for uttering and publishing. *People v. Aguwa*, 245 Mich. App. 1 (2001).

The crime of uttering and publishing includes a "copy" of a document. *People v. Cassadime*, 258 Mich. App. 395 (2003).

# COUNTERFEITING

## Possession of Counterfeit Bills—MCL 750.252

*Any person who shall have in his possession at the same time, 10 or more similar false, altered, forged or counterfeit notes, bills of credit, bank bills or notes of this state, or any of its political subdivisions or municipalities, payable to the bearer thereof, or to the order of any person, such as are mentioned in the preceding sections of this chapter, knowing the same to be false, altered, forged or counterfeit, with intent to utter the same as true, and thereby to injure and defraud as aforesaid, shall be guilty of a felony, punishable by imprisonment in the state prison not more than 7 years.*

### Definition

***Counterfeit:*** To make an unauthorized copy, imitation or forgery of something with the intent to deceive or cheat someone by using the copy, imitation or forgery as it were real. CJI2d 22.13.

## Possession of Counterfeit Bills—MCL 750.254 (felony)

*Any person who shall bring into this state, or shall have in his possession, any false, altered, forged or counterfeit bill or note in the similitude of the bills or notes payable to the bearer thereof, or to the order of any person issued by or for this state, or any of its political subdivisions or municipalities, or any bank or banking company, established in this state, or in any of the British provinces in North America, or in any other state or country, with intent to utter or pass the same, or to render the same current as true, knowing the same to be false, forged or counterfeit, shall be guilty of a felony, punishable by imprisonment in the state prison not more than 5 years, or by fine of not more than 2,500 dollars.*

### Elements

1. The defendant possessed a counterfeit bill,
2. While knowing that the bills are false, forged, or counterfeited, and
3. Did so with the intent to utter or pass.

Ten or more bills fall under MCL 750.252 (7-year felony).

## Counterfeiting and Possession of Coins— MCL 750.260 (felony)

*Any person who shall counterfeit any gold or silver coin, current by law or usage within this state, and every person who shall have in his possession, at the same time, 5 or more pieces of false money or coin, counterfeited in the similitude of any gold or silver coin current as aforesaid, knowing the same to be false and counterfeit, and with intent to utter or pass the same as true, shall be guilty of a felony, punishable by imprisonment in the state prison for life, or for any term of years.*

### Elements

1. The defendant counterfeited any gold or silver coin, and
2. Such coin was current by law or usage within this state.

or

1. The defendant possessed,
2. Five or more pieces of false money or coins,
3. Knowing that the money or coins were false or counterfeit, and
4. Did so with the intent to utter or pass the money or coins as true.

Less than five coins falls under MCL 750.261 (10-year felony).

## Tools for Counterfeiting Bills or Notes— MCL 750.255 (felony)

*Any person who shall engrave, make or mend, or begin to engrave, make or mend, any plate, block, press or other tool, instrument or implement, or shall make or provide any paper or other material, adapted or designed for the forging and making any false or counterfeit note, certificate or other bill of credit in the similitude of the notes, certificates, bills of credit issued by lawful authority for any debt of this state, or any of its political subdivisions or municipalities, or any false or counterfeit note or bill in the similitude of the notes or bills issued by any bank or banking company established in this state, or within the United States, or in any of the British provinces in North America, or in any foreign state or country; and any person who shall have in his possession any such plate or block, engraved in whole or in part, or any press or other tool, instrument or implement, or any paper or other material, adapted and designed as aforesaid, with intent to use the same, or to cause or permit the same to be used in forging or making any such false or counterfeit certificates, bills or notes, shall be guilty of a felony, punishable by imprisonment in the state prison not more than 10 years or by fine of not more than 5,000 dollars.*

## Elements

1. The defendant made or began to make or provided to another person,
2. A tool designed for the forging of a bill or a note, and
3. The bill or note is issued by a public entity.

or

1. The defendant possessed,
2. A tool designed for the forging of a bill or a note,
3. Intending to use the tool or to cause the tool to be used to create a false bill or note, and
4. The bill or note is issued by a public entity.

> A community college district was found to be a public entity for purposes of this statute when the defendant possessed tools for creating forged Delta College checks. *People v. Egleston*, 114 Mich. App. 436 (1982).
>
> Checks drawn on a county's commercial account meet the requirements for this statute. *People v. Beckner*, 92 Mich. App. 166 (1979).
>
> Likewise, checks drawn on a city's commercial account also meet the requirements of this statute. *People v. Jackson*, 98 Mich. App. 735 (1980).
>
> A computer, scanner, and printer fall within this statute when used to make counterfeit bills. *People v. Harrison*, 283 Mich. App. 374 (2009).

## Tools for Counterfeiting Coins—MCL 750.262 (felony)

*Any person who shall cast, stamp, engrave, make or mend, or shall knowingly have in his possession, any mould, pattern, die, puncheon, engine, press or other tool or instrument, adapted and designed for coining or making any counterfeit coin, in the similitude of any gold or silver coin, current by law or usage in this state, with intent to use or employ the same, or to cause or permit the same to be used or employed in coining or making any such false and counterfeit coin as aforesaid, shall be guilty of a felony, punishable by imprisonment in the state prison not more than 10 years, or by a fine of not more than 5,000 dollars.*

## Elements

1. The defendant made or knowingly possessed,
2. A mold, pattern, die, puncheon, engine, press, or other tool,
3. Designed for coining or making a counterfeit coin, and
4. Intending to use the tool or intending to permit its use in the making of a counterfeit coin.

## Defrauding an Innkeeper—MCL 750.292 (90-day misdemeanor)

*Any person who shall put up at any hotel, motel, inn, restaurant or cafe as a guest and shall procure any food, entertainment or accommodation without paying therefor, except when credit is given therefor by express agreement, with intent to defraud such keeper thereof out of the pay for the same, or, who, with intent to defraud such keeper out of the pay therefor, shall obtain credit at any hotel, motel, inn, restaurant or cafe for such food, entertainment or accommodation, by means of any false show of baggage or effects brought thereto, is guilty of a misdemeanor. No conviction shall be had under the provisions of this section unless complaint is made within 60 days of the time of the violation hereof.*

Applies to one of the following:

- The suspect, with the intent to defraud, stayed at a hotel, motel, inn, restaurant, or cafe as a guest and procured food, entertainment, or accommodation without paying and credit was not given by express agreement.
- The suspect, with the intent to defraud, obtained credit at a hotel, motel, inn, restaurant, or cafe for such food, entertainment, or accommodation, by means of a false show of baggage or effects.

No conviction shall be had under the provisions of this section unless complaint is made within 60 days of the time of the violation.

Refusal or neglect to pay is prima facie evidence of intent to defraud under this statute. MCL 750.293.

# FINANCIAL TRANSACTION DEVICE (FTD)

## Definition—750.157m

FTD means any of the following:

- Electronic funds card—ATM card.
- Credit card—e.g., Visa, AmEx, and merchant cards.

- Debit card—e.g., gas cards, cards used in copy machines, and long distance cards.
- Point of sale card—permits the purchase of goods and services where a deduction is made from an account at the time the goods/services are purchased.
- Any instrument, code number, PIN number, and means of access to a credit or deposit account, or a driver's license or identification card that can be used either alone or with another device, to:
  - Obtain money, cash, credit, goods, services, or anything else of value.
  - Certify or guarantee that the device holder has available funds on deposit to honor a draft or check.
  - Provide the device holder with access to an account in order to deposit, withdraw, or transfer funds to obtain information about a deposit account.
- A health insurance card.

A MasterCard check is not an FTD under this statute because the account is accessed by paper. *People v. Kotesky,* 190 Mich. App. 330 (1991).

## FTD Violations

### Stealing, Taking, or Removing an FTD; Possession of Fraudulent or Altered FTD—MCL 750.157n (felony)

> *(1) A person who steals knowingly takes, or knowingly removes a financial transaction device from the person or possession of a deviceholder, or who knowingly retains, knowingly possesses, knowingly secretes, or knowingly uses a financial transaction device without the consent of the deviceholder, is guilty of a felony.*
>
> *(2) A person who knowingly possesses a fraudulent or altered financial transaction device is guilty of a felony.*

### Elements

1. The defendant obtained, retained, hid, or used someone else's FTD.
2. The defendant did so knowingly.
3. The defendant did so without the owner's consent.
4. The defendant intended to defraud or cheat.
CJ12d 30.3.

or

1. The defendant possessed a fraudulent or altered FTD.
2. The defendant knew that the FTD was fraudulent or altered.
3. The defendant intended to defraud or cheat.
CJ12d 30.4.

Under the statute, intent to defraud or cheat is not an element requiring proof separate from knowing possession. *People v. Cohen,* 467 Mich. 874 (2002).

The defendant could not be convicted under MCL 750.157n where she improperly used a company credit card that was issued in her name. Embezzlement would have been a more proper charge. *People v. Anderson,* 268 Mich. App. 410 (2005).

## Possession of Another's FTD with Intent to Use, Deliver, Circulate, or Sell—MCL 750.157p (felony)

### Elements

1. The defendant knowingly possessed someone else's FTD.
2. The defendant did not have the owner's permission and knew that he did not have the owner's permission.
3. The defendant had the intent to use, deliver, circulate or sell the device, or permit or cause someone else to use, deliver, circulate, or sell the device.
4. The defendant intended to defraud or cheat.
CJ12d 30.5.

## Delivery, Circulation, or Sale of an FTD—MCL 750.157q (felony)

> *A person who delivers, circulates, or sells a financial transaction device which was obtained or held by that person under circumstances proscribed under section 157n, 157p, or 157v, or uses, permits, causes, or procures the financial transaction device to be used, delivered, circulated, or sold, knowing the device to have been obtained or held under circumstances proscribed under section 157n, 157p, or 157v is guilty of a felony.*

The defendant's conviction was upheld where she obtained a credit card that was never actually issued to the victim (the credit card was issued in the victim's name, but the victim never applied for or possessed the credit card). This would include cases where the suspect used the victim's personal information to obtain credit cards in the victim's name. *People v. Collins*, 158 Mich. App. 508 (1987).

The defendant's conviction was upheld even though his attempted use of the FTD was not completed. The defendant argued that he was only guilty of an "attempt" crime, but the appellate court disagreed with him, holding that the statute seeks to punish unlawful use of a credit card, not the obtaining of goods and services through unlawful use of a credit card. Thus, the crime was completed when the defendant presented the card for payment regardless of whether or not the transaction was completed. *People v. Hilliard*, 160 Mich. App. 484 (1987).

## Fraud, Forgery, Material Alteration, and Counterfeiting of FTD—MCL 750.157r (felony)

*A person who, with intent to defraud, forges, materially alters, simulates, or counterfeits a financial transaction device is guilty of a felony.*

### Elements

1. The FTD was falsely made, materially altered, forged, counterfeited, or duplicated.
2. It was the defendant who falsely made, materially altered, forged, counterfeited, or duplicated the FTD.
3. The defendant intended to defraud or cheat someone.

CJI2d 30.6.

## Use of a Revolved or Canceled FTD with Intent to Defraud— MCL 750.157s

*A person who, for the purpose of obtaining goods, property, services, or anything of value, knowingly and with intent to defraud uses 1 or more financial transaction devices that have been revoked or canceled by the issuer of the device or devices, as distinguished from expired, and has received notice of the revocation or cancellation is guilty of a crime.*

### Elements

1. The FTD had been revoked or canceled.
2. The FTD had been issued by an issuer to the holder and had been revoked or canceled by the issuer.
3. The defendant received notice of the revocation or cancelation.
4. After receiving the notice, the defendant used the FTD at a business for the purpose of obtaining goods, property, services, or other things of value.
5. The defendant knew when he used the FTD that it had been revoked or canceled.
6. When the defendant used the FTD, he intended to defraud or cheat someone.

CJI2d 30.7.

Penalties:

| Less than $100—First offense | 93-day misdemeanor |
|---|---|
| Less than $100—Second offense or subsequent offense | 1-year misdemeanor |
| $100 to less than $500—First and second offense | 1-year misdemeanor |
| $100 to less than $500—Third or more offense | 2-year felony |
| $500 or more | 2-year felony |

## Use of FTD to Defraud—MCL 750.157w

*A person who knowingly and with intent to defraud uses a financial transaction device to withdraw or transfer funds from a deposit account in violation of the contractual limitations imposed on the amount or frequency of withdrawals or transfers or in an amount exceeding the funds then on deposit in the account is guilty of a crime.*

### Elements

1. The defendant used an FTD to withdraw or transfer money.
2. The defendant did one of the following:
   a. Withdrew more money than he or she had on deposit.
   b. Withdrew more money than he or she was allowed to.
   c. Withdrew money more often than allowed to.
3. The defendant did this knowingly.
4. The defendant intended to defraud or cheat someone.

CJI2d 30.11.

Penalties:

| Less than $200 | 93-day misdemeanor |
|---|---|
| $200 to less than $1,000; or less than $200 if previously convicted | 1-year misdemeanor |
| $1,000 to less than $20,000; or $200 to less than $1,000 if previously convicted | 5-year felony |
| Over $20,000; or $1,000 to less than $20,000 if previously convicted twice | 10-year felony |

# MONEY LAUNDERING

## Definitions

*Controlled substance offense:* A felony controlled substances violation—MCL 333.7401 to 333.7461.

*Knowingly:* In the case of a corporation, means with the approval or prior actual knowledge of the board of directors, a majority of the directors, or persons who together hold a majority of the voting ownership interests in the corporation. In determining whether a majority of the directors approved of or had knowledge of the activity, a director who was not aware of the activity due to his or her own negligence or other fault is regarded as having had knowledge of the activity. This subdivision does not limit the liability of any individual officer, employee, director, or stockholder of a corporation.

*Financial transaction:* A purchase, sale, loan, pledge, gift, transfer, delivery, exchange, or other disposition of a monetary instrument or other property and, with respect to a financial institution, includes a deposit, withdrawal, transfer between accounts, exchange of currency, loan, extension of credit, purchase or sale of any stock, bond, certificate of deposit, or other monetary instrument, or any other payment, transfer, or delivery by, through, or to a financial institution, by whatever means effected.

*Financial institution:* One or more of the following, if located in or doing business in this state:

- An insured bank, as defined in section 3(h) of the federal deposit insurance act, 12 USC 1813(h).
- A commercial bank or trust company.
- A private banker.
- An agency or branch of a foreign bank.
- A savings and loan institution.
- A thrift institution.
- A credit union.
- A broker or dealer registered with the Securities and Exchange Commission under the securities exchange act of 1934, 15 U.S.C. § 78a–78nn.
- A broker or dealer in securities or commodities.
- An investment banker or investment company.
- A currency exchange.
- An insurer, redeemer, or cashier of traveler's checks, checks, or money orders.
- An operator of a credit card system.
- An insurance company.
- A dealer in precious metals, stones, or jewels.
- A pawnbroker.
- A loan, finance, or mortgage company.
- A travel agency.
- A licensed sender of money.
- A telegraph company.

*Monetary instrument:* Coin or currency of the United States or another country, or group of countries, a traveler's check, personal check, bank check, money order, or investment security or negotiable instrument in bearer form or in any other form such that delivery is sufficient to pass title.

*Proceeds of a specified criminal offense:* Any monetary instrument or other real, personal, or intangible property obtained through the commission of a specified criminal offense, including any appreciation in the value of the monetary instrument or property.

*Specified criminal offense:* Any of the following:

- Felony tobacco tax violations. MCL 205.428.
- Felonious disposal of hazardous waste. MCL 324.11151.
- Any controlled substance offense.
- Felony welfare fraud. MCL 400.60.
- Medicaid fraud. MCL 400.604, 400.605, and 400.607.
- Felony gaming violations. MCL 432.218.
- Securities fraud. MCL 451.809.
- Display or dissemination of obscene matter to minors. MCL 722.675 and 722.677.
- Felony arson. MCL 750.72–750.75.
- Bank bond, bill, note or property violations. MCL 750.93–750. 96.
- Bribery. MCL 750.117–750.121, or 750.124.
- Jury tampering. MCL 750.120a.
- Child sexually abusive activity or material violations. MCL 750.145c.
- Felony credit card or financial transaction device offenses. MCL 750.157n, 750.157p–750.157u.
- Racketeering. MCL 750.159i.
- Felony embezzlement offenses. MCL 750.174–750.176, 750.180–750.182.

- Felony explosive or bomb violations. MCL 750.200–750.212a.
- Extortion. MCL 750.213.
- Felony false pretense violations. MCL 750.218.
- A felony forgery and counterfeiting violations. MCL 750.248–750.266.
- Securities fraud violations. MCL 750.271–750.274.
- Gambling offenses. MCL 750.301–750.305a, or 750.313.
- Murder. MCL 750.316 or 750.317.
- Horse racing violations. MCL 750.330–750.332.
- Kidnapping. MCL 750.349, 750.349a, or 750.350.
- Felony larceny. MCL 750.356–750.367c.
- Perjury or subornation of perjury. MCL 750.422–750.425.
- Prostitution. MCL 750.452, 750.455, or 750.457–750.459.
- Robbery. MCL 750.529–750.531.
- Felony stolen, embezzled, or converted property violations. MCL 750.535, 750.535a.
- Terrorism. MCL 750.543a–750.543z.
- Obscenity violations. MCL 752.365.
- A conspiracy, attempt, or solicitation to commit any of the listed offenses.

***Substituted proceeds of a specified criminal offense:*** Any monetary instrument or other real, personal, or intangible property obtained or any gain realized by the sale or exchange of proceeds of a specified criminal offense.

### Money Laundering, Fourth Degree—MCL 750.411l (2-year misdemeanor)

**Elements**

1. The defendant knowingly received or acquired a monetary instrument or other property that constitutes the proceeds or substituted proceeds of a specified criminal offense.
2. The defendant did so with prior actual knowledge that the monetary instrument or other property represents the proceeds or substituted proceeds of a criminal offense.
3. The defendant did so with prior actual knowledge that receipt or acquisition of the proceeds or substituted proceeds meets any of the following criteria:
   a. It will aid that person or another person in promoting or carrying on the criminal offense from which the proceeds or substituted proceeds were derived or any other criminal offense.
   b. It is designed, in whole or in part, to conceal or disguise the nature, location, source, ownership, or control of the proceeds or substituted proceeds of the specified criminal offense or to avoid a transaction reporting requirement under state or federal law.

or

1. The defendant knowingly conducted, attempt to conduct, or participated in conducting or attempting to conduct a financial transaction involving a monetary instrument or other property that constitutes the proceeds or substituted proceeds of a specified criminal offense.
2. The defendant did so with prior actual knowledge that the monetary instrument or other property represents the proceeds or substituted proceeds of a criminal offense.
3. The defendant did so with prior actual knowledge that the financial transaction meets any of the following criteria:
   a. It will aid that person or another person in promoting or carrying on the criminal offense from which the proceeds or substituted proceeds were derived or any other criminal offense.
   b. It is designed, in whole or in part, to conceal or disguise the nature, location, source, ownership, or control of the proceeds or substituted proceeds of the specified criminal offense, or to avoid a transaction reporting requirement under state or federal law.

### Money Laundering, Third Degree—MCL 750.411m (felony)

**Elements**

All of the elements of fourth-degree money laundering and one of the following:

   a. The proceeds or substituted proceeds were $10,000 or more.
   b. The predicate offense was a controlled substance offense or attempt, solicitation, or conspiracy to commit a controlled substance offense.
   c. The laundering is committed with intent to either promote the commission of a criminal offense or conceal or disguise the source, nature, ownership, or control of the proceeds.

Third-degree money laundering is a felony punishable by up to five years in prison. The $10,000 threshold may be aggregated over 30 days.

### Money Laundering, Second Degree—MCL 750.411n (felony)

**Elements**

All of the elements of fourth-degree money laundering where the proceeds or substituted proceeds were $10,000 or more and either of the following:

   a. The predicate offense was a controlled substance offense or attempt, solicitation, or conspiracy to commit a controlled substance offense.

b. The laundering is committed with intent to either promote the commission of a criminal offense or conceal or disguise the source, nature, ownership, or control of the proceeds.

Second-degree money laundering is a felony punishable by up to 10 years in prison. The $10,000 threshold may be aggregated over 30 days.

## Money Laundering, First Degree—MCL 750.411o (felony)

### Elements

All of the elements of fourth-degree money laundering and all of the following:

a. The proceeds or substituted proceeds were $10,000 or more.
b. The predicate offense was a controlled substance offense or attempt, solicitation, or conspiracy to commit a controlled substance offense.
c. The laundering is committed with intent to either promote the commission of a criminal offense or conceal or disguise the source, nature, ownership, or control of the proceeds.

First-degree money laundering is a felony punishable by up to 20 years in prison. The $10,000 threshold may be aggregated over 30 days.

## Money Laundering-Financial Transaction Involving Proceeds of Criminal Offense—MCL 750.411p (felony)

### Elements

1. The defendant conducted, attempted to conduct, or participated in conducting or attempting to conduct a financial transaction.
2. The transaction involved a monetary instrument or other property.
3. The transaction was represented by a law enforcement officer to be the proceeds or substituted proceeds of a specified criminal offense.
4. The defendant did so with the intent to either:

   a. Promote the commission of a criminal offense.
   b. Conceal or disguise the nature, location, source, ownership, or control of a monetary instrument or other property believed to be the proceeds or substituted proceeds of a specified criminal offense or avoid a transaction reporting requirement under state or federal law.

For purposes of this section, a representation of a monetary instrument or other property as the proceeds or substituted proceeds of a specified criminal

offense may be made by a person at the direction of, or with the approval of, a law enforcement official authorized to investigate or prosecute violations of this section.

For purposes of this section, the $10,000.00 threshold for the value of the monetary instrument or other property represented to be proceeds or substituted proceeds may be aggregated over a period of 30 calendar days.

Penalties:

| | |
|---|---|
| Transaction is represented to be the proceeds of a controlled substance offense and has a value of $10,000.00 or more | 20-year felony |
| Transaction is represented to be the proceeds of a controlled substance offense or has a value of $10,000.00 or more | 10-year felony |
| All other violations | 5-year felony |

## Possession, Use, or Transfer of Sales Suppression Device—MCL 750.411w (felony)

*A person shall not knowingly sell, purchase, install, transfer, or possess in this state any automated sales suppression device or zapper, phantom-ware, or a skimming device.*

A person who violates this statute is guilty of a felony punishable by one to five years in prison and is liable for all taxes and penalties due the state as the result of the fraudulent use of an automated sales suppression device and shall disgorge all profits associated with the sale or use of an automated sales suppression device.

This statute does not apply to equipment or technology utilized by a law enforcement officer while the officer is in the lawful performance of his or her duties as a law enforcement officer.

### Definitions

***Automated sales suppression device* or *zapper*:** A software program carried on a memory stick or removable compact disk, accessed through an Internet link, or accessed through any other means, that falsifies the electronic records of electronic cash registers and other point-of-sale systems, including, but not limited to, transaction data and transaction reports.

***Electronic cash register:*** A device that keeps a register or supporting documents through the means of an electronic device or computer system designed to record transaction data for the purpose of computing, compiling, or processing retail sales transaction data in whatever manner.

*Financial transaction device:*  A bank, savings and loan association, or credit union, and includes a corporation wholly owned by a financial institution or by the holding company parent of a financial institution.

*Personal identifying information and personal information:*  A name, number, or other information that is used for the purpose of identifying a specific person or providing access to a person's financial accounts, including, but not limited to, a person's name, address, telephone number, driver license or state personal identification card number, social security number, place of employment, employee identification number, employer or taxpayer identification number, government passport number, health insurance identification number, mother's maiden name, demand deposit account number, savings account number, financial transaction device account number or the person's account password, any other account password in combination with sufficient information to identify and access the account, automated or electronic signature, biometrics, stock or other security certificate or account number, credit card number, vital record, or medical records or information.

*Phantom-ware:*  A hidden, preinstalled, or installed at a later time programming option embedded in the operating system of an electronic cash register or hardwired into the electronic cash register that can be used to create a virtual second till or may eliminate or manipulate transaction records that may or may not be preserved in digital formats to represent the true or manipulated record of transactions in the electronic cash register.

*Skimming device:*  Any combination of devices or methods that are designed or adapted to be placed on the physical property of another person and to obtain the personal information or personal identifying information of another, or any other information that allows access to a person's financial accounts, from a financial transaction device without the permission of the owner of the financial transaction device.

*Transaction data:*  Information regarding items purchased by a customer, the price for each item; a taxability determination for each item; a segregated tax amount for each of the taxed items; the amount of cash or credit tendered; the net amount returned to the customer in change, the date and time of the purchase; the name, address, and identification number of the vendor; and the receipt or invoice number of the transaction.

*Transaction report:*  A report that includes, but need not be limited to, the sales, taxes collected, media totals, and discount voids at an electronic cash register that is printed on cash register tape at the end of a day or shift, or a report documenting every action at an electronic cash register that is stored electronically.

## Violations of the Charitable Organizations and Solicitations Act—MCL 400.293(1) (6-month misdemeanor)

*A person that does any of the following is guilty of a misdemeanor punishable by imprisonment for not more than 6 months or a fine of not more than $5,000.00, or both, for each violation:*

(a) *Knowingly misrepresents or misleads any person in any manner to believe that a person on whose behalf a solicitation effort is conducted is a charitable organization or that the proceeds of a solicitation effort are for charitable purposes.*

(b) *Knowingly diverts or misdirects contributions to a purpose or organization other than for which the funds were contributed or solicited.*

(c) *Knowingly misrepresents that funds solicited or contributed will be used for a specific charitable purpose.*

(d) *Knowingly misrepresents that a donor will receive special benefits or treatment or that failure to make a contribution will result in unfavorable treatment.*

(e) *Employs any device, scheme, or artifice to defraud or obtain money or property from a person by means of a false, deceptive, or misleading pretense, representation, or promise.*

(f) *Knowingly fails to file any materials, information, or report required under this act.*

(g) *Engages in any of the following practices and wrongfully obtains more than $1,000.00 and less than $5,000.00, in the aggregate, as a result of the practice or practices:*

(h) *Knowingly misrepresents that a person soliciting contributions or other funds for a charitable organization has a sponsorship, approval, status, affiliation, or other connection with a charitable organization or charitable purpose that the person does not have.*

(i) *Knowingly uses a name, symbol, or statement so closely related or similar to a name, symbol, or statement used by another charitable organization or governmental agency that use of that name, symbol, or statement is confusing or misleading.*

(ii) *Knowingly uses a bogus, fictitious, or nonexistent organization, address, or telephone number in any solicitation.*

(iii) *Knowingly misrepresents or misleads any person in any manner to believe that a person or governmental agency sponsors, endorses, or approves a solicitation effort if that person or agency has not given written consent to the use of the person's or agency's name for that purpose.*

(iv) *Knowingly misrepresents that the amount or percentage of a contribution that a charitable organization will receive for a charitable program after costs of solicitation are paid is greater than the amount or percentage of the contribution the charitable organization will actually receive.*

(v) *Knowingly solicits contributions, conducts a charitable sales promotion, or otherwise operates in this state as a charitable organization or professional fund raiser unless the information required under this act is filed with the attorney general as required under this act.*

(vi) *Aids, abets, or otherwise permits a person to solicit contributions or conduct a charitable sales promotion in this state unless the person soliciting contributions or conducting the charitable sales promotion has complied with the requirements of this act.*

(vii) *Knowingly solicits or receives a contribution, conducts a charitable sales promotion, or sells memberships in this state for or on behalf of any charitable organization subject to the provisions of this act that is not registered under this act.*

## Violation of the Charitable Organizations and Solicitations Act—MCL 400.293(2) (felony)

*A person that does any of the following is guilty of a felony punishable by imprisonment for not more than 5 years or a fine of not more than $20,000.00, or both, for each violation:*

(a) *Engages in any practice or practices described in subsection (1)(a), (b), (c), (d), or (e) if the amount of money fraudulently collected or wrongfully diverted from the charitable purpose for which the money was solicited exceeds, in the aggregate, $1,000.00.*

(b) *Engages in any practice or practices described in subsection (1)(g) and wrongfully obtains more than $5,000.00, in the aggregate, as a result of the practice or practices.*

(c) *Knowingly submits any of the following in materials or statements required under this act or requested by the attorney general:*

    (i) *Any document or statement purporting to have been signed, certified, attested to, approved by, or endorsed by a person if the signature, certification, attestation, approval, or endorsement is not genuine or has not been given by that person.*

    (ii) *Any document containing any materially false statement.*

## Presumption of Intent—MCL 400.293(3)

*For purposes of this section, a person is presumed to have committed a violation knowingly if the attorney general provided written notice identifying alleged violations to the person before the acts or omissions in violation of subsection (1) or (2) occurred.*

## Civil Actions—MCL 400.293(4)

*In addition to pursuing a criminal action under this section, the attorney general may bring a civil action for damages or equitable relief to enforce the provisions of this act.*

## Prosecution for Other Crimes—MCL 400.293(5)

*This section does not limit or restrict prosecution under the general criminal statutes of this state.*

# CRIMES AGAINST PROPERTY: SELECTED STATUTES

## RECEIVING OR CONCEALING STOLEN PROPERTY

### Receiving or Concealing Stolen Property—MCL 750.535(1)

*A person shall not buy, receive, possess, conceal, or aid in the concealment of stolen, embezzled, or converted money, goods, or property knowing, or having reason to know or reason to believe, that the money, goods, or property is stolen, embezzled, or converted.*

### Elements

1. The property was stolen, embezzled, or converted or was represented to the defendant as being stolen.
2. The defendant bought, received, possessed, concealed, or aided in the concealment of the property.
3. The defendant knew or had reason to know or believe the property was stolen.

CJ12d 26.1.

Penalties:

| | |
|---|---|
| Less than $200 | 93-day misdemeanor |
| $200 to less than $1,000; or less than $200 if previously convicted | 1-year misdemeanor |
| $1,000 to less than $20,000; or $200 to less than $1,000 if previously convicted | 5-year felony |
| Over $20,000; or $1,000 to less than $20,000, if previously convicted twice | 10-year felony |

When there are separate incidents that are part of a common scheme or plan, the total amount can be aggregated over a 12-month period for a total.

The value of stolen property is based on the value of the item on the open market with the prices fixed to those prevailing in the locality where the item was stolen, at the time it was stolen. The value of stolen goods is their market value at the time of the receiving or possession by the defendant. Thus, when thieves damaged vending machines while stealing them, the value was prefaced on the condition of the machines when the thieves sold the machines to the defendant, not the condition before the theft. *People v. Fishel*, 270 Mich. 82 (1935).

The special value to the owner of property stolen is not the proper basis for proving its value. *People v. Gilbert*, 163 Mich. 511 (1910).

A conviction under this statute was upheld where the defendant purchased two silver candelabras, later learned they were stolen, and then retained the candelabras. *People v. Fortuin*, 143 Mich. App. 279 (1985).

## Receiving or Concealing Stolen Motor Vehicle—MCL 750.535(7) (felony)

*A person shall not buy, receive, possess, conceal, or aid in the concealment of a stolen motor vehicle knowing that the motor vehicle is stolen, embezzled, or converted. A person who violates this subsection is guilty of a felony punishable by imprisonment for not more than 5 years or a fine of not more than $10,000.00 or 3 times the value of the motor vehicle purchased, received, possessed, or concealed, whichever is greater, or both imprisonment and a fine. A person who is charged with, convicted of, or punished for a violation of this subsection shall not be convicted of or punished for a violation of another provision of this section arising from the purchase, receipt, possession, concealment, or aiding in the concealment of the same motor vehicle. This subsection does not prohibit the person from being charged, convicted, or punished under any other applicable law.*

### Elements

1. The property was stolen, embezzled, or converted or was represented to the defendant as being stolen.
2. The defendant bought, received, possessed, concealed, or aided in the concealment of the property.
3. The defendant knew or had reason to know or believe the property was stolen.
4. The property was a motor vehicle.
CJ12d 26.1.

Evidence was sufficient to show that a car was stolen where the subject took his ex-girlfriend's vehicle without permission. *People v. Pratt*, 254 Mich. App. 425 (2002).

## Transporting Stolen Firearm—MCL 750.535b(1) (felony)

*A person who transports or ships a stolen firearm or stolen ammunition, knowing that the firearm or ammunition was stolen, is guilty of a felony, punishable by imprisonment for not more than 10 years or by a fine of not more than $5,000.00, or both.*

## Receiving and Concealing Stolen Firearm—MCL 750.535b(2) (felony)

*A person who receives, conceals, stores, barters, sells, disposes of, pledges, or accepts as security for a loan a stolen firearm or stolen ammunition, knowing that the firearm or ammunition was stolen, is guilty of a felony, punishable by imprisonment for not more than 10 years or by a fine of not more than $5,000.00, or both.*

Concealing or storing stolen firearms is a continuing crime. The statute of limitations does not run during the concealment or storage. *People v. Owen*, 251 Mich. App. 76 (2002).

The defendant was a getaway driver in a breaking and entering of a home in Lapeer County. She was subsequently convicted of home invasion in Lapeer County and of receiving and concealing a stolen firearm (which was stolen during the Lapeer County home invasion) in Oakland County. The court held that the dual convictions were not a Double Jeopardy violation because the statutes do not contain the same elements. *People v. Nutt*, 469 Mich. 565 (2004).

Convictions for receiving and concealing a stolen firearm and possession of a firearm during a felony ("felony-firearm") do not violate the Double Jeopardy Clause. *People v. Mitchell*, 456 Mich. 693 (1998).

## Knowledge that Property Was Stolen

Mere possession is not enough. There must be other facts or circumstances that show the defendant knew or should have known or had reason to believe the property was stolen. Examples include the following:

- The circumstances surrounding the taking.
- The way the suspect acted.
- The price that was paid.
- What the suspect said about the property.

- The time between when the property had been taken and when it was found in the defendant's possession.
- Any other circumstances that would allow the person to know the property was stolen. CJI2d 26.3.

# TRESPASS

## Trespass Upon the Lands or Premises of Another—Forbidden Entry—MCL 750.552(1)(a) (30-day misdemeanor)

*A person shall not enter the lands or premises of another without lawful authority after having been forbidden to do so by the owner or occupant or the agent of the owner or occupant.*

### Elements

1. The defendant willfully entered upon,
2. The land of another, and
3. Had been forbidden to do so.

A refusal to leave is not a necessary element when the defendant had already been forbidden from being on the premises. *People v. Bell*, 182 Mich. App 181 (1989).

A criminal trespass conviction was upheld where the defendants moved into a vacant city-owned house and made it habitable. *People v. Johnson*, 16 Mich. App. 745 (1969).

## Trespass Upon the Lands or Premises of Another—Refusal to Leave—MCL 750.552(1)(b) (30-day misdemeanor)

*A person shall not remain without lawful authority on the land or premises of another after being notified to depart by the owner or occupant or the agent of the owner or occupant.*

### Elements

1. The defendant was on the premises of another, and
2. After being notified to depart, refused to do so.

## Trespass Upon the Lands or Premises of Another—Fenced or Posted Farm Property—MCL 750.552(1)(c) (30-day misdemeanor)

*A person shall not enter or remain without lawful authority on fenced or posted farm property of another person without the consent of the owner*

*or his or her lessee or agent. A request to leave the premises is not a necessary element for a violation of this subdivision. This subdivision does not apply to a person who is in the process of attempting, by the most direct route, to contact the owner or his or her lessee or agent to request consent.*

### Elements

1. The defendant entered or remained on,
2. The fenced or posted farmland of another person,
3. Without lawful authority, and
4. Without the landowner's consent.

## Process Server Exception—MCL 750.552(2)

**Process server:**   A person authorized under MCL 600.101 to 600.9947 or Supreme Court rule to serve process.

The trespass statute does not apply to a process server who is on the land or premises of another while in the process of attempting, by the most direct route, to serve process upon any of the following:

- An owner or occupant of the land or premises.
- An agent of the owner or occupant of the land or premises.
- A lessee of the land or premises.

## Trespassing on a State Correctional Facility—MCL 750.552b (felony)

*A person who willfully trespasses by entering or remaining upon the property of a state correctional facility without authority or permission to enter or remain is guilty of a felony punishable by imprisonment for not more than 4 years or a fine of not more than $2,000.00, or both.*

**State correctional facility:**   A facility or institution that houses a prisoner population under the jurisdiction of the Department of Corrections. State correctional facility does not include a community corrections center or a community residential home.

## Trespass on Key Facilities—MCL 750.552c (felony)

*A person shall not intentionally and without authority or permission enter or remain in or upon premises or a structure belonging to another person that is a key facility if the key facility is completely enclosed by a physical barrier of any kind, including, but not limited to, a significant water barrier that prevents pedestrian access, and is posted with [required] signage as prescribed under subsection (2).*

*Key facility:* One or more of the following:

- A chemical manufacturing facility.
- A refinery.
- An electric utility facility, including, but not limited to, a power plant, a power generation facility peaker, an electric transmission facility, an electric station or substation, or any other facility used to support the generation, transmission, or distribution of electricity. Electric utility facility does not include electric transmission land or right-of-way that is not completely enclosed, posted, and maintained by the electric utility.
- A water intake structure or water treatment facility.
- A natural gas utility facility, including, but not limited to, an age station, compressor station, odorization facility, main line valve, natural gas storage facility, or any other facility used to support the acquisition, transmission, distribution, or storage of natural gas. Natural gas utility facility does not include gas transmission pipeline property that is not completely enclosed, posted, and maintained by the natural gas utility.
- Gasoline, propane, liquid natural gas (LNG), or other fuel terminal or storage facility.
- A transportation facility, including, but not limited to, a port, railroad switching yard, or trucking terminal.
- A pulp or paper manufacturing facility.
- A pharmaceutical manufacturing facility.
- A hazardous waste storage, treatment, or disposal facility.
- A telecommunication facility, including, but not limited to, a central office or cellular telephone tower site.
- A facility substantially similar to a facility, structure, or station listed in subdivisions (a) to (k) or a resource required to submit a risk management plan under 42 U.S.C. § 7412(r).

A key facility shall be posted in a conspicuous manner against entry. The minimum letter height on the posting signs shall be one inch. Each posting sign shall be not less than 50 square inches, and the signs shall be spaced to enable a person to observe not less than one sign at any point of entry upon the property.

This section does not prohibit and shall be not construed to prevent lawful assembly or a peaceful and orderly petition for the redress of grievances, including, but not limited to, a labor dispute between an employer and its employees.

# RECREATIONAL TRESPASS

## Recreational Trespass on Non-Farm Property— MCL 324.73102(1) (90-day misdemeanor)

A person shall not enter or remain upon the property of another person, other than farm property or a wooded area connected to farm property, to engage in any recreational activity or trapping on that property without the consent of the owner or his or her lessee or agent, if either of the following circumstances exists:

- The property is fenced or enclosed and is maintained in such a manner as to exclude intruders.
- The property is posted in a conspicuous manner against entry. The minimum letter height on the posting signs shall be one inch. Each posting sign shall be not less than 50 square inches, and the signs shall be spaced to enable a person to observe not less than one sign at any point of entry upon the property.

### Elements

1. The defendant entered or remained,
2. On someone else's property that is not farm property or woods connected to farm property,
3. To engage in recreational or trapping activities,
4. Without the owner's consent, and
5. The property is either of the following:
   a. Fenced or enclosed and is maintained to keep out intruders.
   b. Posted in a conspicuous manner against entry.

## Recreational Trespass on Farm Property— MCL 324.73102(2) (90-day misdemeanor)

A person shall not enter or remain upon farm property or a wooded area connected to farm property for any recreational activity or trapping without the consent of the owner or his or her lessee or agent, whether or not the farm property or wooded area connected to farm property is fenced, enclosed, or posted.

## Exceptions to Recreational Trespass

- *Fisherman:* On fenced or posted property or farm property, a fisherman wading or floating a navigable public stream may, without written or oral consent, enter upon property within the clearly defined banks of the stream or, without damaging farm products, walk a route as closely proximate to the clearly defined bank as possible when necessary to avoid a natural or artificial hazard or obstruction, including, but not limited to, a dam, deep hole, or a fence or other exercise of ownership by the riparian owner.

- *Retrieval of Hunting Dogs:*   A person other than a person possessing a firearm may, unless previously prohibited in writing or orally by the property owner or his or her lessee or agent, enter on foot upon the property of another person for the sole purpose of retrieving a hunting dog. The person shall not remain on the property beyond the reasonable time necessary to retrieve the dog. In an action under section 73109 or 73110, the burden of showing that the property owner or his or her lessee or agent previously prohibited entry under this subsection is on the plaintiff or prosecuting attorney, respectively.

The defendant was fishing in the Grand River near a dam. The defendant hooked a fish that swam into a gap in the dam's structure. The defendant stood on a below-water section of the dam and attempted to land the fish. A DNR officer cited the defendant for recreational trespass. The defendant appealed his conviction. The court held that the fisherman exception to the recreational trespass only applies when the fisherman enters the property to avoid an obstruction or hazard in the water; a fisherman cannot simply enter the property of another to continue fishing. Additionally, Michigan's recreational trespass laws are preempted by federal law. Public navigable rivers are the property of the United States. The Federal Energy Regulatory Commission license to the Consumer's Energy Dam provided that the facility may reserve from public access such portions of the project waters, adjacent lands, and project facilities as may be necessary for the protection of life, health, and property. Recreational trespass was superseded by the FERC license on the dam. *People v. Gatski*, 260 Mich. App. 360 (2004).

## Consent

Consent to enter or remain upon the property of another person pursuant to this section may be given orally or in writing. The consent may establish conditions for entering or remaining upon that property. Unless prohibited in written consent, a written consent may be amended or revoked orally. If the owner or his or her lessee or agent requires all persons entering or remaining upon the property to have written consent, the presence of the person on the property without written consent is prima facie evidence of unlawful entry.

© 2014, Shutterstock, Inc.

# 15

# CONTROLLED SUBSTANCES

## SCHEDULES

Michigan and federal law both classify controlled substances, placing known chemical compounds on lists (called schedules) according to several factors. Substances are placed on Michigan's schedules as follows (some substances may appear in multiple schedules depending on weight or mixture):

### Schedule 1

Substances with high potential for abuse and no accepted medical use. MCL 333.7211.

Specific compounds, examples: Mescaline, Cat, Peyote, GHB, Ecstasy, Psilocybin, Marihuana, Lysergic acid diethylamide (LSD), K-2, Spice, BZP, Khat, Bath Salts, Synthetic Marihuana. MCL 333.7212, Mich. Admin. Code R. 338.3112-338.3114a.

### Schedule 2

Substances with high potential for abuse and accepted medical uses. Abuse may lead to severe psychic or physical dependence. MCL 333.7213.

Specific compounds, examples: Opium, Morphine, Fentanyl, Methadone, Cocaine, Oxycodone. MCL 333.7214, Mich. Admin. Code R. 338.3116-338.3118.

### Schedule 3

Substances with potential for abuse but less than schedules 1 and 2 and with currently accepted medical uses. Abuse may lead to moderate or low physical dependence or high psychological dependence. MCL 333.7215.

Specific compounds, examples: Codeine, Lysergic acid, Opium or Morphine mixtures, Ketamine, Anabolic steroids. MCL 333.7216, Mich. Admin. Code R. 338.3122.

### Schedule 4

Substances with low potential for abuse and currently accepted medical uses. Abuse may lead to limited physical dependence or psychological dependence compared to schedule 3. MCL 333.7217.

Specific compounds, examples: Phenobarbital, Diazepam. MCL 333.7218, Mich. Admin. Code R. 338.3123.

### Schedule 5

Substances with low potential for abuse and currently acceptable medical uses. The substance has limited physical dependence or psychological dependence liability compared to schedule 4. MCL 333.7219.

Specific compounds, examples: Opium or Codeine mixtures, Ephedrine. MCL 333.7220, Mich. Admin. Code R. 338.3125.

### Manufacture, Delivery, or Possession with the Intent to Deliver a Controlled Substance—MCL 333.7401 (felony)

*Except as otherwise authorized by law, it is a felony to "manufacture, create, deliver, or possess with*

Penalties:

| Drug Type | Amount | Punishment |
|---|---|---|
| Schedule 1 or 2 narcotic or cocaine | 1,000 grams or more | Life felony, $1,000,000 fine |
| | 450 grams or more, but less than 1,000 grams | 30-year felony, $500,000 fine |
| | 50 grams or more, but less than 450 grams | 20-year felony, $250,000 fine |
| | Less than 50 grams | 20-year felony, $25,000 fine |
| Ecstasy or methamphetamine | Any amount | 20-year felony, $25,000 fine |
| Any other schedule 1 or 2, or any schedule 3 (except marihuana) | Any amount | 7-year felony, $10,000 fine |
| Schedule 4 | Any amount | 4-year felony, $2,000 fine |
| Marihuana | 45 kilograms or more, or 200 plants or more | 15-year felony, $10,000,000 fine |
| | 5 kilograms or more, but less than 45 kilograms, or 20 plants or more, but less than 200 plants | 7-year felony, $500,000 fine |
| | Less than 5 kilograms or less than 20 plants | 4-year felony, $20,000 fine |
| Schedule 5 | Any amount | 2-year felony, $2,000 fine |
| Prescription form or counterfeit form | | 7-year felony, $5,000 fine |

*intent to manufacture, create, or deliver a controlled substance, a prescription form, or a counterfeit prescription form. A practitioner licensed by the administrator under this article shall not dispense, prescribe, or administer a controlled substance for other than legitimate and professionally recognized therapeutic or scientific purposes or outside the scope of practice of the practitioner, licensee, or applicant."*

## Manufacture

**Elements**

1. The defendant produced or processed a controlled substance. This may include extraction from natural substances, chemical synthesis, packaging or repackaging the substance, or labeling or relabeling the container.
2. The defendant knew he was manufacturing the controlled substance.
CJI2d 12.1.

The conversion of powdered cocaine into crack cocaine constitutes manufacturing. *People v. Hunter*, 201 Mich. App. 671 (1993).

## Delivery

**Elements**

1. The defendant delivered a controlled substance.
2. The defendant knew he was delivering the controlled substance.
CJI2d 12.2.

Delivery does not include the use of cocaine by a pregnant woman where the substance is passed to her unborn child. *People v. Hardy*, 188 Mich. App. 305 (1991).

Delivery includes the transferring of drugs during social sharing of drugs. *People v. Schultz*, 246 Mich. App. 695 (2001).

Two charges for delivery were proper when two separate deliveries were made and each was bargained for separately. *People v. Manning*, 163 Mich. App. 641 (1987).

Two charges for delivery were improper when both deliveries stemmed from a single transaction. *People v. Miller*, 182 Mich. App. 482 (1990).

Knowledge of the amount of drug delivered is not an element of the delivery charge. However, to be convicted of conspiracy to deliver a controlled substance, the prosecution must prove beyond a reasonable doubt that the defendant knew the quantity of the controlled substance to be delivered. The defendant did not have to know the exact amount to be delivered, just that the amount met the threshold for the amount charged in the conspiracy, i.e., if the defendant is charged with conspiracy to deliver at least 225 grams but less than 650 grams of cocaine, it need not be proved that the conspiracy was planning to deliver 450 grams of cocaine, just that the defendant knew it was at least 225 grams. However, the court also held "if a conspiracy to deliver and a delivery charge are coupled (and the proofs for the delivery demonstrate the weight of the substance delivered) such proofs may suffice to demonstrate defendant's knowledge of the amount for the conspiracy charge. This is because a prosecutor is free to argue, and the jury would be free to find, if it was persuaded, given all the circumstances, that defendant had knowingly conspired to deliver the same amount that was actually delivered." *People v. Mass*, 464 Mich. 615 (2001).

## Attempt to Deliver

### Elements

1. Intent to deliver a controlled substance or mixture of substance to someone else.
2. The defendant must have taken some action toward delivering the substance, but failed to complete the delivery. It is not enough to prove that the defendant made preparations for delivering the substance. Things like planning the crime or arranging how it will be committed are just preparations; they do not qualify as an attempt. In order to qualify as an attempt, the action must go beyond mere preparation, to the point where the crime would have been completed if it hadn't been interrupted by outside circumstances.

CJI2d 12.2.

## Possession with the Intent to Deliver

1. The defendant knowingly possessed a controlled substance or mixture of the substance.
2. The defendant intended to deliver the substance to someone else.

CJI2d 12.3.

Intent to deliver may be determined by circumstantial evidence. For example, even though only two usable doses of heroin were seized in a raid, the presence of pre-cut pieces of aluminum foil and two heroin cookers was sufficient to allow a jury to infer intent to deliver. *People v. Tolbert*, 77 Mich. App. 162 (1977).

## Includes Controlled Substance or Mixture

The amount determines the severity of the punishment.

For total weight of a drug mixture to be charged, the drug and the filler must be "mixed" together to form a "mixture" that is reasonably uniform. A sample from anywhere in the mixture should reasonably approximate in purity a sample taken elsewhere in the mixture. It should be reasonably difficult to separate the drug from the filler material because of the mixing or blending of the two substances. *People v. Barajas*, 198 Mich. App. 551 (1993).

The term mixture precludes the weight of the controlled substance and filler material from being aggregated to punish the defendant more severely unless both the controlled substance and filler are mixed together to form a homogeneous or reasonably uniform mass. In this case, a cocaine mixture was suspended in water. The water was easily evaporated by chemical analysts; thus, the defendant could only be charged with the weight of the remaining solid residue. *People v. Hunter*, 201 Mich. App. 671 (1993).

## Delivery of Marihuana without Remuneration— MCL 333.7410(7) (1-year misdemeanor)

*A person who distributes marihuana without remuneration and not to further commercial distribution and who does not violate subsection (1) is guilty of a misdemeanor punishable by imprisonment for not more than 1 year or a fine of not more than $1,000.00, or both, unless the distribution is in accordance with the federal law or the law of this state.*

## Operating or Maintaining a Laboratory— MCL 333.7401c (felony)

A person shall not do any of the following:

(a) Own, possess, or use a vehicle, building, structure, place, or area that he or she knows or has reason to know is to be used as a location to manufacture a controlled substance in violation of [MCL 333.7401] or a counterfeit substance or a controlled substance analog in violation of [MCL 333.7402].

(b) Own or possess any chemical or any laboratory equipment that he or she knows or has reason to know is to be used for the purpose of manufacturing a controlled substance in violation of [MCL 333.7401] or a counterfeit substance or a controlled substance analog in violation of [MCL 333.7402].

(c) Provide any chemical or laboratory equipment to another person knowing or having reason to know that the other person intends to use that chemical or laboratory equipment for the purpose of manufacturing a controlled substance in violation of [MCL 333.7401] or a counterfeit substance or a controlled substance analog in violation of [MCL 333.7402].

This statute does not apply to a violation involving cocaine or marihuana, or both.

## Definitions

*Hazardous waste:*   Waste or a combination of waste and other discarded material including solid, liquid, semisolid, or contained gaseous material that because of its quantity, quality, concentration, or physical, chemical, or infectious characteristics may cause or significantly contribute to an increase in mortality or an increase in serious irreversible illness or serious incapacitating but reversible illness, or may pose a substantial present or potential hazard to human health or the environment if improperly treated, stored, transported, disposed of, or otherwise managed. Hazardous waste does not include material that is solid or dissolved material in domestic sewage discharge, solid or dissolved material in an irrigation return flow discharge, industrial discharge that is a point source subject to permits under [federal law], or is a source, special nuclear, or by-product material as defined [under federal law].

*Laboratory equipment:*   Any equipment, device, or container used or intended to be used in the process of manufacturing a controlled substance, counterfeit substance, or controlled substance analog.

*Manufacture:*   The production, preparation, propagation, compounding, conversion, or processing of a controlled substance, directly or indirectly by extraction from substances of natural origin, or independently by means of chemical synthesis, or by a combination of extraction and chemical synthesis. Manufacture does not include any of the following:

- The packaging or repackaging of the substance or labeling or relabeling of its container.

- The preparation or compounding of a controlled substance by any of the following:
   - A practitioner as an incident to the practitioner's administering or dispensing of a controlled substance in the course of his or her professional practice.
   - A practitioner, or by the practitioner's authorized agent under his or her supervision, for the purpose of, or as an incident to, research, teaching, or chemical analysis and not for sale.

*Minor:*   An individual less than 18 years of age.

*Response activity costs:*   All costs incurred in taking or conducting a response activity, including enforcement costs.

*School property:*   A building, playing field, or property used for school purposes to impart instruction to children in grades kindergarten through 12, when provided by a public, private, denominational, or parochial school, except those buildings used primarily for adult education or college extension courses.

*Vehicle:*   Every device in, upon, or by which any person or property is or may be transported or drawn upon a highway, except devices exclusively moved by human power or used exclusively upon stationary rails or tracks.

Penalties:

| | |
|---|---|
| Violation involves the possession, placement, or use of a firearm or any other device designed or intended to be used to injure another person | 25-year felony |
| Violation is committed in the presence of a minor | 20-year felony |
| Violation involves the unlawful generation, treatment, storage, or disposal of a hazardous waste | 20-year felony |
| Violation occurs within 500 feet of a residence, business establishment, school property, or church or other house of worship | 20-year felony |
| Violation involves or is intended to involve the manufacture of a methamphetamine | 20-year felony |
| All other violations | 10-year felony |

## Possession—MCL 333.7403

*A person shall not knowingly or intentionally possess a controlled substance, a controlled substance analog, or a prescription form unless the controlled substance, controlled substance analog, or prescription form was obtained directly from, or pursuant to, a valid prescription or order of a practitioner while acting in the course of the practitioner's professional practice, or except as otherwise authorized by this article.*

### Elements

1. The defendant possessed a controlled substance.
2. The defendant knew that he was possessing the controlled substance.

CJI2d 12.5.

- Possession does not necessarily mean ownership. Possession means that either:
    - The person has actual physical control of the substance or thing.
    - The person has the right to control the substance or thing, even though it is in a different room or place.
- Possession may be sole, where one person alone possesses the substance or thing.
- Possession may be joint, where two or more people each share possession.
- It is not enough if the defendant merely knew about the substance or thing; the defendant possessed the state substance or thing only if he has control of it or the right to control it, either alone or together with someone else.

CJI2d 12.7.

Penalties:

| | |
|---|---|
| LSD, peyote, mescaline, dimethyltryptamine, psilocyn, psilocybin, or controlled substances in schedule 5 | 1-year misdemeanor |
| Marihuana | 1-year misdemeanor |
| Unlawful possession of an unofficial prescription form | 1-year misdemeanor |
| Unlawful possession of an official prescription form | Felony |
| Possession of schedule 1, 2, 3, or 4 | Felony |

### Knowingly Possess

The suspect knowingly possessed a controlled substance or a mixture of a controlled substance for personal use. A person may be in possession even if the substance is in a different room. Also, more than one person may be in possession. It is not enough that the person merely knows about the substance, but he or she did possess the substance if he or she had control of it or the right to control it either alone or together with someone else.

The defendant's probation officer went to defendant's home for an unscheduled residence visit. During a consensual search, a plate was found under defendant's bed, which held a white powdery substance, an assortment of pills and tablets, a straw, defendant's driver's license, and a "baggie" containing a white powdery substance. The officers also found an empty baggie coated with a white powdery residue. The defendant stated that he used the substances to "get high." Subsequent forensic testing negated the presence of any controlled substances in the pills, tablets, and powder on the plate and in the full baggie. However, the white powdery residue found on the otherwise empty baggie was analyzed and found to contain less than one milligram of ketamine. The defendant argued that in order for the ketamine residue to fall within the definition of a controlled substance, the prosecution was required to establish that the residue was not so diluted by other substances as to vitiate its potential for abuse. However, the court held that once the prosecution presented a prima facie case that defendant knowingly or intentionally possessed ketamine, defendant had the burden to affirmatively defend his innocence by presenting competent evidence that the ketamine discovered within the subject residue was "in a proportion or concentration to vitiate the potential for abuse. In short, defendant presented no evidence that the white powder that tested as ketamine fell outside the definition of a controlled substance. *People v. Hartuniewicz*, 294 Mich. App. 237 (2011).

The defendant was a passenger in a vehicle. Undercover officers observed that the vehicle had a headlight out and attempted to stop it. While the vehicle fled, the officers observed the passenger door open and a package was thrown from the vehicle. The vehicle was stopped one block later. The package was recovered and contained five kilograms of heroin. Because the prosecution was able to show that the defendant was the passenger in the vehicle, the package was thrown from the passenger-side door, the vehicle was continuously under police observation from the time the package was thrown until it was stopped, and police testified that no other persons were on the street at the time the package was thrown, there was sufficient evidence to allow the jury to conclude that the defendant threw the package from the vehicle; thus, the defendant's possession conviction was proper. *People v. Eaves*, 4 Mich. App. 457 (1966).

The defendant was asked by his passenger if the passenger could place a suitcase full of marihuana in the trunk of the defendant's car. The defendant consented. This consent was sufficient to support possession charges against the defendant. *People v. Harper*, 365 Mich. 494 (1962).

Possession may be either actual or constructive. A person's presence where drugs are found is insufficient, by itself, to prove constructive possession. Some additional connection between the defendant and the contraband must be shown. *People v. Hardiman*, 466 Mich. 417 (2002).

## Fraudulently Obtaining a Controlled Substance or Prescription—MCL 333.7403a (felony)

*A person shall not fraudulently obtain or attempt to obtain a controlled substance or a prescription for a controlled substance from a health care provider.*

## Use—MCL 333.7404(1)

*A person shall not use a controlled substance or controlled substance analog unless the substance was obtained directly from, or pursuant to, a valid prescription or order of a practitioner while acting in the course of the practitioner's professional practice, or except as otherwise authorized by this article.*

### Elements

1. The defendant used a controlled substance.
2. At the time he used it, the defendant knew the substance was the controlled substance. CJI2d 12.6.

Penalties:

| Marihuana | 90-day misdemeanor |
|---|---|
| LSD, peyote, mescaline, dimethyltryptamine, psilocin, psilocybin, or controlled substances in schedule 5 | 6-month misdemeanor |
| Schedule 1, 2, 3, or 4 | 1-year misdemeanor |

## Date Rape Drugs—MCL 333.7401a (felony)

*A person is guilty of violating this statute if they, without an individual's consent, deliver a controlled substance or a substance described in MCL 333.7401b or cause a controlled substance or a substance described in MCL 333.7401b to be delivered to that individual to commit or attempt to commit criminal sexual conduct or assault with intent to commit criminal sexual conduct.*

This section applies regardless of whether the person is convicted of a CSC violation or attempted violation.

## Gamma Hydroxybutyrate (GHB)—MCL 333.7212(g)

This date rape drug falls under schedule 1.

## Gamma Butyrolactone (GBL)—MCL 333.7401b

GBL is a precursor to and can be readily converted to gamma hydroxybutyrate (GHB), also known as the "date rape drug" when taken orally. The manufacture, delivery, or possession of GBL for human consumption is prohibited. GBL can be possessed for use in a commercial application such as industrial solvent and floor stripper.

Penalties:

| Possession of GBL | 2-year felony |
|---|---|
| Penalty for manufacture, delivery, or intent to manufacture or deliver | 7-year felony |
| GBL used to commit CSC | 20-year felony |

## Use or Possession in Hotels—MCL 750.411g(2) (90-day misdemeanor)

*An individual or group that does 1 or more of the following on the premises or property of a hotel or bed and breakfast, or an individual or group* *that rents or leases a hotel room or bed and break-fast room with reason to know that another individual or group will do 1 or more of the following on the premises or property of a hotel or bed and breakfast, is guilty of a misdemeanor, punishable by imprisonment for not more than 90 days, community service, or by a fine of not more than $500.00, or a combination of any of these punishments:*

(a) *Uses or possesses a controlled substance in violation of MCL 333.7403 and 333.7404, or a local ordinance substantially similar to those sections.*

## Drug Paraphernalia—MCL 333.7453 (90-day misdemeanor)

A person shall not sell or offer for sale drug paraphernalia knowing that it is drug paraphernalia. Before a person can be arrested, the attorney general or prosecuting attorney shall notify the person in writing not less than two days before arrest for the violation.

Additional Penalty:

| | |
|---|---|
| Suspect is older than 18 and sells to a person less than 18 years old | 1-year misdemeanor |

Because anything designed for the smoking of marihuana, such as a dugout pipe or a bong, may also be used to smoke tobacco, such items are not prohibited paraphernalia. *Gauthier v. Alpena County Prosecutor*, 267 Mich. App. 167 (2005).

## Prescription Misuse—MCL 333.17766 (90-day misdemeanor)

This statute is violated when a person does any of the following:

(a) *Obtains or attempts to obtain a prescription drug by giving a false name to a pharmacist or other authorized seller, prescriber, or dispenser.*

(b) *Obtains or attempts to obtain a prescription drug by falsely representing that he or she is a lawful prescriber, dispenser, or licensee, or acting on behalf of a lawful prescriber, dispenser, or licensee.*

(c) *Falsely makes, utters, publishes, passes, alters, or forges a prescription.*

(d) *Knowingly possesses a false, forged, or altered prescription.*

(e) *Knowingly attempts to obtain, obtains, or possesses a drug by means of a prescription for other than a legitimate therapeutic purpose, or as a result of a false, forged, or altered prescription.*

(f) *Possesses or controls for the purpose of resale, or sells, offers to sell, dispenses, or gives away, a drug, pharmaceutical preparation, or chemical that has been dispensed on prescription and has left the control of a pharmacist, or that has been damaged by heat, smoke, fire, water, or other cause and is unfit for human or animal use.*

(g) *Prepares or permits the preparation of a prescription drug, except as delegated by a pharmacist.*

(h) *Sells a drug in bulk or in an open package at auction, unless the sale has been approved in accordance with rules of the board.*

## Imitation Controlled Substance—MCL 333.7341

*A person shall not manufacture, distribute, or possess with intent to distribute an imitation controlled substance.*

This section does not apply to any person who is authorized by the administrator or the federal food and drug administration to manufacture, distribute, prescribe, or possess an imitation controlled substance for use as a placebo for legitimate medical, therapeutic, or research purposes.

***Imitation controlled substance:*** A substance that is not a controlled substance or is not a drug for which a prescription is required under federal or state law, which by dosage unit appearance including color, shape, size, or markings, and/or by representations made, would lead a reasonable person to believe that the substance is a controlled substance. However, this subsection does not apply to a drug that is not a controlled substance if it was marketed before the controlled substance that it physically resembles. An imitation controlled substance does not include a placebo or registered investigational drug that was manufactured, distributed, possessed, or delivered in the ordinary course of professional practice or research. All of the following factors shall be considered in determining whether a substance is an imitation controlled substance:

- Whether the substance was approved by the Federal Food and Drug Administration (FDA) for over-the-counter sales and was sold in the FDA approved packaging along with the FDA approved labeling information.

- Any statements made by an owner or another person in control of the substance concerning the nature, use, or effect of the substance.
- Whether the substance is packaged in a manner normally used for illicit controlled substances.
- Whether the owner or another person in control of the substance has any prior convictions under state or federal law related to controlled substances or fraud.
- The proximity of the substance to controlled substances.
- Whether the consideration tendered in exchange for the substance substantially exceeds the reasonable value of the substance considering the actual chemical composition of the substance and, if applicable, the price at which the over-the-counter substances of like chemical composition sell.

Penalties:

| Use or possession with the intent to use, first offense | $100.00 fine |
| Use or possession with the intent to use, second offense | 90-day misdemeanor |
| Advertise or solicit distribution of imitation controlled substance | 1-year misdemeanor |
| Manufacture, distribute, and possess with intent to distribute | 2-year felony |

## Selling Falsely Represented Products— MCL 333.7417 (felony)

*A person who knows that a named product contains or previously contained an ingredient that was designated to be a schedule 1 controlled substance shall not sell or offer to sell any other product while representing that it contains an ingredient that produces the same or a substantially similar physiological or psychological effect as that scheduled ingredient.*

**Named product:** Means either of the following:

- A product having a designated brand name.
- A product having a street or common name with application sufficient to identify the product as a specific product within this state or within a local unit of government.

This subsection does not apply to a product approved by the Federal Food and Drug and Administration.

A person who violates this section is guilty of a four-year felony.

## Controlled Substance Analog— MCL 333.7402 (felony)

An analog has a similar chemical structure to that of a schedule 1 or 2 controlled substance and has a narcotic, stimulant, depressant, or hallucinogenic effect on the nervous system. MCL 333.7104(3).

A person shall not manufacture, deliver, or possess with intent to deliver a controlled substance analog intended for human consumption.

## Counterfeit Substance—MCL 333.7402 (felony)

A counterfeit substance is a controlled substance that bears the trademark, trade name, or other identifying marks of a manufacturer other than the person who in fact manufactured the substance. MCL 333.7104(5).

A person shall not manufacture, deliver, or possess with intent to deliver a counterfeit substance intended for human consumption.

## Possession of Ephedrine—MCL 333.17766c

It is a 93-day misdemeanor to purchase more than 3.6 grams of ephedrine or pseudoephedrine within a single calendar day or purchase more than 9 grams of ephedrine or pseudoephedrine within a 30-day period.

It is a two-year felony to possess more than 12 grams of ephedrine or pseudoephedrine alone or in a mixture.

*This section does not apply to any of the following:*

(a) *A person who possesses ephedrine or pseudoephedrine pursuant to a license issued by this state or the United States to manufacture, deliver, dispense, possess with intent to manufacture or deliver, or possess a controlled substance, prescription drug, or other drug.*

(b) *An individual who possesses ephedrine or pseudoephedrine pursuant to a prescription.*

(c) *A person who possesses ephedrine or pseudoephedrine for retail sale pursuant to a license issued under the general sales tax act, 1933 PA 167, MCL 205.51 to 205.78.*

(d) *A person who possesses ephedrine or pseudoephedrine in the course of his or her business of selling or transporting ephedrine or pseudoephedrine to a person described in subdivision (a) or (c).*

(e) *A person who, in the course of his or her business, stores ephedrine or pseudoephedrine for sale or distribution to a person described in subdivision (a), (c), or (d).*

(f) *Any product that the state board of pharmacy, upon application of a manufacturer, exempts from this section because the product has been formulated in such a way as to effectively prevent the conversion of the active ingredient into methamphetamine.*

(g) *Possession of any pediatric product primarily intended for administration to children under 12 years of age according to label instructions.*

## Sale, Distribution, or Delivery of Ephedrine—MCL 333.7340 (felony)

*It is unlawful to sell, distribute, deliver, or furnish ephedrine or pseudoephedrine through the use of the mail, Internet, telephone, or other electronic means. This does not apply to pediatric products designed for children under 12, a liquid product in which ephedrine is not the only active ingredient, a product that cannot be converted into methamphetamine, products dispensed pursuant to a prescription, and products distributed by licensed manufacturers.*

## Unlawful Containers for Anhydrous Ammonia—MCL 750.502d (felony)

*It is unlawful to transport or possess anhydrous ammonia in a container other than a container approved by law, or to unlawfully tamper with a container approved by law.*

***Container approved by law:*** Means a container that was manufactured to satisfy the requirements for the storage and handling of anhydrous ammonia pursuant to R408.17801 of the Michigan administrative code or its successor rule.

## Use of Inhalants—MCL 752.272 (90-day misdemeanor)

This statute makes it unlawful to do the following:

- For the purpose of causing a condition of intoxication, euphoria, excitement, exhilaration, stupefaction, or dulling senses,
- Intentionally smell, or inhale the fumes of a chemical agent, or
- Drink, eat, or otherwise introduce any chemical agent into one's respiratory or circulatory system.

This section does not prohibit inhaling anesthesia for medical or dental purposes.

## Sale of Nitrous Oxide—MCL 752.272a

A person shall not sell or otherwise distribute to another person any device that contains any quantity of nitrous oxide (also known as laughing gas) for the purpose of causing a condition of intoxication, euphoria, excitement, exhilaration, stupefaction, or dulling of the senses or nervous system. Law targets novelty "head" shops, making it more difficult for persons to obtain the gas for recreational use.

Exemptions:  Persons who sell or distribute catering supplies, persons who sell compressed gases for industrial or medical use, pharmacists or health care professionals, and persons licensed under the Food Processing Act of 1977.

Penalties:

| First Violation | 93-day misdemeanor |
|---|---|
| Second Violation | 1-year misdemeanor |
| Two or more prior convictions | 4-year felony |

## Licensing Requirement—MCL 333.7303

A person who manufactures, distributes, prescribes, or dispenses a controlled substance in this state or who proposes to engage in the manufacture, distribution, prescribing, or dispensing of a controlled substance in this state shall obtain a license issued by the administrator in accordance with the rules. The following persons need not be licensed and may lawfully possess controlled substances or prescription forms under this article:

- An agent or employee of a licensed manufacturer, distributor, prescriber, or dispenser of a controlled substance, if acting in the usual course of the agent's or employee's business or employment.
- A common or contract carrier or warehouseman or an employee thereof, whose possession of a controlled substance or prescription form is in the usual course of business or employment.
- An ultimate user or agent in possession of a controlled substance or prescription form pursuant to a lawful order of a practitioner or in lawful possession of a schedule 5 substance.
- The administrator may waive or include by rule the requirement for licensure of certain manufacturers, distributors, prescribers, or dispensers, if it finds the waiver or inclusion is consistent with public health and safety.
- A separate license is required at each principal place of business or professional practice where the applicant manufactures, distributes, prescribes, or dispenses controlled substances.

The requirement of licensure is waived for the following persons in the circumstances described:

- An officer or employee of the Drug Enforcement Administration while engaged in the course of official duties.
- An officer of the United States Customs Service while engaged in the course of official duties.
- An officer or employee of the United States Food and Drug Administration while engaged in the course of official duties.
- A federal officer who is lawfully engaged in the enforcement of a federal law relating to controlled substances, drugs, or customs and who is authorized to possess controlled substances in the course of that person's official duties.
- An officer or employee of this state, or a political subdivision or agency of this state who is engaged in the enforcement of a state or local law relating to controlled substances and who is authorized to possess controlled substances in the course of that person's official duties.
- An official exempted from licensure by this section, when acting in the course of that person's official duties, may possess a controlled substance and may transfer a controlled substance to any other official who is exempt and who is acting in the course of that person's official duties.
- An official exempted by this section may procure a controlled substance in the course of an administrative inspection or investigation or in the course of a criminal investigation involving the person from whom the substance was procured.
- A law enforcement officer exempted by this section may distribute a controlled substance to another person in the course of that officer's official duties as a means to detect criminal activity or to conduct a criminal investigation.

## Drug-Free School Zones—MCL 333.7410

This statute provides enhanced sentences for the following:

- Delivery of a controlled substance by a person 18 or older to a person under 18 and at least three years younger than the person delivering the substance.
- Delivery, by a person 18 or older, of a schedule 1 or 2 narcotic drug or cocaine to any person on or within 1,000 feet of school property or a library.
- Possessing with intent to deliver, by a person 18 or older, a schedule 1 or 2 narcotic drug or cocaine to any person on or within 1,000 feet of school property or a library.
- Possession of any controlled substance on school property or a library.

*Library:* A library that is established by the state; a county, city, township, village, school district, or other local unit of government or authority or combination of local units of government and authorities; a community college district; a college or university; or any private library open to the public.

*School property:* A building, playing field, or property used for school purposes to impart instruction to children in grades kindergarten through 12, when provided by a public, private, denominational, or parochial school, except those buildings used primarily for adult education or college extension courses.

## Maintaining a Drug House—MCL 333.7405(d) (2-year misdemeanor)

*A person shall not knowingly keep or maintain a store, shop, warehouse, dwelling, building, vehicle, boat, aircraft, or other structure or place, that is frequented by persons using controlled substances in violation of this article for the purpose of using controlled substances, or that is used for keeping or selling controlled substances in violation of this article.*

### Elements

1. The defendant knowingly kept or maintained a building, dwelling, vehicle, vessel, or other place.
2. This building, dwelling, vehicle, vessel, or other place was any of the following:
   a. Frequented by persons for the purpose of illegally using controlled substances.
   b. Used for illegally keeping controlled substances.
   c. Used for illegally selling controlled substances.
3. The defendant knew that the building, dwelling, vehicle, vessel, or other place was frequented or used for such illegal purposes.

CJI2d 12.8.

If the evidence only shows that a defendant used a vehicle to keep or deliver drugs on one occasion, and there is no other evidence of continuity, the evidence is insufficient to establish that a defendant kept or maintained a drug vehicle in violation of MCL 333.7405(1)(d). However, "while the statute precludes a conviction for an isolated incident without other evidence of continuity, the statute does not require the prosecution to show that a defendant's actions occurred 'continuously for an appreciable period.'" *People v. Thompson*, 477 Mich. 146 (2007).

# THE MICHIGAN MEDICAL MARIHUANA ACT—MCL 333.26421–333.26430; MICH. ADMIN. CODE R. 333.101–333.133

The Michigan Medical Marihuana Act (MMMA) is an exception to the statutes governing the manufacture, delivery, possession and use of marihuana and it does not create a general right for individuals to engage in any of these activities. Manufacture, delivery, possession, and use of marihuana are still prohibited by the Public Health Code; however, under the MMMA, certain individuals are protected from arrest, prosecution, and penalty if they meet certain requirements set forth in the MMMA. The Michigan Department of Licensing and Regulatory Affairs is responsible for administering the MMMA.

## Definitions—MCL 333.26423

*Debilitating medical condition:* One or more of the following:

- Cancer, glaucoma, positive status for human immunodeficiency virus, acquired immune deficiency syndrome, hepatitis C, amyotrophic lateral sclerosis, Crohn's disease, agitation of Alzheimer's disease, nail patella, or the treatment of these conditions.
- A chronic or debilitating disease or medical condition or its treatment that produces one or more of the following: cachexia or wasting syndrome; severe and chronic pain; severe nausea; seizures, including but not limited to those characteristic of epilepsy; or severe and persistent muscle spasms, including but not limited to those characteristic of multiple sclerosis.
- Any other medical condition or its treatment approved by the Department of Licensing and Regulatory Affairs, as provided for in section 333.26426(k).

*Enclosed, locked facility:* A closet, room, or other comparable, stationary, and fully enclosed area equipped with secured locks or other functioning security devices that permit access only by a registered primary caregiver or registered qualifying patient.

Marihuana plants grown outdoors are considered to be in an enclosed, locked facility if all of the following:

- They are not visible to the unaided eye from an adjacent property when viewed by an individual at ground level or from a permanent structure.
- They are grown within a stationary structure that is enclosed on all sides, except for the base, by chain-link fencing, wooden slats, or a similar material that prevents access by the general public and that is anchored, attached, or affixed to the ground.
- They are located on land that is owned, leased, or rented by either the registered qualifying patient or a person designated through the Medical Marihuana Program registration process as the primary caregiver for the registered qualifying patient or patients for whom the marihuana plants are grown.
- There are equipped with functioning locks or other security devices that restrict access to only the registered qualifying patient or the registered primary caregiver who owns, leases, or rents the property on which the structure is located.

Enclosed, locked facility includes a motor vehicle if both of the following conditions are met:

- The vehicle is being used temporarily to transport living marihuana plants from one location to another with the intent to permanently retain those plants at the second location.
- An individual is not inside the vehicle unless he or she is either the registered qualifying patient to whom the living marihuana plants belong or the individual designated through the departmental registration process as the primary caregiver for the registered qualifying patient.

Possession of marihuana occurs when a person exercises dominion and control over the drug with knowledge of its presence and character. To determine whether or not a defendant "possessed" the marihuana in the supposed enclosed, locked facility, the court considers whether a "sufficient nexus" exists between the defendant and the marihuana, including whether he exercised "dominion and control" over it. Other factors considered include:

- Could he remove the marihuana plants if he wanted to?
- Was he involved with all or some of the plants?
- How often was he around the plants?
- Was the gate locked or just latched?
- Was there free access to the plants?

*People v. Bylsma*, 493 Mich. 17 (2012).

*Marihuana:* All parts of the plant Cannabis sativa L., growing or not; the seeds thereof; the resin extracted from any part of the plant; and every compound, manufacture, salt, derivative, mixture, or preparation of the plant or its seeds or resin. It does not include the mature stalks of the plant, fiber produced from the stalks, oil or cake made from the seeds of the plant, any other compound, manufacture, salt, derivative, mixture, or preparation of the mature stalks, except the resin extracted therefrom, fiber, oil or cake, or the sterilized seed of the plant which is incapable of germination.

*Medical use:*   The acquisition, possession, cultivation, manufacture, use, internal possession, delivery, transfer, or transportation of marihuana or paraphernalia relating to the administration of marihuana to treat or alleviate a registered qualifying patient's debilitating medical condition or symptoms associated with the debilitating medical condition.

> Possession may be actual or constructive (a person need not have actual physical possession of a controlled substance to be guilty of possessing it) and may be joint (with more than one person actually or constructively possessing the controlled substance) or exclusive. *State v. McQueen*, 493 Mich. 135 (2013).
>
> "Transfer" includes sales of marihuana. Because a transfer is "any mode of disposing of or parting with an asset or an interest in an asset, including the payment of money, the word 'transfer,' as part of the statutory definition of 'medical use,' also includes sales." *State v. McQueen*, 493 Mich. 135 (2013).

*Primary caregiver:*   A person who is at least 21 years old and who has agreed to assist with a patient's medical use of marihuana and who has not been convicted of any felony within the past 10 years and has never been convicted of a felony involving illegal drugs or a felony that is an assaultive crime as defined in MCL 770.9a.

*Qualifying patient or patient:*   A person who has been diagnosed by a physician as having a debilitating medical condition.

*Registry identification card:*   A document issued by the Department of Licensing and Regulatory Affairs that identifies a person as a registered qualifying patient or registered primary caregiver.

> Michigan residency is a prerequisite to the valid possession of a registry identification card. *People v. Jones*, 301 Mich. App. 566 (2013).

*Usable marihuana:*   The dried leaves and flowers of the marihuana plant, and any mixture or preparation thereof, but does not include the seeds, stalks, and roots of the plant.

> Marihuana resin is not usable marihuana under the MMMA. The only "mixture" or "preparation" that falls within the definition of "usable marihuana" is a mixture or preparation of "the dried leaves and flowers of the marihuana plants." Edibles, therefore, are permitted under the MMMA so long as they are consistent with this requirement. Brownies prepared or mixed with the dried leaves or flowers of the marihuana plants are permitted, whereas those prepared with marihuana resin or its extraction, THC, are not permitted under the MMMA. *People v. Carruthers*, 301 Mich. App. 590 (2013).

*Visiting qualifying patient:*   A patient who is not a resident of this state or who has been a resident of this state for less than 30 days.

*Written certification:*   A document signed by a physician, stating all of the following:

- The patient's debilitating medical condition.
- The physician has completed a full assessment of the patient's medical history and current medical condition, including a relevant, in-person, medical evaluation.
- In the physician's professional opinion, the patient is likely to receive therapeutic or palliative benefit from the medical use of marihuana to treat or alleviate the patient's debilitating medical condition or symptoms associated with the debilitating medical condition.

## Protections for Medical Use of Marihuana

### Legal Amounts—MCL 333.26424

#### Qualifying Patients

The qualifying patient must present *both* his registry identification card and a valid government issued identification card that bears a photographic image of the qualifying patient to utilize the privilege from arrest. A qualifying patient may:

- Legally possess not more than 2.5 ounces of usable marihuana.
- Legally cultivate not more than 12 marihuana plants kept in an enclosed, locked facility, provided the qualifying patient has not specified that a primary caregiver will be allowed to cultivate the plants for him or her.
- Incidental amounts of seeds, stalks, and unusable roots.

### Primary Caregivers

The primary caregiver must present *both* his registry identification card and a valid government issued identification card that bears a photographic image of the caregiver to utilize the privilege from arrest. A primary caregiver who has been issued and possesses a registry identification card may legally assist a qualifying patient to whom he or she is connected through the Medical Marihuana Program registry with the medical use of marihuana. A qualifying patient can only have one primary caregiver. A primary caregiver may assist not more than five qualifying patients. A primary caregiver may:

- Legally possess not more than 2.5 ounces of usable marihuana for each patient connected to him or her through the Medical Marihuana Program registry.
- Legally cultivate not more than 12 marihuana plants kept in an enclosed, locked facility, provided the qualifying patient has specified that the primary caregiver will be allowed to cultivate the plants for him or her.
- Incidental amounts of seeds, stalks, and usable roots.

## Possession of More than the Authorized Amount of Plants

The defendant is a registered primary caregiver under the MMMA and was charged with manufacturing marihuana. He moved to dismiss the charge, asserting that as the registered primary caregiver of two registered qualifying patients, he was allowed to possess 24 marihuana plants and that the remainder of the 88 plants seized by the police from his leased unit in a building belonged to other registered primary caregivers and registered qualifying patients whom defendant had offered to assist in growing and cultivating the plants.

The MMMA incorporates the definition of possession of controlled substances used in long-standing Michigan law. The essential inquiry is whether there is a sufficient nexus between the defendant and the contraband, including whether the defendant exercised dominion and control over it. In this case, defendant exercised dominion and control over all the marihuana plants seized from the warehouse space that he leased, given that he was actively engaged in growing all the marihuana in the facility; used his horticultural knowledge and expertise to oversee, care for, and cultivate all the marihuana growing there; and had the ability to remove any or all of the plants given his unimpeded access to the warehouse space. The court held that under the MMMA, only one of

two people may possess a patient's 12 marihuana plants for purposes of immunity under § 4(a) and 4(b): either the registered qualifying patient if the patient has not specified that a primary caregiver be allowed to cultivate the patient's plants or the patient's registered primary caregiver if the patient has specified that a primary caregiver be allowed to cultivate the patient's plants. Because defendant clearly possessed more plants than allowed under § 4 and possessed plants on behalf of patients with whom he was not connected through the state's registration process, defendant was not entitled to § 4 immunity." *People v. Bylsma,* 493 Mich. 17 (2012).

## Immunity—MCL 333.26424

A person shall not be subject to arrest, prosecution, or penalty for:

- Providing a registered qualifying patient or a registered primary caregiver with marihuana paraphernalia for purposes of a qualifying patient's medical use of marihuana. MCL 333.2424(g).
- Solely being in the presence or vicinity of the medical use of marihuana in accordance with the MMMA or for assisting a registered qualifying patient with using or administering marihuana. MCL 333.2424(i).

A registered primary caregiver may receive compensation for costs associated with assisting a registered qualifying patient in the medical use of marihuana. Such compensation does not constitute sale of controlled substances. MCL 333.2424(e).

There is a presumption that a qualifying patient or primary caregiver is engaged in the medical use of marihuana (and thus, not subject to arrest) if the qualifying patient or primary caregiver:

- Is in possession of a registry identification card; and
- Is in possession of an amount of marihuana that does not exceed the amount allowed under the MMMA. See above section on allowed amounts for qualifying patients and primary caregivers.

This presumption may be rebutted by evidence that the conduct related to marihuana, i.e., the sale, use, transfer, etc., was not for the purpose of alleviating the qualifying patient's debilitating medical condition or symptoms associated with the debilitating medical condition.

## Local Ordinance Cannot Conflict with the MMMA

Section 4(a) of the MMMA is not preempted by the Federal Controlled Substances Act. The broad power of cities to enact ordinances is subject to the laws of Michigan. A city cannot enact an ordinance in direct conflict with a Michigan statutory scheme; i.e., a city cannot enact an ordinance conflicting with the MMMA. *Ter Beek v. City of Wyoming*, 495 Mich. 1 (2014).

## No Immunity for Patient-to-Patient Transfers

A dispensary that permits a registered qualifying patient who transfers marihuana to another registered qualifying patient for the transferee's use is illegal and the patients are not entitled to a dispensary that permits a registered qualifying patient who transfers marihuana to another registered qualifying patient for the transferee's use is illegal and the patients are not entitled to immunity. Per the MMMA terms, "using" and "administering" are limited to conduct involving the actual ingestion of marihuana. Section 4 permits, for example, the spouse of a registered qualifying patient to assist the patient in ingesting marihuana, regardless of the spouse's status. However, section 4 does not permit a MMMA patient to transfer marihuana to another qualifying patient. Transfer includes both sales and gifts. Section 4 immunity does not extend to a registered primary caregiver who transfers marihuana for any purpose other than to alleviate the condition or symptoms of a specific patient with whom the caregiver is connected through the Medical Marihuana Program registration process. Therefore, the prosecuting attorney was entitled to injunctive relief to enjoin the operation of the defendants' business because it constituted a public nuisance. *State v. McQueen*, 493 Mich. 135 (2013).

## No Immunity When Card Obtained After the Offense

Undercover officers observed marihuana plants growing at the defendant's residence. Prior to officers observing the marihuana, the defendant had not obtained certification from a physician stating the defendant was likely to receive benefit from the medical use of marihuana. After the marihuana was observed, but before the defendant was arrested, the defendant obtained written certification, and he also obtained a registry identification card. Ten days after receiving the registry identification card, the defendant was arrested and charged with the manufacture of marihuana. The defendant has no immunity under MCL 333.26424 because defendant did not possess a registry identification card at the time of the purported offense. *People v. Reed*, 294 Mich. App. 78 (2011).

## Mere Possession of a Card Does Not Guarantee Immunity

The defendant argued that mere possession of the registry identification card entitled him to immunity from prosecution under section 4 of the MMMA. The court rejected the defendant's argument. The court noted that the defendant possessed 77 plants—five more than permitted to him by Section 4(b)(2). "Mere possession of a state-issued card—even one backed by a state investigation—does not guarantee that the cardholder's subsequent use and production of marihuana was 'for the purpose of alleviating the qualifying patient's debilitating medical condition or symptoms associated with the debilitating medical condition.' Indeed, defendant's testimony provided ample evidence that he was not holding true to the medical purposes of the statute. He failed to introduce evidence of: (1) some of his patients' medical conditions; (2) the amount of marihuana they reasonably required for treatment and how long the treatment should continue; and (3) the identity of their physicians. . . . Possession of a registry identification card indicates that the holder has gone through the requisite steps in § 6 required to obtain a card. It does not indicate that any marihuana possessed or manufactured by an individual is *actually* being used to treat or alleviate a debilitating medical condition or its symptoms. In other words, prior state issuance of a registry identification card does not guarantee that the holder's subsequent behavior will comply with the MMMA. The defendant's theory is akin to stating that possession of a Michigan driver's license establishes that the holder of the license always obeys state traffic laws." *People v. Hartwick*, 303 Mich. App. 247 (2013).

## Card Must be Reasonably Accessible to be Immune From Arrest

The defendant was arrested for possession of marihuana. At the time of his arrest, he was a passenger in a parked vehicle and had approximately one ounce of marihuana in his possession. He verbally informed the police officer that he was a medical marihuana patient. The defendant indicated that he had been approved for medical marihuana, but that he had not yet received his registry identification card. The defendant claimed to have paperwork showing his approval for use of marihuana for medical purposes, but the paperwork was in his own car. The police officer arrested the defendant and he was subsequently charged with possession of marihuana in violation of MCL 333.7403(2)(d).

On appeal, the defendant argued that a qualifying patient may not be arrested or prosecuted for the medical use of marihuana so long as that patient has a registry identification card somewhere, and that a patient is not required to produce the card immediately or carry the card on his or her person in order to qualify for the immunity set forth in § 4(a). The court held that because the defendant possessed marihuana without having his registry card in an area reasonably accessible to him, he was not entitled to immunity at the time of arrest; thus, the arrest for possession of marihuana was proper. However, the defendant's presentation of a registry card to the district court that was valid at the time of his arrest may entitle him to immunity from prosecution if he can also prove that he was engaged in the medical use of marihuana in accordance with the MMMA at the time of his arrest. *People v. Nicholson*, 297 Mich. App. 191 (2012).

## Affirmative Defense—MCL 333.26428

The MMMA contains an affirmative defense that may be asserted by a patient and a patient's primary caregiver, if any, in any prosecution involving marihuana. The defense is not limited to registered patients and registered primary caregivers so it may be asserted by anyone. Affirmative defenses have no impact on a decision to arrest. The affirmative defense will be presumed valid and charges will be dismissed if the evidence proves all of the following:

- A physician has stated that the patient is likely to receive a therapeutic or palliative benefit from the medical use of marihuana.

- The patient or caregiver did not possess more than reasonably necessary to ensure uninterrupted availability for the purpose of treating or alleviating the patient's condition or symptoms.
- The patient or caregiver had the marihuana or paraphernalia to treat the patient's medical condition or symptoms.

To assert an affirmative defense under § 8, a person must obtain a physician's statement before violating the Public Health Code. *People v. Reed*, 294 Mich. App. 78 (2011).

For a caregiver to use the affirmative defense under § 8, he must present evidence that his patients have bona fide physician–patient relationships with their certifying physicians. The defendant was unable to do so; additionally, he was unable to even provide the names of his patients' certifying physicians. The MMMA does not explicitly impose a duty on patients to provide such basic medical information to their primary caregivers; however, § 8 requires such information for a patient or caregiver to effectively assert the affirmative defense in a court of law. *People v. Hartwick*, 303 Mich. App. 247 (2013).

The defendant sold marihuana to a confidential informant he originally met on a website that connects medical marihuana patients with marihuana growers. Before the sales, defendant met with the confidential informant and asked him for various documents to demonstrate that he was a "qualifying patient" under the MMMA. The defendant did not ask the confidential informant (nor did the confidential informant provide) information on how much marihuana he required to treat his debilitating medical condition, or how long this treatment should continue. The defendant was a caregiver for two certified patients under the MMMA. Under Section 4(d), qualifying patients or primary caregivers are presumed to be "engaged in the medical use of marihuana in accordance with the MMMA if they are in possession of: (1) "a registry identification card" and (2) "an amount of marihuana that does not exceed the amount allowed under this act." MCL 333.26424(d). This presumption is rebuttable—if the prosecution provides "evidence that conduct related to marihuana was not for the purpose of alleviating the qualifying patient's debilitating medical condition or symptoms associated with the debilitating medical condition, in accordance with this act" it will not apply. MCL 333.26424(d)(2). In this case, defendant admitted he sold marihuana to an individual outside the parameters of the MMMA. As such, he does not have the privilege to claim immunity under section 4. This action rebuts the presumption as to *all* his conduct involving marihuana—even conduct involving his two other qualifying patients. Additionally, Section 8(a) separately provides a defense to MMMA defendants. The court made clear that a registry card is necessary but not sufficient to comply with the MMMA and clearly does not satisfy the section 8 requirements for a total defense to a charge of violation of this act. To be successful under section 8, defendant must present evidence to satisfy three elements as to every patient possibly using the marihuana at issue:

1.  The existence of a bona fide physician-patient relationship.
2.  Possession of no more marihuana than "reasonably necessary" for the patient's treatment.
3.  The actual medical use of marihuana.

In this case, because defendant did not present evidence demonstrating all three elements of the section 8 affirmative defense, he is not entitled to have the case dismissed under that section, nor was he permitted to make that defense at trial. *People v Tuttle,* 304 Mich App 72 (2014)

## Search and Seizure—MCL 333.26424(h) and MCL 333.26426(g)

Any marihuana, marihuana paraphernalia, or licit (lawful) property that is possessed, owned, or used in connection with the medical use of marihuana shall not be seized or forfeited.

Possession of, or application for, a registry identification card shall not constitute probable cause or reasonable suspicion to search or seize or otherwise subject the person or property to inspection.

Police received information from a roommate that the defendant was growing marihuana in his home. Officers did a trash pull and located marihuana leaves. Based on the information, a search warrant was sought and obtained. The officer did not check to see if the defendant was a qualifying patient or a primary caregiver under the MMMA. During the search officers located eight marihuana plants and two grams of marihuana. The defendant argued the warrant was not valid because the MMMA made it legal to possess and grow certain amounts of marihuana and, thus, the statement in the affidavit that defendant was growing marihuana was insufficient to provide the police officers with probable cause that a crime was committed. Because possession, manufacture, use, creation, and delivery of marihuana are still illegal in Michigan even after passage of the MMMA, a search warrant affidavit need not provide facts that the conduct alleged is specifically not legal under the MMMA. The court declined to impose an affirmative duty on the police to obtain information pertaining to a person's noncompliance with the MMMA before seeking a search warrant for marihuana; however, if the police do have clear and uncontroverted evidence that a person is in full compliance with the MMMA, this evidence must be included as part of the affidavit because such a situation would not justify the issuance of a warrant. *People v. Brown,* 297 Mich. App. 670 (2012).

## Return of Seized Medical Marihuana is Prohibited

However, if marihuana is seized by law enforcement, it cannot subsequently be returned to a qualifying patient or primary caregiver because it is impossible for a law enforcement officer to comply with both federal and state law. "Section 4(h) of the Michigan Medical Marihuana Act, MCL 333.26424(h), which prohibits the forfeiture of marihuana possessed for medical use, directly conflicts with and is thus preempted by, the Federal Controlled Substances Act, 21 USC 801 *et seq.,* to the extent § 4(h) requires a law enforcement officer to return marihuana to a registered patient or primary caregiver upon release from custody." OAG 2011–2012, No. 7, 262, p. 5 (November 10, 2011).

## Out-of-State Cards—MCL 333.26424(j)

Michigan will recognize medical marihuana cards, or the equivalent, that are issued by other states, territories, etc. that allow the medical use of marihuana by a visiting qualifying patient or allow a person to assist a visiting qualifying patient's medical use of marihuana. Out-of-state medical marihuana cards have the same force and effect as a Michigan registry identification card.

## Confidentiality—MCL 333.26426

The Department of Licensing and Regulatory Affairs shall verify to law enforcement whether a registry identification card is valid, without disclosing more than is reasonably necessary to verify the authenticity of the card.

A person, including an employee or official of the Department of Licensing and Regulatory Affairs or another state agency or local unit of government, who discloses confidential information in violation of the MMMA is guilty of a six-month misdemeanor.

## Limitations—MCL 333.26427

The MMMA does not permit any person to do any of the following:

- Undertake any task under the influence of marihuana when doing so would constitute negligence or professional malpractice.
- Possess marihuana or otherwise engage in the medical use of marihuana:
  - In a school bus.
  - On the grounds of any preschool or primary or secondary school.
  - In any correctional facility.
- Smoke marihuana:
  - On any form of public transportation.
  - In any public place.
- Operate or be in actual physical control of any motor vehicle, aircraft, or motorboat while under the influence of marihuana.
- Use marihuana if that person does not have a serious or debilitating medical condition.

The MMMA shall not be construed to require either of the following:

- A government medical assistance program or commercial or non-profit for costs associated with the medical use of marihuana.

- An employer to accommodate the ingestion of marihuana in any workplace or any employee working while under the influence of marihuana."

## Illegal Sale of Medical Marihuana— MCL 333.26424(k) (felony)

*Any registered qualifying patient or registered primary caregiver who sells marihuana to someone who is not allowed to use marihuana for medical purposes under this act shall have his or her registry identification card revoked and is guilty of a felony punishable by imprisonment for not more than two years or a fine of not more than $2,000.00, or both, in addition to any other penalties for the distribution of marihuana.*

## Fraudulent Representation to Law Enforcement— MCL 333.26427(d)

*Fraudulent representation to a law enforcement official of any fact or circumstance relating to the medical use of marihuana to avoid arrest or prosecution is a $500 fine in addition to any other applicable penalties.*

## Medical Marihuana, Improper Transportation in a Vehicle—MCL 750.474 (93-day misdemeanor)

A person shall not transport or possess usable marihuana as defined in MCL 333.26423, in or upon a motor vehicle or any self-propelled vehicle designed for land travel, unless the usable marihuana is one or more of the following:

- Enclosed in a case that is carried in the trunk of the vehicle.
- Enclosed in a case that is not readily accessible from the interior of the vehicle, if the vehicle in which the person is traveling does not have a trunk.

# 16

# EXPLOSIVES AND WEAPONS

## EXPLOSIVES

### Concealment of Explosives as Baggage or Freight—MCL 750.201 (felony)

A person shall not send, order, or transport an explosive on any vehicle used for transporting passengers or articles of commerce.

### Explosives as Implements of Terrorism—MCL 750.204 (felony)

A person shall not send or deliver to another person an explosive, or cause an explosive to be taken or received by any person, with one of the following intents:

- To frighten, terrorize, intimidate, injure or kill another person.
- To damage or destroy property of another.

Penalties:

| If no damage or injury | 15-year felony |
| --- | --- |
| If causes damage | 20-year felony |
| If causes physical injury | 25-year felony |
| If causes serious injury | Up to life felony |
| If causes death | Mandatory life without possibility of parole |

### Sending Fake Bombs—MCL 750.204a (felony)

A person shall not possess, deliver, send, transport, or place a device constructed to represent or presented as an explosive with the intent to frighten, terrorize, harass, threaten, or annoy another person.

### Placing Bombs—MCL 750.207 (felony)

*A person shall not place an explosive substance in or near any real or personal property with the intent to frighten, terrorize, intimidate, threaten, harass, injure, or kill any person, or with the intent to damage or destroy any real or personal property without the permission of the property owner or, if the property is public property, without the permission of the governmental agency having authority over that property. MCL 750.207(1).*

Penalties:

| Placing bombs with the intent to frighten, threaten, or harass | 15-year felony |
| --- | --- |
| If causes damage | 20-year felony |
| If causes physical injury | 25-year felony |
| If causes serious injury | Up to life felony |
| If causes death | Mandatory life without possibility of parole |

## Placing Offensive or Injurious Substances in or Near Real or Personal Property—MCL 750.209 (felony)

A person shall not place an offensive or injurious substance or compound in or near to any real or personal property with any of the following intents:

- To injure or coerce another person.
- To injure the property or business of another.
- To interfere with the person's use or management of his or her property.

Penalties:

| | |
|---|---|
| If the suspect places offensive or injurious substance in or near any real or personal property with intent to annoy or alarm | 5-year felony |
| If no damage or injury | 15-year felony |
| If causes damage | 20-year felony |
| If causes physical injury | 25-year felony |
| If causes serious injury | Up to life felony |
| If causes death | Mandatory life without possibility of parole. |

## Possessing Explosives in a Public Place—MCL 750.209a (felony)

*A person who, with the intent to terrorize, frighten, intimidate, threaten, harass, or annoy any other person, possesses an explosive substance or device in a public place is guilty of a felony punishable by imprisonment for not more than 10 years or a fine of not more than $10,000.00, or both.*

## Possession of Substance with Explosive Capability—MCL 750.210 (felony)

*A person shall not carry or possess an explosive or combustible substance or a substance or compound that when combined with another substance or compound will become explosive or combustible or an article containing an explosive or combustible substance or a substance or compound that when combined with another substance or compound will become explosive or combustible, with the intent to frighten, terrorize, intimidate, threaten, harass, injure, or kill any person, or with the intent to damage or destroy any real or personal property without the permission of the property owner or, if the property is public property, without the permission of the governmental agency having authority over that property.*

Penalties:

| | |
|---|---|
| If no damage or injury | 15-year felony |
| If causes damage | 20-year felony |
| If causes physical injury | 25-year felony |
| If causes serious injury | Up to life felony |
| If causes death | Mandatory life without possibility of parole |

## Carry, Manufacture, Buy, Sell or Furnish Explosive Compounds with Intent to Frighten, Terrorize, Harass, and Injure—MCL 750.211a (felony)

*(1) A person shall not do either of the following:*

*(a) Except as provided in subdivision (b), manufacture, buy, sell, furnish, or possess a Molotov cocktail or any similar device.*

*(b) Manufacture, buy, sell, furnish, or possess any device that is designed to explode or that will explode upon impact or with the application of heat or a flame or that is highly incendiary, with the intent to frighten, terrorize, intimidate, threaten, harass, injure, or kill any person, or with the intent to damage or destroy any real or personal property without the permission of the property owner or, if the property is public property, without the permission of the governmental agency having authority over that property.*

Penalties:

| | |
|---|---|
| If no damage or injury | 15-year felony |
| If causes damage | 20-year felony |
| If causes physical injury | 25-year felony |
| If causes serious injury | Up to life felony |
| If causes death | Mandatory life without possibility of parole |

## Vulnerable Targets—MCL 750.212a (felony)

An additional 20-year penalty will be added if explosion occurs in or is directed at one of the following vulnerable targets and death or serious injury results:

- A child care or day care center.
- A health care facility or agency.
- A building or structure open to the general public.
- A church, synagogue, mosque, or other place of religious worship.
- A school, K-12.
- An institution of higher education.
- A stadium.
- Critical transportation infrastructures.

- Public service facilities.
- A building, structure, or other facility owned or operated by the government.

## Possessing Information of Vulnerable Targets—MCL 750.543r (felony)

A person shall not obtain or possess a blueprint, an architectural or engineering diagram, security plan, or other similar information of a vulnerable target with the intent to commit a prohibited offense.

# HARMFUL BIOLOGICAL, CHEMICAL, OR RADIOACTIVE SUBSTANCES OR DEVICES

## Definitions—MCL 750.200h

*Harmful biological substance:*   A bacteria, virus, or other microorganism or toxic substance derived from microorganism that can cause death, injury, or disease in humans, animals, or plants.

*Harmful chemical substance:*   A solid, liquid, or gas that, alone or in combination with one or more other chemical substances, can cause death, injury, or disease in humans, animals, or plants.

*Harmful radioactive material:*   Material that is radioactive that can cause death, injury, or disease in humans, animals, or plants.

*Chemical irritant:*   A solid, liquid, or gas that, through its chemical or physical properties alone or in combination with other substances, can be used to produce an irritant effect in humans, animals, or plants.

*For an unlawful purpose:*   To frighten, terrorize, intimidate, threaten, harass, injure, or kill any person or to damage or destroy any real or personal property without the permission of the property owner.

## Manufacture, Deliver, Possess, Use—MCL 750.200i (felony)

A person shall not manufacture, deliver, possess, transport, use or release *for an unlawful purpose* any of the following:

- A harmful biological substance or device.
- A harmful chemical substance or device.
- A harmful radioactive material or device.

Hot cooking oil used to injure another person is not a harmful substance under this statute because oil's chemical properties alone cannot cause injury, death, or disease. *People v. Blunt,* 282 Mich. App. 81 (2009).

## Other Harmful Substances—MCL 750.200j (felony)

*A person shall not manufacture, deliver, possess, transport, place, use, or release for an unlawful purpose any of the following:*

(a) *A chemical irritant or a chemical irritant device.*
(b) *A smoke device.*
(c) *An imitation harmful substance or device.*

## False Exposure to Harmful Substance—MCL 750.200l (felony)

*A person shall not commit an act with the intent to cause an individual to falsely believe that the individual has been exposed to a harmful biological substance, harmful biological device, harmful chemical substance, harmful chemical device, harmful radioactive material, or harmful radioactive device.*

*The court also shall impose costs on a person who violates this subsection to reimburse any governmental agency for its expenses incurred.*

# MICHIGAN FIREWORKS SAFETY ACT

## Definitions—MCL 28.452

*Agricultural and wildlife fireworks:*   Fireworks devices distributed to farmers, ranchers, and growers through a wildlife management program administered by the United States *Department of the Interior or the Michigan Department of Natural Resources.*

*Articles pyrotechnic:*   Pyrotechnic devices for professional use that are similar to consumer fireworks in chemical composition and construction but not intended for consumer use, that meet the weight limits for consumer fireworks but are not labeled as such, and that are classified as UN0431 or UN0432 under 49 CFR 172.101.

*Consumer fireworks:*   Fireworks devices that are designed to produce visible effects by combustion, that are required to comply with the construction, chemical composition, and labeling regulations promulgated by the United States consumer product safety commission under 16 CFR parts 1500 and 1507, and that are listed in APA standard 87-1, 3.1.2, 3.1.3, or 3.5. Consumer fireworks does not include low-impact fireworks.

*Department:*   The Department of Licensing and Regulatory Affairs.

*Display fireworks:*   Large fireworks devices that are explosive materials intended for use in fireworks displays and designed to produce visible or audible effects by combustion, deflagration, or detonation, as provided in 27 CFR 555.11, 49 CFR 172, and APA standard 87-1, 4.1.

*Firework or fireworks:* Any composition or device, except for a starting pistol, a flare gun, or a flare, designed for the purpose of producing a visible or audible effect by combustion, deflagration, or detonation. Fireworks consist of consumer fireworks, low-impact fireworks, articles pyrotechnic, display fireworks, and special effects.

*Local unit of government:* A city, village, or township.

*Low-impact fireworks:* Ground and handheld sparkling devices as that phrase is defined under APA standard 87-1, 3.1, 3.1.1.1 to 3.1.1.8, and 3.5.

*Minor:* An individual who is less than 18 years of age.

*Novelties:* That term as defined under APA standard 87-1, 3.2, 3.2.1, 3.2.2, 3.2.3, 3.2.4, and 3.2.5 and all of the following:

- Toy plastic or paper caps for toy pistols in sheets, strips, rolls, or individual caps containing not more than .25 of a grain of explosive content per cap, in packages labeled to indicate the maximum explosive content per cap.
- Toy pistols, toy cannons, toy canes, toy trick noisemakers, and toy guns in which toy caps as described in subparagraph (i) are used, that are constructed so that the hand cannot come in contact with the cap when in place for the explosion, and that are not designed to break apart or be separated so as to form a missile by the explosion.
- Flitter sparklers in paper tubes not exceeding 1/8 inch in diameter.
- Toy snakes not containing mercury, if packed in cardboard boxes with not more than 12 pieces per box for retail sale and if the manufacturer's name and the quantity contained in each box are printed on the box; and toy smoke devices.

*Person:* An individual, agent, association, charitable organization, company, limited liability company, corporation, labor organization, legal representative, partnership, unincorporated organization, or any other legal or commercial entity.

*Retailer:* A person who sells consumer fireworks or low-impact fireworks for resale to an individual for ultimate use.

*Serious impairment of a body function:* That term as defined in MCL 257.58c which includes, but is not limited to, one or more of the following:

- Loss of a limb or loss of use of a limb.
- Loss of a foot, hand, finger, or thumb or loss of use of a foot, hand, finger, or thumb.
- Loss of an eye or ear or loss of use of an eye or ear.

- Loss or substantial impairment of a bodily function.
- Serious visible disfigurement.
- A comatose state that lasts for more than three days.
- Measurable brain or mental impairment.
- A skull fracture or other serious bone fracture.
- Subdural hemorrhage or subdural hematoma.
- Loss of an organ.

*Serious violation:* A violation of this act, an order issued under this act, or a rule promulgated or adopted by reference under this act for which a substantial probability exists that death or serious impairment of a body function to a person other than the violator may result unless the violator did not and could not, with the exercise of reasonable diligence, know of the presence of the violation.

*Special effects:* A combination of chemical elements or chemical compounds capable of burning independently of the oxygen of the atmosphere and designed and intended to produce an audible, visual, mechanical, or thermal effect as an integral part of a motion picture, radio, television, theatrical, or opera production or live entertainment.

*Wholesaler:* Any person who sells consumer fireworks or low-impact fireworks to a retailer or any other person for resale. Wholesaler does not include a person who sells only display fireworks or special effects.

## Novelties—MCL 28.453

*This act does not apply to novelties. Nothing in this act allows a local unit of government to enact or enforce an ordinance, code, or regulation pertaining to, or in any manner regulating, the sale, storage, display for sale, transportation, use, or distribution of novelties.*

## Consumer Fireworks—MCL 28.454

*(1) A person shall not sell consumer fireworks unless the person annually obtains and maintains a consumer fireworks certificate from the department under this section. A person who knows, or should know, that he or she is required to comply with this subsection and who fails or neglects to do so is guilty of a misdemeanor punishable by imprisonment for not more than 2 years or a fine, or both.*

. . . .

*(7) The holder of a consumer fireworks certificate shall prominently display the original or copy of the certificate in the appropriate retail location. A person that violates this subsection is*

*responsible for a civil fine of $100.00. Each day that the consumer fireworks certificate is not displayed as required under this subsection is a separate violation.*

*....*

(9) *The face of the consumer fireworks certificate shall indicate the location or address for which it was issued.*

## Low-Impact Fireworks—MCL 28.456

*....*

(2) *Beginning February 1, 2012, a person shall not sell low-impact fireworks unless he or she registers with the low-impact fireworks retail registry not less than 10 days before selling the fireworks in each calendar year.*

(3) *A person who sells low-impact fireworks at retail and who fails to register as described in this section shall cease the sale of low-impact fireworks until the person complies with subsection (2).*

## Articles Pyrotechnic or Display Fireworks—MCL 28.466

(1) *The legislative body of a city, village, or township, upon application in writing on forms provided by the department and payment of a fee set by the legislative body, if any, may grant a permit for the use of agricultural or wildlife fireworks, articles pyrotechnic, display fireworks, or special effects manufactured for outdoor pest control or agricultural purposes, or for public or private display within the city, village, or township by municipalities, fair associations, amusement parks, or other organizations or individuals approved by the city, village, or township authority, if the applicable provisions of this act are complied with. After a permit has been granted, sales, possession, or transportation of fireworks for the purposes described in the permit only may be made. A permit granted under this subsection is not transferable and shall not be issued to a minor.*

## Local Ordinances—MCL 28.457

(1) *Except as provided in this act, a local unit of government shall not enact or enforce an ordinance, code, or regulation pertaining to or in any manner regulating the sale, display, storage, transportation, or distribution of fireworks regulated under this act.*

(2) *A local unit of government may enact an ordinance regulating the ignition, discharge,*

*and use of consumer fireworks, including, but not limited to, an ordinance prescribing the hours of the day or night during which a person may ignite, discharge, or use consumer fireworks. If a local unit of government enacts an ordinance under this subsection, the ordinance shall not regulate the ignition, discharge, or use of consumer fireworks on the day preceding, the day of, or the day after a national holiday except as follows:*

(a) *A local unit of government with a population of 50,000 or more or a local unit of government located in a county with a population of 750,000 or more may regulate the ignition, discharge, or use of consumer fireworks between the hours of 12 midnight and 8 a.m. or between the hours of 1 a.m. and 8 a.m. on New Year's day.*

(b) *A local unit of government with a population of less than 50,000 located in a county with a population of less than 750,000 may regulate the ignition, discharge, or use of consumer fireworks between the hours of 1 a.m. and 8 a.m.*

(3) *An ordinance under subsection (2) shall only impose a civil fine of not more than $500.00 for each violation of the ordinance and no other fine or sanction.*

## Prohibited Acts—MCL 28.462

(1) *A person shall not ignite, discharge, or use consumer fireworks on public property, school property, church property, or the property of another person without that organization's or person's express permission to use those fireworks on those premises. Except as otherwise provided in this section, a person that violates this subsection is responsible for a state civil infraction and may be ordered to pay a civil fine of not more than $500.00.*

(2) *Consumer fireworks shall not be sold to a minor. A person that violates this subsection shall be ordered to pay a civil fine of not more than $500.00, or, for a second or subsequent violation of this subsection, a civil fine of not more than $1,000.00. In addition, the person's consumer fireworks certificate shall be suspended for 90 days after the civil fine is ordered for a second or subsequent violation. This age requirement shall be verified by any of the following:*

(a) *An operator's or chauffeur's license issued under the Michigan vehicle code, 1949 PA 300, MCL 257.1 to 257.923.*

(b) An official state personal identification card issued under 1972 PA 222, MCL 28.291 to 28.300.

(c) An enhanced driver license or enhanced official state personal identification card issued under the enhanced driver license and enhanced official state personal identification card act, 2008 PA 23, MCL 28.301 to 28.308.

(d) A military identification card.

(e) A passport.

(f) Any other bona fide photograph identification that establishes the identity and age of the individual.

(3) An individual shall not discharge, ignite, or use consumer fireworks or low-impact fireworks while under the influence of alcoholic liquor, a controlled substance, or a combination of alcoholic liquor and a controlled substance. As used in this subsection:

(a) "Alcoholic liquor" means that term as defined in section 1d of the Michigan vehicle code, 1949 PA 300, MCL 257.1d.

(b) "Controlled substance" means that term as defined in section 8b of the Michigan vehicle code, 1949 PA 300, MCL 257.8b.

(4) An individual who violates the smoking prohibition under NFPA 1124, 7.3.11.1 is guilty of a misdemeanor punishable by imprisonment for not more than 1 year or a fine of not more than $1,000.00, or both.

---

- NFPA 7.3.11.1 prohibits smoking inside or within 50 feet of a Consumer Fireworks Retail Sales (CFRS) area. The CFRS area is the portion of a consumer fireworks retail sales facility or store, including the immediately adjacent aisles, where consumer fireworks are located for the purpose of retail displays and sale to the public.

## Permissible Acts—28.467

---

Except as otherwise provided in this act, this act does not prohibit any of the following:

(a) A wholesaler, retailer, commercial manufacturer, or importer from selling, storing, using, transporting, or distributing consumer fireworks or low-impact fireworks.

(b) The use of fireworks by railroads or other transportation agencies or law enforcement agencies for signal purposes or illumination.

(c) The use of agricultural or wildlife fireworks.

(d) The sale or use of blank cartridges for any of the following:

(i) A show or play.

(ii) Signal or ceremonial purposes in athletics or sports.

(iii) Use by military organizations.

(iv) Use by law enforcement agencies.

(e) The possession, sale, or disposal of fireworks incidental to the public display of fireworks by wholesalers or other persons who possess a permit to possess, store, and sell explosives from the bureau of alcohol, tobacco, firearms, and explosives of the United States department of justice.

(f) Interstate wholesalers from selling, storing, using, transporting, or distributing fireworks.

---

## Violations—MCL 28.468

---

(1) Unless otherwise provided in this act, if a person violates this act, the person is guilty of a crime as follows:

(a) Except as otherwise provided in this section, a misdemeanor punishable by imprisonment for not more than 30 days or a fine of not more than $1,000.00, or both.

(b) If the violation causes damage to the property of another person, a misdemeanor punishable by imprisonment for not more than 90 days or a fine of not more than $5,000.00, or both.

(c) If the violation causes serious impairment of a body function of another person, a felony punishable by imprisonment for not more than 5 years or a fine of not more than $5,000.00, or both.

(d) If the violation causes the death of another person, a felony punishable by imprisonment for not more than 15 years or a fine of not more than $10,000.00, or both.

(2) In addition to any other penalty imposed for the violation of this act, a person that is found guilty of a violation of this act shall be required to reimburse the appropriate governmental agency for the costs of storing seized fireworks that the governmental agency confiscated for a violation of this act. This reimbursement shall be in a form and at a time as required by the department and as otherwise required by law.

## Seizure of Fireworks—MCL 28.464

*(1) A governmental or law enforcement agency that identifies a firework that is in violation of this act shall secure the firework and immediately notify the department of the alleged violation. The department or law enforcement agency shall investigate the alleged violation for compliance with this act within a reasonable time.*

*(2) If the department or law enforcement agency determines that a violation of this act has occurred, except for a violation of section 6(2), the department or law enforcement agency may seize the firework as evidence of the violation. Evidence seized under this section shall be stored pending disposition of any criminal or civil proceedings arising from a violation of this act at the expense of the person, if the person is found guilty, responsible, or liable for the violation.*

## Storage of Seized Fireworks—MCL 28.465

*(1) Fireworks seized for an alleged violation of this act shall be stored in compliance with this act and rules promulgated under this act.*

*(2) Following final disposition of a conviction for violating this act, the seizing agency in possession may dispose of or destroy any fireworks retained as evidence in that prosecution.*

*(3) The person from whom fireworks are seized under this act shall pay the actual costs of storage and disposal of the seized fireworks.*

*(4) The department of state police and the department may use fireworks described in subsection (2) for training purposes.*

## Michigan Fireworks Safety Act Administrative Rules

The Michigan Fireworks Safety Act Administrative Rules are contained in R 29.2901–29.2929.

# FIREARMS AND UNLAWFUL WEAPONS

## Definitions

**For purposes of the Firearms Act, MCL 28.421–28.435, and the Firearms chapter of the Michigan Penal Code, MCL 750.222–750.239a, the following terms have the following meaning:**

*Firearm:*  A weapon from which a dangerous projectile may be propelled by an explosive or by gas or air. Firearm does not include a smooth bore rifle or handgun designed to shoot BBs not exceeding .177 caliber.

*Pistol:*  A loaded or unloaded firearm, 26 inches or less in length, or by its construction or appearance conceals the fact that it is a firearm.

- As detailed in MCL 28.421(2), a person may lawfully own, possess, carry, or transport as a pistol a firearm greater than 26 inches in length if all of the following conditions apply:
  - The person registered the firearm as a pistol under MCL 28.422 or MCL 28.422a before January 1, 2013.
  - The person who registered the firearm as a pistol has maintained registration of the firearm since January 1, 2013 without lapse.
  - The person possesses a copy of the license or record issued to him or her under MCL 28.422 or 28.422a.

**For purposes of the Firearms Act, MCL 28.421–28.435, the following terms have the following meaning:**

*Peace officer:*  An individual who is employed as a law enforcement officer, as that term is defined under section 2 of the Commission on Law Enforcement Standards Act, MCL 28.602, by this state or another state, a political subdivision of this state or another state, or the United States, and who is required to carry a firearm in the course of his or her duties as a law enforcement officer.

*Purchaser:*  A person who receives a pistol from another person by purchase or gift.

*Seller:*  A person who sells or gives a pistol to another person.

**For purposes of the Firearms chapter of the Michigan Penal Code, MCL 750.222–750.239a, the following terms have the following meaning:**

*Barrel length:*  The internal length of a firearm as measured from the face of the closed breech of the firearm when it is unloaded, to the forward face of the end of the barrel.

*Purchaser:*  A person who receives a pistol from another person by purchase, gift, or loan.

*Rifle:*  A firearm, designed or redesigned, made or remade, and intended to be fired from the shoulder, which uses the energy of an explosive in a fixed metallic cartridge to fire a single projectile through a rifled bore for each single pull of the trigger.

*Seller:*  A person who sells, furnishes, loans, or gives a pistol to another person.

*Shotgun:*  A firearm, designed or redesigned, made or remade and intended to be fired from the shoulder, which uses the energy of an explosive in a fixed shotgun shell to fire through a smooth bore either ball shot or a single projectile for each single pull of the trigger.

## Pistol Possession and Registration Requirements

Michigan law prohibits a person from purchasing, carrying, possessing, or transporting a pistol in Michigan without first having obtained a License to Purchase a Pistol or completing a Pistol Sales Record, and registering the pistol. A person has to be 18 years of age or older or, if the seller is a federally licensed firearms dealer, 21 years of age or older to purchase a pistol. In general, a person may only possess a pistol that is registered to him or her, unless the person is exempt from the registration requirements. Exemptions to the registration requirements are contained in MCL 28.422 and MCL 28.432.

## License to Purchase a Pistol—MCL 28.422

A person shall not purchase, carry, possess, or transport a pistol in Michigan without first having obtained a License to Purchase a Pistol from a local police or sheriff department. The purchaser shall hand-deliver or mail a copy of the license to the issuing police or sheriff department within 10 days of purchasing a pistol (failure to do so is a state civil infraction). The issuing police or sheriff department is required to forward that copy of the license to the Michigan State Police. The purchaser, when carrying, using, possessing, or transporting the pistol, must have a copy of the license in his or her possession for 30 days after purchase. A license is void unless used within 30 days after the date it is issued. As detailed in MCL 750.232a, a person who obtains a pistol in violation of MCL 28.422 is guilty of a 90-day misdemeanor. Forging any matter on an application for a license is a four-year felony.

## Pistol Sales Record—MCL 28.422a

Michigan Concealed Pistol License holders, federally licensed firearms dealers, and individuals who purchase a pistol from a federally licensed firearms dealer in compliance with 18 U.S.C. § 922(t) are not required to obtain a License to Purchase a Pistol. Instead, they are required to sign a Pistol Sales Record completed by the seller when they purchase or otherwise acquire a pistol. The purchaser shall hand-deliver or mail a copy of the record to the local police or sheriff department having jurisdiction where the purchaser resides within 10 days of purchasing a pistol (failure to do so is a state civil infraction). The local police or sheriff department is required to forward that copy of the record to the Michigan State Police. The purchaser, when carrying, using, possessing, or transporting the pistol, must have a copy of the record in his or her possession for 30 days after purchase.

## Persons Exempt from Registration Requirements— MCL 28.422 and MCL 28.432

MCL 28.422 exempts the following persons from registration requirements:

- Active duty members of the military are exempt for 30 days after returning to Michigan on leave. Persons who have been discharged from active duty with the military are exempt for 30 days after returning to Michigan.
- Licensed dealers when buying a pistol from a wholesaler.
- Non-residents if all of the following apply:
  - The person is licensed in his or her state of residence to purchase, carry, or transport a pistol.
  - The person is in possession of that license.
  - The person owns the pistol carried.
  - The person possesses the pistol for a lawful purpose.
  - The person is in Michigan for fewer than 180 days and does not intend to establish residency.
  - The person presents the license upon demand of a police officer. Failure to present the license upon demand is a 90-day misdemeanor.
- A Michigan resident under 18 possessing another person's pistol if all of the following apply:
  - The person is not otherwise prohibited from possessing the pistol.
  - The person is at a recognized target range.
  - The person possesses the pistol for target practice or instruction in safely using a pistol.
  - The person's parent or guardian is physically present and supervising the use of the pistol.
  - The owner of the pistol is physically present.
- A Michigan resident 18 or older possessing another person's pistol if all of the following apply:
  - The person is not otherwise prohibited from possessing the pistol.
  - The person is at a recognized target range or shooting facility.

- The person possesses the pistol for target practice or instruction in safely using a pistol.
- The owner of the pistol is physically present and supervising the use of the pistol.

MCL 28.432 exempts the following persons from registration requirements:
- Police and correctional agencies.
- The United States Army, Air Force, Navy, or Marine Corps, including reserve and national guard components.
- An organization authorized by law to purchase weapons from the United States or this state.
- Police, corrections, and military members while going to or from those duties.
- A United States citizen holding a concealed pistol license issued by another state.
- Manufacturers and their agents while transporting pistols as merchandise.
- Persons possessing antique firearms as defined in MCL 750.231a.
- Michigan Concealed Pistol License holders or individuals exempt from having to obtain a Michigan Concealed Pistol License under MCL 28.432a when carrying, possessing, using, or transporting a pistol lawfully possessed by the owner.

### Persons Exempt from Registration Requirements—Federal Law

Notwithstanding state law, a person who is not prohibited from possessing a firearm under federal law is permitted to transport a firearm for any lawful purpose from any place where it may be lawfully possessed and carried to any other place where it may be lawfully possessed and carried. During transportation, the firearm must be unloaded and neither the firearm nor ammunition may be readily or directly accessible from the passenger compartment of the vehicle. If the vehicle does not have a compartment separate from the driver's compartment, the firearm and ammunition must be locked in a container other than the glove compartment or console. 18 USC § 926(a).

### Failure to Have Pistol Registered or Making False Statement in Application for License to Purchase—MCL 750.232a

(1) Except as provided in subsection (2), a person who obtains a pistol in violation of section 2 of Act No. 372 of the Public Acts of 1927, as amended, being section 28.422 of the Michigan Compiled Laws, is guilty of a misdemeanor, punishable by imprisonment for not more than 90 days or a fine of not more than $100.00, or both.

(2) Subsection (1) does not apply to a person who obtained a pistol in violation of section 2 of Act No. 372 of the Public Acts of 1927 before the effective date of the 1990 amendatory act that added this subsection, who has not been convicted of that violation, and who obtains a license as required under section 2 of Act No. 372 of the Public Acts of 1927 within 90 days after the effective date of the 1990 amendatory act that added this subsection.

(3) A person who intentionally makes a material false statement on an application for a license to purchase a pistol under section 2 of Act No. 372 of the Public Acts of 1927, as amended, is guilty of a felony, punishable by imprisonment for not more than 4 years, or a fine of not more than $2,000.00, or both.

(4) A person who uses or attempts to use false identification or the identification of another person to purchase a firearm is guilty of a misdemeanor, punishable by imprisonment for not more than 90 days or a fine of not more than $100.00, or both.

Penalties:

| | |
|---|---|
| Obtaining a pistol in violation of the License to Purchase statute, MCL 28.422 | 90-day misdemeanor |
| Use or attempted use of false identification or identification of another to purchase a firearm | 90-day misdemeanor |
| Making a material false statement on application for a License to Purchase a Pistol | Felony |

### Unlawful Weapons—MCL 750.224 (felony)

A person is prohibited from manufacturing, selling, offering for sale or possessing any of the following weapons:

- A *machine gun* or firearm that shoots or is designed to shoot automatically more than one shot without manual reloading by a single function of the trigger.
  - In a related section of law, MCL 750.224e prohibits knowingly manufacturing, selling, distributing, or possessing a device that is designed or intended to convert a semi-automatic firearm into a fully automatic firearm. The penalty for a violation is a felony. Exceptions to this section include police, armed forces, and a licensed dealer if the dealer had the device prior to March 28, 1991.

A person in Michigan may only possess a machine gun if it was lawfully possessed before May 19, 1986, and is properly registered under federal law. A person in Michigan may only transfer possession of a machine gun in Michigan if authorized to do so by the Bureau of Alcohol, Tobacco, Firearms and Explosives. The federal regulatory scheme under 18 U.S.C. § 922(o) and related regulations constitutes a "license" within the meaning of MCL 750.224. OAG, 2005–2006, No. 7,183, p 63 (December 27, 2005).

- A *muffler or silencer.*   Muffler or silencer means a device for muffling, silencing, or deadening the report of a firearm; a combination of parts intended for use in assembling or fabricating a muffler or silence; and a part intended only for use in assembling or fabricating a muffler or silencer.

The possession, manufacture, or sale of a firearm silencer is permitted in Michigan under MCL 750.224(1)(b) if the person is licensed or approved to possess, manufacture, or sell such a device by the federal Bureau of Alcohol, Tobacco, Firearms and Explosives, as required by MCL 750.224(3)(c). Possession, manufacture, or sale of a firearm silencer by an unlicensed or unapproved person is a felony, punishable by up to five years imprisonment under MCL 750.224(2). OAG, 2011-2012, No 7,260, p 11 (September 2, 2011).

- A *bomb or bombshell.*   A bomb or bombshell means a hollow container filled with gunpowder or other explosive or combustible material and designed to be set off by a fuse or other device.
- A *blackjack.*   A blackjack is a weapon consisting of a lead slug attached to a narrow strip, usually of leather.
- A *slungshot*.   A slungshot is a striking weapon consisting of a small mass of metal or stone fixed on a flexible handle or strap.
- A *billy.*   A billy is a small bludgeon that may be carried in the pocket.

A nightstick similar to ones sold at police equipment stores, which was 24 inches long, is too long to be a billy within the meaning of MCL 750.224(1). A billy is a small bludgeon that may be carried in the pocket. *People v. Hassenfratz*, 99 Mich. App. 154 (1980).

A wooden club or "fish billy," carried and used as a fish bonker without wrongful knowledge or intent, is not an unlawful weapon under MCL 750.224(1). *People v. Battles*, 109 Mich. App. 384 (1981).

- A *sand club* or *sand bag.*   A sand club or sandbag is a small narrow bag filled with sand and used as a bludgeon.
- A *bludgeon.*   A bludgeon is a short club, usually weighted at one end or bigger at one end than the other, and designed for use as a weapon.

A nightstick, similar to a policemen's nightstick, which had a circumference of three inches at both the top and bottom, measured 22 inches in length, and had a leather strap and carved handle is not a bludgeon within the meaning of MCL 750.224(1). The object involved in this case did not possess the distinguishing characteristic of having a weighted or thicker end. Rather, the object is one typically referred to as a "nightstick" that may be purchased in police equipment stores or other similar stores. *People v. Beasley*, 198 Mich. App. 40 (1993).

Karate sticks and bludgeons are different instruments with different descriptions. Karate sticks are not dangerous weapons under the "bludgeon" category. *People v. Malik*, 70 Mich. App. 133 (1976).

- *Metallic knuckles.*   Metallic knuckles are pieces of metal designed to be worn over the knuckles in order to protect them in striking a blow and to make the blow more effective.
- *A device that releases a gas or substance that renders a person temporarily or permanently disabled*. A self-defense spray or foam device is not prohibited by this subdivision.
  - *Self-defense spray or foam device* means a device that contains not more than 35 grams of any combination of orthochlorobenzalmalonitrile and inert ingredients or a solution containing not more than 10% oleoresin capsicum. MCL 750.224d.
  - The reasonable use of a self-defense spray or foam device containing not more than 10% oleoresin capsicum is allowed by a person in the protection of a person or

property under circumstances that would justify the person's use of physical force.

- Unlawful use of a self-defense spray or foam device is a two-year misdemeanor.
- If a person uses a self-defense spray or foam device during the commission of another crime or threatens to use a self-defense spray or foam device during the commission of a crime to temporarily or permanently disable another person, the person's sentence may be enhanced.
- Selling a self-defense spray or foam device to a minor is a 90-day misdemeanor.

## Elements

1. The defendant knowingly manufactured, sold, offered for sale, or possessed a prohibited weapon.
2. At the time he or she manufactured, sold, offered for sale, or possessed it, the defendant knew that it was a weapon.

It is not a crime under this act if the firearms, explosives, or munitions of war were being manufactured under a contract with a department of the United States, or if the defendant was licensed by the Secretary of the Treasury of the United States or the secretary's delegate to manufacture, sell or possess them or if the device the defendant is charged with possessing was a self-defense spray device, that is, a device that carries 35 grams or less of orthochlorobenzalmalononitrile and other ingredients or a solution containing not more than 10 percent oleoresin capsicum, but that does not give off any other substance that will disable or injure a person. CJI2d 11.29.

## Tasers and Stun Guns—MCL 750.224a (felony)

(1) Except as otherwise provided in this section, a person shall not sell, offer for sale, or possess in this state a portable device or weapon from which an electrical current, impulse, wave, or beam may be directed, which current, impulse, wave, or beam is designed to incapacitate temporarily, injure, or kill.

(2) This section does not prohibit any of the following:

   (a) The possession and reasonable use of a device that uses electro-muscular disruption technology by a peace officer, or by any of the following individuals if the individual has been trained in the use, effects, and risks of the device, and is using the device while performing his or her official duties:

   (i) An employee of the department of corrections who is authorized in writing by the director of the department of corrections to possess and use the device.

   (ii) A local corrections officer authorized in writing by the county sheriff to possess and use the device.

   (iii) An individual employed by a local unit of government that utilizes a jail or lockup facility who has custody of persons detained or incarcerated in the jail or lockup facility and who is authorized in writing by the chief of police, director of public safety, or sheriff to possess and use the device.

   (iv) A probation officer.

   (v) A court officer.

   (vi) A bail agent authorized under section 167b.

   (vii) A licensed private investigator.

   (viii) An aircraft pilot or aircraft crew member.

   (ix) An individual employed as a private security police officer. As used in this subparagraph, "private security police" means that term as defined in section 2 of the private security business and security alarm act, 1968 PA 330, MCL 338.1052.

   (b) The possession and reasonable use of a device that uses electro-muscular disruption technology by an individual who holds a valid license to carry a concealed pistol under section 5b of 1927 PA 372, MCL 28.425, and who has been trained under subsection (5) in the use, effects, and risks of the device.

   (c) Possession solely for the purpose of delivering a device described in subsection (1) to any governmental agency or to a laboratory for testing, with the prior written approval of the governmental agency or law enforcement agency and under conditions determined to be appropriate by that agency.

(3) A manufacturer, authorized importer, or authorized dealer may demonstrate, offer for sale, hold for sale, sell, give, lend, or deliver a device that uses electro-muscular disruption technology to a person authorized to possess a device that uses electro-muscular disruption technology and may possess a device that uses

*electro-muscular disruption technology for any of those purposes.*

(4) *A person who violates subsection (1) is guilty of a felony punishable by imprisonment for not more than 4 years or a fine of not more than $2,000.00, or both.*

(5) *An authorized dealer or other person who sells a device that uses electro-muscular disruption technology to an individual described in subsection (2)(b) shall verify the individual's identity and verify that the individual holds a valid concealed pistol license issued under section 5b of 1927 PA 372, MCL 28.425b, and shall provide to the individual purchasing the device, at the time of the sale, training on the use, effects, and risks of the device. A person who violates this subsection is guilty of a misdemeanor punishable by imprisonment for not more than 30 days or a fine of not more than $500.00, or both.*

(6) *An individual described in subsection (2) shall not use a device that uses electro-muscular disruption technology against another person except under circumstances that would justify the individual's lawful use of physical force. An individual who violates this subdivision is guilty of a misdemeanor punishable by imprisonment for not more than 2 years or a fine of not more than $2,000.00, or both.*

(7) *As used in this section:*

(a) *"A device that uses electro-muscular disruption technology" means a device to which both of the following apply:*

    (i) *The device is capable of creating an electro-muscular disruption and is used or intended to be used as a defensive device capable of temporarily incapacitating or immobilizing a person by the direction or emission of conducted energy.*

    (ii) *The device contains an identification and tracking system that, when the device is initially used, dispenses coded material traceable to the purchaser through records kept by the manufacturer, and the manufacturer of the device has a policy of providing that identification and tracking information to a police agency upon written request by that agency. However, this subdivision does not apply to a launchable device that is used only by law enforcement agencies.*

(b) *"Local corrections officer" means that term as defined in section 2 of the local corrections officers training act, 2003 PA 125, MCL 791.532.*

(c) *"Peace officer" means any of the following:*

    (i) *A police officer or public safety officer of this state or a political subdivision of this state, including motor carrier officers appointed under section 6d of 1935 PA 59, MCL 28.6d, and security personnel employed by the state under section 6c of 1935 PA 59, MCL 28.6c.*

    (ii) *A sheriff or a sheriff's deputy.*

    (iii) *A police officer or public safety officer of a junior college, college, or university who is authorized by the governing board of that junior college, college, or university to enforce state law and the rules and ordinances of that junior college, college, or university.*

    (iv) *A township constable.*

    (v) *A marshal of a city, village, or township.*

    (vi) *A conservation officer of the department of natural resources or the department of environmental quality.*

    (vii) *A reserve peace officer, as that term is defined in section 1 of 1927 PA 372, MCL 28.421.*

    (viii) *A law enforcement officer of another state or of a political subdivision of another state or a junior college, college, or university in another state, substantially corresponding to a law enforcement officer described in subparagraphs (i) to (vii).*

## Electro-Muscular Disruption Device

To qualify as a device that uses electro-muscular disruption technology, MCL 750.224a requires that the device contain an identification and tracking system that when the device is initially used, dispenses coded material traceable to the purchaser through records kept by the manufacturer, and the manufacturer of the device has a policy of providing that identification and tracking information to a police agency upon written request by that agency (e.g., Taser). Therefore, devices that do not dispense this material are not lawful to possess (e.g., stun guns, stun batons, stun canes, stun flashlights).

## Taser Possession by Michigan Concealed Pistol Licensees

MCL 750.224a allows for the possession and reasonable use of a device that uses electro-muscular disruption technology by a person who possesses a valid

Michigan Concealed Pistol License and who has been trained in the use, effects, and risks of the device.

## Reasonable Use—MCL 750.224a(6) (2-year misdemeanor)

Any individual who may lawfully possess and use a device that uses electro-muscular disruption technology may only use that device against another person under circumstances that would justify the individual's lawful use of physical force. Violation is a two-year misdemeanor.

Various sections of the Firearms Act that apply to carrying a concealed pistol also apply to carrying a device that uses electro-muscular disruption technology:

- Possession of licenses and disclosure requirements, MCL 28.425f.
- Immediate seizure and forfeiture requirements, MCL 28.425g.
- Carrying under the influence, MCL 28.425k.
- Pistol-free zones, MCL 28.425o.

## Training on the Use, Effects, and Risk

An authorized dealer or other person who sells a device that uses electro-muscular disruption technology to a person who possesses a Michigan Concealed Pistol License is required to verify the individual's identity and verify that the person holds a valid Michigan Concealed Pistol License. The dealer or seller must provide the licensee with training on the use, effects, and risks of the device at the time of sale.

## Possession of a Short Barreled Shotgun or Rifle— MCL 750.224b (felony)

*Short-barreled shotgun:* A shotgun with one or more barrels less than 18 inches, or an overall length less than 26 inches.

*Short-barreled rifle:* A rifle with one or more barrels less than 16 inches, or an overall length less than 26 inches.

*A person shall not make, manufacture, transfer, or possess a short-barreled shotgun or short-barreled rifle.*

*Exception:* This prohibition does not apply to a short-barreled shotgun or short-barreled rifle that is lawfully made, manufactured, transferred, or possessed under federal law.

## Registration Requirements

**Short-barreled shotgun or short-barreled rifle that is 26 inches or less in length must be registered as a pistol in Michigan. MCL 750.224b(4).**

*A person, except a manufacturer, lawfully making, transferring, or possessing a short-barreled shotgun or a short-barreled rifle that is 26 inches or less in length shall comply with the registration requirements of MCL 28.422 or 28.422a.*

A short-barreled shotgun or a short-barreled rifle that is 26 inches or less in length is considered a pistol as defined by Michigan law and is subject to all Michigan statutes applicable to pistols.

**Short-barreled shotgun or short-barreled rifle that is greater than 26 inches in length. MCL 750.224b(5).**

*A person who possesses a short-barreled shotgun or a short-barreled rifle that is greater than 26 inches in length shall possess a copy of the federal registration of that short-barreled shotgun or a short-barreled rifle while transporting or using that short-barreled shotgun or a short-barreled rifle and shall present that federal registration to a peace officer upon request by that peace officer.*

Violation of this requirement is a state civil infraction.

## Seizure and Forfeiture of a Short-Barreled Shotgun or a Short-Barreled Rifle

**Seizure and forfeiture of a short-barreled shotgun or a short-barreled rifle greater than 26 inches in length. MCL 750.224b(6).**

*A short-barreled shotgun or short-barreled rifle greater than 26 inches in length possessed by a person who does not possess a copy of the federal registration is subject to immediate seizure by a peace officer. If a peace officer seizes a short-barreled shotgun or short-barreled rifle under this subsection, the person has 45 days to display the federal registration to an authorized employee of the seizing law enforcement agency. If the person displays the federal registration within the 45-day period, the authorized employee shall return the short-barreled shotgun or short-barreled rifle to the person unless the person is prohibited by law from possessing a firearm. If the person does not display the federal registration within the 45-day period, the short-barreled shotgun or short-barreled rifle is subject to seizure and forfeiture under MCL 600.4701 to 600.4709.*

## Armor Piercing Ammunition—MCL 750.224c (felony)

*(1) Except as provided in subsection (2), a person shall not manufacture, distribute, sell, or use armor piercing ammunition in this state.*

*A person who willfully violates this section is guilty of a felony, punishable by imprisonment for not more than 4 years, or by a fine of not more than $2,000.00, or both.*

(2) *This section does not apply to either of the following:*

(a) *A person who manufactures, distributes, sells, or uses armor piercing ammunition in this state, if that manufacture, distribution, sale, or use is not in violation of chapter 44 of title 18 of the United States Code.*

(b) *A licensed dealer who sells or distributes armor piercing ammunition in violation of this section if the licensed dealer is subject to license revocation under chapter 44 of title 18 of the United States Code for that sale or distribution.*

(3) *As used in this section:*

(a) *"Armor piercing ammunition" means a projectile or projectile core which may be used in a pistol and which is constructed entirely, excluding the presence of traces of other substances, of tungsten alloys, steel, iron, brass, bronze, beryllium copper, or a combination of tungsten alloys, steel, iron, brass, bronze, or beryllium copper. Armor piercing ammunition does not include any of the following:*

   (i) *Shotgun shot that is required by federal law or by a law of this state to be used for hunting purposes.*

   (ii) *A frangible projectile designed for target shooting.*

   (iii) *A projectile that the director of the department of state police finds is primarily intended to be used for sporting purposes.*

   (iv) *A projectile or projectile core that the director of the department of state police finds is intended to be used for industrial purposes.*

(b) *"Licensed dealer" means a person licensed under chapter 44 of title 18 of the United States Code to deal in firearms or ammunition.*

## Carrying a Concealed Weapon (CCW)—MCL 750.227 (felony)

(1) *A person shall not carry a dagger, dirk, stiletto, a double-edged nonfolding stabbing instrument of any length, or any other dangerous weapon, except a hunting knife adapted and carried as such, concealed on or about his or her person, or whether concealed or otherwise in any vehicle operated or occupied by the person, except in his or her dwelling house, place of business or on other land possessed by the person.*

(2) *A person shall not carry a pistol concealed on or about his or her person, or, whether concealed or otherwise, in a vehicle operated or occupied by the person, except in his or her dwelling house, place of business, or on other land possessed by the person, without a license to carry the pistol as provided by law and if licensed, shall not carry the pistol in a place or manner inconsistent with any restrictions upon such license.*

## Pistol on a Person

### Elements

1. The defendant knowingly carried a pistol. It does not matter why the defendant was carrying the pistol, but to be guilty of this crime the defendant must have known that he or she was carrying a pistol.

2. This pistol was concealed on or about the person of the defendant. Complete invisibility is not required. A pistol is concealed if it cannot easily be seen by those who come into ordinary contact with the defendant.

CJI2d 11.1.

---

For CCW, complete invisibility is not required. The weapon is concealed if it is not observed by those casually observing the suspect as people do in the ordinary and usual associations of life. *People v. Jones*, 12 Mich. App. 293 (1968).

The carrying of a pistol in a holster or belt outside the clothing is not CCW. However, carrying under a coat would constitute a violation. OAG, 1945-1946, No 3,158, p 237 (February 14, 1945). Note that it is legal to carry a visible pistol in public (often called "open carry").

The Private Security Business and Security Alarm Act does not exempt security guards from the CCW law. *People v. Biller*, 239 Mich. App. 590 (2000).

Motor Carrier Enforcement Officers are not peace officers, therefore, they are not exempt from concealed weapons licensing. OAG, 1987-1988, No 6,530, p 362 (August 5, 1988).

## Pistol in a Vehicle

### Elements

1. A pistol was in a vehicle that the defendant was in.
2. The defendant knew the pistol was there.
3. The defendant took part in carrying or keeping the pistol in the vehicle.

CJI2d 11.1.

The CCW statute does not punish presence in a car where the pistol was found. The point of the statute is to punish "carrying." Thus, to convict one who is merely present in a car necessarily rests upon two inferences (a) an inference that he knows a pistol is present; and (b) an inference that he is carrying the pistol. Therefore, even by showing that someone knew a pistol was present should not lead automatically to a conclusion that he was carrying the pistol.

Hard and fast rules regarding what circumstantial evidence is sufficient to sustain a conviction of carrying a weapon in a motor vehicle have not evolved. The decisions have, however, emphasized the relevancy of the following factors either alone or in combination: (1) the accessibility or proximity of the weapon to the person of the defendant, (2) defendant's awareness that the weapon was in the motor vehicle, (3) defendant's possession of items that connect him to the weapon, such as ammunition, (4) defendant's ownership or operation of the vehicle, and (5) the length of time during which defendant drove or occupied the vehicle. *People v. Butler*, 413 Mich. 377 (1982).

To be convicted of CCW in a vehicle, a defendant's knowledge of the weapon's presence and participation in the carrying of the weapon must be proved. Participation in the act of carrying may be inferred from the fact that the defendant was found carrying ammunition usable in the gun in question, that the defendant was in close proximity to the weapon, or that defendant and others were engaged in a common, unlawful enterprise and the gun was being carried in furtherance of the enterprise. *People v. Stone*, 100 Mich. App. 24 (1980).

A pistol wedged in a space near the engine of a motorcycle was "in" the motorcycle for purposes of the CCW statute, even though it was not completely enclosed in a compartment that was part of the motorcycle or attached to the motorcycle (e.g., a saddlebag). *People v. Nimeth*, 236 Mich. App. 616 (1999).

## Operability Required

It is not against this law to carry a gun that is so out of repair, taken apart with parts missing, welded together, or plugged up that it is totally unusable as a firearm and cannot be easily made operable. CJI2d 11.06.

A "pistol," as defined under the CCW statute, must be operable. The pistol must be capable of propelling a dangerous projectile or be able to be altered to do so within a reasonably short time. It is an affirmative defense to CCW if it is proven that the pistol could not fire and could not be readily made to fire. *People v. Gardner*, 194 Mich. App. 652 (1992).

## Time of Possession

Possession of a pistol, no matter how short the period of time, will satisfy the CCW statute. Momentary possession after disarming another person is not a defense. *People v. Hernandez-Garcia*, 477 Mich. 1039 (2007).

## Other Weapons Under CCW

- Double-edged, nonfolding stabbing instrument (double-edged knives).
  - Does not include a knife, tool, implement, arrowhead, or artifact manufactured from stone by means of conchoidal fracturing (breaking of stone). The item cannot be transported in a vehicle, unless it is in a container and inaccessible to the driver. MCL 750.222a.
- Dirk, dagger, and stiletto.
  - Dirk is a straight knife with a pointed blade.
  - Dagger is a knife with a short-pointed blade.
  - Stiletto is a small dagger with a slender, tapering blade.

CJI2d 11.5.

- Dangerous stabbing instruments.
  - A dangerous stabbing instrument is any object that is carried as a weapon for bodily assault or defense and that is likely to cause serious physical injury or death when used as a stabbing weapon. Some objects, such as guns or bombs, are dangerous because they are specifically designed to be dangerous. Other objects

are designed for peaceful purposes but may be used as dangerous weapons. The way an object is carried determines whether or not it is a dangerous weapon. If an object is carried for use as a stabbing weapon, and is likely to cause serious physical injury or death when used as a stabbing weapon, it is a dangerous stabbing weapon.

CJI2d 11.4.

## Elements

On the person:

1. The defendant knowingly carried a dagger; dirk, stiletto; double-edged, nonfolding stabbing instrument; or dangerous stabbing weapon. It does not matter why the defendant was carrying the weapon, but to be guilty of this crime the defendant must have known that it was a weapon.
2. This dagger; dirk; stiletto; double-edged, nonfolding stabbing instrument; or dangerous stabbing weapon was concealed. Complete invisibility is not required. A weapon is concealed if it cannot easily be seen by those who come into ordinary contact with the defendant.

CJI2d 11.2

In a vehicle:

1. The instrument or item was a dagger; dirk; stiletto; double-edged, nonfolding stabbing instrument; or dangerous stabbing weapon.
2. The instrument or item was in a vehicle that the defendant was in.
3. The defendant knew the instrument or item was in the vehicle.
4. The defendant took part in carrying or keeping the instrument or item in the vehicle.

CJI2d 11.2.

Some implements are dangerous weapons per se while others are not dangerous unless used in a manner intended to cause serious injury or carried for such a purpose. Mere proof that the defendant knew the machete he purchased and placed under the front seat of his car could be used as a dangerous weapon is insufficient to sustain a CCW charge. The prosecution must also show that an item was used for or was intended to be used for an assaultive or defensive purpose by the defendant. *People v. Brown,* 406 Mich. 215 (1979).

A homemade knife, which was pointed and ground down on both edges and discovered in possession of a prison inmate could properly be deemed a dangerous weapon per se. *People v. Grandberry,* 102 Mich. App. 769 (1980).

## Exceptions

A person is not CCW under the following circumstances:

- The person is unaware the weapon is on his person or in his vehicle. CJI2d 11.7.
- The person is carrying a hunting knife. A hunting knife is a large, heavy, wide-bladed knife with a single cutting edge that curves up to a point. It is typically used to skin and cut up game. This law does not apply to hunting knives adapted and carried as hunting knives.

CJI2d 11.9.

The defendant was charged with violating the CCW statute for carrying a five-inch, double-edged, folding knife. The defendant moved for dismissal, claiming the knife was a hunting knife. The court held, "Whether his knife was 'adapted and carried' as a hunting knife, within the meaning of the hunting knife exception to the carrying concealed weapons statute, M.C.L. § 750.227(1); M.S.A. § 28.424(1), is a secondary consideration to be addressed only upon concluding that the knife at issue is a 'hunting knife.' Then, and only then, do facts and circumstances such as, e.g., whether it was hunting season, whether defendant was hunting at the time he or she was arrested, or going to or from a hunting excursion, become relevant. However, in this case, we find that as a threshold matter defendant's knife is not a 'hunting knife.' . . . Webster's [Dictionary] includes diagrams next to its definitions for 'hunting knife,' 'dagger' and 'stiletto.' Both the dagger and stiletto are depicted as double-edged, straight-bladed knives. On the other hand, the hunting knife is shown typically as a heavy, wide-bladed knife with a single cutting edge which curves to a point. . . . To be sure, even a hunting knife can be employed as a weapon, thus, the intent of the statute is plainly to exempt only those hunting knives where defendant can show he or she was using and carrying it as a hunting knife." *People v. Payne,* 180 Mich. App. 283 (1989).

• *The person is in his house.*

In order to qualify for the dwelling house exception, the defendant must present evidence that the location where the concealed pistol was carried was the defendant's dwelling house. The defendant could not be convicted of CCW for possessing a pistol in his home regardless of the fact that he could not lawfully possess a pistol because he was a convicted felon. Lawful ownership of the pistol is not a prerequisite to the dwelling house exception to the CCW statute. The defendant could have been prosecuted under other weapons law, but not CCW. *People v. Pasha*, 466 Mich. 378 (2002).

The CCW statute does not allow a person to carrying a concealed weapon on a public easement. Exceptions to the statute were intended to allow persons to defend those areas in which they have a possessory interest. The public has superior rights over public easements and even the owner of the land beneath that easement can do nothing antagonistic to the public's right. The defendant, who was carrying a concealed handgun on an area of his driveway between the public sidewalk and the public street, was properly convicted of CCW because he did not have a possessory interest in the area between the sidewalk and roadway sufficient to come within the dwelling house exception. The defendant had no need to defend that which all are fee to use. *People v. Marrow*, 453 Mich. 903 (1996).

• *The person is at his place of business.*

A taxicab driver's taxicab is not a place of business within the meaning of the place of business exception to the CCW statute. The place of business exception is limited to business property on land. *People v. Brooks*, 87 Mich. App. 515 (1978).

The defendant was in the business of delivering produce. The defendant's van was not his place of business for purposes of the place of business exception to the CCW statute. *People v. Wallin*, 172 Mich. App. 748 (1988).

A person does not have a right to carry a concealed pistol at his employer's place of business. The defendant was employed by Dana Corporation at the time of his arrest. The nature of his employment was not clear and there was nothing to show that he had the necessary possessory interest in the business to bring him within the place of business exception. *People v. Clark*, 21 Mich. App. 712 (1970).

• *The person is on land he or she owns.*

The defendant was charged with engaging in an illegal occupation and CCW after a raid on an alleged "blind pig." The defendant leased the premises at which the raid was conducted. The defendant claimed he was in his place of business or on other land possessed by him. The undisputed evidence indicated that defendant was in his place of business or on other land possessed by him. Consequently, he was within the exception to the CCW statute. *People v. Gatt*, 77 Mich. App. 310 (1977).

## Exceptions to MCL 750.227(2) (CCW in a Vehicle)—MCL 750.231a

(1) *CCW in a vehicle does not apply to the following:*

(a) *To a person holding a valid license to carry a pistol concealed upon his or her person issued by his or her state of residence except where the pistol is carried in nonconformance with a restriction appearing on the license.*

(b) *To the regular and ordinary transportation of pistols as merchandise by an authorized agent of a person licensed to manufacture firearms.*

(c) *To a person carrying an antique firearm, completely unloaded in a closed case or container designed for the storage of firearms in the trunk of a vehicle.*

(d) *To a person while transporting a pistol for a lawful purpose that is licensed by the owner or occupant of the motor vehicle in compliance with section 2 of 1927 PA 372, MCL 28.422, and the pistol is unloaded in a closed case designed for the storage of firearms in the trunk of the vehicle.*

(e) *To a person while transporting a pistol for a lawful purpose that is licensed by the owner or occupant of the motor vehicle in compliance with section 2 of 1927 PA 372, MCL 28.422, and the pistol is unloaded in a closed case designed for the storage of firearms in a vehicle that does not have a trunk and is not readily accessible to the occupants of the vehicle.*

(2) *As used in this section, "antique firearm" means either of the following:*

(a) *A firearm not designed or redesigned for using rimfire or conventional center fire ignition with fixed ammunition and manufactured in or before 1898, including a matchlock, flintlock, percussion cap, or similar type of ignition system or replica of such a firearm, whether actually manufactured before or after 1898.*

(b) *A firearm using fixed ammunition manufactured in or before 1898, for which ammunition is no longer manufactured in the United States and is not readily available in the ordinary channels of commercial trade.*

Out-of-state concealed carry permits are invalid for Michigan residents. Residency is proved by the totality of the circumstances and can be supported by the purchase of a home in Michigan, registration of a car in Michigan, application for a Michigan driver's license, obtainment of permanent employment in Michigan. The defendant in this case was not held to be a resident because, although he had a Michigan personal identification card, he had retained his residence in Alabama, not pursued Michigan employment, and not changed his vehicle registration or driver's license. Thus, his possession of a valid Alabama concealed carry permit was a defense to CCW conviction. *People v. Williams*, 226 Mich. App. 568 (1997).

MCL 750.231a(1)(a) requires both that a valid concealed pistol license be held by a person seeking its protection and that the license was issued by a state. An out-of-state resident is required to carry a license to carry a concealed pistol when carrying a concealed pistol in Michigan, even if his or her state does not require a license to carry a concealed pistol. Another state's legislative scheme that does not require any license whatsoever being issued is insufficient to trigger the exclusion of MCL 750.231a(1)(a). *People v. Miller*, 238 Mich. App. 168 (1999).

## Self-Defense

Self-defense is not a defense for carrying a concealed weapon. CJI2d 11.8.

## Federal Law on Carrying of Concealed Firearms by Qualified Law Enforcement Officers (Law Enforcement Officers Safety Act, LEOSA)—18 USC 926B

(a) *Notwithstanding any other provision of the law of any State or any political subdivision thereof, an individual who is a qualified law enforcement officer and who is carrying the identification required by subsection (d) may carry a concealed firearm that has been shipped or transported in interstate or foreign commerce, subject to subsection (b).*

(b) *This section shall not be construed to supersede or limit the laws of any State that—*

(1) *permit private persons or entities to prohibit or restrict the possession of concealed firearms on their property; or*

(2) *prohibit or restrict the possession of firearms on any State or local government property, installation, building, base, or park.*

(c) *As used in this section, the term "qualified law enforcement officer" means an employee of a governmental agency who—*

(1) *is authorized by law to engage in or supervise the prevention, detection, investigation, or prosecution of, or the incarceration of any person for, any violation of law, and has statutory powers of arrest or apprehension under section 807(b) of title 10, United States Code (article 7(b) of the Uniform Code of Military Justice);*

(2) *is authorized by the agency to carry a firearm;*

(3) *is not the subject of any disciplinary action by the agency which could result in suspension or loss of police powers;*

(4) *meets standards, if any, established by the agency which require the employee to regularly qualify in the use of a firearm;*

(5) *is not under the influence of alcohol or another intoxicating or hallucinatory drug or substance; and*

(6) *is not prohibited by Federal law from receiving a firearm.*

(d) *The identification required by this subsection is the photographic identification issued by the governmental agency for which the individual is employed that identifies the employee as a police officer or law enforcement officer of the agency.*

(e) *As used in this section, the term "firearm"—*

(1) *except as provided in this subsection, has the same meaning as in section 921 of this title;*

(2) includes ammunition not expressly prohibited by Federal law or subject to the provisions of the National Firearms Act; and

(3) does not include—

    (A) any machinegun (as defined in section 5845 of the National Firearms Act);

    (B) any firearm silencer (as defined in section 921 of this title); and

    (C) any destructive device (as defined in section 921 of this title).

(f) For the purposes of this section, a law enforcement officer of the Amtrak Police Department, a law enforcement officer of the Federal Reserve, or a law enforcement or police officer of the executive branch of the Federal Government qualifies as an employee of a governmental agency who is authorized by law to engage in or supervise the prevention, detection, investigation, or prosecution of, or the incarceration of any person for, any violation of law, and has statutory powers of arrest or apprehension under section 807(b) of title 10, United States Code (article 7(b) of the Uniform Code of Military Justice).

A qualified law enforcement officer from any state who is carrying the required police identification may carry a concealed firearm in Michigan without registering the firearm and without a license to carry the concealed pistol. This federal statute supersedes all Michigan statutes that would prohibit a qualified law enforcement officer from carrying a concealed firearm in Michigan including, but not limited to, Michigan statutes that prohibit firearms on certain premises. This federal statute does not prevent private property owners from prohibiting or restricting firearms on their property.

## Federal Law on Carrying of Concealed Firearms by Qualified Retired Law Enforcement Officers (Law Enforcement Officers Safety Act, LEOSA)—18 USC 926C

(a) Notwithstanding any other provision of the law of any State or any political subdivision thereof, an individual who is a qualified retired law enforcement officer and who is carrying the identification required by subsection (d) may carry a concealed firearm that has been shipped or transported in interstate or foreign commerce, subject to subsection (b).

(b) This section shall not be construed to supersede or limit the laws of any State that—

(1) permit private persons or entities to prohibit or restrict the possession of concealed firearms on their property; or

(2) prohibit or restrict the possession of firearms on any State or local government property, installation, building, base, or park.

(c) As used in this section, the term "qualified retired law enforcement officer" means an individual who—

(1) separated from service in good standing from service with a public agency as a law enforcement officer;

(2) is authorized by law to engage in or supervise the prevention, detection, investigation, or prosecution of, or the incarceration of any person for, any violation of law, and has statutory powers of arrest or apprehension under section 807(b) of title 10, United States Code (article 7(b) of the Uniform Code of Military Justice);

(3) (A) before such separation, served as a law enforcement officer for an aggregate of 10 years or more; or

    (B) separated from service with such agency, after completing any applicable probationary period of such service, due to a service-connected disability, as determined by such agency;

(4) during the most recent 12-month period, has met, at the expense of the individual, the standards for qualification in firearms training for active law enforcement officers, as determined by the former agency of the individual, the State in which the individual resides or, if the State has not established such standards, either a law enforcement agency within the State in which the individual resides or the standards used by a certified firearms instructor that is qualified to conduct a firearms qualification test for active duty officers within that State;

(5) (A) has not been officially found by a qualified medical professional employed by the agency to be unqualified for reasons relating to mental health and as a result of this finding will not be issued the photographic identification as described in subsection (d)(1); or

    (B) has not entered into an agreement with the agency from which the individual is separating from service in which that individual acknowledges he or she is not qualified under this section for reasons relating to mental health and for those reasons will not receive or accept the photographic identification as described in subsection (d)(1);

(6) is not under the influence of alcohol or another intoxicating or hallucinatory drug or substance; and

(7) is not prohibited by Federal law from receiving a firearm.

(d) The identification required by this subsection is—

(1) a photographic identification issued by the agency from which the individual separated from service as a law enforcement officer that identifies the person as having been employed as a police officer or law enforcement officer and indicates that the individual has, not less recently than one year before the date the individual is carrying the concealed firearm, been tested or otherwise found by the agency to meet the active duty standards for qualification in firearms training as established by the agency to carry a firearm of the same type as the concealed firearm; or

(2) (A) a photographic identification issued by the agency from which the individual separated from service as a law enforcement officer that identifies the person as having been employed as a police officer or law enforcement officer; and

(B) a certification issued by the State in which the individual resides or by a certified firearms instructor that is qualified to conduct a firearms qualification test for active duty officers within that State that indicates that the individual has, not less than 1 year before the date the individual is carrying the concealed firearm, been tested or otherwise found by the State or a certified firearms instructor that is qualified to conduct a firearms qualification test for active duty officers within that State to have met—

(i) the active duty standards for qualification in firearms training, as established by the State, to carry a firearm of the same type as the concealed firearm; or

(ii) if the State has not established such standards, standards set by any law enforcement agency within that State to carry a firearm of the same type as the concealed firearm.

(e) As used in this section—

(1) the term "firearm"—

(A) except as provided in this paragraph, has the same meaning as in section 921 of this title;

(B) includes ammunition not expressly prohibited by Federal law or subject to the provisions of the National Firearms Act; and

(C) does not include—

(i) any machinegun (as defined in section 5845 of the National Firearms Act);

(ii) any firearm silencer (as defined in section 921 of this title); and

(iii) any destructive device (as defined in section 921 of this title).

(2) the term "service with a public agency as a law enforcement officer" includes service as a law enforcement officer of the Amtrak Police Department, service as a law enforcement officer of the Federal Reserve, or service as a law enforcement or police officer of the executive branch of the Federal Government.

---

A qualified retired law enforcement officer from any state who is carrying the required retired police identification with an indication of firearms qualification within the past year may carry a concealed firearm in Michigan without registering the firearm and without a license to carry the concealed pistol. This federal statute supersedes all Michigan statutes that would prohibit a qualified retired law enforcement officer from carrying a concealed firearm in Michigan including, but not limited to, Michigan statutes that prohibit firearms on certain premises. This federal statute does not prevent private property owners from prohibiting or restricting firearms on their property.

## Michigan Retired Law Enforcement Officer's Firearm Carry Act—MCL 28.511–28.527

The Michigan Retired Law Enforcement Officer's Firearm Carry Act establishes the requirements and procedures through which a qualified retired law enforcement officer who legally resides in Michigan may be certified by the Michigan Commission on Law Enforcement Standards (MCOLES) to carry a concealed firearm under the federal Law Enforcement Officers Safety Act (LEOSA) and this Act. This Act requires the MCOLES to issue a certificate to a qualified retired officer who complies with the active duty firearms standard and who is eligible to carry a concealed firearm under LEOSA and this Act. This Act prescribes the requirements for persons issued a certificate under the Act and imposes civil and criminal penalties for violations of the Act. Many of these requirements are the same as the requirements that apply to individuals who possess Michigan Concealed Pistol Licenses. The requirements include:

- Disclosure to a peace officer. MCL 28.517.
- Immediate reporting to MCOLES when certain circumstances occur (e.g., arrest, PPO issuance, adjudication of mental illness, positive drug test). MCL 28.518.
- Implied consent and restrictions on carrying under the influence. MCL 28.519.

## Concealed Pistol Licenses (CPL)

A Michigan resident may obtain a license to carry a pistol concealed. The following is a brief review of some of the laws affecting Concealed Pistol License (CPL) holders.

## Requirements of CPL holders when stopped by police—MCL 28.425f

- A CPL holder who is carrying a concealed pistol or a portable device that uses electro-muscular disruption technology must disclose to a peace officer immediately when stopped that he or she is carrying a pistol or a portable device that uses electro-muscular disruption technology on his or her person or in his or her vehicle. A CPL holder is not required to immediately disclose that he or she has a CPL if he or she is not in possession of a concealed pistol or a portable device that uses electro-muscular disruption technology; however, as detailed below, a CPL holder is still required to show certain documentation to a peace officer upon request. MCL 28.425f(3).

Penalties:

| First offense | State civil infraction, CPL suspended for 6 months |
|---|---|
| Second offense within 3 years | State civil infraction, CPL revoked |

- A CPL holder must possess his or her CPL when carrying a concealed pistol. A violation of this subsection is punishable as a state civil infraction and not more than a $100 fine. MCL 28.425f(1).
- Upon request by a peace officer, a CPL holder who is carrying a concealed pistol or a portable device that uses electro-muscular disruption technology shall show his or her (a) CPL and (b) driver license or Michigan personal identification card. A violation of this subsection is punishable as a state civil infraction and not more than a $100 fine. MCL 28.425f(2).

- A pistol or portable device that uses electro-muscular disruption technology carried in violation of MCL 28.425f is subject to immediate seizure by a peace officer; however, a peace officer may not seize a pistol or portable device that uses electro-muscular disruption technology if the CPL holder has his or her driver license or Michigan personal identification card in his or her possession when the violation occurs and the peace officer verified through LEIN that the individual has a valid Michigan CPL. MCL 28.425f(7).
  - If a peace officer seizes a pistol or portable device that uses electro-muscular disruption technology under this subsection, the individual has 45 days to display his or her license or documentation to the seizing law enforcement agency. If displayed within 45 days, the seizing law enforcement agency shall return the pistol or portable device that uses electro-muscular disruption technology to the individual unless the individual is prohibited by law from possessing a firearm or a portable device that uses electro-muscular disruption technology. If the individual does not display his or her license or documentation within the 45-day period, the pistol or portable device that uses electro-muscular disruption technology is subject to forfeiture as provided in MCL 28.425g.

## CPL Prohibited Premises—MCL 28.425o

A CPL holder shall not carry a concealed pistol or a portable device that uses electro-muscular disruption technology on the premises of any of the following (parking lots are excluded):

- Schools or school property, except a parent or legal guardian who is dropping off or picking child up and pistol is kept in the vehicle.
  - "School" means a public, private, denominational, or parochial school offering developmental kindergarten, kindergarten, or any grade from 1 through 12.
  - "School property" means a building, playing field, or property used for school purposes to impart instruction to children or used for functions and events sponsored by a school, except a building used primarily for adult education or college extension courses.
- Public or private child care center or day care center, public or private child caring institution, or public or private child placing agency.
- Sports arena or stadium.

- A bar or tavern where sale and consumption of liquor by the glass and consumed on the premises is the primary source of income of the business.
  - This subsection does not apply to an owner or employee of the business.
- Any property or facility owned or operated by a church, synagogue, mosque, temple, or other place of worship, unless authorized by the presiding official or officials.
- An entertainment facility that has a seating capacity of 2,500 or more.
- A hospital.
- A dormitory or classroom of a community college, college, or university.
  - This subsection only prohibits a CPL holder from carrying in a dorm or classroom; it does not prohibit possession on the entire premises.
- A casino.

Note: This section only applies if the CPL holder is carrying a **concealed pistol** or a portable device that uses electro-muscular disruption technology. If the CPL holder is carrying a non-concealed pistol or any firearm other than a pistol, this section does not apply.

Penalties:

| First offense | State civil infraction, CPL suspended for 6 months |
| Second offense | 90-day misdemeanor, CPL revoked |
| Third and subsequent offenses | 4-year felony, CPL revoked |

The above listed premises do not apply to the CPL holders who are any of the following:

- Retired police officers or retired law enforcement officers.
- Persons employed or contracted by an entity listed above to provide security services and carrying a concealed pistol on the premises is a term of employment.
- Licensed private detectives or investigators.
- Sheriff's department corrections officers.
- State police motor carrier officers or capitol security officers.
- Members of a sheriff's posse.
- Auxiliary officers or reserve officers of a police or sheriff's department.
- Parole or probation officers of the Department of Corrections.
- State court judges or retired state court judges.
- Court officers.

## Carrying While Under the Influence—MCL 28.425k

- Acceptance of a CPL constitutes implied consent to submit to a chemical test for violations of this section. This section also applies to individuals exempt from having to obtain a CPL under MCL 28.432a.
- An individual shall not carry a concealed pistol or portable device that uses electro-muscular disruption technology while he or she is under the influence of alcoholic liquor or a controlled substance or while having a bodily alcohol content of .02 grams or more per 100 milliliters of blood, per 210 liters of breath, or per 67 milliliters of urine.
- EXCEPTION: This section does not prohibit a CPL holder who has any bodily alcohol content from doing any of the following:
  - Transporting a pistol in the locked trunk of his or her motor vehicle or another motor vehicle in which he or she is a passenger. If the vehicle does not have a trunk, from transporting a pistol unloaded in a locked compartment or container that is separated from the ammunition.
  - Transporting a portable device that uses electro-muscular disruption technology in the locked trunk of his or her motor vehicle or another motor vehicle in which he or she is a passenger. If the vehicle does not have a trunk, from transporting a portable device that uses electro-muscular disruption technology in a locked compartment or container.
  - Transporting a pistol on a vessel if the pistol is unloaded in a locked compartment or container that is separated from the ammunition.
  - Transporting a portable device that uses electro-muscular disruption technology on a vessel if the portable device is in a locked compartment or container.
- A peace officer who has probable cause to believe an individual is carrying a concealed pistol or portable device that uses electro-muscular disruption technology in violation of this section may require the individual to submit to a chemical analysis of his or her breath, blood, or urine. The collection and testing of breath, blood, and urine specimens shall be conducted in the same manner alcohol and controlled substances related driving violation under the Michigan Vehicle Code.
  - If the person refuses the chemical test, the peace officer shall report the refusal in writing to the concealed weapon licensing board

that issued the license to the individual. If the person takes the chemical test and the results prove any bodily content, the peace officer shall promptly report the the results to the concealed weapon licensing board that issued the license to the individual.

- Before an individual is required to submit to a chemical analysis, the peace officer shall inform the individual of all of the following:
  - ◆ The individual may refuse to submit to the chemical analysis, but if he or she chooses to do so, the officer may obtain a court order requiring the individual to submit to a chemical analysis and the refusal may result in his or her CPL being suspended or revoked.
  - ◆ If the individual submits to the chemical analysis, he or she may obtain a chemical analysis from a person of his or her own choosing.

Penalties:

| .02 -.079 BAC | State civil infraction, CPL may be revoked for 1 year |
| .08 -.099 BAC | 93-day misdemeanor, CPL may be revoked for 3 years |
| .10 or more BAC | 93-day misdemeanor, CPL permanently revoked |

## Seizure of Pistols—MCL 28.425g

A pistol or portable device that uses electro-muscular disruption technology may be seized and forfeited for any violation of the Firearms Act, MCL 28.421–28.435, except:

- A pistol or portable device that uses electro-muscular disruption technology shall not be seized for a violation of MCL 28.425f if the CPL holder is not in possession of his or her CPL but is in possession of his or her driver's license or Michigan personal identification card and the peace officer can verify through LEIN the existence of a valid CPL. If the license cannot be verified in LEIN, the pistol may be seized and individual has 45 days to produce a license or the weapon may be forfeited.

The seizure and forfeiture of a pistol or portable device that uses electro-muscular disruption technology under this section is conducted in the same manner as property subject to seizure and forfeiture under MCL 600.4701 - 600.4709. Note: This requires that the appropriate persons are given timely notice of the seizure of the property and intent to forfeit and dispose of the property.

## Notice of Suspension—MCL 28.428

The concealed weapon licensing board may order a CPL suspended or revoked as detailed in this section. A suspension or revocation order, or an amendment to a revocation or suspension order, shall be immediately entered into LEIN.

- A suspension or revocation order is effective immediately. However, an individual is not criminally liable for violating the order or amended order unless he or she has received notice of the order or amended order.
- If an officer locates an individual who has not received notice of a suspension or revocation, the officer shall inform the person of the suspension or revocation and give him or her an opportunity to comply before an arrest is made.
- The officer shall immediately enter a statement into LEIN that notice was given.

## Persons Exempt from the Requirement to Obtain a Concealed Pistol License—MCL 28.432a

- Regularly employed police officers.
- MCOLES certified constables.
- Michigan Department of Corrections employees while performing duties, or going to or from those duties (must have written authorization of the MDOC director).
- Local corrections officers while on duty (must have written authorization of sheriff or police chief).
- Members of the military while on duty or while going to or from duty.
- A resident of another state licensed by his or her state of residence to carry a concealed pistol.
- Firearms manufacturers and their agents when the pistol is being transported as merchandise.
- A person transporting an unloaded pistol in a wrapper or container in the trunk of his or her vehicle or, if the vehicle does not have a trunk, from transporting an unloaded pistol in a locked compartment or container that is separated from the ammunition from any of the following:
  - ◆ The place of purchase to his or her home or place of business.
  - ◆ A place of repair or back to his or her home or place of business.
  - ◆ In moving good from one place of abode or business to another place of abode or business.
  - ◆ *See also* MCL 750.231a.
- A Canadian police officer.

## Carrying Dangerous Weapon with Unlawful Intent—MCL 750.226 (felony)

*It is unlawful for a person, with intent to use the same unlawfully against the person of another, to go armed with a pistol or other firearm or dagger, dirk, razor, stiletto, or knife having a blade over 3 inches in length, or any other dangerous or deadly weapon or instrument.*

### Elements

1. The defendant went armed with a dangerous weapon.
2. At that time, the defendant intended to use the weapon unlawfully against someone else.
CJI2d 11.17.

A dangerous weapon is any object that is used in a way that is likely to cause serious physical injury or death. Some objects, such as guns or bombs, are dangerous because they are specifically designed to be dangerous. Other objects are designed for peaceful purposes, but may be used as dangerous weapons. The way an object is used or intended to be used in an assault determines whether or not it is a dangerous weapon. If an object is used in a way that is likely to cause serious physical injury or death, it is a dangerous weapon. CJI2d 11.19.

A dangerous weapon under this statute may be either a weapon designed and used to be dangerous or an object used as a dangerous weapon. An object the victim believes is dangerous, but is otherwise harmless and not employed in a dangerous manner is not a dangerous weapon (e.g., a toy gun shooting caps is not a dangerous weapon merely because the victim believes it to be dangerous, a screwdriver used as a knife to stab someone is a dangerous weapon). *People v. Barkley*, 151 Mich. App. 234 (1986).

In prosecutions under MCL 750.226 involving a knife, an element of the crime is that the blade of the knife be over three inches in length. Lack of such proof invalidates a conviction. *People v. Parker*, 288 Mich. App. 500 (2010).

### Difference between CCW and Carrying with Unlawful Intent

Under the CCW statute, MCL 750.227, the offense is carrying the weapon concealed and the reason for carrying it is immaterial. CCW is also restricted to pistols, double-edged nonfolding knives, and other dangerous stabbing instruments. Under the

carrying with unlawful intent statute, MCL 750.226, the weapon could be any object that may be used as a dangerous weapon. The reason for carrying the weapon is material, as the suspect must have unlawful intent.

## Mechanical Knife—MCL 750.226a (1-year misdemeanor)

*It is unlawful for a person to sell or offer to sell, or have in his or her possession any knife having the appearance of a pocket knife, the blade or blades of which can be opened by the flick of a button, pressure on a handle or other mechanical contrivance.*

*The provisions of this section do not apply to any one-armed person carrying a knife on his person in connection with his living requirements.*

### Elements

1. The defendant sold, offered for sale, or possessed a knife.
2. The knife looked like a pocket knife, but had a blade that could be opened mechanically by the flick of a button, pressure on the handle, or other mechanical device.
3. A pocket knife is a knife that is made so that the blade can be folded into the handle for carrying.
CJI2d 11.28.

A switchblade concealed upon a person may be prosecuted under this statute or under CCW. *People v. Czerwinski*, 99 Mich. App. 304 (1980).

## Long Gun Violations

### Transporting Loaded Firearms in Vehicles—MCL 750.227c (2-year misdemeanor)

*Except as otherwise permitted by law, a person shall not transport or possess in or upon a sailboat or a motor vehicle, aircraft, motorboat, or any other vehicle propelled by mechanical means, a firearm, other than a pistol, which is loaded.*

Knowledge that the weapon is loaded is not a necessary element. The person who transports a firearm must inspect it before transporting it. The defendant was guilty of transporting or possessing a loaded rifle in a vehicle, although, the people presented no evidence regarding who actually placed the rifle in the defendant's vehicle. *People v. Quinn*, 440 Mich. 178 (1992).

## Transporting Unloaded Firearms in Vehicles—MCL 750.227d (90-day misdemeanor)

*Except as otherwise permitted by law, a person shall not transport or possess in or upon a motor vehicle or any self-propelled vehicle designed for land travel a firearm, other than a pistol, unless the firearm is unloaded and is one or more of the following:*

*(a) Taken down.*
*(b) Enclosed in a case.*
*(c) Carried in the trunk of the vehicle.*
*(d) Inaccessible from the interior of the vehicle.*

## Exceptions to Weapons Violations for Certain Individuals—MCL 750.231

- MCL 750.224 (unlawful weapons).
- MCL 750.224a (tasers and stun guns).
- MCL 750.224b (short-barreled shotguns or rifles).
- MCL 750.224d (self-defense spray or foam device).
- MCL 750.226a (mechanical knife).
- MCL 750.227 (CCW).
- MCL 750.227c (transporting or possessing a loaded firearm in a vehicle).
- MCL 750.227d (transporting or possessing an unloaded firearm in a vehicle).

The above listed statutes do not apply to any of the following (for MCL 750.224a(1), the person must be trained on the use, effects, and risks of using the portable device or weapon):

- A police officer of a duly authorized police agency of the United States, of this state, or of any political subdivision of this state, who is regularly employed and paid by the United States, this state, or a political subdivision of this state.
- Department of Corrections officers when given a letter from their director and when on official business (includes private vendors operating a correctional facility).
- Military personnel when in performance of duties.
- An organization authorized by law to purchase or receive weapons from the United States or from this state.
- Michigan State Police Capital Security Officers.
- Michigan State Police Motor Carrier Officers.

## Brandishing a Firearm in Public—MCL 750.234e (90-day misdemeanor)

*Except as provided below, a person shall not knowingly brandish a firearm in public.*

*This statute does not apply to any of the following:*

*(a) A peace officer lawfully performing his or her duties as a peace officer.*
*(b) A person lawfully engaged in hunting.*
*(c) A person lawfully engaged in target practice.*
*(d) A person lawfully engaged in the sale, purchase, repair, or transfer of that firearm.*

A person, when carrying a handgun in a holster in plain view, is not waving or displaying the firearm in a threatening manner. Thus, such conduct does not constitute brandishing a firearm in violation of MCL 750.234e. OAG 2001-2002, No 7,101, p 80 (February 6, 2002).

## Possession of Firearm in Public by Person Under 18 Years Old—MCL 750.234f (90-day misdemeanor)

*An individual less than 18 years of age shall not possess a firearm in pblic except under the direct supervision of an individual 18 years of age or older.*

This section does not apply to the following:

- A person in possession of a valid hunting license and following DNR regulations.
- A person going to a target range or trap or skeet shooting ground if, while going to and from the range or ground, the firearm is enclosed in a case or locked in the trunk.

## Prohibited Places to Possess Firearm—MCL 750.234d (90-day misdemeanor)

A person is prohibited from possessing a firearm on the premises of any of the following:

- A depository financial institution (e.g., bank or credit union).
- A church or other house of religious worship.
- A court.
- A theatre.
- A sports arena.
- A day care center.
- A hospital.
- An establishment licensed under the Liquor Control Code.

This section does not apply to the following persons:

- The owner or a person hired as security, if the firearm is possessed for the purpose of providing security.
- A peace officer.

- A person with a valid CPL issued by any state.
- A person with permission of the owner or an agent of the owner.

Note: Valid CPL holders are exempt from MCL 750.234d and cannot be lawfully arrested for violating MCL 750.234d. Furthermore, the prohibited premises listed in MCL 28.425o only apply to CPL holders when they are carrying <u>concealed</u> pistols or portable devices that use electro-muscular disruption technology.

## Weapon Free School Zone Violations—MCL 750.237a

*School:*   A public, private, denominational, or parochial school offering developmental kindergarten, kindergarten, or any grade from 1 through 12.

*School property:*   A building, playing field, or property used for school purposes to impart instruction to children or used for functions and events sponsored by a school, except a building used primarily for adult education or college extension courses.

*Weapon free school zone:*   School property and a vehicle used by a school to transport students to or from school property.

An individual who possesses a weapon in a weapon free school zone is guilty of a misdemeanor punishable by not more than 93 days imprisonment; however, this prohibition does not apply to the following individuals:

- An individual employed or contracted by the school (if the weapon is possessed for the purposes of providing security).
- A peace officer.
- A person with a valid CPL issued by any state.
- An individual who possess a weapon provided by a school or a school's instructor for purposes of providing or receiving instruction in the use of the weapon.
- An individual who possesses a firearm with the permission of the school's principal or an agent of the school designated by the school's principal or board.
- An individual 18 years of age or older who is not a student at the school and who possesses a firearm on school property while dropping off or picking up a student if certain conditions apply.

Note: Valid CPL holders are exempt from MCL 750.237a(4) and cannot be lawfully arrested for violating this subsection by carrying a firearm in a weapon free school zone. However, a CPL holder carrying a concealed pistol in a school or on school property may be in violation of MCL 28.425o.

An individual who violates MCL 750.224, 750.224b, 750.224c, 750.224e, 750.226, 750.227, 750.227a, 750.227f, 750.234a, 750.234b, or 750.234c, or who violates MCL 750.232(2) for a second or subsequent time, in a weapon free school zone is guilty of a felony punishable by not more than the maximum term of imprisonment authorized for the section violated.

An individual who violates MCL 750.223(1), 750.224d, 750.226a, 750.227c, 750.227d, 750.231c, 750.232a(1), 750.232a(4), 750.233, 750.234, 750.234e, 750.234f, 750.235, 750.236, or 750.237, or 750.223(2) for the first time, in a weapon free school zone is guilty of a misdemeanor punishable by not more than the maximum term of imprisonment authorized for the section violated or 93 days, whichever is greater.

## Parent of Minor and Weapon Free School Zone Violations—MCL 750.235a (90-day misdemeanor)

The parent of a minor (less than 18 years of age) is guilty of a misdemeanor if all of the following apply:

- The parent has custody of the minor.
- The minor violates the Firearms chapter of the Michigan Penal Code in a weapon free school zone.
- The parent knows that the minor would violate the Firearms Chapter of the Michigan Penal Code or the parent acts to further the violation.

It is a complete defense to prosecution under this section if the parent promptly notifies local law enforcement or the school administration that the minor is violating or will violate the Firearms chapter of the Michigan Penal Code in a weapon free school zone.

## Possession of Firearm During Commission of Felony (Felony Firearm)—MCL 750.227b (felony)

*(1) A person who carries or has in his or her possession a firearm when he or she commits or attempts to commit a felony, except a violation of section 223, section 227, 227a or 230, is guilty of a felony, and shall be imprisoned for 2 years. Upon a second conviction under this section, the person shall be imprisoned for 5 years. Upon a third or subsequent conviction under this subsection, the person shall be imprisoned for 10 years.*

*(2) A term of imprisonment prescribed by this section is in addition to the sentence imposed for the conviction of the felony or the attempt to commit the felony, and shall be served con-*

*secutively with and preceding any term of imprisonment imposed for the conviction of the felony or attempt to commit the felony.*

*(3) A term of imprisonment imposed under this section shall not be suspended. The person subject to the sentence mandated by this section is not eligible for parole or probation during the mandatory term imposed pursuant to subsection (1).*

*(4) This section does not apply to a law enforcement officer who is authorized to carry a firearm while in the official performance of his or her duties, and who is in the performance of those duties. As used in this subsection, "law enforcement officer" means a person who is regularly employed as a member of a duly authorized police agency or other organization of the United States, this state, or a city, county, township, or village of this state, and who is responsible for the prevention and detection of crime and the enforcement of the general criminal laws of this state.*

## Elements

1. The defendant committed or attempted to commit a felony. It is not necessary, however, that the defendant be convicted of that crime.
2. At the time the defendant committed or attempted to commit a felony, he or she knowingly carried or possessed a firearm.

CJI2d 11.34.

First-degree home invasion, where there is a larceny of a firearm during a residential breaking and entering, can be the predicate felony for a felony-firearm conviction. *People v. Shipley*, 256 Mich. App. 367 (2003).

## Operability Not Required

There is no requirement that the firearm be "operable" or "reasonably or readily repairable." For purposes of the felony-firearms statute, a weapon is a firearm if it is the type of weapon that was designed or intended to propel a dangerous projectile by an explosive, gas, or air. The design and construction of the weapon, rather than its state of operability, are relevant in determining whether it is a firearm. *People v. Peals*, 476 Mich. 636 (2006).

## Actual or Constructive Possession

Possession of a firearm can be actual or constructive, joint or exclusive. "[A] person has constructive possession if there is proximity to the article together with indicia of control. Put another way, a defendant has constructive possession of a firearm if the location of the weapon is known and it is reasonably accessible to the defendant."

Evidence indicated that the police seized the rifles from the corner of the front room of the house, in the vicinity of where Johnson was seated behind the table that contained marijuana. Johnson admitted that he had been selling marijuana from the house for a month. He contends that there was no evidence that the weapons were in plain sight and no proof that they were his. However, the sizes of the rifles and the testimony describing their location in the corner of the front room, coupled with the fact that Johnson had admittedly been selling drugs from the house for a month, were sufficient to enable the jury to rationally find that he was aware of the rifles and that they were reasonably accessible to him. Thus, there was sufficient evidence that Johnson constructively possessed the rifles to support his felony-firearm conviction. *People v. Johnson*, 293 Mich. App. 79 (2011).

In a prosecution for delivery of a controlled substance and for felony-firearm, with respect to the element of possession of a firearm, the question would be whether the offender possessed a firearm at the time of the delivery. However, when a defendant is prosecuted for possession of a controlled substance and felony-firearm, the inquiry would be whether the offender possessed the firearm at the time he possessed the controlled substance. In this case, felony-firearm charges were upheld where officers located two handguns on top of a dresser and within three feet of a drawer that contained cocaine. *People v. Burgenmeyer*, 461 Mich. 431 (2000).

## Felon in Possession of Firearm or Ammunition— MCL 750.224f (felony)

*(1) Except as provided in subsection (2), a person convicted of a felony shall not possess, use, transport, sell, purchase, carry, ship, receive,*

or distribute a firearm in this state until the expiration of 3 years after all of the following circumstances exist:

(a) The person has paid all fines imposed for the violation.

(b) The person has served all terms of imprisonment imposed for the violation.

(c) The person has successfully completed all conditions of probation or parole imposed for the violation.

(2) A person convicted of a specified felony shall not possess, use, transport, sell, purchase, carry, ship, receive, or distribute a firearm in this state until all of the following circumstances exist:

(a) The expiration of 5 years after all of the following circumstances exist:

(i) The person has paid all fines imposed for the violation.

(ii) The person has served all terms of imprisonment imposed for the violation.

(iii) The person has successfully completed all conditions of probation or parole imposed for the violation.

(b) The person's right to possess, use, transport, sell, purchase, carry, ship, receive, or distribute a firearm has been restored under section 4 of 1927 PA 372, MCL 28.424.

(3) Except as provided in subsection (4), a person convicted of a felony shall not possess, use, transport, sell, carry, ship, or distribute ammunition in this state until the expiration of 3 years after all of the following circumstances exist:

(a) The person has paid all fines imposed for the violation.

(b) The person has served all terms of imprisonment imposed for the violation.

(c) The person has successfully completed all conditions of probation or parole imposed for the violation.

(4) A person convicted of a specified felony shall not possess, use, transport, sell, carry, ship, or distribute ammunition in this state until all of the following circumstances exist:

(a) The expiration of 5 years after all of the following circumstances exist:

(i) The person has paid all fines imposed for the violation.

(ii) The person has served all terms of imprisonment imposed for the violation.

(iii) The person has successfully completed all conditions of probation or parole imposed for the violation.

(b) The person's right to possess, use, transport, sell, purchase, carry, ship, receive, or distribute ammunition has been restored under section 4 of 1927 PA 372, MCL 28.424.

(5) A person who possesses, uses, transports, sells, purchases, carries, ships, receives, or distributes a firearm in violation of this section is guilty of a felony punishable by imprisonment for not more than 5 years or a fine of not more than $5,000.00, or both.

(6) A person who possesses, uses, transports, sells, carries, ships, or distributes ammunition in violation of this section is guilty of a felony punishable by imprisonment for not more than 5 years or a fine of not more than $5,000.00, or both.

(7) Any single criminal transaction where a person possesses, uses, transports, sells, carries, ships, or distributes ammunition in violation of this section, regardless of the amount of ammunition involved, constitutes 1 offense.

(8) This section does not apply to a conviction that has been expunged or set aside, or for which the person has been pardoned, unless the expunction, order, or pardon expressly provides that the person shall not possess a firearm or ammunition.

(9) As used in this section:

(a) "Ammunition" means any projectile that, in its current state, may be expelled from a firearm by an explosive.

(b) "Felony" means a violation of a law of this state, or of another state, or of the United States that is punishable by imprisonment for 4 years or more, or an attempt to violate such a law.

(10) As used in subsections (2) and (4), "specified felony" means a felony in which 1 or more of the following circumstances exist:

(a) An element of that felony is the use, attempted use, or threatened use of physical force against the person or property of another, or that by its nature, involves a substantial risk that physical force against the person or property of another may be used in the course of committing the offense.

(b) An element of that felony is the unlawful manufacture, possession, importation, exportation, distribution, or dispensing of a controlled substance.

(c) An element of that felony is the unlawful possession or distribution of a firearm.

*(d) An element of that felony is the unlawful use of an explosive.*

*(e) The felony is burglary of an occupied dwelling, or breaking and entering an occupied dwelling, or arson.*

Note: As detailed in (9)(b) above, for purposes of this section, a felony means a violation of a law of this state, or of another state, or of the Unites States that is punishable by imprisonment for four or more years, or an attempt to violate a law that is punishable by imprisonment for four or more years. Accordingly, a person convicted of a two-year felony or convicted of attempting to commit a two-year felony is not prohibited from possessing a firearm or ammunition under this section

This section prohibits a person from possessing, using, transporting, selling, or receiving a firearm or ammunition within certain time frames after being convicted of a felony. For a person convicted of a felony, except a specified-felony as discussed below, three years must have passed since all fines were paid, all imprisonment served, and any terms of probation or parole have been completed before the person is eligible to possess a firearm or ammunition. Once the three year time period has passed, the person's rights to possess a firearm or ammunition under Michigan law are automatically restored. For a person convicted of a specified felony, five years must has passed since all fines were paid, all imprisonment served, and any terms of probation or parole have been completed before the person is eligible to possess a firearm or ammunition. In addition to the five-year time period, a person convicted of a specified felony must have his or her rights to possess a firearm or ammunition restored by a concealed weapons licensing board before the person is eligible to possess a firearm or ammunition.

## Elements—3-year time period

1. The defendant possessed, used, transported, sold, or received a firearm or ammunition in this state.
2. The defendant was convicted of a felony as defined in MCL 750.224f(9)(a).
3. Less than 3 years had passed since all fines were paid, all imprisonment was served, and all terms of probation or parole were successfully completed.
CJI2d 11.38.

## Elements—5-year time period

1. The defendant possessed, used, transported, sold, or received a firearm or ammunition in this state.

2. The defendant was convicted of a specified felony as defined in MCL 750.224f(10).
3. Less than 5 years had passed since all fines were paid, all imprisonment was served, and all terms of probation or parole were successfully completed.
4. The defendant's right to possess, use, transport, sell, and receive a firearm or ammunition have not been restored pursuant to Michigan law.
CJI2d 11.38a.

A five-year time period applies to the following specified felonies:

- Element of the felony includes the use, attempted use, or threatened use of physical force against the person or property of another, or substantial risk that physical force against the person or property of another may be used in the course of committed the offense.
- Controlled substance violation.
- Unlawful possession or distribution of firearm.
- Unlawful use of explosive.
- Breaking and entering of occupied dwelling.
- Arson.

## Specified Felony

Attempted breaking and entering of an unoccupied structure, MCL 750.110, is a specified felony in that it involves attempted use or threated use of force against property of another. By its nature, breaking and entering involves the use of physical force, or the substantial risk that physical force may be used, against the property of another in the commission of the offense. *Tuggle v. Dept. of State Police*, 269 Mich. App. 657 (2005).

The defendant was convicted in 1975 of breaking and entering a sporting goods store in violation of MCL 750.110. The defendant was subject to prosecution in 2004 for felon in possession of a firearm because he never had his firearm rights restored by his local county concealed weapons licensing board. *People v. Pierce*, 272 Mich. App. 394 (2006).

By its nature, larceny from the person, MCL 750.357, involves a substantial or considerable risk that physical force will be used and, thus, is a specified felony subjecting persons convicted of such felonies to the additional requirement of obtaining a firearm rights restoration by a concealed weapons licensing board. *People v. Perkins*, 473 Mich. 626 (2005).

If a person is convicted of an attempted violation of law, and that attempt involved the unlawful manufacture, possession, importation, exportation, distribution, or dispensing of a control substance, then the individual has been convicted of a specified felony. The defendant's conviction for attempted possession of cocaine qualifies as a conviction for a specified felony within the meaning of the felon in possession statute. *People v. Parker*, 230 Mich. App. 677 (1998)

## Operability Not Required

A handgun need not be currently operable in order to qualify as a firearm for purposes of the felony-firearm statute. *People v. Brown*, 249 Mich. App. 382 (2002).

A firearm does not have to be operable in order to support a conviction for felon in possession or possession of a firearm during the commission of a felony. The relevant statute (MCL 750.222) does not require that a firearm be operable. Instead, it focuses on what the firearm was designed to do. *People v. Peals*, 476 Mich. 636 (2006).

## Possession

Th defendant was convicted of breaking into the home of a senior couple during which the 70-year-old victim armed himself with a gun after realizing the possibility of an intruder. The defendant assaulted the victim and he jointly possessed the firearm when he placed both hands on the gun as he attempted to take it from the victim. "The essential question is one of control. . . . During the struggle, [the defendant] had both of his hands on the gun, repeatedly tried to take it away, and directed [the victim] to 'give it up.' . . . As [the defendant] attempted to gain sole possession of the gun, it discharged and [the victim] was shot. Viewed in a light most favorable to the prosecution, the evidence was sufficient to permit a rational trier of fact to reasonably infer that [the defendant] possessed the [firearm]." *People v. Strickland*, 293 Mich. App. 393 (2011).

## Return of Convicted Felon's Firearms

During the execution of a search warrant at the defendant's home, police lawfully seized 87 firearms. Of these, the defendant lawfully owned 86, but he illegally possessed one short-barreled shotgun. The defendant was convicted of possession of a short-barreled shotgun and one count of felony-firearm. The defendant moved to have all of his lawfully owned firearms, which were still in the police department's possession, returned to his mother as his Durable Power of Attorney.

MCL 750.224f suspends a convicted felon's ability to actually or constructively possess firearm or engage in any of the other prohibited activities listed in the statute, but it does not sever his or her ownership interest in the firearms. Although not in actual possession, a person has constructive possession if he knowingly has the power and the intention at a given time to exercise dominion or control over a thing, either directly or through another person. If the defendant designates an agent to possess the firearms on his behalf and the agent does so, the defendant is in violation of MCL 750.224f(2) because a sufficient nexus would remain between defendant and the firearms. A power of attorney suggests the existence of an agency relationship.

Unlike an agent, a bailee by definition remains free from the felon's control. In this case, the police department became a constructive bailee of the defendant's lawfully owned firearms. The police department may turn over the firearms to a third party, including the defendant's mother, to assume possession of the firearms as a bailee and not an agent. If the defendant's mother acted as a bailee, and not a power of attorney, the defendant would have no control over the firearms. The circuit court may order the police department to turn the firearms over to an appointed successor bailee as long as the order is clear that the nature of the relationship between defendant and the successor is that of a bailment and that defendant must have no control over or access to the firearms. The successor bailee may not engage in any actions that would destroy defendant's ownership rights in the guns, such as selling them. If no replacement bailee is willing to hold the firearms in accordance with the conditions outlined by the court, then the police department may retain possession as constructive bailee until defendant is lawfully entitled to possession of his firearms. *People v. Minch*, 493 Mich. 87 (2012).

## Possession of Firearm While Intoxicated—MCL 750.237 (93-day misdemeanor)

(1) *An individual shall not carry, have in possession or under control, or use in any manner or discharge a firearm under any of the following circumstances:*

   (a) *The individual is under the influence of alcoholic liquor, a controlled substance, or a combination of alcoholic liquor and a controlled substance.*

   (b) *The individual has an alcohol content of 0.08 or more grams per 100 milliliters of blood, per 210 liters of breath, or per 67 milliliters of urine.*

   (c) *Because of the consumption of alcoholic liquor, a controlled substance, or a combination of alcoholic liquor and a controlled substance, the individual's ability to use a firearm is visibly impaired.*

   . . . .

(5) *A peace officer who has probable cause to believe an individual violated subsection (1) may require the individual to submit to a chemical analysis of his or her breath, blood, or urine. However, an individual who is afflicted with hemophilia, diabetes, or a condition requiring the use of an anticoagulant under the direction of a physician is not required to submit to a chemical analysis of his or her blood.*

(6) *Before an individual is required to submit to a chemical analysis under subsection (5), the peace officer shall inform the individual of all of the following:*

   (a) *The individual may refuse to submit to the chemical analysis, but if he or she refuses, the officer may obtain a court order requiring the individual to submit to a chemical analysis.*

   (b) *If the individual submits to the chemical analysis, he or she may obtain a chemical analysis from a person of his or her own choosing.*

(7) *The failure of a peace officer to comply with the requirements of subsection (6) does not render the results of a chemical analysis inadmissible as evidence in a criminal prosecution for violating this section, in a civil action arising out of a violation of this section, or in any administrative proceeding arising out of a violation of this section.*

(8) *The collection and testing of breath, blood, or urine specimens under this section shall be conducted in the same manner as O.W.I./OUID.*

(9) *Subject may be charged with other violations that arise out of the same transaction.*

Penalties:

| If causes no injury | 93-day misdemeanor |
|---|---|
| If causes serious impairment of a body function of another individual | 5-year felony |
| If causes the death of another individual by the discharge or use in any manner of a firearm | 15-year felony |

Officers were dispatched to a disturbance call where the defendant had been arguing with another subject. Officers were told the defendant had been drinking and was inside his house with a gun. He was subsequently arrested for the possession of a firearm while intoxicated charge. The court held that arresting the defendant for possession of a firearm while intoxicated violated the defendant's Second Amendment rights where the defendant's conduct took place within his home and there was no evidence that he was committing any other crime. The court noted that when he was arrested, the defendant only constructively possessed the handgun; there was no actual possession. The government cannot justify infringing on defendant's Second Amendment right to possess a handgun in his home simply because defendant was intoxicated in the general vicinity of the firearm. *People v. Deroche*, 299 Mich. App. 301 (2013).

## Hunting with Firearm While Intoxicated—MCL 750.167a (90-day misdemeanor)

A person shall not be drunk or intoxicated while hunting with a firearm or other weapon under a valid hunting license. Upon conviction, the firearm must be turned over to DNR and the person's shall not apply for or possess a hunting license for a period of three years.

## Altering, Removing, or Obliterating the Serial Number from a Firearm—MCL 750.230 (felony)

*A person who shall willfully alter, remove, or obliterate the name of the maker, model, manufacturer's number, or other mark of identity of a pistol or other firearm, shall be guilty of a felony, punishable by imprisonment for not more than 2 years or fine of not more than $1,000.00. Possession of a firearm upon which the number shall have been altered, removed, or obliterated, other than an antique* *firearm as defined by section 231a(2)(a) or (b), shall be presumptive evidence that the possessor has altered, removed, or obliterated the same.*

The portion of this statute which makes the possession of a firearm on which identifying numbers altered, removed, or obliterated presumptive evidence that the possessor has altered, removed, or obliterated the identifying numbers is unconstitutional. *People v. Moore*, 402 Mich. 538 (1978).

### Selling Firearms and Ammunition—MCL 750.223

To sell means to transfer possession, give, or loan to someone else. It does not matter whether what is sold has any value. CJI2d 11.32.

To offer to sell means to offer to transfer possession, give, or loan to someone else. It does not matter whether what is offered has any value or whether anything is to be received in exchange. CJI2d 11.33.

### Selling Pistol without Complying with License to Purchase Requirements—MCL 750.223(1) (90-day misdemeanor)

A person shall not knowingly sell a pistol without complying with the license to purchase a pistol requirements proscribed in MCL 28.422.

### Selling a Firearm to a Minor—MCL 750.223(2)

A person shall not knowingly sell a firearm longer than 26 inches in length to a person less than 18 years old.

Penalties:

| First offense | 90-day misdemeanor |
| --- | --- |
| Second or subsequent offense | Felony |

It is an affirmative defense to a prosecution under this subsection that the person who sold the firearm asked to see and was shown a driver's license or identification card issued by a state that identified the purchaser as being 18 years of age or older.

### Selling Firearm or Ammunition under Certain Circumstances—MCL 750.223(3) (felony)

A seller shall not sell a firearm or ammunition to a person if the seller knows the person is under indictment for a felony or the person is prohibited from possessing, using, transporting, selling, purchasing, carrying, shipping, receiving, or distributing a firearm

under MCL 750.224f. For purposes of this subdivision, "felony" means a crime punishable by imprisonment for four years or more.

### Spring Guns—MCL 750.236 (1-year misdemeanor)

A person shall not set any spring or other gun, or any trap or device operated by the firing or explosion of gunpowder or any other explosive, and leave or permit the same to be left, except in the presence of some competent person. If death results from a violation of this section, the person is guilty of manslaughter.

### Signaling Device—MCL 750.231c (90-day misdemeanor)

*Approved signaling device:* A pistol which is a signaling device approved by the U.S. Coast Guard pursuant to regulations issued under former § 4488 of the Revised Statutes of the United States, 46 U.S.C. Appx. 481, or under former § 5 of the Federal Boat Safety Act of 1971, Public Law 92-75, 46 U.S.C. 1454.

A person may possess an approved signaling device only under the following circumstances:

- If the possession is part of marketing or manufacturing and the device is unloaded.
- The device is on a vessel or airplane (a vessel is a watercraft used for transportation on water).
- The device is at a person's residence.
- The person is en route from the place of purchase to his residence, vessel, or aircraft. The device must be unloaded and enclosed in a case and either in a trunk or not readily accessible to the occupants.

A person shall not use an approved signaling device unless he or she reasonably believes that its use is necessary for the safety of the person or of another person on the waters of this state or in an aircraft emergency situation. Violation is a 90-day misdemeanor.

Sections MCL 750.223, 750.227, 750.228, 750.232, 750.232a, and 750.237 do not apply to an approved signaling device

### Intentionally Aiming Firearm without Malice—MCL 750.233 (90-day misdemeanor)

*A person who intentionally but without malice points or aims a firearm at or toward another person is guilty of a misdemeanor punishable by imprisonment for not more than 93 days or a fine of not more than $500.00, or both.*

This section does not apply to a peace officer of this state or another state, or of a local unit of government of this state or another state, or of the United States, performing his or her duties as a peace officer. As used in this section, "peace officer" means that term as defined in MCL 750.215.

The defendant intentionally pointed the gun at or toward another person, but without intending to threaten or harm anyone. CJI2d 11.23.

## Discharge of Firearm While Intentionally Aimed without Malice—MCL 750.234 (1-year misdemeanor)

*A person who discharges a firearm while it is intentionally but without malice aimed at or toward another person, without injuring another person, is guilty of a misdemeanor punishable by imprisonment for not more than 1 year or a fine of not more than $500.00, or both.*

This section does not apply to a peace officer of this state or another state, or of a local unit of government of this state or another state, or of the United States, performing his or her duties as a peace officer. As used in this section, "peace officer" means that term as defined in MCL 750.215.

### Elements

1. The defendant pointed a gun at or towards another person.
2. The defendant intended to point the gun, but did not intend to threaten or harm anyone.
3. While pointing the gun, the defendant discharged it, but no one was injured.

CJI2d 11.24.

## Discharge of Firearm Causing Injury While Intentionally Aimed without Malice—MCL 750.235 (1-year misdemeanor)

*A person who maims or injures another person by discharging a firearm pointed or aimed intentionally but without malice at another person is guilty of a misdemeanor punishable by imprisonment for not more than 1 year or a fine of not more than $500.00, or both.*

This section does not apply to a peace officer of this state or another state, or of a local unit of government of this state or another state, or of the United States, performing his or her duties as a peace officer.

As used in this section, "peace officer" means that term as defined in MCL 750.215.

### Elements

1. The defendant pointed a gun at or towards another person.
2. The defendant intended to point the gun, but did not intend to threaten or harm anyone.
3. While pointing the gun, the defendant discharged it and injured the other person.

CJI2d 11.24.

## Careless, Reckless, or Negligent Use of Firearm Causing Injury or Death—MCL 752.861 (felony)

*Any person who, because of carelessness, recklessness or negligence, but not wilfully or wantonly, shall cause or allow any firearm under his immediate control, to be discharged so as to kill or injure another person, shall be guilty of a misdemeanor, punishable by imprisonment in the state prison for not more than 2 years, or by a fine of not more than $2,000.00, or by imprisonment in the county jail for not more than 1 year, in the discretion of the court.*

### Elements

1. Someone was injured or killed.
2. The injury or death was caused by the discharge of a gun.
3. Either of the following:
   a. The gun was discharged by the defendant.
   b. At the time of the discharge the gun was under the immediate control of the defendant and that the defendant caused or allowed the gun to be discharged.
4. The discharge was the result of the defendant's carelessness, recklessness, or negligence.

CJI2d 11.20.

## Reckless or Wanton Use of Firearm—MCL 752.863a (90-day misdemeanor)

*Any person who shall recklessly or heedlessly or wilfully or wantonly use, carry, handle or discharge any firearm without due caution and circumspection for the rights, safety or property of others shall be guilty of a misdemeanor.*

The defendant recklessly, heedlessly, willfully, or wantonly used, carried, handled, or fired a gun without reasonable caution for the rights, safety, or property of others. CJI2d 11.26.

This statute is not contained in the Firearms chapter of the Michigan Penal Code. The forfeiture provision detailed in MCL 750.239 that provides for the forfeiture of firearms that are carried, possessed, or used contrary to the Firearms chapter of the Michigan Penal Code does not apply to this statute. *People v. Switras*, 217 Mich. App. 142 (1996).

## Discharge of a Firearm From a Motor Vehicle—MCL 750.234a (felony)

*[A]n individual who intentionally discharges a firearm from a motor vehicle, a snowmobile, or an off-road vehicle in such a manner as to endanger the safety of another individual is guilty of a felony, punishable by imprisonment for not more than 4 years, or a fine of not more than $2,000.00, or both.*

This section does not apply to a peace officer of this state or another state, or of a local unit of government of this state or another state, or of the United States, performing his or her duties as a peace officer. As used in this section, "peace officer" means that term as defined in MCL 750.215. This section also does not apply to a person who discharges a firearm in self-defense or defense of another individual.

### Elements

1. The defendant discharged a firearm.
2. The defendant did so intentionally, that is, on purpose.
3. The defendant did so from a motor vehicle, snowmobile, or off-road vehicle.
4. The defendant did so in a way that endangered someone else.

CJI2d 11.37.

## Discharge of Firearm at Dwelling or Occupied Structure—MCL 750.234b (felony)

(1) *[A]n individual who intentionally discharges a firearm at a facility that he or she knows or has reason to believe is a dwelling or an occupied structure is guilty of a felony, punishable by imprisonment for not more than 4 years, or a fine of not more than $2,000.00, or both.*

(2) *An individual who intentionally discharges a firearm in a facility that he or she knows or has reason to believe is an occupied structure in reckless disregard for the safety of any individual is guilty of a felony, punishable by imprisonment for not more than 4 years, or a fine of not more than $2,000.00, or both*

*Dwelling:*    A facility habitually used as a place of abode.

*Occupied structure:*    A facility where one or more persons are present. This section does not apply to a peace officer of this state or another state, or of a local unit of government of this state or another state, or of the United States, performing his or her duties as a peace officer. As used in this section, "peace officer" means that term as defined in MCL 750.215. This section also does not apply to a person who discharges a firearm in self-defense or defense of another individual.

### Elements

1. The defendant discharged a firearm.
2. The defendant did so intentionally, that is, on purpose.
3. The defendant did so at a facility that he or she knew or had reason to believe was a dwelling or occupied structure, or that he or she did so in a facility that he or she knew or had reason to believe was an occupied structure and he or she did so in reckless disregard for the safety of someone else.

CJI2d 11.37.

MCL 750.234b applies where the defendant shot above a house and the victim testified that she feared for her life and thought the house was being shot at. *People v. Wilson*, 230 Mich. App. 590 (1998).

MCL 750.234b applies to a husband who, during an argument with his wife, fired a handgun into the bedroom wall. *People v. Henry*, 239 Mich. App. 140 (1999).

## Discharge of a Firearm at an Emergency or Law Enforcement Vehicle—MCL 750.234c (felony)

(1) *An individual who intentionally discharges a firearm at a motor vehicle that he or she knows or has reason to believe is an emergency or law enforcement vehicle is guilty of a felony, punishable by imprisonment for not more than 4 years, or a fine of not more than $2,000.00, or both.*

(2) *As used in this section, "emergency or law enforcement vehicle" means 1 or more of the following:*

(a) *A motor vehicle owned or operated by a fire department of a local unit of government of this state.*

(b) *A motor vehicle owned or operated by a police agency of the United States, of this state, or of a local unit of government of this state.*

(c) *A motor vehicle owned or operated by the department of natural resources that is used for law enforcement purposes.*

(d) *A motor vehicle owned or operated by an entity licensed to provide emergency medical services under part 192 of article 17 of the public health code, Act No. 368 of the Public Acts of 1978, being sections 333.20901 to 333.20979 of the Michigan Compiled Laws, and that is used to provide emergency medical assistance to individuals.*

(e) *A motor vehicle owned or operated by a volunteer employee or paid employee of an entity described in subdivisions (a) to (c) while the motor vehicle is being used to perform emergency or law enforcement duties for that entity.*

## Elements

1. The defendant discharged a firearm.
2. The defendant did so intentionally, that is, on purpose.
3. The defendant did so at a motor vehicle that he or she knew or had reason to believe was an emergency or law enforcement vehicle.

CJI2d 11.37.

## Forfeiture of Weapons—MCL 750.239 and MCL 750.239a

All pistols, weapons, or devices carried, possessed or used in violation of the Firearms chapter of the Michigan Penal Code, MCL 750.222–750.239a, are forfeited to the state and shall be turned over to the Michigan State Police for disposal; however, a local law enforcement agency may retain a firearm or part of a firearm for certain purposes, instead of forwarding it to the Michigan State Police for disposal.

Before disposing of a firearm under MCL 750.239 or 750.239a, the law enforcement agency shall do both of the following:

• Determine through LEIN whether the firearm has been reported lost or stolen. If the firearm has been reported lost or stolen and the name and address of the owner can be determined, the law enforcement agency shall provide 30 days' written notice of its intent to dispose of the firearm under this section to the owner, and allow the owner to claim the firearm within that 30-day period if he or she is authorized to possess the firearm. If the police agency determines that a serial number has been altered or has been removed or obliterated from the firearm, the police agency shall submit the firearm to the Michigan State Police or a forensic laboratory for serial number verification or restoration to determine legal ownership.

• Provide 30 days' notice to the public on a website maintained by the law enforcement agency of its intent to dispose of the firearm under this section. The notice shall include a description of the firearm and shall state the firearm's serial number, if the serial number can be determined. The law enforcement agency shall allow the owner of the firearm to claim the firearm within that 30-day period if he or she is authorized to possess the firearm. The 30-day period required under this subdivision is in addition to the 30-day period required above.

The defendant was arrested for CCW in violation of MCL 750.227. Police seized the defendant's registered pistol at the time of the defendant's arrest. The defendant motioned the trial court for the return of his pistol. MCL 750.239 provides for an absolute forfeiture of firearms if they are carried, possessed, or used contrary to the Firearms chapter of the Michigan Penal Code. The defendant violated a provision of this chapter, specifically MCL 750.227, and there is no dispute that the pistol was the firearm he possessed while violating MCL 750.227. The trial court had no choice but to deny the defendant's motion to return the pistol. *People v. Thompson*, 125 Mich. App. 45 (1983).

© 2014, Shutterstock, Inc.

# 17

# IMPERSONATION AND OBSTRUCTION OF JUSTICE

## IMPERSONATION

### Definition—MCL 750.215(5)

*Peace officer* means any of the following:

- A sheriff or deputy sheriff of a county of this or another state.
- An officer of the police department of a city, village, or township of this state or another state.
- A marshal of a city, village, or township.
- A constable.
- An officer of the Michigan State Police.
- A conservation officer.
- A security employee employed by the state pursuant to MCL 28.6c.
- A motor carrier officer appointed pursuant to MCL 28.6d.
- A police officer or public safety officer of a community college, college, or university who is authorized by the governing board of that community college, college, or university to enforce state law and the rules and ordinances of that community college, college, or university.
- A park and recreation officer commissioned pursuant to MCL 324.1606.
- A state forest officer commissioned pursuant to MCL 324.83107.

- A federal law enforcement officer.
- An investigator of the state department of attorney general.

### Impersonating a Public Officer—MCL 750.215(1) (1-year misdemeanor)

An individual who is not a peace officer or a medical examiner shall not do any of the following:

- Perform the duties of a peace officer or a medical examiner.
- Represent to another person that he or she is a peace officer or a medical examiner for any unlawful purpose.
- Represent to another person that he or she is a peace officer or a medical examiner with the intent to compel the person to do or refrain from doing any act against his or her will.

### Impersonating a Peace Officer to Commit a Crime—MCL 750.215(3) (felony)

An individual who, in violation of subsection (1), performs the duties of a peace officer to commit or attempt to commit a crime or represents to another person that he or she is a peace officer to commit or attempt to commit a crime is guilty of a felony punishable by imprisonment for not more than four years or a fine of not more than $5,000.00, or both.

## Unlawful Representation as Firefighter or EMS Personnel—MCL 750.217f (felony)

An individual who is not employed as a firefighter or emergency medical service personnel shall not inform another individual or represent to another individual by identification or any other means that he or she is employed in one of those capacities with intent to do one or more of the following:

- Perform the duties of a firefighter or emergency medical service personnel.
- Represent to another person that he or she is a firefighter or emergency medical service personnel for any unlawful purpose.
- Compel a person to do or refrain from doing any act against his or her will.
- Gain or attempt to gain entry to a residence, building, structure, facility, or other property.
- Remain or attempt to remain in or upon a residence, building, structure, facility, or other property.
- Gain or attempt to gain access to financial account information.
- Commit or attempt to commit a crime.
- Obtain or attempt to obtain information to which the individual is not entitled.
- Gain access or attempt to gain access to a person less than 18 years of age or a vulnerable adult.

## Disguising with Intent to Intimidate, Hinder, or Obstruct—MCL 750.217 (1-year misdemeanor)

*Any person who shall, in any manner, disguise himself, with the intent to obstruct the due execution of the law, or with the intent to intimidate, hinder or interrupt any officer, or any other person, in the legal performance of his duty, or the exercise of his rights under the constitution and laws of this state, whether such intent be effective or not, shall be guilty of a 1 year misdemeanor.*

The giving of a false or fictitious name to a police officer by itself does not constitute obstruction by disguise under this statute. *People v. Jones,* 142 Mich. App. 819 (1985).

## FALSE REPRESENTATIONS
### Representation as Public Utility Employee—MCL 750.217b (felony)

An individual who is not employed by a public utility shall not inform another individual or represent to another individual by uniform, identification, or any other means that he or she is employed by that public utility with intent to do one or more of the following:

- Gain or attempt to gain entry to a residence, building, structure, facility, or other property.
- Remain or attempt to remain in or upon a residence, building, structure, facility, or other property.
- Commit or attempt to commit a crime.

As used in this section, "public utility" means a utility that provides steam, gas, heat, electricity, water, cable television, telecommunications services, or pipeline services, whether privately, municipally, or cooperatively owned.

### Representation of an FIA Worker—MCL 750.217e (felony)

An individual who is not employed by the Family Independence Agency shall not inform another individual or represent to another individual by identification, or any other means that he or she is employed by the Family Independence Agency with intent to do one or more of the following:

- Gain or attempt to gain entry to a residence, building, structure, facility, or other property.
- Remain or attempt to remain in or upon a residence, building, structure, facility, or other property.
- Gain or attempt to gain access to financial account information.
- Commit or attempt to commit a crime.
- Obtain or attempt to obtain information to which the individual is not entitled under section 7 of the child protection law.
- Gain access or attempt to gain access to a person less than 18 years of age or a vulnerable adult. As used in this subdivision, "vulnerable adult" means an individual age 18 or older who, because of age, developmental disability, mental illness, or disability, whether or not determined by a court to be an incapacitated individual in need of protection, lacks the cognitive skills required to manage his or her property.

Note: The Family Independence Agency is now the Department of Human Services.

## Unauthorized Wearing of Badge or Uniform of State Police—MCL 750.216 (90-day misdemeanor)

*A person who wears, exhibits, displays, or uses, for any purpose, the badge or uniform or a badge or uniform substantially identical to that prescribed by the department of state police for officers of the department, unless he or she is a member of the department, is guilty of a misdemeanor.*

### Exception

- The person is in the "theatrical profession" and wears the item while actually engaged in the profession.

## Law Enforcement Badges, Patches, and Uniforms—MCL 750.216a (93-day misdemeanor)

*A person shall not sell, furnish, possess, wear, exhibit, display, or use the badge, patch, or uniform, or facsimile of the badge, patch, or uniform, of any law enforcement agency.*

### Exceptions

- The person is authorized by the head of the law enforcement agency.
- The person is a member of the agency.
- The person is a retired law enforcement officer possessing a retirement badge.
- The person is next-of-kin, child, or spouse of a deceased law enforcement officer.
- The person is a collector (the badge, patch, uniform, or facsimile must be in a case when transported by a collector.
- The person is in the "theatrical profession" and wears the item while actually engaged in the profession.
- Bailiffs or court officers appointed pursuant to court rule.

A facsimile includes both an exact replica of an existing item and a close imitation of an existing item.

## Law Enforcement Emblems, Insignia, Logos, Service Mark, or Identification—MCL 750.216b (93-day misdemeanor)

A person other than a peace officer shall not wear or display the emblem, insignia, logo, service mark, or other law enforcement identification of any law enforcement agency, or a facsimile of any of those items, if either of the following applies:

- The person represents himself or herself to another person as being a peace officer.
- The wearing or display occurs in a manner that would lead a reasonable person to falsely believe that the law enforcement agency whose emblem, insignia, logo, service mark, or other law enforcement identification or facsimile is being worn or displayed is promoting or endorsing a commercial service or product or a charitable endeavor.

### Definition

*Law enforcement identification:* Any identification that contains the words "law enforcement" or similar words, including, but not limited to, "agent," "enforcement agent," "detective," "task force," "fugitive recovery agent," or any other combination of names that gives the impression that the bearer is in any way connected with the federal government, state government, or any political subdivision of a state government. However, law enforcement identification does not include "bail agent" or "bondsman" when used by a bail agent or bondsman operating in accordance with the law.

This section does not apply to a person appointed by a court of this state to serve as a bailiff or court officer under the court rules.

## Fire or EMS Badges, Patches, or Uniforms—MCL 750.217g (93-day misdemeanor)

This section parallels, and is substantially the same as, the corresponding statute governing peace officer badges (MCL 750.216a) above.

## Fire or EMS Emblems, Insignia, Logos, Service Mark, or Identification—MCL 750.217h (93-day misdemeanor)

This section parallels, and is substantially the same as, the corresponding statute governing peace officer badges (MCL 750.216b) above.

# BRIBERY

## Bribery of a Public Official—MCL 750.117 (felony)

*Any person who shall corruptly give, offer or promise to any public officer, agent, servant or employee, after the election or appointment of such public officer, agent, servant or employee and either before or after such public officer, agent, servant or employee shall have been qualified or shall take his seat, any gift, gratuity, money, property or other valuable thing, the intent or purpose of which is to influence the act, vote, opinion, decision or judgment of such public officer, agent, servant or employee, or his action on any matter, question, cause or proceeding, which may be pending or may by law be brought before him in his public capacity, or the purpose and intent of which is to influence any act or omission relating to any public duty of such officer, agent, servant or employee, shall be guilty of a felony.*

### Elements

1. The defendant intentionally and corruptly,
2. Gave, offered to give, or promised to give,
3. A gift, money, or other valuable thing,
4. To a public official, and
5. Did so with the intent of influencing that official to act or to fail to act.

A defendant is not entitled to a jury instruction on the misdemeanor charge of an improper campaign contribution (MCL 169.241(1)) when he is properly charged with bribery. *People v. Hryshko*, 170 Mich. App. 368 (1988).

### Public Official Accepting Bribe—MCL 750.118 (felony)

*Any executive, legislative or judicial officer who shall corruptly accept any gift or gratuity, or any promise to make any gift, or to do any act beneficial to such officer, under an agreement, or with an understanding that his vote, opinion or judgment shall be given in any particular manner, or upon a particular side of any question, cause or proceeding, which is or may be by law brought before him in his official capacity, or that in such capacity, he shall make any particular nomination or appointment, shall forfeit his office, and be forever disqualified to hold any public office, trust or appointment under the constitution or laws of this state, and shall be guilty of a felony, punishable by imprisonment in the state prison not more than 10 years, or by fine of not more than 5,000 dollars.*

### Elements

1. A public official, accepted a gift, promise of a gift, or promise of an act that would benefit him or her, and
2. Did so with the understanding or agreement that his or her vote, opinion or judgment would be given in a particular manner, or that he or she would make a particular nomination or appointment.

A city water commissioner was found to be a public official and not a mere employee under this statute because his position was created by an ordinance and he had discretionary authority. *People v. Clark*, 134 Mich. App. 324 (1984).

A court clerk in the traffic division was not an official under this statute; rather, she was an employee who accepted bribes and should have been charged under MCL 750.125. *People v. Nankervis*, 330 Mich. 17 (1951).

All of the following are required to be a public official for the purposes of MCL 750.118:

1. The position must be created by the Constitution or by the Legislature or created by a municipality or other body through authority conferred by the Legislature.
2. The position must possess a delegation of a portion of the sovereign power of government, to be exercised for the benefit of the public.
3. The powers conferred, and the duties to be discharged, must be defined, directly or impliedly, by the Legislature or through legislative authority.
4. The duties must be performed independently and without control of a superior power other than the law, unless they be those of an inferior or subordinate office, created or authorized by the Legislature, and by it placed under the general control of a superior officer or body.
5. The position must have some permanency and continuity and not be only temporary or occasional.

*People v. Leve*, 309 Mich. 557 (1944).

# OTHER BRIBE VIOLATIONS

## Jurors, Appraisers, Executors, Auditors, Arbitrators—MCL 750.119 (felony)

*A person who corrupts or attempts to corrupt an appraiser, receiver, trustee, administrator, executor, commissioner, auditor, juror, arbitrator, or referee by giving, offering, or promising any gift or gratuity with the intent to bias the opinion or influence the decision of that appraiser, receiver, trustee, administrator, executor, commissioner, auditor, juror, arbitrator, or referee regarding any matter pending in a court, or before an inquest, or for the decision for which the appraiser, receiver, trustee, administrator, executor, commissioner, auditor, juror, arbitrator, or referee was appointed or chosen, is guilty of a crime.*

Penalties:

| Violation occurs in criminal case where the maximum punishment is more than 10 years | 10-year felony |
| --- | --- |
| All other violations | 4-year felony |

### Elements

1. The defendant gave, offered, or promised to give a gift,
2. To an appraiser, receiver, trustee, administer, executor, commissioner, auditor, juror, arbitrator, or referee, and
3. Did so with the intent to influence the decision of such person.

### Jurors, Appraisers, Executors, Auditors, Arbiters Accepting Bribes—MCL 750.120 (felony)

*Any person summoned as a juror or chosen or appointed as an appraiser, receiver, trustee, administrator, executor, commissioner, auditor, arbitrator or referee who shall corruptly take anything to give his verdict, award, or report, or who shall corruptly receive any gift or gratuity whatever, from a party to any suit, cause, or proceeding, for the trial or decision of which such juror shall have been summoned, or for the hearing or determination of which such appraiser, receiver, trustee, administrator, executor, commissioner, auditor, arbitrator, or referee shall have been chosen or appointed, shall be guilty of a felony.*

### Elements

1. A juror, appraiser, executor, auditor, arbiter,
2. Took or received a gift or gratuity, and
3. Did so in exchange for a verdict, award, or report, in the matter for which the juror, appraiser, executor, auditor, or arbiter was appointed.

### Officials of Public Institutions by Persons with Contracts Therewith—MCL 750.121 (felony)

*Any person interested directly or indirectly in a contract with a state or municipal institution who shall corruptly give, offer or promise to any officer of such institution any bribe, gift, or gratuity whatever, with*

*intent to improperly influence his official action under such contract, shall be guilty of felony.*

### Elements

1. The defendant, while directly or indirectly interested in a contract with a state or municipal institution,
2. Gave, offered, or promised to give any bribe, gift, or gratuity to an officer of such institution, and
3. And did so with the intent of improperly influencing an official action under that contract.

### Peace Officers or Others Authorized to Arrest Offenders of Criminal Law—MCL 750.123 (6-month misdemeanor)

*A sheriff, coroner, constable, peace officer, or any other officer authorized to serve process or arrest or apprehend offenders against criminal law who shall receive from a defendant or from any other person any money or other valuable thing or any service or promise to pay or give money or to perform or omit to perform any act as a consideration, reward, or inducement, for omitting or delaying to arrest any defendant, or to carry him or her before a magistrate, or for delaying to take any person to prison, or for postponing the sale of any property under an execution, or for omitting or delaying to perform any duty pertaining to his or her office, is guilty of a misdemeanor punishable by imprisonment for not more than 6 months or a fine of not more than $750.00. However, if that defendant is charged with an offense against the criminal laws of this state, an officer convicted under this section may be punished by any fine or by any term of imprisonment or both a fine and imprisonment, within the limits fixed by the statute that the defendant is charged with having violated.*

### Elements

1. The defendant is a police officer.
2. The defendant received consideration, reward, or inducement from another person.
3. The defendant omitted or delayed performance of a duty pertaining to his office.

Prosecution of a police officer charged with accepting a bribe to refrain from making a complaint, which was his or her duty to make, should be brought under this section, instead of the general bribery statute. *People v. McDonald*, 216 Mich. 234 (1921).

The defendants were properly charged with felony extortion rather than misdemeanor peace officer accepting a bribe. The officers demanded a bribe and threatened to charge the victim with providing alcohol to minors if the bribe was not paid. The threatening nature of the defendants' conduct made the crime extortion rather than accepting a bribe. *People v. Percin*, 330 Mich. 94 (1951).

## Athlete—MCL 750.124 (felony)

*Any person who corruptly gives, offers or promises to any person engaged in amateur or professional baseball, boxing, wrestling or other competitive athletic pursuits, any gift, gratuity or valuable thing whatever, with intent to influence him to lose or try to lose, or to affect the result in any way of, any contest in which he is participating or expects to participate; or any person engaged in amateur or professional baseball, boxing, wrestling or other competitive athletic pursuits, who corruptly solicits or accepts a gift, gratuity or valuable thing, or a promise to make a gift or to do an act beneficial to himself, under an agreement or with the understanding that he shall lose or try to lose, or to affect the result in any way of, any contest in which he is participating or expects to participate, shall be guilty of a felony.*

## Bribery of Employees to Deceive Employers— MCL 750.125 (1-year misdemeanor)

*(1) A person shall not give, offer, or promise a commission, gift, or gratuity to an agent, employee, or other person or do or offer to do an act beneficial to an agent, employee, or other person with intent to influence the action of the agent or employee in relation to his or her principal's or employer's business.*

*(2) An agent or employee shall not request or accept a commission, gift, or gratuity, or a promise of a commission, gift, or gratuity, for the agent, employee, or another person or the doing of an act or offer of an act beneficial to the agent, employee, or another person according to an agreement or understanding between the agent or employee and any other person that the agent or employee shall act in a particular manner in relation to his or her principal's or employer's business.*

*(3) A person shall not use or give to an agent, employee, or other person, and an agent or employee shall not use, approve, or certify, with intent to deceive the principal or employer, a receipt, account, invoice, or other document concerning which the principal or employer is interested that contains a statement that is materially false, erroneous, or defective or omits to state fully any commission, money, property, or other valuable thing given or agreed to be given to the agent or employee.*

*(4) Evidence is not admissible in any proceeding or prosecution under this section to show that a gift or acceptance of a commission, money, property, or other valuable thing described in this section is customary in a business, trade, or calling. The customary nature of a transaction is not a defense in a proceeding or prosecution under this section.*

*(5) In a proceeding or prosecution under this section, a person shall not be excused from attending and testifying or from producing documentary evidence pursuant to a subpoena on the ground that the testimony or evidence may tend to incriminate him or her or subject him or her to a penalty or forfeiture. Truthful testimony, evidence, or other truthful information compelled under this section and any information derived directly or indirectly from that truthful testimony, evidence, or other truthful information shall not be used against the witness in a criminal case, except for impeachment purposes or in a prosecution for perjury or otherwise failing to testify or produce evidence as required.*

*(6) A person who violates this section is guilty of a misdemeanor punishable by imprisonment for not more than 1 year or a fine of not more than $1,000.00, or both.*

A clerk of a traffic division of a court is not a public official, but rather a mere employee and should be prosecuted under this section rather than MCL 750.118. *People v. Nankervis*, 330 Mich. 17 (1951).

The defendant, who was the director of the city housing commission, was not a city employee under this statute because he did not represent the city in negotiations nor did he receive compensation for tasks under the city's direct control. Therefore, his conviction under this statute was overturned. *People v. Kirstein*, 6 Mich. App. 107 (1967).

"The characteristic of the agent is that he is a business representative. His function is to bring about, modify, affect, accept performance of, or terminate contractual obligations between his principal and third persons. To the proper performance of his functions therefore, it is absolutely essential that there shall be third persons in contemplation between whom and the principal legal obligations are to be thus created, modified, or otherwise affected by the acts of the agent.

The word servant, in our legal nomenclature, has a broad significance, and embraces all persons of whatever rank or position who are in the employ and subject to the direction or control of another in any department of labor or business. The distinction between an agent and a servant is that the former represents his principal in business dealings with another person, and the latter is in the employ of his master and subject to his direction and control in the work intrusted to him to perform." *Saums v. Parfet*, 270 Mich. 165 (1935) (internal citations omitted).

# FALSE REPORTS

## Definitions—MCL 750.411a(9)

*Local unit of government:*  Any of the following:

- A city, village, township, or county.
- A local or intermediate school district.
- A public school academy.
- A community college.

*Medical first responder:*  An individual who has met the educational requirements of a department approved medical first responder course and who is licensed to provide medical first response life support as part of a medical first response service or as a driver of an ambulance that provides basic life support services only. Medical first responder does not include a police officer solely because his or her police vehicle is equipped with an automated external defibrillator.

*Serious impairment of a body function:*  Includes, but is not limited to, one or more of the following:

- The loss of a limb or use of a limb.
- The loss of a hand, foot, finger, or thumb or use of a hand, foot, finger, or thumb.
- The loss of an eye or ear or use of an eye or ear.
- The loss or substantial impairment of a bodily function.
- A serious visible disfigurement.
- A comatose state that lasts for more than three days.
- Any measurable brain damage or mental impairment.
- A skull fracture or other serious bone fracture.
- A subdural hemorrhage or subdural hematoma.

*State:*  Includes, but is not limited to, a state institution of higher education.

*False reports of crimes:*  Includes false reports made to the following:

- Peace officer.
- Police agency of this state or of a local unit of government.
- 911 operator.
- Any other governmental employee or contractor or employee of a contractor who is authorized to receive reports of a crime.

*False reports of medical or other emergencies:* Includes false reports made to the following:

- Peace officer.
- Police agency of this state or of a local unit of government.
- Fire fighter or fire department of this state or a local unit of government of this state.
- 911 operator.
- Medical first responder.
- Any governmental employee or contractor or employee of a contractor who is authorized to receive reports of medical or other emergencies.

## False Report of a Misdemeanor—MCL 750.411a(1)(a) (93-day misdemeanor)

### Elements

1. The defendant reported to a [peace officer] that a crime had been committed.
2. The report was false as to either the fact or the detail[s] of the crime.
3. When the defendant made the report, the defendant knew it was false.
4. The defendant intended to make a false report concerning a crime.
5. The crime reported was a [misdemeanor].
CJI2d 13.19.

## False Report of a Felony—MCL 750.411a (felony)

### Elements

1. The defendant reported to a [peace officer] that a crime had been committed.
2. The report was false as to either the fact or the detail[s] of the crime.
3. When the defendant made the report, the defendant knew it was false.
4. The defendant intended to make a false report concerning a crime.
5. The crime reported was a felony.
CJI2d 13.19.

The defendant's conviction was upheld when he truthfully reported that he had been carjacked, but he lied about where it had occurred to conceal the fact that he was searching out crack cocaine at the time he was carjacked. The court held that "the plain language of the statute is not limited to only those situations where no crime has been committed; it also applies where one reports false details about the crime." *People v. Chavis*, 468 Mich. 84 (2003).

The *corpus delicti* rule precludes the admission of a defendant's confession in the absence of some other evidence that the crime had occurred. In this case, the defendant lost his car driving home from a bar. He reported that an unknown person had carjacked him, but later admitted to police he had no knowledge of how he lost his car. In order to sustain the defendant's conviction of knowingly filing a false police report, the prosecutor would have to prove, independent of the defendant's confession, that a carjacking did not occur. *People v. Borrelli*, 463 Mich. 930 (2000).

## False Report of a Crime Resulting in Physical Injury—MCL 750.411a(1)(c) (felony)

### Elements

1. The defendant reported to a [peace officer] that a crime had been committed.
2. The report was false as to either the fact or the detail[s] of the crime.
3. When the defendant made the report, the defendant knew it was false.
4. The defendant intended to make a false report concerning a crime.
5. The false report resulted in a response to address the reported crime.
6. While responding, a person incurred physical injury as a proximate result of lawful conduct arising out of that response.

## False Report of a Crime Resulting in Serious Impairment of a Body Function—MCL 750.411a(1)(d) (felony)

### Elements

1. The defendant reported to a [peace officer] that a crime had been committed.
2. The report was false as to either the fact or the detail[s] of the crime.
3. When the defendant made the report, the defendant knew it was false.

4. The defendant intended to make a false report concerning a crime.
5. The false report resulted in a response to address the reported crime.
6. While responding, a person incurred a serious impairment of a body function as a proximate result of lawful conduct arising out of that response.

## False Report of a Crime Resulting in Death—MCL 750.411a(1)(e) (felony)

### Elements

1. The defendant reported to a [peace officer] that a crime had been committed.
2. The report was false as to either the fact or the detail[s] of the crime.
3. When the defendant made the report, the defendant knew it was false.
4. The defendant intended to make a false report concerning a crime.
5. The false report resulted in a response to address the reported crime.
6. While responding, a person is killed as a proximate result of lawful conduct arising out of that response.

## False Report of Medical or Other Emergency—MCL 750.411a(4)(a) (93-day misdemeanor)

### Elements

1. The defendant reported to a [peace officer] a medical or other emergency.
2. The report was false as to either the fact or the detail[s] of the medical or other emergency.
3. When the defendant made the report, the defendant knew it was false.
4. The defendant intended to make a false report concerning the medical or other emergency.

## False Report of Medical or Other Emergency Resulting in Physical Injury—MCL 750.411a(4)(b) (felony)

### Elements

1. The defendant reported to a [peace officer] a medical or other emergency.
2. The report was false as to either the fact or the detail[s] of the medical or other emergency.
3. When the defendant made the report, the defendant knew it was false.
4. The defendant intended to make a false report concerning the medical or other emergency.
5. The false report resulted in a response to address the reported medical or other emergency.

6. While responding, a person incurred physical injury as a proximate result of lawful conduct arising out of that response.

## False Report of Medical or Other Emergency Resulting in Serious Impairment of a Body Function—MCL 750.411a(4)(c) (felony)

### Elements

1. The defendant reported to a [peace officer] a medical or other emergency.
2. The report was false as to either the fact or the detail[s] of the medical or other emergency.
3. When the defendant made the report, the defendant knew it was false.
4. The defendant intended to make a false report concerning the medical or other emergency.
5. The false report resulted in a response to address the reported medical or other emergency.
6. While responding, a person incurred a serious impairment of a body function as a proximate result of lawful conduct arising out of that response.

## False Report of Medical or Other Emergency Resulting in Death—MCL 750.411a(4)(d) (felony)

### Elements

1. The defendant reported to a [peace officer] a medical or other emergency.
2. The report was false as to either the fact or the detail[s] of the medical or other emergency.
3. When the defendant made the report, the defendant knew it was false.
4. The defendant intended to make a false report concerning the medical or other emergency.
5. The false report resulted in a response to address the reported medical or other emergency.
6. While responding, a person is killed as a proximate result of lawful conduct arising out of that response.

## False Report or Threat of Bomb or Harmful Device—MCL 750.411a(2)(a)

A person shall knowingly make a false report of a violation or attempted violation or threaten to violate one of the following offenses and communicate or cause the communication of the false report to any other person, knowing the report to be false:

- Explosives—Carrying on Common Carrier. MCL 750.200.
- Harmful Devices—Unlawful Possession or Use. MCL 750.200i.
- Harmful Devices—Imitation/Irritants—Unlawful Possession or Use. MCL 750.200j.
- Harmful Substance/Device-Person Falsely Exposed. MCL 750.200l.
- Explosives—Transportation of Concussion or Friction Type. MCL 750.201.
- Explosives—Shipping with False Markings/Invoice. MCL 750.202.
- Explosives—Sending with Intent to Injure/Destroy. MCL 750.204.
- Explosives—Sending with Intent to Frighten. MCL 750.204a.
- Explosives—Placing Near Property. MCL 750.207.
- Explosives—Placing Offensive Substance with Intent to Alarm Or Injure. MCL 750.209.
- Explosives—Possession with Intent to Terrorize. MCL 750.209a.
- Explosives—Possession of Bombs with Unlawful Intent. MCL 750.210.
- Explosives—Manufacture/Possession of Molotov Cocktail. MCL 750.211a.
- Explosives—Improperly Marked. MCL 750.212.
- Explosives—Vulnerable Target. MCL 750.212a.
- Homicide—Death by Explosives/Common Carrier. MCL 750.327.
- Homicide—By Explosives In or Near Building. MCL 750.328.
- Food—Placing Harmful Objects In. MCL 750.397a.
- Poisoning—Food/Drink/Medicine/Water Supply. MCL 750.436.

Penalties:

| | |
|---|---|
| False report of a misdemeanor or emergency | 93-day misdemeanor |
| False report of a felony | 4-year felony |
| False report or emergency resulting a response and a person incurs a physical injury | 5-year felony |
| False report or emergency resulting a response and a person incurs serious impairment of a bodily function | 10-year felony |
| False report resulting a response and a person dies | 15-year felony |
| False bomb threat | 4-year felony |
| False bomb threat, second conviction | 10-year felony |

A violation or attempted violation occurs if the communication of the false report originates in this state, is intended to terminate in this state, or is intended to terminate with a person who is in this state and may be prosecuted in any jurisdiction in which the communication originated or terminated.

## Ambulance-False Requests for Service— MCL 750.411d (1-year misdemeanor)

*A person who, with the intent not to use the assistance, knowingly causes or makes a request for the assistance of an ambulance service or an advanced mobile emergency care service is guilty of a misdemeanor punishable by imprisonment for not more than 1 year or a fine of not more than $1,000.00, or both.*

## False Report to Police Dispatch Center— MCL 750.509 (1-year misdemeanor)

*Any person who shall willfully make to any radio broadcasting station operated by any law enforcement agency any false, misleading, or unfounded report, for the purpose of interfering with the operation thereof, or with the intention of misleading any peace officer or officers of this state, is guilty of a misdemeanor punishable by imprisonment for not more than 1 year or a fine of not more than $1,000.00.*

## False Report of Abducted Child—MCL 28.754(1) (felony)

*A person shall not intentionally make a false report of the abduction of a child, or intentionally cause a false report of the abduction of a child to be made, to a peace officer, police agency of this state or of a local unit of government, 9-1-1 operator, or any other governmental employee or contractor or employee of a contractor who is authorized to receive the report, knowing the report is false. A person who violates this subsection is guilty of a felony punishable by imprisonment for not more than 4 years or a fine of not more than $2,000.00, or both.*

## False Report that Severely Disabled Child is Missing—MCL 28.754 (1-year misdemeanor)

*A person shall not intentionally make a false report that a child is missing who suffers from severe mental or physical disability that greatly impairs the child's ability to care for himself or herself, or intentionally cause such a report to be made, to a peace officer, police agency of this state*

*or of a local unit of government, 9-1-1 operator, or any other governmental employee or contractor or employee of a contractor who is authorized to receive the report, knowing the report is false. A person who violates this subsection is guilty of a misdemeanor punishable by imprisonment for not more than 1 year or a fine of not more than $1,000.00, or both.*

# ESCAPE

## Aiding an Escape of a Prisoner—MCL 750.183

### Elements

1. A prisoner in a place of confinement was legally committed to or held in this facility.
2. Any of the following is true:

   a. The defendant knowingly took or sent an object into the place of confinement intending to help a prisoner escape and this object could be used to help the prisoner escape.

   b. The defendant intentionally assisted a prisoner who was trying to escape. It does not matter whether the escape itself was made or even attempted, but the defendant must have intended to assist the escape of the prisoner.

   c. The defendant's act helped a prisoner escape and the defendant knew when he did this act that it created a substantial risk that a prisoner would escape.

   d. The defendant helped a prisoner escape by the use of force.

CJI2d 13.7.

Penalties:

| Prisoner is being held on misdemeanor charges | 1-year misdemeanor |
| --- | --- |
| Prisoner is being held on felony charges | 7-year felony |

Aiding an escape of a prisoner is a general intent crime. In a case where two inmates assaulted a guard during an escape, the defendant was properly convicted of aiding the other prisoner's escape even though the defendant claimed that he was only facilitating his own escape. *People v. Potts*, 55 Mich. App. 622 (1974).

By statute, the prisoner that the defendant aids must be lawfully detained at the time of the assistance. *People v. Gardineer*, 334 Mich. 663 (1952).

## Aiding an Escape From an Officer—MCL 750.184 (1-year misdemeanor)

The suspect assisted a prisoner in an escape attempt from an officer or person who had lawful custody.

## Escape From Juvenile Facility—MCL 750.186a (felony)

The suspect was placed in juvenile facility and did one of the following:

- Escaped, or attempted to escape from the facility.
- Escaped or attempted to escape from an employee of the facility.

"Escape" means to leave without lawful authority or to fail to return to custody when required.

## Escape From Prison—MCL 750.193 (felony)

### Elements

1. The defendant was sentenced to imprisonment and was serving that sentence at the time.
2. The facility holding the defendant was a prison.
3. The defendant did one of the following:

   a. Escaped from prison.
   b. Attempted to escape from prison.
   c. Escaped from the custody of a guard or prison employee while outside of the prison.
   d. Left the prison without being legally discharged.
   e. Escaped from a mental health facility where he or she had been admitted from prison.

CJI2d 13.8.

**Prison:**   A facility that houses prisoners committed to the jurisdiction of the department of corrections and includes the grounds, farm, shop, road camp, or place of employment operated by the facility or under control of the officers of the facility, the department of corrections, a police officer of this state, or any other person authorized by the department of corrections to have a prisoner under care, custody, or supervision, either in a facility or outside a facility, whether for the purpose of work, medical care, or any other reason. MCL 750.193(2).

Escape is a general intent crime. *People v. Spalding*, 17 Mich. App. 73 (1969).

Escape from prison is not a strict liability crime. There must be some proof that the defendant intended to escape from known confinement. *People v. Benevides*, 204 Mich. App. 188 (1994).

Attempted escape is a specific intent crime. *People v. Langworthy*, 416 Mich. 630 (1982).

To be convicted of attempt, the prosecution must prove that the defendant intended to commit the crime and the defendant made some overt act beyond mere preparation toward the commission of the crime. The defendant was going through a dry run of his escape plan. He did not intend to escape during the dry run; he intended to make his actual escape two days later. However, in completing his dry run, the defendant removed some barriers to his physical confinement by removing a bar across a light fixture hole. This satisfied both the intent and overt act requirement to sustain a conviction of attempted escape. *People v. Marsh*, 156 Mich. App. 831 (1986).

The defendant could be convicted under MCL 750.193 if the prosecutor could prove the defendant willfully failed to abide by the terms of his confinement, in this case the terms of an electronic tether program. The prosecution did not have to prove the defendant intended not to return to the boundaries of the tether program, only that he knowingly failed to comply with the program's boundaries. *People v. Sheets*, 223 Mich. App. 651 (1997).

This statute applies to any place authorized by the Department of Corrections to have inmates. This includes:

- Halfway houses. *People v. Mayes*, 95 Mich. App. 188 (1980).
- Community corrections centers. *People v. King*, 104 Mich. App. 459 (1981).
- Hospitals to which prisoners are transferred for treatment. *People v. Smith*, 89 Mich. App. 478 (1979).

## Escape From Jail—MCL 750.195 (felony)

### Elements

The defendant was placed in a county jail and did one of the following:

1. Broke out of jail and escaped.
2. Broke out of jail, though he did not actually escape.
3. Left the jail without being legally discharged from it.
4. Attempted to escape from jail.

CJI2d 13.10.

*Jail:* A facility that is operated by a local unit of government for the detention of persons charged with, or convicted of, criminal offenses or ordinance violations, or persons found guilty of civil or criminal contempt. MCL 750.195(4).

A defendant who escapes before he is booked may be convicted of escaping from jail. In this case, the defendant asked to use the restroom; when the door opened, he escaped through the open sally port door. *People v. Taylor*, 238 Mich. App. 259 (1999).

## Day parole

The defendant is not guilty of escape from jail if he or she has been released to go to work, look for work, attend school, or obtain medical treatment, substance abuse treatment, medical health counseling, and was simply late in returning to jail. The prosecutor must prove beyond a reasonable doubt that defendant intended to escape. CJI2d 13.13.

The defendant could not be convicted under this statute when she was not confined to the jail. The defendant in the instant case was released pending sentencing with the requirement that she report to the jail each evening. The defendant failed to report. Because the reporting was for accountability and not to incarcerate her overnight, she could not be convicted under MCL 750.195; however, the court held that she could be charged with violation of MCL 750.197a (see below). *People v. Jones*, 190 Mich. App. 509 (1991).

## Breaking From County Work Farm, Factory or Shop—MCL 750.196 (misdemeanor)

### Elements

1. The defendant was lawfully committed to a work farm, factory, or shop established by law for the confinement of persons sentenced there, and
2. Escaped or broke away with the intent to escape, or attempted by force, violence, or any other manner to escape.

Punishable by double the term of the original sentence, to be served at the end of the original sentence.

## Escape While Awaiting Court Hearing— MCL 750.197 (felony)

The suspect was awaiting examination, trial, arraignment, or sentence for a misdemeanor or a felony and escaped or attempted to escape.

## Escape From Lawful Custody Under Any Criminal Process—MCL 750.197a (1-year misdemeanor)

The suspect escaped from lawful custody under any criminal process, including periods while at large on bail.

This section does not apply to a person who was lawfully arrested without a warrant and escaped from the back seat of the police car because court action had not yet begun. *People v. Lawrence*, 246 Mich. App. 260 (2001).

The defendant could be convicted of under this statute for failing to appear for sentencing while out on bond. However, he could not be charged with absconding on a felony bond because the crime for which he was on bond, resisting arrest, was not itself a felony. *People v. Williams*, 243 Mich. App. 333 (2000).

## Concealing or Harboring a Fugitive—MCL 750.199

Knowingly and willfully concealing or harboring, for the purpose of concealment from a peace officer, another who is wanted on warrants.

Penalties:

| Person wanted on misdemeanor arrest warrant, bench warrant in a civil case, or criminal bench warrant in misdemeanor case | 93-day misdemeanor |
|---|---|
| Person wanted on felony arrest warrant or bench warrant in felony case | 4-year felony |

## Pursuit and Retaking of Escapee—MCL 764.23

If a person who has been lawfully arrested escapes, the person from whose custody he or she escaped may immediately pursue and retake him or her at any time and in any place within the state without a warrant.

If a prisoner escapes from a state correctional facility or willfully fails to remain within the extended limits of his or her confinement, the prisoner may be pursued and arrested, without a warrant, by a person who is either of the following:

- An employee of the Department of Corrections who is designated by the director of the Department of Corrections as having the authority to pursue and arrest escaped prisoners.
- An employee of a private vendor that operates a youth correctional facility who is designated by the director of the Department of Corrections as having the authority to pursue and arrest escaped prisoners.

## Cellular Telephone to Prisoner—MCL 800.283a (felony)

*A person shall not sell, give, or furnish, or aid in the selling, giving, or furnishing of, a cellular telephone or other wireless communication device to a prisoner in a correctional facility, or dispose of a cellular telephone or other wireless communication device in or on the grounds of a correctional facility.*

## Cellular Phone to a Prisoner in Jail—MCL 801.262a (felony)

*A person shall not sell, give, or furnish, or aid in the selling, giving, or furnishing of, a cellular telephone or other wireless communication device to a prisoner in a jail or a building appurtenant to a jail or on grounds used for jail purposes, or dispose of a cellular telephone or other wireless communication device in a jail or a building appurtenant to a jail or on grounds used for jail purposes.*

Violation of either MCL 800.283a or MCL 801.262a is a five-year felony.

A corrections officer searched an inmate room and found a cellular phone in the trash can. The defendant argued that he had not furnished a cellular phone to a "prisoner in a correctional facility" within the meaning of MCL 800.283a because the inmates that he left the phone for were "parolees" rather than prisoners. The court construed the term "prisoner" to include all parolees who have not yet been released and concluded that the Tuscola Residential Reentry Program is a "correctional facility" within the meaning of the law. *People v. Armisted*, 295 Mich. App. 32 (2011).

# PERJURY

## Perjury-Court Proceeding—MCL 750.422 (felony)

*Any person who, being lawfully required to depose the truth in any proceeding in a court of justice, shall commit perjury shall be guilty of a felony, punishable, if such perjury was committed on the trial of an indictment for a capital crime, by imprisonment in the state prison for life, or any term of years, and if committed in any other case, by imprisonment in the state prison for not more than 15 years.*

### Elements

1. The defendant was legally required to take an oath in a proceeding in a court of justice.
2. The defendant took the oath.
3. The defendant made a false statement while under oath.
4. The defendant knew that the statement was false when he or she made it.

CJ12d 14.1.

A showing that the witness had a good faith belief his statement was true negates perjury charges. *Smith v. Hubbell*, 142 Mich. 637 (1906).

Whether the false statement was about a material fact is not an element. *People v. Lively*, 470 Mich. 248 (2004).

Penalties:

| | |
|---|---|
| During trial for a capital crime | Life or any term of years |
| During trial for all other crimes | 15-year felony |

## Perjury, Other Than Court Proceeding—MCL 750.423 (felony)

*Any person authorized by a statute of this state to take an oath, or any person of whom an oath is required by law, who willfully swears falsely in regard to any matter or thing respecting which the oath is authorized or required is guilty of perjury, a felony punishable by imprisonment for not more than 15 years.*

This applies to a person who willfully makes a false declaration in a record that is signed by the person and given under penalty of perjury.

*Record:*   Information that is inscribed on a tangible medium or that is stored in an electronic or other medium and is retrievable in perceivable form.

*Signed:*   The person did either of the following to authenticate or adopt the record:

- Executed or adopted a tangible symbol.
- Attached to or logically associated with the record an electronic symbol, sound, or process.

### Elements

1. The defendant took an oath to tell the truth.
2. The oath was authorized or required by law.
3. The defendant made a false statement while under oath.
4. The defendant knew that the statement was false.

CJI2d 14.2.

Types of oaths that are included:

- An affidavit for a marriage license. *People v. Mankin*, 225 Mich. 246 (1923).
- Signing of an application for a driver's license containing false and incorrect information. *People v. Thompson*, 193 Mich. App. 58 (1992), *implied overruling recognized by People v. Geoghegan*, Mich. App., November 26, 1996 (unreported).
- The signing of an Aid to Dependant Children application is not an oath. An oath, for the purposes of perjury, requires more than a signature following a warning about perjury. "The usual mode of administering oaths now practiced in this state, by the person who swears holding up the right hand, shall be observed *in all cases* in which an oath may be administered by law except in the cases herein otherwise provided." *People v. Ramos*, 430 Mich. 544 (1988) (emphasis in original).

### Subornation of Perjury—MCL 750.424 (felony)

*Any person who shall be guilty of subornation of perjury, by procuring another person to commit the crime of perjury, shall be punished as provided in the next preceding section.*

The suspect persuaded another to make a false statement under a lawful oath that the suspect knew was false.

### Elements

1. The defendant tried to get another person to make a false statement under oath.
2. The defendant knew that the statement was false.

3. The other person made the false statement as a result of the defendant's actions.
4. The oath was authorized or required by law.

CJI2d 14.3.

### Attempted Subornation of Perjury—MCL 750.425 (felony)

*Any person who shall endeavor to incite or procure any person to commit the crime of perjury, though no perjury be committed, shall be guilty of a felony, punishable by imprisonment in the state prison not more than 5 years.*

### Elements

1. The defendant did or said something in an effort to persuade another person to make a false statement under oath. It does not matter whether anyone actually made a false statement under oath. This crime is completed as soon as the defendant tried to persuade another person to make a false statement.
2. The defendant knew that the statement was false at that time.
3. The oath was authorized or required by law.

CJI2d 14.4.

There is no requirement that witness knew that the statement was false, only that the defendant knew that the statement was false; i.e., the witness might not be committing perjury because he or she believes that the statement is true, but the defendant could still be charged with attempted subornation of perjury if the defendant knew that the statement was false. *People v. Mosley*, 338 Mich. 559 (1953).

# JURY TAMPERING

### Jurors, Attempting to Influence—MCL 750.120a(1) (1-year misdemeanor)

*A person who willfully attempts to influence the decision of a juror in any case by argument or persuasion, other than as part of the proceedings in open court in the trial of the case, is guilty of a misdemeanor punishable by imprisonment for not more than 1 year or a fine of not more than $1,000.00, or both.*

## Jurors, Intimidation—MCL 750.120a(2) (felony)

*A person who willfully attempts to influence the decision of a juror in any case by intimidation, other than as part of the proceedings in open court in the trial of the case, is guilty of a crime.*

Penalties:

| | |
|---|---|
| Intimidation involved threat to kill or injure person or damage property | 15-year felony |
| During trial where the maximum penalty is more than 10 years | 10-year felony |
| During trial for all other crimes | 4-year felony |

## Jurors, Retaliating Against—MCL 750.120a(4) (felony)

*A person who retaliates, attempts to retaliate, or threatens to retaliate against another person for having performed his or her duties as a juror is guilty of a felony punishable by imprisonment for not more than 10 years or a fine of not more than $20,000.00, or both.*

**Retaliate:**   Any of the following:

- Committing or attempting to commit a crime against any person.
- Threatening to kill or injure any person or threatening to cause property damage.

# WITNESS TAMPERING

## Definitions

**Official proceeding:**   A proceeding heard before a legislative, judicial, administrative, or other governmental agency or official authorized to hear evidence under oath, including a referee, prosecuting attorney, hearing examiner, commissioner, notary, or other person taking testimony or deposition in that proceeding.

**Threaten or intimidate:**   Does *not* mean a communication regarding the otherwise lawful access to courts or other branches of government, such as the lawful filing of any civil action or police report of which the purpose is not to harass the other person in violation of MCL 600.2907.

## Bribing a Witness—MCL 750.122(1) (felony)

*A person shall not give, offer to give, or promise anything of value to an individual for any of the following purposes:*

(a) *To discourage any individual from attending a present or future official proceeding as a witness, testifying at a present or future official proceeding, or giving information at a present or future official proceeding.*

(b) *To influence any individual's testimony at a present or future official proceeding.*

(c) *To encourage any individual to avoid legal process, to withhold testimony, or to testify falsely in a present or future official proceeding.*

This section does not apply to the reimbursement or payment of reasonable costs for any witness to provide a statement to testify truthfully or provide truthful information in an official proceeding as provided for by statute or court rule, i.e., an expert witness.

This section does not apply to the lawful conduct of an attorney in the performance of his or her duties, such as advising a client or the lawful conduct or communications of a person as permitted by statute or other lawful privilege.

It is an affirmative defense under this section, for which the defendant has the burden of proof by a preponderance of the evidence, that the conduct consisted solely of lawful conduct and that the defendant's sole intention was to encourage, induce, or cause the other person to testify or provide evidence truthfully.

## Threatening or Intimidating a Witness— MCL 750.122(3) (felony)

*A person shall not do any of the following by threat or intimidation:*

(a) *Discourage or attempt to discourage any individual from attending a present or future official proceeding as a witness, testifying at a present or future official proceeding, or giving information at a present or future official proceeding.*

(b) *Influence or attempt to influence testimony at a present or future official proceeding.*

(c) *Encourage or attempt to encourage any individual to avoid legal process, to withhold testimony, or to testify falsely in a present or future official proceeding.*

This section does not apply to the lawful conduct of an attorney in the performance of his or her duties, such as advising a client or the lawful conduct or communications of a person as permitted by statute or other lawful privilege.

It is an affirmative defense under this section, for which the defendant has the burden of proof by a preponderance of the evidence, that the conduct consisted solely of lawful conduct and that the defendant's sole intention was to encourage, induce, or cause the other person to testify or provide evidence truthfully.

### Interfering With a Witness—MCL 750.122(7) (felony)

*A person shall not willfully impede, interfere with, prevent, or obstruct or attempt to willfully impede, interfere with, prevent, or obstruct the ability of a witness to attend, testify, or provide information in or for a present or future official proceeding.*

The defendant could be charged with MCL 750.122(6) where he willfully attempted to interfere with the witness' intention to attend a hearing by telling her explicitly not to attend, playing to her feelings for him, and assuring her that the consequences would be minor, or nonexistent; and this interference attempted to affect her ability to attend the hearing by impairing her ability to choose to do the right thing, which was to obey the subpoena. *People v. Greene*, 255 Mich. App. 426 (2003).

### Retaliating Against a Witness—MCL 750.122(8) (felony)

*A person who retaliates, attempts to retaliate, or threatens to retaliate against another person for having been a witness in an official proceeding is guilty of a felony punishable by imprisonment for not more than 10 years or a fine of not more than $20,000.00, or both. As used in this subsection, "retaliate" means to do any of the following:*

*(a) Commit or attempt to commit a crime against any person.*

*(b) Threaten to kill or injure any person or threaten to cause property damage.*

Penalties:

| Violation involved crime, attempt, or threat to kill or injure person or damage property | 15-year felony |
|---|---|
| Criminal case where the maximum penalty is more than 10 years | 10-year felony |
| Criminal case for all other crimes | 4-year felony |

This section applies regardless of whether an official proceeding actually takes place or is pending or whether the individual has been subpoenaed or otherwise ordered to appear at the official proceeding if the person knows or has reason to know the other person could be a witness at any official proceeding.

## OBSTRUCTION OF JUSTICE

### Definitions—MCL 750.483a(11)

*Official proceeding:* A proceeding heard before a legislative, judicial, administrative, or other governmental agency or official authorized to hear evidence under oath, including a referee, prosecuting attorney, hearing examiner, commissioner, notary, or other person taking testimony or deposition in that proceeding.

*Threaten or intimidate:* Does *not* mean a communication regarding the otherwise lawful access to courts or other branches of government, such as the lawful filing of any civil action or police report of which the purpose is not to harass the other person in violation of MCL 600.2907.

### Interfering with Crime Report—MCL 750.483a(1)

*A person shall not do any of the following:*

*(a) Withhold or refuse to produce any testimony, information, document, or thing after the court has ordered it to be produced following a hearing.*

*(b) Prevent or attempt to prevent through the unlawful use of physical force another person from reporting a crime committed or attempted by another person.*

*(c) Retaliate or attempt to retaliate against another person for having reported or attempted to report a crime committed or attempted by another person. As used in this subsection, "retaliate" means to do any of the following:*

*(i) Commit or attempt to commit a crime against any person.*

*(ii) Threaten to kill or injure any person or threaten to cause property damage.*

Subsection (a) does not apply to the lawful conduct of an attorney in the performance of his or her duties, such as advising a client or the lawful conduct or communications of a person as permitted by statute or other lawful privilege.

Penalties:

| Violation involved crime, attempt, or threat to kill or injure person or damage property | 10-year felony |
|---|---|
| All other violations | 1-year misdemeanor |

To be convicted under MCL 750.483a(1)(b), the prosecution must prove that a defendant prevented or attempted to prevent, through the unlawful use of physical force, someone from reporting a crime committed or attempted by another person. There is no requirement to provide proof that the crime the victim sought to report was committed or attempted. *People v. Holley*, 480 Mich. 222 (2008).

## Interfering with a Police Investigation—MCL 750.483a(3)

*A person shall not do any of the following:*

(a) *Give, offer to give, or promise anything of value to any person to influence a person's statement to a police officer conducting a lawful investigation of a crime or the presentation of evidence to a police officer conducting a lawful investigation of a crime.*

(b) *Threaten or intimidate any person to influence a person's statement to a police officer conducting a lawful investigation of a crime or the presentation of evidence to a police officer conducting a lawful investigation of a crime.*

It is an affirmative defense, for which the defendant has the burden of proof by a preponderance of the evidence, that the conduct consisted solely of lawful conduct and that the defendant's sole intention was to encourage, induce, or cause the other person to provide a statement or evidence truthfully.

Subsection (b) does not apply to the lawful conduct of an attorney in the performance of his or her duties, such as advising a client or the lawful conduct or communications of a person as permitted by statute or other lawful privilege.

Penalties:

| Violation involved crime, attempt, or threat to kill or injure person or damage property | 10-year felony |
|---|---|
| All other violations | 1-year misdemeanor |

## Tampering with Evidence—MCL 750.483a(5) (felony)

*A person shall not do any of the following:*

(a) *Knowingly and intentionally remove, alter, conceal, destroy, or otherwise tamper with evidence to be offered in a present or future official proceeding.*

(b) *Offer evidence at an official proceeding that he or she recklessly disregards as false.*

Subsection (b) does not apply to the lawful conduct of an attorney in the performance of his or her duties, such as advising a client or the lawful conduct or communications of a person as permitted by statute or other lawful privilege.

Penalties:

| Occurred in a case where the maximum penalty is more than 10 years | 10-year felony |
|---|---|
| All other cases | 4-year felony |

# TAKING WEAPONS FROM AN OFFICER

## Definitions—MCL 750.479b(6)

*Corrections officer:* A prison or jail guard or other employee of a jail or a state or federal correctional facility, who performs duties involving the transportation, care, custody, or supervision of prisoners.

*Peace officer:* One or more of the following:

- A police officer of this state or a political subdivision of this state.
- A police officer of any entity of the United States.
- The sheriff of a county of this state or the sheriff's deputy.
- A public safety officer of a college or university who is authorized by the governing board of that college or university to enforce state law

and the rules and ordinances of that college or university.
- A conservation officer of the department of natural resources.
- A conservation officer of the United States department of interior.

## Taking Weapons Other than Firearms—MCL 750.479b(1) (felony)

*An individual who takes a weapon other than a firearm from the lawful possession of a peace officer or a corrections officer is guilty of a felony punishable by imprisonment for not more than 4 years or a fine of not more than $2,500.00, or both, if all of the following circumstances exist at the time the weapon is taken:*

- *(a) The individual knows or has reason to believe the person from whom the weapon is taken is a peace officer or a corrections officer.*
- *(b) The peace officer or corrections officer is performing his or her duties as a peace officer or a corrections officer.*
- *(c) The individual takes the weapon without consent of the peace officer or corrections officer.*
- *(d) The peace officer or corrections officer is authorized by his or her employer to carry the weapon in the line of duty.*

## Taking a Firearm—MCL 750.479b(2) (felony)

*An individual who takes a firearm from the lawful possession of a peace officer or a corrections officer is guilty of a felony punishable by imprisonment for not more than 10 years or a fine of not more than $5,000.00, or both, if all of the following circumstances exist at the time the firearm is taken:*

- *(a) The individual knows or has reason to believe the person from whom the firearm is taken is a peace officer or a corrections officer.*
- *(b) The peace officer or corrections officer is performing his or her duties as a peace officer or a corrections officer.*
- *(c) The individual takes the firearm without the consent of the peace officer or corrections officer.*
- *(d) The peace officer or corrections officer is authorized by his or her employer to carry the firearm in the line of duty.*

### Elements

1. The defendant took a weapon,
2. From a police officer or corrections officer,
3. The defendant knew that the person was an officer,
4. The officer was performing his or her duties at the time,
5. The officer did not consent to the taking of the weapon, and
6. The officer was authorized to carry the weapon.

CJ12d 13.18.

# RESISTING AND OBSTRUCTING

(For Resisting and Obstructing a Police Officer, see Chapter 4)

## Resisting or Obstructing Officers in Discharge of Duty—MCL 750.479 (felony)

It is unlawful to knowingly and willfully assault, batter, wound, obstruct, or endanger any of the following:

- Medical examiner.
- Township treasurer.
- Judge, magistrate, court employee, or court officer.
- Probation or parole officer.
- Prosecutor or City attorney.
- Officers or duly authorized persons serving or attempting to serve process.
- Officers enforcing ordinance, law, rule, order, or resolution of local government.

This section applies when the individual knows, or has reason to know, that any of the above is performing their duties.

### Elements

1. The defendant assaulted, battered, wounded, obstructed, or endangered an officer or other authorized person who was performing his or her duties. "Obstruct" includes the use or threatened use of physical interference or force or a knowing failure to comply with a lawful command.
2. The defendant knew the person was then an officer [or other authorized person] performing his or her duties.
3. The defendant's actions were intended by the defendant, that is not accidental.

CJI2d 13.2.

Penalties:

| Without injury | 2-year felony |
|---|---|
| Causes bodily injury requiring medical attention | 4-year felony |
| Causes serious impairment of bodily function | 10-year felony |
| Causes death | 20-year felony |

The defendant's polite refusal to comply with a search warrant for his blood was held to be sufficient obstruction where the police officer did not force the defendant to comply. *People v. Philabaun*, 461 Mich. 255 (1999).

# LYING TO A POLICE OFFICER—MCL 750.479c

*Except as provided in this section, a person who is informed by a peace officer that he or she is conducting a criminal investigation shall not do any of the following:*

(a) *By any trick, scheme, or device, knowingly and willfully conceal from the peace officer any material fact relating to the criminal investigation.*

(b) *Knowingly and willfully make any statement to the peace officer that the person knows is false or misleading regarding a material fact in that criminal investigation.*

(c) *Knowingly and willfully issue or otherwise provide any writing or document to the peace officer that the person knows is false or misleading regarding a material fact in that criminal investigation.*

This statute does not apply to the following:

- Any statement made or action taken by an alleged victim of the crime being investigated by the peace officer.
- A person who was acting under duress or out of a reasonable fear of physical harm to himself or herself or another person from a spouse or former spouse, a person with whom he or she has or has had a dating relationship, a person with whom he or she has had a child in common, or a resident or former resident of his or her household.

This statute does not prohibit a person from doing either of the following:

- Invoking the person's rights under the Fifth Amendment.
- Declining to speak to or otherwise communicate with a peace officer concerning the criminal investigation.

Penalties:

| Crime being investigated is a "serious misdemeanor" | 93-day misdemeanor |
|---|---|
| Crime being investigated is a misdemeanor punishable by more than 1 year, or a felony punishable by less than 4 years | 1-year misdemeanor |
| Crime being investigated is a felony punishable by 4 years or more | 2-year misdemeanor |
| Crime being investigated is any of the following:<br>• First or second-degree murder<br>• Human trafficking<br>• CSC first degree<br>• Armed robbery<br>• Carjacking<br>• Terrorism<br>• Violations punishable by 20 years or more in prison<br>• Arson<br>• Explosives, bombs, and harmful devices<br>• Kidnapping | 4-year felony |

## Definitions

*Dating relationship:*   Frequent, intimate associations primarily characterized by the expectation of affectional involvement. This term does not include a casual relationship or an ordinary fraternization between two persons in a business or social context.

*Peace officer:*   Any of the following:

- A sheriff or deputy sheriff of a county of this state.
- An officer of the police department of a city, village, or township of this state.
- A marshal of a city, village, or township of this state.
- A constable of any local unit of government of this state.
- An officer of the Michigan State Police.
- A conservation officer of this state.
- A security employee employed by the state under MCL 28.6c.

- A motor carrier officer appointed under MCL 28.6d.
- A police officer or public safety officer of a community college, college, or university within this state who is authorized by the governing board of that community college, college, or university to enforce state law and the rules and ordinances of that community college, college, or university.
- A park and recreation officer commissioned under MCL 324.1606.
- A state forest officer commissioned under MCL 324.83107.
- An investigator of the state department of attorney general.
- An agent of the state department of human services, office of inspector general.
- A sergeant at arms or assistant sergeant at arms commissioned as a police officer under MCL 4.382.

***Serious misdemeanor:*** That term as defined in MCL 780.811 to include the following:

- Assault and battery. MCL 750.81.
- Assault, infliction of serious injury. MCL 750.81a.
- Breaking and entering, or illegal entry. MCL 750.115.
- Child abuse in the fourth degree. MCL 750.136b(6).
- Contributing to the neglect or delinquency of a minor. MCL 750.145.
- Using the Internet or a computer to make a prohibited communication. MCL 750.145d.
- Intentionally aiming a firearm without malice. MCL 750.233.
- Discharging a firearm intentionally aimed at a person. MCL 750.234.
- Discharge of an intentionally aimed firearm resulting in injury. MCL 750.235.
- Indecent exposure. MCL 750.335a.
- Stalking. MCL 750.411h.
- Injuring a worker in a work zone. MCL 257.601b.
- Leaving the scene of a personal injury accident. MCL 257.617a.
- O.W.I. and impaired driving, if the violation involves an accident resulting in injury or death to another person or damage to another's property. MCL 257.625; MCL 257.625a.
- Operating a vessel while under the influence of or impaired by alcoholic liquor or a controlled substance, or with an unlawful blood alcohol content, if the violation involves an accident resulting in damage to another individual's property or physical injury or death to any individual. MCL 324.80176.
- Selling or furnishing alcoholic liquor to an individual less than 21 years of age if the violation results in physical injury or death to any individual. MCL 436.1701.
- A local ordinance substantially corresponding to the above.

# FLEEING AND ELUDING—MCL 750.479A (FELONY)

*An operator of a motor vehicle or vessel who is given by hand, voice, emergency light, or siren a visual or audible signal by a police or conservation officer, acting in the lawful performance of his or her duty, directing the operator to bring his or her motor vehicle or vessel to a stop shall not willfully fail to obey that direction by increasing the speed of the vehicle or vessel, extinguishing the lights of the vehicle or vessel, or otherwise attempting to flee or elude the police or conservation officer. This subsection does not apply unless the police or conservation officer giving the signal is in uniform and the officer's vehicle or vessel is identified as an official police or department of natural resources vehicle or vessel.*

## First Degree—MCL 750.479a(5) (felony)
### Elements

1. A police [or conservation] officer was in uniform and was performing his lawful duties and that any vehicle driven by the officer was adequately marked as a law enforcement vehicle.
2. The defendant was driving a motor vehicle.
3. The officer ordered that the defendant stop his vehicle.
4. The defendant knew of the order.
5. The defendant refused to obey the order by trying to flee or avoid being caught.
6. The violation resulted in the death of another individual.

CJI2d 13.6a.

In a case where a pursuing police officer lost control of his vehicle, crashed, and was killed, the court ruled that the Legislature could have used either "results in the death of another" or "causes the death of another" in the statute. Further, the court held "results" is not the same as "causes," thus, the fleeing need only be the cause in fact of a death and not the proximate cause of a death. The defendant's conviction for first-degree fleeing and eluding was upheld. *People v. Wood*, 276 Mich. App. 669 (2007).

## Second Degree—MCL 750.479a(4) (felony)

### Elements

1. A police [or conservation] officer was in uniform and was performing his lawful duties and that any vehicle driven by the officer was adequately marked as a law enforcement vehicle.
2. The defendant was driving a motor vehicle.
3. The officer ordered that the defendant stop his vehicle.
4. The defendant knew of the order.
5. The defendant refused to obey the order by trying to flee or avoid being caught.
6. Any of the following is also true:

   a. The violation resulted in serious impairment of a body function to an individual.
   b. The defendant has one or more prior convictions for first-, second-, or third-degree fleeing and eluding; attempted first-, second-, or third-degree fleeing and eluding; or fleeing and eluding under a current or former law of this state prohibiting substantially similar conduct.
   c. The defendant has any combination of two or more prior convictions for fourth-degree fleeing and eluding, attempted fourth-degree fleeing and eluding, or fleeing and eluding under a current or former law of this state prohibiting substantially similar conduct.

CJI2d 13.6b.

"Serious impairment of a body function" includes, but is not limited to, one or more of the following: loss of a limb or loss of use of a limb; loss of a foot, hand, finger, or thumb or loss of use of a foot, hand, finger, or thumb; loss of an eye or ear or loss of use of an eye or ear; loss or substantial impairment of a bodily function; serious visible disfigurement; a comatose state that lasts for more than three days; measurable brain or mental impairment; a skull fracture or other serious bone fracture; subdural hemorrhage or subdural hematoma; or loss of an organ. MCL 257.58c.

## Third Degree—MCL 750.479a(3) (felony)

### Elements

1. A police [or conservation officer] was in uniform and was performing his lawful duties and that any vehicle driven by the officer was adequately marked as a law enforcement vehicle.

2. The defendant was driving a motor vehicle.
3. The officer ordered that the defendant stop his vehicle.
4. The defendant knew of the order.
5. The defendant refused to obey the order by trying to flee or avoid being caught.
6. Any of the following is also true:

   a. The violation resulted in a collision or accident.
   b. Some portion of the violation took place in an area where the speed limit was 35 miles per hour or less whether as posted or as a matter of law.
   c. The defendant has a prior conviction for fleeing and eluding in the fourth degree, attempted fleeing and eluding in the fourth degree, or fleeing and eluding under a current or former law of this state prohibiting substantially similar conduct.

CJI2d 13.6c.

There is "no requirement that the defendant's speeding exceed a certain level or that the speeding occur over a long distance in order for the elements of the statute to be met." *People v. Grayer*, 235 Mich. App. 737 (1999).

Since this is a general intent crime, voluntary intoxication is not a valid defense. *People v. Abramski*, 257 Mich. App. 71 (2003).

## Fourth Degree—MCL 750.479a(2) (felony)

### Elements

1. A police [or conservation officer] was in uniform and was performing his lawful duties and that any vehicle driven by the officer was adequately marked as a law enforcement vehicle.
2. The defendant was driving a motor vehicle.
3. The officer ordered that the defendant stop his vehicle.
4. The defendant knew of the order.
5. The defendant refused to obey the order by trying to flee or avoid being caught.

CJI2d 13.6d.

There was sufficient evidence to convict for fleeing and eluding where the officer in a fully marked police car activated his emergency equipment in an attempt to stop the defendant. The defendant refused to stop, drove approximately one mile at speeds of 25–30 mph, stopped his car, and ran up to a house. *People v. Grayer,* 235 Mich. App. 737 (1999).

There is no requirement for fleeing and eluding that the officer be present in an officially identified vehicle. In this case, the uniformed officer was standing away from his car when he ordered the suspect to stop. *People v. Green,* 260 Mich. App. 710 (2004).

Penalties:

| Fleeing and eluding—first degree | 15-year felony |
| Fleeing and eluding—second degree | 10-year felony |
| Fleeing and eluding—third degree | 5-year felony |
| Fleeing and eluding—fourth degree | 2-year felony |

# PEACE BONDS—MCL 772.1

*A district or municipal judge may cause all the laws made for the preservation of the public peace to be kept and, in the execution of this authority, may require a person to give security to keep the peace in the manner provided in this chapter.*

## Complaint—MCL 772.2

*If a complaint is made in writing and on oath to the district court or a municipal court that a person has threatened to commit an offense against the person or property of another, the judge shall examine on oath the complainant and any witnesses who may be produced.*

## Issuance of a Warrant by the Court—MCL 772.3

*If the judge determines from the examination that there is just reason to believe the person will commit an offense described in section 2 of this chapter, the judge may enter an order directing the person to appear on a date certain within 7 days. If the person fails to appear as ordered, the court shall issue a warrant. Alternatively, the court may issue a warrant directed to the sheriff or any peace officer, reciting the substance of the complaint and commanding that the person be promptly apprehended and brought before the court.*

## Arrest Authority—MCL 772.13a

*If a peace officer has reason to believe that the conditions of a recognizance required under this chapter are being violated in his or her presence or were violated, the peace officer shall arrest the person and hold him or her for presentation to the court on the next day.*

# PUBLIC INTEREST CRIMES: SELECTED STATUTES

## GAMBLING

### Gambling—MCL 750.301 (1-year misdemeanor)

*Any person or his or her agent or employee who, directly or indirectly, takes, receives, or accepts from any person any money or valuable thing with the agreement, understanding or allegation that any money or valuable thing will be paid or delivered to any person where the payment or delivery is alleged to be or will be contingent upon the result of any race, contest, or game or upon the happening of any event not known by the parties to be certain, is guilty of a misdemeanor punishable by imprisonment for not more than 1 year or a fine of not more than $1,000.00.*

Money or other valuable items were directly or indirectly taken, received, or accepted from a person. The valuables were taken with the agreement and understanding that they would be paid or delivered to another person contingent upon the result of any race, contest, game, or upon the happening of any uncertain event.

### Other Gambling Statutes

#### Keeping and Occupying a Gambling House—MCL 750.302 (1-year misdemeanor)

(1) *Except as provided in subsection (2), any person, or his or her agent or employee who, directly or indirectly, keeps, occupies, or assists in keeping or occupying any common gambling house or any building or place where gaming is permitted or suffered or who suffers or permits on any premises owned, occupied, or controlled by him or her any apparatus used for gaming or gambling or who shall use such apparatus for gaming or gambling in any place within this state, is guilty of a misdemeanor punishable by imprisonment for not more than 1 year or a fine of not more than $1,000.00.*

(2) *This section does not prohibit the manufacture of gaming or gambling apparatus or the possession of gaming or gambling apparatus by the manufacturer of the apparatus solely for sale outside of this state, or for sale to a gambling establishment operating within this state in compliance with the laws of this state, if applicable, and in compliance with the laws of the United States, provided the*

*manufacturer meets or exceeds federal government requirements in regard to manufacture, storage, and transportation.*

The Michigan Supreme Court overturned the conviction of a landlord who leased property that was used by the tenant as a gambling house. The court found that there was no evidence that the landlord controlled the premises, nor was there evidence that he allowed gambling devices on the premises. *People v. Johnson*, 323 Mich. 573 (1949).

Video poker machines are included under this statute unless they do not pay out money or something of value. *People v. Lopez*, 187 Mich. App. 305 (1991).

## Selling Pools and Registered Bets—MCL 750.304 (1-year misdemeanor)

*Any person or his or her agent or employee who, directly or indirectly, keeps, maintains, operates, or occupies any building or room or any part of a building or room or any place with apparatus, books, or any device for registering bets or buying or selling pools upon the result of a trial or contest of skill, speed or endurance or upon the result of a game, competition, political nomination, appointment, or election or any purported event of like character or who registers bets or buys or sells pools, or who is concerned in buying or selling pools or who knowingly permits any grounds or premises, owned, occupied, or controlled by him or her to be used for any of the purposes aforesaid, is guilty of a misdemeanor punishable by imprisonment for not more than 1 year or a fine of not more than $1,000.00.*

## Frequenting or Attending Gaming Places—MCL 750.309 (90-day misdemeanor)

*Any person who shall attend or frequent any place where gaming or gambling is suffered or permitted, or any place operated or occupied as a common gaming or gambling house or room, shall be guilty of a misdemeanor.*

# BODY ARMOR

## Definitions

*Body armor:* Clothing or a device designed or intended to protect an individual's body or a portion of an individual's body from injury caused by a firearm.

*Security officer:* An individual lawfully employed to physically protect another individual or to physically protect the property of another person.

*Violent felony:* An offense against a person in violation of the following:

- Felonious assault. MCL 750.82.
- Assault with intent to commit murder. MCL 750.83.
- Assault with intent to commit great bodily harm less than murder. MCL 750.84.
- Assault with intent to maim. MCL 750.86.
- Assault with intent to commit felony. MCL 750.87.
- Assault with intent to rob. MCL 750.88.
- Assault with intent to rob while armed. MCL 750.89.
- First-degree murder. MCL 750.316.
- Second-degree murder. MCL 750.317.
- Manslaughter. MCL 750.321.
- Kidnapping. MCL 750.349.
- Prisoner taking hostage. MCL 750.349a.
- Enticing a child under 14. MCL 750.350.
- Mayhem. MCL 750.397.
- CSC first degree. MCL 750.520b.
- CSC second degree. MCL 750.520c.
- CSC third degree. MCL 750.520d.
- CSC fourth degree. MCL 750.520e.
- Assault with intent to commit CSC. MCL 750.520g.
- Armed robbery. MCL 750.529.
- Carjacking. MCL 750.529a.
- Unarmed robbery. MCL 750.530.

## Use of Body Armor during Crime—MCL 750.227f (felony)

*An individual who commits or attempts to commit a crime that involves a violent act or a threat of a violent act against another person while wearing body armor is guilty of a felony, punishable by imprisonment for not more than 4 years, or a fine of not more than $2,000.00, or both.*

Does not apply to either of the following:

- A peace officer of this state or another state, of a local unit of government of this state or another state, or of the United States, performing his or her duties as a peace officer while on or off a scheduled work shift as a peace officer.
- A security officer performing his or her duties as a security officer while on a scheduled work shift as a security officer.

## Felons in Possession of Body Armor—MCL 750.227g (felony)

*A person who has been convicted of a violent felony shall not purchase, own, possess, or use body armor.*

Exception: A person convicted of a felony may petition the chief of a local unit of government of the county sheriff for written permission to purchase, own, possess, or use body armor if the person's employment, livelihood, or safety is dependent on his or her ability to do so. If the chief or sheriff does issue the written permission, the person must carry it at all times he or she is in possession of the body armor. Failure to carry the written permission is a 93-day misdemeanor.

# LIQUOR LAW VIOLATIONS

## License Requirement—MCL 436.1913

A person shall not maintain, operate, lease, or otherwise furnish to any person alcoholic liquor for consideration without a license.

## Inspections—MCL 436.1217(2)

A licensee shall make the licensed premises available for inspection and search by a commission investigator or law enforcement officer empowered to enforce the commission's rules and this act during regular business hours or when the licensed premises are occupied by the licensee or a clerk, servant, agent, or employee of the licensee. Evidence of a violation of this act or rules promulgated under this act discovered under this subsection may be seized and used in an administrative or court proceeding.

## Definitions

*Alcoholic liquor:*   More than half of one percent of alcohol per volume.

*Any bodily alcohol content:*   Either of the following:

- An alcohol content of 0.02 grams or more per 100 milliliters of blood, per 210 liters of breath, or per 67 milliliters of urine.
- Any presence of alcohol within a person's body resulting from the consumption of alcoholic liquor, other than consumption of alcoholic liquor as a part of a generally recognized religious service or ceremony.

*Consideration:*   Any fee, cover charge, the storage of alcoholic liquor, the sale of food, ice, mixers, or other liquids used with alcoholic liquor drinks, or

the furnishing of glassware or other containers for use in the consumption of alcoholic liquor in conjunction with the sale of food.

*Corrective action:*   Action taken by a licensee or a clerk, agent, or employee of a licensee designed to prevent a minor from further possessing or consuming alcoholic liquor on the licensed premises. Corrective action includes, but is not limited to, contacting a law enforcement agency and ejecting the minor and any other person suspected of aiding and abetting the minor.

*Diligent inquiry:*   A diligent good faith effort to determine the age of a person, which includes at least an examination of an official Michigan operator's or chauffeur's license, an official Michigan personal identification card, a military identification card, or any other bona fide picture identification which establishes the identity and age of the person.

*Emergency medical services personnel:*  A medical first responder, emergency medical technician, emergency medical technician specialist, paramedic, or emergency medical services instructor-coordinator.

*Health facility or agency:*   Any of the following:

- An ambulance operation, aircraft transport operation, nontransport prehospital life support operation, or medical first response service.
- A clinical laboratory.
- A county medical care facility.
- A freestanding surgical outpatient facility.
- A health maintenance organization.
- A home for the aged.
- A hospital.
- A nursing home.
- A hospice.
- A hospice residence.
- A facility or agency listed in subdivisions (a) to (h) located in a university, college, or other educational institution.

*Minor:*   A person under 21 years of age.

*School:*   Public school kindergarten through 12th grade.

*School property:*   Buildings, playing fields, vehicles, or other property used for functions and events sponsored by a school. Does not include a building primarily used for adult education or college extension courses.

## Furnishing Alcoholic Liquor to Minors— Generally—MCL 436.1701(1)

*Alcoholic liquor shall not be sold or furnished to a minor. … [A] person who knowingly sells or furnishes alcoholic liquor to a minor, or who fails to make diligent inquiry as to whether the person is a minor, is guilty of a misdemeanor.*

Penalties:

| First offense | 60-day misdemeanor |
|---|---|
| Second or subsequent offense | 90-day misdemeanor |

This section does not apply to a retail licensee or a retail licensee's clerk, agent, or employee

## Furnishing Alcoholic Liquor to Minors—Death—MCL 436.1701(2) (felony)

*A person who is not a retail licensee or the retail licensee's clerk, agent, or employee and who violates subsection (1) is guilty of a felony, punishable by imprisonment for not more than 10 years or a fine of not more than $5,000.00, or both, if the subsequent consumption of the alcoholic liquor by the minor is a direct and substantial cause of that person's death or an accidental injury that causes that person's death.*

This section does not apply to a retail licensee or a retail licensee's clerk, agent, or employee

## Furnishing Alcoholic Liquor to Minors—Retail Licensee or Clerk—MCL 436.1701(1)

*A retail licensee or a retail licensee's clerk, agent, or employee who violates this subsection shall be punished in the manner provided for licensees in [MCL 436.1909] except that if the violation is the result of an undercover operation in which the minor received alcoholic liquor under the direction of the state police, the commission, or a local police agency as part of an enforcement action, the retail licensee's clerk, agent, or employee is responsible for a state civil infraction and may be ordered to pay a civil fine of not more than $100.00.*

Penalties:

| Violation is the result of an undercover operation in which the minor received alcoholic liquor under the direction of the police. | State civil infraction |
|---|---|
| All other offenses | 6-month misdemeanor |

## Furnishing Alcoholic Liquor to Minors—Establishment Licensed for Consumption—MCL 436.1701(3)

*If a violation occurs in an establishment that is licensed by the commission for consumption of alcoholic liquor on the licensed premises, a person who is a licensee or the clerk, agent, or employee of a licensee shall not be charged with a violation of [MCL 436.1701(1)] or [MCL 436.1801(2)] unless the licensee or the clerk, agent, or employee of the licensee knew or should have reasonably known with the exercise of due diligence that a person less than 21 years of age possessed or consumed alcoholic liquor on the licensed premises and the licensee or clerk, agent, or employee of the licensee failed to take immediate corrective action.*

## Minor in Possession of Alcoholic Liquor—MCL 436.1703

*A minor shall not purchase or attempt to purchase alcoholic liquor, consume or attempt to consume alcoholic liquor, possess or attempt to possess alcoholic liquor, or have any bodily alcohol content, except as provided in this section. A minor who violates this subsection is guilty of a misdemeanor.*

Penalties:

| First offense | Misdemeanor–no jail |
|---|---|
| Second offense | 30-day misdemeanor |
| Third or subsequent offense | 60-day misdemeanor |

## Immunity—MCL 436.1703(10)

The following individuals are not considered to be in violation of the statute:

- A minor who has consumed alcoholic liquor and who voluntarily presents himself or herself to a health facility or agency for treatment or for observation including, but not limited to, medical examination and treatment for any condition arising from a CSC offense committed against a minor.
- A minor who accompanies an individual who has consumed alcohol and who voluntarily presents himself or herself for treatment or for observation including, but not limited to, medical examination and treatment for any

condition arising from a CSC offense committed against a minor.

- A minor who initiates contact with a peace officer or emergency medical services personnel for the purpose of obtaining medical assistance for a legitimate health care concern.

## Exceptions—MCL 436.1703(13)-(15)

The consumption of alcoholic liquor by a minor who is enrolled in a course offered by an accredited post-secondary educational institution in an academic building of the institution under the supervision of a faculty member is not prohibited by this act if the purpose of the consumption is solely educational and is a requirement of the course.

The consumption by a minor of sacramental wine in connection with religious services at a church, synagogue, or temple is not prohibited by this act.

Statute does not apply to a minor who participates in either or both of the following:

- An undercover operation in which the minor purchases or receives alcoholic liquor under the direction of the person's employer and with the prior approval of the local prosecutor's office as part of an employer-sponsored internal enforcement action.
- An undercover operation in which the minor purchases or receives alcoholic liquor under the direction of the state police, the commission, or a local police agency as part of an enforcement action unless the initial or contemporaneous purchase or receipt of alcoholic liquor by the minor was not under the direction of the state police, the commission, or the local police agency and was not part of the undercover operation.

## Affirmative Defense-MCL 436.1703(17)

In a criminal prosecution for a violation concerning a minor having any bodily alcohol content, it is an affirmative defense that the minor consumed the alcoholic liquor in a venue or location where that consumption is legal.

The defendant was a passenger in a vehicle that was stopped for speeding. After the driver of the vehicle was given a Breathalyzer test that indicated the driver had consumed

alcohol, the police officers tested defendant, who also tested positive for alcohol consumption. The defendant moved to dismiss the charges alleging that he drank legally in Canada. The court held that "minors who legally ingest alcohol in a jurisdiction outside Michigan and then return to Michigan (e.g., as passengers in a vehicle) with the alcohol in their bodies have not violated the minor in possession statute." *People v Rutledge*, 250 Mich. App. 1 (2002)

## Preliminary Breath Test (PBT)—MCL 436.1703(7)

The constitutionality of the provisions of the subsection of the minor in possession statute requiring minors to submit to a PBT has been called into question by the United States District Court for the Eastern District of Michigan. That Court has enjoined the Michigan State Police and the Thomas Township Police Department from enforcing that subsection. While that injunction only binds those two agencies, it is advisable that all officers consult with their prosecutors before enforcing that subsection. PBTs may still be administered with a minor's consent by any officer. *Platte v. Thomas Twp.*, 504 F. Supp. 2d 227 (E.D. Mich. 2007).

A PBT administered to a minor constituted a search within the meaning of the Fourth Amendment, to which defendant did not consent. None of the exceptions to the search warrant requirement applied, and the police officers were accordingly required to seek and obtain a valid search warrant before administering the PBT to defendant. *People v. Chowdhury*, 285 Mich. App. 509 (2009).

## Authority to Detain—MCL 436.1705

A peace officer may stop and detain a person and obtain satisfactory identification for a violation of MCL 436.1703.

## Parental Notice—MCL 436.1703(8)

*A law enforcement agency, upon determining that an individual less than 18 years of age who is not emancipated under 1968 PA 293, MCL 722.1 to 722.6, allegedly consumed, possessed, purchased alcoholic liquor, attempted to consume, possess, or purchase alcoholic liquor, or had any bodily alcohol content in violation of subsection (1) shall notify the parent or parents, custodian, or guardian of the individual as to the nature of the violation if the name of a parent, guardian, or custodian is reasonably ascertainable by the law enforcement agency. The law enforcement agency shall notify the parent, guardian, or custodian not later than 48 hours after the law enforcement agency determines that the individual who allegedly violated subsection (1) is less than 18 years of age and not emancipated under 1968 PA 293, MCL 722.1 to 722.6. The law enforcement agency may notify the parent, guardian, or custodian by any means reasonably calculated to give prompt actual notice including, but not limited to, notice in person, by telephone, or by first-class mail. If an individual less than 17 years of age is incarcerated for violating subsection (1), his or her parents or legal guardian shall be notified immediately as provided in this subsection.*

### Undercover Operations and Recruiting Minors— MCL 436.1705(16)

*The state police, the commission, or a local police agency shall not recruit or attempt to recruit a minor for participation in an undercover operation at the scene of a violations involving minors in possession of alcohol and furnishing alcohol to minors.*

### Furnishing Fraudulent Identification to a Minor— MCL 436.1703(2) (93 day-misdemeanor)

*An individual who furnishes fraudulent identification to a minor, or notwithstanding subsection (1) a minor who uses fraudulent identification to purchase alcoholic liquor, is guilty of a misdemeanor punishable by imprisonment for not more than 93 days or a fine of not more than $100.00, or both.*

### Possessing or Consuming Alcoholic Liquor in Certain Places—MCL 436.1915 (90-day misdemeanor)

Alcoholic liquor shall not be consumed on public highways.

Alcoholic liquor may be consumed in public parks, public places of amusement, or publicly owned areas unless prohibited by local governments or state agencies with authority over the lands.

### Consuming Alcoholic Liquor on School Property— MCL 436.1904

*A person shall not consume alcoholic liquor or possess with the intent to consume alcoholic liquor on school property.*

Penalties:

| 1st offense | 93-day misdemeanor/$250 |
|---|---|
| 2nd offense | 93-day misdemeanor/$500 |
| 3rd offense or more | 1-year misdemeanor/$1,000 |

This section does not apply to a recognized religious event or if allowed by the superintendent or administrator of the school.

This section does not prohibit additional charges arising out of the same transaction, except violations under MCL 436.1703.

## POLICE SCANNERS—MCL 750.508

It is unlawful for a person to possess a police scanner in any of the following circumstances:

| The person has been convicted of a felony within the preceding 5 years | 1-year misdemeanor |
|---|---|
| The person is committing a crime punishable by at least 93 days but less than 1 year | 1-year misdemeanor |
| The person is committing a crime punishable by 1 year or more | 2-year felony |

It is not a crime to possess a scanner while committing a crime punishable by less than 93 days.

## PEDDLER LICENSE VIOLATIONS

### Transient Merchant—MCL 445.372 (misdemeanor, fine only)

*It is unlawful for any person, either as a principal or agent, to engage in a business as a transient merchant in the State of Michigan without having first obtained a license.*

***Transient merchant:*** Any person, firm, association, or corporation engaging temporarily in a retail sale of goods, wares, or merchandise, in any place in this state and who, for the purpose of conducting business, occupies any lot, building, room, or structure of any kind. The term shall not apply to any of the following:

- A person selling goods, wares, or merchandise of any description raised, produced, or manufactured by the individual offering the same for sale.
- A person soliciting orders by sample, brochure, or sales catalog for future delivery or making sales at residential premises pursuant to an invitation issued by the owner or legal occupant of the premises.
- A person handling vegetables, fruits, or perishable farm products at any established city or village market.
- A person operating a store or refreshment stand at a resort or having a booth on or adjacent to the property owned or occupied by him or her.
- A person operating a stand on any fairgrounds.
- A person selling at an art fair or festival or similar event at the invitation of the event's sponsor, if all of the following conditions are met:
  - The sponsor is a governmental entity or non-profit organization.
  - The person provides the sponsor with the person's sales tax license number.
  - The sponsor provides a list of the event's vendors and their sales tax license numbers to the county treasurer and the state treasurer.

***Confiscation of goods:*** If the county sheriff or local law enforcement officer has probable cause to believe that a person is engaging in business as a transient merchant without having first obtained a license, the officer shall immediately impound all goods offered for sale until the matter has been adjudicated by court.

### Restrictions on Items to be Sold at Flea Markets and Swap Meets—MCL 750.411r (93-day misdemeanor)

An unused property merchant is a person who sells, offers, displays, or exchanges tangible personal property at an unused property market, such as swap meets, indoor swap meets, or flea markets.

An unused property merchant may not sell one or more of the following:

- Food manufactured, packaged, and labeled specifically for sale or consumption by a child less than two years of age.
- A non-prescription drug that is past its expiration date.
- A medical device.

This section does not apply a merchant who has written authorization from the manufacturer of the product. Use of a false or forged authorization is a 93-day misdemeanor.

An unused property merchant shall retain for two years a purchase receipt for each new and unused property the merchant acquires. The following are 93-day misdemeanors:

- Falsifying a receipt.
- Refusing or failing to make a receipt available for inspection by a law enforcement officer within a reasonable time after the request.
- Destroying the receipt before the end of the two-year period.

## ANIMAL OFFENSES
### Definitions—MCL 750.50

***Adequate care:*** The provision of sufficient food, water, shelter, sanitary conditions, exercise, and veterinary medical attention in order to maintain an animal in a state of good health.

***Animal:*** Any vertebrate other than a human being.

***Animal protection shelter:*** A facility operated by a person, humane society, society for the prevention of cruelty to animals, or any other nonprofit organization, for the care of homeless animals.

***Animal control shelter:*** A facility operated by a county, city, village, or township to impound and care for animals found in streets or otherwise at large contrary to any ordinance of the county, city, village, or township or state law.

***Licensed veterinarian:*** A person licensed to practice veterinary medicine under MCL 333.16101 to 333.18838.

***Livestock:*** Those species of animals used for human food and fiber or those species of animals used for service to humans. Livestock includes, but is not limited to, cattle, sheep, new world camelids, goats, bison, privately owned cervids, ratites, swine, equine, poultry, aquaculture, and rabbits. Livestock does not include dogs and cats.

***Person:*** An individual, partnership, limited liability company, corporation, association, governmental entity, or other legal entity.

***Neglect:*** To fail to sufficiently and properly care for an animal to the extent that the animal's health is jeopardized.

***Sanitary conditions:*** Space free from health hazards including excessive animal waste, overcrowding of animals, or other conditions that endanger the animal's health. This definition does not include any condition resulting from a customary and reasonable practice pursuant to farming or animal husbandry.

*Shelter:* Adequate protection from the elements and weather conditions suitable for the age, species, and physical condition of the animal so as to maintain the animal in a state of good health. Shelter, for livestock, includes structures or natural features such as trees or topography. Shelter, for a dog, includes one or more of the following:

- The residence of the dog's owner or other individual.
- A doghouse that is an enclosed structure with a roof and of appropriate dimensions for the breed and size of the dog. The doghouse shall have dry bedding when the outdoor temperature is or is predicted to drop below freezing.
- A structure, including a garage, barn, or shed, that is sufficiently insulated and ventilated to protect the dog from exposure to extreme temperatures or, if not sufficiently insulated and ventilated, contains a doghouse as provided above that is accessible to the dog.

*State of good health:* Freedom from disease and illness, and in a condition of proper body weight and temperature for the age and species of the animal, unless the animal is undergoing appropriate treatment.

*Tethering:* The restraint and confinement of a dog by use of a chain, rope, or similar device.

*Water:* Potable water that is suitable for the age and species of animal that is made regularly available unless otherwise directed by a licensed veterinarian.

## Cruelty to Animals—MCL 750.50

*An owner, possessor, or person having the charge or custody of an animal shall not do any of the following:*

(a) *Fail to provide an animal with adequate care.*
(b) *Cruelly drive, work, or beat an animal, or cause an animal to be cruelly driven, worked, or beaten.*
(c) *Carry or cause to be carried in or upon a vehicle or otherwise any live animal having the feet or legs tied together, other than an animal being transported for medical care, or a horse whose feet are hobbled to protect the horse during transport or in any other cruel and inhumane manner.*
(d) *Carry or cause to be carried a live animal in or upon a vehicle or otherwise without providing a secure space, rack, car, crate, or cage, in which livestock may stand, and in which all other animals may stand, turn around, and lie down during transportation, or while awaiting slaughter. As used in this subdivision, for purposes of transportation of sled dogs, "stand" means sufficient vertical distance to allow the animal to stand without its shoulders touching the top of the crate or transportation vehicle.*
(e) *Abandon an animal or cause an animal to be abandoned, in any place, without making provisions for the animal's adequate care, unless premises are vacated for the protection of human life or the prevention of injury to a human. An animal that is lost by an owner or custodian while traveling, walking, hiking, or hunting is not abandoned under this section when the owner or custodian has made a reasonable effort to locate the animal.*
(f) *Negligently allow any animal, including one who is aged, diseased, maimed, hopelessly sick, disabled, or nonambulatory to suffer unnecessary neglect, torture, or pain.*
(g) *Tether a dog unless the tether is at least 3 times the length of the dog as measured from the tip of its nose to the base of its tail and is attached to a harness or nonchoke collar designed for tethering.*

This section does not prohibit the lawful killing or other use of an animal, including the following:

- Fishing.
- Hunting, trapping, or wildlife control regulated under MCL 324.101 to 324.90106.
- Horse racing.
- The operation of a zoological park or aquarium.
- Pest or rodent control regulated under MCL 324.8301 to 324.8336.
- Farming or a generally accepted animal husbandry or farming practice involving livestock.
- Activities authorized under MCL 16.109.
- Scientific research under MCL 287.381 to 287.395.
- Scientific research under MCL 333.2226, 333.2671, 333.2676, and 333.7333.

This section does not apply to a veterinarian or a veterinary technician lawfully engaging in the practice of veterinary medicine under MCL 333.18801 to 333.18838.

Penalties:

| Injury to 1 animal | 93-day misdemeanor |
|---|---|
| Injury of 2–3 animals or the death of any animal | 1-year misdemeanor |
| Injury to 4–9 animals or a prior conviction under MCL 750.50 | 2-year felony |
| Injury to 10 or more animals or 2 or more prior convictions under MCL 750.50 | 4-year felony |

The defendants were the owners and the caretakers of 69 lice-ridden horses that did not have access to adequate food and water. The court held that there was sufficient evidence that a crime was committed and that the defendants committed that crime. The prosecution is not required to prove that the defendants intended to harm the horses. Further, forfeiture of the horses was justified under subsection (3) of the statute because a preponderance of the evidence showed the owner failed to provide the horses with adequate care. The forfeiture may occur before disposition of the criminal charges. *People v. Henderson*, 282 Mich. App. 307 (2009).

## Killing/Torturing Animals—MCL 750.50b (felony)

*Except as otherwise provided in this section, a person shall not do any of the following without just cause:*

(a) *Knowingly kill, torture, mutilate, maim, or disfigure an animal.*
(b) *Commit a reckless act knowing or having reason to know that the act will cause an animal to be killed, tortured, mutilated, maimed, or disfigured.*
(c) *Knowingly administer poison to an animal, or knowingly expose an animal to any poisonous substance, with the intent that the substance be taken or swallowed by the animal.*

This section does not prohibit the lawful killing of livestock or a customary animal husbandry or farming practice involving livestock.

This section does not prohibit the lawful killing of an animal pursuant to any of the following:

- Fishing.
- Hunting, trapping, or wildlife control regulated under MCL 324.101 to 324.90106.
- Pest or rodent control regulated under MCL 324.8301 to 324.8336.
- Activities authorized under MCL 16.109.
- Killing of dog pursuing, worrying, or wounding livestock or poultry, or attacking person under MCL 287.279.
- Scientific research under MCL 287.381 to 287.395.
- Scientific research under MCL 333.2226, 333.2671, 333.2676, and 333.7333.

This section does not prohibit the lawful killing or other use of an animal, including the following:

- Scientific research under MCL 287.381 to 287.395.
- Scientific research under MCL 333.2226, 333.2671, 333.2676, and 333.7333.

This section does not apply to a veterinarian or a veterinary technician lawfully engaging in the practice of veterinary medicine under MCL 333.18801 to 333.18838.

A subject could be charged with animal cruelty when he threw firecrackers into a barn that subsequently caught on fire, killing 19 horses. Animal cruelty is a general intent crime. *People v. Fennell*, 260 Mich. App. 261 (2004).

The defendant admitted shooting and killing his neighbor's dog because it was attacking his dogs. He argued that this shooting was justified under MCL 287.279, which allows a person to kill a dog that is attacking livestock, poultry, or person. The court held that dogs are not livestock so the defendant could be charged under MCL 750.50b. *People v. Bugaiski*, 224 Mich. App. 241 (1997).

## Fighting Animals—MCL 750.49

It is a felony for a person to knowingly do any of the following:

- Own, possess, use, buy, sell, offer to buy or sell, import, or export an animal for fighting or baiting, or as a target to be shot at as a test of skill in marksmanship.
- Be a party to or cause the fighting, baiting, or shooting of an animal.

- Rent or otherwise obtain the use of a building, shed, room, yard, ground, or premises for fighting, baiting, or shooting an animal.
- Permit the use of a building, shed, room, yard, ground, or premises belonging to him or her or under his or her control for any of the purposes prohibited by this statute.
- Organize, promote, or collect money for the fighting, baiting, or shooting of an animal.
- Be present at a building, shed, room, yard, ground, or premises where preparations are being made for an exhibition described above, or be present at the exhibition, knowing that an exhibition is taking place or about to take place.
- Breed, buy, sell, offer to buy or sell, exchange, import, or export an animal (or offspring) the person knows has been trained or used for fighting (except when animal is kept for agricultural purposes).
- Own, possess, use, buy, sell, offer to buy or sell, transport, or deliver any device or equipment intended for use in the fighting, baiting, or shooting of an animal.

It is also a felony to incite an animal trained or used for fighting, or an animal that is the first or second generation offspring of an animal trained or used for fighting, to attack a person. This does not apply if the person attacked was committing a crime.

If an animal trained or used for fighting or an animal that is the first or second generation offspring of an animal trained or used for fighting attacks a person without provocation, the owner is guilty of a felony if the person dies and a one-year misdemeanor if the person does not die. This does not apply if the person attacked was committing a crime.

If an animal trained or used for fighting or an animal that is the first or second generation offspring of a dog trained or used for fighting goes beyond the property limits of its owner without being securely restrained, the owner is guilty of a 90-day misdemeanor.

If an animal trained or used for fighting or an animal that is the first or second generation offspring of a dog trained or used for fighting is not securely enclosed or restrained on the owner's property, the owner is guilty of a 90-day misdemeanor.

The statute contains exceptions for police dogs, leader dogs, or dogs used by licensed private security.

## Confiscation and forfeiture

An animal that has been used to fight in violation of this section shall be confiscated as contraband by a law enforcement officer and shall not be returned to the owner, trainer, or possessor of the animal. The animal shall be taken to a local humane society or other animal welfare agency.

All animals being used or to be used in fighting, equipment, devices, and money involved shall be forfeited to the state. All other instrumentalities, proceeds, and substituted proceeds of a violation of subsection (2) are subject to forfeiture under chapter 47 of the revised judicature act of 1961, 1961 PA 236, MCL 600.4701 to 600.4709.

> This statute was not unconstitutionally vague where the defendant was observed training his two dogs to fight, and then they subsequently escaped their pen and killed a person. *People v. Beam*, 244 Mich. App. 103 (2000).

## Beat or Impede Service Dog—MCL 750.50a (90-day misdemeanor)

*An individual shall not do either of the following:*

(a) *Willfully and maliciously assault, beat, harass, injure, or attempt to assault, beat, harass or injure a dog that he or she knows or has reason to believe is a guide or leader dog for a blind individual, a hearing dog for a deaf or audibly impaired individual, or a service dog for a physically limited individual.*

(b) *Willfully and maliciously impede or interfere with, or attempt to impede or interfere with duties performed by a dog that he or she knows or has reason to believe is a guide or leader dog for a blind individual, a hearing dog for a deaf or audibly impaired individual, or a service dog for a physically limited individual.*

## Definitions

*Audibly impaired:*   The inability to hear air conduction thresholds an average of 40 decibels or greater in the individual's better ear.

*Blind:*   Having a visual acuity of 20/200 or less in the individual's better eye with correction, or having a limitation of the individual's field of vision such that the widest diameter of the visual field subtends an angular distance not greater than 20 degrees.

*Deaf:*   The individual's hearing is totally impaired or the individual's hearing, with or without amplification, is so seriously impaired that the primary means of receiving spoken language is through other sensory input, including, but not limited to, lip reading, sign language, finger spelling, or reading.

*Harass:* To engage in any conduct directed toward a guide, leader, hearing, or service dog that is likely to impede or interfere with the dog's performance of its duties or that places the blind, deaf, audibly impaired, or physically limited individual being served or assisted by the dog in danger of injury.

*Injure:* To cause any physical injury to a dog that he or she knows or has reason to believe is a guide or leader dog for a blind individual, a hearing dog for a deaf or audibly impaired individual, or a service dog for a physically limited individual.

*Maliciously:* Any of the following done to a dog that he or she knows or has reason to believe is a guide or leader dog for a blind individual, a hearing dog for a deaf or audibly impaired individual, or a service dog for a physically limited individual:

- With intent to assault, beat, harass or injure a dog.
- With intent to impede or interfere with duties performed by the dog.
- With intent to disturb, endanger, or cause emotional distress to a blind, deaf, audibly impaired, or physically limited individual being served or assisted by a dog.
- With knowledge that the individual's conduct will, or is likely to harass or injure a dog.
- With knowledge that the individual's conduct will, or is likely to impede or interfere with duties performed by a dog.
- With knowledge that the individual's conduct will, or is likely to disturb, endanger, or cause emotional distress to a blind, deaf, audibly impaired, or physically limited individual being served or assisted by a dog.

*Physically limited:* Having limited ambulatory abilities and includes but is not limited to having a temporary or permanent impairment or condition that does one or more of the following:

- Causes the individual to use a wheelchair or walk with difficulty or insecurity.
- Affects sight or hearing to the extent that an individual is insecure or exposed to danger.
- Causes faulty coordination.
- Reduces mobility, flexibility, coordination, or perceptiveness.

## Killing, Harming, Harassing or Interfering with a Police Dog or Horse or Search and Rescue Dog— MCL 750.50c

A person shall not intentionally do any of the following:

- Kill or cause serious physical harm to a police dog or police horse or a search and rescue dog.

- Cause physical harm to a police dog or police horse or a search and rescue dog.
- Harass or interfere with a police dog or police horse or search and rescue dog lawfully performing its duties.

## Definitions

*Dog handler:* A peace officer who has successfully completed training in the handling of a police dog pursuant to a policy of the law enforcement agency that employs that peace officer.

*Physical harm:* Any injury to a dog's or horse's physical condition.

*Police dog:* A dog used by a law enforcement agency of this state or of a local unit of government of this state that is trained for law enforcement work and subject to the control of a dog handler.

*Police horse:* A horse used by a law enforcement agency of this state or of a local unit of government of this state for law enforcement work.

*Search and rescue dog:* A dog that is trained for, being trained for, or engaged in a search and rescue operation.

*Search and rescue operation:* An effort conducted at the direction of an agency of this state or of a political subdivision of this state to locate or rescue a lost, injured, or deceased individual.

*Serious physical harm:* Any injury to a dog's or horse's physical condition or welfare that is not necessarily permanent but that constitutes substantial body disfigurement, or that seriously impairs the function of a body organ or limb.

Penalties:

| | |
|---|---|
| Cause physical harm or harass or interfere with a police dog, police horse, or search and rescue dog | 1-year misdemeanor |
| Cause physical harm or harass or interfere with a police dog, police horse, or search and rescue dog while committing a crime | 2-year felony |
| Kill or cause serious physical harm to a police dog, police horse, or search and rescue dog | 5-year felony |

## Dog Bites—MCL 750.66 (93-day misdemeanor)

*If a person 18 years of age or older is responsible for controlling the actions of a dog or wolf-dog cross and the person knows or has reason to know that the dog or wolf-dog cross has bitten another person, the person shall immediately provide the person who was bitten with all of the following information:*

*(a) His or her name and address and, if that person does not own the dog or wolf-dog cross, the name and address of the dog's or wolf-dog cross's owner.*

*(b) Information, if known by that person, as to whether the dog or wolf-dog cross is current on all legally required vaccinations.*

This section does not apply if the person is bitten by a police dog.

As used in this section, "*dog*" and "*wolf-dog cross*" mean those terms as defined in MCL 287.1002.

If a person who is responsible for a dog or wolf-dog knows or has reason to know that the animal has bitten another person, then he or she must immediately provide the bitten person with both of the following:

- His or her name and address and the dog owner's name and address.
- Information on the dog's vaccinations.

## Dangerous Animals

### Definitions—MCL 287.321

*Dangerous animal* means a dog or other animal that bites or attacks a person, or a dog that bites or attacks and causes serious injury or death to another dog while the other dog is on the property or under the control of its owner. However, a dangerous animal does not include any of the following:

- An animal that bites or attacks a person who is knowingly trespassing on the property of the animal's owner.
- An animal that bites or attacks a person who provokes or torments the animal.
- An animal that is responding in a manner that an ordinary and reasonable person would conclude was designed to protect a person if that person is engaged in a lawful activity or is the subject of an assault.
- Livestock.

*Livestock:* Animals used for human food and fiber or animals used for service to human beings. Livestock includes, but is not limited to, cattle, swine, sheep, llamas, goats, bison, equine, poultry, and rabbits. Livestock does not include animals that are human companions, such as dogs and cats.

*Owner:* A person who owns or harbors a dog or other animal.

*Provoke:* To perform a willful act or omission that an ordinary and reasonable person would conclude is likely to precipitate the bite or attack by an ordinary dog or animal.

*Serious injury:* Permanent, serious disfigurement, serious impairment of health, or serious impairment of a bodily function of a person.

*Torment:* An act or omission that causes unjustifiable pain, suffering, and distress to an animal, or causes mental and emotional anguish in the animal as evidenced by its altered behavior, for a purpose such as sadistic pleasure, coercion, or punishment that an ordinary and reasonable person would conclude is likely to precipitate the bite or attack.

### Dangerous Animal Causing Death—MCL 287.323(1) (felony)

*The owner of an animal that meets the definition of a dangerous animal that causes the death of a person is guilty of involuntary manslaughter, punishable under MCL 750.321.*

### Dangerous Animal Causing Serious Injury—MCL 287.323(2) (felony)

*If an animal that meets the definition of a dangerous animal attacks a person and causes serious injury other than death, the owner of the animal is guilty of a felony, punishable by imprisonment for not more than 4 years, a fine of not less than $2,000.00, or community service work for not less than 500 hours, or any combination of these penalties.*

### Elements

1. The defendant owned or harbored a dog or other animal.
2. That the dog or other animal met the definition of a dangerous animal provided under MCL 287.321(a) prior to and throughout the incident at issue.
3. The defendant knew that the dog or other animal met the definition of a dangerous animal within the meaning of MCL 287.321(a) prior to the incident at issue.
4. The animal attacked a person and caused a serious injury other than death.

### Dangerous Animal Causing Injury—MCL 287.323(3) (90-day misdemeanor)

*If an animal previously adjudicated to be a dangerous animal attacks or bites a person and causes an injury that is not a serious injury, the owner of* *the animal is guilty of a misdemeanor, punishable by imprisonment for not more than 90 days, a fine of not less than $250.00 nor more than $500.00, or community service work for not less than 240 hours, or any combination of these penalties.*

## Allowing Dangerous Animal to Run at Large—MCL 287.323(4) (90-day misdemeanor)

*If the owner of an animal that is previously adjudicated to be a dangerous animal allows the animal to run at large, the owner is guilty of a misdemeanor, punishable by imprisonment for not more than 90 days, a fine of not less than $250.00 nor more than $500.00, or community service work for not less than 240 hours, or any combination of these penalties.*

# DISORDERLY CONDUCT

## Disorderly Person—MCL 750.167 (90-day misdemeanor)

Includes any of the following:

- A person with sufficient ability who refuses to or neglects to support his or her family.

The prosecutor has discretion to charge this offense under the misdemeanor disorderly statute or under the felony desertion and nonsupport statute (MCL 750.161). OAG, 1943–1944, No. 2,096, p 705 (April 13, 1944).

Support includes sufficient funds to provide for shelter, clothing, and medical expenses, not just sufficient funds for food. *People v. Beckman*, 239 Mich. 590 (1927).

- A common prostitute.
- A window peeper.

Conduct: The defendant's conviction under a Grand Rapids ordinance similar to the Michigan statute was affirmed where, at night, the defendant left the sidewalk, proceeded to a lighted residence, and stood six feet away. He then looked into the window where the shade was raised. *City of Grand Rapids v. Williams*, 112 Mich. 247 (1897).

- A person involved in illegal occupation or business.

The defendant's conviction was upheld where he was running an illegal "mutuels" gaming system (i.e., a "numbers" lottery). *People v. Singer*, 304 Mich. 70 (1942).

- A person intoxicated in a public place who either:
  - Directly endangers the safety of another person or of property,
  - Acts in a manner that causes a public disturbance.

The public disturbance provision of the disorderly statute requires a finding that the accused, while intoxicated, directly endangered the safety of another person or another person's property. *People v. Gagnon*, 129 Mich. App. 678 (1983).

To convict a defendant under MCL 750.167(1)(e), the statute requires not only that the disturbance be in a public place, but that the defendant also be in public and intoxicated. Thus, the defendant's conviction was overturned because, although his noise could be heard in public, he made the loud noises inside a hotel room. *People v. Favreau*, 255 Mich. App. 32 (2003).

Preliminary Breath Test results were admissible to impeach the defendants who claimed that they were not intoxicated when they were arrested for disorderly conduct at a wedding reception. *City of Westland v. Okopski*, 208 Mich. App. 66 (1994). Note: This case involves a Westland ordinance that mirrors MCL 750.167(1)(e).

Whether the defendant is voluntarily or involuntarily intoxicated is immaterial. Therefore, a defendant's alcoholism is not an affirmative defense. *People v. Hoy*, 3 Mich. App. 666 (1966).

- A person engaged in indecent or obscene conduct in a public place.

This must be an indecent or obscene act. The use of this statute to regulate speech is unconstitutional. *Leonard v. Robinson*, 477 F.3d 347 (6th Cir. 2007).

The defendant who exposed himself to a 13-year-old female from his front porch was found to be in a public place; thus, his conviction was upheld. *People v. De Vine*, 271 Mich. 635 (1935).

However, the defendant who urinated in a national forest in view of a hidden United States Department of Agriculture Forest Service officer was not in a public place for purposes of this statute. The court reasoned that the defendant had no reason to believe that others might view him. *United States v. Whitmore*, 314 F. Supp. 2d 690 (E.D. Mich. 2004).

- A vagrant.

Even early Michigan case law recognized that an arrest without a warrant for this violation should be rare since the offense generally will not involve a danger to public or private security where an immediate arrest is needed. *In re May*, 41 Mich. 299 (1879).

- A person begging in a public place.

Begging, or the soliciting of alms, is a form of solicitation that the First Amendment protected; therefore, MCL 750.167(1)(h) is unconstitutional. *Speet v. Schuette*, 726 F.3d 867 (6th Cir. 2013).

- Loitering in house of ill fame or prostitution.

To establish this charge, it must be proven that the house was kept as a place for prostitution and that the person found loitering had no lawful purpose to be there. *People v. Cox*, 107 Mich. 435 (1895).

- Loitering in a place where an illegal occupation or business is being conducted.

The court ruled that the defendants were properly convicted when they were present in a home where illegal drugs were being sold. Because of the "knowing" requirement, this statute is not unconstitutionally vague nor does it infringe on the First Amendment. *People v. Dombe*, 133 Mich. App. 179 (1984).

- Soliciting legal services or services of sureties at a police station, hospital, or court building.
- Jostling or roughly crowding people in a public place.

The defendant's conviction was upheld where he grabbed the chief of police by the arm during attempts to disperse a disorderly crowd. *People v. Bishop*, 30 Mich. App. 204 (1971).

## Disorderly Conduct at Funerals—MCL 750.167d (felony)

*A person shall not do any of the following within 500 feet of a building or other location where a funeral, memorial service, or viewing of a deceased person is being conducted or within 500 feet of a funeral procession or burial:*

(a) *Make any statement or gesture or engage in any conduct that would make a reasonable person attending that funeral, memorial service, viewing, procession, or burial under the circumstances feel intimidated, threatened, or harassed.*

(b) *Make any statement or gesture or engage in any conduct intended to incite or produce a breach of the peace among those attending that funeral, memorial service, viewing, or burial or traveling in that procession and that causes a breach of the peace among those attending that funeral, memorial service, viewing, or burial or traveling in that procession.*

(c) *Make any statement or gesture or engage in any conduct intended to disrupt the funeral, memorial service, viewing, procession, or burial and that disrupts the funeral, memorial service, viewing, procession, or burial.*

Penalties:

| First offense | 2-year felony |
|---|---|
| Second offense | 4-year felony |

## Disturbing the Peace—MCL 750.170 (90-day misdemeanor)

*Any person who shall make or excite any disturbance or contention in any tavern, store or grocery, manufacturing establishment or any other business place or in any street, lane, alley, highway, public building, grounds or park, or at any election or other public meeting where citizens are peaceably and lawfully assembled, shall be guilty of a misdemeanor.*

## Elements

The defendant made or excited a disturbance at one of the following:

- A business.
- An election place.
- A street, lane, alley, highway, public grounds, or park.
- A public building.
- A public meeting where citizens were peaceably and lawfully assembled.

In order to justify a conviction under this section, there must be a disturbance or contention. Two individuals merely jostling others at a bus stop did not fall under this section. Contention is actual or threatened violence. *People v. O'Keefe*, 218 Mich. 1 (1922).

The court held that "no reasonable officer would have found probable cause to arrest [the defendant] solely for uttering 'God damn' while addressing the township board . . ." He incited no disturbance and advocacy of an idea cannot be prohibited merely because the idea are themselves offensive to some of their hearers. *Leonard v. Robinson*, 477 F.3d 347 (6th Cir. 2007).

"'Any act causing annoyance, disquiet, agitation, or derangement to another, or interrupting his peace, or interfering with him in the pursuit of a lawful and appropriate occupation or contrary to the usages of a sort of meeting and class of persons assembled that interferes with its due progress or irritates the assembly in whole or in part.' From the above definition it is clear that the statutory prohibition, framed in the disjunctive, embraces more than actual or threatened violence. Violence, actual or threatened, is proscribed by the use of the word 'contention.' The statute, however, does not require both a disturbance and a contention to sustain a conviction. Either is sufficient. A disturbance, which is something less than threats of violence, is an interruption of peace and quiet; a violation of public order and decorum; or an interference with or hindrance of one in pursuit of his lawful right or occupation." *People v. Weinberg*, 6 Mich. App. 345 (1967).

The court upheld the defendant's conviction under this statute where the defendant took part in a "sit-in" at a university. The court also held that this statute is not unconstitutionally vague. *People v. Mash*, 45 Mich. App. 459 (1973).

# RIOTS

## Riots—MCL 752.541 (felony)

*It is unlawful and constitutes the crime of riot for 5 or more persons, acting in concert, to wrongfully engage in violent conduct and thereby intentionally or recklessly cause or create a serious risk of causing public terror or alarm.*

Requires all of the following:

- Five or more persons working together who are engaging in violent conduct.
- Intentionally or recklessly creating a serious risk of causing public terror or alarm.

Public terror or alarm is "caused any time a segment of the public is put in fear of injury either to their persons or their property." *People v. Garcia*, 31 Mich. App. 447 (1971).

The defendant and five others could be charged under MCL 752.541 when during a KKK rally they ran up the stairs of city hall and threw rocks at the police and the building. Prohibited conduct under the statute includes violent acts that intentionally alarm the public or create a serious risk of alarming the public. *People v. Kim*, 245 Mich. App. 609 (2001).

## Inciting to Riot—MCL 752.542 (felony)

*It is unlawful and constitutes incitement to riot for a person or persons, intending to cause or to aid or abet the institution or maintenance of a riot, to do an act or engage in conduct that urges other persons to commit acts of unlawful force or violence, or the unlawful burning or destroying of property, or the unlawful interference with a police officer, peace officer, fireman or a member of the Michigan national guard or any unit of the armed services officially assigned to riot duty in the lawful performance of his duty.*

Includes one of the following:

- Acts that encourage other people to riot.
- Aiding or abetting the maintenance of rioting.
- Unlawful interference with police officers, firemen, or military personnel assigned to riot duty.

## Riotously Destroying Dwelling House or Other Property—MCL 750.528 (felony)

*Any of the persons so unlawfully assembled, who shall demolish, pull down, destroy or injure, or who shall begin to demolish, pull down, destroy or injure any dwelling house or any other building, or any ship or vessel, shall be guilty of a felony, and shall be answerable to any person injured, to the full amount of the damage, in an action of trespass.*

### Elements

1. During an unlawful assembly.
2. The defendant demolished, pulled down, destroyed, or injured a dwelling house, other building, ship, or vessel.

## Refusal to Aid Officer—MCL 750.523 (felony)

*If any person present, being commanded by any of the magistrates or officers aforesaid, to aid and assist in seizing and securing such rioters, or persons so unlawfully assembled, or in suppressing such riot or unlawful assembly, shall refuse or neglect to obey such command, or when required by any such magistrate or officer to depart from the place of such riotous or unlawful assembly, shall refuse or neglect so to do, he shall be deemed to be 1 of the rioters or persons unlawfully assembled, and shall be liable to be prosecuted and punished accordingly.*

If a person present at a riot refuses an order from an officer to assist in suppressing the riot, then that person will be considered to be one of the rioters.

## Disobeying a Firefighter or Persons Working During a Riot—MCL 750.241

*(1) Any person who, while in the vicinity of any fire, willfully disobeys any reasonable order or rule of the officer commanding any fire department at the fire, when the order or rule is given by the commanding officer or a firefighter there present, is guilty of a misdemeanor.*

*(2) During a riot or other civil disturbance, any person who knowingly and willfully hinders, obstructs, endangers, or interferes with any person who is engaged in the operation, installation, repair, or maintenance of any essential public service facility, including a facility for the transmission of electricity, gas, telephone messages, or water, is guilty of a felony.*

Penalties:

- It is a misdemeanor to disobey a firefighter's reasonable order at a fire.
- It is a felony to knowingly hinder a person operating or repairing an essential public service facility at a riot.

# LITTERING

## Littering—MCL 324.8902(1) (state civil infraction)

*A person shall not knowingly, without the consent of the public authority having supervision of public property or the owner of private property, dump, deposit, place, throw, or leave, or cause or permit the dumping, depositing, placing, throwing, or leaving of, litter on public or private property or water other than property designated and set aside for such purposes.*

### Definitions—MCL 324.8901

***Litter:*** Rubbish, refuse, waste material, garbage, offal, paper, glass, cans, bottles, trash, debris, or other foreign substances or a vehicle that is considered abandoned under section 252a of the Michigan vehicle code, 1949 PA 300, MCL 257.252a.

***Public or private property or water:*** Includes, but is not limited to, any of the following:

- The right-of-way of a road or highway, a body of water or watercourse, or the shore or beach of a body of water or watercourse, including the ice above the water.
- A park, playground, building, refuge, or conservation or recreation area.
- Residential or farm properties or timberlands.

***Vehicle:*** A motor vehicle registered or required to be registered under the Michigan vehicle code, 1949 PA 300, MCL 257.1 to 257.923.

***Vessel:*** A vessel registered under part 801.

A person shall not knowingly, without consent, leave litter on public or private property.

Penalties (state civil infraction):

| Less than 1 cubic foot volume | $800 fine |
|---|---|
| 1 to 3 cubic feet | Up to $1,500 fine |
| Over 3 cubic feet, 1 offense | $2,500 fine |
| Over 3 cubic feet, 2 offense | $5,000 fine |
| An abandoned vehicle | $500–$2,500 fine |

## Presumptions

The following are presumed responsible for litter that comes from a vehicle:

- The driver of the vehicle.
- The registered owner or lessee of the vehicle.
- In the case of abandoned vehicles, the registered owner or lessee of the vehicle.

## Wreckers—MCL 324.8902(2) (state civil infraction)

*A person who removes a vehicle that is wrecked or damaged in an accident on a highway, road, or street shall remove all glass and other injurious substances dropped on the highway, road, or street as a result of the accident.*

## Throwing Litter in Front of Vehicle—MCL 324.8903 (1-year misdemeanor)

*A person shall not knowingly cause litter or any object to fall or to be thrown into the path of or to hit a vehicle traveling upon a highway.*

## Throwing Dangerous Objects at Vehicles—MCL 750.394

*A person shall not throw, propel, or drop a stone, brick, or other dangerous object at a passenger train, sleeping car, passenger coach, express car, mail car, baggage car, locomotive, caboose, or freight train or at a street car, trolley car, or motor vehicle.*

Penalties:

| Absent other factors | 93-day misdemeanor |
|---|---|
| Property damage is caused | 1-year misdemeanor |
| Injury to a person is caused | 4-year felony |
| Serious impairment of person's bodily function is caused | 10-year felony |
| A person's death is caused | 15-year felony |

***Serious impairment of a body function:*** Includes, but is not limited to, one or more of the following:

- Loss of a limb or loss of use of a limb.
- Loss of a foot, hand, finger, or thumb or loss of use of a foot, hand, finger, or thumb.
- Loss of an eye or ear or loss of use of an eye or ear.
- Loss or substantial impairment of a bodily function.

- Serious visible disfigurement.
- A comatose state that lasts for more than three days.
- Measurable brain or mental impairment.
- A skull fracture or other serious bone fracture.
- Subdural hemorrhage or subdural hematoma.
- Loss of an organ.

MCL 257.58c.

## Dumping on Property of Another—MCL 750.552a (90-day misdemeanor)

*Any person who shall dump, deposit or place any filth, garbage or refuse on the grounds or premises of another, without the specific permission of the owner thereof, shall be guilty of a misdemeanor.*

# GANG OFFENSES

## Definitions

***Gang:*** An ongoing organization, association, or group of five or more people, other than a non-profit organization, that identifies itself by all of the following:

- A unifying mark, manner, protocol, or method of expressing membership, including a common name, sign or symbol, means of recognition, geographical or territorial sites, or boundary or location.
- An established leadership or command structure.
- Defined membership criteria.

***Gang member or member of a gang:*** A person who belongs to a gang.

## Gangs, Committing Felonies—MCL 750.411u (felony)

*If a person who is an associate or a member of a gang commits a felony or attempts to commit a felony and the person's association or membership in the gang provides the motive, means, or opportunity to commit the felony, the person is guilty of a felony punishable by imprisonment for not more than 20 years.*

## Gangs, Recruitment—MCL 750.411v(1) (felony)

*A person shall not cause, encourage, recruit, solicit, or coerce another to join, participate in, or assist a gang in committing a felony. A person who violates this subsection is guilty of a felony punishable by* *imprisonment for not more than 5 years or a fine of not more than $5,000.00, or both.*

## Gangs, Retaliation for Withdrawing—MCL 750.411v(2) (felony)

*A person shall not communicate, directly or indirectly, to another person a threat of injury or damage to the person or property of that person or to an associate or relative of that person with the intent to do either of the following:*

*(a) Deter the other person from assisting a gang member or associate of a gang to withdraw from the gang.*

*(b) Punish or retaliate against the other person for having withdrawn from a gang.*

A person who violates this section is guilty of a felony punishable for not more than 20 years or a fine of not more than $20,000.00, or both.

# RACKETEERING

## Definitions—MCL 750.159f-750.159h

*Enterprise:* An individual, sole proprietorship, partnership, corporation, limited liability company, trust, union, association, governmental unit, or other legal entity or a group of persons associated in fact although not a legal entity. Enterprise includes illicit as well as licit enterprises.

*Instrumentality:* An interest, real or personal property, or other thing of value, the use of which contributes directly and materially to the commission of an offense included in the definition of racketeering.

*Pattern of racketeering activity:* Not less than two incidents of racketeering to which all of the following characteristics apply:

- The incidents have the same or a substantially similar purpose, result, participant, victim, or method of commission, or are otherwise interrelated by distinguishing characteristics and are not isolated acts.
- The incidents amount to or pose a threat of continued criminal activity.
- At least one of the incidents occurred within this state on or after the effective date of the amendatory act that added this section, and the last of the incidents occurred within 10 years after the commission of any prior incident, excluding any period of imprisonment served by a person engaging in the racketeering activity.

*Person:* An individual, sole proprietorship, partnership, cooperative, association, corporation, limited liability company, personal representative, receiver, trustee, assignee, or other legal or illegal entity.

*Proceeds:* Any real, personal, or intangible property obtained through the commission of an offense included in the definition of racketeering, including any appreciation in the value of the property.

*Prosecuting agency:* The attorney general of this state, or his or her designee, or the prosecuting attorney of a county, or his or her designee.

*Racketeering:* Committing, attempting to commit, conspiring to commit, or aiding or abetting, soliciting, coercing, or intimidating a person to commit an offense for financial gain, involving any of the following:

- Tobacco tax felonies. MCL 205.428.
- Hazardous waste felonies. MCL 324.11151.
- Controlled substances felonies. MCL 333.7401 to 333.7461.
- Welfare fraud felonies. MCL 400.60.
- Medicaid fraud felonies. MCL 400.604, 400.605, and 400.607.
- Gaming felonies. MCL 432.218.
- Securities fraud. MCL 451.2508.
- Display or dissemination of obscene matter to minors. MCL 722.675 and 722.677.
- Animal fighting. MCL 750.49.
- Arson felonies. MCL 750.72–750.75, 750.77.
- Bank bonds, bills, notes, and property. MCL 750.93–750.96.
- Breaking and entering or home invasion. MCL 750.110 or 750.110a.
- Bribery. MCL 750.117–750.121, 750.124.
- Jury tampering. MCL 750.120a.
- Child sexually abusive activity or material. MCL 750.145c.
- Internet or computer crimes. MCL 750.145d.
- Credit cards or financial transaction devices. MCL 750.157n, 750.157p–750.157u.
- Felony embezzlement. MCL 750.174–750.176, 750.180–750.182.
- Explosive and bomb felonies. MCL 750.200–750.212a
- Extortion. MCL 750.213.
- False pretenses felonies. MCL 750.218.
- Firearms or dangerous weapons felonies. MCL 750.223(2), 750.224(1)(a), (b), or (c), 750.224b, 750.224c, 750.224e(1), 750.226, 750.227, 750.234a, 750.234b, or 750.237a.
- Forgery and counterfeiting felonies. MCL 750.248–750.266.
- Securities fraud. MCL 750.271–750.274.

- Food stamp fraud. MCL 750.300a.
- Gambling. MCL 750.301–750.305a, 750.313.
- Murder. MCL 750.316 or 750.317.
- Horse racing. MCL 750.330–750.332.
- Kidnapping. MCL 750.349–750.350.
- Larceny felonies. MCL 750.356–750.367c.
- Money laundering. MCL 750.411k.
- Perjury and subornation of perjury. MCL 750.422–750.425.
- Prostitution. MCL 750.452, 750.455, 750.457-750.479.
- Human trafficking. MCL 750.462a–750.462j.
- Robbery. MCL 750.529–750.531.
- Receiving and concealing felonies. MCL 750.535–750.535a.
- Terrorism. MCL 750.543a–750.543z.
- Obscenity. MCL 752.365.
- Felony identity theft. MCL 445.61–445.77.
- Liquor control felonies. MCL 436.1909.
- An offense committed within this state or another state that constitutes racketeering activity as defined in 18 U.S.C. § 1961(1).
- An offense committed within this state or another state in violation of a law of the United States that is substantially similar to a violation listed above.
- An offense committed in another state in violation of a statute of that state that is substantially similar to a violation listed above.

*Records or documentary materials:* A book, paper, document, writing, drawing, graph, chart, photograph, phonorecord, magnetic tape, computer program or printout, any other data compilation from which information can be obtained or translated into usable form, or any other functionally similar tangible item.

*Substituted proceeds:* Any real, personal, or intangible property obtained or any gain realized by the sale or exchange of proceeds.

## Criminal Enterprises, Conducting—MCL 750.159i(1) (felony)

*A person employed by, or associated with, an enterprise shall not knowingly conduct or participate in the affairs of the enterprise directly or indirectly through a pattern of racketeering activity, or conspire or attempt to do so.*

Penalty:
Violation of this section is a 20-year felony and any real, personal, or intangible property used in furtherance or acquired by conduct in violation of the racketeering statute is subject to forfeiture to the state.

### Elements

In order to find the defendant guilty of racketeering, the jury needed to find beyond a reasonable doubt that:

1. An enterprise existed.
2. The defendant was employed by or associated with the enterprise.
3. The defendant knowingly conducted or participated, directly or indirectly, in the affairs of the enterprise.
4. A pattern of racketeering activity consisted of the commission of at least two racketeering offenses that:

   a. Had the same or substantially similar purpose, result, participant, victim, or method of commission, or were otherwise interrelated by distinguishing characteristics and are not isolated acts.
   b. Amounted to or posed a threat of continued criminal activity, and
   c. Were committed for financial gain.

While the federal racketeering statutes require the prosecution prove that an enterprise exists by proving (1) the existence of a common purpose, (2) a formal or informal organization of participants who function as a unit, and (3) an ascertainable structure distinct from that inherent in the conduct of a pattern of racketeering activity, the Michigan racketeering statutes do not. The prosecution was not required to demonstrate that defendant held a position of authority within the enterprise, but only that he conducted *or participated* in its affairs through a pattern of racketeering activity. *People v. Martin*, 271 Mich. App. 280 (2006).

## Criminal Enterprises, Acquiring or Maintaining—MCL 750.159i(2) (felony)

*A person shall not knowingly acquire or maintain an interest in or control of an enterprise or real or personal property used or intended for use in the operation of an enterprise, directly or indirectly, through a pattern of racketeering activity, or conspire or attempt to do so.*

Penalty:

Violation of this section is a 20-year felony and any real, personal, or intangible property used in further-ance or acquired by conduct in violation of the rack-eteering statute is subject to forfeiture to the state.

## Criminal Enterprises, Racketeering Proceeds—MCL 750.159i(3) (felony)

*A person who has knowingly received any proceeds derived directly or indirectly from a pattern of rack-eteering activity shall not directly or indirectly use or invest any part of those proceeds, or any proceeds derived from the use or investment of any of those proceeds, in the establishment or operation of an enterprise, or the acquisition of any title to, or a right, interest, or equity in, real or personal prop-erty used or intended for use in the operation of an enterprise, or conspire or attempt to do so.*

Penalty:

Violation of this section is a 20-year felony and any real, personal, or intangible property used in further-ance or acquired by conduct in violation of the rack-eteering statute is subject to forfeiture to the state.

# DUTY TO REPORT

## Failure to Report Wounds of Violence—MCL 750.411 (90-day misdemeanor)

Hospitals, pharmacies, and treating physicians have a duty to immediately report to the head of the police force with jurisdiction over the treat-ment facility when a patient arrives or is admitted for treatment of a knife wound, gunshot wound, or other wound caused by a deadly weapon or other means of violence.

The hospital, pharmacy, or treating physician must notify police of:

- The name and residence of the patient, if known.
- The patient's whereabouts.
- The cause, character, and extent of the wounds.
- The identification of the perpetrator if known.

Reports under this section are assumed to be in good faith and do not violate physician-patient privilege. Good faith reports are immune from civil and crimi-nal liability.

## Failure to Report or Investigate Asphyxia or Death by Drowning—MCL 750.411c (90-day misdemeanor)

*Every physician or surgeon, having under his care a person who suffers from asphyxia or dies due to submersion in water, shall report same to any peace officer, the nearest state police post or the sheriff of the county in which the injury or death occurred. Every coroner or medical examiner who completes a death certificate attributing death to drowning shall make a like report to the appropriate officers hereinabove named.*

Officers receiving the report shall investigate the circumstances surrounding the injury or death and shall submit a complete report to the director of state police on forms prescribed by him. The Department of Natural Resources shall receive from the director of state police a copy of the officer's report where the asphyxia or death occurred in waters under the jurisdiction of that department.

## Failure to Report the Discovery of a Dead Body— MCL 333.2841(2) (1-year misdemeanor)

*An individual who discovers the body of an indi-vidual he or she knows or has reason to know is dead and fails to inform a law enforcement agency, a funeral home, or a 9-1-1 operator of the discovery is guilty of a misdemeanor punishable by impris-onment for not more than 1 year or a fine of not more than $1,000.00, or both.*

This subsection does not apply to an individual who knows or has reason to know that a law enforcement agency, a funeral home, or a 9-1-1 operator has been informed of the discovery of the body.

## Concealing the Death of an Individual—MCL 333.2841(3) (felony)

*An individual who discovers the body of an indi-vidual he or she knows or has reason to know is dead and fails to inform a law enforcement agency, a funeral home, or a 9-1-1 operator of the discovery with the purpose of concealing the fact or cause of death of the individual is guilty of a felony punish-able by imprisonment for not more than 5 years or a fine of not more than $5,000.00, or both.*

© 2014, Shutterstock, Inc.

# 19

# LAWS OF ARREST

## FOURTH AMENDMENT TO THE CONSTITUTION

*The right of the people to be secure in their persons, houses, papers, and effects against unreasonable searches and seizures, shall not be violated and no Warrants shall issue, but upon probable cause, supported by Oath or affirmation, and particularly describing the place to be searched, and the persons or things to be seized.*

An arrest is legal if it is any of the following:

- Made by an officer relying on an arrest warrant for the defendant issued by a court.
- Made by an officer for a crime that he reasonably believed was committed in his presence, if it was made as soon as reasonably possible afterward.
- Made by an officer who had reasonable cause to believe that the crime was committed by the defendant. "Reasonable cause" means having enough information to lead an ordinarily careful person to believe that the defendant had committed the crime.
CJI2d 13.5.

### Three Levels of Contacts Between Police and Citizens

**Informational/voluntary**, where no level of suspicion is needed.

**Investigatory detention**, where the officer has **reasonable suspicion** that a crime is afoot.

**Arrest**, where the officer has **probable cause** to believe a crime has occurred and that the person being arrested committed the crime.

The Michigan Supreme Court in *People v. Freeman*, 413 Mich. 492 (1982) suppressed evidence located when officers approached a parked car and ordered the occupant to exit and produce ID. The court held that, by ordering the occupant to exit, a detention occurred, which required reasonable suspicion that crime was afoot. Since there was no suspicion articulated by the officer, the seizure was unlawful, and therefore, the evidence suppressed.

The Court of Appeals distinguished that case in *People v. Shankle*, 227 Mich. App. 690 (1998), where the officer "asked" for ID. "Unlike *Freeman*, [the arresting officer] did not order defendant from his car. There is nothing in the record to suggest that intimidating circumstances compelled defendant to cooperate." The record shows that the officer "merely made a voluntary request to defendant to produce identification." No suspicion was required for this contact. *Shankle* is further differentiated from *Freeman* because the officer in *Freeman* specifically told the defendant that he was not allowed to leave until he presented identification.

A witness saw three men moving something over a golf course at 3:00 a.m. When he confronted them, they ran. An officer responded and found a pile of equipment and three sets of prints leading toward an apartment complex. The officer radioed to another officer to watch out for three white males. The defendants were located and stopped. The investigating officer followed the tracks to a locker facility and found that it had been broken into. The officer then checked and found that the boots of the three defendants matched the tracks he had been following. This took 20 minutes. The initial detention was valid because the officers had reasonable suspicion that a crime was occurring. They also diligently investigated the facts to build up to probable cause to make an arrest within a reasonable amount of time. *People v. Chambers*, 195 Mich. App. 118 (1992).

## Length of Detention During an Investigatory Stop

An investigative detention must be temporary and must last no longer than what is necessary to effectuate the purpose of the stop. In determining if the detention is too lengthy, the court must examine whether the police diligently pursued a means of investigation that was likely to confirm or dispel their suspicions quickly. Here, the court determined that a 20-minute traffic stop that led to a narcotics arrest was not too lengthy under the circumstances. *United States v. Sharpe*, 470 U.S. 675 (1985).

When police actions go beyond checking out the suspicious circumstances that led to the original stop, the detention becomes an arrest that must be supported by probable cause. *United States v. Obasa*, 15 F.3d 603 (6th Cir. 1994).

## What Is Probable Cause?

Police have probable cause to arrest an individual when the facts and circumstances within their knowledge and of which they have reasonably trustworthy information are sufficient to cause a person of reasonable caution to believe the person to be arrested is committing or has committed a crime. *Brinegar v. United States*, 338 U.S. 160 (1949).

Probable cause is a practical, nontechnical, common sense concept. *People v. Keller*, 479 Mich. 467 (2007).

To determine whether or not probable cause exists a court must objectively to assess the agent's or officer's actions in light of the facts and circumstances confronting him at the time without regard to his underlying intent or motive. *Scott v. United States*, 436 U.S. 128 (1978).

Probable cause is assessed from the perspective of a reasonable officer on the scene; thus, probable cause determinations involve an examination of all facts and circumstances within an officer's knowledge at the time of arrest. *Klein v. Long*, 275 F.3d 544 (6th Cir. 2001).

Probable cause is not a point, but a zone in which reasonable mistakes can be made. The endless scenarios confronting police officers make it impossible to reduce the concept of probable cause to a neat set of legal rules. OAG 1993–1994, No 6,822, p 201 (November 23, 1994).

Under Michigan law, probable cause and reasonable cause are the same standard.

## Elements of a Valid Arrest

1. **Authority:** The lawful authority granted to a peace officer.
2. **Intent:** The arresting party must have the intent to arrest. The arrested subject should be so informed of this intent.
3. **Force:** Some amount of force must be used, but only to the extent necessary to make the arrest. That force may be a verbal command or physical.
4. **Custody:** Verbal or physical custody or control must be exercised by the arresting officer.
5. **Submission:** There must be a submission to the arrest by the arrested subject. This may be voluntary or forced. Submission is present when custody or control is gained.

An arrest is the taking, seizing, or detaining of another person by either touching or putting hands on that person, or by any act that indicates an intention to take him or her into custody and subjects the person arrested to the actual control and will of the person making the arrest and must be so understood by the person arrested. *People v. Gonzales,* 356 Mich. 247 (1959).

# ARRESTS PURSUANT TO ARREST WARRANT

## Arrest Warrants

Steps for obtaining an arrest warrant:

1. During the investigation, the officer must establish probable cause that a crime was committed and that the suspect committed it.
2. A warrant request must be completed by the officer and submitted to the prosecutor.
3. The prosecutor authorizes, if criteria are met.
4. A complaint is prepared.
5. A complaint is presented to the judge.
6. An officer swears, under oath, that the facts presented are true to the best of his or her knowledge.
7. A judge reviews whether probable cause exists.
8. If the judge finds that there is probable cause, a warrant is issued with the judge's signature.
9. An arrest is made.
10. The suspect is processed (fingerprinting, photos, and local paperwork).
11. The suspect is offered bond, if appropriate.
12. The suspect is lodged, if judge is unavailable for arraignment.
13. The suspect is brought before judge, without unnecessary delay.

## A Judge's Command

Once issued, the warrant shall command an officer to arrest the person. MCL 764.1b.

## Authority to Enter Residence

Officers may break the door of a suspect's residence to make an arrest if there is reason to believe he or she is in the residence. MCL 764.21.

Forcible entry requires:

- Probable cause that the suspect lives there (*Steagald v. United States,* 451 U.S. 204 (1981), and
- Reasonable suspicion that the suspect is in the house. MCL 764.21.

See "ENTRY INTO RESIDENCE TO MAKE AN ARREST" later in this chapter for a more in-depth explanation.

## Where Can the Arrest with a Warrant Be Made?

An officer with a warrant may arrest anywhere in the state. MCL 764.2.

## Possession of the Warrant at the Time of Arrest

It shall not be necessary for the arresting officer to have the warrant in possession at the time of the arrest. The officer must, if possible, inform the person arrested of the warrant for his or her arrest and, after the arrest is made, shall show the person the warrant, if required, as soon as practicable. MCL 764.18.

## The Warrant Is Valid on Its Face

Under ordinary circumstances, an officer has no obligation to inquire about the legality of a warrant if it appears valid on its face. An arrest warrant is valid on its face and will protect an officer from liability for false arrest and false imprisonment. If the officer should have known or doubted the validity of the warrant, the warrant will not shield the officer from liability. *Hollis v. Baker*, 45 Mich. App. 666 (1973).

# ARRESTS WITHOUT A WARRANT

## Arrests Without a Warrant—MCL 764.15

### Basic Crimes

- A felony, misdemeanor, or ordinance violation committed in the officer's presence.

Offenses are committed in the presence of the officer if ascertainable through sight, sound, smell, or touch. *People v. Wolfe,* 5 Mich. App. 543 (1967).

- A felony that is not committed in the officer's presence.
- A felony was committed and the officer has reasonable cause to believe the person committed it.

Police may not arrest someone for questioning unless there is probable cause to believe that the person to be questioned actually committed the crime. *People v. Kelly*, 231 Mich. App. 627 (1998).

- The officer has reasonable cause to believe a felony was committed and reasonable cause to believe the person committed the felony.
- The officer has reasonable cause to believe a misdemeanor punishable by imprisonment for more than 92 days or a felony has been committed and reasonable cause to believe the person committed it.

A defendant's "OWI" arrest was upheld when he was found sleeping in his vehicle at a fairgrounds and he admitted to the officer that he had driven there. *People v. Stephen*, 262 Mich. App. 213 (2004).

- When the officer receives positive information from an authoritative source that another officer or a court holds a warrant for the person's arrest.
- The officer receives positive information by broadcast from a recognized police or other governmental radio station or teletype that affords the peace officer reasonable cause to believe a misdemeanor punishable by imprisonment for more than 92 days or a felony has been committed and reasonable cause to believe the person committed it.
- The peace officer has reasonable cause to believe the person is an escaped convict, has violated a condition of parole from a prison, has violated a condition of a pardon granted by the executive, or has violated one or more conditions of a conditional release order or probation order imposed by a court of this state, another state, Indian tribe, or United States territory.

## Accidents and O.W.I.

- The officer has reasonable cause to believe that a person was at the time of an accident in this state, the operator of a vehicle involved in an accident and was in violation of MCL 257.625(1), (3), (6), (7) or 257.625m.

The officer responded to a report of a vehicle-mail box accident. The witnesses gave the officer a description of the vehicle and a plate number and also said the diver appeared to be injured and holding his head as he drove away. The officer went to the house, observed the described vehicle with fresh damage and mud. He received no answer when he rang the doorbell. He went to a window, shined in his flashlight, and observed the defendant lying on a bed, bleeding and unmoving. The officer entered the house through an unlocked door, roused the defendant, ascertained the defendant was not seriously injured, and arrested the defendant on suspicion of OUIL based on the damage to the defendant's car, the eye-witness accounts, an odor of alcohol, and his slurred speech. The officer's warrantless entry was justified on probable cause based on specific articulable facts that the entry was necessary to assist a person who may be in serious need of medical assistance and the warrantless arrest was also justified by probable cause that the defendant violated the OUIL statute. *City of Troy v. Ohlinger*, 438 Mich. 477 (1991). *See also* MCL 257.625a(1)(a) and MCL 764.15(1)(h).

- The person is found in the driver's seat of a vehicle parked or stopped on a highway or street and any part of the vehicle intrudes into the roadway and the officer has reasonable cause to believe the person was operating the vehicle in violation of MCL 257.625(1), (3), (6) or (7). MCL 257.625a(1)(b) and MCL 764.15(i).
- The officer has reasonable cause to believe the person was the driver of a snowmobile and was intoxicated or OUID, when involved in an accident. MCL 324.82136(1) and MCL 764.15(1)(j).
- The officer has reasonable cause to believe that the person was the driver of an off-road vehicle (ORV) and was intoxicated or OUID, when involved in an accident. MCL 324.81144 and MCL 764.15(1)(k).

## Retail Fraud

The officer has reasonable cause to believe that a violation of MCL 750.356c and 750.356d has taken place or is taking place, and reasonable cause to believe that person committed or is committing the violation, regardless if it was committed in the officer's presence. MCL 764.15(1)(m).

## School Property

The officer has reasonable cause to believe a misdemeanor has taken place or is taking place on school property and reasonable cause to believe the person committed or is committing the violation, regardless of whether the violation was committed in the officer's presence. MCL 764.15(1)(n).

As used in this section, "school property" means a building, playing field, or property used for school purposes to impart instruction to children in grades kindergarten through 12, when provided by a public, private, denominational, or parochial school, except those buildings used primarily for adult education or college extension courses. MCL 333.7410.

## Domestic Violence—MCL 764.15a

A peace officer may arrest an individual for assault, assault and battery, and aggravated assault regardless of whether the peace officer has a warrant or whether the violation was committed in his or her presence, if the peace officer has or receives positive information that another peace officer has reasonable cause to believe both of the following:

- The violation occurred or is occurring.
- The individual has had a child in common with the victim, resides or has resided in the same household as the victim, has or has had a dating relationship with the victim, or is a spouse or former spouse of the victim. As used in this subdivision, dating relationship means frequent, intimate associations primarily characterized by the expectation of affectional involvement. This term does not include a casual relationship or an ordinary fraternization between two individuals in a business or social context.

## Narcotic Arrests—MCL 333.7501

A sheriff, deputy sheriff, or local or state police officer who has reasonable cause to believe that a violation of this article punishable by imprisonment for one year or more has taken place or is taking place and reasonable cause to believe that an individual has committed or is committing the violation, may arrest that individual without a warrant for that violation whether or not the violation was committed in the law enforcement officer's presence.

The controlled substances portion of the Public Health Code specifically authorizes a police officer to arrest a person upon reasonable cause

to believe that the person is committing or has committed a felony, regardless of whether the violation was committed in the officer's presence. *People v. Jones*, 162 Mich. App. 675 (1987).

## Personal Protection Orders— MCL 600.2950 and MCL 764.15b

A peace officer, without a warrant, may arrest and take into custody an individual, when the peace officer has or receives positive information that another peace officer has reasonable cause to believe all of the following apply:

- A personal protection order or valid foreign protection order has been issued.
- The individual named in the personal protection order is violating or has violated the order.
  - Assaulting, attacking, beating, molesting, or wounding a named individual.
  - Removing minor children from an individual having legal custody of the children, except as otherwise authorized by a custody or parenting time order issued by a court of competent jurisdiction.
  - Entering onto premises.
  - Engaging in stalking conduct.
  - Threatening to kill or physically injure a named individual.
  - Purchasing or possessing a firearm.
  - Interfering with petitioner's efforts to remove petitioner's children or personal property from premises that are solely owned or leased by the individual to be restrained or enjoined.
  - Interfering with petitioner at petitioner's place of employment or education or engaging in conduct that impairs petitioner's employment or educational relationship or environment.
  - Any other act or conduct specified by the court in the personal protection order.
- The person has *received notice*. A peace officer may serve a personal protection order at any time. If the officer responds to a violation and the LEIN reports that the subject had not yet been served, the officer should serve the order by specifically stating what the order prohibits. After service, the suspect must be given a reasonable opportunity to comply. Failure to comply is grounds for immediate arrest. If the suspect does comply, the LEIN entry should be changed to show that service was completed.

- The personal protection order states on its face that a violation of its terms subjects the individual to immediate arrest *and* the following:
  - If the individual restrained or enjoined is 17 years of age or older, to criminal contempt of court and, if found guilty of criminal contempt, to imprisonment of not more than 93 days and a fine of not more than $500.00.
  - If the individual restrained or enjoined is less than 17 years of age, to the dispositional alternatives listed in section 18 of chapter XIIA of the probate code of 1939, 1939 PA 288, MCL 712A.18.
  - If the respondent violates the PPO in a jurisdiction other than this state, the respondent is subject to the enforcement procedures and penalties of that jurisdiction.
- An individual arrested under this section shall be brought before the family division of the circuit court having jurisdiction in the cause within 24 hours after arrest. If the circuit court judge is unavailable, then the individual must be brought before the district court judge. If the district court judge is unavailable, then the individual must be brought before the magistrate.

## Violation of a Condition of Release—MCL 764.15e

A peace officer, without a warrant, may arrest and take into custody a suspect whom the peace officer has or receives positive information that another peace officer has reasonable cause to believe is violating or has violated a condition of release imposed by a court of this state, another state, Indian Tribe, or United States territory. The arresting officer must fill out a violation of condition of release report.

The officer must bring the defendant before the court within one business day. If the violation occurred outside the jurisdiction of the court that issued the order, the defendant must be brought before the court that has jurisdiction where the incident occurred.

If, in the opinion of the arresting police agency or officer in charge of the jail, it is safe to release the defendant before the defendant is brought before the court, that agency or officer may release the defendant on interim bond of not more than $500.00, requiring defendant to appear at the opening of court the next business day. If the defendant is held for more than 24 hours without being brought before the court under subsection (2), the officer in charge of the jail shall note in the jail records why it was not safe to release the defendant on interim bond under this subsection.

## Violation of a Child Protective Order—MCL 764.15f

A peace officer, without a warrant, may arrest and take into custody a person if the officer has reasonable cause to believe all of the following exist:

- A child protective order has been issued by the probate court before January 1, 1998 or the family division of circuit court on or after January 1, 1998.
- A true copy of the order and proof of service has been filed with the law enforcement agency having jurisdiction.
- The person named in the order *has received notice of the same*.
- The person named is acting in violation of the order.
- The order states on its face that a violation of its terms subjects the person to criminal contempt of court and, if found guilty, the person shall be imprisoned for not more than 90 days and may be fined not more than $500.00.
- If a peace officer arrests a person under this section, the peace officer shall do all of the following:
  - Prepare a complaint of a violation of a child protective order.
  - Provide one copy of the complaint to the person subject to the order and the original and one copy to the court that imposed the conditions. The law enforcement agency shall retain one copy.
  - Bring the person before the family division of circuit court having jurisdiction in the cause within 24 hours after arrest to answer a charge of contempt. If the circuit court judge is unavailable, then to the district court judge.

## Protective Custody—MCL 330.1427

A peace officer may take a person into custody if it is shown that he or she is a person requiring treatment. If an officer takes a person into protective custody, he must transport the person to a preadmission screening unit designated by a community mental health services program for examination or for mental health intervention services.

A *person requiring treatment* means a person:

- Who has mental illness, and who as a result of that mental illness can reasonably be expected within the near future to intentionally or unintentionally seriously physically injure himself, herself, or another individual, and who has engaged in an act or acts or made significant threats that are substantially supportive of the expectation. MCL 333.1401(a).

- Who has mental illness, and who as a result of that mental illness is unable to attend to those of his or her basic physical needs such as food, clothing, or shelter that must be attended to in order for the individual to avoid serious harm in the near future, and who has demonstrated that inability by failing to attend to those basic physical needs. MCL 333.1401(b).

An officer may use the same degree of force that would be lawful if the officer was arresting for a misdemeanor without a warrant. The officer may conduct a pat-down search to the extent necessary to remove dangerous weapons, but the pat-down may only be extensive enough to discover and seize weapons. The officer shall inform the person that he or she is in protective custody and not under arrest. Immunity will be granted to the officer unless he is grossly negligent or acts with willful and wanton misconduct. MCL 330.1427a.

# PRIVATE PERSON'S AUTHORITY TO ARREST WITHOUT A WARRANT— MCL 764.16

A private person may make an arrest under the following circumstances:

- A felony committed in his or her presence.
- The suspect committed a felony, although not in the person's presence.
- When summoned by a peace officer to assist in making an arrest.
- If the private person is a merchant, is employed by a merchant, or works security for a merchant and has reasonable cause to believe the person to be arrested violated 750.356c or 750.356d, regardless of whether it was committed in the presence of the private person (retail fraud).

After an arrest, the private person must, without unnecessary delay, deliver the person to a peace officer.

Bail bondsmen are considered private citizens and can be held liable for making an arrest of a subject listed on a warrant who was not the actual person who had committed the crime. Here, the person they arrested had not actually committed a felony. Because private citizens only have arrest powers if the person they arrested actually committed a felony, the bounty hunters were liable for their actions in connection with the arrest. *Bright v. Ailshie,* 465 Mich. 770 (2002).

# MISCELLANEOUS INFORMATION

## When Can Arrest Be Made?

Arrests can be made anytime, day or night. MCL 764.17.

Arrests with a warrant at night are frowned upon unless good cause is shown. *Malcomson v. Scott,* 56 Mich. 459 (1885).

### Prosecuting Certain Crimes

Any offense committed on a county boundary or within one mile of a boundary may be prosecuted in either county. MCL 762.3.

Continuing crimes, i.e., kidnapping moving through state, may be prosecuted in any county through which the crime continues. MCL 762.3.

If fatal wound or poison is administered in one county and the victim dies in another county, prosecution may be held in either county. MCL 762.5.

A homicide conviction in one county was upheld where the defendant claimed that the court lacked jurisdiction because the murder occurred 2/10 of mile into another county. *People v. Lundberg,* 364 Mich. 596 (1961).

The defendant's homicide conviction in Michigan was upheld where he assaulted the victim in Cass County, Michigan, but the victim died in an Indiana hospital. *People v. Duffield,* 387 Mich. 300 (1972).

# RESISTING ARREST

A person may not resist a police officer who is *lawfully* performing his or her duties.

MCL 750.81d does not abrogate the common-law right to resist illegal police conduct, including unlawful arrests and unlawful entries into constitutionally protected areas. Thus, in a resisting case, the prosecution must prove the officers' actions were lawful. *People v. Moreno,* 491 Mich. 38 (2012).

## Biometric Data Requirement—MCL 28.243

### Biometric Data—MCL 28.241a

---

*"Biometric data" means all of the following:*

   (i) *Fingerprint images recorded in a manner prescribed by the department.*

  (ii) *Palm print images, if the arresting law enforcement agency has the electronic capability to record palm print images in a manner prescribed by the department.*

 (iii) *Digital images recorded during the arrest or booking process, including a full-face capture, left and right profile, and scars, marks, and tattoos, if the arresting law enforcement agency has the electronic capability to record the images in a manner prescribed by the department.*

 (iv) *All descriptive data associated with identifying marks, scars, amputations, and tattoos.*

---

## Collection—MCL 28.243

### DNA, Fingerprints, and Biometric Data

---

(1) *Except as provided in subsection (3), upon the arrest of a person for a felony or for a misdemeanor violation of state law for which the maximum possible penalty exceeds 92 days' imprisonment or a fine of $1,000.00, or both, or a misdemeanor authorized for DNA collection under section 6(1)(b) of the DNA identification profiling system act, 1990 PA 250, MCL 28.176, or for criminal contempt under section 2950 or 2950a of the revised judicature act of 1961, 1961 PA 236, MCL 600.2950 and 600.2950a, or criminal contempt for a violation of a foreign protection order that satisfies the conditions for validity provided in section 2950i of the revised judicature act of 1961, 1961 PA 236, MCL 600.2950i, or for a juvenile offense, other than a juvenile offense for which the maximum possible penalty does not exceed 92 days' imprisonment or a fine of $1,000.00, or both, or for a juvenile offense that is a misdemeanor authorized for DNA collection under section 6(1)(b) of the DNA identification profiling system act, 1990 PA 250, MCL 28.176, the arresting law enforcement agency in this state shall collect the person's biometric data and forward the biometric data to the department within 72 hours after the arrest. The biometric data shall be sent to the department on forms furnished by or in a manner prescribed by the department, and the department shall forward the biometric data to the director of*

*the federal bureau of investigation on forms furnished by or in a manner prescribed by the director.*

(2) *A law enforcement agency shall collect a person's biometric data under this subsection if the person is arrested for a misdemeanor violation of state law for which the maximum penalty is 93 days or for criminal contempt under section 2950 or 2950a of the revised judicature act of 1961, 1961 PA 236, MCL 600.2950 and 600.2950a, or criminal contempt for a violation of a foreign protection order that satisfies the conditions for validity provided in section 2950i of the revised judicature act of 1961, 1961 PA 236, MCL 600.2950i, if the biometric data have not previously been collected and forwarded to the department under subsection (1). A law enforcement agency shall collect a person's biometric data under this subsection if the person is arrested for a violation of a local ordinance for which the maximum possible penalty is 93 days' imprisonment and that substantially corresponds to a violation of state law that is a misdemeanor for which the maximum possible term of imprisonment is 93 days. If the person is convicted of any violation, the law enforcement agency shall collect the person's biometric data before sentencing if not previously collected. The court shall forward to the law enforcement agency a copy of the disposition of conviction, and the law enforcement agency shall forward the person's biometric data and the copy of the disposition of conviction to the department within 72 hours after receiving the disposition of conviction in the same manner as provided in subsection (1). If the person is convicted of violating a local ordinance, the law enforcement agency shall indicate on the form sent to the department the statutory citation for the state law to which the local ordinance substantially corresponds.*

(3) *A person's biometric data are not required to be collected and forwarded to the department under subsection (1) or (2) solely because he or she has been arrested for violating section 904(3)(a) of the Michigan vehicle code, 1949 PA 300, MCL 257.904, or a local ordinance substantially corresponding to section 904(3)(a) of the Michigan vehicle code, 1949 PA 300, MCL 257.904.*

(4) *The arresting law enforcement agency may collect the biometric data of a person who is arrested for a misdemeanor punishable by imprisonment for not more than 92 days or a fine of not more than $1,000.00, or both, and who fails to produce satisfactory evidence of identification as required by section 1 of 1961 PA 44, MCL*

*780.581. These biometric data shall be forwarded to the department immediately. Upon completion of the identification process by the department, the biometric data shall be destroyed.*

(5) *An arresting law enforcement agency in this state may collect the person's biometric data upon an arrest for a misdemeanor other than a misdemeanor described in subsection (1), (2), or (4), and may forward the biometric data to the department.*

## DNA Sampling—MCL 750.520m

(1) *A person shall provide samples for chemical testing for DNA identification profiling or a determination of the sample's genetic markers and shall provide samples for chemical testing if any of the following apply:*

(a) *The individual is arrested for a violent felony as that term is defined in section 36 of the corrections code of 1953, 1953 PA 232, MCL 791.236.*

(b) *The person is found responsible for a violation of section 83, 91, 316, 317, or 321, a violation or attempted violation of section 349, 520b, 520c, 520d, 520e, or 520g, or a violation of section 167(1)(c) or (f) or 335a, or a local ordinance substantially corresponding to section 167(1)(c) or (f) or 335a.*

(c) *The person is convicted of a felony or attempted felony, or any of the following misdemeanors, or local ordinances that are substantially corresponding to the following misdemeanors:*

   (i) *A violation of section 145a, enticing a child for immoral purposes.*

   (ii) *A violation of section 167(1)(c), (f), or (i), disorderly person by window peeping, engaging in indecent or obscene conduct in public, or loitering in a house of ill fame or prostitution.*

   (iii) *A violation of section 335a, indecent exposure.*

   (iv) *A violation of section 451, first and second prostitution violations.*

   (v) *A violation of section 454, leasing a house for purposes of prostitution.*

   (vi) *A violation of section 462, female under the age of 17 in a house of prostitution.*

(2) *Notwithstanding subsection (1), if at the time the person is arrested for, convicted of, or found responsible for the violation the investigating law enforcement agency or the department of state police already has a sample from the person that meets the requirements of the DNA*

*identification profiling system act, 1990 PA 250, MCL 28.171 to 28.176, the person is not required to provide another sample or pay the fee required under subsection (6).*

(3) *The county sheriff or the investigating law enforcement agency shall collect and transmit the samples in the manner required under the DNA identification profiling system act, 1990 PA 250, MCL 28.171 to 28.176. However, a sample taken under subsection (1)(a) may be transmitted to the department of state police upon collection.*

(4) *An investigating law enforcement agency, prosecuting agency, or court that has in its possession a DNA identification profile obtained from a sample of a person under subsection (1) shall forward the DNA identification profile to the department of state police at or before the time of the person's sentencing or disposition upon that conviction or finding of responsibility unless the department of state police already has a DNA identification profile of the person.*

(5) *The DNA profiles of DNA samples received under this section shall only be disclosed as follows:*

(a) *To a criminal justice agency for law enforcement identification purposes.*

(b) *In a judicial proceeding as authorized or required by a court.*

(c) *To a defendant in a criminal case if the DNA profile is used in conjunction with a charge against the defendant.*

(d) *For an academic, research, statistical analysis, or protocol developmental purpose only if personal identifications are removed.*

## Admissibility of Evidence

Evidence obtained as a result of an illegal arrest will not be admissible in court. *Wong Sun v. United States,* 371 U.S. 471 (1963).

## LEIN Check Requirements—MCL 764.1g and MCL 764.15g

Police officers must conduct LEIN checks to determine whether a person is on parole when police make an arrest or prior to seeking an arrest warrant. If the person is found to be on parole, the officer must promptly notify the Department of Corrections of the person's identity, the fact that LEIN indicates the person is a parolee, and the charges for which the person has been arrested or the charges in the warrant. If a court delays entry of a warrant into

LEIN, it becomes the court's responsibility to notify the Department of Corrections.

## OFFICER'S AUTHORITY OUTSIDE JURISDICTION—MCL 764.2a

(1) A peace officer of a county, city, village, township, or university of this state may exercise the authority and powers of a peace officer outside the geographical boundaries of the officer's county, city, village, township, or university under any of the following circumstances:

(a) If the officer is enforcing the laws of this state in conjunction with the Michigan state police.

(b) If the officer is enforcing the laws of this state in conjunction with a peace officer of any other county, city, village, township, or university in which the officer may be.

(c) If the officer has witnessed an individual violate any of the following within the geographical boundaries of the officer's county, city, village, township, or university and immediately pursues the individual outside of the geographical boundaries of the officer's county, city, village, township, or university:

  (i) A state law or administrative rule.
  (ii) A local ordinance.
  (iii) A state law, administrative rule, or local ordinance, the violation of which is a civil infraction, municipal civil infraction, or state civil infraction.

(2) The officer pursuing an individual under subsection (1)(c) may stop and detain the person outside the geographical boundaries of the officer's county, city, village, township, or university for the purpose of enforcing that law, administrative rule, or ordinance or enforcing any other law, administrative rule, or ordinance before, during, or immediately after the detaining of the individual. If the violation or pursuit involves a vessel moving on the waters of this state, the officer pursuing the individual may direct the operator of the vessel to bring the vessel to a stop or maneuver it in a manner that permits the officer to come beside the vessel.

A Mt. Morris Township police officer who was deputized by Genessee County could extend his authority to another Mt. Morris officer who made a traffic stop at the first officer's request. *People v. Oliver*, 192 Mich. App. 201 (1991).

## FORCE USED TO EFFECTUATE ARRESTS

### Case Law on the Use of Force

The use of force must be *necessary*.

The use of force is discretionary for the officer. *Firestone v. Rice*, 71 Mich. 377 (1888).

Neither law nor morality can tolerate the use of needless violence, even upon the worst criminals. If crime can be readily prevented without injuring the criminal, every wanton injury is a trespass and may become a crime. The same is true of an arrest. *People v. McCord*, 76 Mich. 200 (1889).

An officer may use such force as he or she deems *necessary* in forcibly arresting an offender, or in preventing an escape after an arrest. The reasonableness of a use of forces is tested using the reasonable person in like or similar circumstances test. *Werner v. Hartfelder*, 113 Mich. App. 747 (1982).

In effecting a lawful arrest for a misdemeanor, a peace officer may use only that degree of force reasonably necessary to effect the arrest, short of deadly force. In effecting a lawful arrest for a felony, a peace officer may use that degree of force reasonably necessary to effect that arrest including deadly force. A peace officer may use deadly force in defense of his own life, in defense of another, or in pursuit of a fleeing felon. If the police officers make an arrest for a misdemeanor only, the arrest must be reasonably immediate after the misdemeanor was observed. A police officer is not liable for injuries inflicted by him in the use of reasonably necessary force. *Jenkins v. Starkey*, 95 Mich. App. 685 (1980).

The use of deadly force for a fleeing felon has been limited by the case of *Tennessee v. Garner*, which is discussed further below.

No one can be justified in taking a life in an attempt to arrest a subject on suspicion only, without incurring serious responsibilities, thus, where the life of a felon is taken by one who does not know, or believe in his or her guilt, the slaying involves criminal liability. *People v. Burt*, 51 Mich. 199 (1883).

### What is Deadly Force?

Any force used by an officer that has a reasonable probability to cause death. *Michigan Law Enforcement Officer—Subject Control Continuum*. A court must determine if the use of force was *objectively reasonable* under the circumstances.

An officer's use of force will be judged in light of an objective reasonableness standard. Reasonableness will be determined by balancing the nature and quality of the intrusions with the countervailing governmental interests. The standard takes into consideration the severity of the crime, whether the suspect poses an immediate threat to the safety of the officers or others and whether the suspect is actively resisting arrest or attempting to evade arrest by flight. The reasonableness will be judged on the scene and at the moment the force was used, rather than from 20/20 hindsight, and will take into consideration the fact that police officers are often forced to make split-second decisions in circumstances that are tense, uncertain, and rapidly evolving. *Graham v. Connor*, 490 U.S. 386 (1989).

## Deadly Force and Fleeing Felon

The suspect must have threatened the officer with a weapon, or the officer must have probable cause to believe that the suspect has committed a crime involving the infliction or threatened infliction of serious physical harm. If feasible, some warning must be given.

"Where the officer has *probable cause* to believe that the suspect *poses a threat of serious physical harm*, either to the officer or others, it is not constitutionally unreasonable to prevent escape by using deadly force." However, the use of deadly force must be reasonably necessary to prevent the suspect's escape and alternative steps are not likely to lead to the safe control of the subject. *Tennessee v. Garner*, 471 U.S. 1 (1985) (emphasis added).

An officer may not use fatal force to effect a misdemeanor arrest.

To retake an escapee, an officer may utilize that force authorized for the crime that person has escaped from. MCL 764.24.

## FRESH PURSUIT

### Fresh Pursuit—MCL 780.101

The **fresh pursuit** statute allows an officer from another state to pursue felons into Michigan and make the arrest with the same arrest powers as those of Michigan peace officers. Once arrested, the person must be brought before the magistrate in the judicial district where the arrest was made pending extradition.

"Fresh pursuit . . . shall not necessarily imply instant pursuit, but pursuit without unreasonable delay." MCL 780.105.

### Police Officers from Adjacent States— MCL 764.2b

A law enforcement officer of an adjacent state (Indiana, Ohio, Minnesota, or Wisconsin) has the same authority and immunity as a law enforcement officer of Michigan if he or she is on duty, is authorized to arrest in his or her home state, and notifies a law enforcement agency of this state that he or she is in Michigan for one of the following reasons:

- The officer is engaged in pursuing, arresting, or attempting to arrest an individual for a violation of a law in an adjacent state.
- The officer is in Michigan at the request of a Michigan officer.
- The officer is working in conjunction with a Michigan officer.
- The officer is responding to an emergency.

## PERSONS EXEMPT FROM ARREST

*Diplomats, their families, official staff, and servants* are immune from criminal arrest and civil proceedings. Vienna Convention on Diplomatic Relations and Optional Protocols arts. 29–37, Apr. 18, 1961, 23 U.S.T. § 3227. 22 U.S.C. §§ 254b–254d.

*Consular officers, but not their families*, have limited immunity from arrest, except for grave crimes. Vienna Convention on Consular Relations and Optional Protocol on Disputes arts. 41–45, *done* Apr. 24, 1963, 21 U.S.T. § 77.

*Federal legislators* are immune from arrest in all cases except treason, felony, and breach of peace, when they are in session or when going to and from session. U.S. Const. art. I, § 6.

*State legislators* are immune from civil arrest and civil process during session and for five days before the commencement and five days after the termination of session. Mich. Const. art. IV, § 11. However, they may be issued citations for civil infraction violations of the Michigan Vehicle Code. MCL 600.1865.

# ARRESTEE'S RIGHTS

## Arrest by a Private Person—MCL 764.14

A private person, who has made an arrest, shall, without unnecessary delay, deliver the person arrested to a peace officer. The officer shall, without unnecessary delay, take that person before a magistrate of the judicial district in which the offense charged is alleged to have been committed. The peace officer or private person shall present to the magistrate a complaint stating the charge against the person arrested. If arrested by a private person, the person arrested *must* be delivered to a peace officer.

## Arrest by a Peace Officer

An arresting officer shall inform the suspect of his or her authority and the cause for the arrest at the time of the arrest unless the person is committing a crime, fleeing, or resisting arrest. MCL 764.19.

A peace officer who has arrested a person without a warrant shall, without unnecessary delay, take the person arrested before a magistrate of the judicial district in which the offense has been committed, and shall present to the magistrate a complaint stating the charge against the person arrested. MCL 764.13.

A delay of more than 48 hours between a warrantless arrest and a judicial determination of probable cause is presumptively unreasonable. Conversely, when the delay is less than 48 hours, the burden is on the plaintiff to prove that the delay was unreasonable. *County of Riverside v. McLaughlin*, 500 U.S. 44 (1991).

## Notice to Appear—MCL 764.9c

For minor offenses of 93-day misdemeanors or less, an appearance ticket may be issued in lieu of custodial arrest except in cases of domestic violence and PPO violations.

# SEARCH INCIDENT TO ARREST

## Search Incident to Arrest—MCL 764.25

Any person making an arrest shall take from the person arrested all offensive weapons or incriminating articles that may be on his or her person. Case law has expanded the area to be searched to include items within the "wingspan" of the person being arrested.

Officers arrested defendant at his home, based on a warrant, and searched the entire three-bedroom house as well as the attic, garage, and small workshop. During this search, they found incriminating evidence. Under this circumstance, the search cannot go beyond areas outside the defendant's reach. The police may search the area within the arrested person's immediate control for destructible evidence and weapons. *Chimel v. California*, 395 U.S. 752 (1969).

A search incident to arrest was upheld where a motorist was arrested on a warrant and officers located tinfoil packets containing heroin and cocaine in his mouth. *People v. Holloway*, 416 Mich. 288 (1982).

## Accompanying Arrestees into the Dwelling

Officers went to the defendant's house with an arrest warrant. He answered the door wearing pajamas. It was suggested that he get dressed. When he approached his dresser to get socks, an officer checked the drawers and found a blackjack. Because the defendant voluntarily chose to dress, seizing the blackjack was valid as a search incident to arrest. When making an arrest, officers may make a reasonable search for weapons in order to prevent the accused's use thereof and to protect their own lives by exposing any dangerous weapons which might be concealed by the accused and subject to use against the police officers. *People v. Giacalone*, 23 Mich. App. 163 (1970).

## Vehicles

The defendant was arrested for driving while his license was suspended. After he was handcuffed and secured in a patrol car, officers searched the vehicle he had been driving and found cocaine. Police may search the passenger compartment of a vehicle incident to a recent occupant's arrest only if it is reasonable to believe that the arrestee might access the vehicle at the time of the search or that the vehicle contains evidence of the offense of arrest. The defendant was arrested for driving on a suspended license; once he was secured in the patrol car, he could not have accessed a weapon from the car nor could a search of the car turn up further evidence of driving on a suspended license. Without more probable cause to justify a search, the search was unreasonable and the cocaine suppressed. *Arizona v. Gant*, 556 U.S. 332 (2009).

The officers in *Gant* were presumably relying on the long-standing rule that allowed officers to search a vehicle without a warrant *every* time an occupant was arrested. With the court's opinion in *Gant,* that is no longer the rule.

The rule only allows police to conduct a vehicle search incident to the arrest of an occupant when either of two circumstances exists:

- Officers may search if the arrestee is within "reaching distance of the passenger compartment." When the arrestee has been secured in a patrol car, he or she is not within reach of the vehicle.
- Officers may search a vehicle incident to arrest if they reasonably believe the vehicle contains evidence of the crime for which the person was arrested. Gant had been arrested for DWLS, and the cocaine was not evidence of DWLS. It appears the court would not have suppressed the cocaine had Gant been arrested for a drug crime.

## What If the Suspect Voluntarily Leaves the Vehicle?

A police officer observed a vehicle with improper license plates. Before the officer was able to stop the vehicle, the driver parked the car and began to walk away. The officer made contact with the driver and, after patting him down, located drugs on him. The officer then searched the vehicle the driver left and found a firearm.

The court held that once a police officer makes a lawful custodial arrest of an automobile's occupant, the officer may search the vehicle's passenger compartment as a contemporaneous incident of arrest, even when an officer does not make contact until the person arrested has already left the vehicle. An arrestee is no less likely to attempt to lunge for a weapon or to destroy evidence if he is outside of, but still

in control of, the vehicle. So long as the arrestee is a recent occupant of a vehicle and next to the vehicle, the vehicle may be searched as a search incident to arrest. *Thornton v. United States,* 541 U.S. 615 (2004).

NOTE: The authority to search in these instances is limited by the court's holding in *Gant.* Therefore, officers may only search in this instance if the arrestee is within reaching distance of the passenger compartment, or the officer reasonably believes the vehicle contains evidence of the crime for which the person was arrested.

### Strip Search—MCL 764.25a

A strip search includes the removal of clothing exposing underclothing, breasts, buttocks, or genitalia of another person. A person arrested for a misdemeanour or civil infraction shall not be subject to a strip search unless both of the following occur:

- The person is lodged on a court order or there is reasonable cause to believe the person is concealing a weapon, controlled substance, or evidence.
- The person conducting the search has obtained prior written authorization of the chief law enforcement officer of that agency or his designee; or if the strip search is conducted upon a minor in a juvenile detention facility which is not operated by a law enforcement agency, the strip search is conducted by a person who has obtained prior written authorization from the chief administrative officer of that facility, or from that officer's designee.

The search must be conducted by an officer of the same sex and, if assisted, by an assistant of the same sex as the person searched. The search must be conducted privately so that others do not observe it. After completing the search, the officer shall prepare a report containing the following information:

- Name and sex of:
  - The person searched.
  - The person conducting search.
  - A person assisting.
- Date, time, and place of search.
- Reason for search.
- List of items recovered.
- A copy of the written authorization.

Unauthorized strip searches are punishable as a misdemeanor.

## Body Cavity Search—MCL 764.25b

A *body cavity*, under this section, includes the interior of the human body, stomach, rectal cavity, and vagina of females.

A *body cavity search* includes the physical intrusion into the body cavity to discover any object concealed therein.

Except as otherwise provided, a body cavity search shall not be conducted without a search warrant. Warrantless body cavity searches may be conducted on:

- A person serving a sentence for a criminal offense in a detention facility or a state correctional facility housing prisoners under the jurisdiction of the Department of Corrections, including a youth correctional facility operated by the Department of Corrections or a private vendor.
- A person lodged by court order in mental institutions if that person is self-abusive and the search is necessary for his protection.
- A person who, as the result of a dispositional order entered after adjudication by the juvenile division of probate court before January 1, 1998, or by the family division of the circuit court on or after January 1, 1998, is residing in a juvenile detention facility.

NOTE: For the exceptions listed above, the person conducting the search must have "prior written authorization from the chief administrative officer of the facility or from that officer's designee."

A body cavity search shall be conducted by a licensed physician, or any of the following with the approval of a licensed physician:

- Physician's assistant.
- LPN.
- RN.

If the search is conducted by a person of the opposite sex, a person of the same sex as the person searched must be present.

The defendant was arrested and officers noticed a string protruding from his rectum. The defendant repeatedly denied having anything and resisted efforts to search. Officers brought the defendant to a hospital to have a physician examine the defendant. The physician gave him injections of sedatives and a muscle relaxer, then later an intravenous paralytic agent which required intubation of the defendant. The physician removed a crack rock of more than five grams from the defendant's rectum. The Court held that because the physician was acting on request of the sheriff, examining a person in custody in the presence of police officers, his conduct was attributable to the state. The Court further held that the use of paralytics, sedatives, and intubation of the defendant against his will, so shocked the conscience as to be unreasonable, especially since less intrusive and less dangerous means of examination were available. Because of the unreasonableness of the search, the crack rock should have been excluded from evidence at trial. If officers require a medical means to extricate evidence from a suspect, be it bullet, drugs, blood, etc., they should attempt to gain the consent of the suspect for the procedure and ensure the doctor performs the least intrusive procedure possible. In this case, an X-ray to confirm the presence of an item in the defendant's rectum followed by a monitored bowel movement would have comported with the Fourth Amendment. The Court frowns on non-consensual, non-emergency procedures involving surgery, probing, anesthesia, and stomach-pumping. Officers should also avoid using the same doctors for medical searches. In this case, the Court sought to deter the police use of willing independent doctors to conduct searches that a government-directed investigating physician could not do. The repeated use of the same doctor by the sheriff's department increased, in the Court's view, the nexus between the state and the physician. *United States v. Booker*, 728 F.3d 535 (6th Cir. 2013).

Surgical intrusion into attempted robbery suspect's left chest area to recover bullet fired by victim was unreasonable under the Fourth Amendment where surgery would require suspect to be put under general anesthesia, where medical risks, although apparently not extremely severe, were subject of considerable dispute, and where there was no compelling need to recover the bullet in light of other available evidence. *Winston v. Lee*, 470 U.S. 753 (1985).

A report is required for all body cavity searches conducted. The report must include:

- Copies of the search warrant or the written authorization to conduct the search.
- The name of the person who conducted the search.

- The time, date, and place of the search.
- A list of all items recovered.
- The name and sex of all law enforcement officers or other personnel present at the search.

# BOND

## Interim Bond—MCL 780.581

If a person is arrested without a warrant for a misdemeanor or a violation of a city, village, or township ordinance punishable by imprisonment for not more than one year, or by a fine or both, the officer making the arrest shall take, without unnecessary delay, the person arrested before the most convenient magistrate of the county in which the offense was committed to answer to the complaint.

If a magistrate is not available or an immediate trial cannot be held, the person arrested may deposit an interim bond to guarantee his or her appearance. The bond shall be a sum of money, as determined by the officer who accepts the bond, not to exceed the amount of the maximum possible fine, but not less than 20 percent of the amount of the minimum possible fine that may be imposed for the offense for which the person was arrested. The person shall be given a receipt.

If, in the opinion of the arresting officer or department, the arrested person falls under any of the following, bond may be denied:

- The person is under the influence of alcoholic liquor, a controlled substance or a combination of both.
- The person is wanted by police authorities to answer to another charge.
- The person is unable to establish or demonstrate his or her identity.
- It is otherwise unsafe to release him or her.

If bond is denied, the suspect shall be held until he or she is in a proper condition to be released, or until the next session of court.

The interim bond statute does not deprive the arresting officer of the ability to do a search subsequent to a lawful custodial arrest. *People v. Chapman*, 425 Mich. 245 (1986).

Interim bond is violated when a search incident to incarceration occurs. *People v. Dixon*, 392 Mich. 691 (1974).

## Exception to Interim Bond for Domestic Violence Arrests—MCL 780.582a(1)

*A person shall not be released on an interim bond as provided in section 1 or on his or her own recognizance as provided in section 3a, but shall be held until he or she can be arraigned or have interim bond set by a judge or district court magistrate if either of the following applies:*

(a) *The person is arrested without a warrant under section 15a of chapter IV of the code of criminal procedure, 1927 PA 175, MCL 764.15a, or a local ordinance substantially corresponding to that section.*

(b) *The person is arrested with a warrant for a violation of section 81 or 81a of the Michigan penal code, 1931 PA 328, MCL 750.81 and 750.81a, or a local ordinance substantially corresponding to section 81 of that act and the person is a spouse or former spouse of the victim of the violation, has or has had a dating relationship with the victim of the violation, has had a child in common with the victim of the violation, or is a person who resides or has resided in the same household as the victim of the violation. As used in this subdivision, "dating relationship" means that term as defined in section 2950 of the revised judicature act of 1961, 1961 PA 236, MCL 600.2950.*

# CUSTODIAL TRAFFIC ARRESTS—MCL 257.727 AND MCL 257.728

Officers are authorized to make custodial arrests for the following traffic violations:

- Moving violation causing death. MCL 257.601d.
- OWI, UBAC, OUID, Impaired Driving. MCL 257.625.
- Reckless driving. MCL 257.626.
- Failure to stop and identify at a serious injury accident or death. MCL 257.617.
- Failure to give aid and information at a personal injury accident. MCL 257.619.
- Failure to have a valid operator's or chauffeur's license in possession. MCL 257.727(d).

# ENTRY INTO RESIDENCE TO MAKE AN ARREST

## Right to Break Open Inner or Outer Door—MCL 764.21

*A private person, when making an arrest for a felony committed in his or her presence, or a peace officer or federal law enforcement officer, when making an arrest with a warrant or when making a felony arrest without a warrant as authorized by law, may break open an inner or outer door of a building in which the person to be arrested is located or is reasonably believed to be located if, after announcing his or her purpose, he or she is refused admittance.*

This statute has been modified through case law that is discussed below.

There is no requirement that officers be affirmatively denied entry; however, they must have a justifiable belief based on the circumstances that they have been denied entry. There is no explicit requirement the officers identify themselves prior to entry, but even if there were, declaration of purpose implicitly declares identity. *United States v. Harris*, 391 F.2d 384 (6th Cir. 1968).

Officers, acting on a tip, went to the defendant's door, identified themselves as federal drug agents to the person inside, then broke the door to gain entry when they were refused admittance. Because the tip gave the agents reasonable grounds to believe the defendant was on the premises, the agents identified themselves to the party inside the door, and the agents waited until they were denied entry, they complied with the requirements of MCL 764.21 and the entry was lawful. *United States v. Alexander*, 346 F.2d 561 (6th Cir. 1965).

## Entry Is Not Allowed for Routine Felony Arrests

The physical entry of the home is the chief evil against which the wording of the Fourth Amendment is directed. This is a substantial invasion to allow without a warrant, in the absence of exigent circumstances, even when it is accomplished under statutory authority and when probable cause is present.

For Fourth Amendment purposes, an arrest warrant founded on probable cause implicitly carries with it the limited authority to enter a dwelling in which the suspect lives, when there is reason to believe the suspect is within. *Payton v. New York*, 445 U.S. 573 (1980).

## Officer Cannot Enter for Warrantless Misdemeanors

Officers chased subject into his house for fleeing and eluding, which was a misdemeanor at the time. The court held the arrest to be unlawful. While MCL 764.21 authorizes a peace officer to break and enter any outer or inner door of any building for purpose of making an arrest with a warrant or a felony without a warrant, this section does not authorize a non-consensual entry into a person's home or other building for purpose of making a warrantless misdemeanor arrest. *People v. Reinhardt*, 141 Mich. App. 173 (1985).

Although the statute says nothing about misdemeanors, at a minimum, these same protections apply to breaking doors to effectuate an arrest for misdemeanors. Hot pursuit may justify breaking doors to enter residences while in hot pursuit of a felon, but breaking doors in pursuit of a fleeing misdemeanant is not justified. *People v. Strelow*, 96 Mich. App. 182 (1980).

## Arrest Warrants Do Not Authorize Entry into a Third Party Residence

DEA agents had an arrest warrant for a subject with the last name of Lyons. They had information that he was at Steagald's house. They went to the residence and entered without a search warrant or consent. The officers did not find Lyons, but did seize cocaine and subsequently charged Steagald. The U.S. Supreme Court suppressed the evidence. When a magistrate issues a search warrant, the interest in privacy in the areas to be searched are directly considered. When issuing an arrest warrant, however, the magistrate does not generally consider third party interests. Therefore, the arrest warrant issued for Lyons offered no protection to Steagald's expectation of privacy and the entry was unlawful. Absent exigent circumstances or consent, law enforcement officers could not legally search for subject of arrest warrant in home of third party, without first obtaining search warrant for those premises. *Steagald v. United States*, 451 U.S. 204 (1981).

Officers entered a third party residence to arrest a subject for outstanding warrants. The person with the warrants was not a resident of the house. A scuffle with the occupants broke out and the officers charged them with resisting and obstructing. The charges were dismissed on the basis that the officers did not first seek a search warrant before entry into the house. *People v. Stark*, 120 Mich. App. 350 (1982).

## Exigent Circumstances May Authorize Entry without a Warrant

Police suspected the defendant of being the driver of the getaway car used in a robbery and murder. After recovering the murder weapon and arresting the suspect, they surrounded the home of two women with whom they believed the defendant had been staying. When police telephoned the home and told one of the women that the defendant should come out, a male voice was heard saying, "Tell them I left." Without seeking permission and with weapons drawn, they entered the home, found the defendant hiding in a closet, and arrested him. Shortly thereafter, he made an inculpatory statement.

An entry may be justified by hot pursuit of a fleeing felon where there is the imminent destruction of evidence, the need to prevent a suspect's escape, or the risk of danger to police or others. In the absence of hot pursuit, there must be at least probable cause to believe that one or more of the other factors were present and, in assessing the risk of danger, the gravity of the crime and likelihood that the suspect is armed should be considered. Although a grave crime was involved, the defendant was known not to be the murderer, the murder weapon had been recovered, and there was no suggestion of danger to the women. Several police squads surrounded the house, and it was evident that the suspect was going nowhere and that if he came out of the house he would have been promptly apprehended. Both the arrest and the statement were held invalid. *Minnesota v. Olson*, 495 U.S. 91 (1990).

An officer responded to a shooting at a hotel at 10:00 p.m. where two people had been murdered. Officers learned that the suspect had been staying in the motel. After completing their investigation at the scene, they informed the night manager to contact them if the suspect returned. At 4:00 a.m., the manager informed the

officers that the suspect had returned and was in his room. The officers responded and after not receiving a response to their knocks, entered to make the arrest. The entry and arrest was valid. "Here, the police were justified in concluding that [the defendant]'s armed presence in the hotel endangered the lives of the other guests. Further, the police were justified in concluding that any delay in arresting [the defendant] while obtaining an arrest warrant would be unreasonable in light of the danger that [the defendant] posed to the other guests. Therefore, we find that there were exigent circumstances known to the police that excused them from taking time to obtain an arrest warrant. The police were confronted with what can only be classified as an emergency situation: a murder suspect, whom they had every reason to believe was armed, located in a hotel room under circumstances that very probably might put the lives and safety of others at risk." *People v. Snider*, 239 Mich. App. 393 (2000).

Officers were investigating a breaking and entering and received a tip that the defendant may have been involved. There were no indications that the suspect was armed or that there was a danger to anyone. There was no concern that evidence would be lost or destroyed. Police entered the defendant's residence an hour after the crime. Based on these facts, there were no exigent circumstances for hot pursuit, loss of evidence, preventing escape, or protecting public safety. All evidence flowing from the illegal entry was suppressed. *People v. Love*, 156 Mich. App. 568 (1986).

Police were dispatched to a robbery/murder that had just occurred. A tracking dog led officers to a nearby house. The officers entered and discovered the defendant and the murder weapon. The court held that the entry was valid because the dog track constituted probable cause and the entry was within minutes of the murder. The circumstances here qualified for a warrantless search under the hot pursuit exception to normal warrant requirements. *People v. Joyner*, 93 Mich. App. 554 (1979).

## Protective Sweeps

Two men committed an armed robbery of a pizza restaurant, and one of them was wearing a red running suit. Two days later, six or seven officers went to the suspect's home with an arrest warrant. One of the officers shouted into the basement and ordered that anyone in the basement come out. The defendant came out and was arrested. An officer went into the basement "in case there was someone else" down there. There was a red running suit in plain view, and the officer seized it.

The court upheld the search as a protective sweep. "The Fourth Amendment permits a properly limited protective sweep in conjunction with an in-home arrest when the searching officer possesses a reasonable belief based on specific and articulable facts that the area to be swept harbors an individual posing a danger to those on the arrest scene." However, the court also stated, "We should emphasize that such a protective sweep, aimed at protecting the arresting officers, if justified by the circumstances, is nevertheless not a full search of the premises, but may extend only to a cursory inspection of those spaces where a person may be found. The sweep lasts no longer than is necessary to dispel the reasonable suspicion of danger and in any event no longer than it takes to complete the arrest and depart the premises." *Maryland v. Buie*, 494 U.S. 325 (1990).

The validity of an entry for a protective search without a warrant depends on the reasonableness of the response, as perceived by police. Officers were conducting a raid on a marihuana farm using air support. The helicopter crew reported a man exiting a mobile home with what appeared to be a weapon. Two other officers pursued him while one conducted a protective sweep of the mobile home to make sure there were no other armed persons inside. At trial, the officer testified that he considered this to be a hostile setting and that he wanted to conduct a protective search. He used the front door and identified himself as a police officer. He was inside for no more than 45 seconds. As soon as he determined that no one was there, he left. He had observed weapons and marijuana in the dwelling but did not confiscate anything. The court held that this was a reasonable protective sweep. *People v. Cartwright*, 454 Mich. 550 (1997).

# KNOCK AND ANNOUNCE—MCL 780.656

*The officer to whom a warrant is directed, or any person assisting him, may break any outer or inner door or window of a house or building, or anything*

*therein, in order to execute the warrant, if, after notice of his authority and purpose, he is refused admittance, or when necessary to liberate himself or any person assisting him in execution of the warrant.*

## Fourth Amendment Requires Knock and Announce

The Fourth Amendment requires that police officers must announce their identity and purpose before attempting forcible entry into a dwelling unless an unannounced entry is reasonable. Countervailing law enforcement interests, including the threat of physical harm to police; the fact that an officer is pursuing a recently escaped arrestee; or the existence of reason to believe that evidence would likely be destroyed if advance notice were given, may establish the reasonableness of an unannounced entry. *Wilson v. Arkansas*, 514 U.S. 927 (1995).

In order to justify a "no-knock" entry, the police must have a *reasonable suspicion* that knocking and announcing would be one of the following:

- Dangerous,
- Futile, or
- Inhibit the effective investigation of the crime (i.e., lead to destruction of evidence).

*Richards v. Wisconsin,* 520 U.S. 385 (1997).

Note, however, that there is not a blanket exception allowing an unannounced entry with search warrants for drugs: an unannounced entry must be reasonable under the circumstances of the specific case.

*Announce:* There must be substantial compliance with the statute.

"We hold that the 'knock-and-announce' statute requires a person attempting to execute a search warrant to proclaim his presence and purpose in a manner reasonably calculated to provide notice to the occupants under the circumstances. In order to comply with the statute, it is not necessary that the inhabitants of a dwelling actually hear the person's announcement, as long as the announcement was reasonably calculated to provide notice under the circumstances. Factors that indicate whether an officer's announcement was reasonably calculated to provide notice under the circumstances include whether the announcement was made with sufficient volume for an average person inside to hear and the time between the announcement and a subsequent forcible entry." When five people, including neighbors, within earshot of the forced entry point, there was no notice; thus, the announcement was inadequate. People v. Ortiz, 224 Mich. App. 468 (1997).

"Police officers, open up" was held to be in compliance with the statute. Declaration of purpose is implicit in declaration of identity, and vice versa. *People v. Doane*, 33 Mich. App. 579 (1971).

"Police officers. I have a search warrant. Open the door," was also held to comply with the statute. *People v. Mayes*, 78 Mich. App. 618 (1977).

## How Long to Wait

A warrant was properly served where an officer knocked on a door and clearly announced authority and purpose and waited long enough for inhabitants to reach the door from the room farthest away before kicking in the door. *People v. Harvey*, 38 Mich. App. 39 (1972).

The length of time is flexible and is determined by the "totality of the circumstances." In drug cases, the appropriate measure of how long to wait may be determined by how long it would take to dispose the evidence as opposed to how long it would take an occupant to get to the door. However, if the search warrant is for a piano then the officers may be required to wait until the occupants actually answer the door and refuse entry. *United States v. Banks*, 540 U.S. 31 (2003).

## No Exclusionary Rule

The court has held that the exclusionary rule does not apply when the police do not wait long enough under the knock and announce rule. Thus, evidence was not suppressed after police waited three to five seconds before forcing entry after announcing their presence. *Hudson v. Michigan*, 547 U.S. 586 (2006).

© 2014, Shutterstock, Inc.

# ADMISSIONS AND CONFESSIONS

## BASIC CONSIDERATIONS

The defendant's own confession is probably the most probative and damaging evidence that can be admitted against him. . . . The admissions of a defendant come from the actor himself, the most knowledgeable and unimpeachable source of information about his past conduct. Certainly, confessions have a profound impact on the jury. Bruton v. United States, 391 U.S. 123 (1968).

### The Fifth Amendment

*No person shall be held to answer for a capital, or otherwise infamous crime, unless on a present-ment or indictment of a Grand Jury, except in cases arising in the land or naval forces, or in the Militia, when in actual service in time of War or public danger; nor shall any person be subject for the same offence to be twice put in jeopardy of life or limb; nor shall be compelled in any criminal case to be a witness against himself, nor be deprived of life, liberty, or property, without due process of law; nor shall private property be taken for public use, without just compensation.*

The Fifth Amendment is applicable to the states via the Fourteenth Amendment.

The question, when a Fifth Amendment viola-tion is alleged is: Based on the totality of the circumstances, was the suspect's confession freely and voluntarily made? The totality of the circumstances includes the age of the accused; his lack of education or his intelligence level; the extent of his previous experience with the police; the repeated and prolonged nature of the questioning; the length of the deten-tion of the accused before he gave the state-ment in question; the lack of any advice to the accused of his constitutional rights; whether there was an unnecessary delay in bringing him before a magistrate before he gave the confession; whether the accused was injured, intoxicated or drugged, or in ill health when he gave the statement; whether the accused was deprived of food, sleep, or medical attention; whether the accused was physically abused; and whether the suspect was threatened with abuse. The absence or presence of any one of these factors is not necessarily conclusive on the issue of voluntariness. The ultimate test of admissibility is whether the totality of the circumstances surrounding the making of the confession indicates that it was freely and vol-untarily made. *People v. Cipriano*, 431 Mich. 315 (1988).

### "Witness Against Himself"

The privilege only protects *testimonial evidence*. It does not include physical evidence, voice or hand-writing exemplars, or blood samples taken from the defendant

An in-custody suspect does *not* have a Fifth Amendment right against self-incrimination that would allow him to refuse to stand in a lineup. If an in-custody suspect refuses to cooperate, this can be used at trial to show knowledge of guilt. *United States v. Wade*, 388 U.S. 218 (1967).

A suspect can be compelled to repeat words spoken by the culprit at the crime scene as well as to make gestures or wear certain clothing, without violating the Fifth Amendment. *People v. Hall*, 396 Mich. 650 (1976); *United States v. Dionisio*, 410 U.S. 1 (1973).

The privilege protects a defendant from testifying against himself at a criminal trial.

A person may refuse to answer any official questions put to him in any other proceeding, whether criminal or civil, formal or informal, *if the answers might incriminate him* in future criminal proceedings. *Minnesota v. Murphy*, 465 U.S. 420 (1984).

### The Difference between an Admission and a Confession

- An admission is a partial admittance to criminal involvement.
- A confession is the complete admittance to criminal involvement.

## THE *MIRANDA* WARNINGS

### The *Miranda* Case

In 1963, the Phoenix police arrested Ernesto *Miranda* for raping and kidnapping a mildly retarded 18-year-old woman. After two hours in a police interrogation room, *Miranda* signed a written confession, but he was not told that he had the right to remain silent, to have a lawyer, and to be protected against self-incrimination.

Despite his lawyer's objections, the confession was presented as evidence at *Miranda's* trial, and he was convicted and sentenced to

20 years. His appeal went all the way to the Supreme Court, where it was joined with three other similar cases. In a landmark ruling, the court established that an accused has the right to remain silent and that prosecutors may not use statements made by defendants during custodial interrogations unless the police have advised them of their rights. The court found custodial interrogations to be *an inherently coercive environment* where the suspect's rights must be explained and waived. *Miranda v. Arizona*, 384 U.S. 436 (1966).

### The *Miranda* Warnings

Rights warnings generally include the following:

- You have the right to remain silent and refuse to answer questions.
- Anything you do say may be used against you in a court of law.
- You have the right to consult with an attorney before speaking to the police and to have an attorney present during questioning now or in the future.
- If you cannot afford an attorney, one will be appointed for you before any questioning, if you wish.
- If you decide to answer questions without an attorney present, you will still have the right to stop answering at any time until you talk to an attorney.
- Knowing and understanding your rights as I have explained them to you, are you willing to answer my questions at this time?

## ADVISEMENT OF RIGHTS

"The wording must reasonably convey the *Miranda* rights. The wording does not have to be precise, but failure to read is fertile grounds for defense arguments." The advisement of rights does not need to be given in the exact form described in the *Miranda* decision. The question that will be asked is whether the advisement reasonably conveys to the suspect his or her rights as required by *Miranda*. *Duckworth v. Eagan*, 492 U.S. 195 (1989).

Informing the suspect that he had "the right to have an attorney present" without saying "during questioning" was sufficient to inform the suspect of his right to counsel during interrogation. *People v. Johnson*, 90 Mich. App. 415 (1979).

The police advised the defendant of his right to have an attorney present by stating, "You have the right to talk to a lawyer before answering any of our questions" and "You have the right to use any of these rights at any time you want during this interview." The defendant then confessed to being a felon in possession of a firearm. He appealed his subsequent conviction by arguing that he was not adequately advised of his right to have an attorney present during questioning. The court held that the warning had adequately conveyed both his right to have an attorney present and his right to request an attorney at any point during the interview. *Florida v. Powell*, 559 U.S. 50 (2010).

The court in *Powell* stated, "The standard warnings used by the Federal Bureau of Investigation are exemplary. They provide, in relevant part: 'You have the right to talk to a lawyer for advice before we ask you any questions. You have the right to have a lawyer with you during questioning.'"

It is better, as a rule of thumb, to read the *Miranda* warnings from a departmentally approved *Miranda* card.

### When Are *Miranda* Warnings Required?

For many years, the Michigan courts followed a focus test for determining when *Miranda* warnings were required. *Miranda* warnings were to be given when an officer focused his or her attention on a person as a possible criminal suspect. This test was difficult to apply and the Michigan Supreme Court rejected it in the case of *People v. Hill*, 429 Mich. 382 (1987). The court instead ruled that *Miranda* warnings have to be given when a person is in custody and subjected to interrogation.

Custody + Interrogation = *Miranda* warnings

### Custody

Custody means:

- The person is under arrest, or
- The person's freedom has been deprived in any significant way. The deciding factor will be whether the defendant felt that he was free to leave.

Custody arises when a person has been deprived of his freedom of action in a meaningful way. *People v. Belanger*, 120 Mich. App. 752 (1982).

To determine whether a defendant was in custody at the time of interrogation, the totality of the circumstances must be examined. The key question is whether the defendant could reasonably believe that he was not free to leave. *People v. Blackburn*, 135 Mich. App. 509 (1984).

The defendant was interviewed in his motel room. Though the police testified he would not have been able to walk out freely, this information was not relayed to the the defendant. In fact, he was told that he was not under arrest. This was held not to be custodial and *Miranda* warnings did not have to be given. *People v. Zahn*, 234 Mich. App. 438 (1999).

Statements made at the *police station* may be non-custodial, especially when the suspect voluntarily goes to the station.

A trooper asked the defendant, a burglary suspect, to come into the post. The defendant went to the post and was told that he was not under arrest. The officer told him that he wanted to talk about a burglary at which the defendant's fingerprints were found (no prints were actually found). The defendant confessed and left the post a half an hour later. The court held that the defendant was not in custody because his freedom was not restricted in any way. He had gone to the post voluntarily and was immediately informed that he was not under arrest. He then left within half an hour without hindrance. *Oregon v. Mathiason*, 429 U.S. 492 (1977).

A detective suspected that the defendant had raped and killed a 10-year-old girl. He informed the defendant that he believed he may have *witnessed* the girl's disappearance. The officer asked the the defendant to accompany him to the station. The suspect agreed. The court held that "A police officer's *subjective view* that the individual under questioning is a suspect, if undisclosed, does not bear upon the question whether the individual is in custody for purposes of *Miranda*. . . . An officer's knowledge or beliefs may bear upon the custody issue if they are conveyed, by word or deed, to the individual being questioned." The test for custody will be determined by the objective conditions surrounding the interrogation. *Stansbury v. California*, 511 U.S. 318 (1994) (emphasis added).

The court found custody where officers picked up an individual they wanted to question about a murder. The officers did not have a warrant or probable cause to make an arrest. They informed the subject that *he was not under arrest, but he would be physically restrained* if he tried to leave. *Dunaway v. New York*, 442 U.S. 200 (1979).

Police suspected that the defendant had committed a murder. They went to his house and asked him to accompany them to the precinct. He voluntarily went with them to the station. The court held that this was not custody. The question to be asked is whether that person reasonably believed that he or she was not free to leave. *People v. Marbury*, 151 Mich. App. 159 (1986).

Police believed that the defendant had information about a recent murder. The officers went to his house and asked him to accompany them to the station for questioning. The suspect was searched prior to entering an unmarked patrol car but was not handcuffed. He was questioned at the station. He gave an incriminating statement. As a result of the statement, the defendant was placed under arrest and read his *Miranda* rights 40 minutes after the interrogation began. The court held that the defendant was not in custody prior to his arrest. *People v. Williams*, 171 Mich. App. 234 (1988).

There was no custody where the defendant picked the time for the interview, drove himself to the station, was told that he was not under arrest, was unrestrained and alone for periods of time, and after giving a written statement, was allowed to leave. *People v. Mendez*, 225 Mich. App. 381 (1997).

The defendant was questioned at a homicide scene by police. He agreed to go to the station and give a statement. At the station, the defendant was told that he was not under arrest and was free to leave at any time. The defendant initially denied any involvement during his first statement. Later, he was confronted with a number of inconsistencies between his statement and the statements of two others from the scene. At this time, he stated that the gun fell from the victim's hand and discharged when it hit the floor. He asked to talk to his father and was told that he would be able to later. He agreed to take a polygraph test. Prior to the test, he was advised of his *Miranda* rights. He waived his rights. During the exam, he was told that he was not being truthful. He then confessed to intentionally shooting the victim. He arrested and again advised of his *Miranda* rights. He then gave a recorded statement. At some point during the defendant's questioning, his father and attorney came to see him. They were denied access to the defendant and the attorney demanded questioning stop until he saw the defendant.

The court upheld the confession: "The trial court found that defendant was treated fairly by the investigating officers throughout his interrogation. The defendant was provided with food and water and was told on at least two occasions that he was not under arrest and could leave at any time. The defendant himself testified that he was treated fairly by the officers and that he was not coerced in any manner into making the challenged statements. The defendant was also advised of his *Miranda* rights and. . . voluntarily waived those rights before making the challenged statements. Although there was evidence that the defendant suffers from an auditory processing disorder and that he has below average intelligence, the trial judge, who was in the best position to observe defendant's demeanor, noted that defendant, while testifying in this matter, understood the questions presented to him and responded to those questions in an appropriate manner. Finally, although the police failed to inform defendant that he had counsel available during his interrogation, failed to disclose defendant's whereabouts to defense counsel, and failed to heed defense counsel's demands that the interrogation be stopped, [we are] not prepared to say that, under the totality of the circumstances, these factors alone rendered defendant's otherwise voluntary statements involuntary." *People v. Sexton*, 461 Mich. 746 (2000).

## Generally, Questions at the Home or Office Is Not Considered Custodial

The defendant was questioned while in his office. The defendant owned the building and was surrounded by people he was familiar with. The court held that the defendant was not in custody, nor was his freedom significantly deprived. *People v. Hill*, 429 Mich. 382 (1987).

Because officers entered the defendant's room at 4:00 am and immediately began questioning him about incriminating facts without first informing him of his *Miranda* rights and because the testimony of the officers at trial revealed that the defendant was under arrest once they entered his room, the defendant's confession was invalid. *Orozco v. Texas*, 394 U.S. 324 (1969).

## Generally, Phone Conversations Do Not Constitute Custody

A pre-arrest telephone conversation between a police officer and the defendant did not require *Miranda* warnings because the defendant was not in custody. The defendant had called the police officer and made incriminating statements. The court reasoned that there was no coercive police pressure and no custody when a suspect is on the phone at his home speaking with police. *People v. Fisher*, 166 Mich. App. 699 (1988).

## Generally, Traffic Stops Do Not Constitute Custody Because a Traffic Stop Does Not Significantly Deprive a Person of His or Her Freedom

Roadside questioning during a traffic stop does not constitute custodial interrogation. However, once an arrest is made, questioning about the driving requires *Miranda* warnings, even if the arrest is for a misdemeanor traffic violation. Routine traffic stops are analogous to *Terry* stops. They do not bear the coerciveness of custodial interrogation; thus, *Miranda* warnings are generally not required. *Berkemer v. McCarty*, 468 U.S. 420 (1984).

*Miranda* warnings were not required prior to an officer conducting roadside questioning as to whether the defendant had been drinking and how much he had been drinking as the defendant was not in custody. The questioning occurred within minutes of stop, at a time when officer had an insufficient basis for concluding that the defendant was operating his automobile under influence of intoxicants, and the defendant was never informed prior to

questioning that he was under arrest or that the detention would be other than brief. *People v. Chinn*, 141 Mich. App. 92 (1985).

On a traffic stop for a civil infraction, an officer asked the driver if there were any weapons in the car. The driver admitted to having a gun. The gun was admissible, even though the questions about the gun were unrelated to the purposes of the stop, as a traffic stop is not custody for purposes of *Miranda*. The court further held where an officer makes a routine stop of a vehicle for a traffic offense which is a civil infraction, there is no obligation to give *Miranda* warnings where the questions asked relate to the existence of weapons in the vehicle. *People v. Edwards*, 158 Mich. App. 561 (1987).

A traffic stop is reasonable as long as the driver is detained only for the purpose of allowing an officer to ask reasonable questions concerning the violation of law and its context for a reasonable period. These questions may include the destination and travel plans. The determination whether a traffic stop is reasonable must necessarily take into account the evolving circumstances with which the officer is faced. *People v. Williams*, 472 Mich. 308 (2005).

It was reasonable for police to extend a traffic stop to confirm or dispel suspicions that a car was stolen. However, extending the stop was unreasonable for purposes of confirming the identity of a passenger who was under no obligation to provide identification in the first place. *People v. Burrell*, 417 Mich. 439 (1983).

## Generally, Pat-Down Searches Do Not Constitute Custody

During a non-custodial pat-down, an officer felt a hard object in defendant's chest pocket. The officer believed the object to be a weapon and asked the defendant what it was. The defendant replied that it was marijuana. The court held that "The limited constraint placed upon defendant's freedom by the officer's conducting the pat-down search does not rise to the level of a custodial interrogation and precludes a finding that defendant's admission was compelled by police action." *People v. Harmelin*, 176 Mich. App. 524 (1989).

## Generally, Questioning at a Hospital Room Does Not Constitute Custody

During the defendant's attempt to commit murder with a bomb, she was seriously injured when the bomb exploded. She lost her hands and was in the hospital when she was interviewed and made incriminating statements. She first argued that she should have been given her *Miranda* rights. The court disagreed because she was not in custody. She also claimed that her statements were not voluntary because of the medicine she was on. The court disagreed by looking at the doctor's statements that her ability to remain silent was not impaired. *People v. Peerenboom*, 224 Mich. App. 195 (1997).

## An Arrest Under a Warrant Will Be Custody, Even If the Suspect Will Soon Be Released on Bond

The defendant was arrested on a warrant. She was told that she would be released after posting bond. She was then questioned about drug paraphernalia found in her vehicle. She made a number of admissions. The court held that even though she was going to be released on bond, she was still in custody at the time of the questioning and *Miranda* warnings should have been given. *People v. Roark*, 214 Mich. App. 421 (1995).

## An Individual Does Not Have to be Arrested When Sufficient Probable Cause Exists

The defendant was being investigated for jury tampering but was not in custody. The defendant made some incriminating statements. At trial, he argued that he should have been taken into custody as soon as probable cause was established. The court held that a defendant has no right to be arrested. Police do not have to stop the investigation and make an arrest the moment they have probable cause. *Hoffa v. United States*, 385 U.S. 293 (1966).

## Custody and Unrelated Charges?

Questioning a prisoner in an area isolated from the general inmate population does not necessarily render the interrogation custodial.

Technical custody, i.e., incarceration, does not automatically mean "custody" for *Miranda* purposes. Questioning of an inmate is noncustodial if the totality of the circumstances indicate the inmate was free to terminate questioning and return to the general population. Here, the facts that the defendant was not "invited" to the interview, was not advised he did not have to speak with deputies, was interviewed for five to seven hours, was interviewed well past the time he normally went to bed, was questioned by armed deputies, and was spoken to in a sharp tone militate toward a finding of custody. However, the repeated reminders that the defendant could return to his cell whenever he wanted, was not physically restrained by any means, was offered food and water, and the conference room door was usually left open created an environment that a reasonable person would have felt free to leave; thus, *Miranda* warnings were not required because there was no custody. *Howes v. Fields*, 132 S. Ct. 1181 (2012).

## Evidence Obtained in Violation of *Miranda* Does Not Automatically Have to Be Suppressed If the Confession Was Voluntarily Made

Officers were investigating the defendant for a violation of a temporary restraining order. They also had information that he was a convicted felon and illegally possessed a pistol. The officers proceeded to his home and arrested him for violating the restraining order. One officer was attempting to advise him of his rights when the defendant interrupted, asserting that he knew his rights. The officer then asked about the pistol and the defendant told him where it was. The pistol was retrieved and the defendant was indicted for possession of a firearm by a convicted felon in violation of federal law. He argued on appeal that the firearm should be suppressed as a violation of *Miranda*.

The court held that:

1. Failure to give a suspect warnings does not require suppression of physical fruits of a suspect's unwarned but voluntary statements.
2. Officers' failure to give warnings in conjunction with restraining order arrest did not require suppression of weapon at

firearms trial, since weapon was recovered based on the defendant's voluntary statement that he possessed it.

3. *Miranda* rights are prophylactic trial rights. Their protections are only triggered when the prosecution seeks to enter into evidence the defendant's statements or the fruits of defendant's statements obtained in violation of *Miranda*.

*United States v. Patane*, 542 U.S. 630 (2004).

# INTERROGATION

Interrogation consists of one of the following:

- Express questioning.
- Any words or actions that the police know or reasonably should know are likely to elicit an incriminating response.

## Michigan Requires Audio-Visual Recording of Interrogations—MCL 763.7-10

### Definitions—MCL 763.7

*As used in this section and sections 8 to 10 of this chapter:*

(a) *"Custodial detention" means an individual's being in a place of detention because a law enforcement official has told the individual that he or she is under arrest or because the individual, under the totality of the circumstances, reasonably could believe that he or she is under a law enforcement official's control and is not free to leave.*

(b) *"Interrogation" means questioning in a criminal investigation that may elicit a self-incriminating response from an individual and includes a law enforcement official's words or actions that the law enforcement official should know are reasonably likely to elicit a self-incriminating response from the individual.*

(c) *"Law enforcement official" means any of the following:*

   (i) *A police officer of this state or a political subdivision of this state as defined in section 2 of the commission on law enforcement standards act, 1965 PA 203, MCL 28.602.*

   (ii) *A county sheriff or his or her deputy.*

   (iii) *A prosecuting attorney.*

   (iv) *A public safety officer of a college or university.*

   (v) *A conservation officer of the department of natural resources and environment.*

   (vi) *An individual acting under the direction of a law enforcement official described in subparagraphs (i) to (v).*

(d) *"Major felony" means a felony punishable by imprisonment for life, for life or any term of years, or for a statutory maximum of 20 years or more, or a violation of section 520d of the Michigan penal code, 1931 PA 328, MCL 750.520d.*

(e) *"Major felony recording" means the interrogation recording required under section 8 of this chapter or a duplicate of that recording.*

(f) *"Place of detention" means a police station, correctional facility, or prisoner holding facility or another governmental facility where an individual may be held in connection with a criminal charge that has been or may be filed against the individual.*

## Audiovisual Recording—MCL 763.8

(1) *This section applies if the law enforcement agency has audiovisual recording equipment that is operational or accessible as provided in section 11(3) or (4) or upon the expiration of the relevant time periods set forth in section 11(3) or (4), whichever occurs first.*

(2) *A law enforcement official interrogating an individual in custodial detention regarding the individual's involvement in the commission of a major felony shall make a time-stamped, audiovisual recording of the entire interrogation. A major felony recording shall include the law enforcement official's notification to the individual of the individual's Miranda rights.*

(3) *An individual who believes the individual's interrogation is being recorded may object to having the interrogation recorded. The individual's objection shall be documented either by the individual's objection stated on the recording or the individual's signature on a document stating the objection. If the individual refuses to document the objection either by recording or signature, a law enforcement official shall document the objection by a recording or signed document. A major felony recording may be made without the consent or knowledge of, or despite the objection of, the individual being interrogated.*

(4) A major felony recording shall be produced using equipment and procedures that are designed to prevent alteration of the recording's audio or visual record.

(5) Pursuant to any request of discovery, the prosecutor shall provide a copy of the recorded statement to the defense counsel of record or to the defendant if he or she is not represented by defense counsel. The court shall not require the police or the prosecutor to prepare or pay for a transcript of a recorded statement. A court or the defense may have a transcript prepared at its own expense.

(6) Prior to conviction or acquittal, a statement recorded under this section is exempt from disclosure under the freedom of information act, 1976 PA 442, MCL 15.231 to 15.246.

## Failure to Record—MCL 763.9

Any failure to record a statement as required under section 8 of this chapter or to preserve a recorded statement does not prevent any law enforcement official present during the taking of the statement from testifying in court as to the circumstances and content of the individual's statement if the court determines that the statement is otherwise admissible. However, unless the individual objected to having the interrogation recorded and that objection was properly documented under section 8(3), the jury shall be instructed that it is the law of this state to record statements of an individual in custodial detention who is under interrogation for a major felony and that the jury may consider the absence of a recording in evaluating the evidence relating to the individual's statement.

## Requirement Is a Directive—MCL 763.10

A failure to comply with sections 8 and 9 of this chapter does not create a civil cause of action against a department or individual. The requirement in section 8 of this chapter to produce a major felony recording is a directive to departments and law enforcement officials and not a right conferred on an individual who is interrogated.

## Implementation—MCL 763.11

(1) The commission on law enforcement standards created under section 3 of the commission on law enforcement standards act,

1965 PA 203, MCL 28.603, shall set quality standards for the audiovisual recording of statements under section 8 of this chapter and standards for geographic accessibility of equipment in the state. The commission shall also conduct an assessment of the initial cost necessary for law enforcement agencies to purchase audiovisual recording equipment. The first assessment shall be conducted within 120 days after the effective date of the amendatory act that added this section. The commission on law enforcement standards shall conduct subsequent assessments regarding the necessary costs of purchasing, upgrading, or replacing the equipment every 2 years.

(2) The commission on law enforcement standards shall recommend to the legislature each year an annual appropriation amount to be determined by the commission's assessment performed under this section. The legislature shall annually appropriate funds to the commission on law enforcement standards for distribution to law enforcement agencies throughout the state to allow the agencies to purchase audiovisual recording equipment for purposes of this chapter. Any funds appropriated for this purpose shall be in addition to the appropriations provided to the commission on law enforcement standards and the department of state police in the immediately preceding fiscal year and shall not be appropriated from the Michigan justice training fund created in section 5 of 1982 PA 302, MCL 18.425, or the department of state police budget.

(3) Except as otherwise provided in subsection (4), law enforcement agencies shall implement sections 7 to 10 of this chapter and this section within 120 days after receiving funds under this section from the commission on law enforcement standards or acquiring access to audiovisual recording equipment as directed by the standards set forth by that commission.

(4) Notwithstanding subsection (3), a law enforcement agency shall comply with the provisions of the amendatory act that added this subsection within 60 days after the date the commission adopts the standards for audiovisual recording equipment required by this section if the law enforcement agency has audiovisual recording equipment that complies with those standards on that date, or within 60 days after the date the law enforcement agency subsequently obtains audiovisual recording equipment that complies with the adopted standards.

## MCOLES Recording Standards

The Michigan Commission on Law Enforcement Standards (MCOLES) is required by the Act to set quality standards for the audiovisual recording of statements and standards for the geographic accessibility of equipment in this state. The MCOLES adopted the following standards on September 18, 2013.

### Standard 1: Recording Capability

Audiovisual equipment shall:

- Use a digital recording format.
- Capture at least 24 frames per second.
- Be compatible with a universal playback system.
- Have the capability for an authorized user to redact a copy of the original digital evidence.
- Export duplicate recordings in the original format.
- Allow for a compressed file sharing copy without loss of picture/audio quality.
- Record, without user intervention, at least a continuous 6-hour event.
- Playback recordings in original quality, without loss of picture/audio integrity.

### Standard 2: Camera

Video cameras must:

- Record in color.
- Have a minimum of 452 horizontal lines of resolution.
- Be positioned so all individuals within the interrogation room are captured.

### Standard 3: Microphone

Audio recording equipment shall:

- Record simultaneously with the video for recording and archiving.
- Be positioned to capture voices of individuals within the interrogation room.
- Be of a quality to accurately record all verbal communication taking place in the interrogation room.

### Standard 4: Date/Time Stamp

Recording systems shall:

- Continually record the time/date stamp as metadata.
- Be administrator-configurable to allow or disallow visual display.

### Standard 5: Agency Policy and Procedure

Michigan law enforcement agencies shall establish operational guidelines for the audiovisual recording of interrogations identified in law. The guidelines shall include:

- Procedures for audiovisual recordings.
- *Miranda* rights within the recording.
- The treatment of recordings as evidence.
- The secured storage of audiovisual recordings.
- Procedures for the copying of recordings.
- Procedures for the retention and/or destruction of recordings.
- How the recording equipment is tested and verified.

### Standard 6: Geographic Accessibility

The geographic accessibility requirement shall be met by an agency if all of the following occur:

- Equipment meeting MCOLES audiovisual standards is reasonably accessible by an agency.
- There is a mutual agreement in place for use of another agency's audiovisual equipment in effect.
- The location housing the audiovisual equipment is considered to be a place of detention as defined in the Act.

## Held to Be Interrogation

The defendant was arrested in connection with the disappearance of a 10-year-old girl. He invoked his rights. As he rode in the police car, the detective began to converse with him. The detective knew that the defendant was deeply religious and so presented what is now known as the "Christian Burial Speech" in an attempt to recover the little girl's body. "Reverend, . . . I want to give you something to think about while we're traveling down the road. . . . Number one, I want you to observe the weather conditions, it's raining, it's sleeting, it's freezing, driving is very treacherous, visibility is poor, it's going to be dark early this evening. They are predicting several inches of snow for tonight, and I feel that you yourself are the only person that knows where this little girl's body is, that you yourself have only been there once, and if you get a snow on top of it you yourself may be unable to find it. And, since we will be going right past the area on the way into Des Moines, I feel that we could stop and locate the body, that the parents of this little girl should be entitled to a Christian burial for the little girl who was snatched away from them on Christmas (E)ve and murdered. And I feel we should stop and locate it on the way in rather than waiting until morning and trying to come back out after a snow storm and possibly not being able to find it at all." The court held that this to be interrogation because the officer knew or should have known that the statements about the Christian burial would elicit incriminating statements. The officer knew the defendant was deeply religious and used that to obtain the confession. *Brewer v. Williams,* 430 U.S. 387 (1977).

## Functional Equivalent of Interrogation

The term "interrogation" refers to any words or action on the part of the police, other than those normally attendant on arrest and custody, that the police should know are reasonably likely to elicit an incriminating response from the suspect. *Rhode Island v. Innis,* 446 U.S. 291 (1980).

After the defendant was arrested for murder, he was provided his *Miranda* warnings and he asserted his right to remain silent. After asserting his right, a colloquy immediately ensued between the detective and the defendant which included the following:

"Defendant: I don't even want to speak.

Detective: I understand. I understand Kadeem. Okay then. The only thing I can tell you Kadeem, is good luck man. Okay. Don't take this personal. It's not personal. It's not personal between me and you, I think I may have had one contact with you on the street. Okay. I've got to do my job. And I understand you've got to do what you've got to do to protect your best interests. Okay. The only thing that I can tell you is this, and I'm not asking you questions, I'm just telling you. I hope that the gun is in a place where nobody can get a hold of it and nobody else can get hurt by it, okay? All right?

Defendant: I didn't even mean for it to happen like that. It was a complete accident.

Detective: I understand. I understand. But like I said, you, uhh, you get your attorney, man. Hey, look dude, I don't think you're a monster, all right? I don't think that. You could have came down to me and turned yourself in and there ain't no damn way I'd beat you up....

Defendant: I know that I didn't mean to do it. I guarantee that, I know I didn't mean to do it."

The defendant moved to suppress his statement arguing that the detective's statement constituted the functional equivalent of interrogation under *Innis*. The court held that the defendant was not subjected to express questioning or its functional equivalent after he invoked his right to remain silent. The term "interrogation" refers not only to express questioning, but also to any words or actions on the part of the police, other than those normally attendant to arrest and custody, that the police should know are reasonably likely to elicit an incriminating response from the suspect. In this case, the defendant was in custody. He was not, however, subjected to express questioning. A question asks for or invites a response. The officer's comment concerning the location of the gun did not ask for or invite a response, but was a mere expression of hope and concern. Nor did the addition of the words "okay" and "all right" at the end of the comment transform it into a question. The officer used the words repeatedly during the colloquy to indicate when he had finished a thought. Additionally, before making the comment, the officer informed the defendant that he was not asking the defendant questions. The officer's statement in that regard made it less likely that the officer would have reasonably expected the defendant to answer with an incriminating response. Further, the defendant's subsequent statement did not concern the gun's location, reinforcing the conclusion that the officer's comment was not a question. That conclusion is also reinforced by the fact that the officer seemed surprised by the defendant's inculpatory statements. *People v. White,* 493 Mich. 187 (2013).

## Held Not to Be Interrogation

Two officers were transporting a murder suspect who they suspected had just killed a taxi cab driver with a shotgun. They were in the front seat and the suspect was sitting in the back. During the drive, the officers had a conversation that they knew was being overheard by the suspect. They mentioned that they wished they could find the missing gun because there was a school for handicapped children nearby, and it would be tragic if any of the children were injured. The suspect spoke up and told them he would show them where the gun was so the children would not be injured. The court held that this did not constitute express interrogation nor was it the functional equivalent of interrogation. . . There was no showing that the officers knew or should have known that their conversations would lead to incriminating statements. The officers did not know that the suspect had a "consciousness" for children's safety. *Rhode Island v. Innis,* 446 U.S. 291 (1980).

The suspect in this case killed his son and was being held in jail. His wife was making a statement about the murder in another interrogation room and insisted on talking to her husband. The police attempted to dissuade her from doing so, but eventually permitted her to speak to her husband as long as she did so with an officer present. The wife talked to her husband in the presence of an officer who they knew was taping the conversation. There was no direct questioning or psychological ploys used, even though the officer knew that the suspect was in an emotional state making it likely he would confess. The court held that this did not constitute interrogation. The officer did nothing that he knew or should have known may lead to incriminating response. Any spousal privilege was lost when the husband talked to his wife in front of a third party, here the officer. *Arizona v. Mauro,* 481 U.S. 520 (1987).

The suspect was taken to the booking room, where the officer informed him that he was going to be fingerprinted. The defendant stated, "It was like a bad dream." The officer responded, "What was like a bad dream?" The defendant replied, "To shoot a man six times and see him still try to get up." The officer said nothing else. Another time, while in a patrol car, defendant mumbled something at which the officer asked, "What did you say?" The defendant responded, "How would you feel in my situation?" The officer said, "I'd probably feel pretty depressed." The defendant then stated, "I didn't mean to reload the gun, but I was afraid my dad was going to get me." The court held that the officer's questions were not interrogation and the defendant's answers were purely voluntary and unsolicited. The questioning was not likely to elicit an incriminating response. *People v. Giuchici,* 118 Mich. App. 252 (1982).

The defendant was in custody and being transported from one county to another. During a conversation, the officers informed him that he was being taken to Monroe County to answer questions about a murder. The defendant said he would cooperate and then suddenly blurted out, "I shot him." The officers stopped the car and advised him of his *Miranda* warnings. He subsequently gave a full confession. Informing the defendant of the charges was not likely to elicit incriminating response, and thus there was no interrogation requiring *Miranda* warnings. *People v. Raper,* 222 Mich. App. 475 (1997).

During an arrest for a home invasion, the defendant resisted, and it took five uniformed officers to subdue him. After the defendant was arrested, a silver handgun was found on the ground near where the struggle took place. As he was being transported to jail, the officer asked the defendant if he would be willing to submit a DNA sample. In response to a question from the defendant as to why a DNA sample was being requested, the officer explained that it would be used to determine if the defendant's DNA was on the gun. The defendant then agreed to submit a DNA sample. According to the officer, after three or four minutes passed, the defendant admitted that he had touched the gun with his elbow while "wrestling" with the officers. The court held that the officer's request for a DNA sample and his explanation in regard to why a DNA sample was being requested, which the officer provided only because of the defendant's inquiry, were not words that the officer knew or should have known were reasonably likely to elicit the somewhat incriminating response given by the defendant. Indeed, the defendant's statement, which came after a period of silence with no commentary by the officer, was essentially volunteered by the defendant. And statements that are entirely volunteered, lacking any compelling influences, are not constitutionally barred from admission into evidence. Further, the DNA question posed by the officer can also be viewed as the type of question 'normally attendant to arrest and custody' and thus not interrogational. *People v. McDonald,* 303 Mich. App. 424 (2013).

## Police Communication versus Interrogation

Co-defendants were being questioned separately about a shooting that had occurred at a gas station. After being advised of his *Miranda* rights, one defendant asked to speak to an attorney. The questioning immediately ceased. He was taken to another room and left alone.

He had access to a phone, but was not free to leave. The defendant called a friend and asked for help in locating an attorney. His friend never called back. About an hour and a half later, the detective returned and informed him that the co-defendant had made a statement and asked him if he "would still like to talk to an attorney." The detective did not discuss the substance of the statement or what effect it had on the defendant. The defendant then told the detective, "If Ron doesn't want an attorney, than neither do I." He then gave a statement. He was then given his *Miranda* rights again and specifically asked if he wanted to talk to an attorney. He agreed to be interviewed and gave another statement. The Michigan Court of Appeals refused to apply the U.S. Supreme Court's decision of *Edwards v. Arizona*, 451 U.S. 477 (1981), to this case, distinguishing between police interrogation and police communication. The *Edwards* case does not "prohibit[] all communication between the police and a suspect who has requested an attorney. Rather, a careful reading of *Edwards* reveals that what is prohibited is further 'police-initiated custodial interrogation'. . . . We further conclude that Detective Lister's remark informing defendant that codefendant Sands had given a statement did not constitute interrogation. The remark did not involve any express questioning, but merely described an event that transpired since Lister last saw the defendant. Significantly, Detective Lister made no attempt to discuss the substance of Sands' statement with defendant or to discuss what effect, if any, Sands' statement might have on defendant's case. In this context, the remark was not likely to elicit an incriminating response." *People v. Kowalski*, 230 Mich. App. 464 (1998).

## Interrogation Does Not Apply to

### Voluntary Statements Not in Response to Police Interrogation

The defendant was taken into custody for murder. While handcuffed and riding in the back of a police car with two officers, but before being advised of his *Miranda* rights, the officers were conversing with the defendant on a range of topics. During the conversation, it came out that defendant had been in the town for about four days. The officers then began discussing the case and informed the defendant that he was being taken back for questioning regarding the homicide investigation. The defendant said that he was going to cooperate and that he would tell them a little bit that he knew. The defendant informed the officers that he was recently with the deceased. Then defendant suddenly blurted out, "I shot him" and became upset. Since the apparent purpose of the officer's conversation was to provide information rather than elicit a response, the court held that the defendant's voluntary statements made other than under interrogation are admissible even though no *Miranda* warning has been given. *People v. Raper*, 222 Mich. App. 475 (1997)

### Prompt, On the Scene Questions

General on-the-scene questioning as to the facts surrounding a crime or other general questioning of citizens in the fact-finding process is not affected by the holding of *Miranda*. *People v. Dunlap*, 82 Mich. App. 171 (1978).

### Normal Arrest and Booking Procedures

The defendant was taken to a booking center where, as was the routine practice, he was told that his actions and voice would be videotaped. He then answered seven questions regarding his name, address, height, weight, eye color, date of birth, and current age, stumbling over two responses. He was also asked, and was unable to give, the date of his sixth birthday. In addition, he made several incriminating statements while he performed physical sobriety tests and when he was asked to submit to a breathalyzer test. He refused to take the breathalyzer test and was advised, for the first time, of his *Miranda* rights.

Only testimonial responses are afforded *Miranda* protections, i.e., using the un-*Mirandized* statements made during the sobriety test as evidence that the defendant's speech was slurred is proper while the content of his oral statements may be protected. *Miranda* warnings are not required for routine booking questions. However, the defendant's response to the sixth birthday question was incriminating not just because of his delivery but also because the content of his answer supported an inference that his mental state was confused. His response was testimonial because he was required to communicate an express or implied assertion of fact or belief and, thus, was confronted with the "trilemma" of truth, falsity, or silence, the historical abuse against which the privilege against self-incrimination was aimed. *Pennsylvania v. Muniz*, 496 U.S. 582 (1990).

| Consequences of Invoking *Miranda* Rights | |
|---|---|
| Right to Remain Silent | Right to an Attorney |
| Questioning must stop | Questioning must stop |
| Officers may reinitiate questioning after a reasonable period of time | Officers may not reinitiate questioning on any crime |

# RIGHT TO REMAIN SILENT

If a person invokes his or her right to remain silent, officers must stop questioning. Officers may reinitiate questioning, after a *reasonable time,* if they scrupulously honor the person's rights.

Once a suspect states he or she wishes to remain silent, the questioning must stop. This right must be *scrupulously* honored. However, the re-initiation of questioning two hours later by a different detective on an unrelated matter after re-*Mirandizing* the defendant was permissible. *Michigan v. Mosley*, 423 U.S. 96 (1975).

A suspect was arrested for murder and was advised of her rights. She invoked her right to remain silent. Officers initiated questioning 22 hours later on the same charges. The court held that where the officers *scrupulously honor* the defendant's rights by stopping the questioning when she requested them to stop, officers could reinitiate questioning 22 hours later. The key is whether the "police scrupulously honored the assertion of the right to cut off questioning" and did not persist in "repeated efforts to wear down her resistance." *People v. Slocum*, 219 Mich. App. 695 (1996).

## Tacit Admission

A tacit admission is an acknowledgment of guilt inferred from silence. Silence in response to accusation of criminal activity is generally not admissible. *People v. Bobo*, 390 Mich. 355 (1973).

Admission of evidence of a defendant's silence as a tacit admission of guilt is prohibited, unless the defendant has shown his adoption of or belief in the truth of the accusation. *People v. Greenwood*, 209 Mich. App. 470 (1995).

## Silence and Demeanor during Custodial Interrogation

The Fifth Amendment does not preclude use of testimony concerning a defendant's behavior and demeanor after a valid waiver of rights. When a defendant speaks after receiving his or her warnings, a momentary pause or even a failure to answer a question will not be construed as an assertion of the right to remain silent.

The use for impeachment purposes of a suspect's silence after the suspect received *Miranda* warnings, violates the Due Process Clause of the Fourteenth Amendment. Post-arrest silence following such warnings is insolubly ambiguous, i.e., it is impossible to tell if the reason for silence is guilt, reflection, caution, etc. The court held that it would be fundamentally unfair to allow an arrestee's silence to be used to impeach an alibi given at trial after he had been impliedly assured by the *Miranda* warnings that his silence would carry no penalty. *Doyle v. Ohio*, 426 U.S. 610 (1976).

When a defendant's silence is attributable to his invocation of Fifth Amendment privilege or reliance on *Miranda* warnings, that silence may not be used against him at trial. However, when there is no basis to conclude that a suspect's unresponsiveness is attributable to invocation of Fifth Amendment privilege or reliance on *Miranda* warnings, there is no violation of the Fifth Amendment to use that unresponsiveness as substantive evidence of the suspect's demeanor during interrogation and to give context to his responses.

Here, the suspect was *Mirandized* and agreed to talk. He answered some questions from the investigators while he did not respond to others. The court held that after a valid *Miranda* waiver, the suspect's unresponsiveness to some questions during the interrogation was not a selective invocation of the right to silence and the unresponsiveness and demeanor could be used as evidence. However, if a defendant "manifested a total revocation of his earlier waiver" or "answered several questions and then invoked his right to remain silent," the prosecutor would not be entitled to introduce evidence of that silence at trial or to comment on it during summation. *People v. McReavy*, 436 Mich. 197 (1990).

In another case, the defendant was arrested for armed robbery. He invoked his *Miranda* rights by refusing to speak to the police. He also asked for an attorney. At trial, the defendant attempted to explain why he had been hiding in an abandoned building. His testified that he was waiting for a taxi when he heard gunshots. He then ran into the abandoned building to hide. He claimed that he tried to offer this explanation to the police after he was arrested. The prosecutor made extensive use of the defendant's post-*Miranda* silence to impeach him. Although his conviction was upheld, the court did hold that this use of post-*Miranda* silence was a constitutional violation. *People v. Borgne*, 483 Mich. 178 (2009).

# FIFTH AMENDMENT RIGHT TO COUNSEL

**Once the Fifth Amendment right to counsel has been invoked, all questioning must stop!**

The right to an attorney cannot be found in the wording of the Fifth Amendment but has been gleaned from the *Miranda* decision. The *Miranda* decision held that to protect a person from being compelled to incriminate him or herself during a custodial interrogation he or she must be informed of his right to an attorney. For these reasons, a "Fifth Amendment right to counsel" during custodial interrogation was created. In the case of *United States v. Dickerson*, 530 U.S. 428 (2000), the U.S. Supreme Court held that the *Miranda* decision was based on the Constitution and that an act of Congress could not overturn it.

Once a suspect has invoked his or her right to counsel under *Miranda*, the suspect may not be subjected to further interrogation until counsel is present, unless:

- The suspect voluntarily initiates further conversation, and
- Waives the previous request for counsel after a fresh set of warnings.

After being arrested on a state criminal charge and after being informed of his *Miranda* rights, the suspect was questioned by the police on January 19, 1976, until he said that he wanted an attorney. Questioning then ceased, but on January 20, police officers came to the jail and, after stating that they wanted to talk to him and again informing petitioner of his *Miranda* rights, obtained his confession after he said that he was willing to talk. The court held that the use of the defendant's confession against him at his trial violated his right under the Fifth and Fourteenth Amendments to have counsel present during custodial interrogation, as declared in *Miranda*. Having exercised his right on January 19 to have counsel present during interrogation, petitioner did not validly waive that right on the 20th. Once the right to counsel is invoked, police may not reinitiate contact with the suspect until the suspect has counsel present or voluntarily reinitiates contact with police himself. After invocation, a subsequent waiver of the right to counsel must be voluntary, knowing, and intelligent. *Edwards v. Arizona*, 451 U.S. 477 (1981).

A suspect was arrested and advised of his *Miranda* rights prior to questioning. He requested an attorney and the questioning stopped. *Three days later*, a different officer advised the defendant of his rights and questioned him about an unrelated crime. The officer was unaware of the defendant's earlier request for counsel. During this interrogation, the suspect incriminated himself. The court held that when a suspect in police custody requests an attorney after *Miranda*, *no further questioning can be conducted regarding the present charge or any other charge*. The right to the continued assistance of counsel can likewise be waived, but the prosecution has a very heavy burden to show a valid waiver. *Arizona v. Roberson*, 486 U.S. 675 (1988).

The suspect was arrested for armed robbery and requested counsel. Nine days later, officers, without notifying the suspect's court appointed attorney and against the suspect's wishes not to talk to police, initiated questioning about the charge and the suspect confessed. The confession was inadmissible as it violated both the Fifth and Sixth Amendments. *People v. Paintman,* 412 Mich. 518 (1982).

## After a Suspect Has Requested an Attorney Under *Miranda*, the Police Must Wait Two Weeks Before Reinitiating Questioning

Invoking the right to counsel at an arraignment is an invocation of Sixth Amendment rights. That protection only applies to subsequent interrogation relating to the same case. The right to silence during a subsequent interrogation by police on an unrelated charge is a Fifth Amendment right and may be validly waived following *Miranda* warnings. *People v. Crusoe,* 433 Mich. 666 (1989); but see *Maryland v. Shatzer,* 130 S. Ct. 1213 (2010), below.

A suspect requested an attorney after being informed of his *Miranda* rights. An attorney was obtained for him, and they were allowed to meet privately. After the attorney left, the officers told the suspect that he had been allowed to speak to his attorney and now he had to talk to them. The court held that when counsel is requested, interrogation must cease. Officials may not reinitiate interrogation without counsel present, even if the accused has consulted with his or her attorney. *Minnick v. Mississippi,* 498 U.S. 146 (1990).

*Miranda* rights apply while a suspect remains in custody and does not extend to where there is a break in the custodial period. *People v. Harris,* 261 Mich. App. 44 (2004).

A detective attempted to interrogate a prison inmate about allegations that the inmate had sexually abused his own son. The inmate stated that he wanted an attorney. He was subsequently returned to the general prison population. Two and a half years later, another detective contacted the inmate about the same allegations. This time the inmate waived his *Miranda* rights. The inmate denied that he had forced his son to perform fellatio on him, but he admitted that he had masturbated in front of his son. The inmate failed a polygraph

examination five days later. He then stated, "I didn't force him. I didn't force him." The court ruled that these statements were admissible. *Maryland v. Shatzer,* 130 S. Ct. 1213 (2010).

The rule from the *Shatzer* case is that police officers may reinitiate contact with a subject who has invoked his right to an attorney once two weeks have passed. During those two weeks, the suspect must be returned to his normal life to allow any residual coercive effects from custody to wear off. Even though the defendant was never actually released from custody because of his incarceration, the break in time from one custodial interrogation to the next was sufficient to allow him to resume his normal incarcerated life in general population. After the requisite non-custodial time has passed, officers must re-*Mirandize* the defendant and obtain a valid waiver of those rights to pursue further interrogation.

## What Constitutes Initiating by the Defendant?

The defendant was arrested for first-degree manslaughter, DUI, and driving without a license. The defendant was arrested, *Mirandized*, and invoked his right to counsel. Questioning stopped immediately. Later, the defendant was transported to a county jail. During the transport, the defendant asked an officer, "What's going to happen to me now?" The officer told that the defendant "You do not have to talk to me. You have requested an attorney and I don't want you talking to me unless you so desire because . . . you have requested an attorney, you know, it has to be at your own free will." The defendant said that he understood and later agreed to take a polygraph. He was again *Mirandized* and then given the polygraph test. He confessed after being told that he failed the test. The court ruled that by asking, "What's going to happen to me now?" the defendant effectively reinitiated contact with police and subsequently knowing and intelligently waived his right to an attorney. *Oregon v. Bradshaw,* 462 U.S. 1039 (1983).

The defendant invoked his right to counsel. Sometime later, he had a brief conversation with a police officer he recognized while waiting for a medical appointment. The court ruled that the brief conversation with the officer did not indicate a desire to speak generally about his case and a subsequent interrogation without counsel three weeks later was a violation of the defendant's rights. *United States v. Whaley*, 13 F.3d 963 (6th Cir. 1994).

## A Confession Obtained in Violation of *Miranda* May Still Be used for Impeachment Purposes

Statements taken in violation of *Miranda* may be used for impeachment purposes, as long as they were voluntarily given. They cannot be used in the prosecutor's case-in-chief. *People v. Stacy*, 193 Mich. App. 19 (1992).

## Consent to Search May Be Sought after a Suspect Has Invoked His Rights under *Miranda*

The defendant was a suspect in the murder of a DNR officer. After being questioned for a while, the defendant stated, "I'm no match for you. I want to talk to an attorney." The officers then asked him for consent to search his home. He agreed and signed the waivers. He argued on appeal that the officers violated his Fifth and Sixth Amendment rights and that the evidence seized during the search should be suppressed. The court held that the defendant was not in custody because he voluntarily came down to the station and was free to leave at any time. Also, the Fifth Amendment protects testimonial evidence and evidence seized during the search was real and physical evidence. "Fifth Amendment rights were not violated when police asked the defendant to sign a consent form after he asked for an attorney." The defendant also argued that his agreement to the search was coerced mainly because he was not provided with an attorney. The court again disagreed. "The situation and circumstances surrounding defendant's questioning by the officers does not suggest that defendant was coerced into agreeing to the searches. The defendant fully cooperated with the police and never indicated any reluctance or that he was pressed into cooperating or consenting to the searches." The Sixth Amendment had not yet attached because the

formal judicial proceeding had not yet begun. (See discussion on Sixth Amendment right to an attorney.) *People v. Marsack*, 231 Mich. App. 364 (1998).

# SIXTH AMENDMENT RIGHT TO COUNSEL
## The Sixth Amendment

*In all criminal prosecutions, the accused shall enjoy the right to a speedy and public trial, by an impartial jury of the State and district wherein the crime shall have been committed, which district shall have been previously ascertained by law, and to be informed of the nature and cause of the accusation; to be confronted with the witnesses against him; to have compulsory process for obtaining witnesses in his favor, and to have the Assistance of Counsel for his defence.*

The Sixth Amendment applies the right to counsel when a defendant becomes accused in a formal judicial proceeding. The accused is entitled to counsel not only at trial, but at *all critical stages of the prosecution* i.e., those stages where counsel's absence might derogate from the defendant's right to a fair trial. *Miranda* still controls to different charges.

The Sixth Amendment provides a right to counsel in all felony cases and any misdemeanor case in which incarceration is actually imposed. *Scott v. Illinois*, 440 U.S. 367 (1979).

Neither request nor appointment of counsel creates a presumption that subsequent waiver of rights by a defendant during a police-initiated interrogation is invalid. *Montejo v. Louisiana*, 556 U.S. 778 (2009).

The Sixth Amendment is offense specific, not fact specific. When the Sixth Amendment right to counsel attaches at the initiation of judicial proceedings, it applies only to the offenses charged and additional uncharged offenses that would be considered the same offense as those charged under *Blockburger*. It does not attach to other crimes, even though they may be factually related to a charge offense. Thus, even though the defendant was charged with burglary and at his arraignment he requested an attorney, he could still be questioned without counsel present, after a valid *Miranda* waiver, regarding a double murder that occurred during the burglary because burglary and homicide are not part of the same offense under *Blockburger*. *Texas v. Cobb*, 532 U.S. 162 (2001).

The defendant was arrested for CCW and retained an attorney at his arraignment. Despite invoking his Sixth Amendment rights, the police were not precluded from questioning him about a murder charge where his Sixth Amendment rights had not yet attached. Before interrogation on the murder charge, the defendant still had to be advised of his *Miranda* rights since he was in custody. *People v. Butler*, 193 Mich. App. 63 (1992).

## Polygraph

Where the defendant demanded a post-indictment polygraph, waiver of the pre-examination *Miranda* warnings was sufficient to waive his Sixth Amendment right to counsel as well. *People v. McElhaney*, 215 Mich. App. 269 (1996).

Officers violated a subject's Sixth Amendment right to counsel where, after his arraignment, they contacted him to see if he still wanted to take a polygraph on the same charge. *People v. Harrington*, 258 Mich. App. 703 (2003).

## When Does the Sixth Amendment Attach?

The Sixth Amendment has not attached even though formal adversarial proceedings have started if the defendant is not yet represented by an attorney and has not requested the assistance of counsel. *Patterson v. Illinois*, 487 U.S. 285 (1988).

"The Sixth Amendment right to counsel is triggered at or after the time that judicial proceedings have been initiated whether by way of formal charge, preliminary hearing, indictment, information, or arraignment. We have held that an accused is denied the basic protections of the Sixth Amendment when there is used against him at his trial evidence of his own incriminating words, which federal agents . . . *deliberately elicited* from him after he had been indicted and in the absence of his counsel." *Fellers v. United States*, 540 U.S. 519 (2004).

## How Long Does the Sixth Amendment Right Last?

The defendant was charged with killing her husband. The charges were eventually dismissed at the preliminary examination and the prosecutor appealed over the next two years. During that time, she became involved in the drug trade, and during a discussion with an undercover DEA agent, she made some incriminating statements about the murder. She was recharged and convicted. She claimed on appeal that the officers violated her Sixth Amendment right to counsel because she still had an attorney appealing the initial charges. The court refused to extend the Sixth Amendment right to counsel through the appellate process, holding that following dismissal of charges by the trial court the right to counsel was no longer necessary because the defendant was no longer accused for Sixth Amendment purposes. The independent nature of the federal investigation further weakened the defendant's argument for counsel. *People v. Riggs*, 223 Mich. App. 662 (1997).

## Waiver After a Request for Attorney Is Made

A defendant may waive his or her Sixth Amendment right to counsel after he or she has made a request for one; however, the waiver will be viewed with suspicion and the prosecutor carries a heavy burden of showing that it done knowingly and voluntarily. *Brewer v. Williams*, 430 U.S. 387 (1977).

## Informant in Jail

### Sixth Amendment

The use of an informant to deliberately elicit incriminating statements on a crime where the Sixth Amendment rights have attached is improper. *Massiah v. United States*, 377 U.S. 201 (1964).

The government violates a suspect's Sixth Amendment rights when it intentionally creates a situation likely to induce the suspect into making incriminating statements after his right to counsel had attached. In this case, a paid government informant was in a holding cell with the defendant. Even though his handlers instructed him to listen for incriminating information and not to ask questions, the court found that, because of the contingency fee arrangement with the informant, it was highly likely the informant would engage in conduct to elicit information so he could get paid. The informant's testimony established that, in fact, he had not been a passive listener and had asked the defendant questions. The court held "[c]onversation stimulated in such circumstances may elicit information that an accused would not intentionally reveal to persons known to be Government agents," thus there could not have been a knowing and intelligent waiver of Sixth Amendment protections. *United States v. Henry*, 447 U.S. 264 (1980).

*Massiah* and *Henry* were intended to protect suspects against secret interrogation and investigation by government agents after the right to counsel had attached.

Use of an informant is allowed if the informant is acting as a "listening post" only and not initiating any conversations to obtain incriminating statements. *Kuhlmann v. Wilson*, 477 U.S. 436 (1986).

## Fifth Amendment

The Fifth Amendment right to counsel is not violated by outfitting another inmate with a wire to have a conversation with an unarraigned defendant in a jail cell. This does not fall under a coercive police atmosphere where *Miranda* rights would need to be read. Remember though, if the suspect were arraigned on the charge, the informant could not question him on that charge. *People v. Fox*, 232 Mich. App. 541 (1998).

# AMBIGUOUS OR LIMITED ASSERTION OF RIGHTS

## Right to Remain Silent

After being read his rights, the defendant stated, "the less I say, the better I think I'll be." The court held that this was not an invocation of the right to remain silent, but an expression of a desire to limit responses. *People v. Spencer*, 154 Mich. App. 6 (1986).

The defendant stating that "he didn't want to say anything about the gun" at that time was not an invocation of the right to remain silent, but an indication that the defendant did not want to discuss a particular subject. *People v. Hicks*, 158 Mich. App. 544 (1987).

A defendant must "unambiguously" invoke the right to remain silent. While incarcerated in Ohio, the defendant was interrogated by Michigan officers about his role in a shooting. The officers read the defendant his *Miranda* warnings, but he refused to sign the *Miranda* form. The dfendant never said that he wanted to remain silent nor did he indicate he wanted an attorney. The defendant was almost entirely silent during a nearly three hour interrogation. One of the officers then asked, "Do you pray to God to forgive you for shooting that boy down?" The defendant answered, "Yes." The defendant argued that the police should not have questioned him until he had affirmatively waived his rights. The court disagreed. The court ruled that a defendant must unambiguously invoke his right to remain silent before questioning must stop, simply remaining silent is not enough. Further, by answering the question, the defendant waived his right to remain silent. *Berghuis v. Thompkins*, 560 U.S. 370 (2010).

## Ambiguous Request for Counsel

When the suspect was asked if he wanted an attorney, he wrote on the rights form "yesan no." The officer asked him to clarify his answer. The defendant then crossed out the "yesan." The court held that the police may attempt to clarify an ambiguous request for counsel and that the suspect in this case did not invoke his rights. *People v. Giuchici*, 118 Mich. App. 252 (1982).

The defendant properly waived his rights. An hour and a half into the interrogation he stated, "Maybe I should talk to an attorney." The officers clarified whether he wanted an attorney and, after he said no, the questioning continued and he eventually confessed. He argued on appeal that he had requested an attorney by his statement and that the questioning should have stopped. The court held that after a defendant waived his rights, the right to counsel under *Miranda* does not come into play unless the suspect makes a statement that a reasonable interrogator under the circumstances would interpret as a request for counsel. An ambiguous request for counsel does not require the interrogator to either stop the questioning or attempt to clarify whether the suspect desires counsel. The court added that it would be *good police practice to clarify* if the suspect was requesting counsel but did not require it. *Davis v. United States*, 512 U.S. 452 (1994).

The defendant was arrested on a murder charge. During the reading of his rights, the detective stated that if the defendant wanted an attorney and could not afford one, the state will pay for an attorney. The defendant then stated, "Yeah, I'm—I'm ah need that cause I can't afford none." The bottom of the waiver read, "I do not want an attorney at this time." The defendant indicated that he understood the statement and was willing to speak to the police that day about the murder. The court held that this was an ambiguous request for counsel and, under *Davis*, the police do not have to stop questioning. If the defendant had been requesting an attorney, he had only to clarify his words at which time all police questioning would have ceased. *People v. Granderson*, 212 Mich. App. 673 (1995).

A suspect did not clearly invoke his rights to an attorney when, during an interview, he asked when he could talk to an attorney. The officer responded that the interview could stop immediately. The suspect than asked, "Can I talk to him right now?" The detective stated yes, and the suspect then stated that he wanted to think about it for five minutes. *People v. Adams*, 245 Mich. App. 226 (2001).

## Requests to Talk to Non-Attorney

A request by a defendant to talk with his father is not the equivalent of a request for counsel. *People v. White*, 191 Mich. App. 296 (1991).

## Failure to Advise Rights May Require Suppression of a Second Confession

The defendant feared charges of neglect when her son, afflicted with cerebral palsy, died in his sleep. She was present when two of her sons and their friends discussed burning her family's mobile home to conceal the circumstances of her son's death. Donald, an unrelated mentally ill 18-year-old living with the family, was left to die in the fire, in order to avoid the appearance that Seibert's son had been unattended. Five days later, the police arrested the defendant but did not read her rights under *Miranda*. At the police station, an officer questioned her for 30–40 minutes, obtaining a confession that the plan was for Donald to die in the fire. He then gave her a 20-minute break, returned to give her warnings, and obtained a signed waiver. He resumed questioning, confronting her pre-warning statements, and getting her to repeat the information. She moved to suppress both her pre-warning and post-warning statements. The officer testified that he made a conscious decision to withhold warnings, question first, then give the warnings, and then repeat the question until he got the answer previously given. The confession was suppressed. "Warnings given mid-interrogation, after defendant gave unwarned confession, were ineffective, and thus confession repeated after warnings were given was inadmissible at trial." *Missouri v. Seibert*, 542 U.S. 600 (2004).

Two-step interrogations, i.e., interrogating without *Miranda* warnings to gain a confession, then giving the warnings to re-elicit the confession, are unconstitutional. However, an unwarned statement made voluntarily can be cured of the taint of a Fifth Amendment violation by proper administration of the *Miranda* warnings, a knowing and intelligent waiver, and a voluntary repetition of the inculpatory statements by the suspect.

"But the *Miranda* presumption does not require that fruits of otherwise voluntary statements be discarded as inherently tainted. It is an unwarranted extension of *Miranda* to hold that a simple failure to administer the warnings, unaccompanied by any actual coercion or other circumstances calculated to undermine the suspect's ability to exercise his free will, so taints the investigatory process that a subsequent voluntary and informed waiver is ineffective for some indeterminate period. The failure of police to administer *Miranda* warnings does not mean that the statements received have actually been coerced, but only that courts will presume the privilege against compulsory self-incrimination has not been intelligently exercised. Absent deliberate coercion or improper tactics in obtaining an unwarned statement, a careful and thorough administration of *Miranda* warnings cures the condition that rendered the unwarned statement inadmissible." *Oregon v. Elstad*, 470 U.S. 298 (1985).

# WAIVER OF RIGHTS

## What Constitutes a Valid Waiver?

After advising a person of his rights, officers should ask the person if he understands the rights that have just been read and if he is willing to give up those rights at this time.

The defendant may waive his rights, provided the waiver is *voluntarily, knowingly and intelligently made. Miranda v. Arizona*, 384 U.S. 436 (1966).

A suspect's waiver must be the product of a *free and deliberate* choice rather than intimidation, coercion, or deception.

"First, the relinquishment of the right must have been voluntary in the sense that it was the product of a free and deliberate choice rather than intimidation, coercion, or deception. Second, the waiver must have been made with a full awareness of both the nature of the right being abandoned and the consequences of the decision to abandon it. Only if the 'totality of the circumstances surrounding the interrogation' reveal both an uncoerced choice and the requisite level of comprehension may a court properly conclude that the *Miranda* rights have been waived." *Moran v. Burbine*, 475 U.S. 412 (1986).

The waiver of rights must not only be voluntary, there must also be a knowing and intelligent relinquishment or abandonment of a known right or privilege. *People v. Paintman*, 412 Mich. 518 (1982).

## Mental Condition: Whether the Suspect Knowingly Waived His Rights

The defendant had an IQ of 62. He was charged with and convicted of murder based in part on his confession. A psychologist testified that the defendant was not competent to waive his rights. The court held that the test for a valid waiver is the *totality of the circumstances*. The court held that the suspect does not need to understand the consequences of choosing to waive or exercise his rights. It must be shown he understood that he did not have to speak, he had the right to the presence of counsel, and his statements could be used against him. In this case, the officers asked the defendant if he understood his rights. The officer had no problem communicating with the defendant. The defendant could not read so his rights were read to him. A second officer was present to verify this. The defendant provided appropriate answers to the questions asked. Under the totality of the circumstances, the confession was admissible. Low IQ is only one factor of many considered. *People v. Cheatham*, 453 Mich. 1 (1996).

The defendant suffered from a delusion that the police work for God and that if he confessed to killing his mother, he would be set free. The question presented was whether the suspect knowingly waived his rights. The court held that a knowing and intelligent waiver of *Miranda* rights does not equate with a wise or lawyer-inspired decision to waive those rights. "Rather, the only inquiry with regard to a 'knowing and intelligent' waiver of *Miranda* rights is whether the defendant understood 'that he did not have to speak, that he had the right to the presence of counsel, and that the state could use what he said in a later trial against him.'" *People v. Daoud*, 462 Mich. 621 (2000).

## A Waiver Does Not Have to Be in Writing

After advising a person of his rights, officers should ask the person if he understands the rights that have just been read and if he is willing to give up those rights at this time.

The defendant may waive his rights, provided the waiver is *voluntarily, knowingly and intelligently made. Miranda v. Arizona*, 384 U.S. 436 (1966).

The waiver need not be in writing and may be implied from conduct, but not from silence alone. The question is not one of form, but rather, whether the defendant in fact knowingly and voluntarily waived his rights. *North Carolina v. Butler*, 441 U.S. 369 (1979). *See also Berghuis v. Thompkins*, 560 U.S. 370 (2010) (the defendant's conduct implied a waiver where he was generally silent during the interrogation, but did answer some officers' questions).

An oral confession does not have to be suppressed where a suspect agreed to speak, but refused to give a written statement without an attorney. The defendant's specific refusal to give a written confession without counsel present was an invocation only for that purpose. Request for counsel must be honored for all purposes only when the defendant flatly invokes his right to counsel or when the purposes for his invocation are ambiguous. The defendant clearly and unequivocally was willing to speak about the CSC, but was only unwilling to make a written statement. *Connecticut v. Barrett*, 479 U.S. 523 (1987).

Many criminal suspects are under the misconception that a confession or inculpatory statement is attributable to them or binding only when it is reduced to writing. Police are under no duty to correct this misconception as a suspect may have any number of reasons to speak but refuse to make a writing. As long as the statement is not improperly induced by police conduct, it is probably admissible; the court has never embraced the theory that a defendant's ignorance of the full consequences of his decision runs against voluntariness.

## A Suspect Does Not Have to Have Knowledge of All the Subjects of Interrogation

A suspect's advance awareness of all possible subjects of questioning is not relevant to the validity of the waiver. Police may question him about crimes he may not have known he was suspected of committing. *Colorado v. Spring*, 479 U.S. 564 (1987).

## Waiver Is Valid for a Reasonable Time

*Miranda* rights are not a litany that must be read every time a suspect is interrogated. After a break in interrogation, it was sufficient for

purposes of protecting the defendant's Fifth Amendment rights to ask whether he still understood his rights and if so if he would talk. *People v. Godboldo*, 158 Mich. App. 603 (1986).

## Validity of Waiver Where Officers Fail to Tell Defendant His Attorney Is Available

The United States Supreme Court held that the police have no duty to inform a defendant, prior to a valid waiver, of attempts by an attorney to contact the defendant. If a defendant waives his right to an attorney, there is no need to inform him that an attorney is available. Events occurring outside of a suspect's presence and entirely unknown to him can have no bearing on the capacity to comprehend and knowingly relinquish a constitutional right. *Moran v. Burbine*, 475 U.S. 412 (1986).

The defendant was read his *Miranda* rights and invoked his right to counsel, but then reinitiated contact with the police when he indicated that he wanted to "get something off of his chest." He was again afforded his *Miranda* rights, and waived them, choosing not to reassert his right to counsel. The court found that the defendant's lack of awareness of the appointed attorney's presence at the jail did not invalidate his *Miranda* waiver. The court held that "[o]nce it is determined that a suspect's decision not to rely on his rights was uncoerced, that he at all times knew he could stand mute and request a lawyer, and that he was aware of the State's intention to use his statements to secure a conviction, the analysis is complete and the waiver is valid as a matter of law." *People v. Tanner*, ___ Mich. ___ (2014) (Docket #146211)

## Reassertion of Rights

A defendant who has waived his or her rights may reassert them at any time. *Miranda v. Arizona*, 384 U.S. 436 (1966).

# VOLUNTARINESS STANDARD
## Determination of Voluntariness

The privilege against self-incrimination protects compelled statements, not voluntary ones. The court, rather than the jury, will determine if a statement was voluntarily given by looking at the "totality of the circumstances." This is determined in a *Walker* hearing. The standard used is a preponderance of the evidence. The defendant may testify at a *Walker* hearing as to his or her version of the facts surrounding the alleged statements without waiving his or her right to remain silent at trial or any other right.

> If the judge finds on a proper record made the confession to be involuntary, the matter ends there and the jury never considers it. However, if the judge determines it to have been voluntarily made, it is admitted. The issue of voluntariness is not submitted to the jury. Jury consideration is limited to its weight and credibility. *People v. Walker*, 374 Mich. 331 (1965).

## "Totality of the Circumstances"

> In *People v. Cipriano*, 431 Mich. 315 (1988), the Michigan Supreme Court provided guidance to assist in determining if a statement is voluntary. The court held that a trial court should consider the totality of the circumstances, which include the following:
>
> - Age.
> - Education.
> - Intelligence.
> - Criminal experience.
> - Lack of advice of constitutional rights.
> - Unnecessary delay.
> - Injuries.
> - Intoxication/drugs.
> - Ill health.
> - Deprivation of food, sleep, or medical attention.
> - Physical abuse.
> - Threats of abuse.
>
> A statement was voluntarily made where evidence showed that the defendant permitted the police officers to enter her apartment building and further permitted them to enter her apartment. The officers did not display weapons, and an officer indicated that he informed the defendant several times that she was not under arrest. The officer also told the defendant that if she wanted them to leave, they would go. Contrary to the defendant's contention, her subjective belief that she was not free to leave because the officer asked her about the murder is not dispositive because an objective assessment of the totality of the circumstances indicates that she was not in custody or under arrest when she gave her oral statement. The defendant proceeded to give a statement, largely in narrative form, with little police questioning. She fully acknowledged that she was not compelled or coerced to give a statement. *People v. Coomer*, 245 Mich. App. 206 (2001).

## Coercive Police Activity

> While the defendant's mental condition suggesting that the "voice of God" compelled him to confess to a murder may be a significant factor in determining voluntariness, it alone cannot violate the voluntariness standard. For a finding of an involuntary statement, there must be some indicia of governmental coercion. *Colorado v. Connelly*, 479 U.S. 157 (1986).

> Coercive police activity is a necessary predicate to a finding that a confession is not voluntary. Coercive police conduct may be psychological, as well as physical. *People v. DeLisle*, 183 Mich. App. 713 (1990).

## Pre-Arraignment Delay

> Where the purpose in delaying a suspect's arraignment is to obtain a confession, the confession will be suppressed. *People v. Hamilton*, 359 Mich. 410 (1960).

> "A defendant's unlawful detention does not mandate suppression of the defendant's confession unless there exists a causal nexus between the illegal arrest and the confession. Whether the connection between a defendant's detention and confession is sufficiently attenuated to purge the confession of its primary taint is determined by focusing upon (1) the temporal proximity between arrest and confession; (2) the flagrancy of official misconduct; (3) any intervening circumstances occurring after arrest; and (4) any circumstances antecedent to arrest. . . . While an arrestee must be arraigned without unnecessary delay, such delay is but one factor in the determination of voluntariness, and an otherwise competent confession should not be excluded solely because of delayed arraignment. Defendant's delayed arraignment, when viewed in light of

the totality of the circumstances surrounding her confessions, does not lead us to conclude that the confessions were involuntary." People v. Feldmann, 181 Mich. App. 523 (1989) (citations omitted).

When an arrested individual does not receive a probable cause determination within 48 hours, the burden of proof shifts to the government to demonstrate the existence of a bona fide emergency or other extraordinary circumstance justifying the delay. This cannot include intervening weekends or the fact that a particular case may take longer to consolidate pretrial proceedings. *County of Riverside v. McLaughlin*, 500 U.S. 44 (1991).

A confession was still admissible under the totality of the circumstances where an 81-hour delay in arraignment was due to difficulty in getting the paperwork done and a change in the detective assignments due to vacations. Prior to getting the paperwork together, the suspect asked to talk to the officer in charge. The court held "The record indicates that [suspect], who was nineteen years old at the time of her arrest, received *Miranda* warnings prior to giving her inculpatory statement. [She] testified that she both read and understood her rights. She further testified that the police did not deprive her of food, water, or sleep. [The detective] testified that [she] did not appear to be under the influence of any drug or other intoxicant, and that she did not appear to need medical attention. Finally, we note that [the suspect], rather than the police, initiated the discussion that resulted in her giving the inculpatory statement." Neither *Riverside County* nor Michigan case law requires automatic suppression of a statement because of unnecessary delay. However, it is possible that in some situations the length of the delay alone may be a sufficient ground to suppress a defendant's statement, particularly where the delay is so inexplicably long that it raises an inference of police misconduct. *People v. Manning*, 243 Mich. App. 615 (2000).

## Physical Abuse

A confession was inadmissible when it was obtained by the whipping and hanging of a defendant. *Brown v. Mississippi*, 297 U.S. 278 (1936).

The defendant was convicted of two counts of armed robbery. He argued that the police obtained his confession by physical compulsion. The court held that, under the totality of the circumstances, the defendant made a voluntary confession to the police. The court reasoned that, although the police told the defendant that "rapists get kicked around in jail," there was no actual physical abuse by the police, nor was the defendant in fear of physical abuse by the police. *People v. Hardy*, 151 Mich. App. 605 (1986).

## Injury

A detective interrogated the defendant while he was in the intensive care unit of a hospital. The defendant was wounded, had partial paralysis of his right leg, was receiving drugs, and had tubes in his mouth, arms, and bladder. The defendant was unable to talk, but could communicate with paper and pencil. The detective advised the defendant of his rights and continued to question him until midnight, ceasing questioning whenever the defendant would lose consciousness.

"Due process requires that the statements obtained from petitioner in the hospital not be used in any way against him at his trial, where it is apparent from the record that they were not 'the product of his free and rational choice,' but to the contrary that he wanted not to answer his interrogator, and that while he was weakened by pain and shock, isolated from family, friends, and legal counsel, and barely conscious, his will was simply overborne." Because the defendant's statements were involuntary, they may not be used for any purpose at trial. *Mincey v. Arizona*, 437 U.S. 385 (1978).

## Intoxication/Drugs

The defendant and his brother beat the victim to death during a drug deal. The defendant made inculpatory statements after he was taken into custody. He later testified that he drank four to five 40-ounce beers, taken 25 Vicodin pills, and smoked 12 marijuana cigarettes in the 24 hours preceding the interview. The court weighed the defendant's alleged intoxication against several other factors including his age (mid-20's), his education (he possessed a GED), his previous police contacts, the short time between being taken into custody and being interviewed, and the three-hour break between his two interviews. The trial court made findings that cast doubt on the defendant's credibility. Considering the totality of the circumstances, the court ruled that the trial court had not erred in finding that the defendant had made the statements willingly, knowingly, and intelligently. *People v. Gipson*, 287 Mich. App. 261 (2010).

## Threats

Confessions obtained by threats or playing on fears, real or imagined, are inadmissible; i.e., "If you don't talk, we'll see you lose your child." *People v. Richter*, 54 Mich. App. 598 (1974).

A statement obtained from a defendant who was informed that his pregnant wife would be jailed if he did not confess is inadmissible. *People v. Robinson*, 386 Mich. 551 (1972).

The defendant was charged with first-degree murder. At a preliminary hearing, he moved to suppress his oral and written confessions due to threats by police. Specifically, the defendant was told he "needed his ass beat for going around shooting people." The court held that under the totality of the circumstances, the confession the police obtained from the defendant was involuntary and should have been suppressed. *People v. Jordan*, 149 Mich. App. 568 (1986).

## Promises

To warrant suppression of a statement, inducements offered must overcome the defendant's ability to make a voluntary decision to make a statement. *People v. Hardy*, 151 Mich. App. 605 (1986).

Statements are inadmissible if obtained by any direct or implied promises, however slight. *Bram v. United States*, 168 U.S. 532 (1897).

"Confessions are inadmissible when induced by threats, or by a promise of favor, made by persons apparently acting by authority." *People v. Clarke*, 105 Mich. 169 (1895).

An officer's statement that he would do what he could to help and that cooperation was usually taken into account at sentencing did not amount to an improper promise that would render the confession involuntary. *People v. Ewing*, 102 Mich. App. 81 (1980).

A promise to release a third person who is not a relative of the defendant's does not alone constitute coercion which would render a confession inadmissible. A promise to release a relative, though, may result in a finding that the confession was involuntarily made. *People v. Smith*, 124 Mich. App. 723 (1983).

## The Two-Part Test for Promises

- Did the suspect reasonably understand the statements by the police to be promises of leniency?
- Did the defendant rely upon the promise in deciding to make a confession and prompted by the promise to give the statement?

*People v. Conte*, 421 Mich. 704 (1984).

## Plea Bargaining

Statements made by the defendant to a prosecuting attorney during plea negotiations cannot be used if:

- The defendant had an actual subjective expectation to negotiate a plea during the discussion, and
- The expectation was reasonable given the totality of the objective circumstances.

*People v. Dunn*, 446 Mich. 409 (1994); See also MRE 410.

If a plea bargain is the basis of an inculpatory statement but the defendant violates the plea bargain, the statement is still inadmissible as involuntary under MRE 410. Statements made during plea negotiations are of induced by promises of leniency. *People v. Conte*, 421 Mich. 704 (1984).

## Rights Under Plea Negotiations May Be Waived

A defendant may waive the protections under plea bargaining. Under a waiver, an agreement extracted as a condition of plea bargaining may be used for impeachment purposes if the bargain fails, unless the defendant made the waiver without knowledge or under coercion. *United States v. Mezzanatto*, 513 U.S. 196 (1995).

During plea negotiations, Defendant admitted to being involved in a robbery and murder. At each of the interviews, he was given warnings about the use of statements that he might make. A plea arrangement was reached, but when he was in front of the judge, he changed his mind and stated that he no longer wanted to take the plea bargain. The question then arose whether the admissions he made during the plea negotiations could be used against him during the trial since MRE 410 provides that "[a]ny statement made in the course of plea discussions with an attorney for the prosecuting authority which do not result in a plea of guilty or which result in a plea of guilty later withdrawn" is not admissible.  The Michigan Supreme Court held that the statements are not rendered inadmissible by MRE 410, and, if otherwise admissible, can be introduced in the prosecutor's case in chief.  The court retained the protections afforded by MRE 410, but allowed criminal defendants to "waive those protections, as long as they are appropriately advised and as long as the statements admitted into evidence are voluntarily, knowingly, and understandingly made." *People v. Stevens*, 461 Mich. 655 (2000).

## Deception, Trick, or Fraud

Use of deception, trick, or fraud to induce a statement will not alone render that statement inadmissible. *People v. Dunnigan*, 163 Mich. 349 (1910).

KEY: If it tends to induce a *false* statement, that statement will be excluded.

Falsely telling a defendant that his co-conspirator had confessed would not, in itself, make a confession involuntary. *Frasier v. Cupp*, 394 U.S. 731 (1969).

The fact that the police misrepresented to defendant that his fingerprints were discovered on an article retrieved from the crime scene is insufficient, by itself, to render the statement

involuntary. *People v. Hicks*, 185 Mich. App. 107 (1990).

During a custodial interrogation that lasted from midnight to 3:00 am, a detective lied to the suspect, first by telling him that a witness had placed him at the scene of the crime. The officer then showed the suspect phony charts and photographs purporting to indicate a fingerprint expert's determination that the suspect's prints were at the scene. Finally, the officer staged an identification by a female officer posing as the victim. The court held that the confession was admissible as voluntarily given and the trickery did not tend to induce a false statement. An officer must remember, though, that he or she will have to testify in court about the process used to obtain a statement. *Ledbetter v. Edwards*, 35 F.3d 1062 (6th Cir. 1994).

A defendant is entitled to have the jury hear the circumstances of the confession, even if the judge has determined it to be given voluntarily. *Crane v. Kentucky*, 476 U.S. 683 (1986).

## Corpus Delecti

*Corpus delecti* applies to every crime. The prosecutor must present prima facie evidence (i.e., sufficient to establish a fact or raise a presumption, if uncontested) that a crime has been committed before the prosecution can introduce the defendant's confession.

A confession by itself cannot establish *corpus delecti*. A voluntary confession, made extra-judicially, is only received as evidence of guilt and by itself cannot establish guilt. The purpose of this rule is to prevent a person's confession from convicting him of a crime he did not commit. *People v. Ish*, 252 Mich. App. 115 (2002).

A woman disappeared without a trace in 1985. In 1990, police were investigating the defendant when he confessed to killing her. He stated that he had cut the body up and had thrown it into a dumpster. Aside from the confession, there was no other evidence. The court reversed the defendant's second-degree murder conviction and held that there must be evidence independent of the confession to uphold the murder conviction. *People v. McMahan*, 451 Mich. 543 (1996).

# JUVENILES—MCL 712A.14

A juvenile under the age of 17 must, on being arrested, be immediately taken before the family division of the circuit court or released to a parent.

The court should look at the following when determining the *totality of the circumstances* as it relates to juvenile confessions:

- Whether the juvenile was advised of his or her rights and clearly understood those rights.
- The degree of police compliance with applicable statutes and juvenile rules (i.e., MCL 764.27).
- The presence of an adult, parent, custodian, or guardian.
- The juvenile background.
- The juvenile's age, education, and intelligence level and extent of defendant's prior experience with police.
- The length of detention before statement is made.
- The repeated and prolonged nature of the questioning.
- Whether the juvenile was injured, intoxicated, in ill health, physically abused or threatened with abuse, or deprived of food, sleep, or medical attention.

*People v. Good*, 186 Mich. App. 180 (1990); *People v. Hana*, 443 Mich. 202 (1993).

Police received a tip that the defendant was involved in an armed robbery. They interviewed him in a detention center where he was being held. Since he was 16 years old, the officers contacted his mother. She had no objections to the interview. The officers ascertained that the defendant could read and write and was not taking medication. He was then advised of his rights and signed a waiver that he would talk without an attorney. Initially, he denied involvement, but then asked if he could make a deal with the prosecutor. The officers said that his cooperation would be noted in their reports to the prosecutor. During the interview, the officers asked if there was any way that the defendant's fingerprints could have been left

on the cash register. In fact, no prints had been obtained. The defendant stated that this could have happened as he was reaching for one of the clerks that had been shot. He eventually confessed to the crime. The court upheld the confession under the "totality of the circumstances." His mother had given her permission to interview him. There was a determination that he could read and write and was not under the influence of any substance. Also, there was no promise of leniency made. "We do not believe that the mere pledge to note defendant's cooperation in a police report, without more, could reasonably be considered a promise of leniency." Also, the statement about the fingerprints did not make the defendant's statement involuntary. It may have been a misrepresentation, but it did not, under the totality of the circumstances, make the confession involuntary. *People v. Givans*, 227 Mich. App. 113 (1997).

The defendant, an 11-year-old, was charged with first-degree murder. During a police interrogation where his mother was present, the defendant confessed to the shooting. The trial court suppressed the confession claiming that, due to his age, the defendant could not intelligently waive his rights. The court looked at the facts and disagreed. The court held that the officers asked the defendant to explain the rights they had read to him. In reference to his right to an attorney, he stated, "That—that when the police talk to me that I can talk with my lawyer with the police." Also, "If we don't got no money, the Court give me one." Finally, as to the fact that his statements may be used against him, he replied "If you say something you go to Court for it." In ruling the confession was admissible, the court also found as a matter of "great significance that defendant's mother was present for, and participated in, the entire *Miranda*-waiver process." *People v. Abraham*, 234 Mich. App. 640 (1999).

A 13-year-old boy was accused of sexually touching two girls, ages four and seven. The officer asked the 13-year-old and his mother to come to the station. The officer first talked to the mother and advised her of the charges and asked to talk to the 13-year-old alone. The mother agreed. The officer also advised her that she could contact an attorney for her son if she wanted to but she declined. Without advising the 13-year-old of his rights, the officer interviewed him for 30–40 minutes during which time the juvenile confessed to the charges. The trial court suppressed the statements but the Court of Appeals reversed. "A juvenile's confession is admissible if, given the totality of the circumstances, the statement was voluntarily made." Under these circumstances, *Miranda* warnings were not required and failure to give them did not result in an involuntary statement. The court further noted that there was no claim made that either the statute or court rules pertaining to juveniles were violated. "In addition, we find that the separation of [the defendant] from his mother, although potentially troublesome in an analysis of the voluntariness of a statement, under the totality of the circumstances here, does not merit a finding that [defendant's] statement was involuntary. [The defendant] knew his mother had consented to his talking alone with the officer and that she was readily available to him. No manipulation of [defendant] or his mother by the police is established by the circumstances. To the contrary, everything was done openly and with the knowledge and consent of [defendant] and his mother." *In re SLL*, 246 Mich. App. 204 (2001).

A statement obtained in violation of MCL 764.27 and MCR 5.934 is not subject to automatic suppression because of the violation. Rather, the violation is considered as part of the totality of the circumstances to determine whether the statement was voluntary. *People v. Hall*, 249 Mich. App. 262 (2002).

J.D.B. was a 13-year-old, seventh-grade student suspected of breaking and entering and larceny. J.D.B. was removed from class and interviewed at his school in a closed-door conference room by two police officers and two school administrators. Before beginning the interview, the officers did not give him *Miranda* warnings, the opportunity to call his legal guardian, or tell him he was free to leave the room. J.D.B. was interrogated about the crimes, and he confessed his involvement. The U. S. Supreme Court reviewed the test for custody: whether a reasonable person in the suspect's position would believe he or she was free to leave. The court noted, in some circumstances, a reasonable child subjected to police questioning will feel pressured to answer questions even though a reasonable adult would feel free to go. The court held that so long as a child's age was known to the officer at the time of questioning or would have been objectively apparent to a reasonable officer, the child's age must be included as part of the custody analysis. In addition, the court noted that this does not mean the child's age will be a significant factor in every case, but it must be included in the analysis. Officers are required to consider a juvenile suspect's age in determining whether *Miranda* warnings must be given to a juvenile during an interrogation. Additionally, officers are reminded to properly advise all in-custody suspects of their *Miranda* warnings before questioning. *J.D.B. v. North Carolina*, 131 S.Ct. 2394 (2011).

# QUESTIONING BY PERSONS OTHER THAN LAW ENFORCEMENT

Generally, questioning by persons other than law enforcement will not require *Miranda*, unless the individual is working with the police.

## Security Guards

Private investigators are not officers of the law and therefore are not required to comply with *Miranda*. *People v. Omell*, 15 Mich. App. 154 (1968).

Incriminating statements made by a defendant to private retail security personnel may be admitted at trial as long as the security officer did not act at the instigation of the police nor function with their assistance or cooperation. *Grand Rapids v. Impens*, 414 Mich. 667 (1982).

However, the court ruled that private security police officers licensed by the state under MCL 388.1079 and performing duties under MCL 388.1080 are State actors as a matter of law. Though this was a § 1983 case and the court did not explicitly say so, it suggests that security guards licensed and acting under these statutes must comply with *Miranda*. *Romanski v. Detroit Entm't, L.L.C.*, 428 F.3d 629 (6th Cir. 2005).

## Corrections Officers

The defendant was held in a juvenile facility in South Carolina. He was being held on a homicide that had occurred in Michigan. During his stay, he made a statement to a correction supervisor. The court held that clearly, the defendant was in custody, but the supervisor had no arrest or detention authority and was not shown to be acting at the behest of the police. *Miranda* warnings were not required. *People v. Anderson*, 209 Mich. App. 527 (1995).

The defendant was an MDOC inmate and during a search of his cell, officers discovered two weapons. Pursuant to MDOC policy, the defendant transferred to a segregation unit until his misconduct report was heard. Approximately an hour later, the shift lieutenant requested to interview the defendant in the control room. Without *Mirandizing* the defendant, the lieutenant told the defendant that the evidence against him was "pretty damaging," that the defendant should disclose what he knew about the recent violence in the prison, and that the defendant should explain why he was in possession of the shanks. The defendant began to talk and the lieutenant openly brought out a tape recorder and began recording the interview. The defendant continued to discuss the matter. Here, the court found no coercive circumstances that required *Miranda* warnings. The defendant was interviewed following a procedural search and removal to segregation. These restraints would have been imposed on the defendant regardless of the interview because of MDOC policy. Additionally, the defendant spoke freely during the interview, even after he knew the interview was being recorded. There was no evidence that the defendant was threatened in any way; his sleep schedule was not interrupted nor was he made uncomfortable in any way. Additionally, the court found that the fact that the defendant was isolated from the general population for the purposes of the interview may have been comforting rather than coercive because inmates are reluctant to speak openly in front of others. *People v. Cortez*, 299 Mich. App. 679 (2013).

## Parole Officer

The defendant was taken into custody by police pursuant to a warrant for failing to report, and the next day, his parole officer served the defendant with a notice of parole violation pertaining to that failure. On the same day, after advising defendant of his *Miranda* rights, detectives questioned the defendant concerning a robbery that

had occurred the previous day at a gas station. After voluntarily answering several questions, the defendant requested an attorney. The police then discontinued the interrogation. Four days later, while the defendant was still incarcerated, a parole officer went to the jail to serve defendant with an amended notice of parole violation that identified three additional parole violations. During this meeting, the parole officer questioned the defendant about his involvement with the robbery and he confessed. These statements were used to convict him of armed robbery.

The court held that when a parolee is incarcerated for an alleged parole violation, 'custodial' means more than just the normal restrictions that exist as a result of the incarceration; incarceration alone is not enough to create a custodial situation for *Miranda* purposes. In this case, the meeting took place in the jail library, it lasted only 15 to 25 minutes, the defendant was not physically restrained, and a reasonable person in the defendant's position, a parolee, would be aware that a parole officer acts independently of the police who placed him or her in custody and that the parole officer has no control over the jail, its staff, or the individuals incarcerated there. On balance, these facts were consistent with an environment in which a reasonable person would have felt free to terminate the interview and leave. Thus, the defendant's freedom of movement was not curtailed. Because the defendant was not subjected to custodial interrogation by the parole officer, even if she was a law enforcement officer, neither the defendant's right to be given a series of warnings before custodial interrogation nor his right to have counsel present during custodial interrogation was violated. Accordingly, the trial court did not err by admitting the defendant's confession." *People v. Elliott*, 494 Mich.

## Inmates

A jailed suspect is not entitled to *Miranda* warnings when he makes a voluntary statement to an undercover agent he believes to be another inmate. A police-dominated atmosphere and compulsion are not present. *Illinois v. Perkins*, 496 U.S. 292 (1990).

KEY: Undercover agent cannot ask questions about crime that a defendant was charged, arraigned, and requested an attorney on. Mere listening is okay. *Kuhlmann v. Wilson*, 477 U.S. 436 (1986).

## Protective Service Workers

Statements made by a defendant to a protective service worker are admissible where the worker was not charged with enforcing any criminal laws nor acting at the behest of the police. *People v. Porterfield*, 166 Mich. App. 562 (1988).

# REMEDIES FOR VIOLATION OF RIGHTS
## Exclusionary Rule

A confession illegally obtained will be excluded. Also, any evidence obtained through that confession will also be excluded under the Fruit of the Poisonous Tree Doctrine. For example, in the Christian Burial case, the defendant was arrested in connection with the disappearance of a 10-year-old girl. He invoked his rights. As he rode in the police car, the detective began to converse with him. The detective knew that the defendant was deeply religious and so presented what is now called the "Christian Burial" speech in an attempt to recover the little girl's body. The defendant confessed and led the officer to the body. Because of the due process violations, not only was the confession suppressed, but the body and all the evidence that was located through the unlawful confession were suppressed as well. *Brewer v. Williams*, 430 U.S. 387 (1977).

"A seizure of the person within the meaning of the Fourth and Fourteenth Amendments occurs when, 'taking into account all of the circumstances surrounding the encounter, the police conduct would "have communicated to a reasonable person that he was not at liberty to ignore the police presence and go about his business."'" In this case, "[a] 17-year-old boy was awakened in his bedroom at three in the morning by at least three police officers, one of whom stated 'we need to go and talk.' He was taken out in handcuffs, without shoes, dressed only in his underwear in January, placed in a patrol car, driven to the scene of a crime and then to the sheriff's offices, where he was taken into an interrogation room and questioned. This evidence points to an arrest." Since he was arrested before he was questioned, and because the state does not even claim that the sheriff's department had probable cause to detain him at that point, well-established precedent requires suppression of the confession unless

that confession was an act of free will sufficient to purge the primary taint of the unlawful invasion. *Miranda* warnings, alone and per se, cannot always break, for Fourth Amendment purposes, the causal connection between illegality of arrest and confession. *Kaupp v. Texas*, 538 U.S. 626 (2003).

## Exceptions
### Inevitable Discovery

Evidence obtained through an illegal confession may still be admissible if:

- Police were actively pursuing the evidence, and
- The evidence would have been found as a result of an ongoing investigation, tainted confession notwithstanding. *People v. Kroll*, 179 Mich. App. 423 (1989); *Nix v. Williams*, 467 U.S. 431 (1984).

Generally, the inevitable discovery rule will not apply to confessions taken after an unlawful arrest. *People v. Thomas*, 191 Mich. App. 576 (1991).

## Public Safety

Officers were dispatched to a rape that had just occurred where the suspect had used a gun. As the officers were interviewing the victim, she saw the suspect enter a grocery store. The officers entered the store and attempted to arrest him. The suspect ran and officers lost sight of him for a few minutes before catching him and placing him under arrest. As they searched him, they found an empty holster. They immediately asked him where the gun was. He admitted to having a gun and told the officers where he threw it in the store. The court held that where spontaneous questioning of a suspect results in the gaining of evidence against the defendant, the evidence will be admissible if the unwarned interrogation was done to protect the public from imminent harm. *New York v. Quarles*, 467 U.S. 649 (1984).

Officers obtained an arrest warrant for the defendant after he assaulted his wife with a pistol. They had also received information that he was suicidal and homicidal. He was arrested at his house as he was in the shower. While he was getting dressed, the officers asked him if there were any weapons in the house and he responded, "Not at this time." The officers then asked him where the weapon was that was used in the assault, and he indicated that it was at his brother's house. At no time prior to this conversation were *Miranda* rights advised. The Supreme Court was then asked if the public safety exception to *Miranda* warnings applied to this case. The court held the "defendant easily could have hidden the weapon in one of the dresser drawers to which he had immediate access. . . . [T]he officers' initial attempts to ascertain the location of the gun were directly related to an objectively reasonable need to secure protection from the possibility of immediate danger associated with the gun. Moreover, the pre-*Miranda* questioning in the present case related solely to neutralizing this danger. The officers only asked about the whereabouts of the gun and not other broader questions relating to investigation of the crime. . . . Here,

once the officers were satisfied that defendant posed no immediate threat of danger to them, they informed defendant of the *Miranda* rights and began their general investigation. For all of these reasons, the pre-*Miranda* questioning at issue in this case falls squarely within the public safety exception to *Miranda*." *People v. Attebury*, 463 Mich. 662 (2001).

## Harmless Error

The admission of an involuntary confession at trial is subject to the harmless error analysis. This means that if the confession is admitted, but the defendant can still be convicted on the other evidence presented, the error was harmless and the conviction will be upheld. *Arizona v. Fulminante*, 499 U.S. 279 (1991).

© 2014, Shutterstock, Inc.

# LAWS ON SUSPECT IDENTIFICATION

## THREE IDENTIFICATION METHODS

The courts generally recognize three types of pretrial identification methods whereby witnesses identify suspects. The courts closely guard the identification process because of concerns over possible misidentification. Identification procedures are considered a critical stage since misidentification prior to trial will generally cast the die and crystallize the witnesses' opinion that the person identified was the culprit. The following methods are used:

- Corporeal lineups.
- Photo displays.
- Show-ups.

### Values Protected Through These Methods

#### Right to a Fair Trial

"[I]t is a matter of common experience that, once a witness has selected an accused out of a line-up, he is not likely to go back on his word later on. . . ." *United States v. Wade*, 388 U.S. 218 (1967).

Based on the totality of the circumstances, identification procedures that are unnecessarily suggestive and conducive to irreparable mistaken identification are a denial of due process of law to the defendant. *Stovall v. Denno*, 388 U.S. 293 (1967).

A happenstance or inadvertent encounter between a witness and the accused in the absence of counsel does not violate due process. *People v. Hampton*, 52 Mich. App. 71 (1974).

To protect a person's right to a fair trial, a person who has been indicted generally has a right to counsel at any critical pretrial confrontation with an eyewitness; this includes a post-indictment pretrial lineup. *Gilbert v. California*, 388 U.S. 263 (1967)

The in-court identification at a preliminary hearing was improper because the defendant was not represented by an attorney. *Moore v Illinois*, 434 U.S. 220 (1977).

### Right to Counsel

The Michigan Supreme Court held that the right to counsel attaches only to corporeal identifications conducted at or after the initiation of adversarial judicial proceedings. The court stated that the on-the-scene identification in this case was made before the initiation of any adversarial judicial criminal proceeding; thus, counsel was not required. *People v. Hickman*, 470 Mich. 602 (2004).

In Michigan, the accused has a right to counsel at photo lineups conducted while the accused is in custody. *People v. Anderson*, 389 Mich. 155 (1973).

# CORPOREAL LINEUPS

A corporeal lineup is a police identification procedure by which the suspect in a crime is exhibited in person before the victim or witness to determine if he or she committed the offense.

It is generally recognized that a corporeal identification is more reliable than a photographic identification. *Simmons v. United States*, 390 U.S. 377 (1968).

The defendant was arrested for armed robbery. An attorney was appointed at his arraignment. Fifteen days later, he was placed in a lineup without his counsel being notified. The Supreme Court suppressed the identification because the attorney was not present. Since the suspect was in custody, he had the right to an attorney at the lineup. "Since it appears that there is grave potential for prejudice, intentional or not, in the pretrial lineup, which may not be capable of reconstruction at trial, and since presence of counsel itself can often avert prejudice and assure a meaningful confrontation at trial, there can be little doubt that for Wade the post indictment lineup was a critical stage of the prosecution at which he was 'as much entitled to such aid (of counsel) as at the trial itself.'" *U.S. v. Wade*, 388 U.S. 218 (1967).

Exceptions to the right to counsel include:

- Intelligent waiver of counsel by the accused. *People v. Shipp*, 21 Mich. App. 415 (1970).
- Emergency situations requiring immediate identification. *People v. Adams*, 19 Mich. App. 131 (1969).
- Prompt on-the-scene corporeal identifications within minutes of the crime. Caution: See show-ups for the limits of this exception. *Russell v. United States*, 408 F.2d 1280 (D.C. Cir. 1969).

*People v. Anderson*, 389 Mich. 155 (1973)

A suspect should be advised of his or her right to have counsel at the lineup and should be encouraged to have counsel present or to have counsel appointed.

## Burdens With and Without Counsel Present

If counsel is present, then the defendant has the burden at trial of supporting any claim that the lineup was unfair or improper. If counsel is not present, the burden falls on the officer.

"[W]here a criminal defendant is represented by counsel at a lineup, the burden rests upon the defendant to factually support his claim that the lineup was impermissibly suggestive." *People v. Haisha*, 111 Mich. App. 165 (1981).

"[F]or identifications made at a confrontation out of the presence of defendant's attorney, the burden is on the prosecution to show fairness." *People v. Young*, 21 Mich. App. 684 (1970).

## Counsel's Role at the Lineup

The role of counsel at the lineup is merely that of an observer. The attorney cannot dictate how the lineup should be conducted.

## The Right Against Self-Incrimination Does Not Apply to Lineups

"It has long been held that the compelled display of identifiable physical characteristics infringes no interest protected by the privilege against compulsory self-incrimination. . . . '(B)oth federal and state courts have usually held that (the privilege) it offers no protection against compulsion to submit to fingerprinting, photographing, or measurements, to write or speak for identification, to appear in court, to stand, to assume a stance, to walk, or to make a particular gesture. The distinction which has emerged, often expressed in different ways, is that the privilege is a bar against compelling 'communications' or 'testimony' but that compulsion which makes a suspect or accused the source of 'real or physical evidence' does not violate it." *United States v. Dionisio*, 410 U.S. 1 (1973).

An in-custody suspect does not have a Fifth Amendment right against self-incrimination to allow him to refuse to stand in a lineup. If an in-custody suspect refuses to cooperate with a lineup, this can be used at trial to show knowledge of guilt. *U.S. v. Wade*, 388 U.S. 218 (1967).

A suspect can be compelled to repeat words spoken by the culprit at the crime scene, as well as to make gestures or wear certain clothing. *People v. Hall*, 396 Mich. 650 (1976).

NOTE: All subjects in the lineup must be asked to perform the same actions. For example in *Wade*, each person in the lineup had to put tape on his or her face and state, "Put the money in the bag."

Taking examples of the defendant's handwriting did not violate the Fifth Amendment. Handwriting samples identify a physical characteristic that is not constitutionally protected. In this case, a bank robber wrote a note to the clerk. *Gilbert v. California*, 388 U.S. 263 (1967).

## Fairness and Suggestibility of a Lineup Are to be Determined From the Totality of the Circumstances

Officers should use good judgment in selecting participants as to height, weight, complexion, hair, unique physical features, age, etc. A photo lineup may be necessary if the suspect is so unique that a fair physical lineup is not possible.

Defendant's identification in a photo lineup was held to be admissible even though he was the only person pictured wearing a "trucker's wallet," his image was larger than the other images in the lineup, his image's background was of a different color. The court held that a suggestive lineup is not necessarily constitutionally defective. It is improper where, under the "totality of circumstances," there is a substantial likelihood of misidentification. *People v. Kurylczyk*, 443 Mich. 289 (1993).

The victim identified the defendant in a lineup. The defendant argued that he appeared in the lineup in the same clothing that he wore on the night of the incident. The court held that this did not automatically render the lineup impermissibly suggestive. *People v. Johnson*, 202 Mich. App. 281 (1993).

The victim identified the suspect in the lineup. The suspect asserted that the lineup was suggestive because his skin tone was darker than other participants in the lineup. The court found that there was no indication from the victim's testimony that the tone of the defendant's skin was a factor in the identification. Nothing in the record showed that the defendant's skin tone was substantially distinguished from others in the lineup. *People v. Vaughn*, 200 Mich. App. 611 (1993).

During a lineup that included three people, the suspect was considerably taller than the other two and the only one wearing a leather coat similar to the one the victim stated the suspect had been wearing. The victim could not identify the suspect, so the police allowed the victim to confront the suspect "one-on-one." The victim was still not certain. Finally, the police conducted a third lineup where the suspect was the only person who was also part of the first lineup. The victim finally stated, "Yep, that is him." The court suppressed the identification as overly suggestive. *Foster v. California*, 394 U.S. 440 (1969).

Identification procedure was overly suggestive where officers played an audiotape involving an interview of the primary suspect by two officers. The officers did not tell the witness which voice was the defendant, but the witness admitted that she knew which voices were the officers. *People v. Williams*, 244 Mich. App. 533 (2001).

Physical differences among lineup participants do not necessarily render the procedure defective. Such differences are significant only to the extent that they are apparent to the witness and substantially distinguish the defendant from the other participants. *People v. Hornsby*, 251 Mich. App. 462 (2002).

## Right to a Lineup

Prior to a trial for assault, defendant's attorney requested a lineup. The trial court denied the request, and the Court of Appeals agreed.

"A right to a lineup arises when eyewitness identification has been shown to be a material issue and when there is a reasonable likelihood of mistaken identification that a lineup would tend to resolve. In the present case, eyewitness identification was a material issue; however, a lineup would not have resolved any 'mistaken identification.'" *People v. McAllister*, 241 Mich. App. 466 (2000).

# PHOTOGRAPHIC LINEUPS/PHOTO DISPLAY

## Suspect Is in Custody

In-custody suspects have the same right to counsel at a photo lineup as they would at a physical lineup. Photographic lineups should not be used for suspects who are in custody, since photo lineups are inferior to physical line-ups and are more likely to cause misidentification. *People v. Anderson*, 389 Mich. 155 (1973).

*Exceptions to the rule.* A photo lineup may be used for in-custody suspects, if:

- *It is not possible to arrange a proper lineup.* For example, there are an insufficient number of persons with defendant's physical characteristics. The defendant was a 50-year-old, 6-foot-tall black male, and there were not enough persons available to make a fair lineup. *People v. Hider*, 135 Mich. App. 147 (1984).
- *Nature of the case requires immediate identification*, such as a medical emergency where victim may die during surgery. *People v. Adams*, 19 Mich. App. 131 (1969).
- *Witnesses are very distant* from the in-custody accused. One possible example of this involved a defendant in a Michigan case who was lodged in Tennessee. *People v. Thornton*, 62 Mich. App. 763 (1975).
- *Subject refuses to participate* or acts to destroy the value of the identification procedure. *People v. Anderson*, 389 Mich. 155 (1973).
- *Protecting a child of tender years.* For example, a photo display was proper for identification by a 5-year-old rape victim. *People v. Currelley*, 99 Mich. App. 561 (1980).

*People v. Davis*, 146 Mich. App. 537 (1985).

A victim was robbed and brutally beaten. A suspect was arrested and a photo lineup was done in the hospital room before the victim went in for surgery. She was able to identify the suspect. The next day, another photo display was done after the victim's status had stabilized. Another identification was done three days before the preliminary examination. All of these were done without an attorney. The court upheld the first identification because of exigency (it was unknown whether the victim would survive) but dismissed the other two. *People v. Anderson*, 389 Mich. 155 (1973).

## Suspect Is *Not* in Custody

Corporeal lineups should be used instead of photographic displays when the suspect is not in custody but is readily available. A suspect is *readily available* when he or she could be legally compelled to appear, such as when the police have a warrant or probable cause to obtain a warrant.

Non-custodial, photographic identification procedure was used in a rape case. Police caught the suspect shortly after the crime in the victim's car as he was searching through the victim's purse. The court held that the photo display was improper since strong probable cause existed to arrest the defendant prior to the photo display and the purpose was to "build a case against the defendant by eliciting identification evidence, not to extinguish a case against innocent bystanders." *People v. Eaton*, 114 Mich. App. 330 (1982) (citing *People v. Kachar*, 400 Mich. 78 (1977)).

Some cases have held that the defendant is not readily available unless he is in custody.

"'Readily available' has been construed in narrow terms. In the case at bar, while defendant was apparently cooperative and had talked with the police, we do not find he was available under the applicable case law. 'Readily available' has been strictly construed to mean subject to legal compulsion to appear at a line-up." *People v. Harrison*, 138 Mich. App. 74 (1984).

The suspect has no right to counsel at photo lineup during the pre-custody, pre-questioning, mere suspicion phase. If counsel were required, every person in a mug book would need an attorney since they are all possible suspects. "In the case of photographic identifications, the right of counsel attaches with custody." *People v. Kurylczyk*, 443 Mich. 289 (1993).

NOTE: Defense counsel can always attack the fairness of the lineup on due process grounds, and it is the prosecution's duty to preserve the photographs. Therefore, the officer should preserve and record the lineup procedure. *People v. Wilson*, 96 Mich. App. 792 (1980).

An armed robbery suspect was arrested after a witness picked his photograph from an eight-photo display. Investigating officers viewed the defendant as a possible suspect based on the similarity of his clothing to that worn by the robber. The defendant had not yet been approached or questioned by the police and was not in custody; thus, he had no right to counsel at this stage of the investigation. *People v. Lee*, 391 Mich. 618 (1974).

The defendant was a suspect in a bank robbery. His picture was included with that of five others in a photo lineup. The defendant's picture was identified, and he was arrested and placed in a corporeal lineup. The defendant argued that he should have had counsel present at the photo lineup. A defendant is not entitled to counsel at a photo lineup merely because the investigation was focused on him. Once he was in custody, generally, a corporeal lineup is required. Where a corporeal lineup is not possible for an in-custody defendant, counsel is required for photographic lineup. The Sixth Amendment right to counsel is not required at a photographic lineup unless the accused is in custody; only under unusual circumstances may a suspect who is not in custody have a right to counsel during a pretrial photographic lineup. *People v. Kurylczyk*, 443 Mich. 289 (1993).

The defendant is not entitled to counsel at a pre-custodial investigatory photographic lineup unless the circumstances underlying the investigation are unusual. *People v. McKenzie*, 205 Mich. App. 466 (1994).

Examples of "unusual circumstances":

- The defendant was contacted or questioned and had been taken into custody and released before the lineup was conducted without counsel.
- Where the witness has previously made a positive identification and the clear intent of the lineup is to build a case against the defendant.

The photo should be as similar as possible, but the fact that five of the six pictures were horizontal shots and the suspect's was vertical did not make the display unduly suggestive. *People v. Dean*, 103 Mich. App. 1 (1981).

# SHOW-UPS

Show-ups are one-on-one confrontations done either physically or by photograph.

Show-ups are considered highly suggestive and are likely to cause misidentification. They should not be used except in emergency situations (e.g., victim may die or public safety requires immediate identification) or subject to the on-the-scene exception listed below.

### On-the-Scene Exception

Justifications for the exception:

- Permits police to decide whom to arrest.
- Prompt identification may exculpate an innocent person.

A police officer may conduct an on-the-scene identification without counsel promptly after the crime.

The victim was shot in a parking lot by three men. He managed to escape and collapsed in the doorway of a nearby Subway. He was able to provide a description of the assailants to police while he was waiting for an ambulance. The assailants were arrested and taken to the Subway. The victim confirmed their identities as the men who assaulted him. The court held that the show-up identification was proper. "It is proper and does not offend the *Anderson* requirements for the police to promptly conduct an on-the-scene identification. Such on-the-scene confrontations are reasonable, indeed indispensable, police practices because they permit the police to immediately decide whether there is a reasonable likelihood that the suspect is connected with the crime and subject to arrest, or merely an unfortunate victim of circumstance." *People v. Winters*, 225 Mich. App. 718 (1997).

The victim was robbed at gunpoint by two black males in their twenties. One was wearing a tan cap and the other was wearing a black hood. After the robbery, the victim called 911 to make a report. That report was then broadcast out to surrounding agencies. Within minutes of the robbery, officers observed two subjects that met the description. They stopped the vehicle and brought the two back to the victim where an identification was made. The court held that it may have been suggestive to bring the suspects to the victim. Further, the court found that the fact that suspects were handcuffed during the show up also may have been suggestive. However, the court held that this procedure to be reasonable given the circumstances and upheld the at-scene identification. *People v. Purofoy*, 116 Mich. App. 471 (1982).

The victim in this case was carjacked by two black males. The police were able to locate the car approximately one hour and twenty minutes later and a vehicle pursuit ensued. There were four occupants when the vehicle finally stopped, and two of them fled on foot. The two that fled were located by a canine unit approximately twenty minutes later. The victim was then brought to the scene where he identified the defendants. The on-scene identification occurred approximately two hours after the carjacking.

The defendants argued that too much time had elapsed between the crime and the identification. The court disagreed. "One of the main benefits of prompt on-the-scene identifications is to obtain reliability in the apprehension of suspects, which insures both that the police have the actual perpetrator and that any improvidently detained individual can be immediately released. Here, because [the victim] stated that only two males had been involved in the crime, police were confronted with the possibility that two of the four individuals apprehended from the car were not involved in the carjacking. Moreover, because [the victim] had earlier seen the perpetrators who had committed the crime upon him just two hours earlier, their appearance was still fresh in his mind. Hence, bringing [him] to the two locations where the individuals were being detained accomplished the dual purposes behind holding a prompt on-the-scene identification. The passage of almost two hours is simply not an unreasonable amount of time between the crime and the identification . . . under the facts presented in this case." *People v. Libbett*, 251 Mich. App. 353 (2002).

# REMEDY FOR IMPROPER IDENTIFICATION PROCEDURES

Evidence of identification cannot be used at trial when obtained in violation of suspect's right to counsel or due process. If the witness identifies the suspect at trial after an improper identification, the prosecution must prove that the in-court identification is not tainted by the improper pretrial identification and has an independent basis.

## Independent Basis Test

Whether the in-court identification is due to the perceptions of the witness at the time of the offense or due to the improper suggestiveness of the lineup or show-up?

Factors for the court to consider:

- Prior relationship or knowledge of the defendant.
- Opportunity to observe the offense.
- Length of time between offense and the identification procedure.
- Accuracy of pre-lineup descriptions.
- Any previous proper or improper identifications.
- Any previous identification of another person as the suspect by the witness.
- Nature of the offense and psychological state of the witness.
- Idiosyncratic or special features of the defendant.

A witness was asked to make photo identification several months after the crime. The photos were labeled with suspect's name and the witness was aware of the suspect's name prior to the photo lineup. This was clearly a violation of due process and, thus, an in-court identification could not be used unless it had an independent basis. *People v. Kachar*, 400 Mich. 78 (1977).

The court held that the identification of the defendant was overly suggestive when the victim failed to positively identify the defendant at a lineup, but later identified him when shown only his picture. However, the court examined the independent basis factors and held that there was an independent basis for an in-court identification. The court paid particular attention to the victim's opportunity to observe the defendant and her previous identification of the defendant, although noncommittal, at a corporeal lineup and the length of time that she observed the crime. *People v. Gray*, 457 Mich. 107 (1998).

# INANIMATE OBJECTS

Lineup procedures applicable to people are not applicable to the identification of objects. *People v. Miller*, 211 Mich. App. 30 (1995).

© 2014, Shutterstock, Inc.

# SEARCH AND SEIZURE

## THE FOURTH AMENDMENT, U.S. CONSTITUTION

*The right of the people to be secure in their persons, houses, papers, and effects, against unreasonable searches and seizures, shall not be violated, and no Warrants shall issue, but upon probable cause, supported by Oath or affirmation and particularly describing the place to be searched, and the persons or things to be seized.*

## THE SEARCH WARRANT RULE

A search warrant is required to conduct a search unless the search falls under one of the specifically stated exceptions. *Katz v. United States,* 389 U.S. 347 (1967).

The general rule is that police officers must have a warrant to conduct a search. There are exceptions to the general rule, which are discussed in Chapter 23.

There are two policy reasons for the United States Supreme Court's interpretations requiring a search warrant. The first is to protect citizen's rights from overzealous police officers who are personally involved in the investigations. The second is to ensure that a neutral and detached magistrate makes the determination of probable cause. *Coolidge v. New Hampshire,* 403 U.S. 443 (1971).

## THE EXCLUSIONARY RULE

When evidence has been obtained in violation of the accused's constitutional rights, the evidence will be excluded (also called suppressed) from court proceedings. *Mapp v. Ohio,* 367 U.S. 643 (1961).

When officers violate a defendant's constitutional rights in seizing evidence, it cannot be used against the defendant. Chapter 23 will discuss the exclusionary rule more fully. The purpose of this rule is to deter illegal police conduct. The rule has caused problems where the police officer was acting in good faith, but violated a technical rule resulting in the evidence being suppressed.

## The Good Faith Exception

In the cases of *United States v. Leon,* 468 U.S. 897 (1984) and *Massachusetts v. Sheppard,* 468 U.S. 981 (1984), the United States Supreme Court recognized the good faith exception to the exclusionary rule. The Court held that the purpose of the exclusionary rule was to deter illegal police conduct. As long as the police acted in good faith and did not do anything illegal, the evidence should be admissible.

The Michigan Supreme Court has also adopted the good faith exception to the exclusionary rule in search warrant cases. The court held that the purpose of the rule, i.e., deterring police misconduct, would not be served by applying the exclusionary rule in a case where the police officers' good faith reliance on the search warrant is objectively reasonable, even if the warrant itself was later held to be invalid. *People v. Goldston,* 470 Mich. 523 (2004).

## Statutory Violations Do Not Require Evidence Suppression

Where there is no determination that a statutory violation constitutes an error of constitutional dimensions, application of the exclusionary rule is inappropriate unless the plain language of the statute indicates a legislative intent that the rule be applied. Michigan courts must determine the Legislature's intent from its words, not from its silence. *People v. Hawkins,* 468 Mich. 488 (2003).

# DIFFERENCE BETWEEN THE MICHIGAN CONSTITUTION AND THE UNITED STATES CONSTITUTION

## Article I, Section 11, Michigan Constitution

*The person, houses, papers and possessions of every person shall be secure from unreasonable searches and seizures. No warrant to search any place or to seize any person or things shall issue without describing them, nor without probable cause, supported by oath or affirmation. The provisions of this section shall not be construed to bar from evidence in any criminal proceeding any narcotic drug, firearm, bomb, explosive or any other dangerous weapon, seized by a peace officer outside the curtilage of any dwelling house in this state.*

The Michigan Constitution has no exclusionary rule for narcotic drugs, firearms, bombs, or other dangerous weapons seized outside the curtilage of a dwelling. For example, a gun that was found illegally during a traffic stop would still be admissible under the Michigan Constitution.

However, federal courts have held that the protections of the Fourth Amendment and due process requirements of the Fourteenth Amendment provide that any evidence gained in violation of the U.S. Constitution will be barred by the exclusionary rule. Thus, the gun would be suppressed under the Fourth Amendment. *States can grant more protections but not fewer than those that are granted by the Bill of Rights.*

"On its face, the anti-exclusionary-rule provision does not purport to deprive an individual of a right guaranteed under the federal constitution. . . . No conflict of rights exists between the last sentence of art. 1, § 11 and the Fourth Amendment because the Michigan Constitution as enacted simply failed to extend the federal right to certain categories of evidence. Because the anti-exclusionary rule provision does not purport to deprive a Michigan citizen of a federally guaranteed right, a conflict exists under art. 1, § 11 and the Fourth Amendment only when state courts ignore the rights conferred by the United States Constitution and admit into evidence items unreasonably seized under the Fourth Amendment." *Sitz v. Dep't of State Police,* 443 Mich. 744 (1993).

"Under state search and seizure law, a 'higher standard' is imposed under art. 1, § 11 of the 1963 Michigan Constitution. If, however, the item seized is, *inter alia,* a 'narcotic drug . . . seized by a peace officer outside the curtilage of any dwelling house in this state,' art. 1, § 11 of the 1963 Michigan Constitution, then the seizure is governed by a standard identical to that imposed by the Fourth Amendment." *Michigan v. Long,* 463 U.S. 1032 (1983).

# APPLYING THE FOURTH AMENDMENT

## There Must Be Governmental Conduct

Governmental conduct for Fourth Amendment purposes generally involves a law enforcement officer or his agent. Actions by private citizens do not generally raise Fourth Amendment issues. The Bill of Rights was created to protect the people from the government, not from each other.

Besides law enforcement, another group that the courts have applied the Fourth Amendment to is public school teachers and school administrators.

Teachers are governmental agents, but with the need to maintain order in the schools, they only need reasonable suspicion for a search. In this case, a teacher found TLO in the bathroom and suspected that she had been smoking cigarettes. She was brought to the assistant principal's office where her purse was opened. The principal observed the cigarettes and after removing them observed some rolling papers commonly used for smoking marihuana. The principal then searched further and located the marihuana. The Court held that the principal was a governmental agent for Fourth Amendment purposes. However, due to the need to maintain order and safety in the school, a teacher must only meet the lower level of reasonable suspicion rather than probable cause in order to conduct a search. The reasonableness of a search in this context is determined by the totality of the circumstances including the reasonableness of the teacher or administrator's belief that the student was violating the law or school rule, the intrusiveness of the search, the student's age, sex, and nature of the infraction. In this case, the teacher had the reasonable suspicion based on the rolling papers. *New Jersey v. T.L.O.*, 469 U.S. 325 (1985).

Because of an increased concern for school safety, statutes have also addressed the issue of school searches. For example, MCL 380.1306 provides:
- A pupil who uses a locker that is property of a school district is presumed to have no expectation of privacy in that locker or that locker's contents.
- The school district must adopt a policy on searches of pupil's lockers and the locker contents taking into consideration the pupil's privacy rights in items that are not illegal or against school policy.
- A public school principal or his designee may search the pupil's locker or contents at any time in accordance with the policy.
- A law enforcement agency having jurisdiction of the school may assist school personnel in conducting a search if that assistance is at the request of the principal or his designee and in accordance with the policy.

## A Private Person Search Does Not Violate the Fourth Amendment

The defendant lived in a house with a roommate. Both had separate bedrooms. One day the roommate's boyfriend was over and was "snooping" in the defendant's bedroom when he located a photo album. He opened it and located child pornography. The FBI was called and seized the photos, charging the defendant with possession of child pornography. He argued that the evidence was seized in violation of the Fourth Amendment.

The Sixth Circuit uses a two-factor analysis in determining whether a private party is acting as an agent of the government such that the Fourth Amendment applies. Those two factors require an analysis of "(1) the government's knowledge or acquiescence" to the search and "(2) the intent of the party performing the search." If "*the intent of the private party* conducting the search is *entirely independent* of the government's intent to collect evidence for use in a criminal prosecution," then "the private party is not an agent of the government."

In the instant case, neither party contested the fact that law enforcement agents were not present or involved in the initial discovery of the album. The FBI gained knowledge of the incriminating evidence as a result of the phone call, and it was only after that privately initiated phone call that the agents arrived at the residence. The agents' subsequent viewing of what was freely made available for their inspection did not violate the Fourth Amendment. *United States v. Bowers*, 594 F.3d 522 (6th Cir. 2010).

## There Must Be a Reasonable Expectation of Privacy in the Place Being Searched

A reasonable expectation of privacy is one that society and the courts are prepared to recognize as reasonable.

The defendant used a telephone booth to make illegal bets. The FBI placed a listening device on the outside of the booth. The government argued that the listening device was on the outside, thus, not in a place in which there was a reasonable expectation of privacy. The Supreme Court disagreed and held that the Fourth Amendment protects people, not places. What a person seeks to preserve in private, even in a place accessible to the public, may have Fourth Amendment protections. For there to be an expectation of privacy, a person must have exhibited an actual (subjective) expectation of privacy and, second, that the expectation be one that society is prepared to recognize as "reasonable." *Katz v. United States*, 389 U.S. 347 (1967).

There is no single factor which is determinative of an individual's reasonable expectation of privacy. Among the factors mentioned by various courts are: whether the area is within the curtilage of a residence, whether it is open to view from a public area, whether the property was owned by the defendant or in some way controlled by him, whether the defendant had a subjective expectation of privacy, whether the area was enclosed, whether the area was posted against trespass, whether there were obstructions to vision, or whether the area was in fact frequented by neighbors or strangers. We also recognize that a person may permit or even invite intrusion by friends or neighbors into areas as to which he has a reasonable expectation of privacy regarding intrusion by authorities. *People v Hopko*, 79 Mich. App. 611 (1977).

### Physical Manipulation Invokes the Fourth Amendment

As an officer was exiting a bus, he squeezed soft luggage that passengers had placed in the overhead storage space. In one bag he felt a brick-like object. He then asked the owner for consent to search the bag, which was given. The bag was opened and the officer located a brick of methamphetamine.

The United States Supreme Court suppressed the evidence holding the search violated the owner's expectation of privacy. "Under this Court's Fourth Amendment analysis, a court first asks whether the individual, by his conduct, has exhibited an actual expectation of privacy; that is, whether he has shown that 'he [sought] to preserve [something] as private.' Here, petitioner sought to preserve privacy by using an opaque bag and placing it directly above his seat. Second, a court inquires whether the individual's expectation of privacy is 'one that society is prepared to recognize as reasonable.' Although a bus passenger clearly expects that

other passengers or bus employees may handle his bag, he does not expect that they will feel the bag in an exploratory manner. But this is exactly what the agent did here." *Bond v. United States*, 529 U.S. 334 (2000).

The Sixth Circuit distinguished a case from *Bond* where officers received reliable information from an informant that a subject was transporting drugs in his luggage. The court reasoned that in the *Bond*, the officers had no suspicion to believe the luggage that was handled contained controlled substances. In this case, the officers received information that the defendant was a drug courier. "In other words, unlike the agent in *Bond*, the officers in this case had a reasonable belief that the luggage contained contraband before ever touching it." *United States v. Flowal*, 234 F.3d 932 (6th Cir. 2000).

## OPEN VIEW: NO EXPECTATION OF PRIVACY

What a person knowingly exposes to the public, even in his own home, is not protected under the Fourth Amendment. *Katz v. United States*, 389 U.S. 347 (1967).

When something is visible to the public, the Fourth Amendment does not apply, thus, neither does the search warrant rule. Open view is distinct from plain view, which is discussed in Chapter 23.

### Aiding Vision

An officer used a 300 mm zoom lens from 125 feet to get a picture of the defendant carrying glassine bags containing a white powder. The court held where activities are conducted within the view of passersby and neighbors, there can be no expectation of privacy. *People v. Ward*, 107 Mich. App. 38 (1981).

An off-duty police officer used a pair of binoculars to see the license plate of a car parked in his neighbor's garage. He then requested a LEIN check, which indicated the vehicle as stolen.

A search warrant was then obtained and executed. The defendant argued that the use of the binoculars constituted an unreasonable search and seizure. The court held that there is no protection for things a person knowingly exposes to the public such as the car parked in an open garage, thus, the officer's use of binoculars to read the license plate was not a search. *People v. Clark*, 133 Mich. App. 619 (1983).

## Electronic Tracking Device

If attachment of the device requires entering a Fourth Amendment protected area, this would constitute a search (i.e., entering a garage or similar place to gain access to the vehicle). Also, if the installation requires entering into the vehicle, the Fourth Amendment would be invoked.

An officer placed a tracking device inside a five-gallon container of chloroform that was purchased by the defendant. The defendant was followed by police, who were aided by the device, for over three days before he stopped at a cabin. A search warrant was obtained and executed. The Court held that the monitoring was neither a search nor seizure because it did not invade any legitimate expectation of privacy. "A person traveling in an automobile on public thoroughfares has no reasonable expectation of privacy in his movements from one place to another." *United States v. Knotts*, 460 U.S. 276 (1983).

The Court has held that monitoring a tracking device may sometimes be considered a search when monitoring it discloses information from inside a private residence, a location not open to visual surveillance. However, attaching a device is not necessarily a Fourth Amendment activity because that act alone conveys no information at all and did not infringe any privacy interest. The Court noted that despite this holding, warrants for the installation and monitoring of a tracking device will obviously be desirable since it may be useful, even critical, to monitor the beeper to determine that it is actually located in a place not open to visual surveillance. *United States v. Karo*, 468 U.S. 705 (1984).

The government obtained a search warrant permitting it to install a Global Positioning System (GPS) tracking device on a vehicle registered to the defendant's wife. The warrant authorized installation in the District of Columbia and within 10 days, but agents installed the device on the 11th day and in Maryland. The government then tracked the vehicle's movements for 28 days. It subsequently secured an indictment of the defendant and others on drug trafficking conspiracy charges. The attachment of the GPS device to the vehicle, and its use of that device to monitor the vehicle's movements, constituted a search under the Fourth Amendment. Here, the Court need not address the Government's contention that the defendant had no "reasonable expectation of privacy," because the defendant's Fourth Amendment rights do not rise or fall with the *Katz* formulation. *Katz* did not repudiate the understanding that the Fourth Amendment embodies a particular concern for government trespass upon the areas it enumerates. The *Katz* reasonable expectation of privacy test has been added to, but not substituted for, the common-law trespassory test. *United States v. Jones*, 132 S.Ct. 945 (2012)

## Pinging Cell Phones

Drug Enforcement Administration (DEA) agents suspected that the defendant was driving cross-country in a motorhome with a load of marihuana. The agents obtained a court order that authorized the phone company to release subscriber information, cell site information, GPS real-time location, and "ping" data for a pay-as-you-go cell phone owned by the defendant. By continuously "pinging" his phone, the agents learned that the defendant stopped somewhere near Abilene, Texas, where they eventually found his motorhome parked at a truck stop. After the defendant denied the agents request to search the vehicle, an officer walked his drug-dog around the perimeter of the motorhome. The dog alerted to the presence of narcotics and the agents searched the motorhome where they discovered over 1,100 pounds of marihuana. The defendant argued that the use of the GPS location information emitted from his cell phone was a warrantless search that violated the Fourth Amendment.

The court held that there was no Fourth Amendment violation because the defendant did not have a reasonable expectation of privacy in the data given off by his voluntarily procured pay-as-you-go cell phone as he traveled on public roadways. If a tool used to transport contraband gives off a signal that can be tracked for location, the police may track the signal. The law cannot be that a criminal is entitled to rely on the expected untrackability of his tools. In addition, although not necessary to a finding that there was no Fourth Amendment violation, the government's case was strengthened by the fact that the agents sought court orders to obtain information on the defendant's location because of the GPS capabilities of his cell phone. *United States v. Skinner*, 690 F.3d. 772 (6th Cir. 2012).

## Observation Over Fences, Aerial Observation

Acting on a tip, an officer stood on the bumper of his patrol car to look over a six-foot high fence. From his position, he was able to see marihuana plants. The court held that the defendant could not have had expectation of privacy against someone standing on an object to look over the fence. "We conclude that defendant could have had no reasonable expectation that a wooden fence which is six feet high would shield his back yard activity from observations by tall passersby, from occupants of aircraft traveling through overhead public airspace, or, indeed, from a police officer standing on the bumper of his automobile on the adjacent public thoroughfare." *People v. Smola*, 174 Mich. App. 220 (1988).

The defendant built a six-foot fence around his back yard with a ten-foot fence inside of that. Police, acting on a tip that the defendant was growing marihuana, rented a plane and flew over the the defendant's property. From 1,000 feet, the officers identified numerous marihuana plants within the ten-foot tall enclosure. The Court held that, despite the defendant's efforts to conceal his activities, observation by police from a public vantage point, here the navigable airspace above the defendant's property, is not a search. Further, the defendant's efforts at concealment were clearly aimed at ground-level observation, not all observation. Observation is permissible when the officer can observe the conduct from a public vantage point where he has a right to be. *California v. Ciraolo*, 476 U.S. 207 (1986).

A person has no reasonable expectation of privacy in activities that can be viewed from the air. Police in a helicopter descended to 400 feet and observed marihuana plants growing in the defendant's greenhouse. The Court held that the search was valid because the helicopter was not violating any FAA rules and nothing suggested that helicopters flying at 400 feet were sufficiently rare that the defendant could have reasonably expected that his growing operation would not be observed from that altitude. *Florida v. Riley*, 488 U.S. 445 (1989).

## Use of a Dog

A dog may sniff the outside of luggage without violating a person's expectation of privacy. *United States v. Place*, 462 U.S. 696 (1983).

After an Illinois state trooper stopped the defendant for speeding and radioed in. A second trooper, overhearing the transmission, drove to the scene with his narcotics-detection dog and walked the dog around the defendant's car while the first trooper wrote the defendant a warning ticket. When the dog alerted at the defendant's trunk, officers searched it, found marihuana, and arrested the defendant. The Court held that a dog sniff conducted during a lawful traffic stop that reveals no information other than the location of a substance that no individual has any right to possess does not violate the Fourth Amendment. It is important to note that use of the dog did not prolong the stop longer than necessary for the first officer to complete the citation. Had the stop been prolonged, a Fourth Amendment violation may have occurred. *Illinois v. Caballes*, 543 U.S. 405 (2005).

There is no legitimate interest in possessing contraband and the use of a well-trained narcotics dog to reveal the presence of contraband does not compromise a legitimate privacy interest. Therefore, a canine sniff is not a search as long as the dog is legally present at the vantage point where its sense of smell was aroused. *People v. Jones*, 279 Mich. App. 86 (2008).

The police received an anonymous tip from a person who claimed that the defendant was growing marihuana in his house. After conducting surveillance on the house for 15 minutes, two police officers approached the defendant's house with a drug-detection dog. The dog alerted to the presence of drugs while on the front porch and after sniffing at the base of the front door. Based upon this information, officers obtained a warrant to search the defendant's house where they seized live marihuana plants and equipment used to grow those plants. The Court held that the investigation of the defendant's home was a "search" within the meaning of the Fourth Amendment. A police officer not armed with a warrant may approach a home in hopes of speaking to its occupants, because that is "no more than any private citizen might do." But the scope of a license is limited not only to a particular area, but also to a specific purpose, and there is no customary invitation to enter the curtilage simply to conduct a search. *Florida v. Jardines*, 133 S.Ct. 1409 (2013).

Officers pulled over respondent for a routine traffic stop. The officer sought consent to search the defendant's truck, and when he refused, the officer executed a sniff test with his trained narcotics dog. The dog alerted at the driver's side door handle, leading the officer to conclude that he had probable cause for a search. That search turned up nothing the dog was trained to detect, but did reveal pseudoephedrine and other ingredients for manufacturing methamphetamine. The defendant was arrested and charged with illegal possession of those ingredients. In a subsequent stop while the suspect was out on bail, the dog again alerted on the defendant's truck but nothing of interest was found. The defendant challenged the dog's reliability. The Court held that a probable cause hearing focusing on a dog's alert should proceed much like any other, with the Court allowing the parties to make their best case and evaluating the totality of the circumstances. If the State has produced proof from controlled settings that a dog performs reliably in detecting drugs, and the defendant has not contested that showing, the Court should find probable cause. But a defendant must have an opportunity to challenge such evidence of a dog's reliability, whether by cross-examining the testifying officer or by introducing his own fact or expert witnesses. The defendant may contest training or testing standards as flawed or too lax, or raise an issue regarding the particular alert. The Court should then consider all the evidence and apply the usual test for probable cause—whether all the facts surrounding the alert, viewed through the lens of common sense, would make a reasonably prudent person think that a search would reveal contraband or evidence of a crime. *Florida v. Harris*, 133 S.Ct. 1050 (2013).

## Garbage

Police suspected the defendant of drug trafficking. They requested the trash collector pick up the defendant's trash and keep it separate from the other trash. The collector then turned it over to the police. The trash had been left by the defendant at the curb for pick up. The Court held that a person has no reasonable expectation of privacy in garbage left for collection outside the curtilage of residence. *California v. Greenwood*, 486 U.S. 35 (1988).

The *Greenwood* rule also applies when police, not the trash collector, pick up curbside trash. *People v. Pinnix*, 174 Mich. App. 445 (1989).

## Vehicle Identification Numbers (VINs)

There is no expectation of privacy in the VIN plate. If it is obstructed from view by papers on the dashboard, the papers can be moved if there is no other way to see the VIN. *New York v. Class*, 475 U.S. 106 (1986).

A trooper stopped a motorcycle and discovered that the VIN number on the registration was not the same as on the cycle. The cycle was brought back to the post where two months later electrolysis was done to determine the actual VIN number, which corresponded to a stolen cycle. The court held that there was no privacy interest in the number listed on the motorcycle's fork. Like the *Class* dashboard VIN, the fork serial number was originally in plain view. If defendant Class's efforts to obscure the dashboard VIN with papers, probably inadvertent, created no Fourth Amendment privacy interest, then neither did the guilty efforts of one who defaced the motorcycle fork. *People v. Dinsmore*, 166 Mich. App. 33 (1988).

There is no VIN exemption to the search warrant rule. Officers must rely on the "automobile exception," another exception, or a search warrant to search for *hidden* VINs within the vehicle. *People v. Wilson*, 257 Mich. App 337 (2003).

## Thermal Imaging

Using sense-enhancing technology to obtain information regarding a home's interior that could not otherwise be obtained without physical intrusion is a search where the technology is not in general public use. *Kyllo v. United States*, 533 U.S. 27 (2001).

## Rest Areas

The stall of the rest room is protected, but not the common areas. *People v. Lillis*, 181 Mich. App. 315 (1989).

## Hospital Room

There is no expectation of privacy in a hospital room. A patient does maintain an expectation of privacy in the drawers and closets, but not in the room itself. *People v. Courts*, 205 Mich. App. 326 (1994).

## Jail Cell

A search of the defendant's jail cell did not violate his Fourth Amendment right to privacy. *People v. Phillips*, 219 Mich. App 159 (1996).

Searches of prison cells do not violate the Fourth Amendment right to privacy. *People v. Herndon*, 246 Mich. App. 371 (2001).

## Running Registration Plates

A police officer may properly run a computer check on a license plate number in open view even if the vehicle is not observed to violate any traffic law and there is no other information to suggest that a crime has been or is being committed. That is, there is no probable cause or articulable suspicion requirement to run a computer check of a license plate number in which there is no expectation of privacy. In the absence of evidence to the contrary, a police officer may reasonably suspect that a vehicle is being driven by its registered owner.

Where information gleaned from a computer check provides a basis for the arrest or further investigation of the registered owner of the vehicle, a police officer may initiate an investigatory stop to determine if the driver is the registered owner of the vehicle. In the course of the investigatory stop, the officer may request identification and may act to reasonably secure his own safety. *People v. Jones*, 260 Mich. App. 424 (2004).

## The Workplace

The defendant was convicted for possession of stolen property. He claimed that his office was improperly searched because the officers did not have a warrant. The court disagreed on the basis that the office was shared with another person who could invite anyone into the office. The supervisor also had access to the work area. Also, security, the custodial staff, and one other person had keys to the office. Ultimately, the amount of control a person has over his work space will dictate whether he has a reasonable expectation of privacy in it; the more control the person has, the more likely a court will find he has an expectation of privacy there. *People v. Powell*, 235 Mich. App. 557 (1999).

## Work-Related Searches Must Be Reasonable Under the Fourth Amendment

A city gave some of their employees, including the defendant, who was a police officer, pagers that were able to send and receive text messages. When the defendant and others exceeded their monthly character limits for several months running, the police chief asked for an audit from Arch Wireless to determine whether the existing limit was too low and whether the officers had to pay fees for sending work-related messages or, conversely, whether the overages were for personal messages. The audit discovered that many of the defendant's messages were not work related, and some were sexually explicit and he was disciplined for violating departmental rules. The defendant then sued the chief for violating his Fourth Amendment rights and the federal Stored Communications Act (SCA) by obtaining and reviewing the transcript of the defendant's pager messages and that Arch Wireless violated the SCA by giving the city the transcript.

Because the search of the defendant's text messages was reasonable, the chief did not violate the defendant's Fourth Amendment rights. The warrantless review of the defendant's pager transcript was reasonable because it was motivated by a legitimate work-related purpose, and because it was not excessive in scope. There were reasonable grounds for finding it necessary for a non-investigatory work-related purpose in that the chief had ordered the audit to determine whether the city's contractual character limit was sufficient to meet the city's needs. It was also reasonably related to the objectives of the search because both the city and the department had a legitimate interest in ensuring that employees were not being forced to pay out of their own pockets for work-related expenses or, on the other hand, that the city was not paying for extensive personal communications. Reviewing the transcripts was an efficient and expedient way to determine whether either of these factors caused the defendant's overages and the review was not excessively intrusive. Although the defendant had exceeded his monthly allotment a number of times, the department requested transcripts for only August and September 2002 in order to obtain a large enough sample to decide the character limits' efficaciousness, and all the messages that the defendant sent while off duty were redacted. And from the department's perspective, the fact that the defendant likely had only a limited privacy expectation lessened the risk that the review would intrude on highly private details of the defendant's life. Similarly, because the city had a legitimate reason for the search and it was not excessively intrusive in light of that justification; the

search would be regarded as reasonable and normal in the private-employer context. *City of Ontario v. Quon*, 560 U.S. 746 (2010).

## Abandonment

While on patrol, officers observed a subject running from a dwelling. As they chased him, they observed him throw a bag away. The bag was retrieved and officers located cocaine inside. The court ruled that once the defendant abandoned the bag, he relinquished any reasonable expectation of privacy in the bag and its contents. *People v. Mamon*, 435 Mich. 1 (1990).

A person does not have to give up ownership in property for it to be abandoned for Fourth Amendment purposes. He or she simply needs to give up his or her reasonable expectation of privacy in it, e.g., placing it where anyone could have access to it and/or failing to assert a property interest in it while observing another search the property. *People v. Henry*, 477 Mich. 1123 (2007).

Entry into and contemporaneous search of an abandoned structure is presumptively reasonable because the owner no longer has an expectation of privacy in the property that he or she has abandoned. Determination of whether or not a structure is abandoned is based on totality of the circumstances. *People v. Taylor*, 253 Mich. App. 399 (2002).

A condemned building is considered abandoned for Fourth Amendment purposes. *People v. Antwine*, 293 Mich. App. 192 (2011).

## Open Fields

Open fields beyond the curtilage are not protected by the Fourth Amendment; thus, observation of those areas does not constitute a search. *United States v. Dunn*, 480 U.S. 294 (1987).

A "no trespassing" sign is not an adequate bar to access of an open field as to convey a reasonable expectation of privacy sufficient to trigger Fourth Amendment protections. Common law trespass does not dictate that a government incursion on open fields is a search. Open fields, or woods in this case, are not protected by the Fourth Amendment. *Oliver v. United States*, 466 U.S. 170 (1984).

# THE CURTILAGE SURROUNDING A RESIDENCE IS PROTECTED

DEA agents tracked large quantities of chemicals used for making controlled substances to a barn on the defendant's ranch. The barn was behind the house. The house was completely surrounded by a barbed wire fence. The barn was outside the barbed-fence, but was inside a wooden fence. The agents jumped over the wooden fence and shined a flashlight through a window where they saw a drug laboratory. The agents then secured a warrant based on their observations.

The Court held that the barn was not within the curtilage of the home and not under the home's Fourth Amendment protection where it was located 50 yards from fence surrounding home and 60 yards from home itself, where the barn was not within area surrounding home that was enclosed by fence, where law enforcement officials possessed objective data indicating that barn was not being used for intimate activities of home, and where owner did little to protect barn from observation by those standing in open fields. Further, the fences surrounding the ranch were the type designed to corral livestock, not protect privacy, so when the DEA agents crossed the fences into the fields, they did not intrude on the defendant's right to privacy. *United States v. Dunn*, 480 U.S. 294 (1987).

## Four-Point Test for Determining Curtilage

1. Proximity of area to the home.
2. Whether the area is in an enclosure surrounding the home.
3. The nature of the area's use.
4. Steps taken to protect the area from observation.

## Technical Trespass

Officers received a call that a car was being stripped and that the suspects were taking the parts to a garage located at the rear of a particular address. The police found a stripped auto and approached the garage. The officers entered the backyard from the alley and approached a door on the side of the garage. Through a window, the officers observed the defendants removing parts from a vehicle. Upon entry, they determined the vehicle to be stolen and the subjects were arrested.

The court held that a technical trespass would not automatically make a search unreasonable and that what the police did here did not constitute a search. "The police did not enter defendant's home or peer into the windows of his home. Rather, they looked into an unattached garage which abutted a public alley from a common access route. . . . The route which any visitor to a residence would use is not private in the Fourth Amendment sense, and thus if police take the route 'for the purpose of making a general inquiry' or for some other legitimate reason, they are 'free to keep their eyes open' . . . " *People v. Houze*, 425 Mich. 82 (1986).

Officers had reason to believe that a house contained controlled substances. The officers approached the residence and noticed that the window immediately to the left of the door had its inside blinds pulled up. With the aid of a flashlight, one officer observed what was in the house. Based on these observations, a search warrant was sought and executed. The court upheld the observations made by the officers. Because the officer was properly present on defendant's porch when he observed the objects in defendant's window, his actions were entirely proper. The court focused on the fact that the officer was lawfully on the front porch and that the homeowner left the blinds open. Thus, it was not reasonable for the defendant to expect privacy when anyone on the porch could look through the window. *People v. Custer*, 248 Mich. App. 552 (2001).

Troopers learned that the defendant was a suspect in the murders of two of his co-workers at the Michigan Department of Corrections prison facility and went to his house. The officers went to a door on an enclosed porch and knocked and received no answer. They then opened the unlocked porch door and entered through the porch to knock at the inner residence door. Looking through the window, the officers observed the defendant slumped at a table with his back to the door. A rifle and ammunition were visible next to him. When he did not respond to loud knocking, the troopers entered the residence and took defendant into custody.

The court held that the defendant did not have a reasonable expectation of privacy in the enclosed porch of his parents' home. The porch appeared to be an entryway into the home. There was no doorbell located on the exterior door, which was a screen door, while there was a doorbell on the inner door. The porch did not have the characteristics of a living area. Rather, it was an unheated area used primarily as storage space. Like any other visitor desiring to speak to the occupant of the residence, the police simply entered the porch to access the inner door adjacent to the residence. Police conducting an investigation may go to places visitors may be expected to go (e.g., walkways, driveways, and porches). Therefore, the police actions were reasonable and did not violate the Fourth Amendment. *People v. Tierney*, 266 Mich. App. 687 (2005).

# CRIME SCENES

The United States Supreme Court has consistently held that there is no crime scene exception to the search warrant rule. A person still maintains an expectation of privacy in his residence even if he has committed a crime.

Undercover officers went to buy heroin from a house. While in the house, an altercation arose where an officer was shot and killed. Back-up officers arrived and entered the residence without a warrant to search for other victims. Homicide detectives then arrived and searched the residence for four days. During the search all drawers, cupboards, clothing, closets, etc., were examined and sections of carpet were removed. A total of two to three hundred items were seized as evidence.

The Court invalidated the search. "The police may make warrantless entries and searches when they reasonably believe that a person within is in need of immediate aid and that police officers may enter a homicide scene to see if there are other victims or if the killer is still on the premises. Any evidence found in plain view during these searches is admissible." However, the Court held that a search outside of these parameters is unconstitutional without a warrant. *Mincey v. Arizona*, 437 U.S. 385 (1978).

The defendant shot and killed her husband and then attempted suicide. She was unsuccessful before family and police found her. The responding officers transported her to the hospital and secured the scene. Thirty-five minutes later, two members of the homicide unit arrived and conducted a follow-up investigation and commenced a general exploratory search for evidence finding a suicide note from the wife that included a statement that she had killed her husband. The Court held that the police may make warrantless entry where they reasonably believe a person is in need of immediate attention, and they may make a prompt warrantless search of the area to see if there are other victims or if the killer is on the premise. However, there is no murder scene exception to the search warrant and once the scene was secured, the officers should have obtained a warrant before further searching. *Thompson v. Louisiana*, 469 U.S. 17 (1984).

The defendant and his wife were vacationing at a cabin in a state park. The defendant called 911 to report that they had been attacked. When the officers arrived, they located defendant outside with wounds to his head and feet. They entered the cabin and discovered that the defendant's wife had been killed. The officers then secured the scene and the defendant was taken to the hospital. When investigators arrived, they entered the cabin and searched for over 16 hours. At one point, they opened a briefcase and located pictures of a man who appeared to be taking off his jeans. These pictures were entered into evidence to support the theory that the defendant murdered his wife. The Court suppressed the pictures. "This position squarely conflicts with *Mincey v. Arizona, supra*, where we rejected the contention that there is a 'murder scene exception' to the Warrant Clause of the Fourth Amendment. We noted that police may make warrantless entries onto premises if they reasonably believe a person is in need of immediate aid and may make prompt warrantless searches of a homicide scene for possible other victims or a killer on the premises, but we rejected any general 'murder scene exception' as 'inconsistent with the Fourth and Fourteenth Amendments.'" *Flippo v. West Virginia*, 528 U.S. 11 (1999).

# STANDING: RESIDENCE/VEHICLE

In order to challenge a search, a person must assert that he personally had a reasonable expectation of privacy in the area searched.

Police removed evidence from an apartment that was rented by the defendant's mother after searching with an invalid warrant. Since the defendant did not have an expectation of privacy in the apartment, he could not attack the search. It was the defendant's mother, not the defendant, who had a reasonable expectation of privacy in the apartment. *United States v. Salvucci*, 448 U.S. 83 (1980).

A person may not assert a Fourth Amendment violation unless they have been personally aggrieved by the search or seizure. To raise a Fourth Amendment challenge, the person must assert a possessory interest in the objects seized or a possessory interest sufficient to give him an expectation of privacy in the object or premises searched. A person may not allege a Fourth Amendment violation on behalf of a third party. *Rakas v. Illinois*, 439 U.S. 128 (1978).

The defendant was wanted on an armed robbery where a victim was killed. Police confirmed that the defendant was an overnight guest at a duplex and later received a call that he was there. They surrounded the residence, entered without permission, and arrested the defendant. The Court held that the defendant had a reasonable expectation of privacy as an overnight guest. *Minnesota v. Olson*, 495 U.S. 91 (1990).

The defendants were invited to another person's house to package cocaine. A police officer observed them through a window. The officer stood 12–18 inches away from the apartment when he made his observations. The defendants were there approximately 2 1/2 hours. When they left, they were stopped and arrested for possessing 47 grams of cocaine. They argued that the observations of the police were illegal under the Fourth Amendment. The Court did not answer that question because it held that the defendants had no expectation of privacy to challenge the observations due to their short stay at the apartment. The Court made a distinction between this visit and an overnight guest who does have an expectation of privacy.

In reaching its decision the Court looked at the following factors:

- The purely commercial nature of the transaction.
- The relatively short period of time on the premises.
- The lack of any previous connection between the defendants and the householder.

*Minnesota v. Carter*, 525 U.S. 83 (1998).

The defendant was a passenger in a vehicle where a .22-caliber pistol was located. The mere fact that the defendant was in the car with the owner's permission immediately prior to the search did not endow him with a reasonable expectation of privacy in the area searched. *People v. Smith*, 106 Mich. App. 203 (1981).

## PRIVATE CONVERSATIONS

Warrantless electronic monitoring of conversations is permissible as long as one party consents to the monitoring. *People v. Collins*, 438 Mich. 8 (1991).

MCL 750.539d prohibits civilians from eavesdropping on or recording of conversations of others without the consent of the parties entitled to privacy in a particular place. This statute does not prohibit security monitoring in a residence if conducted by or at the direction of the owner or principal occupant of that residence unless conducted for a lewd or lascivious purpose. MCL 750.539g also grants police and their agents an exception to this rule in the performance of their duties.

## PRETEXT STOPS

Undercover vice officers observed two subjects acting suspiciously in a vehicle. As the officers turned to investigate, the vehicle took off quickly and made a right turn without using a turn signal. The officers stopped the vehicle for failing to use a turn signal. When they approached the car, they observed a plastic baggie in the passenger's hands with a substance believed to be cocaine. The Court held the stop to be valid. The justices refused to look at the officer's subjective reasons for making the stop and instead asked if the officer "could have" made the stop. Failing to use a signal when turning is a violation of law; thus, the stop was reasonable. As long as the officers have probable cause that a traffic violation has occurred, the stop will be reasonable under the Fourth Amendment. *Whren v. United States*, 517 U.S. 806 (1996).

Officers were waiting to obtain a narcotics search warrant for a residence when the defendant approached. He exited his vehicle, went to the house, and exchanged money for a package. He returned to his car and drove off. A marked unit was called to stop him. He failed to use his turn signal and was stopped. When he failed to produce a license, he was arrested. A search subsequent to the arrest revealed narcotics. The court upheld the stop and search. Even though the stop was a pretext for the looking for drugs, the stop was lawful because the defendant failed to use his turn signal. *People v. Haney*, 192 Mich. App. 207 (1991).

The defendant was pulled over while driving his motor home. During a consent search, officers located marihuana. The basis of the stop was that the vehicle crossed the white line separating the emergency lane from the right-hand lane of traffic for an estimated 20–30 feet. The Tennessee code states that a vehicle "shall be driven as nearly as practicable entirely within a single lane." The prosecutor argued that the basis for the stop was probable cause to believe a traffic violation had occurred or a belief the driver was intoxicated. The court denied both these arguments and held the stop was unlawful. The court stated "We can not agree, however, that one isolated incident of a large motor home partially weaving into the emergency lane for a few feet and an instant in time constitutes a failure to keep the vehicle within a single lane 'as nearly as practicable.'" Also, "the motor home's brief entry into the emergency lane does not constitute probable cause that [the driver] was intoxicated." *United States v. Freeman*, 209 F.3d 464 (6th Cir. 2000).

## PRETEXT ARRESTS

Officers stopped the defendant for speeding and having an improperly tinted windshield. Upon seeing the defendant's driver's license, the officer recognized him from intelligence reports that reported the defendant was involved in narcotics. The defendant then opened his car door in an unsuccessful attempt to locate his registration and proof of insurance. At that point, the officer observed a rusty roofing hatchet on the floorboard of the car. The defendant was arrested for speeding, driving without his registration and insurance,

carrying a weapon, and improper window tinting. A subsequent inventory search of the car revealed drugs and the defendant was charged. The defendant moved to suppress the evidence on the basis that the arrest was merely a pretext and sham to search his car. The Arkansas Supreme Court suppressed the evidence, but the United States Supreme Court reversed in a per curiam decision based on the *Whren* decision.

The Supreme Court said, "The Arkansas Supreme Court's holding to that effect cannot be squared with our decision in *Whren*, in which we noted our 'unwilling[ness] to entertain Fourth Amendment challenges based on the actual motivations of individual officers,' and held unanimously that '[s]ubjective intentions play no role in ordinary, probable-cause Fourth Amendment analysis.' That *Whren* involved a traffic stop, rather than a custodial arrest, is of no particular moment; indeed, *Whren* itself relied on *United States v. Robinson*, 414 U.S. 218 (1973), for the proposition that 'a traffic-violation arrest. . . [will] not be rendered invalid by the fact that it was 'a mere pretext for a narcotics search.'"

Officers should be aware of the concern of four Justices, who stated, "[I]f experience demonstrates 'anything like an epidemic of unnecessary minor-offense arrests,' [we] hope the Court will reconsider its recent precedent." *Arkansas v. Sullivan*, 532 U.S. 769 (2001).

## PROTECTIVE SWEEPS

Officers may make a protective sweep of a residence where there is an articulable concern for officer safety.

On February 3, 1986, two men committed an armed robbery of a restaurant. One of the robbers was wearing a red running suit. On February 5, the police executed an arrest warrant for the defendant. They first had a police department secretary telephone the defendant's house to verify that he was home. Six or seven officers then proceeded to the defendant's house. Once inside, the officers fanned out through the first and second floors. With his weapon drawn, one officer shouted into the basement, ordering anyone down there to come out. Eventually, a pair of hands appeared around the bottom of the stairwell and the defendant emerged from the basement. He was arrested, searched, and handcuffed. An officer entered the basement "in case there was someone else" down there. In the process, he noticed a red running suit lying in plain view on a stack of clothing and seized it.

The Court upheld the search as a protective sweep. "The Fourth Amendment permits a properly limited protective sweep in conjunction with an in-home arrest when the searching officer possesses a reasonable belief based on specific and articulable facts that the area to be swept harbors an individual posing a danger to those on the arrest scene. . . . We should emphasize that such a protective sweep, aimed at protecting the arresting officers, if justified by the circumstances, is nevertheless not a full search of the premises, but may extend only to a cursory inspection of those spaces where a person may be found. The sweep lasts no longer than is necessary to dispel the reasonable suspicion of danger and in any event no longer than it takes to complete the arrest and depart the premises." *Maryland v. Buie*, 494 U.S. 325 (1990).

Officers in a helicopter spotted marihuana near a mobile home. As they flew closer, a pickup drove up to the home and the driver, the defendant, jumped out and signaled the helicopter to go away. The helicopter dropped closer, and the driver gave an obscene hand gesture and ran into the trailer. A short time later a woman with some children emerged and fled in the truck. The driver exited the back of the residence with an object wrapped in a blanket. The helicopter crew radioed to the ground crew that the suspect had run into the woods with what might be a weapon. The first officer on the scene entered the residence to see if any more suspects were inside. During the 30–45 second sweep, he observed marihuana and firearms laying in plain view. These observations were used to obtain a search warrant, which revealed that the defendant was operating a marihuana operation.

The court held that it was reasonable for the officer to be concerned that there were armed, hostile suspects in the area. One suspect had fled into the woods with what could have been a weapon, while another fled in the truck. It would be tactically unsound for the officer to watch the doors of the mobile home until a warrant arrived. His concern for safety justified the limited warrantless intrusion. *People v. Cartwright*, 454 Mich. 550 (1997).

Officers went to the defendant's apartment to execute an arrest warrant for delivery of cocaine. The officers knew that another person was involved, but were not sure of his identity. They knocked on the door and the defendant answered. After telling her about the warrant, she stepped back and they entered. They made a protective sweep of her apartment to see if anyone else was present. During the sweep, they found a scale with what appeared to be cocaine residue. The court found that the protective sweep was reasonable pursuant to the execution of an arrest warrant. *People v. Shaw*, 188 Mich. App. 520 (1991).

Based on the facts and circumstances surrounding the arrest, the arresting officer had a reasonable belief there may have been individuals in the defendant's home who posed a danger to the officers. The officers were justified in conducting a protective sweep of the entire house, including the basement, and searching the area immediately around the defendant's girlfriend for weapons. *People v. Gonzalez*, 256 Mich. App. 212 (2003).

## FLEEING FROM POLICE

As officers approached a group of youths in a high crime area, the defendant took off running. As officers pursued, they saw him throw something away. They recovered the object and found it to be rock cocaine and the defendant was arrested. The Court held that at the time the defendant threw the object down he was not seized for Fourth Amendment purposes. Since he was not seized for Fourth Amendment purposes, the cocaine was admissible because the defendant abandoned it and, thus, lost his expectation of privacy. A seizure occurs:

- Whenever, because of a police show of authority or force, a reasonable person would believe that he or she is not free to leave, and submits; or
- Custody of the individual is achieved through the application of physical force.

*California v. Hodari D.*, 499 U.S 621 (1991).

# 48-HOUR RULE

The defendant was held for four days without a judicial determination of probable cause justifying his arrest. On the fourth day, he confessed to the crime. The court was not impressed with this procedure. The court stated, "We emphasize to police authorities across Michigan the importance of securing a judicial determination of probable cause within 48 hours of an arrest without a warrant in all but the most extraordinary situations. Finally, this decision provides a warning that statements made by an accused person during a longer detainment may well be found inadmissible for purposes of securing a conviction at trial." *People v. Whitehead*, 238 Mich. App. 1 (1999).

Inculpatory statements taken in violation of the 48-hour rule are not automatically suppressed. The court will consider the voluntariness of the statement in light of the totality of the circumstances. The court, in addition to considering the length and justification in delay, considers: "the age of the accused; his lack of education or his intelligence level; the extent of his previous experience with the police; the repeated and prolonged nature of the questioning; the length of the detention of the accused before he gave the statement in question; the lack of any advice to the accused of his constitutional rights; whether there was an unnecessary delay in bringing him before the magistrate before he gave the confession; whether the accused was injured, intoxicated or drugged, or in ill health when he gave the statement; whether the accused was deprived of food, sleep, or medical attention; whether the accused was physically abused; and whether the suspect was threatened with abuse." *People v. Manning*, 243 Mich. App. 615 (2000).

# SEARCH WARRANT REQUIREMENTS

Search warrants are written court orders requiring a search of a particular place for particular things. Search warrants are issued by judges or magistrates after they have determined that probable cause exists to believe that the evidence sought will be found in the place to be searched.

There are three documents associated with all search warrants: The warrant itself, an affidavit, and a return and tabulation. Those documents will be discussed in the pages that follow.

## Neutral and Detached Magistrate

Search warrants may only be issued by a magistrate or judge who is neutral and detached. That is, the issuing person must be impartial, having no stake in the outcome of the case, any bias related to the case, or any role in the investigation of the case.

A judge or district court magistrate may issue a written search warrant in person or by any electronic or electromagnetic means of communication, including by facsimile or over a computer network. MCL 780.651(3).

The magistrate was not neutral and detached where he had previously prosecuted the defendant and had been sued by him. *People v. Lowenstein*, 118 Mich. App. 475 (1982).

Officers executed a controlled buy, which was electronically monitored. After the delivery, the officers contacted other officers who were waiting in the magistrate's chambers. A search warrant was signed. The court upheld the warrant. "The mere fact that police wait in court does not mean that the magistrate has injected himself into the investigatory process. We are satisfied that a judge may remain neutral and detached even with the presence of officers in chambers." *People v. Tejeda*, 192 Mich. App. 635 (1992).

## Judge's Signature on Warrant

A search warrant unsigned by magistrate or judge is presumed invalid. However, this presumption may be rebutted with evidence that the magistrate or judge did make a determination that the search was warranted and did intend to issue the warrant before the search. *People v. Barkley*, 225 Mich. App. 539 (1997).

## Affidavit for a Search Warrant—MCL 780.651

An affidavit for a search warrant is a written document prepared by a person called the affiant that contains facts by which the judge or magistrate may determine whether probable cause to search exists. The affiant (usually a police officer) must affirm under oath that the contents of the affidavit are true.

The magistrate's finding of reasonable or probable cause shall be based upon all the facts related within the affidavit made before him or her. An affidavit is an application for a search warrant. The affiant should list facts only, not conclusions. Conclusions are to be determined by magistrate.

> The affidavit must be signed by the affiant before the magistrate. However, failure to sign does not necessarily render a search warrant invalid. The prosecution has the burden of showing that there was an adequate basis for the issuance of a search warrant. If the prosecutor is successful, the affiant may sign the previously written affidavit supporting the warrant. *People v. Mitchell*, 142 Mich. App. 518 (1985).

## "Four Corners of the Affidavit"

The facts establishing probable cause must fall within the "four corners of the affidavit," that is, probable cause is established by facts within the affidavit.

> A magistrate may, and is encouraged to, ask the affiant questions to ensure the affidavit supports sufficient probable cause for a warrant to issue. However, any additional facts not contained in the affidavit that are relied upon by the magistrate in deciding probable cause exists must be recorded to ensure any reviewing court has a trustworthy basis to support a finding of probable cause. The recording may take various forms, including handwritten notes, video or audiotapes, or formal or informal transcripts of testimony. *People v. Sloan*, 450 Mich. 160 (1995).

## Administration of Oath—MCL 600.1432

The affiant for a search warrant must swear or affirm that the information contained in the affidavit is true to the best of his or her belief while holding up his or her right hand.

## Showing of Probable/Reasonable Cause

In determining if probable cause exists, the magistrate should review the facts in a "common sense" manner.

It is not necessary to determine that the items sought are more likely than not in the place to be searched. It is only necessary that the affidavit enable the magistrate to conclude that it would be reasonable to seek the evidence in the place indicated. The courts must have a "common sense" reading of the affidavit. *People v. Russo*, 439 Mich. 584 (1992).

The basis of a search warrant included the following:

"On July 09, 1997, Affiant who is assigned to the Detroit Police Narcotic Division attempted a purchase of narcotics from 18072 Bloom. The above described seller asked the Affiant what the Affiant wanted, Affiant replied 'one' meaning one (1) pack heroin. The above described seller produced from his right front pocket a large bundle of blue folded small coin envelopes wrapped in rubberbands. The seller looked at the Affiant and asked the Affiant who did Affiant know. Affiant was unable to convince the seller to sell illegal narcotics. The described seller stated come back with someone I know and I'll take care of you." The affidavit continued with information that the Affiant had participated in over 100 narcotics raids and had seen heroin in similar coin envelopes on numerous occasions. A warrant to search the address for narcotics was issued. At trial, the evidence was suppressed based on a failure to establish PC in the affidavit.

When reversing on appeal, the court stated: "Considering these facts 'in a common sense and realistic manner,' we are certain the magistrate had a substantial basis for finding probable cause to issue the search warrant because there was a 'fair probability that contraband or evidence of a crime [would] be found [at the home where this conversation took place.]" *People v. Whitfield*, 461 Mich. 441 (2000).

The defendant was wanted on a federal indictment for delivery of cocaine. Surveillance on an apartment showed that the defendant's vehicle was parked there on two different occasions. He was eventually arrested while he was driving in his car. He lied to the officer about where he lived. A search of the vehicle revealed a key to the apartment and a telephone bill to the defendant mailed to the apartment. A dog was also called and cocaine was located inside the vehicle. Based on this information, a search warrant was obtained for the apartment and additional evidence was seized.

The court stated: "Under the totality of these circumstances, a reasonably cautious person could conclude that there was a substantial basis for the magistrate's finding of probable cause. Indeed, defendant was arrested as a drug trafficker, cocaine was found in his vehicle, and there was abundant evidence that he resided at or habitually used the Kentwood apartment and had lied about this to the police. The defendant contends that the affidavit did not support a search of the Kentwood apartment because nothing in the affidavit tied the alleged drug activity to the apartment. However, defendant's denial that he lived at the Kentwood apartment, combined with the reasonable inference that drug traffickers often keep evidence of illicit activity in their homes, provided a sufficient basis for the magistrate's finding of probable cause to search the apartment." *People v. Nunez*, 242 Mich. App. 610 (2000).

## Staleness

Probable cause must exist when the search warrant is sought and executed. The court held that probable cause supporting a search warrant existed even when the facts relied on in the affidavit were nearly 10 years old. A 16-year-old girl reported to police that she had been molested by the defendant from when she was five until she turned 10. She stated that the defendant had taken numerous sexually explicit photos of her and had showed the pictures to her a number of times. Based on an affidavit containing this information, a magistrate issued a search warrant. The court, after consulting studies on how pedophiles maintain their pornography for years, held that probable cause existed even though there was a significant lapse of time. The question to be asked is whether it is reasonable to believe the items are still where the information placed them. If there is a continued criminal enterprise, there is a likelihood the items sought will remain for a longer time. *People v. Russo*, 439 Mich. 584 (1992).

The probable cause may also become stale if the warrant is not executed within a reasonable time after it has been issued. For example, a search warrant for drugs should be executed immediately after it is obtained because the evidence may disappear if there is a delay. One exception to the rule that probable cause must exist when the search warrant is obtained is an anticipatory search warrant.

## Anticipatory Search Warrants are Constitutional

Officers intercepted a package that contained 28 pounds of marihuana. They set up a delivery with an undercover officer. Prior to completing the delivery, they obtained an "anticipatory search warrant." The warrant specifically identified what would have to occur before it would become valid. "The search was subject to the successful delivery of the narcotics which was to be carried out by an undercover police officer. Further, the affidavit clearly indicated that the warrant would not be executed unless the marihuana was successfully delivered." Based on these facts, the court held that anticipatory search warrants are not unconstitutional per se. *People v. Kaslowski*, 239 Mich. App. 320 (2000).

Anticipatory search warrants are constitutionally valid so long as the affidavit establishes probable cause that the triggering event will occur and probable cause that particular evidence will be found when the triggering event occurs. *United States v. Grubbs*, 547 U.S. 90 (2006).

## Named or Unnamed Persons—MCL 780.653

*The magistrate's finding of reasonable or probable cause shall be based upon all the facts related within the affidavit made before him or her. The affidavit may be based upon information supplied by named or unnamed person if the affidavit contains one of the following:*

(a) *If the person is named, affirmative allegations from which the magistrate can conclude that the person spoke with personal knowledge of the information.*

(b) *If the person is unnamed, affirmative allegations from which the magistrate may conclude that the person spoke with personal knowledge of the information and either that the unnamed person is credible or that the information is reliable.*

A mall manager reported to the police that he had received a number of complaints of homosexual activity in the restroom stalls. Based on this information and after obtaining a warrant, police installed a video camera in the restroom and observed the defendant performing sex acts in a public place. The videotape was suppressed, however, as the reports to the mall manager were uncorroborated. To support a warrant based on hearsay within hearsay, the underlying affidavit must offer proof of the credibility of both levels of informant, i.e., there must be some proof that both the mall manager and those who complained to him or their complaints were credible. *People v. Kalchik*, 160 Mich. App. 40 (1987).

## What Can Be Searched For—MCL 780.652

*A warrant may be issued to search for and seize any property or other thing that is 1 or more of the following:*

(a) *Stolen or embezzled in violation of a law of this state.*

(b) *Designed and intended for use, or that is or has been used, as the means of committing a crime.*

(c) *Possessed, controlled, or used wholly or partially in violation of a law of this state.*

(d) *Evidence of crime or criminal conduct.*

(e) *Contraband.*

(f) *The body or person of a human being or of an animal that may be the victim of a crime.*

(g) *The object of a search warrant under another law of this state providing for the search warrant. If there is a conflict between this act and another search warrant law, this act controls.*

*A warrant may be issued to search for and seize a person who is the subject of either of the following:*

(a) *An arrest warrant for the apprehension of a person charged with a crime.*

(b) *A bench warrant issued in a criminal case.*

## Search Warrant: Search and Seizure of Hair, Tissue, Blood, or Other Fluids—MCL 780.652a

*If the court has probable cause to believe that an individual has violated one of the following CSC sections: 520b(1)(b)(ii) or (h)(i), 520c(1)(b)(ii) or (h)(i), 520d(1)(d), or 520e(1)(g) of the Michigan penal code, the court shall, upon proper petition for a search warrant, authorize the search and seizure of hair or tissue, or blood or other fluid samples from all of the following:*

(a) *Any individual whom the court has probable cause to believe committed that violation.*

(b) *If the court has probable cause to believe that the violation resulted in the birth of a child, that child.*

(c) *If the court has probable cause to believe that the violation resulted in a pregnancy that was terminated before the birth of a child, the remains of that unborn child.*

*This section does not prohibit the court from issuing a search warrant for other evidence as considered appropriate by the court.*

## Mistakes on a Warrant

Police executed a warrant where they had the proper address on the affidavit, but due to a computer "error," the wrong address was printed on the warrant. Neither the officer nor the magistrate noticed the error. The officers executed the warrant at the proper residence. The test for determining the sufficiency of the description of the place to be searched is (1) whether the place to be searched is described with sufficient particularity to enable the executing officer to locate and identify the premises with reasonable effort and (2) whether there is any reasonable probability that another premises might be mistakenly searched. Here, although the warrant contained an inaccurate description of the premises to be searched, the court held that the error was harmless as the proper address was in the affidavit, the officers executing the warrant had the proper house under surveillance, and the proper premises was searched. Under these circumstances, there was zero probability of an erroneous search, thus, exclusion of evidence seized was unnecessary. *People v. Hampton*, 237 Mich. App. 143 (1999).

A search warrant that utterly failed to describe the persons or things to be seized was invalid on its face, notwithstanding that requisite particularized description was provided in the search warrant application. A residential search that was conducted pursuant to this facially invalid warrant could not be regarded as "reasonable," though items to be seized were described in the search warrant application and officers conducting search exercised restraint in limiting scope of search to that indicated in the application. The officer who had prepared and executed warrant was not entitled to qualified immunity from liability as "even a cursory reading of the warrant in this case—perhaps just a simple glance—would have revealed a glaring deficiency that any reasonable police officer would have known was constitutionally fatal." *Groh v. Ramirez*, 540 U.S. 551 (2004).

## General Warrants

General warrants are prohibited by the Fourth Amendment; a particular description of things to be seized is required. Here, the court held that a warrant authorizing the "seizure of all books, records, papers, correspondence and tax returns of the business identified in connection with the falsification of the weights and measures of the gasoline purchases" was not a general warrant. The court held that the language of the warrant was specific enough to limit the seizure only to those records connected to the criminal activity being investigated. *People v. Harajli*, 170 Mich. App. 794 (1988).

## The Place to Be Searched

### Search Warrant Contents—MCL 780.654

(1) *A search warrant shall be directed to the sheriff or any peace officer, commanding the sheriff or peace officer to search the house, building, or other location or place, where the person, property, or thing for which the sheriff or peace officer is required to search is believed to be concealed. Each warrant shall designate and describe the house or building or other location or place to be searched and the property or thing to be seized.*

(2) *The warrant shall either state the grounds or the probable or reasonable cause for its issuance or shall have attached to it a copy of the affidavit.*

An officer executing a warrant must be able to reasonably identify the place to be searched. *Steele v. United States*, 267 U.S. 498 (1925).

The address on the warrant stated to search entire apartment located at 242 National, N.W., Apt. 2, City of Grand Rapids, County of Kent, State of Michigan, further described as being a "blue wooden framed 2 story multi-dwelling residence." In reality, the defendant's apartment was No.1 in 246, next to 242. Both were painted blue.

When obtaining the warrant, the officers checked the address using the Secretary of State. The defendant had lived at 242, but failed to change his address.

Even though the address was incorrect, the court held that the description along with the officer's knowledge and the information in the affidavit was adequate to define the premises to be searched. *People v. Westra*, 445 Mich. 284 (1994).

## Other Buildings Within the Curtilage to Be Searched Must Be Included in the Warrant

*Curtilage* is the land, yard, or buildings adjacent to a house, usually within an enclosure, that is protected by the Fourth Amendment just as the house is.

Officers obtained a search warrant for a residence. During a search, they also looked in a shed located near the house. "While it is recognized that rural property does not lend itself readily to precise description, property that is within the curtilage of any dwelling house must be described with specificity in a search warrant to justify a search of that property." *People v. Mackey*, 121 Mich. App. 748 (1982).

A search of a detached garage was not held improper, although, the search warrant did not specifically identify any outbuildings to be searched. The court held that the warrant's description of the home to be searched combined with language in the warrant describing "storage areas" "accessible" from the premises was sufficient to authorize a search of the detached garage. The test for determining sufficiency of description in a search warrant of the place to be searched is:

1. Whether the place to be searched is described with sufficient particularity to enable executing officers to locate and identify the premises with reasonable effort; and
2. Whether there is any reasonable probability that another premises might be mistakenly searched.

*People v. McGhee*, 255 Mich. App. 623 (2003).

## Descriptions of a Building Should Include

- Type of structure, e.g., dwelling, apartment building, business, and storage shed.
- The number of floors or stories.
- The areas within to be searched.
- Type of construction; e.g., white brick and blue-gray aluminum.
- The color of the exterior.
- Any other building within the curtilage to be searched.
- The street name and address.
- The side of the street the property is located.
- The intersecting roadways between which the property is located, e.g., on Canal between Lansing Road and Davis Highway.
- Any unique characteristics of the premises to be searched, e.g., with satellite dish located 20 feet south of dwelling house.
- The political subdivisions within which the premises are located, i.e., city, village, or township; county; and the state of Michigan.

## Descriptions of Vehicles Should Include

- Year, make, and model.
- Body style.
- Color.
- Registration plate number, year, and state where issued.
- VIN number.
- Any known owner, occupant, or operator of vehicle.
- The usual or probable location of the vehicle.

## Objects of Search

A warrant that leaves the objects to be seized blank or open ended is invalid. The application must describe as specifically as possible the items to be seized. *Lo-Ji Sales, Inc. v. New York*, 442 U.S. 319 (1979).

Example of how to describe an item on a search warrant:

Evidence of the cultivation and/or manufacture of the controlled substance marihuana, including but not limited to, a quantity of marihuana, both live plants and processed marihuana; growing devices and supplies, such as grow lights, heaters, reflectors, fans and blowers, motors, timers, irrigation tubs, hoses, pumps, potting soil, nutrients, fertilizers, carbon dioxide exchangers and tanks, and pots or planters; paraphernalia for processing, packaging, and distribution, including dryers, heaters, scales, baggies, and/or other packaging materials; evidence of bills, canceled envelopes, drivers licenses, keys, and deeds or other documents showing ownership; United States Currency, including pre-recorded bills, fingerprints, and palm prints; and weapons to protect the cultivation.

## Search Warrants for Blood

PBT results may be utilized in an affidavit for a search warrant for blood of an O.W.I. suspect. *People v. Tracy*, 186 Mich. App. 171 (1990).

## Search Warrants for Blood; Pain Compliance to Obtain Blood

The defendant was stopped for speeding and admitted to drinking. He failed the sobriety tests and then refused to take a Breathalyzer. A search warrant was obtained, and he was taken to the hospital. At the hospital, he refused to lie down on the table and evaded the lab technician's attempts to draw the blood. An officer then applied Do-Rite sticks to the suspect's wrists, and he subsequently complied with the withdrawal of his blood.

The court upheld the action as reasonable. The Do-Rite sticks were not used to punish the defendant, but were used to subdue him and to ensure his safety as well as that of others. Because the contact was not severe, unnecessary, or unduly intrusive, the officer's actions were proper. *People v. Hanna*, 223 Mich. App. 466 (1997).

## Knock and Announce – MCL 780.656

*The officer to whom a warrant is directed, or any person assisting him, may break any outer or inner door or window of a house or building, or anything therein, in order to execute the warrant, if, after notice of his authority and purpose, he is refused admittance, or when necessary to liberate himself or any person assisting him in execution of the warrant.*

## Fourth Amendment Requirements

Absent exigent circumstances, failure to knock and announce identity and purpose before executing a search warrant may make the subsequent search unreasonable. *Wilson v. Arkansas*, 514 U.S. 927 (1995).

## No Blanket Exception to Knock and Announce

The Wisconsin Supreme Court concluded that officers are never required to knock and announce their presence when executing a search warrant in a felony drug investigation. The United States Supreme Court reversed and disallowed a blanket exception and required the courts to look at a case-by-case analysis.

In order to justify a "no-knock" entry, the police must have a reasonable suspicion that knocking and announcing under the particular circumstances:

- Would be dangerous or futile; or
- Would inhibit the effective investigation of the crime by, for example, allowing the destruction of evidence.

After reviewing the facts in the case, the court did allow a no-knock entry because the defendant saw the police and ran back into his hotel room. *Richard v. Wisconsin*, 520 U.S. 385 (1997).

## Actual Knock Not Required

An Emergency Services Team assisted in executing a search warrant. They entered the driveway with a police vehicle. The emergency lights were activated and an officer announced on the PA system, "This is the police. We have a search warrant." The officers also had "Police" clearly written on their body armor. Once the team arrived at the door, they entered. The officers testified that it took 30–45 seconds to enter the residence after the announcements were made. They did not announce anything at the door. The defendant argued that the officers were required to knock on the door before entering. The Court of Appeals disagreed and upheld the entry as providing sufficient notice to the occupants of the officer's authority and purpose. *People v. Fetterley*, 229 Mich. App. 511 (1998).

## Knock and Announce Violation Will Not Result in Suppression of Evidence

Officers executed a search warrant at 12:32 a.m. There were no lights on, and they did not observe any activity or hear any footsteps. They knocked and announced, waited 11 seconds, and then broke the door down. Under these facts, the court agreed with the lower courts that the officers violated the knock and announce principles. The question presented, however, was whether the evidence found in the house should be suppressed.

The court said that, "The discovery of the evidence in the present case was inevitable, regardless of the illegalities on the police officer's entry into defendant's home. One of the purposes of the statute is to allow a defendant a brief opportunity to put his personal affairs in order before the police enter his home. It is not meant to allow the defendant the time to destroy evidence. In the present case, the police did not exceed the scope of the search warrant. Therefore, they would have discovered the contested evidence, unless the defendant had been afforded the opportunity to destroy the evidence." *People v. Stevens*, 460 Mich. 626 (1999).

Officers should be mindful that a knock-and-announce violation may still result in civil litigation for violating the homeowner's Fourth Amendment rights.

Police obtained a search warrant for the defendant's residence and executed it by knocking, waiting for less than five seconds, and entering the residence. They found drugs and an illegally possessed gun. The Court held that the exclusionary rule does not apply to federal knock-and-announce violations. The exclusionary rule is designed to prevent the use of evidence that was found only because of a violation of the Constitution. However, when police have a warrant they will find evidence lawfully, even when they did not follow the knock-and-announce rule; a rule violation does not lead to discovery of evidence, the warrant does. *Hudson v. Michigan*, 547 U.S. 586 (2006).

## Examples of Litigation

An undercover officer gave a suspect $20.00 to buy crack cocaine. When the suspect returned, he stated he had been robbed. The officers tried to arrest him and the subject took off running. He ran into a house and the officers chased him inside where an altercation arose with a number of the occupants. The officers initially arrested the wrong person and then later found the right suspect hiding in the house. The occupants of the house sued the officers for violating the Fourth Amendment rights because the officers failed to knock and announce their presence before entry. The officers argued that they had a right to enter the house under hot pursuit. The court ruled that it would not give a blanket exception to hot pursuit. It remanded the case to the trial court to determine if to knock and announce would have been dangerous or futile or would have inhibited an investigation. *Ingram v. City of Columbus*, 185 F.3d 579 (6th Cir. 1999).

There is not a higher standard of scrutiny for a no-knock entry that causes property damage. While executing a warrant for a dangerous escaped prisoner, officers broke a single window and pointed a gun inside as they announced that they had a warrant and shouted "police." The defendant thought he was being burglarized and fired a shot from a pistol. He was then arrested. The lower courts dismissed the charges of being a felon in the possession of a firearm because there were insufficient exigent circumstances to allow a no-knock entry. The Supreme Court reversed and held that "The Fourth Amendment does not hold officers to a higher standard when a 'no-knock' entry results in the destruction of property." To conduct a no-knock entry, the officers "must have a reasonable suspicion that knocking and announcing . . . would 'be dangerous or futile, or . . . inhibit the effective investigation of the crime.'" Here, the officers had sufficient reasonable suspicion because of a reliable informant's statement that he was there. This was confirmed by an officer. The defendant had a violent past and had vowed that he would not do federal time. Plus, breaking the window was reasonable as to discourage anyone from rushing to weapons. *United States v. Ramirez*, 523 U.S. 65 (1998).

## Announce: Substantial Compliance with the Statute

"Police officers, open up" was held to be in compliance with the statute. Declaration of purpose is implicit in declaration of identity, and vice versa. *People v. Doane*, 33 Mich. App. 579 (1971).

"Police officers. I have a search warrant. Open the door," was also held to comply with the statute. *People v. Mayes*, 78 Mich. App. 618 (1977).

## How Long to Wait

Officers went to the defendant's apartment to execute a search warrant. They called out "police—search warrant" and knocked on the front door hard enough to be heard by officers at the back door. They waited for 15–20 seconds with no response and then broke open the door. The defendant was in the shower and testified that he heard nothing until the crash of the door. The defendant argued on appeal that the entry was unreasonable and that the evidence found should be suppressed.

The Court stated that "This case turns on the exigency revealed by the circumstances known to the officers after they knocked and announced, which the Government contends was the risk of losing easily disposable evidence.

After 15–20 seconds without a response, officers could fairly have suspected that [the defendant] would flush away the cocaine if they remained reticent. Each of [the defendant]'s counterarguments—that he was in the shower and did not hear the officers and that it might have taken him longer than 20 seconds to reach the door—rests on a mistake about the relevant inquiry. As to the first argument, the facts known to the police are what count in judging a reasonable waiting time, and there is no indication that they knew that [the defendant] was in the shower and thus unaware of an impending search. As to the second, the crucial fact is not the time it would take [the defendant] to reach the door but the time it would take him to destroy the cocaine. It is not unreasonable to think that someone could get in a position to destroy the drugs within 15–20 seconds. Once the exigency had matured, the officers were not bound to learn anything more or wait any longer before entering, even though the entry entailed some harm to the building." *United States v. Banks*, 540 U.S. 31 (2003).

A search warrant was properly served under MCL 780.656, where an officer knocked on the door and clearly announced authority and purpose and waited long enough for inhabitants to reach the door from the room farthest away before kicking in the door. *People v. Harvey*, 38 Mich. App. 39 (1972).

Police do not have to wait if they have a basis to conclude that:

- Evidence will be destroyed,
- Lives will be endangered, or
- Events indicate that knocking and announcing would be useless.

*People v. Williams*, 198 Mich. App. 537 (1993).

## Detention During Execution of Search Warrant

A warrant to search for contraband founded on probable cause implicitly carries with it the limited authority to detain the occupants of the premises while a proper search is conducted. This protects both the officers and occupants of the premises as well as facilitates a speedy search that avoids property damage. *Michigan v. Summers*, 452 U.S. 692 (1981).

The detention authorized by *Summers* is limited to the area within which an occupant poses a real threat to the safe and efficient execution of a search warrant. This ensures that the scope of the detention incident to a search is confined to the place specified in the warrant. *Bailey v. United States*, 133 S.Ct. 1031 (2013).

## Detentions Pending the Issuance of a Search Warrant

Officers assisted a woman in keeping the peace as she removed some belongings from her residence. When she came outside after getting her possessions, she told one officer that her husband had marihuana under the couch. The officers made contact with the husband and requested permission to search the residence, but the husband refused. One officer then left to get a search warrant while the other officer waited with the husband. The husband was told that he could not enter the residence without being accompanied by the officer. A warrant was obtained and executed two hours later. Marihuana was located and the husband was charged with possession of marihuana and drug paraphernalia.

The Court upheld the detention as reasonable, stating, "In light of the following circumstances, considered in combination, the Court concludes that the restriction was reasonable, and hence lawful. First, the police had probable cause to believe that [the defendant]'s home contained evidence of a crime and unlawful drugs. Second, they had good reason to fear that, unless restrained, he would destroy the drugs before they could return with a warrant. Third, they made reasonable efforts to reconcile their law enforcement needs with the demands of personal privacy by avoiding a warrantless entry or arrest and preventing [the defendant] only from entering his home unaccompanied. Fourth, they imposed the restraint for a limited period, which was no longer than reasonably necessary for them, acting with diligence, to obtain the warrant." *Illinois v. McArthur*, 531 U.S. 326 (2001).

## Scope of the Search Under a Search Warrant

The scope of the search is defined by the object of the search and the places in which there is probable cause to believe that it may be found. A lawful search of fixed premises generally extends to the entire area in which the object of the search may be found and is not limited by the possibility that separate acts of entry or opening may be required to complete the search. A warrant that authorizes an officer to search a home for illegal weapons also provides authority to open closets, chests, drawers, and containers in which the weapon might be found. *United States v. Ross*, 456 U.S. 798 (1982).

A warrant authorizing the search of the premises authorizes the search of containers within the premises that might contain the items listed in the warrant. *People v. Coleman*, 436 Mich. 124 (1990).

## Search of Persons at Scene

A search warrant authorizing the search of a particular building or premises does not give the officers the right to search all persons who may be found at that location. *People v. Krokker*, 83 Mich. App. 474 (1978).

During the execution of a search warrant, an officer at the back door heard a knock. He opened the door and admitted the person. He was immediately frisked and the officer located a gun. The court held frisks of this type should be allowed because people present during the execution of a search warrant pose a hazard to the officers. *People v. Jackson*, 188 Mich. App. 117 (1990).

A search of purses was permitted where the owners of the purses had a special relationship to the target of the warrant such that the purses could be considered part of the premises, the purses were not about on the persons of the owners nor were they placed where someone might expect to store personal effects. *People v. Stewart*, 166 Mich. App. 263 (1988).

## Taking Private Citizens on Search Warrant Executions

"It violates the Fourth Amendment rights of homeowners to bring members of the media or other third parties into their home during the execution of a warrant when the presence of the third parties in the home was not in aid of the warrant's execution." In this case, the officers brought along the media. The exception to this rule is when the third party is necessary to assist the police in their task (i.e., identify stolen property). *Wilson v. Layne*, 526 U.S. 603 (1999).

## Tabulation and Receipt—MCL 780.655

*(1) When an officer in the execution of a search warrant finds any property or seizes any of the other things for which a search warrant is allowed by this act, the officer, in the presence of the person from whose possession or premises the property or thing was taken, if present, or in the presence of at least 1 other person, shall make a complete and accurate tabulation of the property and things that were seized. The officer taking property or other things under the warrant shall give to the person from whom or from whose premises the property was taken a copy of the warrant and shall give to the person a copy of the tabulation upon completion, or shall leave a copy of the warrant and tabulation at the place from which the property or thing was taken. The officer is not required to give a copy of the affidavit to that person or to leave a copy of the affidavit at the place from which the property or thing was taken.*

*(2) The officer shall file the tabulation promptly with the court or magistrate. The tabulation may be suppressed by order of the court until the final disposition of the case unless otherwise ordered. The property and things that were seized shall be safely kept by the officer so long as necessary for the purpose of being produced or used as evidence in any trial.*

*(3) As soon as practicable, stolen or embezzled property shall be restored to the owner of the property. Other things seized under the warrant shall be disposed of under direction of the court or magistrate, except that money and other useful property shall be turned over to the state, county or municipality, the officers of which seized the property under the warrant. Money turned over to the state, county, or municipality shall be credited to the general fund of the state, county, or municipality.*

The **tabulation** is a list of the items seized during the execution of a search warrant.

The tabulation should be completed in the presence of the owner or occupant. If the owner or occupant is not available, the tabulation must be taken in the presence of another person. The tabulation may be suppressed on order of the court.

All evidence seized from the premises must be listed on the tabulation, including evidence seized in plain view or not listed on the warrant. *People v. Secrest*, 413 Mich. 521 (1982), *disapproved of* by *People v. Nash*, 418 Mich. 196 (1983).

According to MCL 780.655, property seized during the execution of a search warrant must be tabulated in front of the person from whose possession or premises the property or thing was taken, if present, or in the presence of at least one other person. In applying the literal meaning to the facts of this case the court held that all money seized during the execution of a search warrant must be counted and tabulated before the officer leaves the scene and in front of the owner or another person. In addition, the court held that the money may not be deposited, but must be kept separate so that the defendants have an opportunity to do an independent analysis. *In re Forfeiture of $25,505*, 220 Mich. App. 572 (1996).

## Leave Copy of the Warrant, Affidavit, and Tabulation at Location Searched—MCL 780.655(1)

*The officer taking property or other things under the warrant shall give to the person from whom or from whose premises the property was taken a copy of the warrant and shall give to the person a copy of the tabulation upon completion or shall leave a copy of the warrant and tabulation at the place from which the property or thing was taken. The officer is not required to give a copy of the affidavit to that person or to leave a copy of the affidavit at the place from which the property or thing was taken.*

## Suppression of the Affidavit—MCL 780.654(3)

*Upon a showing that it is necessary to protect an ongoing investigation or the privacy or safety of a victim or witness, the magistrate may order that the affidavit be suppressed and not be given to the person whose property was seized or whose premises were searched until that person is charged with a crime or named as a claimant in a civil forfeiture proceeding involving evidence seized as a result of the search.*

## Disclosure of the Affidavit—MCL 780.651(8)

*On the fifty-sixth day following the issuance of a search warrant, the search warrant affidavit contained in any court file or court record retention system is public information unless, before the fifty-sixth day after the search warrant is issued a peace officer or prosecuting attorney obtains a suppression order from a magistrate upon a showing under oath that suppression of the affidavit is necessary to protect an ongoing investigation or the privacy or safety of a victim or witness. The suppression order may be obtained ex parte in the same manner that the search warrant was issued. An initial suppression order issued under this subsection expires on the fifty-sixth day after the order is issued. A second or subsequent suppression order may be obtained in the same manner as the initial suppression order and shall expire on a date specified in the order. This subsection does not affect a person's right to obtain a copy of a search warrant affidavit from the prosecuting attorney or law enforcement agency under the freedom of information act.*

### File Tabulation with the Court—MCL 780.655(2)

After executing a search warrant, officers must file the tabulation of property seized with the issuing court (often called the return). This must be done even if there was no property seized. The tabulation may be suppressed by order of the court until the final disposition of the case unless otherwise ordered. MCL 780.655(2).

### Police Must Safe Keep Property for Trial— MCL 780.655(1)

The property seized shall be safely kept by the officer so long as necessary for the purpose of being produced or used as evidence in trial. MCL 780.655(2).

The defendant's blood was taken via a search warrant. The blood was held for two months and then destroyed accordingly to lab policy. The defendant argued that under MCL 780.655 the officers were required to "safe keep" the evidence until after trial for a test of his own.

The court disagreed. The court held the statute in question protects evidence that will be presented to the jury at trial and the sample of blood will not be used for this purpose. Under this logic, there was no violation of MCL 780.655 or the Michigan or Federal Constitutions. *People v. Jagotka*, 461 Mich. 274 (1999).

### Disposition of Property—MCL 750.655(3)

Property must be properly disposed of once the proceedings are complete. As soon as practicable, stolen or embezzled property shall be restored to the owner of the property.

### Once the Search Is Complete Under a Warrant, Officers Need a Second Warrant to Re-enter

Officers may take as long as "reasonably necessary" to execute the warrant and generally may continue to search the premises described in the warrant until they are satisfied that all available evidence has been located. Once the execution of the warrant is complete, the authority conferred by the warrant terminates. A single warrant might authorize more than one entry into a premise as long as the second entry is a "reasonable continuation" of the original search. *United States v. Keszthelyi*, 308 F.3d 557 (6th Cir. 2002).

### Penalty for Exceeding Authority When Executing a Search Warrant—MCL 780.657

- $1,000 fine.
- One year in jail.

### Penalty for Unlawfully Procuring a Search Warrant—MCL 780.658

- $1,000 fine.
- One year in jail.

# 23

# WARRANTLESS SEARCHES

## SEARCH INCIDENT TO A LAWFUL ARREST

### Elements

1. A lawful, custodial arrest.
2. The search is for weapons and evidence located within reach of the arrestee.
3. The search must occur contemporaneously with the arrest.

Rationales for the search incident arrest exception:

- The need to disarm the suspect in order to take him or her into custody, and
- The need to preserve evidence for later use at trial.

### Arrest in a Home

Officers arrested the defendant at his home based on a warrant. Based upon the lawful arrest, the officers searched the entire three-bedroom house including the attic, garage, and small workshop. The Court held that a warrantless search of the defendant's entire house incident to his arrest was unreasonable. An arresting officer may search the person arrested in order to remove any weapons and to seize evidence on the arrestee's person, an area into which arrestee might reach in order to grab a weapon or evidentiary items. Exceeding the scope of this exemption will result in evidence obtained being excluded. *Chimel v. California*, 395 U.S. 752 (1969).

### Accompanying Arrestees into the Dwelling

Officers went to the defendant's house with an arrest warrant. He answered the door wearing his pajamas. It was suggested that he get dressed. When he approached his dresser to get socks, an officer checked the drawers and found a blackjack. The court held that the search of the drawer and seizure of the blackjack was valid because an officer may search anywhere where an arrestee may reach in order to grab a weapon. The fact that the defendant was not in the area at the time of arrest has no bearing on the fact that he later had access to the area while still under arrest. *People v. Giacalone*, 23 Mich. App. 163 (1970).

### Vehicles

The defendant was arrested for driving while his license was suspended. After he was handcuffed and secured in a patrol car, officers searched the vehicle he had been driving and found cocaine. The Court held that the search violated the Fourth Amendment, which required suppression of the cocaine. Police may search the passenger compartment of a vehicle incident to a recent occupant's arrest only if it is reasonable to believe that the arrestee might access the vehicle at the time of the search or that the vehicle contains evidence of the offense of arrest. Here, the defendant could not access the passenger compartment of his car, thus, neither he nor the contents of his care were a safety risk. Further, a search of the car could not turn up any additional evidence of the defendant driving with a suspended license. The search of the defendant's vehicle violated the Fourth Amendment. *Arizona v. Gant*, 556 U.S. 332 (2009).

The officers in *Gant* were presumably relying on the long-standing rule that allowed officers to search a vehicle without a warrant *every* time an occupant was arrested. With the Court's opinion in *Gant*, that is no longer the rule.

The rule only allows police to conduct a vehicle search incident to the arrest of an occupant when either of two circumstances exists:

1. Officers may search if the arrestee is within "reaching distance of the passenger compartment." When the arrestee has been secured in a patrol car, he or she is not within reach of the vehicle.
2. Officers may search a vehicle incident to arrest if they reasonably believe the vehicle contains evidence of the crime for which the person was arrested. Gant had been arrested for DWLS, and the cocaine was not evidence of DWLS. It appears that the Court would not have suppressed the cocaine had Gant been arrested for a drug crime.

## The Exclusionary Rule Is not a Remedy for pre-*Gant* Vehicle Searches That Are now Unreasonable Under *Gant*

When the police conduct a search in objectively reasonable reliance on binding appellate precedent, the exclusionary rule does not apply. *Davis v. United States*, 131 S.Ct. 2419 (2011).

## Suspect Voluntarily Leaving the Vehicle

A police officer observed a vehicle with improper license plates. Before the officer was able to stop the vehicle, the driver parked the car and began to walk away. The officer made contact with the driver and, after patting him down, located drugs on him. The officer then searched the vehicle the driver left and found a firearm.

The Court held that once a police officer makes a lawful custodial arrest of an automobile's occupant, the officer may search the vehicle's passenger compartment as a contemporaneous incident of arrest, even when an officer does not make contact until the person arrested has already left the vehicle. An arrestee is no less likely to attempt to lunge for a weapon or to destroy evidence if he is outside of, but still in control of, the vehicle. *Thornton v. United States*, 541 U.S. 615 (2004).

Note: The authority to search in these instances is limited by the Court's holding in *Gant*. Therefore, officers may only search in this instance if the arrestee is within reaching distance of the passenger compartment, or the officer reasonably believes the vehicle contains evidence of the crime for which the person was arrested.

## Cell Phones

The United States Supreme Court considered two cases which raised a common question: Whether the police may, without a warrant, search digital information on a cell phone from an individual who has been arrested. In the first case, the defendant was arrested for carrying a concealed firearm. During a search incident to arrest, the defendant's cell phone, a "smart phone," was seized and searched by the officers incident to arrest. Officers found evidence of gang involvement and photographs that tied the defendant to an earlier shooting. The defendant was charged in connection with the earlier shooting. In the second unrelated case, a different defendant was arrested after police witnessed him engaged in an apparent drug deal. At the police station, officers seized two cell phones from the defendant, one of which was a "flip phone." This phone was repeatedly receiving calls. Officers opened the phone and, by pressing two buttons, accessed the phone's call log and obtained the phone number associated with the "my house" label on the defendant's cell phone. Officers used this information to assist in determining where the defendant lived. Officers responded to the defendant's apartment, gathered additional information, and obtained a search warrant for the apartment. The defendant was charged with drug and weapon violations.

The Court held that police officers are generally required to obtain a search warrant before conducting a search of digital information on a cell phone seized incident to arrest. In reaching this holding, the Court examined the traditional justifications for allowing warrantless searches incident to arrest: to remove weapons from the arrestee's person and to prevent concealment or destruction of evidence from the arrestee's person. The Court found these justifications did not apply to a search of the digital information on a cell phone.

The Court stressed that cell phones are different than other physical objects that might be kept on an arrestee's person. The Court noted that a person's entire private life can be reconstructed due to a cell phone's immense capacity to store many different types of highly personal information.

The Court noted that police officers may examine the physical aspects of a cell phone to ensure it will not be used as a weapon (e.g., to determine whether there is a razor blade hidden between the phone and its case), but once the officer has secured the phone and eliminated potential physical threats, the data on the phone cannot endanger anyone. In addressing the prosecution's argument that evidence could be destroyed or hidden by remote wiping or data encryption, the Court noted that the problem did not appear to be prevalent and could be prevented by other means (e.g., turn the phone off, remove the battery, place the phone in an enclosure that isolates the phone from radio waves (e.g., Faraday bags)).

The Court recognized that, even though the search incident to arrest exception does not apply to cell phones, the exigent circumstances exception may apply when the exigencies of the situation make the needs of law enforcement so compelling that a warrantless search is objectively reasonable under the Fourth Amendment (e.g., a child abductor who may have information about the child's location on his cell phone). The Court concluded its opinion with the following: Our answer to the question of what police need to do before searching a cell phone seized incident to arrest is accordingly simple - get a warrant. *Riley v. California*, ___ S.Ct. ___(2014).

## Interim Bond

The defendant was arrested based on a warrant. Before offering him the opportunity to post bond, the officer completed a search and discovered a vial containing a controlled substance in the defendant's trousers. In upholding the search, the court held that the interim bail provisions may not be judicially extended to limit the constitutionally permissible scope of searches incident to arrest. *People v. Chapman*, 425 Mich. 245 (1986).

## Search Subsequent to a Citation

Police officers in Iowa were authorized by statute to search vehicles where a citation was issued in lieu of arrest. The Iowa Supreme Court interpreted this statute to mean that officers had the authority to "conduct a full-blown search of an automobile and driver in those cases where police elect not to make a custodial arrest and instead issue a citation—that is, a search incident to citation." The United States Supreme Court found this practice to violate the Fourth Amendment. Although the Court realized the dangerousness involved in traffic stops, a search incident to citation does not fall under either of the above rationales for search incident to arrest. The Court did suggest that where there is an articulable concern for safety, the officer is justified in performing a *Terry* search. *Knowles v. Iowa*, 525 U.S. 113 (1998).

## Arrestee Swallowing Evidence

During an arrest, officers believed the defendant was attempting to swallow something. He refused to open his mouth and continued to chew. Eventually pressure was applied to his jaws under the cheekbones, and nine tinfoil packets of heroin were seized from his mouth. The court upheld the seizure and stated that the police may use a reasonable method and a reasonable amount of force to prevent the destruction of evidence of a crime. *People v. Holloway*, 416 Mich. 288 (1982).

The court upheld a seizure where the police were acting to save the defendant from harm as well as to obtain evidence of a crime. An officer arrested the defendant after he put a baggie in his mouth. The officers and the defendant went to the police station and officers awaited a warrant to search the defendant's mouth. Before the warrant arrived, the defendant began to act as if he might lose consciousness. The defendant then collapsed, and the officer held that the defendant's nose closed and placed his hand over defendant's mouth, forcing him to spit out the bag. The court noted that police officers were content to wait until a proper warrant was issued and that the plan was aborted only after an apparent life-threatening situation arose. *Wayne County Prosecutor v. Recorder's Court Judge*, 149 Mich. App. 183 (1986).

## An Officer Does Not Violate the Fourth Amendment if He or She Makes a Lawful Arrest of a Person with Probable Cause, Even if the Offense is Minor

An officer arrested a woman for not wearing her seatbelt; a misdemeanor punishable by fine only in the state of Texas. The warrantless arrest of anyone violating these provisions is expressly authorized by Texas law, but the police may issue citations in lieu of arrest. The question presented before the Court was whether the officer violated the woman's Fourth Amendment rights against unreasonable search and seizure. In a 5–4 decision, the Court held that the woman could not sue the officers.

The Court found that the woman's arrest satisfied constitutional requirements. It was undisputed that the officer had probable cause to believe that the woman committed a crime in his presence. Because she admitted that neither she nor her children were wearing seat belts, the officer was authorized, though not required, to make a custodial arrest without balancing costs and benefits or determining whether her arrest was in some sense required or necessary. Whether a search or seizure is "extraordinary" turns, above all else, on the manner in which it is executed. The defendant's arrest and subsequent booking, though surely humiliating, were no more harmful to her interests than a normal, custodial arrest. *Atwater v. City of Lago Vista*, 532 U.S. 318 (2001).

### Probable Cause to Make an Arrest

At 3:16 a.m. a Baltimore County Police officer stopped a car for speeding. There were three occupants in the car. The defendant was the front-seat passenger. The officer asked the driver for his license and registration. When the driver opened the glove compartment to retrieve the vehicle registration, the officer observed a large amount of rolled-up money. A computer check did not reveal any violations, and the officer gave the driver a verbal warning. A second patrol car arrived, and the first officer asked the driver if he had any weapons or narcotics in the vehicle. The driver indicated that he did not, and he consented to a search of the vehicle. The search yielded $763 from the glove compartment and five plastic glassine baggies containing cocaine from behind the back-seat armrest. The officer questioned all three men about the ownership of the drugs and money and told them that if no one admitted to ownership of the drugs he was going to arrest them all. The men offered no information regarding the ownership of the drugs or money. All three were placed under arrest and transported to the police station. The defendant admitted to owning the drugs while at the station.

The officer, upon recovering the suspected cocaine, had probable cause to believe a felony had been committed. To determine whether an officer had probable cause to make an arrest, a court must examine the events leading up to the arrest, and then decide whether these historical facts, viewed from the standpoint of an objectively reasonable police officer, amount to probable cause.

The Court held that it was an entirely reasonable inference from these facts that any or all three of the occupants had knowledge of, and exercised dominion and control over, the cocaine. Thus, a reasonable officer could conclude that there was probable cause to believe the defendant committed the crime of possession of cocaine, either solely or jointly and his arrest was proper. *Maryland v. Pringle*, 540 U.S. 366 (2003).

## PROBABLE CAUSE AND EXIGENT CIRCUMSTANCES

### Elements

1. Probable cause that items sought are in a specific location.
2. Exigent circumstances occur when a delay to get a warrant will result in the loss of evidence.

## Vehicle-Automobile Exception

Exigent circumstances automatically occur with a vehicle owing to its mobility.

Police received reliable information that an individual known as "Bandit" was in front of a certain address and selling drugs from the trunk of his car. The informant stated that he had just purchased drugs from "Bandit" and that "Bandit" informed him that additional drugs were in the car. A detailed description of "Bandit" and the vehicle were also given. Officers responded to the address and observed the vehicle. A few minutes later, a man meeting "Bandit's" description was observed driving the vehicle away. The vehicle was stopped and officers searched the vehicle locating a gun in the glove compartment. The defendant was then arrested and the trunk was searched where officers located a brown bag containing heroin. The vehicle was taken to the station where a more thorough search revealed a red-leather pouch containing $32,000.

The Court upheld the searches. A search of this sort is not unreasonable if based on objective facts that would justify the issuance of a warrant, even though a warrant has not actually been obtained. The search may include closed containers if it is possible that the evidence being searched for could be hidden in those containers. *United States v. Ross*, 456 U.S. 798 (1982).

The police may open and search any container placed or found in an automobile as long as they have the requisite probable cause with regard to the container, even if the probable cause focuses specifically on the container and arises before the container is placed in the automobile. *People v. Bullock*, 440 Mich. 15 (1992).

If a car is readily mobile and probable cause exists to believe it contains contraband, the Fourth Amendment permits police to search the vehicle without more. *Pennsylvania v. Labron*, 518 U.S. 938 (1996).

Two months after officers observed the defendant use his vehicle to deliver cocaine, he was arrested on unrelated charges. At that time, his vehicle was seized under the forfeiture laws of Florida. Officers searched the vehicle, locating additional cocaine.

The Court held that the police are not required to obtain a warrant before seizing an automobile from a public place when the police have probable cause to believe that the vehicle itself is forfeitable contraband. Applying this rule to the case, the Court held that police were not required to obtain a warrant before seizing and searching the vehicle. The Court recognized the need to seize readily movable contraband before it is "spirited away." *Florida v. White*, 526 U.S. 559 (1999).

During a traffic stop, a Wyoming Highway Patrol officer noticed a hypodermic syringe in the driver's shirt pocket. The driver admitted to taking drugs. The officer then searched the vehicle including a purse that belonged to the passenger. Drugs were found inside the purse.

The Court held that with probable cause to search a car, a police officer may inspect passengers' belongings found in the car that are capable of concealing the object of the search, in this case drugs. *Wyoming v. Houghton*, 526 U.S. 295 (1999).

Officers executed a search warrant on a residence and located a large amount of cash and illicit drugs. The owner of the residence attempted to flee. After searching the residence, the officers also searched the defendant's vehicle, which was located outside the residence (the vehicle was not listed in the warrant). The defendant argued that the search of his vehicle was illegal because it was not listed on the warrant, and the officers had no other reason to search it.

The court disagreed and examined the issue under the totality of the circumstances. The court found that the defendant's presence in a drug house with a large amount of cash was sufficient for concluding that the defendant was a drug dealer and that there was a fair probability that their search of his vehicle would locate more contraband. The court found that the police had probable cause, plus exigent circumstances to search the defendant's vehicle. *People v. Garvin*, 235 Mich. App. 90 (1999).

An anonymous tip may lead to probable cause if the information is corroborated by independent sources.

An undercover officer received information from an informant that a drug transaction was going to occur at a specific residence. This information was relayed to another officer who began surveillance 45 minutes later. The officer verified the residence and the names of the two people that were supposed to be there. The officer was also familiar with the subject from previous dealings. The officer watched three vehicles arrive and three vehicles leave within a 20-minute period. She then observed a man leave with dark clothing carrying a black bag, which he placed into the trunk of a car. A marked unit then stopped the vehicle and searched the trunk. Marihuana was located inside the bag.

In looking at the officer's training and experience, the court held that there was sufficient probable cause to justify the search. The information provided by the undercover police officer was sufficiently corroborated and supplemented by the officer's own investigation and observations to warrant a finding of probable cause. *People v. Levine*, 461 Mich. 172 (1999).

## Vehicle Destroyed by Fire Is Still Readily Mobile

At approximately 4:00 a.m., a fire department extinguished an automobile fire. After examining the car, they determined that the fire had started in the engine compartment, and since they were unable to find any accidental cause of the fire, it was reported that the fire was of "suspicious" origin. At approximately 8:00 p.m. on the same date, an expert arson investigator went to investigate the defendant's burned car, which was still parked on the street. Without a search warrant, the arson investigator searched the vehicle and discovered evidence of arson. The defendant was subsequently charged. The lower courts dismissed the charges on the grounds that since the vehicle was not mobile, the automobile exception no longer was applicable.

The Court of Appeals disagreed with the premise that the defendant's vehicle was immobile. Although the motor of the automobile was inoperable after the fire, the vehicle was capable of mobility. During the time interval between the first and second search, the defendant could have moved the automobile by summoning a tow truck. The defendant's automobile could have been hauled to any location while the police were preoccupied in court seeking a search warrant. *People v. Carter*, 250 Mich. App. 510 (2002).

## Search at Police Station

If police have probable cause that evidence will be found in an automobile, the automobile can be taken to a station house and searched without a warrant. *Chambers v. Maroney*, 399 U.S. 42 (1970).

Where there is probable cause, the officers may conduct a search of a vehicle without a warrant even after it has been impounded and is in police custody. *People v. Wade*, 157 Mich. App. 481 (1987).

The defendant was arrested for a sexual battery. Police searched his vehicle at the time of his arrest and it was impounded. Eight hours later, a detective returned to the impound lot and searched the vehicle again. The detective had not obtained a search warrant. Additional evidence was seized.

The Court upheld the search because the vehicle was still readily mobile even though it was parked in an impound lot and the officer had probable cause to believe the vehicle contained evidence of the crime. *Florida v. Meyers*, 466 U.S. 380 (1984).

## Motor Homes

The police had information that the defendant was exchanging marihuana for various sex acts from his motor home, parked in a parking lot. At the time, the defendant was using the motor home as his residence. An officer went to the motor home, entered it, and observed marihuana. The Court held that since a motor home is readily mobile, exigent circumstances exist. So long as probable cause also exists, officers do not need a warrant. *California v. Carney*, 471 U.S. 386 (1985).

## Residence

It is more difficult to establish exigent circumstances in a residence. The court developed a two-part test:

1. Is there probable cause?
2. For immediate entry, officers must show the existence of actual emergency and articulate specific and objective facts that reveal a necessity for immediate action.

*More than a mere possibility of destruction or removal of evidence is necessary.*

The threshold question is whether the police can produce specific facts supporting a reasonable and objective belief that there is imminent risk of the removal or destruction of evidence.

If an officer enters a home without a warrant under probable cause and exigent circumstances, the courts prefer the residence be secured to prevent the removal or destruction of evidence rather than a full warrantless search. Officers should then obtain a search warrant before searching the property. *People v. Blasius*, 435 Mich. 573 (1990).

An officer responded to a shooting at a hotel. Upon arrival, he located a victim in the parking lot who was still responsive. The officer asked the victim who shot him, and the victim provided the name "Eric." When asked for a last name, the victim gave no reply. The officer asked where Eric lived, and the victim responded "here" and nodded toward the hotel. The officer also observed a white van with its doors open and located the body of a female who apparently died from a gunshot wound inside. The officer recovered a spent red 12-gauge shotgun shell near the driver's side front tire. The officer then went to the hotel's office and determined that "Eric Snider," in room 412, was the only Eric registered. He went back to the victim who was being loaded in the ambulance and asked if Eric Snider was the one who had shot him, and the victim stated "yes." The officer then obtained a room key and entered room 412. No one was present, but he did observe a red 12-gauge shotgun shell that was similar to the one found near the van. The room was secured and a search warrant was obtained. The warrant was executed and officers recovered the shell, as well as defendant's identification. Officers then left the scene and informed the night clerk to call if the defendant returned. At approximately 4:00 a.m., the clerk called and advised the defendant had returned. The officers obtained the key and, after knocking and getting no response, they entered and found the defendant sitting on the bed holding a shotgun. He was then arrested.

The court upheld all three of the entries as reasonable under the Fourth Amendment. The initial warrantless entry into room 412 was justified under the exigent circumstances exception to the warrant requirement. The officer had probable cause to believe that a crime had just been committed and justification for a search of the room to prevent the destruction of any evidence, to protect the police or others, and to prevent the defendant's escape or to determine if he were wounded. The second entry based on the search warrant was also valid.

The final entry without a warrant was also valid. The court held that the police were justified in concluding that the defendant's armed presence in the hotel endangered the lives of the other guests. Further, the police were justified in concluding that any delay in arresting the defendant while obtaining an arrest warrant would be unreasonable in light of the danger that the defendant posed to the other guests. Therefore, there were exigent circumstances known to the police that excused them from taking time to obtain an arrest warrant. The police were confronted with what can only be classified as an emergency situation: a murder suspect, whom they had every reason to believe was armed, located in a hotel room under circumstances that very probably might put the lives and safety of the others at risk. *People v. Snider*, 239 Mich. App. 393 (2000).

Police officers set up a controlled buy of crack cocaine outside an apartment complex. After the deal occurred, the officer radioed uniformed officers to move in on the suspect. Just as they entered the breezeway, they heard a door shut and detected a very strong odor of burnt marijuana. At the end of the breezeway, the officers saw two apartments, one on the left and one on the right, and they did not know which apartment the suspect had entered. Because they smelled marijuana smoke emanating from the apartment on the left, they approached the door of that apartment banged on the left apartment door and announced, "This is the police" or "'Police, police, police.'" As soon as the officers started banging on the door, they could hear people inside moving, and it sounded as though things were being moved inside the apartment. These noises led the officers to believe that drug-related evidence was about to be destroyed. At that point, the officers announced that they "were going to make entry inside the apartment." One officer then kicked in the door, and they entered the apartment. They found three people in the front room who were smoking marihuana. The officers performed a protective sweep of the apartment during which they saw marijuana and powder cocaine in plain view. Police eventually entered the apartment on the right. Inside, they found the suspected drug dealer who was the initial target of their investigation.

The United States Supreme Court held that the need "to prevent the imminent destruction of evidence" has long been recognized as a sufficient justification for a warrantless search and concluded that the exigent circumstances rule applies when the police do not gain entry to premises by means of an actual or threatened violation of the Fourth Amendment. This holding provides ample protection for the privacy rights that the Amendment protects. When law enforcement officers who are not armed with a warrant knock on a door, they do no more than any private citizen might do. And whether the person who knocks on the door and requests the opportunity to speak is a police officer or a private citizen, the occupant has no obligation to open the door or to speak. Occupants who choose not to stand on their constitutional rights, but instead, elect to attempt to destroy evidence have only themselves to blame for the warrantless exigent-circumstances search that may ensue. "Because the officers in this case did not violate or threaten to violate the Fourth Amendment prior to the exigency, we hold that the exigency justified the warrantless search of the apartment." *Kentucky v. King*, 131 S.Ct.1849 (2011)

# PLAIN VIEW

## Elements

1. Police are lawfully in an area protected by the Fourth Amendment.
2. While in the protected area, they locate items that they have probable cause to believe are contraband or evidence.
3. The fact that the items may be contraband or evidence must be readily apparent to the officer.

During a traffic stop at night, an officer shined his flashlight into the car and observed a green party balloon, knotted at the tip, fall from the driver's hand. Based on his training and experience, the officer knew that drugs were often carried in similar balloons. The officer then shined his flashlight into the glove compartment that the driver had opened. He noticed small plastic vials, loose powder, and an open bag of party balloons. The officer seized the knotted balloon, which seemed to contain a powdery substance.

The Court held that if a police officer is lawfully performing his or her duties and observes an incriminating object for which he or she has probable cause to believe is contraband, that object may be seized. The seizure of property in plain view is not an invasion of privacy and was presumptively reasonable, assuming that there was probable cause to associate the property with criminal activity. In this case, the arresting officer had lawfully viewed the green balloon in connection with a lawful encounter by the officer. The officer also had probable cause to believe that the balloon was subject to seizure; therefore, the seizure was proper. The level needed to seize the item is merely probable cause, the officer need not be certain that the item is contraband. *Texas v. Brown*, 460 U.S. 730 (1983).

The defendant was stopped for a traffic violation. The officer observed several partially smoked marihuana cigarettes in the ashtray. The officer seized the evidence. The court held that police have a right to look inside a properly stopped vehicle and to seize any evidence inside the vehicle that is in plain view. *People v. Julkowski*, 124 Mich. App. 379 (1983).

Officers stopped a car for speeding. Bending down in order to speak with the driver, one of the officers noticed "an alligator clip with a roach attached to it" between the two sun visors. He asked the defendant to get out of the car, confiscated the item, and placed defendant under arrest for possession of marihuana. The officer on the passenger side testified that she also noticed the metal clip above the rearview mirror. She testified that she was not absolutely certain what the cigarette was, but told her partner that it was possibly a controlled substance. After escorting the defendant to the police vehicle and seating him in the back seat, the vehicle's passenger compartment was searched and a small black bag on the front passenger seat was located. The bag was opened and the officer located four small glass vials containing a powdery residue later determined to be cocaine.

The court upheld the search as a valid under the plain view exception. The police had probable cause to believe that the item contained marihuana. Therefore, the subsequent search that lead to the discovery of cocaine was justified as a search incident to lawful arrest. *People v. Alfafara*, 140 Mich. App. 551 (1985).

## Plain View Does Not Have to be Inadvertent

The defendant and an accomplice used a stun gun and machine gun to commit an armed robbery. Jewelry and cash were taken. Police obtained a warrant to search for the jewelry at the defendant's residence, knowing that they may also find the weapons used. During the search, the police discovered an Uzi, a .38-caliber revolver, and two stun guns. The Court allowed the weapons into evidence under the plain view exception. The Court held that discovery of evidence does not have to be inadvertent. *Horton v. California*, 496 U.S. 128 (1990).

Officers responded to a report of shots fired at a known drug house. When they knocked on the door, they observed a subject run downstairs with a package they believed from their training and experience to be a kilo of cocaine. The subject came back upstairs and opened the door. The officers entered and went directly downstairs. They were looking for shooting victims, but they were also aware that the defendant had taken a kilo of cocaine downstairs. They found the cocaine and seized it. The court held that the cocaine was found in plain view. *People v. Moore*, 186 Mich. App. 551 (1990).

## Moving Objects Do Not Fall under Plain View

Police officers cannot move objects to develop probable cause under plain view. In this case, the officers moved some stereo components, turning them around, in order to read the serial numbers. The Court held that this was not plain view because the officer had to manipulate the items to determine they were contraband. Because the officer only had reasonable suspicion, the stereo components were stolen before he manipulated them, they fell outside the plain view exception. Although a cursory inspection would have been permitted, manipulation of the object for the purpose of determining its status as contraband goes beyond the permissible bounds of the plain view exception. *Arizona v. Hicks*, 480 U.S. 321 (1987).

## Plain Feel

Officers may seize contraband discovered during a *Terry* stop and frisk based on plain feel if the identity of the object is immediately apparent to the officer and the officer has probable cause to believe the

item is contraband. An object that a police officer detects on a suspect during the course of a pat-down may be seized without a warrant, if the officer's sense of touch makes it readily apparent that the object, though not threatening in nature, is contraband.

An officer may not manipulate the item to determine what it is. The fact that it is contraband must be readily apparent through the mass or counter of the object. It was not plain feel where officer had to roll the object in his fingers before he could determine it was rock cocaine. Once the officer concludes an item felt during a frisk is not a weapon, he cannot manipulate it further without probable cause that the item is contraband or evidence of a crime. *Minnesota v. Dickerson*, 508 U.S. 366 (1993).

During a valid pat-down, an officer felt a pill bottle in the subject's pants. The pill bottle was removed and the officer found cocaine inside. The court upheld the search because the officer had probable cause to believe the pill bottle contained contraband. The probable cause consisted of the following:

- The defendant walked away from the officers as they approached.
- One of the officers knew defendant from previous drug and weapon convictions.
- The officers were in a high drug crime area.
- The defendant had his hands tucked inside the front of his sweat pants and refused to remove his hands after being requested to do so by the officers.
- The officer knew from his experience that controlled substances were often transported in pill bottles.

Based on the totality of the circumstances, officers had probable cause to believe the pill bottle contained contraband, thus, the plain feel exception to the warrant requirement authorized the removal of the pill bottle from the defendant's sweat pants. The opening of the bottle was justified as a search incident to arrest because, based on the suspect's behavior prior to the *Terry* stop and discovery of the pill bottle in the suspect's pants, the officers had probable cause to arrest the defendant. *People v. Champion*, 452 Mich. 92 (1996).

During a valid pat-down, the officer felt what he believed to be blotter acid in the defendant's pocket. He removed it and placed it on the roof of the car before completing the pat-down. He then retrieved the objects, which turned out to be three photographs facing down. He turned the pictures over and observed that they depicted a subject in a house containing large quantities of marihuana. The question presented was whether the officer could lawfully turn the pictures over under the plain feel doctrine.

The court upheld the seizure of the pictures as valid under plain feel. When conducting a *Terry* stop, officers may seize non-contraband objects that they have probable cause to believe feel like contraband. Once the officer lawfully seized the photographs, the cursory examination of the exterior of the object is not a search for Fourth Amendment purposes. "We conclude that the exterior of an item that is validly seized during a patdown search may be examined without a search warrant, even if the officer subsequently learns that the item is not the contraband the officer initially thought that it was before the seizure." *People v. Custer*, 465 Mich. 319 (2001).

### Plain Smell: Odor of Marihuana

During a traffic stop, an officer testified that he detected "'a very strong smell of marijuana emanating from the vehicle' that was 'overpowering.'" The officer further testified that he had previously participated in 15–20 cases involving marihuana. The driver denied having any marihuana, and the officer then searched the car, locating a brick of marihuana in the trunk. The officer testified that the only basis for searching the trunk was the odor of marihuana.

The court upheld the search. "[T]he smell of marijuana alone by a person qualified to know the odor may establish probable cause to search a motor vehicle, pursuant to the motor vehicle exception to the warrant requirement." *People v. Kazmierczak*, 461 Mich. 411 (2000).

# CONSENT

Key: Voluntarily Given by a Proper Party
Test: Totality of the Circumstances

Police may conduct a search without a warrant or probable cause if they receive consent from the subject of the search to do so. The only requirement is that consent must be voluntarily made without threat or compulsion. Voluntariness is based on the totality of the circumstances. There is no requirement to inform the subject of their right to refuse. *Schneckloth v. Bustamonte*, 412 U.S. 218 (1973).

The Fourth Amendment does not require that a lawfully seized defendant be advised that he is "free to go" before his consent to search will be recognized as voluntary. The Amendment's touchstone is reasonableness, which is measured in objective terms by examining the totality of the circumstances.

The defendant was stopped for speeding. He was given a verbal warning after the officer checked his license and found no previous violations. The officer returned his driver's license to him and asked "Are you carrying any illegal contraband in your car? Any weapons of any kind, drugs, anything like that?" The defendant answered no, and the officer asked for consent to search the car. The defendant agreed and the officer found drugs. The Court held that the police are not required to tell suspects that they are "legally free to go" before asking for consent to search. *Ohio v. Robinette*, 519 U.S. 33 (1996).

Plainclothes officers boarded a bus looking for drug couriers. Officers gave the passengers no reason to believe that they were required to answer questions or that they were not free to leave. The officers did not brandish weapons or make any intimidating movements; they left the aisle free so that passengers could exit, and spoke to them one by one in a polite, quiet voice. An officer asked the defendants if they objected to a search. Even after arresting one defendant, the officer addressed the second defendant politely and gave no indication that he was required to answer questions or consent to a search. Although the officer did not inform the defendants of their right to refuse the search, he did request permission to search. The totality of the circumstances indicated that the consent was voluntary.

Officers need not always inform citizens of their right to refuse when seeking permission to conduct a warrantless consent search. Instead, the totality of the circumstances control, without giving extra weight to whether this type of warning was given. *United States v. Drayton*, 536 U.S. 194 (2002).

## Scope of Search

The scope of a search under a consent search turns on whether it is objectively reasonable for the officer to believe that the scope of the consent permits the officer to open a particular closed container.

The defendants were suspected of selling drugs from their car. They were stopped for not using a turn signal, and the officers asked for consent to search the car for drugs. The driver gave consent, and, during the search, the officer opened up a rolled paper bag, which was on the floor, and located a kilo of cocaine. The Court held that, because the officers asked to search the car for drugs and the defendants placed no restrictions on the search, the officers were allowed to open the bag as it was within the scope of the consented search. *Florida v. Jimeno*, 500 U.S. 248 (1991).

Troopers arrested the defendant for a sex offender registration violation. The troopers obtained a signed consent form that authorized a complete search of his vehicle and any containers therein. The defendant unlocked the vehicle and allowed the troopers access. A laptop computer was located and a cursory search of the computer files revealed child pornography. The computer was secured and a search warrant was obtained. The defendant argued that he did not give consent to search the computer. The court held that the scope of consent to search given by the defendant authorized the search of the computer. The word "complete" included the files. In addition, the defendant did not restrict the search when the computer was seized. *People v. Dagwan*, 269 Mich. App. 338 (2005).

An officer stopped a vehicle and obtained consent from the driver to search the vehicle. The officer did not ask the other occupants for consent, and during the search found marihuana in a backpack belonging to a passenger. The passenger who owned the backpack did not object, nor did she make any attempt to remove the bag from the car when she exited prior to the search. The court held that when police have authority to search the entire passenger compartment of a vehicle, that authority extends to any unlocked containers within the vehicle. *People v. Labelle*, 478 Mich. 891 (2007).

## Consent Can be Limited and Revoked

A suspect can revoke his or her consent to a search at any time. Similarly, a suspect can limit the scope of a search at the beginning. If a person revokes consent given to a search, he or she can halt further police activity that relies on the consent.

An officer asked the defendant if he was carrying any guns, knives, or drugs. When the defendant said no, the officer asked if he could check. The defendant agreed, but when the officer felt small bulges in his pocket and felt plastic baggies, the defendant stepped back and told the officer, "No, you need a warrant for that." The officer nonetheless went into the pocket and retrieved the bag, which contained drugs. The court held that the seizure of the drugs was improper because the defendant limited the search and revoked consent. *People v. Powell*, 199 Mich. App. 492 (1993).

## Consent-Once-Removed Doctrine

The consent-once-removed doctrine applies to the warrantless entry into a residence by backup officers summoned to assist an undercover officer with making an arrest when the undercover officer's initial entry into the residence was based on consent of someone with authority to consent. The doctrine is based on the theory that, because an undercover officer who establishes probable cause to arrest the suspect may in fact arrest the suspect then and there, the undercover officer should be entitled to call in the officer(s) with whom he is working to assist in the arrest.

The plaintiff brought a § 1983 action against Louisville police officers alleging illegal search and seizure following the entry into their home and seizure of their nine dogs. The plaintiffs granted two undercover officers permission to enter the home, ostensibly to view and purchase puppies. The undercover officers spoke with the plaintiff and then left the residence. The undercover officers returned momentarily with several uniformed officers. The uniformed officers knocked, demanded proof of a breeder's license, and entered over the plaintiff's objections and without a warrant or consent. Inside the residence, the officers seized property, but never arrested or intended to arrest anyone.

The consent-once-removed doctrine allows officers to enter a suspect's residence to arrest the suspect without a warrant if: undercover officers entered at the express invitation of someone with authority to consent, at that point the undercover officers established the existence of probable cause to effectuate an arrest or search, and the undercover officers immediately summoned help from other officers. The intent of the entry by the backup officers must be to immediately effectuate an arrest.

The court refused to extend the consent-once-removed doctrine to this case because the undercover officers had left the residence and the backup officers did not rush in to effectuate an arrest nor did they intend to make an arrest inside the residence. One consensual entry does not justify entry at will by law enforcement. *O'Neill v. Louisville/Jefferson Cnty. Metro Gov't*, 662 F.3d 723 (6th Cir. 2011)

## Joint Access or Control

One who possesses authority over premises or effects with one or more other persons has common authority to give consent. A property interest in a premises is not necessarily enough to give consent to search. There must be a showing of mutual use of the property by persons generally having joint access or control so that each person has a right to permit inspection in his or her own right. *United States v. Matlock*, 415 U.S. 164 (1974).

Officers suspected that a husband had killed his girlfriend. They learned that he had written a check to purchase explosives, which were ultimately used to kill his girlfriend. They went to his house and asked his wife for permission to search the house, including the checkbook that they both jointly used. Evidence was located in the checkbook to authorize charges. The court upheld the search because the consent given by the wife included areas that were jointly occupied and used. The area of the search was commonly used between the husband and wife and was not under the exclusive control of the husband. *People v. Chism*, 390 Mich. 104 (1973).

## Joint Access or Control: Disputed Consent

Officers obtained consent to search a home from one spouse, but were denied consent from the other spouse, who was also present. They found drugs which they sought to use

against the refusing spouse. The Court held that a "disputed invitation" cannot overcome the protections guaranteed by the Fourth Amendment. As a result, evidence gathered against a refusing party cannot be used against them. *Georgia v. Randolph*, 547 U.S. 103 (2006).

Officers were investigating arson. They went to the defendant's house and arrested him after he invoked his *Miranda* rights. He was then placed in a patrol car. An officer then asked the defendant's roommate if the officer could enter the residence and use their phone. The roommate agreed, and when the officer entered, he saw evidence of the arson. The defendant claimed that by invoking *Miranda* he had effectively denied consent to search.

The court held that mere invocation of rights does not constitute express objection to entry. The court further noted that police are never under an obligation to seek out an absent tenant to gain approval of consent given by another. However, police may never remove a suspect for the purpose of preventing him from having an opportunity to object. *People v. Lapworth*, 273 Mich. App. 424 (2006).

A person's express refusal to a search is only valid when the person is present at the place to be searched and objecting. Police officers cannot remove a person who may or does refuse a consent to search simply to overcome his express refusal. The removal must be objectively reasonable under the circumstances. If a person is present, objects to the search, but is then lawfully removed from the scene, a person with common authority, such as a roommate or co-owner, can give the officers valid consent to search. A person's objection does not remain in place after his lawful arrest. *Fernandez v. California*, 134 S.Ct. 1126 (2014).

## Parental Consent

Officers were looking for a runaway when they went to the defendant's house. The defendant's mother allowed the officers to search the house for the runaway, including the defendant's bedroom. In the bedroom, they seized a pan on the floor containing four sandwich bags of marihuana. The district court dismissed the charges on the basis that the mother did not have the authority to consent to the search of the defendant's room. That court based its decision on a sign that read

"Keep Out" and that the door was closed and the defendant did not allow anyone into the room.

The Court of Appeals reversed. There was sufficient evidence presented to the officers that the mother had common authority over the bedroom. She had "ready access" to clean his room and gather his laundry. The sign by itself would not stop the consent because kids routinely put similar signs on their doors, nor were there any indications that defendant had exclusive control over the room, such as locks where the parents had no keys. Even if the mother did not have actual authority to search, she had apparent authority to allow the search by the officers. *People v. Goforth*, 222 Mich. App. 306 (1997).

## Apparent Authority

A woman claimed her boyfriend assaulted her. She had a key to the apartment, and she referred to the residence as "our place." She opened the door and officers found cocaine in plain view on a table. The trial court held that the woman did not live there and, therefore, could not have given consent. The Court held that the entry was valid because the officers at the time of the entry reasonably believed that the person who allowed them entry had common authority over the premises. *Illinois v. Rodriguez*, 497 U.S. 177 (1990).

Police were asked to do periodic checks on a residence because the former owner had died. Over an eight-month period, the officers made 33 checks. Unbeknownst to the officers, the house was sold. One day, an officer found a strange car in the garage. A LEIN check revealed that the car was stolen. The court upheld the search because consent had been given and the officers had no reason to know that the consent was no longer valid. *People v. Grady*, 193 Mich. App. 721 (1992).

## Requesting an Attorney Under *Miranda* Does Not Invoke the Fourth Amendment for Purposes of Consent

The defendant was a suspect in the murder of a DNR officer. After being questioned for a while, the defendant stated, "I'm no match for you. I want to talk to an attorney." The officers then asked him for consent to search his home. He agreed and signed the waivers. He argued on appeal that the officers violated his Fifth and Sixth Amendment rights and that the evidence seized during the search should be suppressed.

The court held that the defendant was not in custody because he voluntarily came down to the station and was free to leave at any time. In addition, the Fifth Amendment covers only testimonial evidence, but evidence seized during the search was tangible, physical evidence. The court then found that the defendant's Fourth Amendment rights were not violated when police asked the defendant to sign a consent form after he asked for an attorney. The defendant's consent to the search was freely and voluntarily given. *People v. Marsack*, 231 Mich. App. 364 (1998).

## Use of a Fake Warrant May Invalidate Consent

Officers went to the defendant's house. When he opened the door, one of the detectives opened up a leather folder to get a business card. A form bearing the label of a search warrant was inside the folder. The officers then asked to come in and, as he stepped back, the officers entered. He was then asked if there were any drugs in the house. The defendant went to a freezer and got a bag of marihuana, which he gave to the officers.

The defendant testified that there was a warrant and that he could not refuse them the opportunity to search. Based on the testimony of the defendant and the officers, the court held that the consent was invalid, because it was not freely, voluntarily, or intelligently given. *People v. Farrow*, 461 Mich. 202 (1999).

## "Knock and Talk" Is a Valid Procedure if Done Properly

Officers received information that the defendant may have controlled substances on his property. Since there was not sufficient evidence to obtain a search warrant, the officers decided to do a "knock and talk." That is, going to the suspect house, engaging in conversation, and attempting to gain consent to search.

The court held in the context of a "knock and talk" the mere fact that the officers initiated contact with a citizen does not implicate constitutional protections. It is unreasonable to think that simply because one is at home that he or she is free from having the police come to his or her house and initiate a conversation. The fact that the police's motive for the contact is an attempt to secure permission to conduct a search does not change that reasoning. The police may still obtain consent to search, so long as it is freely, voluntarily, and intelligently given.

A "knock and talk" may, however, run afoul of constitutional protections against unreasonable search and seizure. Any time the police initiate a procedure, whether by search warrant or otherwise, the particular circumstances surrounding the incident are subject to judicial review to ensure compliance with general constitutional protections. Therefore, what happens within the context of a "knock and talk" and any resulting search is certainly subject to judicial review. For example, a person's Fourth Amendment right to be free of unreasonable searches and seizures may be implicated where a person does not feel free to leave or where consent to search is coerced. *People v. Frohriep*, 247 Mich. App. 692 (2001).

Officers received an anonymous tip that the defendant was growing marihuana. During a helicopter fly-over, they observed pots and potting materials in the backyard of the house. This information was relayed to a ground crew, which went to the residence. The first officer to arrive proceeded around the side of the house into the one word backyard, where he observed marihuana plants growing in a lean-to attached to the back of the house. The officer then saw the defendant at the rear of the property entering the lean-to. When he refused to obey the officer's commands to stop, he was placed in handcuffs. Officers then went to the front of the house and knocked on the front door. The defendant's wife answered and officers did a protective sweep of the house and then took the defendant's wife to a patrol car to be questioned. The wife eventually signed a consent form and 122 marihuana plants were seized.

The court suppressed the evidence, holding that this was not a valid "knock and talk." The officer who discovered the marihuana did not wait for the other officers to conduct the purported "knock and talk," but instead proceeded directly to the back of the defendant's home. The police report stated that according to the anonymous tip, the marihuana was in a six-foot by four-foot container right behind the defendant's house. The officer saw the marihuana plants inside the lean-to in a large container. At that point, the defendant was coming out of the woods at the back of the property. The police did not first approach the front door of home, they did not proceed along a path that the public could be expected to travel in visiting the defendant's home, nor did they simply approach the defendant as he was standing in his yard to ask permission to "look around." Only after the marihuana was discovered did the officers go to the door of the home and knock, at which point the defendant's wife answered the door. The court held that "[s]uch intrusions cannot be sanctioned under the guise of knock and talk and 'ordinary citizen contact.'" *People v. Galloway*, 259 Mich. App. 634 (2003).

After receiving a tip that the defendant was storing marihuana, officers went to his residence to conduct a "knock and talk." The defendant admitted them into his residence. The police informed the defendant that they were police officers and that they had received a tip that marihuana was stored at the site. Although the defendant did not deny that there was any marihuana, he denied the officer's request to search. Further, the defendant asked the officers to leave. However, officers did not leave and began to question him further and subsequently narcotics and money were seized.

The court held that, although police are free to employ the knock and talk procedure, they have no right to remain in a home without consent, absent some other legal justification. A person is seized for purposes of the Fourth Amendment when the police fail to promptly leave the person's home following the request that they do so, absent a legal basis for the police to remain independent of the person's consent. Therefore, the evidence was suppressed. *People v. Bolduc*, 263 Mich. App. 430 (2004).

# *TERRY* ENCOUNTERS

## Stop and Frisk

Reasonable suspicion to believe a crime is afoot and that a person is involved allows police to **stop** that person.

Reasonable suspicion to believe person is armed allows police to conduct a pat-down or **frisk** of that person to ensure the safety of the officer, subject, and third parties during the encounter.

Investigative detention must be temporary and last no longer than is necessary to effectuate purpose of stop, and similarly, investigative methods employed should be the least intrusive means reasonably available to verify or dispel officer's suspicion in short period of time. *Florida v. Royer*, 460 U.S. 491 (1983).

An officer with 39 years on the force observed three subjects he thought were "casing" a store for a robbery. The suspects would walk by the store, look in, and then pass by. When the officer stopped them, he was concerned that they may have weapons. He then patted down the outer surface of the defendant's clothing and felt a pistol.

The Court held that the search was valid. A police officer who has reason to believe that he is dealing with an armed and dangerous individual may make a reasonable search for weapons, even though he is not absolutely certain that individual is armed. Reasonableness of the action depends not on his subjective and unparticularized suspicion or hunch but on specific reasonable inferences which he is entitled to draw from facts in light of his experience. *Terry v. Ohio*, 392 U.S. 1 (1968).

The police picked up a murder suspect from a neighbor's home. He was not told that he was under arrest. He was taken to the police station, *Mirandized*, then, after being interrogated for an hour, he confessed. The State conceded that the police lacked probable cause when they picked up the suspect, but sought to justify the warrantless detention and interrogation as an investigative stop. The Court rejected this argument, concluding that the defendant's detention was less like a *Terry* stop than it was "in important respects indistinguishable from a traditional arrest." Instead, he was taken from a neighbor's home to a police car, transported to a police station, and placed in an interrogation room. He was never informed that he was "free to go;" indeed, he would have been physically restrained if he had refused to accompany the officers or had tried to escape their custody. *Dunaway v. New York*, 442 U.S. 200 (1979).

Officers were patrolling near a high school when they observed three juveniles on a sidewalk in front of the school. As the officers approached, one officer noticed a bulge in the waistband of one of the subjects. The officers patted the defendant down and found a loaded 9 mm pistol. The trial court suppressed the gun, but the

Court of Appeals reversed. The court held that because the defendant was in a public place the officer was justified in approaching him. Because of the officer's observation of a bulge in the defendant's pocket combined and the officer's four and a half years of experience, it was reasonable for him to conclude that the defendant may be armed. This provided the reasonable suspicion to justify a *Terry* stop and frisk. *People v. Taylor*, 214 Mich. App. 167 (1995).

A pat-down search conducted merely as a routine precautionary measure for officer's personal safety is unreasonable under the Fourth Amendment.

A pistol was suppressed when, at the time of the pat-down, the defendant was not under arrest, nor was there probable cause to arrest, and the officer had no articulable suspicion that the defendant was armed. The court held that officers cannot search people as a matter of routine but must be able to articulate facts that lead the officer to suspect the individual is armed. *People v. Parham*, 147 Mich. App. 358 (1985).

## *Terry* Search of an Auto

*Terry* does not restrict the search for weapons to the body of a person suspected of criminal activity. If the officer conducting the stop possesses an articulable and objectively reasonable belief that the suspect is potentially dangerous, then a protective sweep for weapons may include the vehicle. *Michigan v. Long*, 463 U.S. 1032 (1983).

An argument was witnessed by a security guard. One of the men ran up to the guard and stated that the other man had a gun and was going to kill him. The suspect then drove off in a car. Police were called, and as the guard was explaining to the officer what happened, the suspect's car drove by. The officers stopped the car and observed the driver reach over and place something in the glove box. The officers opened the glove box and found a gun. Citing *Long*, the court held that the officers had an articulable and objectively reasonable belief that the defendant was armed and potentially dangerous, thus, the seizure was valid. *People v. Vandiver*, 140 Mich. App. 484 (1985).

## Ordering Occupants from Vehicles

The Fourth Amendment is not violated when officers order occupants from a lawfully stopped vehicle.

## Drivers

During a valid traffic stop, a police officer ordered the driver out of the vehicle. As the driver exited, the officer noticed a large bulge under the driver's coat. The driver was frisked, and a gun was discovered. The Court held that ordering the defendant out of the car was a minimal intrusion and did not violate the Fourth Amendment. Once an officer legitimately stops a vehicle, the officer has the right to order the driver out of the vehicle for any purpose. However, without supporting testimony that the suspect is potentially dangerous and may be armed, the police are prohibited from conducting a pat-down search. *Pennsylvania v. Mimms*, 434 U.S. 106 (1977).

## Passengers

The Court held that danger to an officer from a traffic stop is likely to be greater when there are passengers in addition to the driver in the stopped car. While there is not the same basis for ordering the passengers out of the vehicle as there is for ordering the driver out, the additional intrusion on the passenger is minimal. Therefore, an officer making a traffic stop may order passengers to get out of the car pending completion of the stop. *Maryland v. Wilson*, 519 U.S. 408 (1997).

## Police May "Stop and Frisk" a Passenger in a Motor Vehicle on a Traffic Stop

Officers from Arizona's gang task force were on patrol in Tucson near a neighborhood associated with the Crips gang. They stopped a vehicle for a civil infraction that contained three occupants. In making the stop, officers had no reason to suspect anyone of criminal activity. The defendant was the rear seat passenger. The officer who attended to the defendant noticed that he looked back and always kept his eyes on the officers. The officer further noticed that the defendant was wearing clothing that she considered consistent with Crips membership. The

officer also noticed that the defendant had a scanner in his back pocket, which caused her concern because "most people would not carry around a scanner unless they are involved in criminal activity." The defendant informed the officer that he had served time in prison for burglary. The defendant was asked to get out of the car and he complied. Based upon the officer's observations and the defendant's statements, the officer suspected that the defendant might have weapon on his person. Therefore, when the defendant exited the vehicle she conducted a pat-down for her safety. During the pat-down, she felt the butt of gun near the defendant's waist. The defendant was charged with possession of a weapon by a prohibited possessor.

The Court upheld "stop and frisk" as permissible if two conditions are met. First, the stop must be lawful. Second, to proceed from a stop to a frisk, the officer must reasonably suspect that the person stopped is armed and dangerous. In *Brendlin v. California*, 551 U.S. 249 (2007), the Court confirmed that a police officer effectively seizes "everyone in the vehicle" when conducting a traffic stop.

Accordingly, the Court held that, in a traffic-stop setting, the first *Terry* condition—a lawful investigatory stop is met whenever it is lawful for police to detain an automobile and its occupants pending inquiry into a vehicular violation. The police need not have cause to believe any occupant of the vehicle is involved in criminal activity. To justify a pat-down of the driver or passenger during a traffic stop, the must harbor reasonable suspicion that the person subjected to the frisk is armed and dangerous, just as in the case of a pedestrian suspected of criminal activity. *Arizona v. Johnson*, 555 U.S. 323 (2009).

## *Terry* Stops: Reasonable Suspicion

Officers can make a stop based on reasonable suspicion that a crime may be occurring. The stop must be no longer than is necessary to extinguish their suspicions or build up to probable cause.

## Reasonable Suspicion Is not Needed if the Contact Is Voluntary

At 1:40 a.m., an officer observed a vehicle with Arkansas plates parked in a private driveway. The vehicle was running and its parking lights were on. The officer approached and observed the defendant sleeping in the driver's seat with a pillow over his head. The officer testified that he tapped on the window to make sure the driver was okay. When the driver woke up, the officer asked if he lived at the residence and he said no. The officer then asked for identification. As the driver exited the vehicle, the officer could see the grips of a handgun between the passenger seat and the center console.

The district court and circuit court dismissed the charges on the grounds that the officer did not have reasonable suspicion that criminal activity was afoot to justify the request for identification. The Court of Appeals reinstated the charges.

While the Michigan Supreme Court in *People v. Freeman*, 413 Mich. 492 (1982), suppressed evidence located when officers approached a parked car, ordered the occupant to exit, and produce identification because there was no reasonable suspicion for the detention, the Court of Appeals distinguished this case because here the officer "asked" for ID. Unlike the officer in *Freeman*, the arresting officer here did not order the defendant from his car. There was nothing on the record to suggest that intimidating circumstances compelled defendant to cooperate. The record showed that the officer "merely made a voluntary request to defendant to produce identification." The court held that no suspicion was required for this contact. *People v. Shankle*, 227 Mich. App. 690 (1998).

Officers were dispatched to a housing complex, which was known to the police as a high crime and drug area, in response to a loud gathering. Upon their arrival, they found a group of 15–20 people drinking and talking loudly. The defendant was seated on stairs leading to one of the housing units. An officer approached the defendant and the two engaged in a general conversation about the party. At that point, a woman emerged from the attached housing unit and, using profane language, asked the defendant who he was and why he was seated on her porch. After hearing this, the officer asked the defendant if he lived in the housing complex. The defendant said that he did not and the officer asked to see his identification.

When the defendant handed over his state identification card, the officer used his radio and started to run the subject via LEIN. The

defendant's behavior immediately changed. He became obviously nervous and made furtive gestures toward a large pocket on the side of his pants. He began to walk away, despite the fact that the officer still held his identification card and was speaking to him. At that point, the officer and his partner walked alongside the defendant, encouraging him to wait for the results of the LEIN inquiry. When the defendant did not stop, one officer placed a hand on the defendant's back and told him that he was not free to leave. The LEIN inquiry revealed an outstanding warrant for the defendant's arrest. As the officer was placing defendant in handcuffs, a gun fell from the defendant's waistband to the ground. The defendant argued that he had been stopped without any reasonable suspicion and that the gun should be suppressed.

The court held that the officer's initial encounter with defendant was consensual. The officer did not seize the defendant when he asked whether the defendant lived in the housing complex, nor did he seize the defendant when he asked for identification. The Fourth Amendment was not implicated until the officer actually hindered the defendant's attempt to leave the scene, thereby seizing him within the meaning of the Fourth Amendment. Specifically, this seizure occurred when the officer followed the defendant as he tried to walk away, orally discouraged him from leaving, and, finally, put a hand on his back and told him to wait for the results of the LEIN inquiry. At this point, when the officer physically hindered defendant's departure and instructed him to stay in the officer's presence, is when a reasonable person might have concluded that he was not free to leave. By this point, however, the officer had a reasonable suspicion to make an investigatory stop. *People v. Jenkins*, 472 Mich. 26 (2005).

## The Smell of Intoxicants by Themselves May Provide the Basis for an Investigatory Detention

During a traffic stop for a broken taillight, the officer detected a strong odor of intoxicants on the driver's breath. Based solely on the odor, the officer requested the driver to exit and perform sobriety tests. The driver was ultimately arrested. The court upheld the arrest. The court held that the presence of an odor of intoxicants may give rise to a reasonable suspicion that the motorist has recently consumed alcoholic liquor, which may have affected his or her ability to operate a motor vehicle. *People v. Rizzo*, 243 Mich. App. 151 (2000).

## Drug Checkpoints Are Unconstitutional

Indianapolis set up vehicle checkpoints on its roads in an effort to interdict unlawful drugs. The vehicles were systematically stopped and a drug dog would walk around them while an officer would ask the occupants a few questions.

The Court held that this practice violated the Fourth Amendment. The primary purpose of the Indianapolis narcotics checkpoints was to advance the general interest in crime control. The Court declined to suspend the usual requirement of individualized suspicion where the police seek to employ a checkpoint primarily for the ordinary enterprise of investigating crimes. Stops justified only by the generalized and ever-present possibility that interrogation and inspection may reveal that any given motorist has committed some crime are not permitted. *City of Indianapolis v. Edmond*, 531 U.S. 32 (2000).

## Informational Checkpoints May Be Constitutional

Police set up a highway checkpoint to obtain information from motorists about a hit-and-run accident occurring about one week earlier at the same location and time of night. Officers stopped each vehicle for 10–15 seconds, asked the occupants whether they had seen anything happen there the previous weekend, and handed each driver a flyer describing and requesting information about the accident. As the defendant approached, his minivan swerved, nearly hitting an officer. The driver was ultimately arrested for O.W.I. He argued on appeal that the checkpoint was unconstitutional.

The Court held that the checkpoint stop did not violate the Fourth Amendment. The checkpoint in *Edmond* was designed to ferret out drug crimes committed by the motorists themselves. Here, the stop's primary law enforcement purpose was not to determine whether a vehicle's occupants were committing a crime but to ask the occupants, as members of the public, for help in providing information about a crime in all likelihood committed by others.

Information-seeking highway stops are less likely to provoke anxiety or to prove intrusive, since they are likely brief, the questions asked are not designed to elicit self-incriminating information, and citizens will often react positively when police ask for help. In judging its reasonableness, hence, its constitutionality, the Court looks to the gravity of the public concerns served by the seizure, the degree to which the seizure advances the public interest, and the severity of the interference with individual liberty. The relevant public concern was grave, as the police were investigating a crime that had resulted in a human death, and the stop advanced this concern to a significant degree given its timing and location. Most important, the stops interfered only minimally with liberty of the sort the Fourth Amendment seeks to protect. Viewed objectively, each stop required only a brief wait in line and contact with police for only a few seconds. Viewed subjectively, the systematic contact provided little reason for anxiety or alarm, and there is no allegation that the police acted in a discriminatory or otherwise unlawful manner. *Illinois v. Lidster*, 540 U.S. 419 (2004).

## DUI Checkpoints Are Unconstitutional in Michigan

Although permissible under the federal Constitution, sobriety checkpoints are unconstitutional searches and seizures under the Michigan Constitution. "Because there is no support in the constitutional history of Michigan for the proposition that the police may engage in warrantless and suspicionless seizures of automobiles for the purpose of enforcing the criminal law, we hold that sobriety checklanes violate article 1, § 11 of the Michigan Constitution." *Sitz v. Dep't of State Police*, 443 Mich. 744 (1993).

## Vehicle *Terry* stops

Officers saw a vehicle traveling without the use of headlights at 3:30 a.m. in a dark parking lot where stores were located. The vehicle was stopped, and the driver was arrested for O.W.I. The court held that to justify the stop and search of a vehicle, the court examines the reasonableness of the stop based on the facts and circumstances of the case. Moreover, there are fewer facts require to justify the stop and search of a vehicle than a house and an investigatory stop of a vehicle requires fewer substantiating facts than does a stop and search of a vehicle. The court held that the officers had sufficient reasonable suspicion to make the stop. *People v. Peebles*, 216 Mich. App. 661 (1996).

Plainclothes officers observed a Trans Am drive into the parking lot of a Holiday Inn. The vehicle drove up to a Ford Taurus, then the two vehicles drove off together. The vehicles pulled into a plaza about a mile from the Holiday Inn and went to an unlit parking area where the passenger of the Trans Am entered the Taurus. The driver of the Trans Am got out and looked around. After two to three minutes, the passenger returned to the Trans Am and the vehicles departed. A marked unit was called and stopped the Trans Am. Open intoxicants were found and a search incident to arrest revealed crack cocaine and marihuana.

The officer testified to the following: "Upon the basis of the meeting at the Holiday Inn, . . . together driving to the Tel-X Plaza, both vehicles parking separate, the drivers, one passenger getting out, the driver getting out and moving, I believe that there was . . . a possible drug transaction occurring."

The court suppressed the evidence because the officer failed to articulate enough to justify the original traffic stop. All the court had was a "bald assertion" by the officer that the situation looked like a drug transaction.

The court said the officers failed to indicate any of the following:

- Prior experience with the defendants.
- Whether the area was a high crime area.
- Did the suspect act evasively or engage in furtive gestures?
- Prior experiences that persons looping in the back of the Holiday Inn or similar lots were a carbon copy of drug activity.
- There was no extended surveillance.
- There was no tip concerning the activity.
- There was no testimony explaining the reason or type of undercover surveillance.

*People v. LoCicero*, 453 Mich. 496 (1996).

An officer responded to a bank robbery involving two black males. Near the scene, he drove to an apartment complex, which was a location that he believed would be a good place to hide a getaway car. The officer testified that during his nineteen years of experience as a police officer he investigated about 20 bank robberies, and it had been his experience that there usually was another person involved who drives the getaway car. Based on this, he was looking for more than two subjects in a car. As he pulled into the complex, a car with four black male occupants was pulling out of the driveway. The officer testified that "[A]s I was passing by them, I turned and looked over at them, and all four subjects looked directly ahead. They would not, any of them, look over at me." The officer found this very unusual because, based on his experience as a police officer, "people always look at the cops." The officer saw the car within ten or fifteen minutes of the dispatch regarding the bank robbery and he passed within six to eight feet of the car when they passed by each other at the entrance to the apartment complex. The officer called for backup and followed the car as it took a circular route instead of a more direct route that would have taken them directly by the bank. The vehicle was stopped and evidence of the robbery was located. The defendants argued that there was no reasonable suspicion to allow the stop.

The court disagreed. The police stopped a car that contained at least three people in a situation where the police were looking for two bank robbers and expecting to find a getaway driver as well. Because the car had at least two black male occupants, its occupants were consistent with the description of the bank robbers. After the officer eliminated the direction north of the bank, he found the car leaving a secluded area close to the bank from what was a logical hiding place. The occupants of the car drew further suspicion by appearing to a trained law enforcement officer to be evasive by declining to look in the direction of his marked police car as it passed nearby. Finally, the car followed a circuitous route that avoided the site of the bank robbery before the traffic stop. While one or more of these factors in isolation may not have constituted reasonable suspicion to stop the car, the court held that there was reasonable suspicion to justify the traffic stop in this case under the totality of the circumstances. *People v. Oliver*, 464 Mich. 184 (2001).

A trooper stopped a vehicle for speeding. Upon questioning, the driver stated that he was going to Cheboygan and was staying at the Holiday Inn. The trooper was aware that there was no Holiday Inn in Cheboygan and asked the driver to step from the vehicle for further questioning. The driver advised that he was from Detroit and was going to be staying in Cheboygan for a couple of days but he had no luggage. Upon further questioning, the driver admitted that he had been arrested for marihuana-related offenses in the past. The passengers also provided inconsistent stories and a K-9 unit was called and drugs were located in the vehicle.

The defendant argued that the trooper had "unlawfully exceeded the initial stop when he asked the defendant to step from the vehicle to answer questions when he only possessed a generalized hunch that criminal activity was afoot." The defendant further argued that the trooper had no reasonable suspicion of criminal activity to warrant the questioning and had insufficient grounds for pursuing an investigatory stop.

The court held that the traffic stop was reasonable in both scope and duration. The Fourth Amendment is not violated when an officer asks reasonable questions to obtain additional information about the underlying offense and the circumstances leading to its commission. For example, in addition to asking for necessary identification, an officer may ask questions relating to the driver's destination and travel plans. Implicit in this authority to ask questions is the authority to ask follow-up questions when the initial answers given are suspicious. Likewise, there is no constitutional prohibition against asking similar questions of any passengers in the vehicle. In response to questions about his travel plans, the defendant provided an explanation that was implausible. Therefore, the trooper was presented with suspicious circumstances that warranted further investigation. *People v. Williams*, 472 Mich. 308 (2005).

## Detaining Pedestrians

Police learned that the defendant had paid $2,100 for two airplane tickets from Honolulu, Hawaii, to Miami, Florida, with a roll of $20 bills. Miami was known as a source city for illegal drugs. He traveled under a name that did not match the name under which his telephone number was listed and he appeared nervous during the trip. The defendant only spent 48 hours in Miami and did not check any of his baggage during the flights. Based on these facts, the Court felt that there was reasonable suspicion to make the stop. Police may briefly detain a person for investigatory purposes if they have reasonable suspicion that criminal activity may be afoot even if the officer lacks probable cause. *United States v. Sokolow*, 490 U.S. 1 (1989).

## Length of Detention

An investigative detention must be temporary and last no longer than is necessary to achieve the purpose of the stop. In determining if the detention is too long, the Court must examine whether police diligently pursued a means of investigation that was likely to confirm or dispel their suspicions quickly. *United States v. Sharpe*, 470 U.S. 675 (1985).

A witness saw three men moving something over a golf course at 3:00 a.m. When he confronted them, they took off running. An officer responded and found a pile of equipment and three sets of footprints leading toward an apartment complex. Based on this and the witness description, the officer radioed to another officer to watch out for three white males. The defendants were located and stopped. The investigating officer followed the tracks to a locker facility and found that it had been broken into. The officer then checked and found that the boots of the defendants matched the tracks he had been following. This took 20 minutes. The court held that the detention was valid because the officers diligently investigated facts available to them, which led to the reasonable suspicion and eventually probable cause to make the arrest. *People v. Chambers*, 195 Mich. App. 118 (1992).

Officers stopped a car after receiving reliable information that it contained narcotics. After searching the car and its occupants for drugs, the officers placed the occupants into their patrol car and drove them to the police department. The drugs were ultimately located at the police station, after the defendant had been held, against her will, for over an hour.

The court dismissed the charges, holding that the officers unreasonably seized the defendant by placing her in the police car and questioning her, transporting her to the police station, detaining her while at the police station, and questioning her further once there. Although the officers properly relied upon the bulletin from the undercover officers indicating that the defendant was suspected as being involved in drug trafficking, once the defendant identified herself, answered the officer's questions, and consented to the pat-down, which did not reveal anything suspicious, the officers were required under the Fourth Amendment to allow the defendant to go free. The officer's continued detention of the defendant in the back of the locked patrol car ripened the investigatory stop into an arrest, and, because the officers did not have probable cause to arrest the defendant at that time, the seizure was illegal. *United States v. Butler*, 223 F.3d 368 (6th Cir. 2000).

The defendant was stopped for a vision obstruction, weaving within the lane of traffic, and speeding. Upon contacting him, the officer requested to see his driver's license and vehicle information, which were produced. When he was checked in LEIN, there were several warrants for the defendant's arrest. Following his arrest for the warrants, the officer searched the car and found 261 grams of cocaine. The defendant argued that since he cooperated with the officer in providing his information, the stop should have lasted no longer than what was necessary to issue a citation and release him. The officer should not have taken the additional time to file check him in LEIN.

The court disagreed, holding that a LEIN check is an unobtrusive investigative tool employed by the police to retrieve information regarding an individual's driving record and to determine whether there are any outstanding warrants for his arrest, all matters of public record. As such, a LEIN check does not involve an unlawful disregard for individual liberties. Accordingly, because this amount of time is a minimal invasion in light of the substantial government interest in arresting citizens wanted on outstanding warrants, the court found that the officer's use of LEIN does not violate the defendant's constitutional rights. *People v. Davis*, 250 Mich. App. 357 (2002).

## Information from an Unidentified Citizen informant Is Reliable for Purposes of Establishing Reasonable Suspicion of Illegal Activity

After a 911 caller reported that a vehicle had run her off the road, a police officer located the vehicle she identified during the call and executed a traffic stop. Officers smelled marihuana and located 30 pounds of marihuana during a subsequent search. The Court held that the stop complied with the Fourth Amendment because, under the totality of the circumstances, the officer had reasonable suspicion that the driver was intoxicated. An anonymous tip *alone* seldom demonstrates the informant's basis of knowledge or veracity but under appropriate circumstances, an anonymous tip can demonstrate sufficient indicia of reliability to provide reasonable suspicion to make an investigatory stop. "The 911 caller in this case reported more than a minor traffic infraction and more than a conclusory allegation of drunk or reckless driving. Instead, she alleged a specific and dangerous result of the driver's conduct: running another car off the highway. That conduct bears too great a resemblance to paradigmatic manifestations of drunk driving to be dismissed as an isolated example of recklessness. Running another vehicle off the road suggests lane-positioning problems, decreased vigilance, impaired judgment, or some combination of those recognized drunk driving cues. . . . And the experience of many officers suggests that a driver who almost strikes a vehicle or another object—the exact scenario that ordinarily causes "running [another vehicle] off the roadway"—is likely intoxicated. . . . As a result, we cannot say that the officer acted unreasonably under these circumstances in stopping a driver whose alleged conduct was a significant indicator of drunk driving." *Navarette v California*, 134 S. Ct. 1683 (2014)

While on patrol at approximately 2:00 a.m. in Detroit, two officers were flagged down by a man who was pumping gas at a gas station. The man told the officers that a black male driving a burgundy Chevrolet Caprice was at the gas pumps at another gas station down the road, which was approximately one mile away. He further told the officers that the man was waving an "Uzi type weapon" with a long clip. Finally, he told the officers that the man was approximately 30 years old and he looked nervous and upset. The citizen informant refused to give his name to the officers.

Less than five minutes passed before the officers arrived at the gas station and observed a burgundy Chevrolet Caprice sitting at the gas pump. The officers activated their lights, ordered the defendant out of the vehicle, and asked for license, registration, and insurance. When the defendant got out of the car, the officers observed a Glock semi-automatic pistol with an extended magazine on the driver's seat.

The officers had no information about the defendant other than the information provided by the unidentified citizen-informant. The defendant moved to suppress the evidence.

Information from an unidentified citizen-informant may be used by officers to establish reasonable suspicion of illegal activity if they have considered three criteria: (1) the reliability of the particular informant, (2) the nature of the particular information given to police, and (3) the reasonability of the suspicion in light of the facts. *People v. Tooks*, 403 Mich. 568 (1978).

Reasonable suspicion of criminal activity is determined on a case-by-case basis, considering the totality of the circumstances. *People v. Jenkins*, 472 Mich. 26 (2005).

The court held that the totality of the circumstances provided reasonable suspicion for the officers to briefly detain the defendant. The citizen-informant's descriptive information was detailed in nature, and the officers corroborated the information in less than five minutes. Further, the information provided by the citizen informant was accurate. The requirements established in *Tooks* were satisfied by the officers in this case. *People v. Horton*, 283 Mich. App. 105 (2009).

## Anonymous Tip

An anonymous caller reported that a young black male standing at a particular bus stop and wearing a plaid shirt was carrying a gun. Officers responded and observed three black males. Absent the tip, the officers had no reason to suspect any of the three of illegal conducts. The officers did not see a firearm or observe any unusual movements. The officers approached the subjects and frisked them, finding a gun on the defendant. The Court held that an anonymous tip that a person is carrying a gun is not, without more, sufficient to justify a police officer's stop and frisk of that person. Because the officers' suspicion that the defendant was carrying a weapon arose not from their own observations but solely from a call made from an unknown location by an unknown caller, the tip lacked sufficient indicia of reliability to provide reasonable suspicion to make a *Terry* stop. It provided no predictive information and, therefore, left the police without means to test the informant's knowledge or credibility. *Florida v. J.L.*, 529 U.S. 266 (2000).

## Pat-Down of Individuals before Placing Them in a Patrol Car

A trooper contacted a man and woman walking on the freeway. He gave them a warning and then offered them a ride to the next exit. They agreed and, before being seated in the patrol car, they were patted down by the trooper. A gun was located. Since the officer had no authority to arrest the couple, and leaving them on the freeway would be dangerous and allow the offense to continue, the court held that the officer was justified in conducting a pat-down despite absence of any showing of specific and articulable facts that the defendant was armed and dangerous. *People v. Otto*, 91 Mich. App. 444 (1979).

## Fleeing from Police May Establish Reasonable Suspicion for a *Terry* Stop

The defendant fled upon seeing police vehicles converge on an area of Chicago known for drug trafficking. The officers stopped him and conducted a pat-down for weapons locating a pistol. The Court held that the defendant's unprovoked flight from officers in an area of heavy narcotics trafficking supported reasonable suspicion that the defendant was involved in criminal activity and justified a *Terry* stop. "[N]ervous, evasive behavior is a pertinent factor in determining reasonable suspicion." *Illinois v. Wardlow*, 528 U.S. 119 (2000).

## Handcuffing During *Terry* Stops

The defendant parked his car across several visitor parking spaces at a Ford plant after traveling over the grass and causing damage to a front tire. After noticing the smell of alcohol on the defendant's breath, security personnel called the Wixom police, who arrived in uniform and in fully marked police cars to investigate. As the police officers approached the defendant, he appeared to be preparing for a fight, then became belligerent and approached a female officer with clenched fists. After momentarily following instructions to place his hands on the trunk of the vehicle, the defendant pushed away then turned toward the officers. As a result, the defendant was handcuffed. The defendant then began to fight, scream obscenities and threats, and became totally out of control. The fight lasted several minutes, during which time additional officers were called to assist. The defendant was eventually restrained, but continued to thrash violently and make threats for several hours thereafter. Officers searched the car after he was restrained and found a loaded 9 mm handgun, several dozen additional rounds of ammunition, and a number of documents in an unlocked briefcase in the trunk. The defendant claimed that he was placed under arrest as soon as the officers handcuffed him and that the arrest was illegal because the officers did not have probable cause.

The court held that a defendant's restraint is not necessarily an arrest. Police conduct in trying to restrain a defendant during the investigation may be a reasonable intrusion on a defendant's liberty if the safety of the officers is at risk during their lawful attempt to investigate the situation. In this case, the defendant appeared intoxicated and led the officers to believe that he planned to fight them. He was aggressive and hostile, and the officers were unaware whether he possessed a weapon. They were not required to take unnecessary risks when dealing with the defendant. After the officers validly attempted to restrain the defendant for safety reasons, he committed the charge of resisting and obstructing the officers. The police then had probable cause to arrest the defendant. *People v. Green*, 260 Mich. App. 392 (2004).

## Searches of Probationers May be Based on Reasonable Suspicion

The defendant was placed on probation for drug violations. Part of the probation order required him to submit to a search at any time, with or without a warrant, by any probation or law enforcement officer. Later, officers suspected that he was involved in a number of arsons against a power company. At one point, a detective who was investigating him observed a Molotov cocktail and other explosive devices in a pickup truck parked in his driveway. The detective then entered the apartment to search under the probation order. Inside the residence, the officer located incriminating evidence against the defendant. The trial court dismissed the charges holding that although the detective had "reasonable suspicion" to believe that he was involved with incendiary materials, the search was for "investigatory" rather than "probationary purposes."

The United States Supreme Court reversed, holding that the Fourth Amendment's touchstone is reasonableness, and a search's reasonableness is determined by assessing, on one hand, the degree to which it intrudes upon an individual's privacy and, on the other, the degree to which it is needed to promote legitimate governmental interest. In this case, the defendant's status as a probationer subject to a search condition informs both sides of that balance. Therefore, his reasonable expectation of privacy was significantly diminished. In assessing the governmental interest, it must be remembered that the very assumption of probation is that the probationer is more likely than others to violate the law. On balance, no more than reasonable suspicion was required to search the defendant's residence. "Although the Fourth Amendment ordinarily requires probable cause, a lesser degree satisfies the Constitution when the balance of governmental and private interest makes such a standard reasonable." *United States v. Knights*, 534 U.S. 112 (2001).

# INVENTORIES

## Vehicles

The inventory of a vehicle must be reasonable and completed in compliance with departmental policy.

A car was parked in a tow-away zone and impounded. During an inventory of the car, officers located marihuana in the glove compartment. The Court held that routine inventory searches of automobiles lawfully impounded by the police are reasonable. *South Dakota v. Opperman*, 428 U.S. 364 (1976).

Officers arrested the driver for O.W.I. The passenger also was under the influence and unable to drive. The passenger asked if he could arrange for his wife to get the car. The officers refused and towed the vehicle. Before it was towed, the officers conducted an inventory search on the vehicle and found cocaine. The departmental policy stated that a vehicle could be impounded where it would be left unattended. The court held that impounding the vehicle under these circumstances was reasonable. Obviously, the officers could not turn it over to the passenger and the police do not have to make alternative arrangements to avoid impoundment. Police may make routine, warrantless searches of contents of any vehicle that lawfully comes into police custody as part of police caretaking. The purposes of an inventory search are to:

- Protect the owner's property while in police custody.
- Protect the police against claims or disputes over lost or stolen property.
- Protect the police from potential dangers.
- The search cannot be a pretext.

*People v. Toohey*, 438 Mich. 265 (1991)

The defendant was arrested for O.W.I. After the arrest, but before the arrival of the tow truck, the officer searched the vehicle and found a closed knapsack, opened it, and found controlled substances. Departmental regulations allowed police to either impound the vehicle or lock and park it in a public place. The exercise of police discretion is not prohibited so long as that discretion is exercised according to standard criteria and on the basis of something other than suspicion of evidence of criminal activity. The Court held that because the department had a reasonable written inventory procedure for towing the vehicle that was followed in good faith, the search was valid. *Colorado v. Bertine*, 479 U.S. 367 (1987).

Florida Highway Patrol had no policy specifically requiring the opening of closed containers during a legitimate inventory search. The Court suppressed marihuana located in a suitcase in the trunk of a vehicle. The Court held that an inventory search must be conducted based on a department policy in order to restrict officer's discretion so that inventory searches are not turned into ruses for general rummaging to discover incriminating evidence. *Florida v. Wells*, 495 U.S. 1 (1990).

## Arrestee's Personal Effects

The defendant was arrested and brought to the police station for booking. He was required to empty his pockets and turn over the bag he was carrying at the time of arrest. The booking officer examined the contents of the bag and found amphetamine pills. The Court ruled that this was a valid inventory search. It did not fall under the search incident to arrest exception because the search was not done contemporaneous with the arrest. *Illinois v. Lafayette*, 462 U.S. 640 (1983).

# EMERGENCIES
## Elements

Reasonable suspicion that an emergency exists.

### Injury: Community Care-Taking Function

During a fire call, fireman entered the defendant's residence and garage to extinguish the fire. In the process, they located a number of dead deer that had been illegally shot hanging in the garage. The court held that the fire was sufficient as an emergency to authorize the entry and, once inside, the deer carcasses in plain view could be seized as evidence. *People v. Chapman*, 73 Mich. App. 547 (1977).

The defendant was involved in a hit-and-run crash. A witness saw his plate and officers went to his house. They located a vehicle with front-end damage and observed a subject lying unconscious and bleeding in the house. Officers knocked and had dispatch attempt to make contact with telephone calls, with no response. Officers entered the residence to check on his well-being. Subject was not injured but was intoxicated.

The court upheld the entry into the home and the arrest as valid under the emergency exception.

"Where the police have probable cause, based on specific, articulable facts, to believe that immediate entry is necessary to assist a person who may be in serious need of medical aid, they may enter without a warrant. The entry must be limited to the justification therefor, and the officer must be motivated primarily by the 'perceived need to render aid or assistance.' The officer may not do more than is reasonably necessary to determine whether a person is in need of assistance, and to provide that assistance." *People v. Ohlinger,* 438 Mich. 477 (1991).

Officers were dispatched to "Belmar Motel, Room 33 or 34, desk clerk says shots fired." The officers went directly to Room 33 because it was closer and banged on the door. They observed a female looking through the curtains. She shut them and, after three to five minutes, opened the door. The officers entered and observed drug paraphernalia and the butt of a gun underneath the mattress.

The court held that police may enter a location if they have reasonable belief or suspicion that a person inside is in need of immediate aid. In applying this analysis to the facts of this case, the court held that the officers did not have reasonable suspicion that someone was in need. Therefore, the entry and search were invalid. The court found that the 911 call unreliable as the basis of an emergency to enter the room. The caller, despite claiming to be the hotel manager, improperly named the hotel and could not name the cross streets where the hotel was located. Further, the call only stated shots had been fired, not that there were any injuries. *People v. Davis*, 442 Mich. 1 (1993).

Officers were dispatched to respond to a domestic disturbance in progress, possibly involving guns and knives. The officers knocked on the door, but no one answered. They then tried to gain entry, but the door was locked. They heard a lot of wrestling or moving around inside the house. A woman then answered the door and the officers entered. Once inside, they observed the defendant in the back bedroom and ordered him out. The officers then conducted a protective sweep and observed cocaine on the kitchen floor, in the front room, and on a tray in the bedroom.

The Court of Appeals upheld the entry into the home, the protective sweep of the home, and the seizure of the drugs. "[P]olice may enter a dwelling without a warrant when they reasonably believe that a person within is in need of immediate aid. They must possess specific and articulable facts that lead them to this conclusion. In addition, the entry must be limited to the justification therefore, and the officer may not do more than is reasonably necessary to determine whether a person is in need of assistance, and to provide that assistance." *People v. Beuschlein*, 245 Mich. App. 744 (2001).

Officers may enter a residence to prevent injury or restore order (e.g., to break up a fight). An officer's motivation for entry is irrelevant, as long as entry is reasonable as viewed by an objective person. *Brigham City v. Stuart*, 547 U.S. 398 (2006).

Police officers responded to a disturbance and as officers approached the area, a couple directed them to a residence where a man was "going crazy." When they arrived, the officers found a household in considerable chaos. There was a pickup truck in the driveway with its front smashed, damaged fence posts along the side of the property, and three broken house windows, the glass still on the ground outside. The officers also noticed blood on the hood of the pickup and on clothes inside of it, as well as on one of the doors to the house. Through a window, the officers could hear the defendant screaming and throwing things. The back door was locked, and a couch had been placed to block the front door.

The officers knocked on the door, but the defendant refused to answer. They could see that the defendant had a cut on his hand, and they asked him whether he needed medical attention. The defendant ignored these questions and demanded, with accompanying profanity, that the officers go to get a search warrant. The officers then pushed open the door and entered into the house. Inside they saw the defendant pointing a long gun at them. The officers withdrew and the defendant was charged under Michigan law with assault with a dangerous weapon and possession of a firearm during the commission of a felony.

The Michigan courts dismissed the charges on the grounds that the officers entered the house unlawfully, holding that there was not sufficient enough evidence to show that a true emergency existed and that the defendant needed medical attention.

The United States Supreme Court held that, because officers were responding to reports of a disturbance and they encountered signs of possible injury and destructive, violent behavior upon arriving at the scene, the entry was reasonable. The officers' failure to contact an emergency medical team prior to confronting the defendnat is not dispositive, as the officers were justified in ensuring no other person in the house was injured or at risk of injury from the defendnat's tirade. The test is "whether there was 'an objectively reasonable basis for believing' that medical assistance was needed, or persons were in danger." *Michigan v. Fisher*, 558 U.S. 45 (2009).

Police were dispatched to the defendant's condominium to respond to a report that the front door was open and blowing in the wind. The officers arrived at the residence and confirmed that the door indeed was open and blowing in the wind. There was no observable damage to the door. The officers announced their presence, knocked on the door several times, and rang the doorbell. No one came to the door. Because the door to the residence was open, the officers suspected there may have been a recent home invasion. The officers entered the residence in order to ascertain if anyone was inside the condominium and to secure the residence. As soon as the officers entered the kitchen, they smelled a strong odor of marijuana and observed marijuana residue on the counter. They continued to search the house looking for persons and to ensure that the house was secure. When the officers proceeded to the basement, they found two large bags of suspected marihuana in plain view. They did not locate anyone in the residence. The police then sought a search warrant. Detectives arrived at the residence and executed the search warrant. They seized cocaine, marijuana, clear plastic bags, a scale, and paperwork from the kitchen. They also discovered cocaine in one of the bedrooms and marijuana from the basement. An energy bill with the defendant's name on it was located. When the defendant drove near the residence, the police executed a stop on the vehicle. While the defendant admitted that the marihuana belonged to him, he disavowed any knowledge of the cocaine. The defendant argued that the search was illegal because the police entered the condominium without a search warrant and without proper justification. The court held that the officers behaved reasonably in entering the defendant's residence pursuant to the emergency aid exception to the warrant requirement. *People v. Lemons*, 299 Mich. App. 541 (2013).

Officers were sent to the defendant's home shortly after midnight as part of a "welfare check" after the defendant's neighbor called police with concerns about the defendant's well-being. When the officers arrived, the neighbor approached them and indicated that, in the last few days to a week, she had not seen or heard from the defendant and that, for the same time period, the defendant's vehicle had not moved from his property even though the defendant would typically come and go in the vehicle on a regular basis. The neighbor also informed the officers that the defendant usually worked in his house during the night which she could generally hear, but she had not heard him working for several nights. The neighbor mentioned that the interior lights in the defendant's house had been on for awhile and that the defendant's cats had been looking out of the home's windows. Officers noticed that an interior house light was turned on, that there were six to eight pieces of mail in the mailbox, which were a few days old at most, that a phonebook was sitting on the front porch, and that the defendant's car, which was cold and covered with some leaves, was sitting in the driveway. The officers knocked on the defendant's door several times, but there was no answer. The officers also contacted dispatch and asked the dispatcher to make a phone call to the defendant's home. Officers proceeded to knock on back windows and yell out, asking if anyone was present, but there was no response. Officers were able to slide open an unlocked window and yelled inside several times in an attempt to locate anybody, but still did not receive an answer. The officers entered the house and eventually they opened a bedroom closet and found marihuana plants. The closet was tall enough for a person. Officers testified that they did not enter the home to investigate criminal activity.

The court upheld the entry and search. "We conclude that the community-caretaker exception to the warrant requirement was implicated after consideration of all of the surrounding circumstances taken together.... Although there were no signs of forced entry or sounds of someone in distress, the circumstances were such that an officer could reasonably conclude that defendant may be in need of aid or assistance.... Given the reasonable conclusion that defendant may be in the home (the lights were on and the car was parked outside), and considering the lack of response to the police officers' aggressive efforts to communicate, it was be reasonable to conclude that defendant was not only present but in need of attention, aid, or some kind of assistance. This becomes even more apparent when one considers the presence of the phonebook on the porch and the few days of mail that had accumulated in the mailbox. Moreover, the neighbor informed the officers that she was worried about defendant and that the situation at defendant's home was unusual. When all of the pieces of information are considered together and not individually, the sum of their parts equates to specific and articulable facts that would lead an officer to reasonably conclude that defendant was in need of aid." *People v. Hill*, 299 Mich. App. 402 (2013).

"We conclude that the community caretaking exception to the warrant requirement applies when a firefighter, responding to an emergency call involving a threat to life or property, reasonably enters a private residence in order to abate what is reasonably believed to be an imminent threat of fire inside. . . . Application of the community caretaking exception does not provide firefighters with a blank check to enter private residences; rather, it only authorizes *reasonable* intrusions." *People v. Slaughter*, 489 Mich. 302 (2011) (emphasis in original).

# HOT PURSUIT

## Elements

1. Pursuit of a fleeing felon.
2. Exigent circumstances requiring immediate arrest.

Hot pursuit requires that there must be some form of flight by the defendant. *Johnson v. United States*, 333 U.S. 10 (1948).

Undercover officers had probable cause to arrest the defendant for drug dealing from observations they made as she was standing in front of her house. As the officers approached, she retreated into her house. The officers entered and while arresting her, the paper bag she had been carrying fell to the floor and envelopes, later determined to contain heroin, were seized. The Court upheld the arrest and seizure of the evidence. The Court held that the defendant could not commit a crime in a public place, her porch, and retreat into a private place, her home, to avoid capture. Here, police had probable cause that a crime had been committed by the defendant and a reasonable belief that evidence be destroyed sufficient to justify a warrantless entry and arrest. Further, there was hot pursuit based on the fact that police observed the public drug transactions and the defendant retreated into her house upon seeing the approaching officers. There is no requirement that the chase be an extended public one; the extremely short chase in this circumstance was sufficient to justify the arrest of the defendant and the evidence was seized after a valid search incident to arrest. *United States v. Santana*, 427 U.S. 38 (1976).

A 10 1/2-year-old was taken from her apartment at knifepoint. She was taken to another apartment where she was forced to perform fellatio, and the defendant attempted penetration using petroleum jelly. About an hour and a half later, she was released and officers found her wandering outside. The officers broke into the apartment to arrest the defendant, but were unable to locate him. However, in the process, they found the jar of petroleum jelly and seized it. The court held that, because the victim was found in close proximity to the scene of the crime and told police he was still there, the entry fell into the "hot pursuit" exception to the warrant requirement. Upon entry, the tub of petroleum jelly was in plain view, thus properly seized as evidence of the crime. *People v. Lynn*, 91 Mich. App. 117 (1979).

Police were dispatched to a robbery/murder that had just occurred. A tracking dog led officers to a nearby house. The officers entered and discovered defendant and the murder weapon. The court held that the entry was valid because the dog track constituted probable cause. The court further held that the rapid follow-up by police and unbroken chain of immediate pursuit of the perpetrator brought the warrantless entry within the hot pursuit exception. *People v. Joyner*, 93 Mich. App. 554 (1979).

## Warrantless Misdemeanors: Police Cannot Enter under Michigan Statute

Officers chased a subject into his house for fleeing and eluding, which was a misdemeanor at the time. The court held that the arrest violated state law. The court held that Michigan's statute allowing breaking and entering of outer or inner door of any building by a police officer to make an arrest applied only when the officer possessed a warrant or in cases of a felony without a warrant. The statute did not authorize nonconsensual entry into a person's home or other building for purpose of making a warrantless misdemeanor arrest. *People v. Reinhardt*, 141 Mich. App. 173 (1985). See Chapter 19, Laws of Arrest, for further information and explanation.

## Exigent Circumstances Needed for Warrantless Entry

"We hold that the police may enter a dwelling without a warrant if the officers possess probable cause to believe that a crime was recently committed on the premises, and probable cause to believe that the premises contain evidence or perpetrators of the suspected crime. The police must further establish the existence of an actual emergency on the basis of specific and objective facts indicating that immediate action is necessary to (1) prevent the imminent destruction of evidence, (2) protect the police officers or others, or (3) prevent the escape of a suspect. If the police discover evidence of a crime following the entry without a warrant, that evidence may be admissible." *In re Forfeiture of $176,598*, 443 Mich. 261 (1993).

"Exigent circumstances are present as a matter of law (1) to engage in hot pursuit of a fleeing felon; (2) to prevent the imminent destruction of evidence; (3) to prevent a suspect from escaping; and (4) to prevent imminent harm to police or third parties." *United States v. Washington*, 573 F.3d 279 (6th Cir. 2009).

After two days of intense investigation, New York detectives determined that the defendant had murdered the manager of a gas station. At approximately 7:30 a.m. on a Saturday morning, six officers went to the defendant's apartment without either an arrest warrant or a search warrant. Although music was coming from the apartment, there was no answer to their knocks. They used crowbars and forced entry into the residence. Police intended to enter the home and effectuate an arrest of the defendant based on a New York law that permitted warrantless entry, even with force, for the purpose of making a routine felony arrest. They were unable to find the defendant, but they did locate and seize a .30-caliber shell casing that was later admitted into evidence at the

defendant's trial. The Court held that the entry was unlawful and suppressed the evidence.

The Court has consistently held that the "physical entry of the home is the chief evil against which the wording of the Fourth Amendment is directed." In this case, the entry was too substantial an invasion to allow without a warrant, in the absence of exigent circumstances, even when it is accomplished under statutory authority and when probable cause is present. For Fourth Amendment purposes, an arrest warrant founded on probable cause implicitly carries with it the limited authority to enter a dwelling in which the suspect lives when there is reason to believe the suspect is within. The Court held that the New York statute authorizing warrantless entry for routine felony arrests was contrary to the Fourth Amendment. Therefore, the warrantless entry here was improper and the seized evidence was suppressed. *Payton v. New York*, 445 U.S. 573 (1980).

Officers investigated a double homicide that had occurred at 10:00 p.m. At 4:00 a.m., they received information that the suspect was in a motel room. At that point, the murder weapon, a shotgun, had not yet been recovered. The officers went to the room without a warrant and knocked and announced their presence. When there was no answer, they entered, locating the subject and the weapon lying on the bed.

The court held that exigent circumstances justified the entry into the suspect's hotel room as the officers probable cause to believe that a crime had just been committed and had justification for a search of the room to prevent the destruction of any evidence, to protect the police or others, to prevent the suspect's escape, or to determine if the suspect was wounded. Therefore, there were exigent circumstances known to the police that excused them from taking time to obtain an arrest warrant. *People v. Snider*, 239 Mich. App. 393 (2000).

## Held Not to Be Exigent Circumstances

Officers were investigating a B&E, during which the 65-year-old victim was physically assaulted, raped, and robbed in her home. Officers had received a tip that the defendant may have been involved, and he was currently at his apartment. Several officers went to the home and entered it, searched it, and found evidence.

The court held that the entry and search were not valid, because there were no exigent circumstances. There was no concern that evidence would be lost or destroyed while the police obtained a warrant. Further, there was no threat that the defendant would escape, and if there was, the police could have prevented it by posting officers outside of the apartment while others obtained a warrant. *People v. Love*, 156 Mich. App. 568 (1986).

Police suspected the defendant of being the driver of the getaway car used in a robbery-murder. After recovering the murder weapon and arresting the suspected murderer, they surrounded the home of two women with whom they believed that the defendant had been staying. When police telephoned the home and told one of the women that the defendant should come out, a male voice was heard saying, "Tell them I left." Without seeking permission and with weapons drawn, they entered the home, found the defendant hiding in a closet, and arrested him. Shortly thereafter, he made an inculpatory statement.

The Court held that an entry may be justified by hot pursuit of a fleeing felon, the imminent destruction of evidence, the need to prevent a suspect's escape, or the risk of danger to the police or others. However, in the absence of hot pursuit, there must be at least probable cause to believe that one or more of the other factors were present and, in assessing the risk of danger, the gravity of the crime and likelihood that the suspect is armed should be considered. In this case, although a grave crime was involved, the defendant was known not to be the murderer and the murder weapon had been recovered. There was no suggestion of danger to the women; several police squads surrounded the house, it was evident that the suspect was not leaving; and if he came out of the house he would have been promptly apprehended. In light of all of these factors, the Court held that the police should have obtained a warrant before they entered the home. *Minnesota v. Olson*, 495 U.S. 91 (1990).

### Third Party Residence: Police May Not Enter Solely under the Authority of an Arrest Warrant

DEA agents had an arrest warrant for a subject with the last name of Lyons. They received information from an informant that he was at the defendant's house. They went to the residence and entered without a search warrant or consent. The officers did not find Lyons, but did seize cocaine and subsequently charged the defendant for possession of cocaine.

The Court suppressed the evidence. The Court reasoned that, when issuing an arrest warrant, the magistrate does not generally consider privacy interests of third parties as is the case when a search warrant is issued. The arrest warrant issued for Lyons offered no protection to the defendant's expectation of privacy, he was not even contemplated by the magistrate at the time of issuance. The Court held that the entry was unlawful. An arrest warrant may only be used to search the residence of the person for whom the warrant is issued. For other third party residences, police must obtain a search warrant, unless another exemption to the search warrant requirement exists. *Steagald v. United States*, 451 U.S. 204 (1981).

Officers entered a third party residence to arrest a fugitive on an outstanding warrant for traffic violations. A scuffle between the police and the occupants of the home ensued and the officers charged the occupants with resisting and obstructing. The court dismissed the charges because no exigent circumstances could justify the entry and the officers did not first seek a search warrant before entry into the house. *People v. Stark*, 120 Mich. App. 350 (1982).

## ADMINISTRATIVE SEARCHES

Searches conducted pursuant to a statutory scheme to regulate a particular industry or business.

Generally, there is implied consent for the inspections.

A court uses the following balancing test, to determine if an administrative search is permissible, using the following *Tallman* factors:

- The existence of express statutory authorization for search or seizure.
- The importance of the governmental interest at stake.
- The pervasiveness and longevity of industry regulation.
- The inclusion of reasonable limitations on searches in statutes and regulations.
- The government's need for flexibility in the time, scope, and frequency of inspections in order to achieve reasonable levels of compliance.

- The degree of intrusion occasioned by a particular regulatory search.
- The degree to which a business person may be said to have impliedly consented to warrantless searches as a condition of doing business, so that the search does not infringe upon reasonable expectations of privacy.

*Tallman v Dep't. of Natural Resources*, 421 Mich. 585 (1984).

Some industries are pervasively regulated to ensure safety, such as fire codes, public health codes, and buildings. In this case, an inspector attempted to force his way into an apartment without a warrant to check for fire code violations. The Court held that the entry was illegal without a warrant; but the standard for getting the warrant would be less than the probable cause needed for a search warrant. The inspectors should have sought a warrant based on reasonable legislative or administrative standards. The Court held that administrative entry, without consent, upon the portions of commercial premises which are not open to the public may only be compelled through prosecution or physical force within the framework of a warrant procedure. *See v. City of Seattle*, 387 U.S. 541 (1967).

### Warrantless Administrative Searches Are Valid as Long as the Primary Purpose of the Search is for Administrative Purposes and not Detection of Criminal Activity

The defendant was the owner of a business called the Arabian Market. An officer assigned to the state police's tobacco tax team received an anonymous tip that there were illegal tobacco products in the Arabian Market. The officer arrived at the store and identified himself and told the defendant that he was there to conduct an administrative inspection. In the course of the inspection, it was discovered that the defendant did not hold a Michigan tobacco license. The inspection yielded 300-plus cases of tobacco, which were seized by the officers. The defendant moved to quash the charges brought against him.

The court considered the search in light of the *Tallman* factors. The statutory provision here clearly established a legislative intent to give executive agencies the power to search for and seize untaxed tobacco products. The state has a strong interest in collecting revenue from the tobacco tax and there is a long history of taxing and regulating tobacco in Michigan. The statute expressly limits the scope and conditions of search and seizure, and the search at issue here comported with those requirements. Because of the easily disposable nature of tobacco products, the state is justified in promoting flexible searching options to ensure compliance. Based on these factors, the court held that the state interest in conducting warrantless searches in compliance with the Tobacco Products Tax Act (TPTA) outweighs the retailers' privacy interests. The search at issue was proper because the searching agents were interested in enforcing the TPTA and not locating evidence of criminal activity. *People v. Beydoun*, 283 Mich. App. 314 (2009).

### Department of Natural Resources

DNR officers attempted to board several licensed commercial fishing vessels on a number of different occasions to see if there was a violation of commercial fishing laws. Some, but not all, of the attempted boardings were with probable cause. The court held that searches could be conducted without a showing of probable cause to determine if there has been a violation of a pervasively regulated industry. Searches must be done pursuant to a statutory scheme to regulate a particular industry or business that gives authority to search. Implied consent is given as a condition of doing business. In this case, the searches fit within the parameters of an administrative search. *Tallman v. DNR*, 421 Mich. 585 (1984).

### Liquor Inspections

Officers received a tip that defendant was selling cocaine out of a party store. The information was that cocaine was located in a wooden box with a smoked glass top on a shelf in the back of the store. The officers went to the store and found the box. When they were not given consent to open it, they obtained a search warrant to open the box and found cocaine. The

Court of Appeals held that the search locating the box was legal and, further, the officers did not need a warrant to open the box once it was found. The Liquor Control Act provides that a "commission investigator or law enforcement officer" can inspect licensed premises. The inspections must take place during regular business hours. The search fit within the parameters of the statutory authorization; therefore, it was proper. *People v. Jones*, 180 Mich. App. 625 (1989).

## Junk Yards

During an inspection of a salvage yard, officers discovered that the owner had neither a license nor the required records. The officers checked some of the parts and found that they were stolen. The court held, since state law requires the inspection, that the search was valid. *People v. Barnes*, 146 Mich. App. 37 (1985).

## Fire Scenes

Firefighters may enter a scene of a fire within a reasonable time after the fire has been extinguished without a warrant. The entry may be to ensure the fire is extinguished and there is no pending danger. The Court held that an entry to fight a fire required no warrant and additional entries after the fire to investigate the cause may be made under the warrant procedures for administrative searches. In this case, because arson was suspected, the officials needed to obtain a warrant to gather evidence for the prosecution of the crime. *Michigan v. Tyler*, 436 U.S. 499 (1978).

Officers at the scene of a fire may enter to search for the origin of the fire, to prevent further damage. Once in the building, they need no warrant to remain for a reasonable time to investigate the cause of a blaze after it has been extinguished. After determining the point of origin of a fire, the search for a cause is limited to that area and may not be expanded absent probable cause. However, reasonable expectations of privacy may remain in the fire-damaged property. Therefore, additional investigations after the blaze has been extinguished and the fire and police units have left the scene,

a subsequent post-fire search must be conducted pursuant to a warrant, consent, or the identification of some new exigency. So long as the primary purpose is to ascertain the cause of the fire, an administrative warrant will suffice. *Michigan v. Clifford*, 464 U.S. 287 (1984).

## Other Businesses or Industries Affected

- Precious metal and gem dealers.
- Pawn shops.
- Junk and scrap metal dealers.
- Tobacco retailers and wholesalers.

# BORDER SEARCHES EXCEPTION

The Supreme Court has recognized a broad exception to the Fourth Amendment's requirement of probable cause or a warrant for routine searches conducted at the border because of the Government's interest in preventing the entry of unwanted persons and effects. Under this exception, searches of people and their property at the borders are per se reasonable, meaning that they typically do not require a warrant, probable cause, or even reasonable suspicion.

## Authority to Conduct a Border Search

Border searches may only be conducted by persons with lawful authority to do so.

- ICE, Border Patrol, U.S. Coast Guard, cross-designated officers, etc.

## Time, Place, and Scope of a Border Search

A checkpoint for border searches must be a fixed checkpoint at the border or its functional equivalent, such as searches of international flight passengers and cargo or searches conducted at the intersection of two or more roads that extend from the border and intersect a reasonable distance from the border. Roving checkpoints that conduct searches or seizures without probable cause are not proper. *Alemida-Sanchez v. United States*, 413 U.S. 266 (1973).

It is permissible for roving patrols at the border or its functional equivalent to make stops if the officer has reasonable suspicion based on articulable facts and rational inferences from them that the vehicle may contain illegal aliens. The officer may briefly stop such vehicles and question the occupants about their citizenship, immigration status, and the suspicious circumstances that led to the stop. Any search or detention going beyond this must be based on probable cause. *United States v. Brignoni-Ponce*, 422 U.S. 873 (1975).

At a border checkpoint, an inspector stopped a car and requested the driver to step out. The vehicle was taken to a secondary inspection station where the gas tank was tapped. It produced a different sound than expected, which piqued the inspector's interest. A mechanic was called in to remove the tank. He arrived 20–30 minutes later and after the tank was removed, the inspector located 37 kilograms of marihuana. The Court held that the government's authority to conduct suspicion less inspections at the border includes the authority to remove, disassemble, and reassemble a gas tank. The Court held that such searches were reversible without damaging the vehicle or jeopardizing the vehicles safe operation. The Court further held that a disassembly search that resulted in property damage would entitle the owner to recovery. United *States v. Flores-Montano*, 541 U.S. 149 (2004).

© 2014, Shutterstock, Inc.

# 24

# LAWS OF EVIDENCE

## INTRODUCTION

### Definition of Evidence

Any means by which an issue, fact, or the truth of the matter is proved or disproved.

### Purpose of the Rules of Evidence—MRE 102

*To secure fairness in administration, elimination of unjustifiable expense and delay, and promotion of growth and development of the law of evidence to the end that the truth may be ascertained and proceedings justly determined.*

### General Descriptive Terms

*Circumstantial Evidence*:   A group of facts that, when linked together, gives rise to a certain conclusion. Includes presumptions, inferences, habit, custom, and many types of physical evidence. It is equally competent with direct evidence, and its relative weight is for the fact-finder to decide.

*Cumulative Evidence*:   Additional evidence tending to prove the same point. May be excluded from trial.

*Demonstrative Evidence*:   Evidence used to illustrate something to the jury (i.e., photograph, sketches, maps, models of crime scene).

*Direct Evidence*:   Evidence that, if believed, proves existence of fact in issue without inference or presumption (i.e., witness identification, written statements by suspect).

*Real Evidence*:   Tangible items (i.e., fingerprint, document, gun).

*Testimonial Evidence*:   Evidence received from a witness. Witness testifies to what he or she directly saw or indirectly saw as to habit, custom, circumstantial evidence, etc.

### Judging Credibility and Weight of Evidence

Weight and credibility are questions for the jury to decide alone. The judge decides the admissibility of the evidence. *Knowles v. People*, 15 Mich. 408 (1867).

The jury, or the judge in a bench trial, must:

- Decide what the facts of this case are.
- Decide which witnesses are credible and how important their testimony is.

The jury does not have to accept or reject everything a witness says; jury members are free to believe all, none, or part of any person's testimony.

In deciding which testimony to believe, the trier of fact should rely on his or her own common sense and every-day experience. However, the believability of a witness shall not be predicated on any bias or prejudice based on the race, gender, or national origin of the witness.

There is no fixed set of rules for determining whether a witness should be believed. The court provides lay jurors the following factors to help them determine whether they should believe a witness. CJI2d 3.6.

- Was the witness able to see or hear clearly?
- How long was the witness watching or listening?
- Was anything else going on that might have distracted the witness?
- Does the witness seem to have a good memory?
- How does the witness look and act while testifying? Does the witness seem to be making an honest effort to tell the truth, or does the witness seem to evade the questions or argue with the lawyers?
- Does the witness's age or maturity affect how you judge his or her testimony?
- Does the witness have any bias or prejudice or any personal interest in how this case is decided?
- Have there been any promises, threats, suggestions, or other influences that affect how the witness testifies?
- In general, does the witness have any special reason to tell the truth, or any special reason to lie?
- All in all, how reasonable does the witness's testimony seem when you think about all the other evidence in the case?

# PROOF

## Burden of Proof

- *Burden of Producing Evidence*: Party has to produce enough evidence so that reasonable people viewing the evidence in the light most favorable to that party could find in that party's favor.
- *Burden of Persuasion*: A party must persuade the trier of fact to accept his or her argument.

## Standard of Proof

- **Criminal Trial—***Beyond a reasonable doubt:* A reasonable doubt is a fair, honest doubt growing out of the evidence or lack of evidence. It is not merely an imaginary or possible doubt, but a doubt based on reason and common sense. A reasonable doubt is just that—a doubt that is reasonable, after a careful and considered examination of the facts and circumstances of this case. CJI 2d 3.2.
- **Civil Trial, Informal Hearings, Formal Hearings—***Preponderance of the evidence:* Evidence that, as a whole, shows the fact sought to be proven is more probable than not. It is the greater weight of the evidence. This also is the standard used for evidentiary hearings.
- **Stricter Civil Standard—***Clear and convincing:* This standard requires the trier of fact

to have less doubt and a firmer conviction about decision than the usual civil standard of preponderance of the evidence. Party is usually relying upon a theory that is disfavored upon policy grounds (i.e., Mental Commitment Hearings).

# *CORPUS DELICTI*

## Definition

- Literally defined means "body of the crime" or "substance of the crime."
- When using *corpus delicti* to refer to all of the elements of a crime, the *corpus delicti* must be proven beyond a reasonable doubt.
- *Corpus delicti* is an evidentiary rule that requires the prosecutor to produce evidence that a crime has been committed before the prosecution can introduce the defendant's confession.

## Burden of Proof

- On prosecutor.
- An extrajudicial confession by itself cannot establish the *corpus delicti*.

A voluntary confession, made extrajudicially, is only received as evidence of guilt and by itself cannot establish guilt.

Carolyn Kenyon disappeared without a trace in 1985. In 1990, police were investigating the defendant when he confessed to killing Kenyon. He stated that he had cut the body up and thrown it into a dumpster. Other than the confession, the prosecution produced no other evidence. The defendant's conviction for second-degree murder was reversed. Evidence of the murder must exist independent of the confession. *People v. McMahan*, 451 Mich. 543 (1996).

"The *corpus delicti* rule is satisfied and a defendant's confession may be admitted into evidence when the prosecutor presents direct or circumstantial evidence, independent of the confession, establishing (1) the occurrence of the specific injury and (2) some criminal agency as the source of the injury. Once this showing is made, a defendant's confession may be used to establish identity, intent, or aggravating circumstances." *People v. Cotton*, 191 Mich. App. 377 (1991).

# RES GESTAE

The *res gestae* include circumstances, facts, and declarations that surround the commission of a crime. The evidence should be contemporaneous with the crime and serve to illustrate its character.

## *Res Gestae* Witness

### Definition

- An eyewitness to a criminal event whose testimony will aid in developing a full disclosure of all the facts.
- Also includes all witnesses having contact with the defendant reasonably contemporaneous with the crime, whose testimony tends to show the state of mind in which the criminal act was done.

## Purpose of *Res Gestae* Witness Rule

- Shield defendant from false accusations.
- Prevent suppression of testimony favorable to accused.
- Ensure disclosure of all circumstances.

*People v. Norwood,* 123 Mich. App. 287 (1983).

## Requirements—MCL 767.40a

- Prosecutor must list all known *res gestae* witnesses.
- Prosecutor must list all known witnesses that might be called at trial.
- Prosecutor must produce a list of witnesses he intends to produce at trial not less than 30 days before the trial.
- Prosecutor and police must provide to the defendant, or defense counsel, upon request, reasonable assistance, including investigative assistance, as may be necessary to locate and serve process upon a witness.

# CHAIN OF CUSTODY

## Definition

The one who offers real evidence must account for the custody of the evidence from the moment it reaches his or her custody until the moment it is offered into evidence.

## Purpose

To ensure the integrity of evidence and that it is, in fact, the item or evidence that is a part of the criminal charges being litigated.

## Effect

Chain of custody goes toward the weight of evidence and not admissibility.

A perfect chain of custody is not always required. Items of evidence may be admitted where the absence of a mistaken exchange, contamination, or tampering has been established to a reasonable degree of probability or certainty. *People v. White*, 208 Mich. App. 126 (1994).

# JUDICIAL NOTICE—MRE 201

## Definition

Judicial notice is an evidentiary shortcut. The court accepts certain facts without requiring formal proof. It is only permissible when the matter is not subject to reasonable dispute because the issue is:

- Generally known within the territorial jurisdiction of the court, or
- Capable of accurate and ready determination by sources whose accuracy cannot reasonably be questioned.

For example, the City of Lansing is located in Ingham County and the State of Michigan.

## Effect

- Civil trial: A jury must accept as conclusive.
- Criminal trial: A jury may, but is not bound to, accept as conclusive.

Judicial notice was taken regarding the reliability of bloodstain interpretation evidence. The Court of Appeals held that a trial court may take judicial notice of the general acceptance of certain forensic evidence by the scientific community. *People v. Haywood*, 209 Mich. App. 217 (1995).

It was improper for the trial judge to take judicial notice of the time it takes the toilet to cycle because the fact was not generally known within the court's jurisdiction and was not readily ascertainable. *People v. United States Currency*, 158 Mich. App. 126 (1986).

# PRESUMPTIONS AND INFERENCES
## Presumption

A legal inference or assumption that a fact exists, based on the known or proven existence of some other fact or group of facts. *Black's Law Dictionary* (9th Edition, 2009).

## Presumptions in Civil Actions—MRE 301

In a civil trial, the jury is bound to accept a presumption. However, the presumption may be rebutted by the opposing party.

## Presumptions in Criminal Cases—MRE 302

In a criminal trial, the jury is not bound to accept a presumption. The jury may, but need not, infer the existence of a presumed fact. The prosecution still bears the burden of proof beyond a reasonable doubt of all elements.

## Presumption of Innocence

A person accused of a crime is presumed to be innocent. This means that you must start with the presumption that the defendant is innocent. This presumption continues throughout the trial and entitles the defendant to a verdict of not guilty unless you are satisfied beyond a reasonable doubt that he or she is guilty. CJI2d 1.9

Per MCL 750.535, it is a rebuttable presumption that a dealer who received property with an altered registration number knowingly received the stolen property. This does not violate the presumption of innocence or the requirement to prove all the elements beyond a reasonable doubt. A presumption is permissible when there is a substantial assurance that a rational connection exists between the proven facts and the fact presumed based on common experience; however, the jury should be instructed that it may, but need not, infer the existence of the presumed fact from the proven fact. *People v. Gallagher*, 404 Mich. 429 (1979).

In a prosecution for stalking, evidence that the defendant continued to engage in repeated contact without consent after being asked to stop, gives rise to a rebuttable presumption that the continuation of conduct caused the victim to feel frightened, intimidated, threatened, harassed, or molested. *People v. White*, 212 Mich. App. 298 (1995).

## Inference

A conclusion reached by considering other facts and deducting a logical consequence from them. *Black's Law Dictionary* (9th Edition, 2009).

The jury is entitled to draw inferences from circumstantial evidence adduced at trial. *People v. Lauzon*, 84 Mich. App. 201 (1978).

Where there was testimony that a battered child was in exclusive custody of the defendant at the time the child suffered the injuries, the jury could infer that the defendant caused the injuries. *People v. Barnard*, 93 Mich. App 590 (1979).

# ADMISSIBILITY OF EVIDENCE
## Relevancy of Evidence—MRE 402

- All relevant evidence is admissible.
- All irrelevant evidence is not admissible.

## Definition of Relevant Evidence—MRE 401

*Evidence having any tendency to make the existence of any fact that is of consequence to the determination of the action more probable or less probable than it would be without the evidence.*

## Relevant Evidence is Both Probative and Material

- *Probative*: Evidence that tends to prove or disprove points in issue. *Black's Law Dictionary* (9th Edition, 2009).

  **Example:** Adam is accused of a crime. He asserts he was not present at the scene of the crime when the crime took place. Prosecutor Bob enters into evidence a security camera tape that shows Adam at the crime scene just before the crime took place. The tape has probative value because it shows Adam was at or near the scene of the crime just before it took place.
- *Material*: Evidence having some logical connection with the facts of consequence or the issues. *Black's Law Dictionary* (9th Edition, 2009).

  **Example:** In an O.W.I. case, evidence that Adam bought four beers at a bar an hour before he was pulled over would be material. Evidence that Adam paid for beer relates to an element of the O.W.I. charge.

Evidence that the defendant borrowed a set of books titled *How to Kill*, the change in his behavior, including constantly talking about perfect crime, and his suggestion to another person that they help him carry out murder was relevant to the element of premeditation. *People v. Burgess,* 153 Mich. App. 715 (1986).

## Exclusion of Relevant Evidence—MRE 403

*Although relevant, evidence may be excluded if its probative value is substantially outweighed by the danger of unfair prejudice, confusion of the issues, or misleading the jury, or by considerations of undue delay, waste of time, or needless presentation of cumulative evidence.*

## Unfair Prejudice

Evidence of the defendant's guilt is always prejudicial, but where the evidence is relevant and probative, it should be excluded only where it is unfairly prejudicial. *People v. Siler,* 171 Mich. App. 246 (1988), *superseded by rule as stated in People v. Drew,* 2009 WL 3757440.

*Prejudice* means more than simply damage to the opponent's cause. It means an undue tendency to move the tribunal to decide on an improper basis, commonly, an emotional one. *People v. Vasher,* 449 Mich. App. 494 (1995).

The defendant in a gruesome murder admitted guilt and only contested his sanity. Therefore, photographs of the victim, a bloodstained sheet, and other items used in the attack had little, if any, probative value. *People v. Murphy,* 100 Mich. App. 413 (1980).

Evidence is unfairly prejudicial when there exists a danger that marginally probative evidence will be given undue or preemptive weight by the jury. The defendant was charged with possession of cocaine with intent to deliver. The prosecution sought to introduce evidence that defendant had previously committed a similar drug crime. The court ruled that even if the evidence was admissible under other rules of evidence, the evidence would be unfairly prejudicial to the defendant because it created a severe risk that the jury would consider it over other more probative evidence. There was no probative value to the prior conviction evidence; the only purpose the prior conviction evidence could serve was to convince the jury that because he had previously sold cocaine, he did so again. *People v. Crawford,* 458 Mich. 376 (1998).

## Confusion of the Issues

In a civil suit founded on police brutality, evidence that drug paraphernalia was found at the scene was properly excluded because the danger of confusion outweighed the probative value. The court opined that the narcotics evidence would cause the jury to focus on side issues rather than the brutality charges alleged in the complaint. *Gainey v. Sieloff,* 163 Mich. App. 538 (1987).

## Misleading the Jury

In a negligence action against city and railroad for car–train collision that occurred at a railroad crossing, the railroad sought to introduce evidence from a Department of Transportation official suggesting that railroad's failure to install crossing gates was solely the result of the city's delay in performing certain roadwork. Although this might have been the case, it was an issue to be decided by the jury. The trial court properly excluded this evidence as prejudicial because it might have misled the jury into believing that the city was solely responsible for the collision. *Houston v. Grand Trunk Western R. Co.,* 159 Mich. App. 602 (1987).

## By Considerations of Undue Delay, Waste of Time, or Needless Presentation of Cumulative Evidence

The trial court properly excluded as cumulative the testimony of officials, including several commissioners, district court judges, mayors, police chiefs, and county sheriffs. *Wayne County Sheriff v. Wayne County Commissioners,* 148 Mich. App. 702 (1983).

# BEST EVIDENCE RULE (ORIGINAL DOCUMENT RULE)

## Requirement of Original—MRE 1002

*To prove the content of a writing, recording, or photograph, the original writing, recording, or photograph is required, except as otherwise provided by the rules or by the statute.*

## KEY

- When the actual contents of the document are an issue in controversy.
- Only when the contents have to be proven.

## Definitions—MRE 1001

*Writings and recordings:* Consist of letters, words, or numbers, or their equivalent, set down by handwriting, typewriting, printing, photostating, photographing, magnetic impulse, mechanical or electronic recording, or other form of data compilation.

*Photographs:* Include still photographs, X-ray films, videotapes, and motion pictures.

*Originals:* The writing or recording itself or any counterpart intended to have the same effect by a person executing or issuing it. An "original" of a photograph includes the negative or any print therefrom. If data are stored in a computer or similar device, any printout or other output readable by sight, shown to reflect the data accurately, is an "original."

*Duplicates:* A counterpart produced by the same impression as the original, or from the same matrix, or by means of photography, including enlargements and miniatures, or by mechanical or electronic re-recording, or by chemical reproduction, or by other equivalent techniques, which accurately reproduces the original.

## Admissibility of Duplicates—MRE 1003

*A duplicate is admissible to the same extent as the original, unless:*

(a) *A genuine question is raised as to the authenticity of the original, or*
(b) *In the circumstances it would be unfair to admit the duplicate in lieu of the original.*

The trial court properly admitted a filtered copy of a tape recording after the court determined it to be an accurate reproduction of the original.

The difficulty in understanding the tape justified filtering out the background noise. *People v. Schram*, 98 Mich. App. 292 (1980).

## Admissibility of Other Evidence of Contents—MRE 1004

*The original is not required, and other evidence of the contents of writing, recording, or photograph is admissible if:*

(a) *Originals lost or destroyed: All originals have been lost or destroyed, unless the proponent lost or destroyed them in bad faith,*
(b) *Original not obtainable: No original can be obtained by any available judicial process or procedure,*
(c) *Original in possession of opponent: At a time when an original was under the control of the party against whom offered, that party was put on notice, by the pleadings or otherwise, that the contents would be a subject of proof at the hearing, and the party does not produce the original at the hearing, or*
(d) *Collateral matters: The writing, recording, or photograph is not closely related to a controlling issue.*

The victim of an assault received numerous threatening letters from defendant because of her refusal to smuggle drugs to defendant while he was incarcerated. The victim threw out the letters while preparing to move. This occurred several months before the trial. The court held it was proper under MRE 1004 to permit the victim to testify to the content of these letters as there was no evidence that the letters were destroyed in bad faith on her part or the part of the prosecutor. *People v. Thompson*, 111 Mich. App. 324 (1981).

## Public Records—MRE 1005

*The contents of an official record or of a document authorized to be recorded or filed and actually recorded or filed. Including data compilations in any form, if otherwise admissible, may be proved by copy, certified in accordance with Rule 902 or testified to be correct by a witness who has compared it with the original. If a copy which complies with the foregoing cannot be obtained by the exercise of reasonable diligence, then other evidence of the contents may be given.*

## Present Memory Refreshed—MRE 612

A witness may use any writing or object to refresh his or her memory when testifying. If the witness refreshes his or her memory while testifying, the adverse party is entitled to have the writing or object produced. If the witness refreshes his or her memory before testifying, the court, at its discretion, can determine whether justice so requires that an adverse party is entitled to have the writing or object produced. For example, a police officer may have to review his or her notes during testimony. If the notes were used to refresh the memory, the defense would have access to review the notes.

Terms and conditions of production and use:

- Party can inspect the object.
- Party can cross-examine the witness regarding the object.
- Party can introduce into evidence those portions relating to the testimony of the witness.

# HEARSAY

## Definition of Hearsay—MRE 801

*Hearsay is a statement, other than the one made by the declarant while testifying at the trial or hearing, offered in evidence to prove the truth of the matter asserted.*

**Statement:**   Either the oral or written assertion of a person, or the nonverbal conduct of a person if it is intended by the person as an assertion.

**Declarant:**   A person who makes a statement.

For example, an officer responds to an accident. Upon arrival, a witness informs the officer that one of the drivers ran a red light, which caused the accident. It would be hearsay for the officer to testify in court as to what the witness observed. The officer can base his report and enforcement action on what the witness told him. However, if there is a trial, the witness must describe their observations in their own words so the jury may determine the credibility of the witness.

Nonverbal conduct may be hearsay if intended as an assertion.

Verbal acts are not hearsay. For example, "this is a stick-up" is part of the act and thus not considered a statement.

The victim began to cry when she saw the suspect's picture in a mug book. Crying does not qualify as a statement because it was not intended as an assertion. *People v. Gwinn*, 111 Mich. App. 223 (1981).

## The Hearsay Rule-MRE 802

*Hearsay is not admissible except as provided by these rules.*

Although hearsay statements are generally not admissible, the Rules of Evidence provide some exceptions in those situations where the risk in considering hearsay statements have been neutralized. There are other situations where the hearsay rule does not apply.

The court ruled it was not hearsay when a police officer testified as to a radio dispatcher stating robbery was in progress at a particular location because the statement was used to prove why officer proceeded to that location, rather than for the truth of the matter asserted. The statement was properly admitted. *People v. Jackson*, 113 Mich. App. 620 (1982).

There is no "radio run" exception to the hearsay rule for information communicated over police radios. The statement made by the police dispatcher that a person called and reported screaming and a horn honking was admitted through the testimony of the responding officer as substantive proof that the victim did not consent and had resisted the defendant's sexual advances. Because the statement was intended to prove the truth of the matter asserted, it was inadmissible hearsay. *People v. Eady*, 409 Mich. 356 (1980).

## Confrontation Clause—Sixth Amendment

The Confrontation Clause of the Sixth Amendment provides: "In all criminal prosecutions, the accused shall enjoy the right . . . to be confronted with the witnesses against him." The U.S. Supreme Court has held that this provision bars "admission of testimonial statements of a witness who did not appear at trial unless he was unavailable to testify, and the defendant had had a prior opportunity for cross-examination." It is the testimonial character of the statement that separates it from other hearsay that, while subject to traditional limitations upon hearsay evidence, is not subject to the Confrontation Clause. Statements are testimonial in nature when the circumstances objectively indicate that the primary purpose of the statement is to establish or prove past events potentially relevant to later criminal prosecution. *Davis v. Washington*, 547 U.S. 813 (2006).

## Statements Which Are Not Hearsay

### A Prior Statement of a Witness—MRE 801(d)(1)

*A statement is not hearsay if the declarant testifies at the trial or hearing and is subject to cross-examination concerning the statement, and the statement is:*

(a) *Inconsistent with the declarant's testimony, and was given under oath subject to the penalty of perjury at a trial, hearing, or other proceeding, or in a deposition,*

(b) *Consistent with the declarant's testimony and is offered to rebut an express or implied charge against the declarant of recent fabrication or improper influence or motive, or*

(c) *One of identification of a person made after perceiving the person.*

### Admission by Party–Opponent—MRE 801(d)(2)

*A statement is not hearsay if the statement is offered against a party and is:*

(a) *The party's own statement, in either an individual or a representative capacity, except statements made in connection with a guilty plea to a misdemeanor motor vehicle violation or an admission of responsibility for a civil infraction under laws pertaining to motor vehicles,*

(b) *A statement of which the party has manifested an adoption or belief in its truth,*

(c) *A statement by a person authorized by the party to make a statement concerning the subject,*

(d) *A statement by the party's agent or servant concerning a matter within the scope of the agency or employment, made during the existence of the relationship, or*

(e) *A statement by a co-conspirator of a party during the course and in furtherance of the conspiracy on independent proof of the conspiracy.*

### A Party's Own Statement

*An officer could testify that defendant stated he had no need to rob the Stop and Go because he made a lot of money selling drugs and that he was robbed of $80,000 worth of heroin just after the convenience store robbery. Officer's testimony to defendant's statement was admissible as admission by a party opponent. People v. Smith, 120 Mich. App. 429 (1982).*

*The defendant's statement to his mother that he was going to kill her was not hearsay because the statement was offered against the defendant and was his own statement. People v. Kowalak, 215 Mich. App. 554 (1996).*

Though the Fifth Amendment prohibits evidence of a defendant's silence after he has invoked his right to silence, it does not preclude use of testimony concerning defendant's behavior and demeanor after a valid waiver of rights. After waiving, defendant's lack of responsiveness during the interview with police was not evidence of silence. Rather, it was admissible as non-verbal, non-assertive conduct admissible with defendant's later admissions to allow the finder of fact to more fully understand the significance of defendant's statement. *People v. McReavy*, 436 Mich. 197 (1990).

### Statement Adopted by a Party as True

The defendant was a Salvation Army truck driver and went to the victim's house to pick up a donation. The next day, the victim noticed her ring was missing. She reported it and the detective called the defendant and asked him to come to the station. The defendant never appeared. At trial, the prosecutor stated that defendant must be guilty of the crime because he did not accept the invitation to discuss the crime with the detective. The Court of Appeals held that admission of evidence of defendant's silence as a tacit admission of guilt is prohibited, unless defendant has shown his adoption of or belief in the truth of the accusation. Because there was no evidence that defendant refused to come to the station because he took the ring, the statements were improper. *People v. Greenwood*, 209 Mich. App. 470 (1995).

### Statement by a Co-Conspirator

A co-defendant made a statement to the police that implicated the defendant. Since this statement was made immediately after and at the scene of the drug transfer, it was sufficiently connected to the conspiracy to be admissible. *People v. Johnson*, 103 Mich. App. 825 (1981).

## Hearsay Exceptions—Availability of Declarant Immaterial—MRE 803

There are exceptions to the hearsay rule. The exceptions are based on a presumed trustworthiness of the statement. The following statements are *not* excluded by the hearsay rule, even though the declarant is available as a witness:

### Present Sense Impression—MRE 803(1)

*A statement describing or explaining an event or condition made while the declarant was perceiving the event or condition, or immediately thereafter.*

For example, "Look at those fools speeding" or "That guy looks drunk."

During a 911 call, the victim stated, "I have just had the living s- beat out of me." Her live-in boyfriend was subsequently arrested and charged with domestic violence. The victim then requested that the charges be dropped and refused to testify. The question presented to the court was whether the 911 tape could be entered as a present sense impression exception to the hearsay rule. To qualify for the present sense impression exception, the following criteria must be met: (1) the statement provides an explanation or description of the perceived event, (2) the declarant personally perceives the event, and (3) the explanation or description must be substantially contemporaneous with the event.

The court held the three criteria for present sense impression were satisfied, but held independent proof that the assault occurred was required to properly lay a foundation for the admission of the tape. The court held the photographs of the victim's injuries provided the independent evidence of the assault which enabled the 911 tape to be admitted into evidence. *People v. Hendrickson*, 459 Mich. 229 (1998).

### Excited Utterance—MRE 803(2)

*A statement relating to a startling event or condition made while the declarant was under the stress of excitement caused by the event or condition.*

For example, "My wife just shot me!"

To come within the excited utterance exception to the hearsay rule, a statement must meet three criteria: (1) it must arise out of a startling occasion, (1a) the occasion must be startling enough to produce nervous excitement and to render the utterance spontaneous and unreflecting; (2) it must be made before there has been time to contrive and misrepresent; and (3) it must relate to the circumstances of the startling occasion. *People v. Gee*, 406 Mich. 279 (1979).

An out-of-court statement by a child made one month after alleged sexual misconduct did not fit within the excited utterance exception because it was not sufficiently established that declarant spoke while still under the stress caused by the startling event. The court held that the statements may have been a result of the stress of the event or could have been a result of a pelvic examination and repeated questioning by the parents. Because it was unclear whether the statement was a spontaneous statement from the stress of the assault or a reflected upon statement made in response to the repeated questioning by the victim's parents, it was inadmissible as an excited utterance. *People v. Straight*, 430 Mich. 418 (1988).

A statement made by a 16-year-old to his mother 10 hours after being sexually assaulted was an excited utterance where the circumstances preceding and surrounding the statement showed he was still under the stress of the event when he made the statement. *People v. Smith*, 456 Mich. 543 (1998).

### Then Existing Mental, Emotional, or Physical Condition—MRE 803(3)

*A statement of the declarant's then existing state of mind, emotion, sensation, or physical condition (such as intent, plan, motive, design, mental feeling, pain, and bodily health), but not including a statement of memory or belief to prove the fact remembered or believed unless it relates to the execution, revocation, identification, or terms of declarant's will.*

For example, "I plan to travel to Lansing tomorrow."

In a first-degree murder prosecution, a page from the victim's appointment book was admissible under the state-of-mind exception to the hearsay rule as a declaration of where the victim intended to go. *People v. Howard*, 226 Mich. App. 528 (1997).

## Statements Made for Purposes of Medical Treatment or Medical Diagnosis in Connection with Treatment—MRE 803(4)

*Statements made for purposes of medical treatment or medical diagnosis in connection with treatment and describing medical history, or past or present symptoms, pain, or sensations, or the inception or general character of the cause or external source thereof insofar as reasonably necessary to such diagnosis and treatment.*

An inherent truthfulness exists when a person describes a pain, symptom, or problem to medical personnel. The statement can be made to a nurse, ambulance driver, doctor, etc.

In combined cases, the court held that identification of an abuser in the course of an examination is reasonably necessary to effectuate treatment of the victim. Identification of the abuser helps the doctor initiate a course of physical and psychological treatment. The physical symptoms in these cases required examinations by the physicians for purposes of medical diagnosis and treatment. These statements identifying the assailants were also descriptions of the external sources of these victims' injuries. The statements were made in response to inquiries concerning how the victims were injured. The court held that statements of two of the three victims bore indicia of trustworthiness, i.e., that the victims understood the need to tell the truth to the doctor, the victims were not asked leading questions, and the descriptions of the assaults and assailants were phrased with childlike genuineness. The court examined the following factors related to the trustworthiness guarantees surrounding the actual making of the statement:

(1) The age and maturity of the declarant.
(2) The manner in which the statements are elicited (leading questions may undermine the trustworthiness of a statement).
(3) The manner in which the statements are phrased (childlike terminology may be evidence of genuineness).

(4) Use of terminology unexpected of a child of similar age.
(5) Who initiated the examination (prosecutorial initiation may indicate that the examination was not intended for purposes of medical diagnosis and treatment).
(6) The timing of the examination in relation to the assault (the child is still suffering pain and distress).
(7) The timing of the examination in relation to the trial (involving the purpose of the examination).
(8) The type of examination (statements made in the course of treatment for psychological disorders may not be as reliable).
(9) The relation of the declarant to the person identified (evidence that the child did not mistake the identity).
(10) The existence of or lack of motive to fabricate.

*People v. Meeboer*, 439 Mich. 310 (1992).

## Recorded Recollection—MRE 803(5)

*A memorandum or record concerning a matter about which a witness once had knowledge but now has insufficient recollection to enable the witness to testify fully and accurately, shown to have been made or adopted by the witness when the matter was fresh in the witness' memory and to reflect that knowledge correctly. If admitted, the memorandum or record may be read into evidence but may not itself be received as an exhibit unless offered by an adverse party.*

A record of something that the witness once had knowledge about, but now has insufficient recollection. Record must have been made or adopted by the witness when the matter was fresh in his memory (i.e., list of stolen property in a complaint).

## Records of Regularly Conducted Activity—MRE 803(6)

*A memorandum, report, record, or data compilation, in any form, of acts, transactions, occurrences, events, conditions, opinions, or diagnoses, made at or near the time by, or from information transmitted by, a person with knowledge, if kept in the course of a regularly conducted business activity, and if it was the regular practice of that business activity to make the memorandum, report, record, or data compilation, all as shown by the testimony of the custodian or other qualified witness, or by certification that complies with a rule promulgated by the supreme court or a statute permitting certification, unless the source of information or the method or circumstances of preparation indicate lack of trustworthiness.*

A police officer lifted prints from the scene of a breaking and entering. He prepared fingerprint cards and ran them though the Automated Fingerprint Identification System. A print was matched to the defendant and he was arrested and subsequently charged with breaking and entering with intent to commit larceny. The Court of Appeals held that, though prepared as part of an investigation, the fingerprint card would be admissible under MRE 803(6). The cards were prepared as a matter of routine police investigation with the intent of identifying a suspect, not in anticipation of litigation. Furthermore, at the time the cards were prepared, no adversarial relationship between the defendant and the police existed. Thus, the cards bore sufficient indicia of trustworthiness to permit their admission at trial. Additionally, the cards only contained objective information and did not need detailed explanation to understand how they were recovered. Because they bore only the objective information and were prepared as part of routine police work, the cards would be admissible under 803(8) as well. *People v. Jambor*, 273 Mich. App. 477 (2007).

Plainclothes officers were making an arrest outside of a home. A person came out of the home with a gun. The officers killed the person, who turned out to be the arrestee's father. The decedent's estate filed a wrongful death action against the officers. At trial, defendants sought to admit police reports prepared after the shooting to show their conduct was proper. On plaintiff's appeal, the court held the reports should not have been admitted at trial because the reports were made following *Miranda* warnings with the assistance of counsel and in anticipation of litigation and department discipline. These circumstances indicate a lack of trustworthiness in the reports sufficient that they should not have been admitted under the business record exception to the rule against hearsay. *Solomon v. Shuell*, 435 Mich. 104 (1990).

The report of a medical exam in a CSC case was not admissible where the report was prepared solely for litigation purposes and thus lacked trustworthiness. *People v. Huyser*, 221 Mich. App. 293 (1997).

## Public Records and Reports—MRE 803(8)(B)

*Records, reports, statements, or data compilations, in any form, of public offices or agencies, setting forth the activities of the office or agency, or matters observed pursuant to duty imposed by law as to which matters there was a duty to report, excluding, however, in criminal cases matters observed by police officers and other law enforcement personnel.*

A police lab report establishing that a substance found on defendant was heroin was inadmissible. Because the report helped establish an element of the crime by use of hearsay observations made by police officers investigating the crime, the report cannot be admitted under MRE 803(8). *People v. McDaniel*, 469 Mich. 409 (2003).

The trial court did not err by admitting a police report concerning the location of another suspect at the time of the offense. A police report of routine matters observed by police officers made in a non-adversarial setting may be admissible under MRE 803(8)(B). Matters observed by police officers at a scene of a crime or while investigating a crime are not admissible. *People v. Stacy*, 193 Mich. App. 19 (1992).

## Hearsay Exception—Child's Statement About Sexual Act—MRE 803A

### "Tender Years Rule"

*A statement describing an incident that included a sexual act performed with or on the declarant by the defendant or an accomplice is admissible to the extent that it corroborates testimony given by the declarant during the same proceeding, provided:*

(a) *The declarant was under the age of 10 when the statement was made,*

(b) *The statement is shown to have been spontaneous and without indication of manufacture,*

(c) *Either the declarant made the statement immediately after the incident or any delay is excusable as having been caused by fear or other equally effective circumstance, and*

(d) *The statement is introduced through the testimony of someone other than the declarant.*

*If the declarant made more than one corroborative statement about the incident, only the first is admissible under this rule.*

A delay of several days in reporting an incident was excusable because the complainant feared reprisal by the defendant. In this case, a father placed his finger in his 9-year-old daughter's vagina. *People v. Hammons*, 210 Mich. App. 554 (1995).

## Hearsay Exceptions—Declarant Unavailable—MRE 804

### Definition—MRE 804(a)

*"Unavailability as a witness"* includes situations in which the declarant:

(a) *Is exempted by ruling of the court on the ground of privilege from testifying concerning the subject matter of the declarant's statement,*

(b) *persists in refusing to testify concerning the subject matter of the declarant's statement despite an order of the court to do so,*

(c) *has a lack of memory of the subject matter of the declarant's statement,*

(d) *is unable to be present or to testify at the hearing because of death or then existing physical or mental illness or infirmity, or*

(e) *is absent from the hearing and the proponent of a statement has been unable to procure the declarant's attendance (or in the case of a hearsay exception under subdivision (b)(2), (3), or (4), the declarant's attendance or testimony) by process or other reasonable means, and in a criminal case, due diligence is shown.*

*A declarant is not unavailable as a witness if exemption, refusal, claim of lack of memory, inability, or absence is due to the procurement or wrongdoing of the proponent of a statement for the purpose of preventing the witness from attending or testifying.*

## Statements not Excluded as Hearsay if the Declarant is "Unavailable."

### Former Testimony—MRE 804(b)(1)

*Testimony given as a witness at another hearing of the same or a different proceeding, if the party against whom the testimony is now offered, or, in a civil action or proceeding, a predecessor in interest, had an opportunity and similar motive to develop the testimony by direct, cross, or redirect examination.*

Former testimony is when a witness at another hearing gives a statement and the opposing side has a prior opportunity and similar motive to cross-examine. For example, a murder trial is overturned on appeal 10 years after the trial. During that time, a witness at the trial passed away. That testimony at the second trial could be admissible under former testimony.

The trial court held a hearing to determine whether or not a witness who had previously testified against the defendant was available to testify at his retrial. The court found the witness unavailable to testify, largely because her doctor testified, though she could physically come to court and testify, it would be hazardous to her health. Her prior testimony, taken at trial where the defendant and counsel had a similar motive and opportunity to examine the witness, was properly admitted under 804(a)(4). *People v. Murray*, 106 Mich. App. 257 (1981).

## Statement Under Belief of Impending Death—MRE 804(b)(2)

### "Dying declaration"

*In a prosecution for homicide or in a civil action or proceeding, a statement made by a declarant while believing that the declarant's death was imminent, concerning the cause or circumstances of what the declarant believed to be impending death.*

### Elements

1. The declarant is unavailable.
2. The statement was made by the declarant while under the belief that his or her death was imminent.
3. The statement concerned the cause or circumstances of what he or she believed to be impending death.
4. The case involves a prosecution for homicide or a civil action or proceeding.

A victim was shot nine times including once between the eyes and made statements naming the defendant as the shooter. The victim recovered from his injuries and defendant was charged in the shooting, but police could not locate him at the time. Approximately five months later, the victim was shot and killed at a gas station. The defendant was arrested and charged with victim's murder. Although the victim's statement naming the defendant as his assailant after the first shooting did not relate to the circumstances of his death from the second shooting, the statements were admitted as dying declarations at defendant's trial. The Court of Appeals held that the plain language of MRE 804(b)(2) did not retain the traditional requirement that the declarant actually died in order for a statement to be admissible as a dying declaration. *People v. Orr*, 275 Mich. App. 587 (2007)

A dying declaration did not occur where a statement was made a month after the shooting and that the victim was recuperating at the time it was made. *People v. Parney*, 98 Mich. App. 571 (1979).

## Statement Against Interest—MRE 804(b)(3)

*A statement which was at the time of its making so far contrary to the declarant's pecuniary or proprietary interest, or so far tended to subject the declarant to civil or criminal liability, or to render invalid a claim by the declarant against another, that a reasonable person in the declarant's position would not have made the statement unless believing it to be true. A statement tending to expose the declarant to criminal liability and offered to exculpate the accused is not admissible unless corroborating circumstances clearly indicate the trustworthiness of the statement.*

### Elements

- The declarant is unavailable.
- The statement was against the declarant's penal interest.
- A reasonable person in the declarant's position would have believed the statement to be true.
- Corroborating circumstances clearly indicated the trustworthiness of the statement.

A police officer was allowed to testify to the contents of a telephone call that the officer listened to involving an informant and the defendant arranging the sale of drugs. A person is unlikely to attempt to arrange the purchase drugs unless he actually wanted the drugs. *People v. Lucas*, 188 Mich. App. 554 (1991).

Following a murder, the brother of defendant told his friend that he cleaned up his grandparents' house because defendant was incapacitated and there had been blood in the bathtub. The friend testified to these statements at trial. The court held the statements were properly admitted under MRE 804(b)(3). Here, the declarant was unavailable because he invoked his Fifth Amendment privilege. The statements were against his interest because they indicated he was aware of a murder that took place and

assisted with covering it up. He would not have made the statements to his friend unless he believed they were true. The statements were made voluntarily and to a person he considered a friend. *People v. Ortiz-Kehoe*, 237 Mich. App. 508 (1999).

The defendant was convicted of murder. The key evidence was a statement that his co-defendant, Andre Freeman, had made. Freeman told his ex-girlfriend that he and Beasley went to the victim's house to purchase drugs. At the residence, they found more drugs than expected and decided to take advantage of the situation by shooting the woman and man at the residence. The ex-girlfriend testified that Freeman told her this information because he had to get it off his chest and that she was the only one he could talk to.

Beasley argued on appeal that the ex-girlfriend's statement to Freeman was not admissible against him. The Court of Appeals disagreed. "Freeman's statement was voluntarily given to Townsend (his ex-girlfriend), who was someone to whom Freeman would likely speak truthfully. Furthermore, Freeman sought out Townsend to initiate the making of the statement. In addition, as stated earlier, Freeman's statement was clearly against his penal interest, and does not shift the blame, but makes reference to defendant only in the context of his narration of the events of the incident." *People v. Beasley*, 239 Mich. App. 548 (2000).

Law enforcement officers should record the facts and circumstances surrounding all statements. The documentation of such information may be necessary for the prosecutor to introduce evidence that might otherwise have gone unheard.

## Hearsay Statements in Domestic Violence Cases— MCL 768.27c

Statements made by victims of domestic violence are admissible in court, even if the victim is not present, if the victim's statement:

- Is made to a law enforcement officer,
- Describes the infliction or threat of physical injury,
- Is made at or near the time of the infliction or threat of physical injury, and
- Is made under circumstances indicating trustworthiness.

## Statement By Declarant Made Unavailable by Opponent—MRE 804(b)(6)

### "Forfeiture by Wrongdoing"

*A statement offered against a party that has engaged in or encouraged wrongdoing that was intended to, and did, procure the unavailability of the declarant as a witness.*

### Elements

1. The defendant engaged in or encouraged wrongdoing.
2. The wrongdoing was intended to procure the declarant's unavailability.
3. The wrongdoing did procure the unavailability.

The forfeiture-by-wrongdoing rule is also an exception to defendant's constitutional right of confrontation. Both the Sixth Amendment and the court rule incorporate a specific-intent requirement. Thus, for the forfeiture-by-wrongdoing rule to apply, the defendant must have specifically intended his wrongdoing to render the witness unavailable to testify. *People v Roscoe*, 303 Mich App 633 (2014).

## TESTIMONY

### Competency—MRE 601

*Unless the court finds after questioning a person that the person does not have sufficient physical or mental capacity or sense of obligation to testify truthfully and understandably, every person is competent to be a witness except as otherwise provided in these rules.*

### Personal Knowledge—MRE 602

*The witness may not testify unless he or she has personal knowledge of the crime. Evidence to prove personal knowledge may, but need not, consist of testimony of the witness.*

This rule is subject to MRE 702 which may allow opinion testimony by expert witnesses.

### Oath or Affirmations—MRE 603

*Before testifying, every witness shall be required to declare that the witness will testify truthfully, by oath or affirmation administered in a form calculated to awaken the witness' conscience and impress the witness' mind with the duty to do so.*

## Exclusion of Witnesses—MRE 615

*At the request of a party the court may order witnesses excluded so that they cannot hear the testimony of other witnesses, and it may make the order of its own motion. This rule does not authorize exclusion of:*

(a) *A party who is a natural person,*
(b) *An officer or employee of a party which is not a natural person designated as its representative by its attorney, or*
(c) *A person whose presence is shown by a party to be essential to the presentation of the party's cause.*

The law enforcement officer assisting the prosecutor is usually allowed to stay in the courtroom during the proceedings.

## OPINION EVIDENCE

### Lay Opinion—MRE 701

*If the witness is not testifying as an expert, the witness' testimony in the form of opinions or inferences is limited to those opinions or inferences which are:*

(a) *Rationally based on the perception of the witness, and*
(b) *Helpful to a clear understanding of the witness' testimony or the determination of a fact in issue.*

Witnesses were allowed to give opinions about the visible intoxication of the defendant. *Heyler v. Dixson*, 160 Mich. App. 130 (1987).

A police officer, who was not an expert in drug enforcement, was allowed to give an opinion based on his observations of the defendant selling crack cocaine. *People v. Daniel*, 207 Mich. App. 47 (1994).

### Expert Opinion—MRE 702

*If the court determines that scientific, technical, or other specialized knowledge will assist the trier of fact to understand the evidence or to determine a fact in issue, a witness qualified as an expert by knowledge, skill, experience, training, or education may testify thereto in the form of an opinion or otherwise if:*

(a) *The testimony is based on sufficient facts or data,*
(b) *The testimony is the product of reliable principles and methods, and*

*(c) The witness has applied the principles and methods reliably to the facts of the case.*

An officer properly qualified as an expert on the basis of his training and experience with observing drug use and drug trafficking may give an opinion that the quantity of crack cocaine, its street price, and the fact that it was evenly cut clearly indicated an intent to sell the crack cocaine and not simply use it for personal consumption. *People v. Ray*, 191 Mich. App. 706 (1991).

An officer trained in accident reconstruction was qualified as an expert to give an opinion about results of tests that he had performed after an accident. *Osner v. Boughner*, 180 Mich. App. 248 (1989).

# IMPEACHMENT

## Definition

To impeach is to attack the credibility of a witness.

## Who May Impeach—MRE 607

*The credibility of a witness may be attacked by any party, including the party calling the witness.*

## Evidence of Character and Conduct of Witness—MRE 608

### Opinion and Reputation Evidence of Character—MRE 608(a)

*The credibility of a witness may be attacked or supported by evidence in the form of opinion or reputation, but subject to these limitations:*

*(a) The evidence may refer only to character for truthfulness or untruthfulness, and*

*(b) Evidence of truthful character is admissible only after the character of the witness for truthfulness has been attacked by opinion or reputation evidence or otherwise.*

This includes evidence about a witness's reputation for truth and veracity from someone who is familiar with the witness in the community where he or she lives. For example, "He's lived in our neighborhood for four years. Everyone knows he is dishonest."

A party's present personal opinion of witness's ability to tell the truth. There must be a reasonable basis for the opinion. For example, "I've worked with Jones for five years and he has lied to me a number of times."

A county jail correctional officer was allowed to testify about a defense witness's reputation for untruthfulness among county jail employees. *People v. Bieri*, 153 Mich. App. 696 (1986).

## Specific Instances of Conduct—MRE 608(b)

*Specific instances of the conduct of a witness, for the purpose of attacking or supporting the witness' credibility, other than conviction of crime as provided in Rule 609, may not be proved by extrinsic evidence. They may, however, in the discretion of the court, if probative of truthfulness or untruthfulness, be inquired into on cross-examination of the witness:*

*(a) Concerning the witness' character for truthfulness or untruthfulness, or*

*(b) Concerning the character for truthfulness or untruthfulness of another witness as to which character the witness being cross-examined has testified.*

## Impeachment by Evidence of Conviction—MRE 609

### General Rule—MRE 609(a)

*For the purpose of attacking the credibility of a witness, evidence that the witness has been convicted of a crime shall not be admitted unless the evidence has been elicited from the witness or established by public record during cross-examination, and*

*(a) The crime contained an element of dishonesty or false statement, or*

*(b) The crime contained an element of theft, and*

- *The crime was punishable by imprisonment in excess of one year or death under the law under which the witness was convicted, and*

- *The court determines that the evidence has significant probative value on the issue of credibility and, if the witness is the defendant in a criminal trial, the court further determines that the probative value of the evidence outweighs its prejudicial effect.*

### Determining Probative Value and Prejudicial Effect—MRE 609(b)

*For purposes of the probative value determination required above, the court shall consider only the age of the conviction and the degree to which a conviction of the crime is indicative of veracity. If a determination of prejudicial effect is required, the court shall consider only the conviction's similarity to the charged offense and the possible effects on the decisional process if admitting the evidence causes the defendant to elect not to testify. The court must articulate, on the record, the analysis of each factor.*

## Time Limit—MRE 609(c)

*Evidence of a conviction under this rule is not admissible if a period of more than ten years has elapsed since the date of the conviction or of the release of the witness from the confinement imposed for that conviction, whichever is the later date.*

Because armed robbery contains an element of theft, evidence of such prior conviction is admissible under MRE 609, if it satisfies the balancing test. *People v. Cross*, 202 Mich. App. 138 (1993).

"In sum, the trial judge's first task, under the amended MRE 609, will be to determine whether the crime contains elements of dishonesty or false statement. If so, it would be admitted without further consideration. If not, then the judge must determine whether the crime contains an element of theft. If it is not a theft crime, then it is to be excluded from evidence without further consideration. If it is a theft crime and it is punishable by more than one year's imprisonment, the trial judge would exercise his discretion in determining the admissibility of the evidence by examining the degree of probativeness and prejudice inherent in the admission of the prior conviction. For purposes of the probativeness side of the equation, only an objective analysis of the degree to which the crime is indicative of veracity and the vintage of the conviction would be considered, not either party's need for the evidence. For purposes of the prejudice factor, only the similarity to the charged offense and the importance of the defendant's testimony to the decisional process would be considered. The prejudice factor would, of course, escalate with increased similarity and increased importance of the testimony to the decisional process. Finally, unless the probativeness outweighs the prejudice, the prior conviction would be inadmissible." *People v. Allen*, 429 Mich. 558 (1988).

# CHARACTER EVIDENCE
## Character Evidence Generally—MRE 404(a)

*Evidence of a person's character or a trait of character is not admissible for the purpose of proving action in conformity therewith on a particular occasion, except:*

(a) *Character of accused: Evidence of a pertinent trait of character offered by an accused, or by the prosecution to rebut the same; or if evidence of a trait of character of the alleged victim of the crime is offered by the accused and admitted as provided below, evidence of a trait of character for aggression of the accused offered by the prosecution.*

(b) *Character of alleged victim of homicide: When self-defense is an issue in a charge of homicide, evidence of a trait of character for aggression of the alleged victim of the crime offered by an accused, or evidence offered by the prosecution to rebut the same, or evidence of a character trait of peacefulness of the alleged victim offered by the prosecution in a charge of homicide to rebut evidence that the alleged victim was the first aggressor.*

(c) *Character of alleged victim of sexual conduct crime: In a prosecution for criminal sexual conduct, evidence of the alleged victim's past sexual conduct with the defendant and evidence of specific instances of sexual activity showing the source or origin of semen, pregnancy, or disease.*

(d) *Character of witness: Evidence of the character of a witness, as provided in MRE 607, 608, and 609.*

## Other Crimes, Wrongs, or Acts—MRE 404(b)

*Evidence of other crimes, wrongs, or acts is not admissible to prove the character of a person in order to show action in conformity therewith. It may, however, be admissible for other purposes, such as proof of motive, opportunity, intent, preparation, scheme, plan, or system in doing an act, knowledge, identity, or absence of mistake or accident when the same is material, whether such other crimes, wrongs, or acts are contemporaneous with or prior or subsequent to the conduct at issue in the case.*

The policy underlying MRE 404(b) is the desire to avoid the danger of conviction based on the defendant's history of other misconduct rather than on evidence of his or her conduct in the case at issue. *People v. Golochowicz*, 413 Mich. 298 (1982).

MRE 404(b) only limits evidence of other acts introduced solely to show criminal propensity. Evidence of other acts may be introduced for any other purpose provided that it is logically relevant to a disputed material issue and is not substantially more prejudicial than probative. *People v. VanderVliet*, 444 Mich. 52 (1993) *amended*, 445 Mich. 1205 (1994).

Evidence of uncharged prior sexual abuse of defendant's half sister over a period of years by defendant was admissible in his trial for criminal sexual conduct involving his minor, adopted daughter. This evidence was admissible because it was offered to rebut his claim of fabrication by the victim's mother and explains why the victim was questioned regarding her father's conduct. *People v. Starr*, 457 Mich. 490 (1998).

Evidence that there had been previous altercations between the victim and defendant was admissible to contradict the argument that the altercation was an accident. *People v. Morris*, 139 Mich. App. 550 (1984).

## Use of Other Bad Acts Evidence

The defendant was charged with sexual assault of his 13-year-old daughter. During his CSC trial, the victim's step-sister was allowed to testify to similar activity by the defendant. The defendant's alleged assault of the complainant and alleged abuse of his stepdaughter shared sufficient common features to infer a plan, scheme, or system to do the acts. *People v. Sabin*, 463 Mich. 43 (2000).

The defendant, a teacher, was charged with having sexual contact with a student. During his trial, the prosecutor was allowed to enter into evidence the defendant had previously engaged in sexual penetration of a student as it showed a common plan in approaching and molesting his victims. *People v. Knapp*, 244 Mich. App. 361 (2001).

Evidence of assaults against the defendant's former girlfriends was admissible to establish common scheme, plan, or system in perpetrating a particular type of physical assault. *People v. Hine*, 467 Mich. 242 (2002).

Testimony of several girls that the defendant allowed his pants to fall down in front of them, or that the defendant otherwise exposed his genitals, was admissible because this evidence was relevant to the defendant's plan, scheme, or system. All three complainants described incidents in which the defendant's overalls fell to the floor while they were present. The frequency with which this happened in front of girls was relevant to show the improbability that the defendant's overalls accidentally fell and exposed his genitals and supported an inference that the defendant's actions were part of a system of desensitizing girls to sexual misconduct. *People v. Ackerman*, 257 Mich. App. 434 (2003).

## Other Bad Acts Against Minors—MCL 768.27a

If a defendant is accused of committing a listed offense against a person under the age of 18, evidence that the defendant committed another listed offense against a minor is admissible and may be considered for its bearing on any matter to which it is relevant. A "listed offense" is any offense that would require registration on Michigan's sex offender registry.

## Other Bad Acts, Domestic Violence—MCL 768.27b

If a defendant is accused of an offense involving domestic violence, evidence of the defendant's commission of other acts of domestic violence is admissible for any purpose for which it is relevant, if it is not otherwise excluded under Michigan rule of evidence 403, if the other acts were committed within the previous 10 years.

## Rape Shield Statute—MCL 750.520j

*Evidence of specific instances of the victim's sexual conduct, opinion evidence of the victim's sexual conduct, and reputation evidence of the victim's sexual conduct shall not be admitted in CSC cases unless and only to the extent that the judge finds that the following proposed evidence is material to a fact at issue in the case and that its inflammatory or prejudicial nature does not outweigh its probative value:*

(a) *Evidence of the victim's past sexual conduct with the actor, or*
(b) *Evidence of specific instances of sexual activity showing the source or origin of semen, pregnancy, or disease.*

The rape shield statute not only bars evidence of the complainant's sexual activities before the alleged rape, but it also bars evidence of all sexual activity by the complainant not incident to the alleged rape. Evidence that the complainant had consented to sex with a stranger seven hours after the rape was not admissible to show she had consented to sex with the defendant. *People v. Stull*, 127 Mich. App. 14 (1983).

If a victim's statement regarding sex does not constitute specific sexual conduct, it is not precluded from admission by the rape shield statute. In this case, the victim made a statement earlier in the day to a friend that she was ready to have sex. Later that night, she had a sexual encounter with the defendant that she argued was rape, while his defense was consent. The statement to the friend was admissible on the issue of consent. *People v. Ivers*, 459 Mich. 320 (1998).

The rape shield statute bars evidence of all sexual activity by the complainant that is not incident to the alleged rape, except evidence of the victim's past sexual conduct with the defendant. Past sexual conduct includes acts that occur between the alleged rape and trial. *People v. Adair*, 452 Mich. 473 (1996).

The rape shield statute barred evidence that the complainant was a topless dancer and had been seen with prostitutes. *People v. Powell*, 201 Mich. App. 516 (1993).

## Method to Prove Character—MRE 405

*Reputation or opinion:* *In all cases in which evidence of character or a trait of character of a person is admissible, proof may be made by testimony as to reputation or by testimony in the form of an opinion. On cross-examination, inquiry is allowable into reports of relevant specific instances of conduct.*

*Specific instances of conduct:* *In cases in which character or a trait of character of a person is an essential element of a charge, claim, or defense, proof may also be made of specific instances of that person's conduct.*

## Habit—MRE 406

*Evidence of the habit of a person or of the routine practice of an organization, whether corroborated or not and regardless of the presence of eyewitnesses, is relevant to prove that the conduct of the person or organization on a particular occasion was in conformity with the habit or routine practice.*

Habit is a regular response to a repeated specific situation, a regular practice of meeting a particular kind of situation with a specific type of conduct, a set pattern, or evidence of something that is done routinely or has been performed on countless occasions. *Cook v. Rontal*, 109 Mich. App. 220 (1981).

# PRIVILEGES—MRE 501

Certain confidential communications are considered privileged and cannot be used against a person. Only the holder can waive the privilege. The purpose of maintaining privileged communication is to encourage parties under certain circumstances to have open communication without concern of reprisal. Types of privileges are listed below.

Communications that take place in the presence of a third party are not privileged. The privilege protects only confidential communications. *People v. Biggs*, 202 Mich. App. 450 (1993).

## Attorney–Client—MCL 767.5a(2)

*Any communications between attorneys and their clients . . . are hereby declared to be privileged and confidential when those communications were necessary to enable the attorneys . . . to serve as such attorney.*

In the course of investigation and trial of a murder case, defense counsel came into the possession of a number of pieces of incriminating evidence from defendant. Defense counsel contacted police, who obtained a warrant, and then received the evidence. Admission of the evidence and a police officer's testimony that incriminating evidence had been seized from the defense counsel's office did not violate defendant's attorney–client privilege. *People v. Nash*, 418 Mich. 196 (1983).

Either the client or the attorney may assert the privilege, but only the client may waive it. *Kubiak v. Hurr*, 143 Mich. App. 465 (1985).

There was no attorney–client privilege where a defendant chose to communicate with counsel by speaking in a manner that could be overheard by a third person rather than covering his mouth and quietly whispering or communicating in writing. *People v. Compeau*, 244 Mich. App. 595 (2001).

## Spouse as Witness—MCL 600.2162

There are two types of privileges between a husband and wife. There is the spousal privilege and the confidential communications privilege. These privileges do not apply in any the following:

- Divorce, separate maintenance, or annulment cases.
- Bigamy prosecutions.
- Crimes against individuals under 18 years of age.
- Causes of action for a wrong or injury done by one spouse to the other, or for non-support.
- Desertion or abandonment cases.
- Certain property actions.

In a criminal prosecution, a party may consent to testify against his or her spouse. Thus, the testifying party holds the privilege.

## Spousal Privilege—MCL 600.2162(2)

*In criminal prosecution, a husband shall not be examined as a witness for or against his wife without his consent, or a wife for or against her husband without her consent, except in the above causes of action.*

The defendant took a rifle into the home where his estranged wife and her three children lived. A man was in the house with the wife. Subsequently, the gun was fired and the man was shot in the arm, but the wife was not shot. The police were called and spoke to the wife, who appeared visibly upset. There were bullet holes in two walls of the house. Later, the wife attempted to assert her spousal privilege to avoid testifying against her husband. The court held that the spousal privilege statute specifically denies the victim-spouse a testimonial privilege in a case that grew out of a personal wrong or injury done by the defendant-spouse to the victim-spouse. *People v Szabo*, 303 Mich App 737 (2014).

## Confidential Communication Privilege—MCL 600.2162(7)

*Except as otherwise provided above, a married person or a person who has been married previously shall not be examined in a criminal prosecution as to any communication made between that person and his or her spouse or former spouse during the marriage without the consent of the person to be examined.*

The defendant and his fiancé participated in a crime together two weeks before getting married. The defendant's fiancé testified against him at trial. By the time of trial, the two had divorced. The court held the spousal privilege did not apply because the parties were not married at the time of trial and the confidential communication privilege did not apply because the parties were not married at the time of the communications. *People v. Zak*, 184 Mich. App. 1 (1990).

## Physician–Patient—MCL 600.2157, MCL 767.5a(2)

*Except as otherwise provided by law, a person duly authorized to practice medicine or surgery shall not disclose any information that the person has acquired in attending a patient in a professional character, if the information was necessary to enable the person to prescribe for the patient as a physician, or to do any act for the patient as a surgeon. MCL 600.2157.*

*Any communications between . . . physicians and their patients are hereby declared to be privileged and confidential when those communications were necessary to enable the . . . physicians to serve as such . . . physician. MCL 767.5a(2).*

The purpose of MCL 600.2157 is to protect the confidential nature of the physician–patient relationship. The privilege belongs to the patient and can only be waived by the patient. *Gaertner v. Michigan*, 385 Mich. 49 (1971).

In a drug prosecution, the defendant's doctor was not precluded from testifying about the defendant's altered prescription. Legitimate confidential communications are protected, but not communications that further an unlawful purpose. *People v. Johnson*, 111 Mich. App. 383 (1981).

The defendant was charged with the involuntary manslaughter of her three children who died as a result of a house fire caused by defendant leaving an empty pot on a lit burner while intoxicated. The Court of Appeals held that information acquired from a patient while the patient is unconscious falls within the physician–patient privilege and that since the blood test results were not the only means of proving intoxication, the results were not "demonstrably relevant" enough to the case at issue so as to overcome the claim of privilege. The court also held that the test results did not fall within the statutorily created physician–patient privilege exceptions for blood drawn after car accidents (MCL 257.625a(6)(e)) or a hospital's duty to report patients wounded by violent means (MCL 750.411). The Court of Appeals denied the subpoena on the basis of the physician–patient privilege. *People v. Childs*, 243 Mich. App. 360 (2000).

## Psychologist–Patient—MCL 333.18237

*A psychologist licensed or allowed to use that title under this part or an individual under his or her supervision cannot be compelled to disclose confidential information acquired from an individual consulting the psychologist in his or her professional capacity if the information is necessary to enable the psychologist to render services.*

The purpose of the psychologist–patient privilege statute is to protect the confidential nature of the psychologist–patient relationship. *People v. Lobaito*, 133 Mich. App. 547 (1984).

## Clergy—MCL 600.2156, MCL 767.5a(2)

*No minister of the gospel, or priest of any denomination whatsoever, or duly accredited Christian Science practitioner, shall be allowed to disclose any confessions made to him in his professional character, in the course of discipline enjoined by the rules or practice of such denomination. MCL 600.2156.*

*Any communications between . . . members of the clergy and the members of their respective churches . . . are hereby declared to be privileged and confidential when those communications were necessary to enable the . . . members of the clergy . . . to serve as such . . . member of the clergy. . . . MCL 767.5a(2).*

The privilege of the confessional belongs to the penitent. *People v. Lipsczinska*, 212 Mich. 484 (1920).

The victim of a CSC told her mother of the rape. The mother reported the incident to the pastor, who was also the pastor for the suspect. The minister called the suspect into his office at night with the suspect's parent and questioned him about the allegation. He asked the suspect whether the incident occurred and the suspect confessed. Later, the minster testified in court about the statement. The Court of Appeals held that "the parent's presence does not destroy the confidentiality of the conversation between defendant and the pastor. The defendant was a minor when the pastor summoned him and [the parent] to the church office. . . . Moreover, there is no record indication that defendant, or even the pastor, believed [the parent's] presence destroyed the confidentiality of their communication. The meeting occurred at night behind closed doors. These conditions support an understanding of confidentiality. As the evidentiary privilege of MCL 767.5a(2) applies under the circumstances, and defendant did not waive that privilege, the pastor's statement cannot be used in trial." *People v. Bragg*, 296 Mich. App. 433 (2012).

## Traffic Crash Reports—MCL 257.624

*A report of a traffic crash required by the Michigan Vehicle Code [UD-10] shall not be available for use in a court action, but a report shall be for the purpose of furnishing statistical information regarding the number and cause of accidents.*

## Consultation Between Victim and Sexual Assault or Domestic Violence Counselor—MCL 600.2157a

*A confidential communication, or any report, working paper, or statement contained in a report or working paper, given or made in connection with a consultation between a victim and a sexual assault or domestic violence counselor, shall not be admissible as evidence in any civil or criminal proceeding without the prior written consent of the victim.*

## News Informants—MCL 767.5a(1)

*A reporter or other person who is involved in the gathering or preparation of news for broadcast or publication shall not be required to disclose the identity of an informant, any unpublished information obtained from an informant, or any unpublished matter or documentation, in whatever manner recorded, relating to a communication with an informant, in any inquiry authorized by this act, except an inquiry for a crime punishable by imprisonment for life when it has been established that the information which is sought is essential to the purpose of the proceeding and that other available sources of the information have been exhausted.*

## Criminal Informants

Disclosure of an informant's identity must be determined according to the circumstances of each case. The trial court should require production of the informant and conduct a hearing in chambers out of the presence of the defendant, if the government invokes the informer's privilege following a defense request for disclosure and the accused is able to demonstrate a possible need for the informer's testimony. At the hearing, the court can examine the informant to determine whether any testimony could be offered that would be helpful to the defense. If the testimony would be helpful to the defense, the informant's identity will be revealed to the defense. A record should be made of the hearing with the contents sealed, and access must be limited to appellate review. *People v. Underwood*, 447 Mich. 695 (1994).

## Social Worker—MCL 333.18513

A social worker may be an affiant on a search warrant. The social worker privilege does not apply to actions taken under the Child Protection Law. *People v. Wood*, 447 Mich. 80 (1994).

## Circuit Court Family Counselors—MCL 551.339

*A communication between a counselor in the family counseling service and a person who is counseled is confidential. The secrecy of the communication shall be preserved inviolate as a privileged communication which privilege cannot be waived. The communication shall not be admitted in evidence in any proceedings. The same protection shall be given to communications between spouses and counselors to whom they have been referred by the court or the court's family counseling service.*

Exception: A family referred by the court with custody or parenting time problems whose adult members sign an agreement indicating the purpose of the referral is exempt from confidentiality may consent to a report of an evaluation of those families being submitted to the court with indicated recommendations.

## Self-Incrimination—MCL 600.2154

*Any competent witness in a cause shall not be excused from answering a question relevant to the matter in issue, on the ground merely that the answer to such question may establish, or tend to establish, that such witness owes a debt, or is otherwise subject to a civil suit; but this provision shall not be construed to require a witness to give any answer which will have a tendency to accuse himself of any crime or misdemeanor, or to expose him to any penalty or forfeiture, nor in any respect to vary or alter any other rule respecting the examination of witnesses.*

## Polygraph Results or Reports—MCL 338.1728(3)

*Any recipient of information, report, or results from a polygraph examiner, except for the person tested, shall not provide, disclose, or convey such information, report, or results to a third party except as may be required by law.*

A polygraph result or the refusal to take a polygraph may not be used by the prosecution.

The mention of taking a polygraph by a witness during trial may require a mistrial if it unfairly prejudices the defendant. In considering the matter, the court weighs the following factors:

- whether defendant objected and/or sought a cautionary instruction.
- whether the reference was inadvertent.
- whether there were repeated references.
- whether the reference was an attempt to bolster a witness's credibility.

- whether the results of the test were admitted rather than merely the fact that a test had been conducted.

*People v. Nash*, 244 Mich. App. 93 (2000).

## Accountant–Client—MCL 339.732

*The information derived from or as the result of professional service rendered by a certified public accountant is confidential and privileged.*

Exception: This privilege does not prohibit a licensee, or a person employed by a licensee, from disclosing information otherwise privileged and confidential to appropriate law enforcement or governmental agencies when the licensee, or person employed by the licensee, has knowledge that forms a reasonable basis to believe that a client has committed a violation of federal or state law or a local governmental ordinance.

The privilege ceases to operate when the advice sought refers to future wrongdoing. The privilege does protect past wrongdoing. *People v. Paasche*, 207 Mich. App. 698 (1994).

## Privileged Communications and Mandatory Reporting of Child Abuse—MCL 722.631

*Any legally recognized privileged communication except that between attorney and client or that made to a member of the clergy in his or her professional character in a confession or similarly confidential communication is abrogated and shall not constitute grounds for excusing a report otherwise required to be made or for excluding evidence in a civil child protective proceeding resulting from a report made pursuant to this act. This section does not relieve a member of the clergy from reporting suspected child abuse or child neglect under [The Child Protection Act] if that member of the clergy receives information concerning suspected child abuse or child neglect while acting in any other capacity listed under the [law].*

Marital communications privilege is abolished in civil child protective proceedings. *Matter of Stricklin*, 148 Mich. App. 659 (1986).

Statutory abrogation of physician–patient privilege in proceedings under Child Protection Law does not require that proceedings result from report of suspected abuse by someone obligated to make such report; report made by someone not under obligation to report, such as neighbor, is also "report" made pursuant to Child Protection Law. *In Re Brock*, 442 Mich. 101 (1993).

In the absence of indication that psychologist meeting with mother was result of any action under the Child Protection Law, provision of this section abrogating the psychologist–patient privilege was not applicable. *Matter of Atkins*, 112 Mich. App. 528 (1982).

# EXCLUSIONARY RULE

The purpose of the exclusionary rule is to deter police activity that violates the rights of a citizen. Illegally seized evidence may be excluded from trial.

Evidence gained by violating defendant's federal constitutional rights will not be admitted into evidence in a criminal proceeding. *Weeks v. United States*, 232 U.S. 383 (1914).

Fourth Amendment standards are applied to the states via the Fourteenth Amendment. The exclusionary rule is applicable to the states. *Mapp v. Ohio*, 367 U.S. 643 (1961).

The Michigan Supreme Court also applies the exclusionary rule against evidence seized in violation of the Michigan Constitution. *People v. Case*, 220 Mich. 379 (1922).

## "Fruit of the Poisonous Tree" Doctrine

Evidence obtained after illegal governmental action will be excluded. This includes not only materials subject to the Exclusionary Rule, but also subsequent confessions, admissions, identifications, and testimony obtained as a result of the primary taint. These "fruits" of the illegality will be excluded. *Wong Sun v. United States*, 371 U.S. 471 (1963).

# O.W.I. LAW

## O.W.I. STATUTE—MCL 257.625(1)

*A person, whether licensed or not, shall not operate a vehicle upon a highway or other place open to the general public or generally accessible to motor vehicles, including an area designated for the parking of vehicles, within this state if the person is operating while intoxicated.*

**Operating while intoxicated** means any of the following:

- The person is under the influence of alcoholic liquor, a controlled substance, or other intoxicating substance or a combination of alcoholic liquor, a controlled substance, or other intoxicating substance.
- The person has an alcohol content of 0.08 grams or more per 100 milliliters of blood, per 210 liters of breath, or per 67 milliliters of urine.
- The person has an alcohol content of 0.17 grams or more per 100 milliliters of blood, per 210 liters of breath, or per 67 milliliters of urine.

### Elements

1. The defendant was operating a motor vehicle. Operating means driving or having actual physical control of the vehicle.
2. The defendant was operating a vehicle on a highway or other place open to the public or generally accessible to motor vehicles.

3. While operating a motor vehicle, the defendant:
   (a) Was under the influence of alcohol, a controlled substance, or other intoxicating substance;
   (b) Had a bodily alcohol level of 0.08 grams or more per 100 milliliters of blood, 210 liters of breath, 67 milliliters of urine; or
   (c) Had a bodily alcohol level of 0.17 grams or more per 100 milliliters of blood, 210 liters of breath, 67 milliliters of urine.

CJI2d 15.1–15.3.

### What Does It Mean To Operate?

"*Operate or Operating*" means one or more of the following:

- Being in actual physical control of a vehicle.
- This subdivision applies regardless of whether or not the person is licensed under this act as an operator or chauffeur.

MCL 257.35a.

"*Operator*" means a person, other than a chauffeur, who does either of the following:

- Operates a motor vehicle upon a highway or street.
- Operates an automated motor vehicle upon a highway or street.

MCL 257.36.

The defendant was found slumped over the steering wheel in the lane of a drive-through restaurant. The vehicle's engine was running, the vehicle was in gear, and the defendant's foot was on the brake. The court held the driver was operating the vehicle, stating "[o]nce a person using a motor vehicle as motor vehicle has put the vehicle in motion, or in a position posing significant risk of causing a collision, such a person continues to operate it until the vehicle is returned to a position posing no such risk." Because the defendant's foot could have slipped off the brake and the vehicle could have then rolled causing a collision, he had not returned it to a position of safety, thus, he was still operating the vehicle. *People v. Wood*, 450 Mich. 399 (1995).

The defendant was a passenger in a vehicle driven by his girlfriend, with whom he was arguing. The defendant grabbed the steering wheel, causing the vehicle to veer off the road and strike a jogger. The jogger was severely injured and defendant was charged with felonious driving. The court held the Vehicle Code's definition of operate neither requires exclusive nor complete control of a vehicle; nor does it require "control over all the functions necessary to make the vehicle operate." In order to operate a vehicle under the Vehicle Code, "actual physical control" is all that is required, which the court defined as the "power to guide the vehicle." Under that definition, grabbing a steering wheel is enough to exert the control required by the Vehicle Code. *People v. Yamat*, 475 Mich. 49 (2006).

The statute covers areas open to the public, though not open necessarily to vehicular travel. For instance, the lawn of a girl's dormitory at Wayne State University is a place open to the public, and an arrest for O.W.I. on the lawn is valid. *People v. Tracy*, 18 Mich. App. 529 (1969).

An officer observed a vehicle drifting within the lane and driving on the lane markers. The weather was dry and there was no rain or ice on the paved road. The driver of the car activated his left turn signal, traveling past numerous driveways and one side street. He traveled approximately two-tenths of a mile before finally turning. He was stopped and subsequently arrested for O.W.I. The court upheld the stop. Erratic driving can give rise to reasonable suspicion of unlawful intoxication to justify an investigatory stop by a police officer. *People v. Christie*, 206 Mich. App. 304 (1994).

While responding to an anonymous call, a police officer discovered the defendant asleep in his truck at the county fairgrounds. The truck was wedged on a parking lot, with the tires barely touching the ground. The defendant was found asleep in the front seat, covered by a sleeping bag. The truck's engine was not running, the automatic transmission was in park, and the keys to the truck were inside defendant's pocket. The police officer woke up the defendant, observed that he smelled strongly of intoxicants and was confused and unaware of his surroundings. The defendant explained that he had been at a bar earlier that evening, had too much to drink, and drove to the fairgrounds to sleep because he was too intoxicated to drive home. The defendant explained that he struck the parking lot while trying to leave the fairgrounds and, after unsuccessfully attempting to free the truck from the lot, he turned off the engine and went to sleep. The police officer arrested the defendant for O.W.I. The defendant argued that the arrest was illegal.

The court held that the officer's arrest was valid because an officer may arrest a person without a warrant if the officer has reasonable cause to believe a misdemeanor punishable by more than 92 days of imprisonment occurred, and reasonable cause to believe the person committed it. First offense O.W.I. is a misdemeanor punishable by imprisonment for not more than 93 days. Therefore, an officer does not have to observe a defendant operating a vehicle for the defendant to be arrested and prosecuted for O.W.I. under this exception. The officer must have reasonable cause to believe that the crime of O.W.I. had been committed and that defendant committed it.

In this case, the defendant admitted to the police officer that he drove on public roadways to the fairgrounds to sleep off the effects of having too much to drink. According to the defendant, he struck the parking lot while attempting to leave the fairgrounds and turned off the engine and went to sleep after he was unable to dislodge his truck. This is different than the defendant not driving the vehicle, but using the vehicle as a shelter, rather than a motor vehicle, in a parking lot. *People v. Stephen*, 262 Mich. App. 213 (2004).

Officers were alerted that some females in a Pontiac G6 hit a concrete barrier when they entered the parking deck and that they appeared to be drunk as they were leaving the bar. The officer saw the vehicle, which was legally parked. As he approached, the officer noticed that the vehicle's backup lights and brake lights were on. The backup lights then turned off, and it appeared that the transmission had been put back into park because the vehicle "settled a little bit." The tires did not move. The officer activated his overhead lights and blocked the car and the driver was subsequently arrested for O.W.I. The court held that because the defendant applied the brakes of her running vehicle, shifted the vehicle into reverse, and then shifted back into park, the defendant was in "actual physical control" of the vehicle. Thus, she "operated" the vehicle and the fact that it remained stationary is immaterial. *City of Plymouth v. Longeway*, 296 Mich.App. 1 (2012).

## O.W.I.—Under the Influence—Alcohol—MCL 257.625(1)

*"Under the influence of alcohol"* means that, because of drinking alcohol, the defendant's ability to operate a motor vehicle in a normal manner was substantially lessened. To be under the influence, a person does not have to be inebriated to the point of falling down. Conversely, just because the person has consumed alcohol does not prove, by itself, that the person is under the influence of alcohol. The test is whether, because of drinking alcohol, the defendant's mental or physical condition was significantly affected to the point that the ability to operate a vehicle in a normal manner is impacted. CJI2d 15.3.

To prove the offense of operating a motor vehicle under the influence of intoxicating liquor, the prosecution must establish that (1) the defendant was operating a motor vehicle on a highway or other place open to the general public; (2) while so operating the defendant was under the influence of alcohol, controlled substances, or a combination thereof; and (3) as a result of the drinking or taking of a controlled substance, the defendant was substantially deprived of normal control or clarity of mind. *People v. Raisanen*, 114 Mich. App. 840 (1982).

## O.W.I.—Under the Influence—Controlled Substance—MCL 257.625(1)

*"Under the influence of a controlled substance"* means that, because of consuming a controlled substance, the defendant's ability to operate a motor vehicle in a normal manner was substantially lessened. To be under the influence, a person does not have to be inebriated to the point of falling down. Conversely, just because the person has consumed a controlled substance does not prove, by itself, that the person is under the influence of a controlled substance. The test is whether, because of consuming a controlled substance, the defendant's mental or physical condition was significantly affected to the point that the ability to operate a vehicle in a normal manner is impacted.

Police were informed of a disabled vehicle near I-75. Upon arriving at the scene, the officer found the defendant trying to start the vehicle, but there was extensive damage to the vehicle, including damage to the driver's side wheels. The defendant informed the officer that he was driving when he suddenly hit the guardrail. The defendant allegedly told the officer that he took Ritalin, and had not taken the drug in some time, but his mother had given him Xanax, which caused his driving accident. The defendant was transported to a hospital where a blood sample was taken. The lab results from the defendant's blood sample indicated that 250 ng/mL of Zolpidem, a sedative used to treat insomnia sold under the brand name Ambien, was detected. The defendant was charged with operating while under the influence of a controlled substance, MCL 257.625(1). The defendant sought to dismiss the charges since Zolpidem was not listed by statute as a controlled substance, and the O.W.I statute did not incorporate the rules promulgated by the Board of Pharmacy. The court held "the Michigan Vehicle Code requires that for purposes of determining what constitutes a controlled substance, the health code must be examined, and the health code appropriately delegates classification of additional drugs through the use of administrative rules, and administrative rules have the force and effect of law. In the area of drug regulation, resort to the flexibility of administrative rules is necessary because new drugs are developed and introduced at a rapid rate" coupled with the discovery of new methods to abuse drugs. The court held that Zolpidem was a "controlled substance." *Bloomfield Township v. Kane*, 302 Mich. App. 170 (2013).

## O.W.I.—Under the Influence—Intoxicating Substance—MCL 257.625(1)

*"Under the influence of an intoxicating substance"* means that, because of consuming some other intoxicating substance, the defendant's ability to operate a motor vehicle in a normal manner was substantially lessened. To be under the influence, a person does not have to be inebriated to the point of falling down. Conversely, just because the person has consumed some other intoxicating substance does not prove, by itself, that the person is under the influence of an intoxicating substance. The test is whether, because of consuming an intoxicating substance, the defendant's mental or physical condition was significantly affected to the point that the ability to operate a vehicle in a normal manner is impacted.

*"Intoxicating substance"* means any substance, preparation, or a combination of substances and preparations other than alcohol or a controlled substance, that is either of the following:

- Recognized as a drug in any of the following publications or their supplements:
  - The official United States pharmacopoeia.
  - The official homeopathic pharmacopoeia of the United States.
  - The official national formulary.
- A substance, other than food, taken into a person's body, including, but not limited to, vapors or fumes, that is used in a manner or for a purpose for which it was not intended, and that may result in a condition of intoxication.

## Unlawful Bodily Alcohol Content (UBAC)—MCL 257.625(1)(b)

### Elements

1. The defendant was operating a motor vehicle. Operating means driving or having actual physical control of the vehicle.
2. The defendant was operating a vehicle on a highway or other place open to the public or generally accessible to motor vehicles.
3. While operating a motor vehicle, the defendant had a bodily alcohol level of 0.08 grams or more per 100 milliliters of blood, 210 liters of breath, 67 milliliters of urine.

CJI2d 15.2-15.3

## Enhanced Unlawful Bodily Alcohol Content ("Super Drunk")—MCL 257.625(1)(c)

### Elements

1. The defendant was operating a motor vehicle. Operating means driving or having actual physical control of the vehicle.

2. The defendant was operating a vehicle on a highway or other place open to the public or generally accessible to motor vehicles.
3. While operating a motor vehicle, the defendant had a bodily alcohol level of 0.17 grams or more per 100 milliliters of blood, 210 liters of breath, 67 milliliters of urine.

CJI2d 15.2-15.3

## Impaired Driving—MCL 257.625(3)

*A person, whether licensed or not, shall not operate a vehicle upon a highway or other place open to the general public or generally accessible to motor vehicles, including an area designated for the parking of vehicles, within this state when, due to the consumption of alcoholic liquor, a controlled substance, or other intoxicating substance, or a combination of alcoholic liquor, a controlled substance, or other intoxicating substance, the person's ability to operate the vehicle is visibly impaired.*

Note: A person charged with operating while intoxicated may be found guilty of operating while visibly impaired.

### Elements

1. The defendant was operating a motor vehicle. Operating means driving or having actual physical control of the vehicle.
2. The defendant was operating a vehicle on a highway or other place open to the public or generally accessible to motor vehicles. While operating a motor vehicle, the defendant drove with less ability than would an ordinary careful driver due to the use of alcohol or a controlled substance. The defendant's driving ability must have been lessened to the point that it would have been noticed by another person.

CJI2d 15.2 and CJI2d 15.4.

## Operating With The Presence Of Drugs (O.W.P.D.)—MCL 257.625(8)

*A person, whether licensed or not, shall not operate a vehicle upon a highway or other place open to the general public or generally accessible to motor vehicles, including an area designated for the parking of vehicles, within this state if the person has in his or her body any amount of a controlled substance listed in schedule 1 under MCL 333.7212 [including marihuana], or a rule promulgated under that section, or of a controlled substance described in MCL 333.7214(a)(iv) [cocaine].*

Note: If the suspect driver is a patient under the Michigan Medical Marijuana Act (MMMA), he or she

MUST be under the influence of THC for a violation and cannot be prosecuted for simply having the presence of THC in his or her system under this section.

> The defendant was driving on an unlit five-lane road when he struck and killed the victim. The defendant's bodily alcohol content at the time of the accident was between 0.091 and 0.115 grams per 100 milliliters of blood. Furthermore, 11-carboxy-THC was present in his blood. 11-carboxy-THC is a metabolite of THC, the active ingredient in marihuana. The defendant was convicted of O.W.P.D. causing death and he appealed. The court held that 11-carboxy-THC is *not* schedule 1 controlled substance because it is not a derivative of marihuana. *People v. Feezel*, 486 Mich. 184 (2010).

Under current Michigan law, 11-carboxy-THC is no longer sufficient to prove O.W.P.D.; however, the courts have not yet answered whether it could be considered an "other intoxicating substance."

> The defendant was pulled over for speeding 83 miles per hour in a 55-miles-per-hour zone. The arresting officer smelled intoxicants, and the defendant admitted to having consumed one beer sometime within the last couple of hours. The defendant consented to a pat-down of his person, voluntarily removed a pipe, and explained that he had a medical marihuana registry card and had last smoked marihuana five to six hours previously. A blood test showed that the defendant had active THC in his system at 10 ng/mL. The defendant was charged with operating a motor vehicle with a schedule 1 controlled substance in his body under the "zero tolerance" law under MCL 257.625(8). The court held that because the MMMA superseded all statutes inconsistent with its provisions, a MMMA patient with marihuana in their system cannot be charged under MCL 257.625(8) unless they are shown to be under the influence of marihuana. If the patient is shown to be under the influence of marihuana, their MMMA immunity does not apply and they may be convicted of any statute of which they are in violation. Although the MMMA does not define what it means to be under the influence of marihuana, the court considered the MMMA in whole and held that "under the influence of marihuana" required some effect on a person, not simply having any amount of marihuana in one's system. *People v. Koon*, 494 Mich. 1 (2013).

## O.W.I. at the Scene of an Accident/Passed Out Behind The Wheel—MCL 257.625a(1)

A peace officer may arrest a person without a warrant under either of the following circumstances:

- The peace officer has reasonable cause to believe the person was, at the time of an accident in this state, the operator of a vehicle involved in the accident and was operating the vehicle in violation of MCL 257.625.
- The person is found in the driver's seat of a vehicle parked or stopped on a highway or street within this state if any part of the vehicle intrudes into the roadway and the peace officer has reasonable cause to believe the person was operating the vehicle in violation of MCL 257.625.

> Whether an accident has occurred, for purposes of applying the warrantless arrest statute, depends on an examination of all the circumstances surrounding the incident. Factors include:
>
> - Whether there was a collision.
> - Whether personal injury or property damage resulted.
> - Whether the incident was either undesirable for or unexpected by any of the parties involved.
>
> *People v. Keskimaki*, 446 Mich. 240 (1994).

## Disclosure of Blood Tests—MCL 257.625a(6)(e)

*If, after an accident, the driver of a vehicle involved in the accident is transported to a medical facility and a sample of the driver's blood is withdrawn at that time for medical treatment, the results of a chemical analysis of that sample are admissible in any civil or criminal proceeding to show the amount of alcohol or presence of a controlled substance or both in the person's blood at the time alleged, regardless of whether the person had been offered or had refused a chemical test. The medical facility or person performing the chemical analysis shall disclose the results of the analysis to a prosecuting attorney who requests the results for use in a criminal prosecution as provided in this subdivision. A medical facility or person disclosing information in compliance with this subsection is not civilly or criminally liable for making the disclosure.*

The results of blood tests taken by medical facilities for purposes of medical treatment must be disclosed upon request to the prosecutor, even without a warrant, and may be used at trial to prove blood alcohol levels. Neither the taking of blood for medical purposes nor the warrantless acquisition of blood by prosecutors for use at trial violate the state or federal Constitution. The court held that the privacy interest in blood-alcohol test results following car accidents is not one society is prepared to recognize as reasonable. *People v. Perlos*, 436 Mich. 305 (1990).

The subpoena of blood results taken by a medical facility is not limited to persons who are arrested, but may apply to anyone involved in a traffic crash. A person can be "involved in" an accident where the evidence demonstrates that the person was implicated in or connected with the accident in a logical or substantial manner. The person need not have caused the accident in order to have been "involved in" the accident. *People v. Aldrich*, 246 Mich. App. 101 (2001).

Penalties—MCL 257.625(9)

| First conviction O.W.I/UBAC and impaired | 93-day misdemeanor: Court may order immobilization |
|---|---|
| Second conviction within 7 years | 1-year misdemeanor: Vehicle is subject to forfeiture; if not forfeited, must be immobilized |
| Third conviction during lifetime | 5-year felony: Vehicle is subject to forfeiture; if not forfeited, must be immobilized |

## What Constitutes Prior Convictions—MCL 257.625(25)(b)

- All drug and alcohol violations under MCL 257.625 (except allowing an intoxicated person to operate a vehicle under MCL 257.625(2)).
- Murder, manslaughter, and negligent homicide with a vehicle.
- Moving violation which causes the death or serious impairment of another person under 257.601d.
- Child endangerment. MCL 257.625(7).
- Commercial motor vehicle violations under MCL 257.625m.
- Attempted violations and similar laws from other states are also included. MCL 257.625(25)(b).
- Only one zero tolerance violation can be used to enhance. MCL 257.625(26).
- Only one conviction can be used for violations arising out of the same transaction. MCL 257.625(27).

## Enhanced Bodily Alcohol Content ("Super Drunk Law")

- 180-day misdemeanor.
- Mandatory rehabilitation by the court, including mandatory ignition interlock.

# .02/ZERO TOLERANCE—MCL 257.625(6)

*A person who is less than 21 years of age, whether licensed or not, shall not operate a vehicle upon a highway or other place open to the general public or generally accessible to motor vehicles, including an area designated for the parking of vehicles, within this state if the person has any bodily alcohol content. As used in this subsection, "any bodily alcohol content" means either of the following:*

*(a) An alcohol content of 0.02 grams or more but less than 0.08 grams per 100 milliliters of blood, per 210 liters of breath, or per 67 milliliters of urine, or, beginning October 1, 2018, the person has an alcohol content of 0.02 grams or more but less than 0.10 grams per 100 milliliters of blood, per 210 liters of breath, or per 67 milliliters of urine.*

*(b) Any presence of alcohol within a person's body resulting from the consumption of alcoholic liquor, other than consumption of alcoholic liquor as a part of a generally recognized religious service or ceremony.*

## Elements

1. The defendant was less than 21 years of age.
2. The defendant was operating a motor vehicle upon a highway or other place open to the public or generally accessible to motor vehicles.
3. While having any bodily alcohol content as evidenced by either:

   a. An alcohol content of 0.02 grams or more but less than 0.08 grams per 100 milliliters of blood, per 210 liters of breath, or per 67 milliliters of urine.
   b. Any presence of alcohol within a person's body resulting from the consumption of alcoholic liquor, other than consumption of alcoholic liquor as a part of a generally recognized religious service or ceremony.

Penalties—MCL 257.625(12)

| First conviction | Misdemeanor; however, not punishable by imprisonment. |
|---|---|
| Second conviction, if violation occurs within 7 years of one or more prior convictions | 93-day misdemeanor |

A person arrested for violating MCL 750.625(6) may be held by a peace officer under MCL 780.581(3) until the person is in a safe condition to be released. OAG 1993–1994, No. 6,824, p. 206 (December 1, 1994).

## Commercial Motor Vehicle Drivers—MCL 257.625m

*A person, whether licensed or not, who has an alcohol content of 0.04 grams or more but less than 0.08 grams per 100 milliliters of blood, per 210 liters of breath, or per 67 milliliters of urine, shall not operate a commercial motor vehicle within this state.*

### Elements

1. The defendant was operating a commercial motor vehicle. Operating means driving or having actual physical control of the vehicle.
2. The defendant had a bodily alcohol content of 0.04 grams or more but less than 0.08 grams per 100 milliliters of blood, 210 liters of breath, or 67 milliliters of urine when operating the commercial motor vehicle.

CJI2d 15.13.

Penalties:

| | |
|---|---|
| Refusal to take PBT for commercial driver MCL 257.625a(5) | 93-day misdemeanor |
| First conviction impaired driving of a commercial vehicle | 93-day misdemeanor |
| Second conviction within 7 years | 1-year misdemeanor |
| Third conviction within 10 years | 1- to 5-year felony |

## O.W.I., Impaired, or O.W.P.D. Causing Death—MCL 257.625(4) (felony)

*A person, whether licensed or not, who operates a motor vehicle while intoxicated, visibly impaired, or with the presence of a controlled substance, and by the operation of that motor vehicle causes the death of another person is guilty of a crime.*

### Elements

1. That the defendant was operating a motor vehicle. Operating means driving or having actual physical control of the vehicle.
2. That the defendant was operating the vehicle on a highway or other place that was open to the public or generally accessible to motor vehicles, including any designated parking area.
3. That while operating the vehicle, the defendant was intoxicated or visibly impaired.
4. That the defendant voluntarily decided to drive knowing that he or she had consumed alcoholic liquor, a controlled substance, or other intoxicating substance or a combination of alcoholic liquor, a controlled substance, or other intoxicating substance and might be intoxicated or visibly impaired, or operated a vehicle with the presence of a controlled substance.
5. That the defendant's operation of the vehicle caused the victim's death. To "cause" the victim's death, the defendant's operation of the vehicle must have been a factual cause of the death, that is, but for the defendant's operation of the vehicle the death would not have occurred. In addition, operation of the vehicle must have been a proximate cause of death, that is, death or serious injury must have been a direct and natural result of operating the vehicle.

CJI2d 15.11–15.11a.

Violation is a felony, punishable by 15-year imprisonment.

## Second-Degree Murder

After a fatal traffic accident, defendant was charged with second-degree murder. He argued that he did not have sufficient malice for the charge. The court held the mens rea for second-degree murder does not mandate a finding of specific intent to harm or kill. The intent to do an act in obvious disregard of life-endangering consequences is a malicious intent. Second-degree murder is a general-intent crime to which voluntary intoxication is not an available defense.

In this case, the court found there was sufficient evidence to bind the defendant over. First, he tried to evade the police as they drove by on patrol giving the inference that he was aware of his intoxication. Despite this intoxication, he drove recklessly down a main road and, after nearly striking another vehicle, he continued driving. He then sped through a red light before striking the victim.

Here, the defendant was highly intoxicated and, while leaving the bar, backed twice into the same vehicle. This could infer that he should have known that he should not be driving. Still, he drove at a high rate of speed through a residential area. He swerved to miss a car stopped at a stop sign, ran through a stop sign, and nearly hit another car. The occupants of his vehicle told him he was driving too fast and should slow down. He then collided with a vehicle, drove over a curb, across some grass, and struck the victim. The passengers then jumped out and told him he had hit the child. He continued to drive for several blocks before stopping. *People v. Goecke*, 457 Mich. 442 (1998).

Second-degree murder charges were upheld where the defendant had a history of blacking out when drinking, knew he may drive irresponsibly if he drank alcohol, and still went to the bar and drank before driving his vehicle the wrong way on the freeway. *People v. Werner*, 254 Mich. App. 528 (2002).

Causation is a required element for O.W.I. causing death. In the *Feezel* case (discussed in the O.W.P.D. section of this chapter), the defendant was driving on an unlit five-lane road in the rain. The defendant struck and killed the victim, who was walking in the middle of the road. The victim's blood alcohol content was at least 0.268%. The defendant was charged with O.W.I. causing death, O.W.P.D. causing death, and failure to stop at the scene of an accident causing death. The court ruled that evidence of the victim's BAC should have been admissible at trial. This is because the victim's actions may have been a superseding cause of his death. Under the facts of this case, the jury should have been allowed to consider the victim's intoxication. *People v. Feezel*, 486 Mich. 184 (2010).

## O.W.I., Impaired, or O.W.P.D. Causing Serious Impairment of a Body Function—MCL 257.625(5) (felony)

*A person, whether licensed or not, who operates a motor vehicle while intoxicated, visibly impaired, or with the presence of a controlled substance and by the operation of that motor vehicle causes a serious impairment of a body function of another person is guilty of a felony punishable by imprisonment for not more than 5 years or a fine of not less than $1,000.00 or more than $5,000.00, or both.*

### Elements

1. The defendant was operating a motor vehicle.
2. The defendant was operating the vehicle on a highway or other place that was open to the public or generally accessible to motor vehicles, including any designated parking area.
3. While operating the vehicle, the defendant was intoxicated or visibly impaired or had any amount of a schedule 1 or 2 controlled substance in his body.

4. The defendant voluntarily decided to drive knowing that he had consumed alcohol or a controlled substance or a combination of alcohol and a controlled substance and might be intoxicated or visibly impaired or had any amount of a schedule 1 or 2 controlled substance in his body.
5. The defendant's operation of the vehicle caused a serious impairment of a body function to the victim within the definition of MCL 257.58c. To "cause" such injury, the defendant's operation of the vehicle must have been a factual cause of the injury, that is, but for the defendant's operation of the vehicle the injury would not have occurred. In addition, operation of the vehicle must have been a proximate cause of the injury, that is, the injury must have been a direct and natural result of operating the vehicle.
CJI2d 15.12–CJI2d 15.12a.

*"Serious impairment of a body function"* includes, but is not limited to, one or more of the following:

- Loss of a limb or loss of use of a limb.
- Loss of a foot, hand, finger, or thumb or loss of use of a foot, hand, finger, or thumb.
- Loss of an eye or ear or loss of use of an eye or ear.
- Loss or substantial impairment of a bodily function.
- Serious visible disfigurement.
- A comatose state that lasts for more than three days.
- Measurable brain or mental impairment.
- A skull fracture or other serious bone fracture.
- Subdural hemorrhage or subdural hematoma.
- Loss of an organ.

## Child Endangerment—MCL 257.625(7)

*A person, whether licensed or not, shall not operate a vehicle while intoxicated, visibly impaired, causing death, causing serious impairment of a body function, or with the presence of a controlled substance while another person who is less than 16 years of age is occupying the vehicle.*

Penalties:

| First conviction | 1-year misdemeanor |
|---|---|
| Second conviction within 7 years or third conviction | 5-year felony/ immobilization |

Child endangerment is included in the implied consent law. MCL 257.625c(1)(a).

Penalties if a person violates the zero tolerance statute, MCL 257.625(6), with someone less than 16 years old in the vehicle:

| First conviction | 93-day misdemeanor |
|---|---|
| Second conviction within 7 years or third conviction | 1-year misdemeanor |

## Permitting Person Under Influence to Drive—MCL 257.625(2)

### Elements

1. The owner of a vehicle or a person in charge or in control of a vehicle,
2. Shall not authorize or knowingly permit the vehicle to be operated upon the highway or other place open to the public or generally accessible to motor vehicles, and
3. By a person who is visibly impaired or under the influence of alcoholic liquor, a controlled substance, or other intoxicating substance or combination thereof, or who has a UBAC.

Penalties:

| No aggravating factors | 93-day misdemeanor |
|---|---|
| Operation results in serious impairment | 2-year felony |
| Operation results in death | 5-year felony |

## Confiscation of Registration Plate—MCL 257.904c

If a person is being arrested for a second alcohol violation or third D.W.L.S. violation, the Secretary of State will advise the officer via LEIN that the driver is a repeat offender. The officer must then do the following:

- Immediately confiscate the vehicle's registration plate and destroy it. Ownership of the vehicle does not matter.

  - Exceptions: tribal, rental, trailer, manufacture, dealer, U.S. government, out-of-state, or IRP plates.

- The officer must issue a temporary plate and place it on the vehicle. The temporary plate expires on the same date as the original plate.
- The plate shall not be seized if the Secretary of State computer system is not functioning.
- At the station:
  - A copy of the paper plate must be attached to the warrant request and print cards.
  - The SOS screen for confiscated plate must be completed and, if there was no plate on the vehicle, the VIN number shall be entered.

## Immobilization—MCL 257.904c-f

If a vehicle stopped by an officer is supposed to be immobilized, SOS will notify the officer of the dates of immobilization and the offender's driver license number. If the vehicle is being operated in violation of an immobilization order, the vehicle shall be impounded.

**Exception:** If the vehicle is immobilized under tether technology that immobilizes the offender only and the offender is not driving.

The penalty for tampering with or removing an immobilization device is a 93-day misdemeanor. MCL 257.904e.

## Ignition Interlocks—MCL 257.625l

As part of a restricted license, SOS may require ignition interlocks to be installed. Under MCL 257.319, SOS must issue a one-year suspension when a defendant is convicted of a "super drunk" violation. SOS may issue a restricted license after the first 45 days of the suspension, but during that restriction, the defendant may only operate a vehicle that has an ignition interlock device installed in it.

The following violations are 6-month misdemeanors:

- A person required only to use vehicles with an ignition interlock operating a vehicle without an ignition interlock. MCL 257.625l(2).
- Requesting another person to blow into the interlock device. MCL 257.625l(3).
- Blowing into another's interlock device. MCL 257.625l(4).
- Tampering with the device in any way. MCL 257.625(5).

## Registration Denial—MCL 257.219

SOS will cancel and deny registration for following offenders:

- Third offense drunk driving.
- Fourth offense DWLS/DWLR.

Obtaining a car during suspension:

- A person cannot buy, lease, or otherwise acquire a motor vehicle during a period of suspension, revocation, or denial.
- Violation is a 93-day misdemeanor.

## Recouping Costs—MCL 257.625(13)

*The court may order a defendant to pay costs for the arrest, investigation, emergency response, and prosecution of charges of O.W.I.*

## Implied Consent—MCL 257.625c

A person who operates a vehicle upon a public highway or other place open to the general public or generally accessible to motor vehicles, including an area designated for the parking of vehicles, within this state is considered to have given consent to chemical tests of his or her blood, breath, or urine for the purpose of determining the amount of alcohol or presence of a controlled substance or both in his or her blood or urine or the amount of alcohol in his or her breath if the person is arrested for any of the following offenses:

- Murder or manslaughter resulting from the operation of a motor vehicle, if reasonable cause to believe the driver was O.W.I. or impaired.
- Felonious driving, if reasonable cause to believe the driver was O.W.I. or impaired.
- Moving violation causing death, if reasonable cause to believe the driver was O.W.I. or impaired.
- O.W.I.
- O.W.I. causing death.
- O.W.I. causing serious injury.
- Unlawful blood alcohol content.
- Impaired driving.
- O.W.P.D.
- 0.02/Zero tolerance.
- Child endangerment.
- Commercial motor vehicle—refusing to take the PBT.
- Commercial motor vehicle—0.04–0.07 BAC.
- A local ordinance substantially corresponding to any of the above offenses.

## Exception to Implied Consent to Withdrawal of Blood—MCL 257.625c(2)

- Hemophiliacs, diabetics, or persons requiring the use of anticoagulants under the direction of a physician are not considered to have given consent to the withdrawal of blood.
- In cases involving a hemophiliac, a diabetic, or a person using an anticoagulant, officers must either offer a breath test or obtain a search warrant for blood.
- In O.W.P.D. cases involving a hemophiliac, a diabetic, or a person using an anticoagulant, officers should seek a search warrant.

After being arrested for O.W.I., the defendant consented to a blood draw after being improperly informed of his rights as a diabetic under the informed consent law. The arresting officer testified at trial that he had been unaware of the implied consent exception for diabetics. The prosecution argued that the officer would have obtained a search warrant if he had known about the exception. The court ruled that the defendant's Fourth Amendment right against an unreasonable search and seizure had been violated and that the "inevitable discovery" exception did not apply. Therefore, the blood results were suppressed. *People v. Hyde*, 285 Mich. App. 428 (2009).

## Preliminary Breath Tests (PBTs)—MCL 257.625a

### Basis of Arrest

- On reasonable cause, an officer may require a person to submit to a PBT.
- An arrest may be based wholly or in part on a PBT result.
- Results may be used in court for the following reasons:
  - To assist the court or hearing officer in determining a challenge to the validity of an arrest.
  - As evidence of the defendant's breath alcohol content, if offered by the defendant, to rebut testimony elicited on cross-examination of a defense witness that the defendant's breath alcohol content was higher at the time of the charged offense than when a chemical test was administered.
  - As evidence of the defendant's breath alcohol content, if offered by the prosecution, to rebut testimony elicited on cross-examination of a prosecution witness that the defendant's breath alcohol content was lower at the time of the charged offense than when a chemical test was sections.

## Penalty for Refusal to Submit to a PBT—MCL 257.625a(2)(d)

- Civil infraction.
- 93-day misdemeanor for commercial motor vehicle drivers.

A person's refusal to submit to a chemical test as provided in MCL 750.275a(6) is admissible in a criminal prosecution for a crime described in MCL 750.625c(1) only to show that a test was offered to the defendant, but not as evidence in determining the defendant's innocence or guilt. CJI2d 15.9.

## Chemical Tests—MCL 257.625a(6)

A chemical test may be administered at the request of a police officer who has reasonable grounds to believe a person has committed a crime described in MCL 257.625c.

## Admissibility and Presumption—MCL 257.625a(6)(a)

*The amount of alcohol or presence of a controlled substance or both in a driver's blood or urine or the amount of alcohol in a person's breath at the time alleged as shown by chemical analysis of the person's blood, urine, or breath is admissible into evidence in any civil or criminal proceeding and is presumed to be the same as at the time the person operated the vehicle.*

## Advice of Chemical Test Rights—MCL 257.625a(6)(b)

A person arrested for a crime described above shall be advised of all of the following:

- If he or she takes a chemical test of his or her blood, urine, or breath administered at the request of a peace officer, he or she has the right to demand that a person of his or her own choice administer one of the chemical tests.
- The results of the test are admissible in a judicial proceeding as provided under this act and will be considered with other admissible evidence in determining the defendant's innocence or guilt.
- He or she is responsible for obtaining a chemical analysis of a test sample obtained at his or her own request.
- If he or she refuses the request of a peace officer to take a test described above, a test shall not be given without a court order, but the peace officer may seek to obtain a court order.
- Refusing a peace officer's request to take a test described above will result in the suspension of his or her operator's or chauffeur's license and vehicle group designation or operating privilege and in the addition of six points to his or her driver record.

See Appendix for examples of *Advice of Chemical Test Rights* [DI-177 form] and *Officer's Report of Refusal to Submit to Chemical Test* [DI-93].

The defendant was involved in an accident and taken to a hospital. Police determined she had been drinking, but did not arrest her. The officer asked for a blood sample, which she voluntarily provided. Since she was not under arrest, implied consent rights were not read. The court held that implied consent rights are only triggered once arrested. Here, the defendant was never arrested before the request for blood. The case was remanded to determine whether consent was voluntary. *People v. Borchard-Ruhland*, 460 Mich. 278 (1999).

## Collection—MCL 257.625a(6)(c)

*A sample or specimen of urine or breath shall be taken and collected in a reasonable manner. Only a licensed physician, or an individual operating under the delegation of a licensed physician under MCL 333.16215, qualified to withdraw blood and acting in a medical environment, may withdraw blood at a peace officer's request to determine the amount of alcohol or presence of a controlled substance or both in the person's blood, as provided in this subsection. Liability for a crime or civil damages predicated on the act of withdrawing or analyzing blood and related procedures does not attach to a licensed physician or individual operating under the delegation of a licensed physician who withdraws or analyzes blood or assists in the withdrawal or analysis in accordance with this act unless the withdrawal or analysis is performed in a negligent manner.*

"When officers in drunk-driving investigation can reasonably obtain a warrant before having a blood sample drawn without significantly undermining the efficacy of the search, the Fourth Amendment mandates that they do so. Circumstances may make obtaining a warrant impractical such that the alcohol's dissipation will support an exigency, but that is a reason to decide each case on its facts, as in *Schmerber v. California*, 384 U.S. 757 (1966), not to accept the 'considerable overgeneralization' that a per se rule would reflect. *Richards v. Wisconsin*, 520 U. S. 385, 393 (1997).

Because the State sought a per se rule here, it did not argue that there were exigent circumstances in this particular case. The arguments and the record thus do not provide the Court with an adequate framework for a detailed discussion of all the relevant factors that can be taken into account in determining the reasonable of acting without a warrant. It suffices to say that the metabolization of alcohol in the bloodstream and the ensuing loss of evidence are among the factors that must be considered in deciding whether a warrant is required." *Missouri v. McNeely*, 133 S.Ct. 1552 (2013).

## Independent Test—MCL 257.625a(6)(d)

*A chemical test described in this subsection shall be administered at the request of a peace officer having reasonable grounds to believe that the person has committed a crime described in section 625c(1). A person who takes a chemical test administered at a peace officer's request as provided in this section shall be given a reasonable opportunity to have a person of his or her own choice administer one of the chemical tests described in this subsection within a reasonable time after his or her detention. The test results are admissible and shall be considered with other admissible evidence in determining the defendant's innocence or guilt. If the person charged is administered a chemical test by a person of his or her own choice, the person charged is responsible for obtaining a chemical analysis of the test sample.*

---

It is not a denial of a defendant's due process rights to deny the defendant's request for a blood test after the defendant has refused to take a requested breath test. *People v. Dewey*, 172 Mich. App. 367 (1988).

The defendant's blood was drawn following his arrest. The sample was destroyed by the State Police Crime Lab pursuant to a policy to destroy samples two years after receipt unless there is a request to preserve the sample longer. The defendant argued that he was deprived of his right under MCL 257.625a(6) to have an independent chemical test performed on the blood sample. The court held that the defendant had more than an ample opportunity to have his blood sample independently tested; therefore, the trial court did not abuse its discretion in denying the defendant's motion to suppress the test results. *People v. Reid*, 292 Mich. App. 508 (2011).

A police department's policy was reasonable where the defendant was given an opportunity to seek an independent blood test and offered a ride within reason to a hospital of his choice. *People v. Craun*, 429 Mich. 859 (1987).

The suppression of the police-administered chemical analysis or the dismissal of an O.W.I. charge is not the appropriate remedy where a person is denied the opportunity to obtain exculpatory evidence with an independent test. However, the jury may be given an instruction informing them that the defendant was denied an opportunity to obtain an independent test. The jury may decide what weight to give the denial of such a test. *People v. Anstey*, 476 Mich. 436 (2006).

The following are the duties of a peace officer if a person refuses to take the test or results reveal unlawful alcohol content:

- Immediately confiscate the person's license or permit.
- Issue a temporary license or permit.
- Immediately forward a copy of the refusal form to the SOS.
- Notify the SOS of the temporary license via LEIN.
- Destroy the person's license or permit.

MCL 257.625g(1).

The following are the duties of a peace officer if a blood or urine test is taken:

- Immediately confiscate the person's license or permit and issue a temporary license.
- Wait for the results to return from the lab.
- If the results show an unlawful alcohol content, the officer shall destroy the license.
- If there is not an unlawful alcohol content, the officer shall notify the person and immediately return the license or permit via first class mail.

MCL 257.625g(2).

Unlawful alcohol content applies to:

- 0.02/Zero tolerance legislation.
- 0.04–0.08 BAC and commercial motor vehicle drivers.
- 0.08 BAC or more.

MCL 257.625g(4).

## Administering the Test

An administrative rule for Breathalyzer tests requires that the defendant be observed by the operator for 15 minutes prior to the test to prevent the defendant from smoking, regurgitating, or placing anything in his or her mouth. Mich. Admin. Code R325.2655(1)(e).

## Compare

The defendant was observed on a videotape for 35 minutes before the test was administered during which the camera's view was blocked at different times. The test was held to be invalid because he was not watched for the full 15 minutes before the test, the test operator was present for only eight minutes of the observation period and did not observe defendant for all of those eight minutes, and defendant had his hands near his face or in his mouth multiple times during the observation period making it impossible to determine whether he had put anything in his mouth. *People v. Boughner*, 209 Mich. App. 397 (1995).

## With

Prior to performing a breath test on a suspected drunk driver, the officer testified that he continually observed the subject for 18 minutes, except for the few seconds it took him to check the time on the machine. During that time, a corrections officer watched the defendant. The defendant argued that, under the administrative rules and the case of *People v. Boughner*, the results of the test should not be admissible. The court disagreed, finding that the observing officers did not see defendant place anything in his mouth nor regurgitate during the observation period. Nor did defendant dispute the results of the test. Thus, even though this may have been a technical violation, it was a harmless error. *People v. Wujkowski*, 230 Mich. App. 181 (1998).

## Request for an Attorney Prior to the Test

There is no right to counsel under either the U.S. Constitution or the Michigan Constitution before taking a Breathalyzer test. Thus, police may refuse to permit an O.W.I. suspect and his attorney to privately confer over that decision. *City of Ann Arbor v. McCleary*, 228 Mich. App. 674 (1998).

However, it may be unreasonable under due process analysis to refuse him or her a reasonable opportunity to contact a lawyer. *Hall v. Secretary of State*, 60 Mich. App. 431 (1975).

Denial of the right to consult with counsel before an accused decides to take the Breathalyzer test does not violate the Sixth Amendment. *However*, the mere allowing of a reasonable phone call to counsel prior to administering the test would be a more commendable practice on the part of the police. *Holmberg v. 54-A Judicial Dist. Judge*, 60 Mich. App. 757 (1975).

If the officer denies the driver the opportunity to call his or her attorney, it will not affect the criminal charges, but may affect the DLAD hearing.

## DLAD Implied Consent Hearing—MCL 257.625f(4)

If a person received a refusal for taking a chemical test, he or she has the right to an implied consent hearing" so it reads a hearing with the Driver's License Appeal Division (DLAD) to determine whether the refusal was properly taken. The police officer has the burden of proof by a preponderance of the evidence at the hearing. The hearing shall only cover the following issues:

- Whether the police officer had reasonable grounds to believe that the person had committed a crime.
- Whether the person was placed under arrest for the crime.
- If the person refused to submit to the test upon request of the officer, whether the refusal was reasonable.
- Whether the person was advised of the chemical test rights required by MCL 257.625a(6). Submit a copy of the refusal when testifying to this portion.

## *Miranda* Rights and the O.W.I. Arrest

*Miranda* warnings are required when a person is in custody and subject to interrogation. Custody requires that the person be placed under arrest or his or her freedom of movement significantly deprived.

Generally, traffic stops do not involve custody for purposes of *Miranda*. Once an arrest is made, however (i.e., O.W.I.), *Miranda* warnings are required before questioning. *Berkemer v. McCarty*, 468 U.S. 420 (1984).

Failure of a police officer to give *Miranda* warnings prior to conducting roadside questioning as to whether the defendant had been drinking and how much he had been drinking does not mandate suppression of the defendant's answers. Even if the officer intends to arrest a driver from the outset, this does not automatically trigger the *Miranda* rule because an officer's unarticulated plan had no bearing on the question whether a suspect was "in custody" at a particular time. The only relevant inquiry was how a reasonable person in defendant's position would have understood his or her situation. *People v. Chinn*, 141 Mich. App. 92 (1985).

## Forcing Entry Into the Residence

Under MCL 764.21, officers may not forcibly enter a residence for a warrantless misdemeanor arrest if consent or some other lawful means is not present. *People v. Reinhardt*, 141 Mich. App. 173 (1985).

Officers responded to a hit-and-run accident where witnesses observed the driver driving away holding his head. They went to the registered owner's house and, after knocking on his front door, observed him lying in the house with a cut to his forehead. They knocked on the windows and had dispatch call the residence. When the subject did not respond, the officers entered. The court upheld the entry and subsequent arrest for the following reasons:

- A police officer may enter a dwelling without a warrant where it is reasonably believed that a person inside is in need of medical assistance.

- The entry must be limited to the reason for its justification.
- The officer must be motivated primarily by a perceived need to render assistance and may do no more than is reasonably necessary to determine whether assistance is and render it.

Once lawfully inside the residence, the officer may make an arrest without a warrant that is authorized by law and, absent a reason for exclusion, the evidence obtained is admissible. *City of Troy v. Ohlinger*, 438 Mich. 477 (1991).

© 2014, Shutterstock, Inc.

# 26

# JUVENILE LAW

## DIFFERENCES IN TERMINOLOGY

Juvenile proceedings are not considered criminal in nature. "Labeling theory" purports that if we label a juvenile as a criminal, then he or she will grow up to be a criminal. "Labeling theory" is a large part of the basis for the Juvenile Justice and Delinquency Prevention Act (see below). Thus, it is important to know the differences in terminology between juvenile proceedings and criminal proceedings. The focus of the juvenile process is not to punish, as in the adult system, but to rehabilitate. Some examples of the different terminology are:

- An offender is a *delinquent*, not a *criminal*.
- Officers will seek a *petition*, not request an *arrest warrant*.
- Juveniles are *apprehended*, not *arrested*.
- Juveniles must be *forthwith* turned over to their parents or the court, whereas an adult has to be brought to the court without *unnecessary delay*.
- The juvenile's guilt or innocence is determined in *adjudication*, not at a *trial*.
- After adjudication, the court will have a *disposition*, not a *sentencing*.

### Status Offender

A status offender is a person who commits an act that is a violation because of the person's special status, such as the person's age. Certain offenses would not be an offense if an adult committed the act. For example, if a 15-year-old skips school, he would be considered a truant and could fall under the jurisdiction of the court. However, if a 20-year-old skips his college classes, the court would not take notice.

> "[A] juvenile status offense is an offense which is illegal only because of the offender's age (under 18) and which is not serious." *United States v. Cole*, 418 F.3d 592 (6th Cir. 2005).

Examples of status offenders include the following:

- Runaways.
- Curfew violators.
- Truants.
- Minors in possession of alcohol.

## JURISDICTION OF THE FAMILY DIVISION OF CIRCUIT COURT

### Exclusive, Original Jurisdiction—MCL 712A.2(a)

The family division of circuit court has exclusive, original jurisdiction over any children who are less than 17 years old and who:

- Violate any ordinance or law. Exceptions include civil infractions and where the prosecutor charges the juvenile as an adult for a specific juvenile violation.

**401**

- Run away.
- Do not attend school.
- Are repeatedly disobedient to reasonable and lawful demands of parents, guardians, or custodians.

### Exclusive Jurisdiction—MCL 712A.2(b)

The family division of circuit court has exclusive jurisdiction over any child less than 18 years old who has been abused or neglected.

### Concurrent Jurisdiction—MCL 712A.2(d)

The family division of circuit court has concurrent jurisdiction over children between 17 and 18 years old who:

- Are repeatedly addicted to drugs or alcohol.
- Repeatedly associate with criminals.
- Are willfully disobedient to reasonable demands of parents.
- Are willfully and with knowledge in a house of prostitution or ill-fame.

### Other Jurisdiction—MCL 712A.2(c)

The family division of circuit court may accept jurisdiction of children under 18 years old who are subject to a custody battle as a result of a divorce.

### Civil Infractions

MCL 257.741 gives district courts jurisdiction over minors for purposes of civil infractions.

Under MCL 712A.2e, the family division of circuit court may agree with the district court to waive jurisdiction for all civil infractions to the district court.

## CUSTODY

A police officer may take any child into custody without a court order when:
- The child is found violating any criminal law or criminal ordinance. MCR 3.933, MCL 712A.14.
- If there is reasonable cause to believe that a child is at substantial risk of harm or is in surroundings that present an imminent risk of harm and the child's immediate removal from those surroundings is necessary to protect the child's health and safety. MCR 3.963, MCL 712A.14a(1).
- The child is violating or has violated a personal protection order or foreign protection order. MCL 600.2950(11), MCL 712A.14.

Upon such custody:
- Officers must immediately attempt to notify the parent, guardian, or custodian if that person can be found. MCL 712A.14(1), MCR 3.933.
- While awaiting the arrival of the parents, guardian, or custodian, a juvenile taken into custody shall not be held in a detention facility unless the child is completely isolated from verbal, visual, or physical contact with any adult prisoner. MCL 712A.14(1), MCL 712A.16(1), MCR 3.933.
- Unless immediate detention is required, juveniles shall be released once the parent or guardian makes a written promise that the juvenile will appear in court. MCL 712A.14(1).
- Immediate detention is allowed under one or more of the following circumstances:
  - Due to the nature of the violation, releasing the juvenile would not serve the best interest of the juvenile or the public.
  - No parent or guardian can be located.
  - The parent or guardian refuses to take custody.

  MCL 712A.14(1), MCR 3.933(A)(3).

- If the child is not released to the parents, the child shall be immediately brought before the court for a preliminary hearing. If a complaint is authorized, the court shall order where the child shall be placed. MCL 712A.14(2)–(3), MCR 3.935(D).
- For civil infractions, the officer may issue a citation and release. MCR 3.933.

### Juvenile Justice and Delinquency Prevention Act (JJDPA)—42 U.S.C. §§ 5601-5633

In order to receive federal block grants, the federal JJDPA establishes the following mandates:

- *Deinstitutionalization of status offenders*: A juvenile status offender cannot be placed in a secure institution, except those found in contempt of a court order and full due process protections are afforded.
- *Sight and sound separation*: There must be total sight and sound separation between juveniles and adults held in the same facility.
- *Jail removal initiative*: All juveniles shall be removed from the adult jails, except those who are transferred to the adult court and against whom criminal felony charges have been filed.
- *Six-hour rule*: Federal and state guidelines permit locking juveniles in adult facilities for a maximum of six hours, for processing purposes

only. This applies only to those juveniles who are charged with a crime. The sight and sound rule still applies.

The six-hour time frame starts the moment that juvenile is placed in a locked setting or cuffed to a stationary object. The clock does not start when a juvenile is placed in a police vehicle, unless locked in a vehicle parked in a sally port. *Michigan Guide to Compliance with Laws Governing the Placement of Juveniles in Secure Facilities*, Mich. Comm. on Juvenile Justice (Jan. 2000).

**Exception:** The six-hour rule does not apply to *status offenders* and abused or neglected children because they cannot be locked up at all. *Status offenders must be kept under constant supervision or visual contact at all times during their detention.* Soft restraints may be used if necessary.

## Detention Facilities—MCL 712A.16

*If a juvenile under the age of 17 years is taken into custody or detained, the juvenile shall not be confined in any police station, prison, jail, lockup, or reformatory or transported with, or compelled or permitted to associate or mingle with, criminal or dissolute persons . . . the court may order a juvenile 15 years of age or older whose habits or conduct are considered a menace to other juveniles, or who may not otherwise be safely detained, placed in a jail or other place of detention for adults, but in a room or ward separate from adults and for not more than 30 days, unless longer detention is necessary for the service of process.*

Juveniles under 17 years of age may not have contact with adult prisoners. There is an exception allowing a court to order that a dangerous juvenile over 15 years of age be jailed in an adult facility.

## Escape by Juvenile from Facility or Residence—MCL 712A.18j

*If a juvenile escapes from a facility or residence in which he or she has been placed for a violation described in section 2(a)(1) of this chapter, other than his or her own home or the home of his or her parent or guardian, the individual at that facility or residence who has responsibility for maintaining custody of the juvenile at the time of the escape shall immediately notify one of the following of the escape or cause one of the following to be immediately notified of the escape:*

*(a) If the escape occurs in a city, village, or township that has a police department, the*

*police department of that city, village, or township.*

*(b) Except as provided in subdivision (a), one of the following:*

*(i) The sheriff department of the county in which the escape occurs.*

*(ii) The department of state police post having jurisdiction over the area in which the escape occurs.*

*A police agency that receives notification of an escape under subsection (1) shall enter that notification into the law enforcement information network without undue delay.*

*As used in this section, "escape" means to leave without lawful authority or to fail to return to custody when required.*

# WAIVER OF JURISDICTION

## Non-Automatic Waiver Offenses—MCL 712A.4

Under certain circumstances, a prosecutor may request the family division of circuit court waive jurisdiction of a child to the adult court system. Generally, the child must be at least 14 years old. The judge will then decide whether to retain jurisdiction over the child or transfer said child to the adult court. In making this decision, the court will look at a number of factors including the following:

- The child's prior record, physical and mental maturity, and pattern of living.
- The seriousness of the offense charged.
- Whether the offense is part of a repetitive pattern.
- If the child's behavior is likely to render the child dangerous to the public.
- If waiving the child would be in the best interest of the public.

## Automatic Waiver—MCL 712A.4

Under the automatic waiver, the prosecutor will decide whether to authorize a complaint and warrant instead of a petition charging an enumerated life offense. Once this is done, the juvenile becomes subject to the jurisdiction of the court of general criminal jurisdiction automatically. Generally, the child has to be at least 14 years old and must have committed a very serious offense such as murder, first-degree CSC, armed robbery, carjacking, kidnapping, serious assaults, or a controlled substance violation where the amount was 650 grams or more.

# TRANSFER OF JURISDICTION— MCR 3.926

When a minor is brought before a juvenile court in a county other than where the minor resides, the court may transfer the case to the court in the county of residence prior to adjudication.

# RIGHTS OF A CHILD

## Preliminary Hearing—MCR 3.935

- A preliminary hearing is held to determine whether probable cause exists that the child committed the offense.
- The hearing must be within 24 hours of detention, excluding Sundays or holidays, or the juvenile must be released.

### Admission or Confession

For many years, the test for admitting a confession of a juvenile was a per se rule that, if the parent or guardian was not present during the interrogation, the confession was automatically suppressed. This test has now given way to the totality of the circumstances test, which is similar to the test used for adult confessions. This is a balancing test, which requires that the court weigh various factors.

> The Michigan Supreme Court has accepted "totality of the circumstances" test for juvenile confessions. *People v. Hana*, 443 Mich. 202 (1993).

Under the totality of the circumstance test for a juvenile confession, a court must consider:

- Whether *Miranda* requirements were met and whether the juvenile clearly understood his or her rights and properly waived them.
- The degree of police compliance with applicable statutes and court rules.
- The presence of an adult parent, custodian, or guardian.
- The juvenile defendant's personal background.
- The juvenile's age, education, intelligence level, and extent of prior experience with police.
- The length of detention before statement was made.
- The repeated and prolonged nature of the questioning.
- Whether the accused was injured, intoxicated, ill, physically abused, threatened with abuse, or deprived of food, sleep, or medical attention.

> However, the court specifically held that the "failure to take defendant immediately and forthwith before the juvenile division of the probate court does not per se require suppression of the statement." *People v. Good*, 186 Mich. App. 180 (1990).
>
> The defendant, an 11-year-old, was charged with first-degree murder. During a police interrogation where his mother was present, the juvenile confessed to the shooting. Under the totality of the circumstances, the court upheld the admissibility of the confession.
>
> The officers asked the defendant to explain the rights that they had read to him. In reference to his right to an attorney, he stated, "That-that when the police talk to me I can talk with my lawyer with the police." Also, "If we don't got no money, the court give me one." Finally, as to the fact that his statement may be used against him, he replied, "If you say something you go to court for it." In ruling the confession was admissible, the court also found that it was of "great significance," that the defendant's mother was present for and participated in the entire *Miranda* waiver process. *People v. Abraham*, 234 Mich. App. 640 (1999).

# BIOMETRIC DATA—MCL 28.243

## Definitions—MCL 28.241a

*Arrest card*: A paper form or an electronic format prescribed by the department that facilitates the collection and compilation of criminal and juvenile arrest history record information and biometric data.

*Biometric data:* Means all of the following:

- Fingerprint images recorded in a manner prescribed by the department.
- Palm print images, if the arresting law enforcement agency has the electronic capability to record palm print images in a manner prescribed by the department.
- Digital images recorded during the arrest or booking process, including a full-face capture, left and right profile, and scars, marks, and tattoos, if the arresting law enforcement agency has the electronic capability to record the images in a manner prescribed by the department.
- All descriptive data associated with identifying marks, scars, amputations, and tattoos.

*Juvenile history record information:* Name; date of birth; personal descriptions including identifying marks, scars, amputations, and tattoos; aliases and prior names; social security number, driver's license number, and other identifying numbers; and information on juvenile offense arrests and adjudications or convictions.

## Collection of Biometric Data—MCL 28.243

*Officers must collect a person's biometric data upon arrest for a felony or for a misdemeanor violation of state law for which the maximum possible penalty exceeds 92 days' imprisonment or a fine of $1,000.00, or both, or a misdemeanor authorized for DNA collection under MCL 28.176(1)(B), or for criminal contempt, or criminal contempt for a violation of a foreign protection order, or for a juvenile offense, other than a juvenile offense for which the maximum possible penalty does not exceed 92 days' imprisonment or a fine of $1,000.00, or both, or for a juvenile offense that is a misdemeanor authorized for DNA collection, the arresting law enforcement agency in this state shall collect the person's biometric data and forward the biometric data to the department within 72 hours after the arrest.*

A juvenile must be fingerprinted when required by law. The court may permit fingerprinting or photographing, or both, of a minor concerning whom a petition has been filed. Fingerprints and photographs must be placed in the confidential files, capable of being located and destroyed on court order. MCR 3.923(C).

At the time that the court authorizes the filing of a petition alleging a juvenile offense and before the court enters an order of disposition on a juvenile offense, the court shall examine the confidential files and verify that the juvenile has been fingerprinted. If it appears to the court that the juvenile has not been fingerprinted, the court must order the juvenile to go to the police department that apprehended him or order the sheriff to apprehend the juvenile to take the fingerprints of the juvenile. MCR 3.936(B).

## Destruction of Biometric Data and Arrest Card—MCL 28.243

The biometric data and arrest card must be destroyed if the juvenile is not petitioned, is adjudicated and found to be outside of the provisions of the probate code, or is charged as an adult and found not guilty.

However, the required destruction of the biometric data and arrest card does not apply to a juvenile arraigned for any of the following:

- The commission or attempted commission of a crime with or against a child under 16 years of age.
- Rape.
- Criminal sexual conduct in any degree.
- Sodomy.
- Gross indecency.
- Indecent liberties.
- Child abusive commercial activities.
- A person who has a prior conviction, other than a misdemeanor traffic offense, unless a judge of a court of record, except the probate court, by express order on the record, orders the destruction or return of the biometric data and arrest card.
- A person arrested who is a juvenile charged with an offense that would constitute the commission or attempted commission of any of the crimes in this subsection if committed by an adult.

MCL 28.243(7); 28.243(8); 28.243(12).

When a juvenile has been fingerprinted for a juvenile offense, but no petition on the offense is submitted to the court, the court does not authorize the petition, or the court does not take jurisdiction of the juvenile and the records have not been destroyed pursuant to statute, upon the filing of a motion, the court, on motion filed shall issue an order directing the Department of State Police, or other official holding the information, to destroy the fingerprints and arrest card of the juvenile pertaining to the offense, other than an offense as listed above. MCR 3.936(D).

## Restrictions on the Release of Criminal Records—MCL 28.242a

*(1) All criminal history record information that is associated with a state identification number and is supported by biometric data shall be disseminated in response to either a fingerprint-based search or a name-based search of the criminal history record information database. This subsection does not allow the dissemination of criminal history record information that is nonpublic or is prohibited by law from being disseminated.*

*(2) Except as provided in subsection (3), all juvenile history record information that is associated with a state identification number and is supported by biometric data shall be disseminated in response only to a fingerprint-based*

*search of the criminal history record information database. This subsection does not allow the dissemination of juvenile history record information that is nonpublic or is prohibited by law from being disseminated.*

*(3) All juvenile history record information that is associated with a state identification number and that is supported by biometric data shall be disseminated in response to either a name-based or a fingerprint-based search of the criminal history record information database solely to a person or entity authorized to access the law enforcement information network. This subsection does not allow the dissemination of juvenile history record information that is prohibited by law from being disseminated.*

# HEARING PHASES
## Adjudication Phase

Includes the following:

- Determines child's guilt or innocence.
- The child has the right to a jury trial. MCR 3.911.
- The child has the right to an attorney. MCR 3.915.
- The trial must be held within six months after the petition is filed, unless adjourned for good cause, if child is in custody. If the child is detained, the trial must be within 63 days after the child is taken into custody. If longer than 63 days, the court shall order the juvenile released pending trial. MCR 3.942(A).
- The Michigan Rules of Evidence and the standard of proof beyond a reasonable doubt apply at adjudication. MCR 3.942(C).

*Trial*: The fact-finding adjudication of an authorized petition to determine whether the minor comes within the jurisdiction of the court. MCR 3.903(A)(27).

## Dispositional Phase

During the dispositional phase, the court determines what measures the court will take with respect to the juvenile. This is similar to the sentencing phase in adult cases. MCL 3.943, MCL 712A.18.

- After a juvenile has been convicted, the court must conduct a dispositional hearing, unless the hearing is waived. MCR 3.943.
- No right to jury at the dispositional phase. A juvenile only has a right to a jury at a trial. MCR 3.911.
- If convicted as an adult, a dispositional hearing is still required to determine whether the subject should be sentenced as an adult or juvenile, unless he or she must automatically be sentenced as an adult. MCR 3.955(C).
- If the juvenile is to be sentenced as an adult, the burden is on the prosecuting attorney to prove by a preponderance of the evidence that such a sentence is in the best interest of the public. MCR 3.955(B).

© 2014, Shutterstock, Inc.

# LAWS ON USE OF FORCE

It is important that police officers know the use of force laws because the improper use of force can open up both criminal and civil liability.

## MICHIGAN STANDARD

An officer may use such force as he or she deems necessary in forcibly arresting an offender or in preventing his or her escape after an arrest. *Firestone v. Rice*, 71 Mich. 377 (1888).

An officer may use that force necessary to apprehend a criminal, but neither law nor morality can tolerate the use of needless violence, even upon the worst criminals. *People v. McCord*, 76 Mich. 200 (1889).

"Both officers and private persons seeking to prevent a felon's escape must exercise reasonable care to prevent the escape of the felon without doing personal violence, and it is only where killing him is necessary to prevent this escape, that the killing is justified. . . . If the killing is not justifiable, it is either murder or manslaughter." *People v. Gonsler*, 251 Mich. 443 (1930).

Although Michigan has a fleeing felon rule, under the Fourth Amendment, a police officer's use of deadly force is limited to those situations where the officer has probable cause to believe that the felon poses a threat of serious physical harm to either himself or others. *Washington v. Starke*, 173 Mich. App. 230 (1988).

"[N]o one, whether private person or officer, has any right to make an arrest without warrant in the absence of actual belief, based on actual facts creating probable cause of guilt. Suspicion without cause can never be an excuse for such action. The two must both exist and be reasonably well founded. . . . [N]o one can be justified in threatening or taking life, in attempting an arrest on suspicion, without incurring serious responsibilities. And where the life of an actual felon is taken by one who does not know or believe his guilt, such slaying is murder." *People v. Burt*, 51 Mich. 199 (1883).

## FEDERAL STANDARD

A peace officer may use deadly force:

- In defense of his or her own life,
- In defense of another, or
- In pursuit of a fleeing felon where the officer has probable cause to believe that the suspect poses a significant threat of death or serious physical injury to the officer or others. *Tennessee v. Garner*, 471 U.S. 1 (1985).

The courts take an objective view when deciding use of force cases. The question is whether the officer's actions are "objectively reasonable" in light of the facts and circumstances confronting them, regardless of their underlying intent or motivation. *Graham v. Connor*, 490 U.S. 386 (1989).

## Objectively Reasonable Test

The United States Supreme Court applies a reasonableness standard under the Fourth Amendment to use of force actions by police. Reasonableness is determined by balancing "the nature and quality of the intrusion" against "the countervailing governmental interests." Factors include:

- The severity of the crime at issue.
- Whether the suspect poses an immediate threat to the safety of officers and others.
- Whether the suspect is actively resisting arrest or attempting to evade arrest by flight.

Reasonableness is "judged from the perspective of a reasonable officer on the scene, rather than with the 20/20 vision hindsight."

- The reasonableness standard must make an allowance for the fact that police officers are often forced to make split-second judgments in circumstances that are tense, uncertain, and rapidly evolving.
- An officer's use of force will be judged at the moment the force is used.

*Graham v. Connor*, 490 U.S. 386 (1989).

Example: At night, an officer is dispatched to a suspicious situation at an abandoned house. He walks inside and sees an individual pointing a gun at him. The officer draws his gun and shoots the individual. In the aftermath, it turns out that the gun was a toy and that the individual was a 12-year-old. Although tragic, the use of force may be appropriate based on the facts the officer had at the time of the shooting.

"An officer's evil intentions will not make a Fourth Amendment violation out of an objectively reasonable use of force; nor will an officer's good intentions make an objectively unreasonable use of force constitutional." *Graham v. Connor*, 490 U.S. 386 (1989).

Example: An officer knows that the person confronting him is 6'5" tall, has just used PCP, is a martial arts expert, may have a concealed weapon, and has just brutally attacked another officer without provocation. All of this is relevant because they are the facts and circumstances confronting the officer. The officer may be very angry with the subject for the injury to the fellow officer. This anger is irrelevant to the analysis because it is the officer's subjective intent.

# MICHIGAN LAW ON THE USE OF DEADLY FORCE
## Deadly Force Defined

"[D]eadly force has been used where the defendant's acts are such that the natural, probable, and foreseeable consequence of said acts is death." *People v. Pace*, 102 Mich. App. 522 (1980).

Deadly force is "that force which could result in the loss of human life." OAG 1975–1976, No. 5,068, p. 201 (September 3, 1976). This may include batons, saps, flashlights, brass knuckles, and even an officer's fists.

Police were dispatched to an apartment after several calls from a screaming woman about a man with a knife and a gun. Officers arrived and entered the apartment. The defendant, who had a guitar in one hand and a butcher knife in the other, confronted an officer. He advanced toward the officer in a threatening manner. The officer repeatedly told the defendant to drop the knife. When the defendant got within two to five feet, the officer shot him twice.

The court held that the police officer was protected by governmental immunity because he was acting during the course of employment, he reasonably believed that he was acting within the scope of his employment, he acted in good faith, and he was performing a discretionary act. In regards to the "scope of employment" analysis, it was held to be undisputed that the officer possessed the authority to use deadly force in certain circumstances. *Butler v. City of Detroit*, 149 Mich. App. 708 (1986).

Pursuant to a court writ, officers went to the defendant's residence to assist in removing a pickup truck. While the tow truck driver was attempting to hook up the truck, the defendant was observed standing in the doorway carrying a rifle in the port arms position. He yelled, "Leave my truck alone! Get out of here!" He then retreated into his house. He never pointed the gun at any officers or verbally threatened to use it.

After a nearly six-hour standoff, an officer broke a window to see inside. The defendant responded by firing approximately 10 shots. At that point, the chief issued a "shoot to kill order." Subsequently, a sharpshooter shot the defendant in the neck as he was standing in his kitchen.

The excessive force issue was settled out of court. The court did hold, however, that the police violated the plaintiff's Fourth Amendment rights because they should have attempted to obtain either a search warrant or an arrest warrant. The officers argued that there were exigent circumstances. The court ruled that the exigent circumstances no longer existed once the house was surrounded. However, the court also ruled that the police were protected by qualified immunity. Even though there was a Fourth Amendment violation, an objectively reasonable officer could believe that there was an exigency. *O'Brien v. City of Grand Rapids*, 23 F.3d 990 (6th Cir. 1994).

Plaintiff was experiencing a manic episode which made him extremely volatile. He broke into the Forest View Hospital by smashing out a window to the reception area. He then began smashing windows and whatever was in his path while yelling that he was the "baddest [expletive] around." Someone called 911 and deputies from the Kent County Sheriff's Department responded.

Officers entered the hospital armed with ASP batons. The plaintiff took a boxer's stance and began approaching the officers while verbally threatening them. The officers swung and hit plaintiff a number of times, including two strikes to the head. One deputy was picked up and thrown to the floor. Plaintiff even removed a drinking fountain from the wall. Eventually, eight officers were able to subdue and handcuff him.

Applying the objective standard, the court held that the officers did not use excessive force against Plaintiff. Furthermore, "Once the plaintiff started and continued the fight, the officers had no constitutional duty to retreat or to submit." *Nicholson v. Kent County Sheriff's Dept.*, 839 F.Supp. 508 (W.D. Mich. 1993).

Troopers were dispatched to investigate a report of shots being fired. The caller also advised that a man was walking nearby with a long gun. The troopers stated they located the man walking down the street carrying a gun. One trooper yelled very loudly, "State Police— drop the gun." The man reportedly then raised the gun and pointed it directly at an officer.

Three troopers then responded by firing several times. The man died a short time thereafter.

The man's estate filed suit and countered that the man was obviously intoxicated and walking down the street singing and carrying a large bottle of beer. The plaintiff-estate also claimed that even though the man did have an unloaded shotgun, he was not threatening anyone and was carrying it with the barrel down.

Summary judgment was denied because there were facts that had to go to the jury for determination. The key question was whether there was a *material issue of fact* as to reasonableness of the officers' actions. A judge at summary judgment cannot decide issues of fact. At trial, the jury returned a verdict in favor of the troopers. *Roxbury v. Paul*, 838 F.Supp. 1204 (W.D. Mich. 1992) *aff'd*, 7 F.3d 234 (6th Cir. 1993).

Officers responded to a residence where there was a suicidal man. He had cut his arms in a number of places and was carrying a knife. Officers attempted to communicate with him, but he refused to communicate. He also mentioned a gun, and his father confirmed that there were guns in the house. He exited the house but then went back inside. When he re-entered the house, officers followed him into the breezeway. At one point, he approached an officer, who sprayed him with mace. The mace was not effective and the subject was able to re-enter the house.

Approximately 15 minutes after the officers' arrival, the man approached the officers holding two knives. Officers testified that his right arm was raised above his shoulder and a knife was in his hand. Officers told him to drop the knives. When he was between six to nine feet from the officers, two officers shot and killed him.

The trial court granted summary judgment to the officers. The Sixth Circuit Court of Appeals reversed. "The discovery depositions, affidavits, exhibits, and other material demonstrate clearly that the two sides do not agree on the facts. The police claim the man threatened to get a gun and then charged at them through the kitchen door with the knives on the porch. The man's estate filed suit and denied this version of what happened. The plaintiff-estate claimed the man never said anything about a gun and was shot before he ever stepped out of the kitchen doorframe. Our resolution of this case therefore turns upon whether it was proper for the district court to grant the officers qualified immunity in the face of such a factual dispute. . . . This court has established that summary judgment is *inappropriate* where there are contentious factual disputes over the reasonableness of the use of deadly force." In short, the jury must decide factual issues.

The court did uphold the summary judgments granted to the police department because "a plaintiff who sues a city and its police department for constitutional violations under 42 U.S.C. § 1983 must establish that a governmental policy or custom caused the alleged injury" and the plaintiff failed to meet that burden. The suit against the officers was eventually settled out of court. *Sova v. The City of Mt. Pleasant*, 142 F.3d 898 (6th Cir. 1998).

# FLEEING FELONS

## Tennessee v. Garner

Officers responded to a "prowler" complaint. One officer went to the rear of the house, heard a door slam, and saw someone run across the backyard. The suspect stopped at a 6-foot-high fence. The officer could see the suspect's face and hands and was reasonably sure that the suspect was not armed. The officer walked toward the suspect and yelled, "[P]olice, halt." The suspect then began to climb the fence. The officer then shot and killed the suspect. There was a purse and $10 from the house on the suspect's body.

The United States Supreme Court stated that when the fleeing felon rule was established, there were very few felonies, all of which were punishable by death. There are now many more felonies, and many of today's felonies are not considered to be dangerous. The Court found that a fleeing felon statute that authorized the use of deadly force to prevent the escape of all felony suspects, whatever the circumstances, is constitutionally unreasonable. *Tennessee v. Garner*, 471 U.S. 1 (1985).

## *Garner* Requirements: Deadly Force and Fleeing Felon

"Where the officer has probable cause to believe that the suspect poses a threat of serious physical harm, either to the officer or to others, it is not constitutionally unreasonable to prevent escape by using deadly force. Thus, if the suspect

threatens the officer with a weapon or there is probable cause to believe that he has committed a crime involving the infliction or threatened infliction of serious physical harm, deadly force may be used if necessary to prevent escape, and if, where feasible, some warning has been given."

The use of deadly force must be reasonably necessary to prevent the suspect's escape and alternative steps to prevent the suspect's escape and alternative steps are not likely to lead to the safe control of the subject. "We conclude that such force may not be used unless it is necessary to prevent the escape and the officer has probable cause to believe that the suspect poses a significant threat of death or serious physical injury to the officer or others." *Tennessee v. Garner*, 471 U.S. 1 (1985).

## Fleeing Vehicles

An officer attempted to stop a vehicle for speeding, and the driver fled. The pursuit was on a two-lane road and, at times, was at speeds over 85 mph. The driver crossed the centerline multiple times, ran red lights, and, at one point, went through a parking lot and struck a police car. The pursuit ended when the officer rammed the suspect vehicle, causing it to leave the road and overturn. The driver was rendered quadriplegic and sued the officer.

The court analyzed the case under the *Garner* reasonableness standard, which is adopted from the Fourth Amendment, and held that the fleeing driver's actions posed a risk to innocent bystanders, including police officers, and this risk outweighed his Fourth Amendment rights. The driver was the one who created a substantial risk to others, and it was reasonable for the officer to use force to stop him. This is the rule even when the officer's actions place a fleeing motorist at risk of serious injury or death. The court also held that pursuing officers have no constitutional obligation to terminate a pursuit in order to protect innocent bystanders from a fleeing motorist; termination of a pursuit does not guarantee a driver will drive more safely, whereas ramming a fleeing vehicle will end the pursuit, thus making it safer for everyone (except the fleeing driver). *Scott v. Harris*, 550 U.S. 372 (2007).

Note: The plaintiff's account of this incident conflicted with the officers' account. The court held that there was no "genuine" dispute of the facts because the pursuit was recorded on patrol car video, which the court was able to review. The pursuit video is available as of July 7, 2014, on YouTube by searching "*Scott v. Harris.*"

### Case Law in Michigan on Fleeing Felons

Deadly force was justified to prevent the escape of a suspect who was attempting to escape from the scene of a robbery attempt. The suspect was armed with a knife and had demonstrated his willingness to use the knife against store clerks during the robbery. While he was attempting to flee, the suspect slipped, fell, or lunged at one of the clerks and was subsequently shot in the head by an officer. In concluding that the use of force was reasonable, the court noted, "[Suspect] did not become 'unarmed' merely because he placed the weapon in his pants pocket, and was at no point deprived of the availability of the weapon. [He] admits that he had attempted to rob the store and used the knife to effectuate this purpose. Having taken no affirmative step to relinquish the weapon, [his] claim that he was unarmed is not convincing." *Newcomb v. City of Troy*, 719 F.Supp. 1408 (E.D. Mich. 1989).

Two victims were waiting for a bus when the suspects drove up. The passenger in the suspect vehicle brandished a gun, and the victims were robbed. The victims escaped and found two Southfield officers. Later, the officers observed the vehicle in the parking lot. The passenger pointed a gun at a woman who was walking to her car. The officers surrounded the car, and the passenger pointed the gun at one of the officers. The officers fired into the car. The driver exited the car and began to run away. The officers shot and killed him. It was later determined that only the passenger was armed. The passenger was arrested after a short foot pursuit.

The estate brought suit against the officers for excessive force and against the police department for failing to adequately train their officers and for having an unconstitutional deadly force policy.

The Court of Appeals asked the following questions:

"Should objectively reasonable officers have realized that [the driver], in fact, was not armed?"

"Did the officers have probable cause to believe that [the driver] posed a threat of serious bodily harm to them or to others?"

"Did [the driver] commit, or was he in the process of committing, a crime involving the infliction of serious physical harm?"

"Was deadly force necessary to prevent [the driver's] escape?"

"Was [the driver] given warning, or was one necessary under the circumstances?"

The court sent the case back to the jury to determine if an objective police officer should have perceived the driver as unarmed or as "nondangerous." *Washington v. Newsom*, 977 F.2d 991 (6th Cir. 1992).

## PRIVATE CITIZEN USE OF DEADLY FORCE

A split Michigan Supreme Court held that the rule from *Tennessee v. Garner* is not applicable to a private citizen because *Garner* is a Fourth Amendment case and, thus, only applies to governmental agents. Since the fleeing felon rule still exists, it is up to the Legislature, not the court, to change law. *People v. Couch*, 436 Mich. 414 (1990).

The use of deadly force by a private citizen is justified when the following occur:

- The evidence must show that a felony actually occurred.
- The fleeing suspect against whom the force was used must be the person who committed the felony.
- The use of deadly force must have been "necessary" to ensure the apprehension of the felon.

*People v. Hampton*, 194 Mich. App. 593 (1992).

The defendant and his wife had a poor relationship with their neighbors, which resulted in several altercations. During the altercation in this case, the neighbors hurled insults at defendant and his wife and threw rocks and eggs at their home. The defendant's wife responded in kind. At some point, she struck one of the neighbor's in the chest. Fifteen minutes later, the boy's mother arrived with a bat and battered the screen door of the defendant's enclosed front porch. She claimed that she did it in reaction to the defendant's wife, who was ranting, raving, spitting at her, and threatening to "whoop [her] ass." The defendant was able to get his wife to step inside their home. At some point, another subject showed up who claimed to be trying to escort the mother back home. The defendant felt that he was being threatened and stated he was "getting tired of this shit," pulled out a handgun, and fired six times striking both parties. He was charged with two counts of assault with intent to commit murder, two counts of assault with intent to do great bodily harm less than murder, two counts of felonious assault, and one count of felony-firearm. He claimed self-defense.

At the close of trial, the court read CJI2d 7.16 to the jury. The instruction reads in part:

1. A person can use deadly force in self-defense only where it is necessary to do so. If the defendant could have safely retreated but did not do so, you may consider that fact in deciding whether the defendant honestly and reasonably believed [he/she] needed to use deadly force in self-defense.
2. However, a person is never required to retreat if attacked in [his/her] own home, nor if the person reasonably believes that an attacker is about to use a deadly weapon, nor if the person is subject to a sudden, fierce, and violent attack.

The success of the defendant's self-defense claim hinges not on whether he was required to retreat or stand his ground on his porch. Rather, it hinged on whether he honestly and reasonably believed that it was necessary to use deadly force while standing his ground. After being properly informed that the defendant had no duty to retreat if attacked in his home, the jury concluded that deadly force was still not necessary. It recognized that the evidence showed that the defendant was unharmed and could have continued to stand his ground and remain unharmed without shooting the victims. *People v. Richardson*, 490 Mich. 115 (2011).

# USE OF FORCE IN SELF-DEFENSE
## The Self-Defense Act
### Using Less Than Deadly Force—MCL 780.972(2)

---

*An individual who has not or is not engaged in the commission of a crime at the time he or she uses force other than deadly force may use force other than deadly force against another individual anywhere he or she has the legal right to be with no duty to retreat if he or she honestly and reasonably believes that the use of that force is necessary to defend himself or herself or another individual from the imminent unlawful use of force by another individual.*

---

## Elements

A person has the right to use force to defend himself or another person under certain circumstances. If a person acts in lawful self-defense or defense of others, his actions are justified and he is not guilty of a crime.

1. The actor's conduct is judged according to how the circumstances appeared to him at the time he acted.
2. At the time he acted, the actor must not have been engaged in the commission of a crime.
3. When he acted, the actor must have honestly and reasonably believed that he had to use force to protect himself or a third party from the imminent unlawful use of force by another. If his belief was honest and reasonable, he could act at once to defend himself or the third party, even if it turns out later that he was wrong about how much danger he or the third party was in.
4. A person is only justified in using the degree of force that seems necessary at the time to protect himself or the other person from danger. The actor must have used the kind of force that was appropriate to the attack made and the circumstances as he saw them. In deciding whether the force used was what seemed necessary, whether the defendant knew about any other ways of protecting himself or a third party and how the excitement of the moment affected the choice the defendant made may be considered.
5. The right to defend oneself or another person only lasts as long as it seems necessary for the purpose of protection.
6. The person claiming self-defense must not have acted wrongfully and brought on the assault.

However, if the defendant only used words, that does not prevent him from claiming self-defense if he was attacked. CJI2d 7.22.

## Using Deadly Force—MCL 780.972(1)

*An individual who has not or is not engaged in the commission of a crime at the time he or she uses deadly force may use deadly force against another individual anywhere he or she has the legal right to be with no duty to retreat if either of the following applies:*

(a) *The individual honestly and reasonably believes that the use of deadly force is necessary to prevent the imminent death of or imminent great bodily harm to himself or herself or to another individual.*

(b) *The individual honestly and reasonably believes that the use of deadly force is necessary to prevent the imminent sexual assault of himself or herself or of another individual.*

## Elements

1. At the time he acted, the actor must have honestly and reasonably believed that he was in danger of being killed, seriously injured, or sexually assaulted. If the actor's belief was honest and reasonable, he could act immediately to defend himself even if it turned out later that he was wrong about how much danger he was in. In deciding if the actor's belief was honest and reasonable, consider all the circumstances as they appeared to the actor at the time.

2. An actor may not kill or seriously injure another person just to protect himself against what seems like a threat of only minor injury. The actor must have been afraid of death, serious physical injury, or sexual assault. In deciding if the actor was afraid of one or more of these, consider all the circumstances: the condition of the people involved, including their relative strength; whether the other person was armed with a dangerous weapon or had some other means of injuring the actor; the nature of the other person's attack or threat; or whether the actor knew about any previous violent acts or threats made by the other person.

3. At the time he acted, the actor must have honestly and reasonably believed that what he did was immediately necessary. Under the law, a person may only use as much force as he thinks is necessary at the time to protect himself.

In determining whether the amount of force used seemed to be necessary, whether the actor knew about any other ways of protecting himself and how the excitement of the moment affected the choice the actor made may be considered. CJI2d 7.15.

## Presumptions: Honest and Reasonable Belief—MCL 780.951

There is a rebuttable presumption that a person using force has an honest and reasonable belief that imminent death, great bodily harm, or sexual assault will occur if the person using force honestly and reasonably believes the person against whom force is used is any of the following:

- In the process of breaking and entering a dwelling or business.
- In the process of committing a home invasion.
- Has committed a breaking and entering or home invasion and is still present in the dwelling or business.
- Is attempting to unlawfully remove a person from a dwelling, business, or vehicle against his or her will.

The presumption does not apply in the following circumstances:

- The person against whom force was used had a legal right to be in the dwelling, business, or vehicle.
- The person being removed from a dwelling, business, or vehicle was a child in the lawful custody of the person removing the child.
- The person using force was engaged in a crime or was using the business, dwelling, or vehicle to further a crime.
- The person against whom force was used was a police officer attempting to enter a dwelling, business, or vehicle in the performance of the officer's duties.
- The person against whom force was used had a domestic relationship with the person using force and the person using force had a history of domestic violence as the aggressor.

## Duty to Retreat—MCL 780.973
## Elements

1. A person can use deadly force in self-defense only where it is necessary to do so. If the defendant could have safely retreated but did not do so, you may consider that fact in deciding

whether the defendant honestly and reasonably believed he or she needed to use deadly force in self-defense.

2. However, a person is never required to retreat if attacked in his or her own home, nor if the person reasonably believes that an attacker is about to use a deadly weapon, nor if the person is subject to a sudden, fierce, and violent attack.

3. Furthermore, a person is not required to retreat if the person:

    a. Has not or is not engaged in the commission of a crime at the time the deadly force is used.

    b. Has a legal right to be where the person is at that time.

    c. Has an honest and reasonable belief that the use of deadly force is necessary to prevent imminent death, great bodily harm, or sexual assault of the person or another.

CJ12d 7.16.

## Deadly Force in Defense of Others
### Elements

A person has the right to use force or even take a life to defend someone else under certain circumstances. If a person acts in lawful defense of another, his or her actions are justified and he or she is not guilty of a crime. The persons conduct is judged according to how the circumstances appeared to him or her at the time he or she acted. In deciding whether a person acted in lawful defense of another, all of the evidence should be considered while using the following rules:

1. At the time he or she acted, the actor must not have been engaged in the commission of a crime.

2. When he or she acted, the actor must have honestly and reasonably believed that a third party was in danger of being killed, seriously injured, or sexually assaulted. If his or her belief was honest and reasonable, he or she could act at once to defend the third party, even if it turns out later that the actor was wrong about how much danger the third party was in.

3. If the actor was only afraid that the third party would receive a minor injury, then he or she was not justified in killing or seriously injuring the attacker. The actor must have been afraid that the third party would be killed, seriously injured, or sexually assaulted. When you decide if he or she was so afraid, you should consider all of the circumstances: the conditions of the people involved, including their relative strength; whether the other person was armed with a dangerous weapon or had some other means of injuring the third party; the nature of the other person's attack or threat; or whether the actor knew about any previous violent acts or threats made by the other person.

4. At the time he or she acted, the actor must have honestly and reasonably believed that what he or she did was immediately necessary. Under the law, a person may only use as much force as he or she thinks is needed at the time to protect the other person. When you decide whether the force used appeared to be necessary, you may consider whether the actor knew about any other ways of protecting the third party, but you may also consider how the excitement of the moment affected the choice the actor made.

5. The actor does not have to prove that he or she acted in defense of a third party. Instead, the prosecutor must prove beyond a reasonable doubt that the actor did not act in defense of the third party.

CJ12d 7.21.

Deadly force in defense of others includes the use of deadly force to protect an embryo or fetus whether or not viable. However, this defense is available only in the context of an assault against the mother; it does not extend to frozen or other embryos existing outside a woman's body. *Peopie v. Kurr*, 253 Mich. App. 317 (2002).

## Duty of Prosecution—MCL 780.961

If the prosecutor believes that an individual used force that was unjustified (i.e., it was not self-defense), the prosecutor must present evidence to that effect at the time of warrant issuance, preliminary examination, and trial.

# 28

# CIVIL LAW AND LIABILITY

## CIVIL LAW

Civil law is that body of principles that determines private rights and liabilities.

### Civil Law Compared to Criminal Law

#### Civil Law

Laws governing private rights and remedies are designed to adjudicate differences between private persons. Civil law is a truth-seeking process where constitutional limitations against self-incrimination and unreasonable search and seizure have little application.

#### Criminal Law

Criminal acts are wrongs committed against society and not only against the victim. Criminal prosecutions are limited by constitutional protections discussed in previous chapters such as right to counsel, right against self-incrimination, protection against unreasonable searches and seizure, and right to a speedy trial. An act may be both a crime and a civil wrong.

## CIVIL LITIGATION

### Discovery for Civil Litigation

*Discovery* is a pretrial method used to obtain facts and information about the case from the other party.

Methods of discovery include:
- Depositions.
- Interrogatories.
- Production of documents or things.
- Permission to enter on lands or other property.
- Physical or mental examinations.
- Requests for admissions.

MCR 2.300 et seq.

### Scope of Discovery—MCR 2.302

- Parties may obtain discovery regarding any matter, not privileged, *that is relevant* to the subject matter involved in the pending action.
- It does not matter that the information being sought will be admissible at trial, as long as it appears "*reasonably calculated*" to lead to discovery of admissible evidence.
- If the information or item sought is privileged, then it cannot be discovered (e.g., attorney–client, physician–patient, and husband–wife).

### Types of Discovery

#### Depositions—MCR 2.303-2.308

*Deposition:* An interview under oath. A deposition can be taken of any person, whether a party to the action or not. A deposition provides examination and cross-examination of a person, face-to-face, without time to deliberate carefully and fashion a response. A plaintiff cannot take a defendant's deposition until the defendant has had a reasonable amount of time to consult an attorney.

Depositions may be used in later court proceedings:

- To impeach a witness.
- When deponent is an expert witness.
- When the witness is dead.
- When the witness is unable to attend the trial.
- When the witness refuses to testify.
- When the witness has a lack of memory.

If a party decides to use part of a deposition at trial, an adverse party can require any other part of the deposition to be admitted.

A subpoena for a deposed witness not only directs the witness to show up at a particular time and place to be deposed, but it also may direct the witness to produce documents and other tangible things relevant to the case.

*Subpoena:* A writ or order commanding a person to appear before a court or other tribunal, subject to a penalty for failing to appear. *Black's Law Dictionary* 1563 (9th ed. 2009).

## Interrogatories to Parties—MCR 2.309

*Interrogatories:* Written questions, submitted to a party, who is to answer them as part of discovery under oath and signs a sworn statement that the answers are true. Interrogatories can only be required from a party of an action. Answers or objections to interrogatories must be returned within 28 days of receiving them or within 42 days if served with the complaint.

## Failure to Provide or to Permit Discovery—MCR 2.313

A party who requests discovery may make a motion to the court for an order to compel discovery or production when the opposing party fails to respond or responds incompletely or evasively to the request. If the court issues the order to compel discovery, the opposing party must produce the requested items or testimony. Failure to comply with a court order may bring sanctions or other adverse consequences for the party failing to comply; these consequences include:

- A default judgment may be entered or the case may be dismissed.
- A contempt order, which may include a fine or imprisonment, could be imposed.
- The information sought could be found in favor of the party seeking discovery.

## Summons—MCR 2.102

*Summons:* A writing used to notify a person of an action that was commenced against him or her. Upon a complaint being filed, the court clerk issues a summons. A summons contains the following:

- Lists the name and address of the court with jurisdiction.
- Discloses the allegations within the complaint.
- Reveals the names and addresses of the parties.
- Gives notice of the time in which the defendant is required to respond.
- Gives notice that if the respondent fails to answer the complaint within the time allowed, judgment may be entered against him or her.

## Service of Process—MCR 2.103

*Process in civil actions may be served by any legally competent adult who is not a party or an officer of a corporate party.*

## Proof of Service—MCR 2.104

*Proof of service may be made by:*

(1) *Written acknowledgment of the receipt of a summons and a copy of the complaint, dated and signed by the person to whom the service is directed or by a person authorized under these rules to receive the service of process,*

(2) *A certificate stating the facts of service, including the manner, time, date, and place of service, if service is made within the State of Michigan by a*

    (a) *A sheriff,*

    (b) *A deputy sheriff or bailiff, if that officer holds office in the county in which the court issuing the process is held,*

    (c) *An appointed court officer,*

    (d) *An attorney for a party, or*

(3) *An affidavit stating the facts of service, including the manner, time, date, and place of service, and indicating the process server's official capacity, if any.*

## Manner of Service

The manner of service differs by jurisdiction. Service may be made by:

- For a Michigan case:
  - Delivering a summons and copy of complaint to the defendant personally, or
  - Sending a copy of the summons and complaint by registered or certified mail, return receipt requested, and delivery restricted to the defendant.

- For a federal case:
  - ◆ Delivering a summons to the defendant personally, or
  - ◆ By first-class mail.

## Alternative Dispute Resolution

With a rising cost of litigation and increasing case loads, parties often seek to avoid trials. Cases may be resolved before trial by a number of means including:

- Mediation.
- Negotiation.
- Arbitration.
- Third-party case evaluation.

# CIVIL LIABILITY

## Crime Compared to Tort

A civil wrong, or tort, differs from the criminal matters which have been discussed up to this point. A crime is an offense against society that results in punishment, whereas a tort is a wrong against another person. A person convicted of a crime may be sentenced to jail, whereas a person found responsible for a tort will be ordered to financially compensate that person for their injury.

In tort, a person may sue the person who injured him or her for money damages. Generally, the courts will only allow the amount of damages recoverable to the actual amount of injury sustained. Sometimes, the court will allow punitive damages. These damages go beyond the actual injury and have the purpose of punishing the person responsible for the injury.

A crime can also result in civil litigation. For example, a person could strike another in the face, breaking his nose. The state would seek criminal charges for aggravated assault, and the person injured could sue to recover the costs of the injury.

## Three Theories of Tort Affecting Law Enforcement

There are three theories of torts that generally affect law enforcement. They include intentional torts, negligence, and constitutional torts.

- An *intentional tort* is an act that is done with purpose. A typical example is where the officer strikes someone without justification.
- Officers can also be held to be *negligent* in their actions, but in Michigan, officers must be shown to have been grossly negligent before they are held liable.
- A *constitutional tort* is when the officer violates a person's constitutional rights. The officer will not be liable if he or she was acting in good faith.

# INTENTIONAL TORTS

## Intentional Torts Typically Affecting Law Enforcement

### False arrest or false imprisonment.

*False arrest* is an unlawful taking, seizing, or detaining of a person, either by touching or putting hands on him or her, or by any other act that indicates an intention to take him or her into custody and subjects the person arrested to the actual control and will of the person making the arrest. The act must have been performed with the intent to make an arrest and must have been so understood by the person arrested. M Civ JI 116.01.

*False imprisonment* is the unlawful restraint of an individual's personal liberty or freedom of movement. To constitute a false imprisonment, there must be an intentional and unlawful restraint, detention, or confinement that deprives a person of his or her personal liberty or freedom of movement against his or her will. The restraint necessary to create liability for false imprisonment may be imposed either by actual physical force or by an express or implied threat of force. M Civ JI 116.02.

An arrest is lawful if the defendant had probable cause to make the arrest. An arrest is unlawful if the defendant did not have probable cause.

There was probable cause if both of the following:

- The officer was aware of information, facts, or circumstances which were sufficient to lead a reasonable and prudent person to believe that a felony had been committed or was in the process of being committed, and that plaintiff was the person who had committed it or was in the process of committing it.
- The officer believed that the felony had been committed or was in the process of being committed and that plaintiff was the person who had committed it or was in the process of committing it.

An arrest made with probable cause is lawful even if the felony had not actually been committed, nor was it in the process of being committed, or the felony had been committed or was in the process of being committed, but plaintiff was not the person who had committed it or was in the process of committing it. M Civ JI 116.05.

Examples include falsely procuring an arrest warrant, failure to confirm a warrant, and what has sometimes been called an "attitude arrest," i.e., arrest for disrespectful conduct or attitude toward an officer without actual criminal conduct.

## Battery

*Battery* is the willful or intentional touching of a person against that person's will. M Civ JI 115.02.

An arresting officer may use such force as is reasonably necessary to effect a lawful arrest. However, an officer who uses more force than is reasonably necessary to effect a lawful arrest commits a battery upon the person arrested to the extent the force used was excessive. M Civ JI 115.09.

An example is where an officer kicks or hits another person without justification or continues to strike a suspect after the suspect has ceased resisting.

## Intentional Infliction of Mental Distress

An example of this is where officers beat a person in front of a family member. The family member can file suit for emotional distress resulting from witnessing the beating.

## Typical Defenses to Intentional Torts

There are many possible defenses to an intentional tort, including:

- Action was justified: e.g., the person was attacking the officer at the time he was struck.
- Reasonable mistake: An officer may reasonably feel he is being attacked when, in fact, he was not, or an officer makes an arrest based on mistaken facts, but the mistake was reasonable at the time.
- Consent: The person consented to the act, e.g., the person consented to go to the police station.
- Self-defense.
- Defense of others.
- Defense of property.
- Recapture of chattels (reclaiming property).
- Necessity: e.g., shooting of a dog that is rabid.
- Legal process: e.g., officer carrying out legal duties such as an arrest warrant.
- Immunity under MCL 691.1407.

# NEGLIGENCE TORTS

## Negligence Actions Require Proof of Duty, Breach, Injury, and Causation

### Duty

**Public duty doctrine:** Unless there is a *special relationship*, officers do not owe a duty to any one individual.

Before an individual can bring suit against a police officer, a special relationship must exist between the injured party and the officer. To demonstrate a special relationship, the plaintiff must show:

- The police officer *made assurances* of protection verbally or demonstratively.
- The police officer knew that, without his or her action, harm could come to the victim.
- The police officer was in direct contact with the victim.
- The *victim relied* on the officer's assurances of protection.

*White v. Beasley*, 453 Mich. 308 (1996).

Officers did not establish a special relationship with the plaintiffs when the officers did not arrest suspects after the plaintiffs called 911 to report a suspicious situation. During the investigation, the officers took the suspects in the patrol car and parked across the street from the plaintiff's house. No arrests were made and later in the evening, the plaintiff's house was firebombed. The court applied the four factors under *White* and dismissed the suit. *Smith v. Jones*, 246 Mich. App. 270 (2001).

### Breach

The officer breached the duty owed to the plaintiff.

### Causation (Connection)

The breach caused the injury.

### Proximate cause (legal cause)

Proximate cause is an action or omission which in a natural and continuous sequence, unbroken by any new, independent cause, produces the injury, without which such injury would not have occurred. *Weissert v. City of Escanaba*, 298 Mich. 443 (1941).

### Intervening cause

An event that comes between the initial event in a sequence and the end result, thereby altering the natural course of events that might have connected a wrongful act to an injury. *Black's Law Dictionary* 250 (9th ed. 2009).

## Injury

An injury resulted.

> A trooper cocked his revolver while in the process of arresting a driver after a high-speed chase. The driver was not cooperative and the officer placed his left hand on the driver's left shoulder. The driver suddenly swung his left elbow around and struck the officer. The driver's movement placed the side of his head against the muzzle of the gun. The gun discharged and the driver was killed.
>
> *Duty:*  A duty to safeguard persons in custody was created when placing plaintiff under arrest.
>
> *Breach:*  The officer may have breached that duty when he arrested plaintiff with a cocked revolver.
>
> *Causation:*  The cocking of the revolver caused the weapon to accidentally discharge.
>
> *Injury:*  Driver died.
>
> *McMillian v. Vliet*, 422 Mich. 570 (1985).

## Negligence During Pursuits

### State Laws Governing Emergency Vehicle Use

### Exceptions to the Motor Vehicle Code for Emergency Vehicles—MCL 257.603

*The driver of an authorized emergency vehicle when responding to an emergency call, but not while returning from an emergency call, or when pursuing or apprehending a person who has violated or is violating the law or is charged with or suspected of violating the law may exercise the privileges set forth in this section, subject to the conditions of this section. The driver of an authorized emergency vehicle may do any of the following:*

(a) *Park or stand, irrespective of this act.*
(b) *Proceed past a red or stop signal or stop sign, but only after slowing down as may be necessary for safe operation.*
(c) *Exceed the prima facie speed limits so long as he or she does not endanger life or property.*
(d) *Disregard regulations governing direction of movement or turning in a specified direction.*

### Emergency Vehicle Exemption from Speed Limits—MCL 257.632

*The speed limitation set forth in this chapter shall not apply to vehicles when operated with due regard for safety under the direction of the police when traveling in emergencies or in the chase or apprehension of violators of the law or of persons charged with or suspected of a violation, nor to fire department or fire patrol vehicles when traveling in response to a fire alarm, nor to public or private ambulances when traveling in emergencies. This exemption shall apply only when the driver of the vehicle while in motion sounds an audible signal by bell, siren, or exhaust whistle as may be reasonably necessary or when the vehicle is equipped with at least 1 lighted lamp displaying a flashing, oscillating, or rotating red or blue light visible under normal atmospheric conditions from a distance of 500 feet to the front of such vehicles, unless the nature of the mission requires that a law enforcement officer travel without giving warning to suspected law violators. This exemption shall not however protect the driver of the vehicle from the consequences of a reckless disregard of the safety of others.*

### Duty to Yield to Emergency Vehicle—MCL 257.653

*Upon the immediate approach of an authorized emergency vehicle equipped with not less than 1 lighted flashing, rotating, or oscillating lamp exhibiting a red or blue light visible under normal atmospheric condition from a distance of 500 feet to the front of the vehicle and when the driver is giving audible signal by siren, exhaust whistle, or bell:*

(a) *The driver of another vehicle shall yield the right of way and shall immediately drive to a position parallel to and as close as possible to the right-hand edge or curb of the roadway, clear of an intersection, and shall stop and remain in that position until the authorized emergency vehicle has passed, except when otherwise directed by a police officer.*
(b) *The operator of a streetcar shall immediately stop the car, clear of an intersection, and shall keep it in that position until the authorized emergency vehicle has passed, except when otherwise directed by a police officer.*

*This section does not relieve the driver of an authorized emergency vehicle from the duty to drive with due regard for the safety of persons using the highway.*

*A person who violates this section is responsible for a civil infraction.*

### State Standard—MCL 691.1405

*Governmental agencies shall be liable for bodily injury and property damage resulting from the negligent operation by any officer, agent, or employee of the governmental agency, of a motor vehicle of which the governmental agency is owner.*

The Michigan Supreme Court has limited officer liability in this context as it applies negligence liability in police pursuits.

The court held that the police owe a duty to innocent passengers, but not to passengers who are themselves wrongdoers whether they help bring about the pursuit or encourage flight. "A passenger who seeks to recover for injuries allegedly caused by a negligent police pursuit bears the burden of proving personal innocence as a precondition to establishing the duty element of a cause of action."

An officer's physical handling of a motor vehicle during a police chase can constitute "negligent operation . . . of a motor vehicle" within the motor vehicle exception. However, a plaintiff must prove they were an innocent person and owed a duty by police. Then, plaintiff must demonstrate that his or her injuries were the result of the actual operation of the police cars. If the police cars did not hit the plaintiff, cause another vehicle or object to hit the plaintiff, or force the vehicle occupying the plaintiff off the road or into another vehicle or object, the motor vehicle exception to governmental immunity does not apply.

An officer's decision to pursue a vehicle does not constitute the negligent operation of a motor vehicle.

Finally, actions of individual police officers must be the proximate cause of the plaintiff's injuries in order for the individual officer to be liable. The actions of one officer during a pursuit do not make all officers in the pursuit subject to liability. *Robinson v. City of Detroit*, 462 Mich. 439 (2000).

## Federal Standard

Two officers observed two subjects on a motorcycle traveling at a high rate of speed. The officers turned on their emergency lights and yelled for the cyclist to stop. The driver maneuvered around the patrol cars and sped away. The officers activated their emergency equipment and chased the motorcycle. The chase ended when the motorcycle tipped over. One officer slammed on his brakes, but was unable to avoid striking the passenger and caused his death.

The family of the decedent brought a suit in federal court for violating his constitutional rights. The Supreme Court applied the "shock-the-conscience" standard (an extremely high standard of review) for determining liability. "In the circumstances of a high-speed chase aimed at apprehending a suspected offender, where unforeseen circumstances demand an instant judgment on the part of the officer who feels the pulls of competing obligations, only a purpose to cause harm unrelated to the legitimate object of arrest will satisfy the shock-the-conscience standard."

The court also refused to apply the Fourth Amendment to this type of situation. "That Amendment covers only 'searches and seizures,' neither of which took place here. No one suggests that there was a search, and this court's cases foreclose finding a seizure, since Smith did not terminate Lewis's freedom of movement through means intentionally applied." *County of Sacramento v. Lewis*, 523 U.S. 833 (1998).

## Immunity to Negligent Torts—MCL 691.1407

### Individual Tort Immunity for Negligence Actions

Judges, legislators, and highest level executive officials at all levels of government have absolute immunity if acting within scope of authority.

Lower-level officials and employees (police officers) are granted immunity if:

- They are acting or reasonably believe they are acting within scope of authority.
- The agent is engaged in a governmental function (see below).
- The conduct is not *grossly negligent* (not so reckless as to demonstrate a substantial lack of concern for whether an injury results).

### Governmental Agent Immunity

Agent must be performing a governmental function:

- A function expressly or impliedly mandated or authorized by constitution, statute, local charter or ordinance, or other law.
- Governmental function includes any activity for the purpose of public safety, which is performed on public or private property by a sworn law enforcement officer within the scope of the law enforcement officer's authority.

- Government function must not fall under a statutory exception to immunity. Exceptions to immunity include:
    - Maintaining highways in reasonable repair. MCL 691.1402.
    - Negligent operation of government vehicles. MCL 691.1405.
    - Dangerous/defective conditions of public buildings. MCL 691.1406.

Operation of police department is governmental function for immunity purposes. *Isabella County v. Michigan*, 181 Mich. App. 99 (1989).

Governmental employees enjoy qualified immunity for intentional torts. A governmental employee must raise governmental immunity as an affirmative defense and establish that:

(1) The employee's challenged acts were undertaken during the course of employment and that the employee was acting, or reasonably believed he was acting, within the scope of his authority,

(2) The acts were undertaken in good faith, and

(3) The acts were discretionary, rather than ministerial, in nature.

*Odom v. Wayne County*, 482 Mich. 459 (2008).

## Fireman's Rule

Traditionally, police officers were precluded from filing civil suits against someone who injured them while they were performing their duty as a police officer. On-duty injuries at one time were considered "part of the job."

The Michigan Supreme Court held that the fireman's rule is not "a license to act with impunity, without regard for the officer's well being." A suit based on an act that is alleged to have been *wanton, reckless, or grossly negligent* is not precluded by the fireman's rule. In this case, while directing traffic, Officer Gibbons was struck by a reckless driver. The court held that being struck by a reckless driver is not a risk inherent in a police officer's duties. *Gibbons v. Caraway*, 455 Mich. 314 (1997).

Trooper Fields was on a traffic stop on I-94 when he was struck by a vehicle driven by the defendant. The lawsuit was dismissed on the grounds of the fireman's rule. The Michigan Supreme Court reversed. The court held that in instances where the "negligent conduct of the defendant did not result in the officer's presence at the scene of the injury, the fireman's rule does not apply." *Harris-Fields v. Syze*, 461 Mich. 188 (1999).

# CONSTITUTIONAL TORTS— 42 U.S.C. § 1983

## Definition

Any *person* who, *acting under color of law*, subjects any other person to the deprivation of any rights, privileges, or immunities secured by the Constitution and laws is liable to the party injured. Police officers are generally acting under color of state law.

## Person

- A state or state agency is not a "person" and cannot be sued under this section.
- Cities and municipalities can be persons if it is shown that they have a custom or policy of violating constitutional rights.
- Individual officers are considered persons.

## Acting under Color of Law

Police officers are generally acting under color of state law.

## Deprive a Person of Rights, Privileges, or Immunities Secured by the Constitution

The purpose of the Constitution is to protect people from the state, not from one another. *Rogers v. Port Huron*, 833 F.Supp. 1212 (E.D. Mich. 1993).

"[N]othing in the language of the Due Process Clause itself requires the State to protect the life, liberty, and property of its citizens against invasion by private actors. The Clause is phrased as a limitation on the State's power to act, not as a guarantee of certain minimal levels of safety and security. It forbids the State itself to deprive individuals of life, liberty, or property without 'due process of law,' but its language cannot fairly be extended to impose an affirmative obligation on the State to ensure that those interests do not come to harm through other means." *DeShaney v. Winnebago County Department of Social Services*, 489 U.S. 189 (1989).

## General Claims under 42 U.S.C. § 1983

- Freedom of Speech—First Amendment.
- Excessive Force—Fourth Amendment.
- Illegal Search and Seizure—Fourth Amendment.
- False Arrest—Fourth Amendment.
- Cruel and Unusual Punishment—Eighth Amendment.
- Violation of the Equal Protection of Laws—Fourteenth Amendment.
- Violation of Due Process—Fourteenth Amendment.

## Immunity to 42 U.S.C. § 1983 Actions

*Absolute immunity* is given to judges, legislators, and prosecutors when they are performing their respective functions. *Schorn v. Larose*, 829 F.Supp. 215 (E.D. Mich. 1993), aff'd, 16 F.3d 1221 (6th Cir. 1994).

*Qualified immunity* is given to other governmental officials when they:

- Act in good faith, and
- Reasonably believe their actions are constitutional.

State immunity acts are not controlling for violations under § 1983 claims. *Howlett v. Rose*, 496 U.S. 356 (1990).

The general rule of qualified immunity from civil liability is intended to provide government officials the ability to "reasonably" anticipate when their conduct may give rise to liability. Where rule is applicable, officers can know that they will not be liable as long as their actions are "reasonable" under current American law. *Anderson v. Creighton*, 483 U.S. 635 (1987).

The Sixth Circuit denied qualified immunity to a police officer who arrested a man who drove by a group of abortion protesters and yelled obscenities out the window. Because the vehicle was traveling at a fast rate of speed and was located quite a distance away from the protesters, the court would not classify the statement as "fighting words." Thus, the speech was protected under the First Amendment. *Sandul v. Larion*, 119 F.3d 1250 (6th Cir. 1997).

Officers are provided qualified immunity when an officer reasonably believes that his or her conduct complies with the law. Police officers are entitled to rely on existing lower court cases without facing personal liability for their actions. If judges disagree on a constitutional question, it is unfair to subject police to money damages for picking the losing side of the controversy. The relevant inquiry is the objective reasonableness of the officers' action in light of clearly established legal rules. *Pearson v. Callahan*, 555 U.S. 223 (2009).

Government officials in general, and police officers in particular, may not exercise their authority for personal motives, particularly in response to real or personal slights to their dignity. The fighting words doctrine may be limited in the case of communications addressed to a properly trained police officer because police officers are expected to exercise greater restraint in their response than the average citizen. *Greene v. Barber*, 310 F.3d 889 (6th Cir. 2002).

A search warrant that failed to describe the persons or things to be seized was invalid on its face, notwithstanding that requisite particularized description was provided in search warrant application. The residential search that was conducted pursuant to this facially invalid warrant could not be regarded as "reasonable," though items to be seized were described in search the warrant application, and though officers conducting search exercised restraint in limiting scope of search to that indicated in application. Because the warrant was so facially deficient, the officer who had prepared and executed the warrant was not entitled to qualified immunity from liability as he was adequately on notice of the warrant's deficiency by his preparation of the warrant and he was on notice of his liability because of departmental policy in place at the time. *Groh v. Ramirez*, 540 U.S. 551 (2004).

## Theories of Liability under 42 U.S.C. § 1983

### Intentional Torts

### Negligence

A §1983 claim may generally not be prefaced on ordinary negligence or carelessness. The negligent act of a government agent resulting in the loss of life, limb, or property does not rise to the level of a deprivation under the Due Process Clause. *Daniels v. Williams*, 474 U.S. 327 (1986).

"We said again that the substantive component of the Due Process Clause is violated by executive action only when it 'can properly be characterized as arbitrary, or conscience shocking, in a constitutional sense.'" The Court declined to precisely define where shocking the conscience fell on the scale of culpability, they did say it fell somewhere more than negligence but less than intentional conduct, such as recklessness or gross negligence. County of Sacramento v. Lewis, 523 U.S. 833 (1998).

## Good Faith Defense

This defense applies where officer acts in "good faith." Courts look at officer's subjective belief of probable cause.

The good faith defense will apply even if probable cause is absent, so long as the officer has a "good faith" belief his actions are lawful. *Pierson v. Ray*, 386 U.S. 547 (1967).

Government officials performing discretionary functions generally are shielded from liability for civil damages as long as their conduct does not violate clearly established statutory or constitutional rights of which a reasonable person would have known. If the court finds that the officer did violate this test, he or she may plead a "good faith" defense. An officer pleading a good faith defense, where a clearly established right has been violated, must claim extraordinary circumstances and prove that he or she neither knew nor should have known that he or she was violating clearly established statutory or constitutional rights. *Harlow v. Fitzgerald*, 457 U.S. 800 (1982).

# CRIME VICTIM'S RIGHTS ACT

## DEFINITIONS FOR PURPOSES OF THE CRIME VICTIM'S RIGHTS ACT

### Victim–MCL 780.752(1)(m)

*Victim:* Any of the following
- An individual who suffers direct or threatened physical, financial, or emotional harm as a result of the commission of a crime, serious misdemeanor, or juvenile offense.
- Sole proprietorships, partnerships, corporations, associations, governmental agencies, or any other legal entity that has suffered direct physical or financial harm as a result of a crime, serious misdemeanor, or juvenile offense. MCL 780.766, 780.794.

> The legislative intent behind the CVRA permits narcotics enforcement teams as victims to obtain restitution of "buy money" lost to a defendant's criminal act of selling controlled substances. *People v. Crigler*, 244 Mich. App. 420 (2001).

- Any following relations of a deceased victim if the relation is not the defendant:

    - The spouse.
    - A child 18 years of age or older if the victim has no surviving spouse.

- A parent if the victim has no surviving spouse or adult children.
- A guardian or custodian of a child of deceased victim if the child is less than 18 years old and the victim had no surviving spouse, adult children, or parents.
- A sibling if the victim had no surviving spouse, adult children, minor children, or parents.
- A grandparent if the victim had no surviving spouse, adult children, minor children, siblings, or parents.

- A parent, guardian, or custodian of a victim who is less than 18 years of age and who is neither the defendant nor incarcerated if the parent, guardian, or custodian so chooses. For the purpose of making an impact statement only, a parent guardian, or custodian of a victim who is less than 18 years of age at the time of the commission of the crime and who is neither the defendant nor incarcerated, if the parent, guardian, or custodian so chooses.
- A parent, guardian, or custodian of a victim who is so mentally incapacitated that he or she cannot meaningfully understand or participate in the legal process if he or she is neither the defendant nor incarcerated.
- If a victim is physically unable to exercise the privileges and rights under this article, the victim may designate one of the following to act in

place of the victim during the duration of the disability if he or she is neither the defendant nor incarcerated:

- The spouse.
- A child 18 years or older.
- A parent.
- A sibling.
- A grandparent.
- Any other person 18 years or older.

## Crime—MCL 780.752(1)(b)

*Crime:* A violation of a penal law of this state for which the offender may be punished by imprisonment for more than one year, or an offense expressly designated as a felony.

## Juvenile Offense—MCL 780.781

*Juvenile:* A child within the jurisdiction of the Family Division of the Circuit Court.

*Offense:* Either a crime or a serious misdemeanor as described below.

## Serious Misdemeanors—MCL 780.811

*Serious misdemeanors:* Any of the following:

- Assault and battery. MCL 750.81.
- Assault, infliction of serious injury. MCL 750.81a.
- Breaking and entering, or illegal entry. MCL 750.115.
- Child abuse in the fourth degree. MCL 750.136b(6).
- Contributing to the neglect or delinquency of a minor. MCL 750.145.
- Using the Internet or a computer to make a prohibited communication. MCL 750.145d.
- Intentionally aiming a firearm without malice. MCL 750.233.
- Discharging a firearm intentionally aimed at a person. MCL 750.234.
- Discharge of an intentionally aimed firearm resulting in injury. MCL 750.235.
- Indecent exposure. MCL 750.335a.
- Stalking. MCL 750.411h.
- Injuring a worker in a work zone. MCL 257.601b.
- Leaving the scene of a personal injury accident. MCL 257.617a.
- O.W.I. and impaired driving, if the violation involves an accident resulting in serious physical or death to another person or damage to another's property. MCL 257.625-257.625a.
- Operating a vessel while under the influence of or impaired by alcoholic liquor or a controlled substance, or with an unlawful blood alcohol content, if the violation involves an accident resulting in damage to another individual's property or physical injury or death to any individual. MCL 324.80176.
- Selling or furnishing alcoholic liquor to an individual less than 21 years of age if the violation results in physical injury or death to any individual. MCL 436.1701.
- A local ordinance substantially corresponding to the above.

# REQUIREMENTS UNDER THE ACT FOR LAW ENFORCEMENT

## Initial Contact—MCL 780.753, 780.782, 780.813

*Within 24 hours after initial contact* between the victim of a reported "crime," "juvenile offense," or "serious misdemeanor," the law enforcement agency having the responsibility for investigating the incident shall give the victim the following information:

- The availability of emergency and medical services, if applicable.
- The availability of victim's compensation benefits and the address of the crime victims compensation board.
- The address and phone number of the prosecuting attorney whom the victim should contact to obtain information about victim's rights.
- The following statement: "If you would like to be notified of an arrest in your case or the release of the person arrested, or both, you should call [law enforcement agency's telephone number] and inform them. If you are not notified of an arrest in your case, you may call [law enforcement agency's telephone number] for the status of the case at anytime."

## Property—MCL 780.754, MCL 780.783, MCL 780.814

The law enforcement agency investigating a "crime," "juvenile offense," or "serious misdemeanor," shall promptly return to the victim property belonging to the victim that is taken in the course of the investigation, except:

- Contraband.
- When the ownership of the property is in dispute.
- Any weapons used in the commission of a crime or other evidence that the prosecutor certifies that there is a need to retain the evidence in lieu of a photograph or other means of memorializing its possession by the agency.

## Arraignment for a Crime—MCL 780.755

*Within 24 hours of defendant's arraignment* for a "crime," the arresting agency must:

- Give the victim notice of the availability of pretrial release.
- Supply the telephone number of the sheriff or juvenile facility.
- Provide notice that the victim may contact the sheriff to determine whether defendant has been released.
- Promptly notify the victim of the arrest or pretrial release, or both, if the victim requests or has requested the information.

## Preliminary Hearing for a Juvenile— MCL 780.785

*Not later than 48 hours after the preliminary hearing* for a juvenile offense, the prosecuting attorney or court must provide the victim the telephone number of the juvenile facility and notice that the victim may contact the juvenile facility to determine if the juvenile has been released.

The law enforcement agency with responsibility for investigating the crime shall promptly notify the victim of the arrest or pretrial release, or both, if the victim requests or has requested the information.

If the juvenile is released from custody by the sheriff or juvenile facility, the sheriff or juvenile facility shall notify the law enforcement agency having responsibility for investigating the crime.

## Arrest for a Serious Misdemeanor—MCL 780.815

*Not later than 72 hours after the arrest* of the defendant for a "serious misdemeanor," the investigating agency shall give to the victim:

- Notice of the availability of pretrial release for the defendant,
- The phone number of the sheriff,
- Notice that the victim may contact the sheriff to determine whether the defendant has been released from custody, and
- Prompt notice of the arrest or pretrial release, or both, if the victim requests or has requested the information.

## List of Victims of Serious Juvenile Offense or Misdemeanor—MCL 780.784, MCL 780.812

A law enforcement officer investigating a "juvenile offense" or "serious misdemeanor" involving a victim, shall include, with the complaint, appearance ticket, traffic citation, or petition filed with the court a separate written statement including the name, address, and phone number of each victim. This separate statement shall not be a matter of public record.

# APPENDIX

| STATE OF MICHIGAN JUDICIAL DISTRICT JUDICIAL CIRCUIT | WARRANT MISDEMEANOR | CASE NO. |
|---|---|---|
| | ☐ Traffic    ☐ Nontraffic | COURT ORI |

Court address _____ Court telephone no.

---

**THE PEOPLE OF**

☐ The State of Michigan

☐ _____

v

Defendant

---

**TO:**    Any peace officer or court officer authorized to make an arrest.

Upon examination of the citation, I find probable cause to believe the defendant committed the offense set forth.

**THEREFORE, IN THE NAME OF THE PEOPLE OF THE STATE OF MICHIGAN,** I command you to arrest and bring defendant before the court immediately, or defendant may be released when a cash interim bond is posted in the amount of $ _____ for personal appearance before the court.

_____
Date

_____
Judge/Magistrate

**(SEAL)**

Authorized on _____ by:
            Date

_____
Prosecuting official

By virtue of this warrant, the defendant has been taken into custody as commanded.

_____
Date

_____
Arresting official

COPY OF CITATION

| Original complaint - Court<br>Warrant - Court | 2nd Complaint copy - Prosecutor<br>3rd Complaint copy - Defendant |
|---|---|

| STATE OF MICHIGAN<br>JUDICIAL DISTRICT | COMPLAINT<br>MISDEMEANOR | CASE NO. |
|---|---|---|

| ORI<br>MI- | Court address | Court telephone no. |
|---|---|---|

| THE PEOPLE OF<br>☐ The State of Michigan   **v**<br>☐ _____ | Defendant's name and address | Victim or complainant |
|---|---|---|
| | | Complaining witness |

| Codefendant(s) | Date: On or about |
|---|---|

| City/Twp./Village | County in Michigan | Defendant TCN | Defendant CTN | Defendant SID | Defendant DOB |
|---|---|---|---|---|---|

| Police agency report no. | Charge | Maximum penalty |
|---|---|---|

| Witnesses | ☐ Oper./Chauf.<br>☐ CDL | Vehicle Type | Defendant DLN |
|---|---|---|---|

STATE OF MICHIGAN, COUNTY OF _____ .

The complaining witness says that on the date and at the location described, the defendant, contrary to law,

☐ The complaining witness asks that defendant be apprehended and dealt with according to law.

(Peace officers only) I declare that the statements above are true to the best of my information, knowledge, and belief.

| | |
|---|---|
| Warrant authorized on _____ by:<br>        Date<br><br>Prosecuting official | Complaining witness signature<br><br>Subscribed and sworn to before me on _____ .<br>                  Date<br><br>Judge/Court clerk/Magistrate |

DC 225 (3/12) **COMPLAINT, MISDEMEANOR**

| | Original complaint - Court | 2nd Complaint copy - Prosecutor |
|---|---|---|
| | Warrant - Court | 3rd Complaint copy - Defendant |

| STATE OF MICHIGAN JUDICIAL DISTRICT | WARRANT MISDEMEANOR | CASE NO. |
|---|---|---|

| ORI | Court address | Court telephone no. |
|---|---|---|
| MI- | | |

**THE PEOPLE OF**
☐ The State of Michigan

☐ _____

**v**

Defendant's name and address

Victim or complainant

Complaining witness

Codefendant(s)

Date: On or about

| City/Twp./Village | County in Michigan | Defendant TCN | Defendant CTN | Defendant SID | Defendant DOB |
|---|---|---|---|---|---|

| Police agency report no. | Charge | Maximum penalty |
|---|---|---|

| Witnesses | ☐ Oper./Chauf. ☐ CDL | Vehicle Type | Defendant DLN |
|---|---|---|---|

**STATE OF MICHIGAN, COUNTY OF** _____ .

**To any peace officer or court officer authorized to make an arrest:** The complaining witness has filed a sworn complaint in this court stating that on the date and the location described, the defendant, contrary to law,

Upon examination of the complaint, I find probable cause to believe defendant committed the offense set forth. **THEREFORE, IN THE NAME OF THE PEOPLE OF THE STATE OF MICHIGAN,**

☐ a. I order you to arrest and bring defendant before the _____ District Court immediately.
☐ b. I order you to bring defendant before the _____ District Court.
☐ c. The defendant may be released when a cash bond is posted in the amount of $ _____ for personal appearance before the court.

_____ (SEAL)    _____
Date                                              Judge/Magistrate                                   Bar no.

By virtue of this warrant, the defendant has been taken into custody as ordered.

_____    _____
Date                                              Peace officer

**DC 225** (3/12) **WARRANT, MISDEMEANOR**

| Information - Circuit court<br>Original complaint - Court<br>Warrant - Court | Bind over/Transfer - Circuit/Juvenile court<br>Complaint copy - Prosecutor<br>Complaint copy - Defendant/Attorney |
|---|---|

| STATE OF MICHIGAN<br>JUDICIAL DISTRICT<br>JUDICIAL CIRCUIT | COMPLAINT<br>FELONY | CASE NO.<br><br>DISTRICT<br>CIRCUIT |
|---|---|---|

District Court ORI: MI-          Circuit Court ORI: MI-

| THE PEOPLE OF THE STATE OF MICHIGAN   v | Defendant's name and address | Victim or complainant |
|---|---|---|
| | | Complaining witness |
| Codefendant(s) | | Date: On or about |

| City/Twp./Village | County in Michigan | Defendant TCN | Defendant CTN | Defendant SID | Defendant DOB |
|---|---|---|---|---|---|

| Police agency report no. | Charge | | Maximum penalty |
|---|---|---|---|

| Witnesses | ☐ Oper./Chauf.<br>☐ CDL | Vehicle Type | Defendant DLN |
|---|---|---|---|

STATE OF MICHIGAN, COUNTY OF _____ .

The complaining witness says that on the date and at the location described, the defendant, contrary to law,

☐ The complaining witness asks that defendant be apprehended and dealt with according to law.

| Warrant authorized on _____ by: | |
| Date | |
| | _____ |
| _____ | Complaining witness signature |
| Prosecuting official | Subscribed and sworn to before me on _____ . |
| | Date |
| ☐ Security for costs posted | _____ |
| | Judge/Magistrate/Clerk      Bar no. |

MCL 764.1 *et seq.*, MCL 766.1 *et seq.*, MCL 767.1 *et seq.*, MCR 6.110

MC 200 (3/12) **FELONY SET, Complaint**

| Information - Circuit court | Bind over/Transfer - Circuit/Juvenile court |
|---|---|
| Original complaint - Court | Complaint copy - Prosecutor |
| Warrant - Court | Complaint copy - Defendant/Attorney |

| STATE OF MICHIGAN JUDICIAL DISTRICT JUDICIAL CIRCUIT | INFORMATION FELONY | CASE NO. |
|---|---|---|
| | | DISTRICT |
| | | CIRCUIT |

District Court ORI: MI-                     Circuit Court ORI: MI-

| THE PEOPLE OF THE STATE OF MICHIGAN   v | Defendant's name and address | Victim or complainant |
|---|---|---|
| | | Complaining witness |
| Codefendant(s) | | Date: On or about |

| City/Twp./Village | County in Michigan | Defendant TCN | Defendant CTN | Defendant SID | Defendant DOB |
|---|---|---|---|---|---|

| Police agency report no. | Charge | | Maximum penalty |
|---|---|---|---|

| Witnesses | ☐ Oper./Chauf. ☐ CDL | Vehicle Type | Defendant DLN |
|---|---|---|---|

STATE OF MICHIGAN, COUNTY OF _____

**IN THE NAME OF THE PEOPLE OF THE STATE OF MICHIGAN:** The prosecuting attorney for this county appears before the court and informs the court that on the date and at the location described, the defendant:

and against the peace and dignity of the State of Michigan.

Prosecuting Attorney

By: _____

_____
Date

MCL 764.1 *et seq.*, MCL 766.1 *et seq.*, MCL 767.1 *et seq.*, MCR 6.110

**MC 200** (3/12) **FELONY SET, Information**

Information - Circuit court
Original complaint - Court
Warrant - Court

Bind over/Transfer - Circuit/Juvenile court
Complaint copy - Prosecutor
Complaint copy - Defendant/Attorney

| STATE OF MICHIGAN<br>JUDICIAL DISTRICT<br>JUDICIAL CIRCUIT | WARRANT<br>FELONY | CASE NO.<br><br>DISTRICT<br>CIRCUIT |
|---|---|---|

**District Court ORI: MI-**                          **Circuit Court ORI: MI-**

| THE PEOPLE OF THE<br>STATE OF MICHIGAN | v | Defendant's name and address | Victim or complainant |
|---|---|---|---|
| | | | Complaining witness |

| Codefendant(s) | Date: On or about |
|---|---|

| City/Twp./Village | County in Michigan | Defendant TCN | Defendant CTN | Defendant SID | Defendant DOB |
|---|---|---|---|---|---|

| Police agency report no. | Charge | | Maximum penalty |
|---|---|---|---|

| Witnesses | ☐ Oper./Chauf.<br>☐ CDL | Vehicle Type | Defendant DLN |
|---|---|---|---|

**STATE OF MICHIGAN, COUNTY OF** _____ .
**To any peace officer or court officer authorized to make arrest:** The complaining witness has filed a sworn complaint in this court stating that on the date and the location described, the defendant, contrary to law,

Upon examination of the complaining witness, I find that the offense charged was committed and that there is probable cause to believe that defendant committed the offense. THEREFORE, IN THE NAME OF THE PEOPLE OF THE STATE OF MICHIGAN,

☐ a. I order you to arrest and bring defendant before the _____ District Court immediately.
☐ b. I order you to bring defendant before the _____ District Court.
☐ c. The defendant may be released before arraignment if $ _____ is posted as interim bail by _____ .
                                                                                                    Date

_____          (SEAL)          _____
Date                                                                       Judge/Magistrate                                    Bar no.

**See return on reverse side.**

MC 200   (3/12)   **FELONY SET, Warrant**                   MCL 764.1 *et seq.*, MCL 766.1 *et seq.*, MCL 767.1 *et seq.*, MCR 6.110

**RETURN**

As ordered in this warrant, the defendant was arrested on _____ at _____
Date                                                                                                Time

at _____ .
Place of arrest

_____
Date

_____
Peace officer

Information - Circuit court
Original complaint - Court
Warrant - Court

Bind over/Transfer - Circuit/Juvenile court
Complaint copy - Prosecutor
Complaint copy - Defendant/Attorney

| STATE OF MICHIGAN<br>JUDICIAL DISTRICT<br>JUDICIAL CIRCUIT | BIND OVER/TRANSFER AFTER<br>PRELIMINARY EXAMINATION<br>FELONY | CASE NO.<br><br>DISTRICT<br>CIRCUIT |
|---|---|---|

District Court ORI: MI-                                     Circuit Court ORI: MI-

| THE PEOPLE OF THE<br>STATE OF MICHIGAN | Defendant's name and address<br><br>v | Victim or complainant |
|---|---|---|
| | | Complaining witness |
| Codefendant(s) | | Date: On or about |

| City/Twp./Village | County in Michigan | Defendant TCN | Defendant CTN | Defendant SID | Defendant DOB |
|---|---|---|---|---|---|

| Police agency report no. | Charge | | Maximum penalty |
|---|---|---|---|

| Witnesses | ☐ Oper./Chauf.<br>☐ CDL | Vehicle Type | Defendant DLN |
|---|---|---|---|

Date: _____     District judge: _____

Bar no.

| Reporter/Recorder | Cert. no. | Represented by counsel | Bar no. |
|---|---|---|---|

## EXAMINATION WAIVER

1. I, the defendant, understand:
   a. I have a right to employ an attorney.
   b. I may request a court-appointed attorney if I am financially unable to employ one.
   c. I have a right to a preliminary examination where it must be shown that a crime was committed and probable cause exists to charge me with the crime.

2. I voluntarily waive my right to a preliminary examination and understand that I will be bound over to circuit court on the charges in the complaint and warrant (or as amended).

| Defendant attorney | Bar no. | Defendant |
|---|---|---|

## ADULT BIND OVER

☐ 3. Examination was waived on _____ .
   Date

☐ 4. Examination was held on _____ and it was found that probable cause exists to believe both that an offense not cognizable by the district court has been committed and that the defendant committed the offense.

☐ 5. The defendant is bound over to circuit court to appear on _____ at _____ m.
   Date                                                                                          Time

   ☐ on the charge(s) in the complaint.

   ☐ on the amended charge(s) of _____

_____ MCL/PACC Code _____ .

6. Bond is set in the amount of $ _____ . Type of bond: _____ ☐ Posted

| Date | Judge | Bar no. |
|---|---|---|

**Certification of transmittal and bind over/transfer for juvenile are printed on reverse side.**

MCL 764.1 *et seq.*, MCL 766.1 *et seq.*, MCL 767.1 *et seq.*, MCR 6.110

MC 200  (3/12)  **FELONY SET,  Bind Over/Transfer After Preliminary Examination**

## JUVENILE BIND OVER/TRANSFER

☐ 3. Examination was waived on _____ .
                                   Date

☐ 4. Examination was held on _____ and it was found that
                               Date

    ☐ there is probable cause that a life offense occurred and there is probable cause that the juvenile committed the life offense.

    ☐ there is no probable cause that a life offense occurred or there is no probable cause that the juvenile committed the life offense, but some other offense occured that if committed by an adult would constitute a crime, and there is probable cause to believe the juvenile commited that offense.

☐ 5. The juvenile is bound over to circuit court criminal division to appear on _____ at _____ m.
                                                                    Date                     Time

    ☐ on the charge(s) in the complaint.

    ☐ on the amended charge(s) of _____

    _____ MCL/PACC Code _____ .

☐ 6. This case is transferred to the family division of the circuit court for further proceedings
    ☐ immediately.

    ☐ on _____ at _____ m.
              Date                        Time

7. Bond is set in the amount of $ _____ . Type of bond: _____ ☐ Posted

_____                      _____

Date                                       Judge                                     Bar no.

                                                              MCL 766.14(2), MCR 6.911

## CERTIFICATION

I certify that on this date I have transmitted to the _____ circuit court criminal division

the prosecutor's authorization for a warrant application, the complaint, a copy of the register of actions, and any recognizances

received.

_____                      _____

Date                                       Court clerk

NOTE: Send a copy of this bind over to the Michigan State Police Criminal Justice Information Center.

Original - Return
1st copy - Witness
2nd copy - File
3rd copy - Extra

| STATE OF MICHIGAN | SUBPOENA | CASE NO. |
|---|---|---|
| JUDICIAL DISTRICT<br>JUDICIAL CIRCUIT<br>COUNTY PROBATE | Order to Appear and/or Produce | |

| Court address | Court telephone no. |
|---|---|

Police Report No. (if applicable)

| Plaintiff(s)/Petitioner(s) | | Defendant(s)/Respondent(s) |
|---|---|---|
| ☐ People of the State of Michigan<br>☐ _____ | v | |
| ☐ Civil        ☐ Criminal | | Charge |
| ☐ Probate    In the matter of _____ | | |

In the Name of the People of the State of Michigan.    TO:

If you require special accommodations to use the court because of disabilities, please contact the court immediately to make arrangements.

**YOU ARE ORDERED:**

☐ 1. to appear personally at the time and place stated below:   You may be required to appear from time to time and day to day until excused.

   ☐ The court address above   ☐ Other: _____

| Day | Date | Time |
|---|---|---|
| | | |

☐ 2. Testify at trial / examination / hearing.

☐ 3. Produce/permit inspection or copying of the following items:_____

_____

_____

☐ 4. Testify as to your assets, and bring with you the items listed in line 3 above.

☐ 5. Testify at deposition.

☐ 6. MCL 600.6104(2), 600.6116, or 600.6119 prohibition against transferring or disposing of property is attached.

☐ 7. Other: _____

☐ 8.

| Person requesting subpoena | Telephone no. |
|---|---|
| Address | |
| City | State | Zip |

**NOTE:** If requesting a debtor's examination under MCL 600.6110, or an injunction under item 6. this subpoena must be issued by a judge. For a debtor examination, the affidavit of debtor examination on the other side of this form must also be completed. Debtor's assets can also be discovered through MCR 2.305 without the need for an affidavit of debtor examination or issuance of this subpoena by a judge.

**FAILURE TO OBEY THE COMMANDS OF THE SUBPOENA OR APPEAR AT THE STATED TIME AND PLACE MAY SUBJECT YOU TO PENALTY FOR CONTEMPT OF COURT.**

| | Court use only |
|---|---|
| | ☐ Served   ☐ Not served |

Date _____   Judge/Clerk/Attorney _____   Bar no. _____

MC 11  (4/14)  **SUBPOENA, Order to Appear and/or Produce**        MCL 600.1455, 600.1701, 600.6110, 600.6119, MCR 2.506

**TO PROCESS SERVER:** You must make and file your return with the court clerk. If you are unable to complete service, you must return this original and all copies to the court clerk.

## CERTIFICATE / AFFIDAVIT OF SERVICE / NONSERVICE

☐ **OFFICER CERTIFICATE**      **OR**     ☐ **AFFIDAVIT OF PROCESS SERVER**

I certify that I am a sheriff, deputy sheriff, bailiff, appointed court officer, or attorney for a party [MCR 2.104(A)(2)], and that:    (notarization not required)

Being first duly sworn, I state that I am a legally competent adult who is not a party or an officer of a corporate party, and that:    (notarization required)

☐ I served a copy of the subpoena, together with _____ (including any required fees) by
       Attachment

     ☐ personal service     ☐ registered or certified mail (copy of return receipt attached)    on:

| Name(s) | Complete address(es) of service | Day, date, time |
|---|---|---|
| | | |
| | | |

☐ I have personally attempted to serve the subpoena and required fees, if any, together with _____
on the following person and have been unable to complete service.    Attachment

| Name(s) | Complete address(es) of service | Day, date, time |
|---|---|---|
| | | |

| Service fee | Miles traveled Fee | |
|---|---|---|
| $ | $ | |
| Incorrect address fee | Miles traveled Fee | **TOTAL FEE** |
| $ | $ | $ |

Signature _____

Name (type or print) _____

Title _____

Subscribed and sworn to before me on _____ , _____ County, Michigan.
                 Date

My commission expires: _____ Signature: _____
               Date                         Deputy court clerk/Notary public

Notary public, State of Michigan, County of _____

## ACKNOWLEDGMENT OF SERVICE

I acknowledge that I have received service of the subpoena and required fees, if any, together with _____
                                                              Attachment

_____ on _____
                              Day, date, time

_____ on behalf of _____ .
Signature

## AFFIDAVIT FOR JUDGMENT DEBTOR EXAMINATION

I request that the court issue a subpoena which orders the party named on this form to be examined under oath before a judge concerning the money or property of:
for the following reasons:

_____
                 Signature

Subscribed and sworn to before me on _____ , _____ County, Michigan.
                 Date

My commission expires: _____ Signature: _____
               Date                         Deputy court clerk/Notary public

Notary public, State of Michigan, County of _____

MCR 2.105

| BTH TEST OPR NO | LEIN ENTRY | RECORD SEQUENCE NO |
|---|---|---|

DI-93 (03/13) By the authority of P.A. 300 of 1949 as amended

# OFFICER'S REPORT OF REFUSAL TO SUBMIT TO CHEMICAL TEST

| PERSON'S FULL NAME (AS APPEARS ON MICHIGAN DRIVER'S LICENSE) | BIRTH DATE (MM/DD/YY) | SEX |
|---|---|---|
| | | MALE    FEMALE |

| ADDRESS (NUMBER & STREET) | MICHIGAN DRIVER'S LICENSE NUMBER |
|---|---|

| CITY | STATE | ZIP | OTHER STATE DRIVER'S LICENSE NUMBER | STATE |
|---|---|---|---|---|

| HEIGHT | WEIGHT | EYE COLOR | HAIR COLOR | ☐ OPERATOR   ☐ CHAUFFEUR   ☐ MOPED |
|---|---|---|---|---|

| ARREST DATE (MM/DD/YY) | MILITARY TIME | REFUSAL DATE (MM/DD/YY) | MILITARY TIME |
|---|---|---|---|

| COUNTY (OF ARREST) | CITY OR TOWNSHIP (OF ARREST) | CO/CTY/TWP CODE |
|---|---|---|

| *VEHICLE TYPE | Was person involved in an accident? YES   NO | INSTRUMENT # REFUSED | BAC #1 N/A | BAC #2 N/A | BAC #3 N/A | UCR CODE | COMPLAINT NUMBER |
|---|---|---|---|---|---|---|---|

| ARRESTING OFFICER'S NAME | BADGE NUMBER | ORI NUMBER |
|---|---|---|

| BREATH TEST OPERATOR'S NAME, only if not listed above and necessary for hearing | BADGE NUMBER | ORI NUMBER |
|---|---|---|

| OTHER OFFICER, if necessary for hearing | BADGE NUMBER | ORI NUMBER |
|---|---|---|

The above named person was arrested for a violation of section 625(1), (3), (4), (5), (6), (7), (8), 625a(5) or 625m of the Michigan Vehicle Code, as amended, or a local ordinance substantially corresponding to section 625(1), (3), (4), (5), (6), (7), (8), 625a(5) or 625m or for the offense of manslaughter, murder, reckless driving causing death, reckless driving causing serious impairment of a body function, moving violation causing death, or moving violation causing serious impairment of a body function resulting from the operation of a motor vehicle.

The officer had reasonable grounds to believe that the above named person violated section 625(1), (3), (4), (5), (6), (7), (8), 625a(5) or 625m of the Michigan Vehicle Code, as amended, or local ordinance substantially corresponding to section 625(1), (3), (4), (5), (6), (7), (8), 625a(5) or 625m or committed the offense of manslaughter, murder, reckless driving causing death, reckless driving causing serious impairment of a body function, moving violation causing death, or moving violation causing serious impairment of a body function resulting from the operation of a motor vehicle while impaired by or under the influence of alcoholic liquor, a controlled substance, other intoxicating substance, or a combination, or while having an unlawful bodily alcohol content, or if the person is less that 21 years of age while having any bodily alcohol content. [MCL 257.625c(1)(b)]

The above named person was requested to take a chemical test. The person was advised of the chemical test rights as required under section 625a and refused to take a chemical test.

| Michigan Driver's License confiscated? | Yes ☐   No ☐ | Michigan Driver's License destroyed? | Yes ☐   No ☐ | Under 21? Yes ☐   No ☐ | LICENSED OUT OF STATE |
|---|---|---|---|---|---|

Driving status on date of arrest
VALID ☐   EXPIRED ☐   RESTRICTED ☐   SUSPENDED ☐   REVOKED ☐   DENIED ☐   UNLICENSED ☐   UNKNOWN ☐   LICENSED OUT OF STATE ☐

CDL   License ☐   Permit ☐   A ☐   B ☐   C ☐   H ☐   N ☐   X ☐   P ☐   T ☐   CDL restrictions _____   ENDORSEMENT   CY ☐   F ☐   R ☐   Other _____

*VEHICLE TYPES

| CY | Cycle | MD | Med Tr w/wo Trl ovr 10,000# (non CDL) | AP | Group A Passenger | BH | Group B Hazardous | CS | Group C School Bus |
|---|---|---|---|---|---|---|---|---|---|
| MO | Moped | OR | Offroad Vehicle (ATV type) | AS | Group A School Bus | BN | Group B Tank | BB | Group B |
| PA | Pass Car & Sta Wgn | SM | Snowmobile | AT | Group A Double/Triple | BP | Group B Passenger | CX | Group C Tank & Hazardous |
| VA | Van & Motor Home | OO | Other | AX | Group A Tank & Hazardous | BS | Group B School Bus | | |
| PU | Pickup | AA | Group A | AY | Group A Tank & Double/Triple | BX | Group B Tank & Hazardous | | |
| | | AH | Group A Hazardous | AZ | Group A Hazardous Double/Triple | CH | Group C Hazardous | | |
| ST | Sm Tr (un 10,000) | AN | Group A Tank | AL | Grp A Hazard Tank Double/Triple | CP | Group C Passenger | | |

## SERVICE OF NOTICE OF SUSPENSION

I certify that I hand delivered a copy of the document containing the Notice of Suspension and Appeal Rights to the person named above.

Officer's Signature_____     Date (MM/DD/YY)_____

OFFICER'S INSTRUCTIONS
Give two white copies to person
Keep two pink copies

# REQUEST FOR HEARING

DI-93 (03/13)

# Request For Hearing:

I request a hearing before the Administrative Hearings Section to contest issues number(s)._____
*(Issues are listed on the Notice of Suspension.)*

**Affirmative Address Statement:**

☐ The address on my master driving record is correct. Send all correspondence to this address.

☐ The address on the reverse side is only a temporary address. Send all correspondence to this address. Please DO NOT CHANGE the address on my master driving record file.

If you need to inform the Department of State of a permanent address change you may change your address on-line, by mail or in person.

Online: A change of address may be submitted through ExpressSOS.com.

By Mail: The form to change your address can be obtained from the SOS website at Michigan.gov/sos.

In Person: If you are changing your address at a branch office, be sure to bring your driver's license or personal ID card.

Signature _____ Date_____

Driver's License Number _____ Telephone _____

**This request for hearing must be mailed within 14 days of the receipt of the Officer's Report Of Refusal to Submit to Chemical Test containing Notice of Suspension, or your operator's or chauffeur's license and vehicle group designation or operating privilege will be suspended. Send this form. Do not send a photocopy.**

Mail to:      MICHIGAN DEPARTMENT OF STATE
ADMINISTRATIVE HEARINGS SECTION
P O BOX 30196
LANSING MI 48909-7696

DI-93 (03/13) By the authority of P.A. 300 of 1949 as amended

| BTH TEST OPR NO | LEIN ENTRY | RECORD SEQUENCE NO |
|---|---|---|
| | | |

# OFFICER'S REPORT OF REFUSAL TO SUBMIT TO CHEMICAL TEST

| PERSON'S FULL NAME (AS APPEARS ON MICHIGAN DRIVER'S LICENSE) | BIRTH DATE (MM/DD/YY) | SEX | |
|---|---|---|---|
| | | MALE | FEMALE |

| ADDRESS (NUMBER & STREET) | MICHIGAN DRIVER'S LICENSE NUMBER | |
|---|---|---|

| CITY | STATE | ZIP | OTHER STATE DRIVER'S LICENSE NUMBER | STATE |
|---|---|---|---|---|

| HEIGHT | WEIGHT | EYE COLOR | HAIR COLOR | □ OPERATOR   □ CHAUFFEUR   □ MOPED |
|---|---|---|---|---|

| ARREST DATE (MM/DD/YY) | MILITARY TIME | REFUSAL DATE (MM/DD/YY) | MILITARY TIME |
|---|---|---|---|

| COUNTY (OF ARREST) | CITY OR TOWNSHIP (OF ARREST) | CO/CTY/TWP CODE |
|---|---|---|

| *VEHICLE TYPE | Was person involved in an accident? YES □ NO □ | INSTRUMENT # REFUSED | BAC #1 N/A | BAC #2 N/A | BAC #3 N/A | UCR CODE | COMPLAINT NUMBER |
|---|---|---|---|---|---|---|---|

| ARRESTING OFFICER'S NAME | BADGE NUMBER | ORI NUMBER |
|---|---|---|

| BREATH TEST OPERATOR'S NAME, only if not listed above and necessary for hearing | BADGE NUMBER | ORI NUMBER |
|---|---|---|

| OTHER OFFICER, if necessary for hearing | BADGE NUMBER | ORI NUMBER |
|---|---|---|

The above named person was arrested for a violation of section 625(1), (3), (4), (5), (6), (7), (8), 625a(5) or 625m of the Michigan Vehicle Code, as amended, or a local ordinance substantially corresponding to section 625(1), (3), (4), (5), (6), (7), (8), 625a(5) or 625m or for the offense of manslaughter, murder, reckless driving causing death, reckless driving causing serious impairment of a body function, moving violation causing death, or moving violation causing serious impairment of a body function resulting from the operation of a motor vehicle.

The officer had reasonable grounds to believe that the above named person violated section 625(1), (3), (4), (5), (6), (7), (8), 625a(5) or 625m of the Michigan Vehicle Code, as amended, or local ordinance substantially corresponding to section 625(1), (3), (4), (5), (6), (7), (8), 625a(5) or 625m or committed the offense of manslaughter, murder, reckless driving causing death, reckless driving causing serious impairment of a body function, moving violation causing death, or moving violation causing serious impairment of a body function resulting from the operation of a motor vehicle while impaired by or under the influence of alcoholic liquor, a controlled substance, other intoxicating substance, or a combination, or while having an unlawful bodily alcohol content, or if the person is less that 21 years of age while having any bodily alcohol content. [MCL 257.625c(1)(b)]

The above named person was requested to take a chemical test. The person was advised of the chemical test rights as required under section 625a and refused to take a chemical test.

| Michigan Driver's License confiscated? | Yes □ | No □ | Michigan Driver's License destroyed? | Yes □ | No □ | Under 21? | Yes □ | No □ | | | LICENSED OUT OF STATE |
|---|---|---|---|---|---|---|---|---|---|---|---|

| Driving status on date of arrest | VALID □ | EXPIRED □ | RESTRICTED □ | SUSPENDED □ | REVOKED □ | DENIED □ | UNLICENSED □ | UNKNOWN □ | LICENSED OUT OF STATE □ |
|---|---|---|---|---|---|---|---|---|---|

| CDL | License □ | Permit □ | A □ | B □ | C □ | H □ | N □ | X □ | P □ | T □ | CDL restrictions _____ | ENDORSEMENT | CY □ | F □ | R □ | Other _____ |
|---|---|---|---|---|---|---|---|---|---|---|---|---|---|---|---|---|

## MICHIGAN TEMPORARY DRIVING PERMIT

This temporary driving permit is valid only if you have a valid Michigan operator's or chauffeur's license. If your license has a CDL and/or endorsement or restrictions, this permit grants you the same CDL and/or endorsements or restrictions. You may not apply for a replacement photo license. This permit is valid until the criminal charges are dismissed or you are acquitted, or your license or permit is suspended, restricted, or revoked for a conviction. [MCL257.625g(3)]

## SERVICE OF NOTICE OF SUSPENSION

I certify that I hand delivered a copy of the document containing the Notice of Suspension and Appeal Rights to the person named above.

Officer's Signature_____   Date (MM/DD/YY)_____

## Notice to the officer:

Complete this form to record implied consent refusals, including most search warrants. (See DI-177)

Confiscate and destroy arrested person's Michigan driver's license or permit. Do Not confiscate the out of state licenses.

Input arrest data into LEIN Alcohol File (F Breath Screen)

**Note:** This LEIN data is a continuation of the written report prescribed and furnished by the Secretary of the Sate. The encoded information will print at the Secretary of State office and will include the following statement, "The officer had reasonable grounds to believe that the person had committed a crime described in section 625c(1), and that the person had refused to submit to the test upon the request of the peace officer and had been advised of the consequences of the refusal" as required by section 625d.

OFFICER'S INSTRUCTIONS
Give two white copies to person
Keep two pink copies

OFFICER'S COPY

# Notice of Suspension

You have allegedly refused to take a chemical test. Your Michigan operator's or chauffeur's license, vehicle group designation or operating privilege will be suspended and six points will be added to your driving record.

## Appeal Rights:

If you do not appeal within 14 days your operator's or chauffeur's license, vehicle group designation or operating privilege will be automatically suspended. If you wish to request a hearing you must do so within 14 days of the date of service of this Notice of Suspension.

## Hearing Issues:

MCL 257.625f limits the issues appealable at a hearing ONLY to the following:

1. Whether the peace officer had reasonable grounds to believe that you committed a crime described in MCL 257.625c(1).
2. Whether you were placed under arrest for a crime described in MCL 257.625c(1).
3. If you refused to submit to a chemical test upon the request of the officer, whether the refusal was reasonable.
4. Whether you were advised of your rights under MCL 257.625a.

To request a hearing, complete the attached Request for Hearing and mail to the Department of State within 14 days of the date of the service of this notice.

You are not required to have an attorney at this hearing, but an attorney may represent you if you wish.

# CHEMICAL TEST RIGHTS
*(As read by peace officer)*

I am requesting that you take a chemical test to check for alcohol and/or controlled substances or other intoxicating substance in your body. IF YOU WERE ASKED TO TAKE OR TOOK A PRELIMINARY BREATH TEST BEFORE YOUR ARREST, YOU MUST STILL TAKE THE TEST I AM OFFERING YOU.

If you refuse to take this chemical test, it will not be given without a court order, but I may seek to obtain such a court order. Your refusal to take this test shall result in the suspension of your operator's or chauffeur's license and vehicle group designation or operating privilege, and the addition of six points to your driving record.

After taking my chemical test, you have a right to demand that a person of your own choosing administer a breath, blood, or urine test. You will be given a reasonable opportunity for such a test. You are responsible for obtaining a chemical analysis of a test sample taken by a person of your own choosing.

The results of both chemical tests shall be admissible in a judicial proceeding, and will be considered with other admissible evidence in determining your innocence or guilt.

DI-93 (03/13) By the authority of P.A. 300 of 1949 as amended

| BTH TEST OPR NO | LEIN ENTRY | RECORD SEQUENCE NO |
|---|---|---|
| | | |

# OFFICER'S REPORT OF REFUSAL TO SUBMIT TO CHEMICAL TEST

| PERSON'S FULL NAME (AS APPEARS ON MICHIGAN DRIVER'S LICENSE) | BIRTH DATE (MM/DD/YY) | SEX |
|---|---|---|
| | | MALE       FEMALE |

| ADDRESS (NUMBER & STREET) | MICHIGAN DRIVER'S LICENSE NUMBER |
|---|---|

| CITY | STATE | ZIP | OTHER STATE DRIVER'S LICENSE NUMBER | STATE |
|---|---|---|---|---|

| HEIGHT | WEIGHT | EYE COLOR | HAIR COLOR | ☐ OPERATOR   ☐ CHAUFFEUR   ☐ MOPED |
|---|---|---|---|---|

| ARREST DATE (MM/DD/YY) | MILITARY TIME | REFUSAL DATE (MM/DD/YY) | MILITARY TIME |
|---|---|---|---|

| COUNTY (OF ARREST) | CITY OR TOWNSHIP (OF ARREST) | CO/CTY/TWP CODE |
|---|---|---|

| *VEHICLE TYPE | Was person involved in an accident? YES   NO | INSTRUMENT # REFUSED | BAC #1 N/A | BAC #2 N/A | BAC #3 N/A | UCR CODE | COMPLAINT NUMBER |
|---|---|---|---|---|---|---|---|

| ARRESTING OFFICER'S NAME | BADGE NUMBER | ORI NUMBER |
|---|---|---|

| BREATH TEST OPERATOR'S NAME, only if not listed above and necessary for hearing | BADGE NUMBER | ORI NUMBER |
|---|---|---|

| OTHER OFFICER, if necessary for hearing | BADGE NUMBER | ORI NUMBER |
|---|---|---|

The above named person was arrested for a violation of section 625(1), (3), (4), (5), (6), (7), (8), 625a(5) or 625m of the Michigan Vehicle Code, as amended, or a local ordinance substantially corresponding to section 625(1), (3), (4), (5), (6), (7), (8), 625a(5) or 625m or for the offense of manslaughter, murder, reckless driving causing death, reckless driving causing serious impairment of a body function, moving violation causing death, or moving violation causing serious impairment of a body function resulting from the operation of a motor vehicle.

The officer had reasonable grounds to believe that the above named person violated section 625(1), (3), (4), (5), (6), (7), (8), 625a(5) or 625m of the Michigan Vehicle Code, as amended, or local ordinance substantially corresponding to section 625(1), (3), (4), (5), (6), (7), (8), 625a(5) or 625m or committed the offense of manslaughter, murder, reckless driving causing death, reckless driving causing serious impairment of a body function, moving violation causing death, or moving violation causing serious impairment of a body function resulting from the operation of a motor vehicle while impaired by or under the influence of alcoholic liquor, a controlled substance, other intoxicating substance, or a combination, or while having an unlawful bodily alcohol content, or if the person is less that 21 years of age while having any bodily alcohol content. [MCL 257.625c(1)(b)]

The above named person was requested to take a chemical test. The person was advised of the chemical test rights as required under section 625a and refused to take a chemical test.

| Michigan Driver's License confiscated? | Yes ☐ | No ☐ | Michigan Driver's License destroyed? | Yes ☐ | No ☐ | Under 21? | Yes ☐ | No ☐ | LICENSED OUT OF STATE |
|---|---|---|---|---|---|---|---|---|---|

Driving status on date of arrest

| VALID ☐ | EXPIRED ☐ | RESTRICTED ☐ | SUSPENDED ☐ | REVOKED ☐ | DENIED ☐ | UNLICENSED ☐ | UNKNOWN ☐ | STATE ☐ |
|---|---|---|---|---|---|---|---|---|

CDL

| License ☐ | Permit ☐ | A ☐ | B ☐ | C ☐ | H ☐ | N ☐ | X ☐ | P ☐ | T ☐ | CDL restrictions _____ | ENDORSEMENT | CY ☐ | F ☐ | R ☐ | Other _____ |
|---|---|---|---|---|---|---|---|---|---|---|---|---|---|---|---|

## MICHIGAN TEMPORARY DRIVING PERMIT

This temporary driving permit is valid only if you have a valid Michigan operator's or chauffeur's license. If your license has a CDL and/or endorsement or restrictions, this permit grants you the same CDL and/or endorsements or restrictions. You may not apply for a replacement photo license. This permit is valid until the criminal charges are dismissed or you are acquitted, or your license or permit is suspended, restricted, or revoked for a conviction. [MCL257.625g(3)]

## SERVICE OF NOTICE OF SUSPENSION

I certify that I hand delivered a copy of the document containing the Notice of Suspension and Appeal Rights to the person named above.

Officer's Signature_____     Date (MM/DD/YY)_____

OFFICER'S INSTRUCTIONS
   Give two white copies to person
   Keep two pink copies

# Read the complete page to the arrested person.

I am a peace officer. You are under arrest for the offense of: *(Read only the charge that applies)*

- Operating a vehicle while intoxicated due to the consumption of alcoholic liquor, a controlled substance, other intoxicating substance or a combination.

- Operating a vehicle while visibly impaired due to the consumption of alcoholic liquor, a controlled substance, other intoxicating substance or a combination.

- Operating with any presence of schedule 1 drugs or cocaine.

- Causing the death of another while operating a vehicle while intoxicated, or while visibly impaired by alcoholic liquor, a controlled substance, other intoxicating substance or a combination, or with an unlawful bodily alcohol content.

- Causing serious injury to another while operating a vehicle intoxicated, or while visibly impaired by alcoholic liquor, a controlled substance, other intoxicating substance or a combination, or with an unlawful bodily alcohol content.

- Operating a commercial motor vehicle with bodily alcohol content of 0.04 grams or more but less than 0.08 grams per 100 milliliters of blood, per 210 liter of breath, or per 67 milliliters of urine.

- Operating a vehicle while less than 21 years of age and having any bodily alcohol content.

- Murder resulting from the operation of a motor vehicle.

- Manslaughter resulting from the operation of a motor vehicle.

- Reckless driving causing death.

- Reckless driving causing serious impairment of a body function.

- Moving violation causing death.

- Moving violation causing serious impairment of a body function.

- Refusing a Preliminary Breath Test if arrested while operating a commercial motor vehicle.

- Endangerment (Operating while intoxicated or while visibly impaired with person under age of 16.)

## CHEMICAL TEST RIGHTS

I am requesting that you take a chemical test to check for alcohol and/or controlled substances or other intoxicating substance in your body. IF YOU WERE ASKED TO TAKE OR TOOK A PRELIMINARY BREATH TEST BEFORE YOUR ARREST, YOU MUST STILL TAKE THE TEST I AM OFFERING YOU.

If you refuse to take this chemical test, it will not be given without a court order, but I may seek to obtain such a court order. Your refusal to take this test shall result in the suspension of your operator's or chauffeur's license and vehicle group designation or operating privilege, and the addition of six points to your driving record.

After taking my chemical test, you have a right to demand that a person of your own choosing administer a breath, blood, or urine test. You will be given a reasonable opportunity for such a test. You are responsible for obtaining a chemical analysis of a test sample taken by a person of your own choosing.

The results of both chemical tests shall be admissible in a judicial proceeding, and will be considered with other admissible evidence in determining your innocence or guilt.

Will you take a: (Select the appropriate test from the following list)

| Breath Test? | or | *Blood Test? | or | Urine Test? |
|---|---|---|---|---|

*MCL 257.625c(2) provides that a person afflicted with hemophilia, diabetes, or a condition requiring the use of an anticoagulant shall not be considered to have given consent to the withdrawal of blood.

DI-93 (03/13) By the authority of P.A. 300 of 1949 as amended

| BTH TEST OPR NO | LEIN ENTRY | RECORD SEQUENCE NO |
|---|---|---|
| | | |

# OFFICER'S REPORT OF REFUSAL TO SUBMIT TO CHEMICAL TEST

| PERSON'S FULL NAME (AS APPEARS ON MICHIGAN DRIVER'S LICENSE) | BIRTH DATE (MM/DD/YY) | SEX | |
|---|---|---|---|
| | | MALE | FEMALE |

| ADDRESS (NUMBER & STREET) | MICHIGAN DRIVER'S LICENSE NUMBER | |
|---|---|---|

| CITY | STATE | ZIP | OTHER STATE DRIVER'S LICENSE NUMBER | STATE |
|---|---|---|---|---|

| HEIGHT | WEIGHT | EYE COLOR | HAIR COLOR | ☐ OPERATOR  ☐ CHAUFFEUR  ☐ MOPED |
|---|---|---|---|---|

| ARREST DATE (MM/DD/YY) | MILITARY TIME | REFUSAL DATE (MM/DD/YY) | MILITARY TIME |
|---|---|---|---|

| COUNTY (OF ARREST) | CITY OR TOWNSHIP (OF ARREST) | CO/CTY/TWP CODE |
|---|---|---|

| *VEHICLE TYPE | Was person involved in an accident? YES NO | INSTRUMENT # REFUSED | BAC #1 N/A | BAC #2 N/A | BAC #3 N/A | UCR CODE | COMPLAINT NUMBER |
|---|---|---|---|---|---|---|---|

| ARRESTING OFFICER'S NAME | BADGE NUMBER | ORI NUMBER |
|---|---|---|

| BREATH TEST OPERATOR'S NAME, only if not listed above and necessary for hearing | BADGE NUMBER | ORI NUMBER |
|---|---|---|

| OTHER OFFICER, if necessary for hearing | BADGE NUMBER | ORI NUMBER |
|---|---|---|

The above named person was arrested for a violation of section 625(1), (3), (4), (5), (6), (7), (8), 625a(5) or 625m of the Michigan Vehicle Code, as amended, or a local ordinance substantially corresponding to section 625(1), (3), (4), (5), (6), (7), (8), 625a(5) or 625m or for the offense of manslaughter, murder, reckless driving causing death, reckless driving causing serious impairment of a body function, moving violation causing death, or moving violation causing serious impairment of a body function resulting from the operation of a motor vehicle.

The officer had reasonable grounds to believe that the above named person violated section 625(1), (3), (4), (5), (6), (7), (8), 625a(5) or 625m of the Michigan Vehicle Code, as amended, or local ordinance substantially corresponding to section 625(1), (3), (4), (5), (6), (7), (8), 625a(5) or 625m or committed the offense of manslaughter, murder, reckless driving causing death, reckless driving causing serious impairment of a body function, moving violation causing death, or moving violation causing serious impairment of a body function resulting from the operation of a motor vehicle while impaired by or under the influence of alcoholic liquor, a controlled substance, other intoxicating substance, or a combination, or while having an unlawful bodily alcohol content, or if the person is less that 21 years of age while having any bodily alcohol content. [MCL 257.625c(1)(b)]

The above named person was requested to take a chemical test. The person was advised of the chemical test rights as required under section 625a and refused to take a chemical test.

| Michigan Driver's License confiscated? | Yes ☐ | No ☐ | Michigan Driver's License destroyed? | Yes ☐ | No ☐ | Under 21? | Yes ☐ | No ☐ | | | LICENSED OUT OF STATE |
|---|---|---|---|---|---|---|---|---|---|---|---|

| Driving status on date of arrest | VALID ☐ | EXPIRED ☐ | RESTRICTED ☐ | SUSPENDED ☐ | REVOKED ☐ | DENIED ☐ | UNLICENSED ☐ | UNKNOWN ☐ | STATE ☐ |
|---|---|---|---|---|---|---|---|---|---|

| CDL | License ☐ | Permit ☐ | A ☐ | B ☐ | C ☐ | H ☐ | N ☐ | X ☐ | P ☐ | T ☐ | CDL restrictions _____ | ENDORSEMENT | CY ☐ | F ☐ | R ☐ | Other _____ |
|---|---|---|---|---|---|---|---|---|---|---|---|---|---|---|---|---|

## MICHIGAN TEMPORARY DRIVING PERMIT

This temporary driving permit is valid only if you have a valid Michigan operator's or chauffeur's license. If your license has a CDL and/or endorsement or restrictions, this permit grants you the same CDL and/or endorsements or restrictions. You may not apply for a replacement photo license. This permit is valid until the criminal charges are dismissed or you are acquitted, or your license or permit is suspended, restricted, or revoked for a conviction. [MCL257.625g(3)]

## SERVICE OF NOTICE OF SUSPENSION

I certify that I hand delivered a copy of the document containing the Notice of Suspension and Appeal Rights to the person named above.

Officer's Signature_____     Date (MM/DD/YY)_____

OFFICER'S INSTRUCTIONS
    Give two white copies to person
    Keep two pink copies

# MICHIGAN TEMPORARY DRIVING PERMIT
### This permit is only valid if you have a valid Michigan driver's license.
### This permit is not valid if you are unlicensed or your license is expired, suspended, revoked or denied.

## Carry this permit when driving.

DRIVER'S COPY

# Read the complete page to the arrested person.

I am a peace officer. You are under arrest for the offense of: *(Read only the charge that applies)*

- Operating a vehicle while intoxicated due to the consumption of alcoholic liquor, a controlled substance, other intoxicating substance or a combination.

- Operating a vehicle while visibly impaired due to the consumption of alcoholic liquor, a controlled substance, other intoxicating substance or a combination.

- Operating with any presence of schedule 1 drugs or cocaine.

- Causing the death of another while operating a vehicle while intoxicated, or while visibly impaired by alcoholic liquor, a controlled substance, other intoxicating substance or a combination, or with an unlawful bodily alcohol content.

- Causing serious injury to another while operating a vehicle intoxicated, or while visibly impaired by alcoholic liquor, a controlled substance, other intoxicating substance or a combination, or with an unlawful bodily alcohol content.

- Operating a commercial motor vehicle with bodily alcohol content of 0.04 grams or more but less than 0.08 grams per 100 milliliters of blood, per 210 liter of breath, or per 67 milliliters of urine.

- Operating a vehicle while less than 21 years of age and having any bodily alcohol content.

- Murder resulting from the operation of a motor vehicle.

- Manslaughter resulting from the operation of a motor vehicle.

- Reckless driving causing death.

- Reckless driving causing serious impairment of a body function.

- Moving violation causing death.

- Moving violation causing serious impairment of a body function.

- Refusing a Preliminary Breath Test if arrested while operating a commercial motor vehicle.

- Endangerment (Operating while intoxicated or while visibly impaired with person under age of 16.)

## CHEMICAL TEST RIGHTS

I am requesting that you take a chemical test to check for alcohol and/or controlled substances or other intoxicating substance in your body. IF YOU WERE ASKED TO TAKE OR TOOK A PRELIMINARY BREATH TEST BEFORE YOUR ARREST, YOU MUST STILL TAKE THE TEST I AM OFFERING YOU.

If you refuse to take this chemical test, it will not be given without a court order, but I may seek to obtain such a court order. Your refusal to take this test shall result in the suspension of your operator's or chauffeur's license and vehicle group designation or operating privilege, and the addition of six points to your driving record.

After taking my chemical test, you have a right to demand that a person of your own choosing administer a breath, blood, or urine test. You will be given a reasonable opportunity for such a test. You are responsible for obtaining a chemical analysis of a test sample taken by a person of your own choosing.

The results of both chemical tests shall be admissible in a judicial proceeding, and will be considered with other admissible evidence in determining your innocence or guilt.

Will you take a: (Select the appropriate test from the following list)

Breath Test?　　　　　　or　　　　　　*Blood Test?　　　　　　or　　　　　　Urine Test?

*MCL 257.625c(2) provides that a person afflicted with hemophilia, diabetes, or a condition requiring the use of an anticoagulant shall not be considered to have given consent to the withdrawal of blood.

DI-177 (03/13) By the Authority of P.A. 300 of 1949 as amended

# BREATH, BLOOD, URINE TEST REPORT
## LEIN INPUT PROMPT

| BTH TEST OPR NO | LEIN ENTRY | RECORD SEQUENCE NO |
|---|---|---|
| | | |

| PERSON'S FULL NAME (As Appears On Michigan Driver's License) | BIRTH DATE (MMDDYY) | SEX ☐ MALE ☐ FEMALE |
|---|---|---|

| ADDRESS (Number & Street) | MICHIGAN DRIVER'S LICENSE NUMBER |
|---|---|

| CITY | STATE | ZIP | OTHER STATE DRIVER'S LICENSE NUMBER | STATE |
|---|---|---|---|---|

| HEIGHT | WEIGHT | EYE COLOR | HAIR COLOR | ☐ OPERATOR ☐ CHAUFFEUR ☐ MOPED |
|---|---|---|---|---|

| ARREST DATE (MMDDYY) | MILITARY TIME | INCIDENT DATE (MMDDYY) | MILITARY TIME |
|---|---|---|---|

| COUNTY (Of Arrest) | CITY OR TOWNSHIP (Of Arrest) | CO/CTY/TWP CODE | **MICHIGAN** |
|---|---|---|---|

| *VEHICLE TYPE | Was Person Involved In An Accident? ☐ YES ☐ NO | INSTRUMENT NUMBER | BAC #1 | BAC #2 | BAC #3 | UCR CODE | COMPLAINT NUMBER |
|---|---|---|---|---|---|---|---|

| ARRESTING OFFICER'S NAME | BADGE NUMBER | ORI NUMBER |
|---|---|---|

| BREATH TEST OPERATOR'S NAME (Only If Not Listed Above And Necessary For Hearing) | BADGE NUMBER | ORI NUMBER |
|---|---|---|

You have been arrested for a crime described in section 625c of the Michigan Vehicle Code and submitted to a chemical test which revealed an unlawful bodily alcohol content or have a blood or urine test pending.

This temporary driving permit is valid only if you have a valid Michigan driver's license. If your license was restricted, this permit grants the same restrictions. This permit grants you the same CDL and/or endorsements that are on your Michigan license. You may not apply for a replacement photo license.

This permit is to be used until the criminal charges against you are dismissed or until you are acquitted, or your license or permit is suspended, restricted, or revoked for a conviction. [MCL 257.625g(3)]

| | YES | NO | | YES | NO | | | YES | NO | | |
|---|---|---|---|---|---|---|---|---|---|---|---|
| Michigan driver's license confiscated? | ☐ | ☐ | Michigan driver's license destroyed? | ☐ | ☐ | Under 21? | | ☐ | ☐ | | LICENSED OUT OF STATE |

| | VALID | EXPIRED | RESTRICTED | SUSPENDED | REVOKED | DENIED | UNLICENSED | UNKNOWN | |
|---|---|---|---|---|---|---|---|---|---|
| Driving status on date of arrest | ☐ | ☐ | ☐ | ☐ | ☐ | ☐ | ☐ | ☐ | ☐ |

| | License | Permit | A | B | C | H | N | X | P | T | CDL restrictions | | CY | F | R | Other |
|---|---|---|---|---|---|---|---|---|---|---|---|---|---|---|---|---|
| CDL | ☐ | ☐ | ☐ | ☐ | ☐ | ☐ | ☐ | ☐ | ☐ | ☐ | _____ | ENDORSEMENT | ☐ | ☐ | ☐ | _____ |

Officer's Signature _____ Date (MMDDYY) _____

| *VEHICLE TYPES | | | |
|---|---|---|---|
| CY  Cycle | OR  Offroad Vehicle (ATV type) | AT  Group A Double/Triple | BP  Group B Passenger |
| MO  Moped | SM  Snowmobile | AX  Group A Tank & Hazardous | BS  Group B School Bus |
| PA  Pass Car & Sta Wgn | OO  Other | AY  Group A Tank & Double/Triple | BX  Group B Tank & Hazardous |
| VA  Van & Motor Home | AA  Group A | AZ  Group A Hazardous Double/Triple | CH  Group C Hazardous |
| PU  Pickup | AH  Group A Hazardous | AL  Group A Hazard Tank Double/Triple | CP  Group C Passenger |
| ST  Sm Tr (un 10,000#) | AN  Group A Tank | BB  Group B | CS  Group C School Bus |
| MD  Med Tr w/wo Tri ovr 10,000# (non DCDL) | AP  Group A Passenger | BH  Group B Hazardous | CX  Group C Tank & Hazardous |
| | AS  Group A School Bus | BN  Group B Tank | |

Notice to officer: Complete this form when any alcohol test is given.

Confiscate and destroy the arrested person's Michigan driver's license or permit, issue the third copy of this form, and destroy the second copy **if a breath test revealed a bodily alcohol content of:**

  0.08 grams or more per 210 liters of breath while operating a motor vehicle, **or**
  0.04 grams or more per 210 liters of breath while operating a commercial motor vehicle, **or**
  0.02 grams or more per 210 liters of breath while operating a vehicle and less than 21 years of age.

When a voluntary blood or urine test is pending, or in special cases involving an unconscious person where a search warrant has been issued, attach the Michigan driver's license or permit to the second copy of this form and issue the third copy to the arrested person.

If a chemical test is refused, use the Officer's Report of Refusal to Submit to Chemical Test form (DI-93).

For all of the above, input arrest data into the LEIN F Breath Screen, even if the driver is licensed out of state. (Do not confiscate the out of state license.)

Officer's Copy

| BTH TEST OPR NO | LEIN ENTRY | RECORD SEQUENCE NO |
|---|---|---|

# BREATH, BLOOD, URINE TEST REPORT
## NOTICE OF BLOOD OR URINE TEST RESULT

| PERSON'S FULL NAME (As Appears On Michigan Driver's License) | BIRTH DATE (MMDDYY) | SEX ☐ MALE ☐ FEMALE |
|---|---|---|

| ADDRESS (Number & Street) | MICHIGAN DRIVER'S LICENSE NUMBER |
|---|---|

| CITY | STATE | ZIP | OTHER STATE DRIVER'S LICENSE NUMBER | STATE |
|---|---|---|---|---|

| HEIGHT | WEIGHT | EYE COLOR | HAIR COLOR | ☐ OPERATOR ☐ CHAUFFEUR ☐ MOPED |
|---|---|---|---|---|

| ARREST DATE (MMDDYY) | MILITARY TIME | INCIDENT DATE (MMDDYY) | MILITARY TIME |
|---|---|---|---|

| COUNTY (Of Arrest) | CITY OR TOWNSHIP (Of Arrest) | CO/CTY/TWP CODE | MICHIGAN |
|---|---|---|---|

| *VEHICLE TYPE | Was Person Involved In An Accident? ☐ YES ☐ NO | INSTRUMENT NUMBER | BAC #1 | BAC #2 | BAC #3 | UCR CODE | COMPLAINT NUMBER |
|---|---|---|---|---|---|---|---|

| ARRESTING OFFICER'S NAME | BADGE NUMBER | ORI NUMBER |
|---|---|---|

| BREATH TEST OPERATOR'S NAME (Only If Not Listed Above And Necessary For Hearing) | BADGE NUMBER | ORI NUMBER |
|---|---|---|

You have been arrested for a crime described in section 625c of the Michigan Vehicle Code and submitted to a chemical test which revealed an unlawful bodily alcohol content or have a blood or urine test pending.

This temporary driving permit is valid only if you have a valid Michigan driver's license. If your license was restricted, this permit grants the same restrictions. This permit grants you the same CDL and/or endorsements that are on your Michigan license. You may not apply for a replacement photo license.

This permit is to be used until the criminal charges against you are dismissed or until you are acquitted, or your license or permit is suspended, restricted, or revoked for a conviction. [MCL 257.625g(3)]

Michigan driver's license confiscated?   YES ☐   NO ☐       Michigan driver's license destroyed?   YES ☐   NO ☐       Under 21?   YES ☐   NO ☐       LICENSED OUT OF STATE ☐

| Driving status on date of arrest | VALID ☐ | EXPIRED ☐ | RESTRICTED ☐ | SUSPENDED ☐ | REVOKED ☐ | DENIED ☐ | UNLICENSED ☐ | UNKNOWN ☐ | LICENSED OUT OF STATE ☐ |
|---|---|---|---|---|---|---|---|---|---|

| CDL | License ☐ | Permit ☐ | A ☐ | B ☐ | C ☐ | H ☐ | N ☐ | X ☐ | P ☐ | T ☐ | CDL restrictions _____ | ENDORSEMENT | CY ☐ | F ☐ | R ☐ | Other _____ |
|---|---|---|---|---|---|---|---|---|---|---|---|---|---|---|---|---|

Officer's Signature _____   Date (MMDDYY) _____

You were arrested for drunk driving and submitted to a blood or urine test to determine your bodily alcohol content. The blood or urine sample was submitted to a testing laboratory. The results were received and show a bodily alcohol content of _____.

☐ Your bodily alcohol content was unlawful. The Temporary Driving Permit that was issued will be valid until the criminal charges against you are dismissed or you are acquitted, or your license or permit is suspended, restricted, or revoked for a conviction. [MCL 257.625g(3)]

☐ Your bodily alcohol content does not require confiscation of your driver's license. Your license is being returned to you. Please see attached. This does not affect the criminal charges pending against you.

# Notice to officer:

## Use this form when a blood or urine test is given.

## Attach driver's license or permit to this form until test results are received.

## When results are received, complete the "Results Section" of this form and input results into LEIN Alcohol File (F Breath Screen).

If the bodily alcohol content is unlawful, destroy the driver's license or permit and send this form to the driver. If the bodily alcohol content does not require driver's license confiscation, return the driver's license or permit with this form.

## After this form is completed, mail it to the arrested person.

Note: This copy can be discarded if a breath test was given.

DI-177 (03/13) By the Authority of P.A. 300 of 1949 as amended

# BREATH, BLOOD, URINE TEST REPORT
## MICHIGAN TEMPORARY DRIVING PERMIT

| BTH TEST OPR NO | LEIN ENTRY | RECORD SEQUENCE NO |
|---|---|---|
| | | |

| PERSON'S FULL NAME (As Appears On Michigan Driver's License) | BIRTH DATE (MMDDYY) | SEX ☐ MALE ☐ FEMALE |
|---|---|---|

| ADDRESS (Number & Street) | MICHIGAN DRIVER'S LICENSE NUMBER |
|---|---|

| CITY | STATE | ZIP | OTHER STATE DRIVER'S LICENSE NUMBER | STATE |
|---|---|---|---|---|

| HEIGHT | WEIGHT | EYE COLOR | HAIR COLOR | ☐ OPERATOR  ☐ CHAUFFEUR  ☐ MOPED |
|---|---|---|---|---|

| ARREST DATE (MMDDYY) | MILITARY TIME | INCIDENT DATE (MMDDYY) | MILITARY TIME |
|---|---|---|---|

| COUNTY (Of Arrest) | CITY OR TOWNSHIP (Of Arrest) | CO/CTY/TWP CODE | MICHIGAN |
|---|---|---|---|

| *VEHICLE TYPE | Was Person Involved In An Accident? ☐ YES ☐ NO | INSTRUMENT NUMBER | BAC #1 | BAC #2 | BAC #3 | UCR CODE | COMPLAINT NUMBER |
|---|---|---|---|---|---|---|---|

| ARRESTING OFFICER'S NAME | BADGE NUMBER | ORI NUMBER |
|---|---|---|

| BREATH TEST OPERATOR'S NAME (Only If Not Listed Above And Necessary For Hearing) | BADGE NUMBER | ORI NUMBER |
|---|---|---|

You have been arrested for a crime described in section 625c of the Michigan Vehicle Code and submitted to a chemical test which revealed an unlawful bodily alcohol content or have a blood or urine test pending.

This temporary driving permit is valid only if you have a valid Michigan driver's license. If your license was restricted, this permit grants the same restrictions. This permit grants you the same CDL and/or endorsements that are on your Michigan license. You may not apply for a replacement photo license.

This permit is to be used until the criminal charges against you are dismissed or until you are acquitted, or your license or permit is suspended, restricted, or revoked for a conviction. [MCL 257.625g(3)]

| | YES | NO | | YES | NO | | YES | NO | |
|---|---|---|---|---|---|---|---|---|---|
| Michigan driver's license confiscated? | ☐ | ☐ | Michigan driver's license destroyed? | ☐ | ☐ | Under 21? | ☐ | ☐ | LICENSED OUT OF STATE |

| | VALID | EXPIRED | RESTRICTED | SUSPENDED | REVOKED | DENIED | UNLICENSED | UNKNOWN | STATE |
|---|---|---|---|---|---|---|---|---|---|
| Driving status on date of arrest | ☐ | ☐ | ☐ | ☐ | ☐ | ☐ | ☐ | ☐ | ☐ |

| | License | Permit | A | B | C | H | N | X | P | T | CDL restrictions | | CY | F | R | Other |
|---|---|---|---|---|---|---|---|---|---|---|---|---|---|---|---|---|
| CDL | ☐ | ☐ | ☐ | ☐ | ☐ | ☐ | ☐ | ☐ | ☐ | ☐ | _____ | ENDORSEMENT | ☐ | ☐ | ☐ | _____ |

Officer's Signature _____ Date (MMDDYY) _____

Note to officer:

Use this form only when a test of a Michigan licensed driver reveals an unlawful bodily alcohol content or when a blood or urine test is pending.

# MICHIGAN TEMPORARY DRIVING PERMIT

This permit is only valid if you have a valid Michigan driver's license.
This permit is not valid if you are unlicensed or your license is expired,
suspended, revoked or denied.

## Carry this permit when driving.

# Read the complete page to the arrested person.

I am a peace officer. You are under arrest for the offense of: *(Read only the charge that applies)*

- Operating a vehicle while intoxicated due to the consumption of alcoholic liquor, a controlled substance, other intoxicating substance or a combination.
- Operating a vehicle while visibly impaired due to the consumption of alcoholic liquor, a controlled substance, other intoxicating substance or a combination.
- Operating with any presence of schedule 1 drugs or cocaine.
- Causing the death of another while operating a vehicle while intoxicated, or while visibly impaired by alcoholic liquor, a controlled substance, other intoxicating substance or a combination, or with an unlawful bodily alcohol content.
- Causing serious injury to another while operating a vehicle while intoxicated, or while visibly impaired by alcoholic liquor, a controlled substance, other intoxicating substance or a combination, or with an unlawful bodily alcohol content.
- Operating a commercial motor vehicle with a bodily alcohol content of 0.04 grams or more but less than 0.08 grams per 100 milliliters of blood, per 210 liters of breath, or per 67 milliliters of urine.
- Operating a vehicle while less than 21 years of age and having any bodily alcohol content.
- Murder resulting from the operation of a motor vehicle.
- Manslaughter resulting from the operation of a motor vehicle.
- Reckless driving causing death.
- Reckless driving causing serious impairment of a body function.
- Moving violation causing death.
- Moving violation causing serious impairment of a body function.
- Refusing a Preliminary Breath Test if arrested while operating a commercial motor vehicle.
- Endangerment (Operating while intoxicated or while visibly impaired with person under age of 16.)

## CHEMICAL TEST RIGHTS

I am requesting that you take a chemical test to check for alcohol and/or controlled substances in your body. IF YOU WERE ASKED TO TAKE OR TOOK A PRELIMINARY BREATH TEST BEFORE YOUR ARREST, YOU MUST STILL TAKE THE TEST I AM OFFERING YOU.

If you refuse to take this chemical test, it will not be given without a court order, but I may seek to obtain such a court order. Your refusal to take this test shall result in the suspension of your operator's or chauffeur's license and vehicle group designation or operating privilege, and the addition of six points to your driving record.

After taking my chemical test, you have a right to demand that a person of your own choosing administer a breath, blood, or urine test. You will be given a reasonable opportunity for such a test. You are responsible for obtaining a chemical analysis of a test sample taken by a person of your own choosing.

The results of both chemical tests shall be admissible in a judicial proceeding, and will be considered with other admissible evidence in determining your innocence or guilt.

Will you take a: (Select the appropriate test from the following list)

| Breath Test? | or | *Blood Test? | or | Urine Test? |

*MCL 257.625c(2) provides that a person afflicted with hemophilia, diabetes, or a condition requiring the use of an anticoagulant shall not be considered to have given consent to the withdrawal of blood.

## Notice
Destroy all DI-93 and DI-177 forms with revision date before 3/13

## Attention
The enclosed DI-93, Officer's Report of Refusal to Submit to a Chemical Test and/or DI-177 Breath, Blood, Urine Test report forms are to replace the forms currently on hand. Please destroy all forms dated before 3/13. Only the forms dated 3/13 should be used.

New legislation amends the Michigan Vehicle Code to include operating a vehicle while under the influence (OUI) of any intoxicating substance in the definition of "operating while intoxicated" in the drunk/drugged driving statues, effective March 31, 2013.

If you need additional forms, send a written request to Michigan Department of State, Inventory Unit, Richard H. Austin Building, 430 West Allegan Street, Lansing, MI 48918 or Fax (517) 373-1475. You may contact Inventory at (517) 373-2579 if you have questions regarding your order.

## Notice
Destroy all DI-93 and DI-177 forms with revision date before 3/13

## Attention
The enclosed DI-93, Officer's Report of Refusal to Submit to a Chemical Test and/or DI-177 Breath, Blood, Urine Test report forms are to replace the forms currently on hand. Please destroy all forms dated before 3/13. Only the forms dated 3/13 should be used.

New legislation amends the Michigan Vehicle Code to include operating a vehicle while under the influence (OUI) of any intoxicating substance in the definition of "operating while intoxicated" in the drunk/drugged driving statues, effective March 31, 2013.

If you need additional forms, send a written request to Michigan Department of State, Inventory Unit, Richard H. Austin Building, 430 West Allegan Street, Lansing, MI 48918 or Fax (517) 373-1475. You may contact Inventory at (517) 373-2579 if you have questions regarding your order.

## Instructions for Preparing Affidavit and Search Warrant

This packet consists of seven parts. TYPE OR PRESS HARD.

*Alternate procedures may be required for these items when using electromagnetic means for issuing warrants.

1.     In paragraph one FULLY describe the person, place, or thing to be searched and give its EXACT location.

2.     In paragraph two FULLY describe the property/person that is to be searched for and seized.

3.     In paragraph three set forth the facts and observations that establish probable cause. If additional pages are necessary, continue on form MC 231a.

4.     *Present to prosecuting official for review if required locally.

5.     *Present the original of the affidavit and search warrant to the judge/magistrate for review.

6.     *Swear to the contents of the affidavit and sign it before the judge/magistrate.

7.     Have the judge/magistrate sign both the original of the affidavit and the search warrant.

8.     Print names of judge/magistrate and affiant on all copies of the affidavit and/or search warrant where the signatures have not been reproduced by the carbons.

9.     Separate packet, retaining carbons to make duplicate tabulations later.

10.    *Leave original affidavit and last copy of warrant with the issuing judge/magistrate.

11.    *Execute search warrant at location given.

12.    Complete the tabulation (list) of property taken in the presence of the person(s) from whom it is seized, if present, or any other person (including another officer).

13.    Have person before whom the tabulation is completed sign the tabulation as witness.

14.    *Leave a copy of the search warrant and completed tabulation with the person(s) from whom the property was taken, if present, or at the premises.

15.    *Return the original search warrant and complete tabulation to the issuing court indicating the date returned and name of the person(s) served.

## AFFIDAVIT FOR SEARCH WARRANT

*Please type or press hard.*          *See the other side for instructions.*          Police Agency
Report Number: _____

_____ , affiant(s), state that:

1. The person, place, or thing to be searched is described as and is located at:

2. The PROPERTY/PERSON to be searched for and seized, if found, is specifically described as:

3. The FACTS establishing probable cause or the grounds for search are:

This affidavit consists of _____ pages.

_____
Affiant

| | |
|---|---|
| Review on _____<br>　　　　　　Date<br>by _____<br>　Prosecuting official | Subscribed and sworn to before me _____<br>　　　　　　　　　　　　　　　　　Date<br>_____ Court<br>_____<br>Judge/Magistrate　　　　　　　　Bar no. |

**MC 231** (3/10) **AFFIDAVIT FOR SEARCH WARRANT**

Original warrant - Return to issuing court
1st copy - Prosecutor
2nd copy - Serve
3rd copy - Issuing judge

# SEARCH WARRANT

**TO THE SHERIFF OR ANY PEACE OFFICER:**

Police Agency
Report Number: _____

_____ , has sworn to the affidavit regarding the following:

1. The person, place, or thing to be searched is described as and is located at:

2. The PROPERTY/PERSON to be searched for and seized, if found, is specifically described as:

**IN THE NAME OF THE PEOPLE OF THE STATE OF MICHIGAN:** I have found that probable cause exists and you are commanded to make the search and seize the described property/person. Leave a copy of this warrant and a tabulation (a written inventory) of all property taken with the person from whom the property was taken or at the premises. You are further commanded to promptly return this warrant and tabulation to the court.

Issued: _____          _____
          Date                                                                                      Judge/Magistrate                                                                Bar no.

## RETURN AND TABULATION

Search was made_____ and the following property/person was seized:
                     Date

☐ Continued on other side.

_____
Officer

Copy of warrant and tabulation served on: _____
                                  Name

Tabulation filed: _____
              Date

**MC 231** (3/10) **AFFIDAVIT AND SEARCH WARRANT**

Original - Court
1st copy - Law enforcement agency (file) (green)
2nd copy - Respondent (blue)

3rd copy - Petitioner (pink)
4th copy - Return (yellow)
5th copy - Return (goldenrod)

| STATE OF MICHIGAN JUDICIAL CIRCUIT COUNTY | (A) | PERSONAL PROTECTION ORDER ☐ EX PARTE (DOMESTIC RELATIONSHIP) | (B) | CASE NO. |
|---|---|---|---|---|

Court address

Court telephone no.

ORI
MI-

(C) Petitioner's name

Address and telephone no. where court can reach petitioner

v

Respondent's name, address, telephone no., and DLN

(D)

| Height | Weight | Race * | Sex * | Date of birth or age* | Hair color | Eye color | Other identifying information |
|---|---|---|---|---|---|---|---|

*These items **must** be filled in for the police/sheriff to enter on LEIN; the other items are not required but are helpful.     **Needed for NCIC entry.

Date: _____ Judge: _____   ☐ no hearing.  ☐ **after hearing.

☐ 1. A petition requested respondent be prohibited from entry onto the premises, and either the parties are married, petitioner has property interest in the premises, or respondent does not have a property interest in the premises.

☐ 2. Petitioner requested an ex parte order, which should be entered without notice because irreparable injury, loss, or damage will result from the delay required to give notice or notice itself will precipitate adverse action before the order can be issued.

** ☐ 3. Respondent poses a credible threat to the physical safety of the petitioner and/or a child of the petitioner.

☐ 4. Respondent  ☐ **is the spouse or former spouse of the petitioner, had a child in common with the petitioner, or is residing or had resided in the same household as the petitioner.  ☐ has or had a dating relationship with the petitioner.

**IT IS ORDERED:**

5. _____ is prohibited from:

☐ a. entering onto property where petitioner lives.

☐ b. entering onto property at _____ .

** ☐ c. assaulting, attacking, beating, molesting, or wounding _____

☐ d. removing minor children from petitioner who has **legal** custody, except as allowed by custody or parenting-time order provided removal of the children does not violate other conditions of this order.  An existing custody order is dated _____ . An existing parenting-time order is dated _____ .

** ☐ e. stalking as defined under MCL 750.411h and MCL 750.411i that includes but is not limited to:

☐ following petitioner or appearing within his/her sight.   ☐ appearing at petitioner's workplace or residence.

☐ sending mail or other communications to petitioner.   ☐ contacting petitioner by telephone.

☐ approaching or confronting petitioner in a public place or on private property.

☐ entering onto or remaining on property owned, leased, or occupied by petitioner.

☐ placing an object on or delivering an object to property owned, leased, or occupied by petitioner.

☐ f. interfering with petitioner's efforts to remove his/her children/personal property from premises solely owned/leased by respondent.

** ☐ g. threatening to kill or physically injure _____

☐ h. interfering with petitioner at his/her place of employment or education or engaging in conduct that impairs his/her employment or educational relationship or environment.

☐ i. having access to information in records concerning a minor child of petitioner and respondent that will reveal petitioner's address, telephone number, or employment address or that will reveal the child's address or telephone number.

** ☐ j. purchasing or possessing a firearm.

☐ k. other: _____

6. As a result of this order, federal and/or state law may prohibit you from possessing or purchasing ammunition or a firearm.

7. Violation of this order subjects respondent to immediate arrest and to the civil and criminal contempt powers of the court. If found guilty, respondent shall be imprisoned for not more than 93 days and may be fined not more than $500.00.

8. **This order is effective when signed, enforceable immediately, and remains in effect until** _____ . This order is enforceable anywhere in this state by any law enforcement agency when signed by a judge, and upon service, may also be enforced by another state, an Indian tribe, or a territory of the United States. If respondent violates this order in a jurisdiction other than this state, respondent is subject to enforcement and penalties of the state, Indian tribe, or United States territory under whose jurisdiction the violation occurred.

9. The court clerk shall file this order with _____ who will enter it into the LEIN.

10. Respondent may file a motion to modify or terminate this order. For ex parte orders, the motion must be filed within 14 days after being served with or receiving actual notice of the order. Forms and instructions are available from the clerk of court.

11. A motion to extend the order must be filed 3 days before the expiration date in item 8 or a new petition must be filed.

_____     _____     _____
Date and time issued                                        Judge                                                Bar no.

**CC 376** (3/12) **PERSONAL PROTECTION ORDER (Domestic Relationship)** MCL 600.2950, MCR 3.705, MCR 3.706, 18 USC 922(g)(8)(c)

|  |  |
|---|---|
| **PROOF OF SERVICE** | **Personal Protection Order**<br>Case No. |

**TO PROCESS SERVER:** You must serve the personal protection order and file proof of service with the court clerk. If you are unable to complete service, you must return this original and all copies to the court clerk.

### CERTIFICATE / AFFIDAVIT OF SERVICE / NONSERVICE

| ☐ **OFFICER CERTIFICATE** | **OR** | ☐ **AFFIDAVIT OF PROCESS SERVER** |
|---|---|---|
| I certify that I am a sheriff, deputy sheriff, bailiff, appointed court officer, or attorney for a party [MCR 2.104(A)(2)], and that: (notarization not required) | | Being first duly sworn, I state that I am a legally competent adult who is **not** a party or an officer of a corporate party, and that: (notarization required) |

☐ I served a copy of the personal protection order by:
  ☐ personal service   ☐ registered mail, delivery restricted to the respondent (return receipt attached)
  on:

| Name of respondent | Complete address of service | Day, date, time |
|---|---|---|
| | | |
| Law enforcement agency | Complete address of service | Day, date, time |
| | | |

☐ I have personally attempted to serve a copy of the personal protection order on the following respondent and have been unable to complete service.

| Respondent name | Complete address of service |
|---|---|
| | |

I declare that the statements above are true to the best of my information, knowledge, and belief.

| Service fee<br>$ | Miles traveled  Fee<br>$ | |
|---|---|---|
| Incorrect address fee<br>$ | Miles traveled  Fee<br>$ | **TOTAL FEE**<br>$ |

Name (type or print) _____

Signature _____

Title _____

Subscribed and sworn to before me on _____ , _____ County, Michigan.
                                              Date

My commission expires: _____ Signature: _____
                                Date                    Deputy court clerk/Notary public

Notary public, State of Michigan, County of _____

### ACKNOWLEDGMENT OF SERVICE

I acknowledge that I have received a copy of the personal protection order on _____ .
                                                                    Day, date, time

_____
Signature of respondent

MCR 2.105(A)

| STATE OF MICHIGAN JUDICIAL CIRCUIT COUNTY | PERSONAL PROTECTION ORDER (NONDOMESTIC) ☐ EX PARTE | CASE NO. |
|---|---|---|

Court address

ORI
MI-

Court telephone no.

**A** Petitioner's name

Address and telephone no. where court can reach petitioner

**v**

Respondent's name, address, and telephone no.

Address and telephone no. where court can reach respondent

**B** Full name of respondent (type or print) *

Driver's license number (if known)

| Height | Weight | Race * | Sex * | Date of birth or age* | Hair color | Eye color | Other identifying information |
|---|---|---|---|---|---|---|---|
| | | | | | | | |

*These items **must** be filled in for the police/sheriff to enter on LEIN; the other items are not required but are helpful.

Date: _____  Judge: _____

Bar no.

1. This order is entered ☐ without a hearing. ☐ after hearing.

**THE COURT FINDS:**

☐ 2. A petition requesting an order to restrain conduct prohibited under MCL 750.411h and MCL 750.411i and/or MCL 750.411s has been filed under the authority of MCL 600.2950a.

☐ 3. Petitioner requested an ex parte order, which should be entered without notice because irreparable injury, loss, or damage will result from delay required to give notice or notice itself will precipitate adverse action before an order can be issued.

4. Respondent committed the following acts of willful, unconsented contact: (State the reasons for issuance.)

**IT IS ORDERED:**

5. _____ is prohibited from
   Full name of respondent

☐ a. stalking as defined under MCL 750.411h and MCL 750.411i, which includes but is not limited to
   ☐ following or appearing within sight of the petitioner.
   ☐ appearing at the workplace or the residence of the petitioner.
   ☐ approaching or confronting the petitioner in a public place or on private property.
   ☐ entering onto or remaining on property owned, leased, or occupied by the petitioner.
   ☐ sending mail or other communications to the petitioner.
   ☐ contacting the petitioner by telephone.
   ☐ placing an object on or delivering an object to property owned, leased, or occupied by the petitioner.
   ☐ threatening to kill or physically injure the petitioner.
   ☐ purchasing or possessing a firearm.
   ☐ other: _____
☐ b. posting a message through the use of any medium of communication, including the Internet or a computer or any electronic medium, pursuant to MCL 750.411s.

6. Violation of this order subjects the respondent to immediate arrest and to the civil and criminal contempt powers of the court. If found guilty, respondent shall be imprisoned for not more than 93 days and may be fined not more than $500.00.

7. **This order is effective when signed, enforceable immediately, and remains in effect until** _____ .
   This order is enforceable anywhere in this state by any law enforcement agency when signed by a judge, and upon service, may also be enforced by another state, an Indian tribe, or a territory of the United States. If respondent violates this order in a jurisdiction other than this state, respondent is subject to enforcement and penalties of the state, Indian tribe, or United States territory under whose jurisdiction the violation occurred.

8. The court clerk shall file this order with _____ who will enter it into the LEIN.

9. Respondent may file a motion to modify or terminate this order. For ex parte orders, the motion must be filed within 14 days after being served with or receiving actual notice of the order. Forms and instructions are available from the clerk of court.

10. A motion to extend the order must be filed 3 days before the expiration date in item 7, or a new petition must be filed.

_____
Date and time issued

_____
Judge

**CC 380** (3/12) **PERSONAL PROTECTION ORDER (NONDOMESTIC)**

MCL 600.2950a, MCR 3.705, MCR 3.706

| PROOF OF SERVICE | Personal Protection Order (Nondomestic) Case No. |
|---|---|

**TO PROCESS SERVER:** You must serve the personal protection order and file proof of service with the court clerk. If you are unable to complete service, you must return this original and all copies to the court clerk.

## CERTIFICATE / AFFIDAVIT OF SERVICE / NONSERVICE

| ☐ OFFICER CERTIFICATE OR | ☐ AFFIDAVIT OF PROCESS SERVER |
|---|---|
| I certify that I am a sheriff, deputy sheriff, bailiff, appointed court officer, or attorney for a party (MCR 2.104[A][2]), and that: (notarization not required) | Being first duly sworn, I state that I am a legally competent adult who is **not** a party or an officer of a corporate party, and that: (notarization required) |

☐ I served a copy of the personal protection order by
   ☐ personal service on:   ☐ registered mail, delivery restricted to the respondent (return receipt attached) on:

| Name of respondent | Complete address of service | Day, date, time |
|---|---|---|
| | | |
| Law enforcement agency | Complete address of service | Day, date, time |
| | | |

☐ I have personally attempted to serve a copy of the personal protection order on the following respondent and have been unable to complete service.

| Respondent's name | Complete address of service |
|---|---|
| | |

I declare that the statements above are true to the best of my information, knowledge, and belief.

| Service fee $ | Miles traveled Fee $ | | Signature |
|---|---|---|---|
| Incorrect address fee $ | Miles traveled Fee $ | TOTAL FEE $ | Name (type or print) |
| | | | Title |

Subscribed and sworn to before me on _____ , _____ County, Michigan.
                                          Date

My commission expires: _____ Signature: _____
                          Date                        Deputy court clerk/Notary public

Notary public, State of Michigan, County of _____

## ACKNOWLEDGMENT OF SERVICE

I acknowledge that I have received a copy of the personal protection order on _____.
                                                                          Day, date, time

_____
Signature of respondent

MCR 2.105(A)

Original - Court file
Copies as needed

| STATE OF MICHIGAN<br>JUDICIAL CIRCUIT<br>COUNTY | PROOF OF SERVICE/ORAL NOTICE<br>REGARDING<br>PERSONAL PROTECTION ORDER | CASE NO. |
|---|---|---|

Court address _____ Court telephone no. _____

| Petitioner's name | | Respondent's name, address, and telephone no. |
|---|---|---|
| Address and telephone no. where court can reach petitioner | v | |

## AFFIDAVIT OF SERVICE

I certify that on _____ I personally served _____
                                Date                                                Respondent name

at _____
        Address or location of service

with a copy of the personal protection order issued on _____ by the _____
                                                            Date

Circuit Court.

_____          _____
Officer signature                                       Law enforcement agency

_____          _____
Name (type or print)                    ID no.          Address

                                            _____
                                            City, state, zip                    Telephone no.

Subscribed and sworn to before me on _____, _____County, Michigan.
                                            Date

My commission expires: _____ Signature: _____
                            Date                            Deputy court clerk/Notary public

Notary public, State of Michigan, County of _____

## PROOF OF ORAL NOTICE

I certify that on _____ I orally notified _____ of
                        Date                                Respondent name

the existence of a personal protection order issued on _____ by the _____
                                                            Date

Circuit Court. I also certify that the respondent was advised of the following:
- the specific conduct enjoined.
- the penalties for violating the order.
- where the respondent could obtain a copy of the personal protection order.

_____          _____
Date                                                    Officer signature

                                            _____
                                            Name (type or print)                    ID no.

                                            _____
                                            Law enforcement agency

                                            _____
                                            Address

                                            _____
                                            City, state, zip                    Telephone no.

MCL 600.2950(22), MCL 600.2950a(19), MCR 3.706(E)

**CC 386** (3/11) **PROOF OF SERVICE/ORAL NOTICE REGARDING PERSONAL PROTECTION ORDER**

# CLASSIFICATION OF TRAFFIC LAW VIOLATIONS
ALL VIOLATIONS ARE CIVIL INFRACTIONS UNLESS NOTED OTHERWISE

## ALCOHOL VIOLATIONS
| | |
|---|---|
| 8027* | Operating with a High BAC (over0.17%) – 625(1)(c) |
| 8030* | Child endangerment - 625(7) |
| 8041* | Operating while intoxicated - 625(1) |
| 8042* | Permitted an intoxicated person to operate - 625(2) |
| 8043* | Operating while visibly impaired - 625(3) |
| 8028* | Operating with BAC of 08% or more - 625(1) |
| 8045* | Tampering with ignition control device - 625l |
| 8048* | Commercial driver, BAC .04% thru .07% - 625m |
| 8049* | Violation of out of service order: Alcohol - 319d(7) |
| 8050* | Under 21 with any BAC .02% thru .07% - 625(6) |
| 4103* | Transporting open intoxicants - 624a |
| 4104* | Possession of open intoxicants - 624a |
| 4195* | Possession or transporting liquor by a minor in a motor vehicle - 624b |
| 8326 | Refused preliminary breath test - 625a(2)(d) |
| 8327* | Refused preliminary breath test: Commercial driver - 625a(5) |

## BICYCLE VIOLATIONS
| | |
|---|---|
| 8310 | Bicycle violations - 656 through 662 |

## CONTROLLED SUBSTANCE VIOLATIONS
| | |
|---|---|
| 8029* | Operating with any presence of drug (Sch.1 and or Cocaine) – 625(8) |
| 8031* | Operating while intoxicated: controlled substance - 625(1) |
| 8032* | Permitted an intoxicated person to operate: controlled substance - 625(2) |
| 8033* | Operating while visibly impaired - 625(3) |

## EQUIPMENT VIOLATIONS
| | |
|---|---|
| 8191 | No mirror for obstructed view - 708 |
| 8192 | Safety chain violation/defective trailer hitch - 721 |
| 8193 | Unlawful trailer or trailer rig - 721 |
| 8194 | Illegal towing equipment - 721 |
| 8195 | No slow moving vehicle emblem - 688(g) |
| 8202 | Defective tires - 710 |
| 8203 | No flag on projecting load (daytime) - 693 |
| 8204* | Improper or no horn - 706 |
| 8205 | Obstruction to view (non-tint violations) - 709 |
| 8206 | Windshield wiper/washers (none or defective) - 709(4) |
| 8209 | Unauthorized siren - 706(b) |
| 8210 | Noisy muffler and/or excessive fumes or smoke - 707 |
| 8211 | Use of tires damaging highway - 710 |
| 8212 | Failed to maintain equipment - 683♦ |
| 8216 | Window tint violation - 709 |
| 8217 | Bumper/suspension violation - 710c |
| 8220 | Defective or improper brakes - 705 |

## EVADING ARREST
| | |
|---|---|
| 8171* | Attempted to flee or elude police officer - 602a |
| 8172* | Disregarded police officer - 602 |
| 8173* | Refused vehicle inspection - 602 |
| 8174* | Furnished false information to police officer - 324(1)(h) |

## IGNITION CONTROL DEVICES
| | |
|---|---|
| 8045* | Tampering with ignition control device – 625l(5) |
| 8045* | Unauthorized removal of ignition control device – 322a |
| 8045* | Operating w/o ignition control when required – 625l(2) |
| 8045* | Requesting another to blow into ignition control - 625(1)(3) |
| 8045* | Blowing into ignition control for another – 625(l)(4) |

## FOLLOWING TOO CLOSELY
| | |
|---|---|
| 8080 | Following too closely - 643 |

## HIT AND RUN (PI OR PD)
| | |
|---|---|
| 8011* | Accident, failed to stop and identify - 617a through 621 |
| 8012* | Accident, failed to give assistance - 619 |
| 8013* | Refused to stop for weighing - 724(6) |

## LANE USE/WRONG WAY VIOLATIONS
| | |
|---|---|
| 8141 | Drove on wrong side, undivided highway - 634 |
| 8142 | Drove on wrong side, divided highway - 644 |
| 8143 | Drove wrong way, one way road - 641 |
| 8144 | Improper lane driving, multiple lane highway - 642 |
| 8145 | Improper lane use, truck on freeway - 634(3) |

## LICENSE VIOLATIONS
| | |
|---|---|
| 8271* | No operator's license - 301 |
| 8272* | No chauffeur's license - 301 |
| 8273* | Driving on suspended, revoked, or refused license - 904 |
| 8274* | Permitted unlicensed minor to operate - 325 |
| 8275* | Violation of restricted license - 312 |
| 8275 | Failed to change address - 315 |
| 8275+ | Other driver license law violations |
| 8281* | No operator's or chauffeur's license on person - 311♦ |

## LIGHTS
| | |
|---|---|
| 8160 | Failed to dim headlights - 700 |
| 8231 | Headlights (defective, improper or none) - 684, 685 |
| 8232 | Tail lights (defective, improper or none) - 686 |
| 8233 | Turn signal (defective, improper or none) - 686 |
| 8234 | Reflectors/clearance markers (improper or none) - 687 |
| 8235 | Unlighted registration plate - 686(2) |
| 8236 | More than two spot lights / fog lights - 696(a) |
| 8238 | Too many cowl, running board, or back-up lights - 698 |
| 8239* | Unauthorized flashing lights - 698 |
| 8240 | No red light on projecting load (nighttime) - 693 |

## LOAD/WEIGHT VIOLATIONS
| | |
|---|---|
| 8022* | Insecure loads and/or spilling loads on highway - 720 |
| 8023* | Failed to tarp - 720 |
| 8278* | Overweight - 722 (includes sec. 716) |
| 8279 | Overweight - 722 (includes sec. 724) |

## LOW-SPEED VEHICLES
| | |
|---|---|
| 8302 | Helmet violation – 658b |
| 8215 | Operating where prohibited – 660(7) |

## MOTORCYCLE VIOLATIONS
| | |
|---|---|
| 8301 | Motorcycle violations - 658 through 661a |
| 8302 | Helmet violation - 658 |
| 8283* | No motorcycle endorsement - 312a(1) |
| 8285 | No eye protection - 708a |

## MOPED VIOLATIONS
| | |
|---|---|
| 8303 | Moped violations - 657-661 |
| 8304 | Helmet violation - 658 |
| 8284* | No moped license - 312a(2) |

## OTHER VIOLATIONS
| | |
|---|---|
| 3295 | Texting while driving – 602b |
| 8180+ | Other hazardous violations |
| 8181 | Television viewer in motor vehicle - 708b |
| 8250+ | Other non-hazardous violations |
| 8218 | Occupant under age 18 in open bed of pickup truck - 682b |

## OVERTAKING VIOLATIONS
| | |
|---|---|
| 8090 | Overtaking - other - 638 through 640 |
| 8091 | Improper overtaking on a curve - 639 |
| 8092 | Improper overtaking on a hill - 639 |
| 8093 | Failed to give way when overtaken - 636 |
| 8094 | Improper overtaking on the right - 637 |

## PARKING VIOLATIONS
| | |
|---|---|
| 8290 | Improper parking - 674 through 676 |
| 8291 | Parked in handicap space - 674(1)(s) |
| 8292* | Improper use of handicap permit - 675 |
| 8293 | Parking, stopping, or standing on roadway - 672 |

## PEDESTRIAN VIOLATIONS
| | |
|---|---|
| 8321 | Walked in roadway, sidewalks provided - 655 |
| 8322 | Walked in roadway with traffic, no sidewalks - 655 |
| 8323 | Other pedestrian violations - 613 |
| 8325 | Pedestrian on freeway - 679a |

## REGISTRATION, INSURANCE, AND TITLE VIOLATIONS
| | |
|---|---|
| 8276+ | Title law violations - Chapter II |
| 8277 | Unsigned or no registration certificate - 223♦ |
| 8277* | Failed to transfer registration - 233 |
| 8277 | No plate/expired plate/failed to display valid – 255 |
| 8277* | No plate/expired plate/failed to display valid – Commercial Vehicle - 255 |
| 8277* | Improper use of registration plate - 256 |
| 8277 | Improper display of registration plate - 225 |
| 8280 | No proof of insurance - 328 |

## RIGHT-OF-WAY VIOLATIONS
| | |
|---|---|
| 8110 | Failed to yield within intersection; left turn - 650 |
| 8111 | Failed to yield at unsigned intersection - 649 |
| 8112 | Failed to yield at signed intersection - 649 |
| 8113 | Failed to yield to pedestrians - 612 |
| 8114 | Failed to yield - all others |
| 8115 | Failure to yield to emergency responder - 653(1)(a) |
| 8115* | Failure to use due caution for emergency responder - 653a(1)(b) |

## SAFETY BELT VIOLATIONS
| | |
|---|---|
| 8213 | Child restraint violation – 710d♦ |
| 8214 | Failed to properly wear safety belt - 710e |
| 8215 | Failed to wear safety belt: Ages 4-15 - 710e |

## SIGNALING VIOLATIONS
| | |
|---|---|
| 8151 | Failed to sound horn for safe operation - 706 |
| 8152 | Failed to signal/improper signal - 648 |

## SPEED: OTHER / ALL ROADWAYS
| | |
|---|---|
| 8054 | Violation of basic speed - too fast – 627(1) |
| 8055 | Violation of basic speed - too slow – 627(1) |
| 8060 | Speeding in construction zone - 627(9) |
| 8071* | Drag racing - 626a |
| 8072 | Careless driving - 626b |
| 8073* | Reckless driving - 626 |

## SPEED: FREEWAY VIOLATIONS
| | |
|---|---|
| 8057 | Exceeded freeway speed limit – car towing trailer - 627(5) |
| 8057 | Exceeded 55 mph speed limit – trucks over 10,000 lbs – 627(6) |
| 8061 | Exceeded freeway speed limit - 55 zone – 628 |
| 8063 | Exceeded freeway speed limit - 65 zone – 628 |
| 8062 | Exceeded freeway speed limit - 70 zone – 628 |
| 8065 | Below minimum freeway speed - 628 |

## SPEED: NON-FREEWAY VIOLATIONS
| | |
|---|---|
| 8051 | Exceeded posted or unposted maximum speed – 628 |
| 8052 | Exceeded prima facie speed limit – 627 |
| 8057 | Exceeded posted speed - trucks over 10,000 lbs - 627(6) |
| 8057 | Frost Law speed 35 mph – trucks over 10,000 lbs – 627(6) |

## STOP AND GO VIOLATIONS
| | |
|---|---|
| 8121 | Disregarded stop sign - 649(6) |
| 8122 | Disregarded flashing red signal - 614 |
| 8123 | Disregarded steady yellow signal - 612 |
| 8124 | Failed to stop/yield at signed or signalized RR crossing - 667 through 670 |
| 8124 | RR crossing/serious CDL violation - 669a |
| 8125 | Failed to stop for school bus - 682 |
| 8126 | Failed to stop leaving private drive - 652 |
| 8127 | Disregarded stop and go light - 612 |
| 8128 | Improper stop and turn on red - 612 |
| 8129 | Avoided traffic control device - 611 |
| 8180 | RR crossing/HM and Buses - 670 |

## TURNING VIOLATIONS
| | |
|---|---|
| 8131 | Improper right turn - 647, 648 |
| 8132 | Improper left turn - 647, 648 |
| 8133 | Improper turn from wrong lane - 647 |
| 8134 | Other improper turning |
| 8135 | Limited access highway, driving across median – 644 |

* = MISDEMEANOR, + = REFER TO VEHICLE CODE, ♦ = DISMISSIBLE

## MOTOR CARRIER ENFORCEMENT VIOLATIONS
### UNAUTHORIZED TRANSPORTATION (1933 PA 254)
| | |
|---|---|
| 8901* | Haul for hire without authority |
| 8904* | Leasing violations |

### REGISTRATION RULES AND INSURANCE (1933 PA 254)
| | |
|---|---|
| 8910* | Improper use of MPSC plate – 476.1 |
| 8911* | Fail to secure MPSC plate – 479.16 |
| 8912* | No MPSC card and/or plate – 479.16 |
| 8913* | Improper fee paid for MPSC plate – 479.16 |
| 8914* | Failure to display proper special ID card – 479.16 |
| 8915* | Motor Carrier - interstate registration violation – 478.7 |
| 8916* | Public inspection of records – 479.16 |
| 8917* | Name and account records – 479.16 |
| 8918* | Inspection of cargo – 479.16 |
| 8920* | Fail to file PL and PD insurance |
| 8930* | Other violations of commission rules |

### MOTOR CARRIER SAFETY ACT (1963 PA 181)
| | |
|---|---|
| 8950 | Driver violations |
| 8951 | Equipment violations |
| 8953 | Log book violations |
| 8954* | Hazardous materials |
| 8969 | Other motor carrier safety rule violations |

### BUS TRANSPORTATION (1982 PA 432)
| | |
|---|---|
| 8990* | Haul for hire without MDOT authority |
| 8991* | Failure to maintain MDOT passenger insurance |
| 8992* | Failure to pay bus registration fee |
| 8993* | No information displayed on bus |
| 8994* | Other motor bus violations |

### OTHER VIOLATIONS
| | |
|---|---|
| 8971 | Highway permit number |
| 8976 | Overlength – 719 |
| 8977 | Overwidth – 717 |
| 8978 | Overheight – 719 |
| 8981* | Bypassing scale - 724(4) |
| 8982* | Refused to stop for weighing - 724(6) |

### FUEL TAX VIOLATIONS (1980 PA 119)
| | |
|---|---|
| 8999* | Fuel tax permit – 207.225 |
| 8998* | Fuel tax return violation – 207.214 |

### FUEL TAX VIOLATIONS (2000 PA 403)
| | |
|---|---|
| 8999* | Illegal use of dyed diesel fuel – 207.1122 |

## COMMERCIAL MOTOR VEHICLE & COMMERCIAL
## DRIVER LICENSE ENDORSEMENT

Group "A" is any combination of vehicles with a gross combination weight rating (GCWR) of 26,001 lbs. or more when towing a vehicle or trailer that has a gross vehicle weight rating (GVWR) over 10,000 lbs.

| Two position codes | CDL Endorsement Required |
|---|---|
| AA = Group A | A |
| AH = Group A, hazardous | A H |
| AN = Group A, tank | A N |
| AP = Group A, passenger | A P |
| AS – Group A, school bus | A S |
| AT = Group A, double/triple | A T |
| AX = Group A, tank & hazardous | A X |
| AY = Group A, tank & double/triple hazardous | A NT |
| AZ = Group A, double/triple & hazardous | A HT |
| AL = Group A, tank & double/triple & hazardous | A TX |

Group "B" is any single vehicle with a gross vehicle weight rating (GVWR) of 26,001 lbs or more or any such vehicle when towing a vehicle or trailer that has a (GVWR) of 10,000 lbs or less.

| Two position codes | CDL Endorsement Required |
|---|---|
| BB = Group B | B |
| BH = Group B, hazardous | B H |
| BN = Group B, tank | B N |
| BP = Group B, passenger | B P |
| BS – Group B, school bus | B S |
| BX = Group B, tank & hazardous | B X |

Group "C" is any single vehicle with a gross vehicle weight rating (GVWR) of less than 26,001 lbs or a combination of vehicles having a gross combination weight rating (GCWR) under 26,001 lbs and the vehicle being towed has a gross vehicle weight rating (GVWR) of 10,000 lbs. or less and is transporting materials required to be placarded for hazardous materials under C.F.R. 49, parts 100 to 199, or a vehicle designed to transport 16 or more passengers (including driver).

| Two position codes | CDL Endorsement Required |
|---|---|
| CH = Group C, hazardous | C H |
| CP = Group C, passenger | C P |
| CS – Group C, school bus | C S |
| CX= Group C, tank & hazardous | C |

## NON-COMMERCIAL VEHICLE TYPES
| | | | | |
|---|---|---|---|---|
| CY | Cycle | PU | Pickup | |
| MO | Moped | ST | Small trucks (under 10,000 lbs) | |
| PA | Passenger car & station wagon | MD | Medium trucks w/wo trailer over | |
| VA | Van, motor home | | 10,000 lbs GVWR (non-CDL) | |
| GC | Go cart | OR | Off-road vehicle (ATV type) | |
| SM | Snowmobile | | | |

## CRIMINAL VIOLATIONS

### MISCELLANEOUS
| | | |
|---|---|---|
| 28.243a | * | Fail to submit to fingerprinting |
| 500.3102 | * | Operating a Motor Vehicle without Insurance |
| 750.81 | | Assault and battery/domestic assault |
| 750.167 | | Disorderly person |
| 750.337 | | Indecent language in presence of women or children |
| 750.411(h) | | Stalking |
| 750.479 | | Resisting/obstructing police officer |
| 750.508 | | Police scanner in vehicle |
| 750.479a | | Fleeing and Eluding |

### OFFENSES AGAINST PROPERTY
| | |
|---|---|
| 750.110 | Breaking and entering |
| 750.111 | Entering without breaking |
| 750.356 | Larceny (includes gasoline and license plate) |
| 750.356(a) | Larceny from motor vehicle |
| 750.356(c)(d) | Retail fraud |
| 750.377a | Malicious destruction of personal property |
| 750.377b | Malicious destruction of police/fire property |
| 750.380 | Malicious destruction of house, barn, etc. |
| 750.394 | Throwing stone or missile at train, car, or vehicle |
| 750.535 | Receiving/concealing/possession of stolen property |
| 750.552 | Trespassing |
| 324.8902 | Littering |

### ALCOHOL AND NARCOTICS
| | |
|---|---|
| 333.7403 | Possession of marijuana |
| 436.1701 | Furnish or sell alcoholic beverage to minor |
| 436.1703(1) | Purchase or consuming alcoholic beverages by minor |
| 436.1703(2) | Furnish/use fraudulent ID to purchased alcohol by minor |
| 436.1703(5)+ | Minor refuses PBT |
| 436.1915 | Consuming alcoholic liquor on the public highway |
| 750.141a | Furnishing alcoholic beverage to minor |

### FIREARMS AND FIREWORKS
| | |
|---|---|
| 324.40111 | Discharging firearm within 150 yards of dwelling or farm of another |
| 750.227d | Firearm improperly carried in vehicle (loaded, not cased, etc.) |
| 750.227 | Carrying a concealed weapon |
| 750.237 | Possession of firearm by person under influence |
| 750.234d | Possession of firearm on certain premises |
| 480.17c | Firearm as forbidden explosive in a Commercial MV(49 CFR 173.54f) |
| 750.228 | Failure to have pistol safety inspected – Fail to register |
| 750.234e | Brandishing a firearm in public |

### CONCEALED PISTOL LICENSE VIOLATIONS
| | |
|---|---|
| 28.425k(2)(c) | Possession of a firearm with a bodily alcohol content .02-.079 |
| * 28.425k(2)(a)or(b) | Possession of a firearm with a bodily alcohol content greater than .08 |
| 28.425f | Failure to possess or display either driver's license, Michigan ID and concealed pistol license |
| 28.425f(5) | Failure to immediately disclose possession of concealed pistol |
| 28.425o | Possession of a concealed pistol in a "pistol free" zone |

### SNOWMOBILE VIOLATIONS
| | |
|---|---|
| 324.82103 | Unregistered snowmobile |
| 324.82113 | No registration decal displayed on snowmobile |
| 324.82119 | Operation of snowmobile in prohibited area |
| 324.82122 | No headlight or taillight, or inadequate brakes on snowmobile (day or night) |
| 324.82131 | Operation of snowmobile without displaying proper lights (night only) |
| 324.82126 | Operation of snowmobile at unreasonable speed |
| 324.82127 | Operation of snowmobile while under the influence of intoxicating liquor or controlled substance |
| 324.82126 | Snowmobile muffler fails to prevent excessive or unusual noise or excessive smoke |
| 324.82126 | Bow or firearm in snowmobile not securely cased |
| 324.82126 | Operation of snowmobile in nursery, planting area, forest reproduction area |
| 324.82132 | Failure to report a snowmobile accident |

### CONSERVATION LAWS
| | |
|---|---|
| 324.43509 | Hunting without a license |
| 324.43509 | Fishing without a license |
| R 3.103 | Possession of an untagged deer (commission regulation) |

**\* = MISDEMEANOR, + = REFER TO VEHICLE CODE, ♦ = DISMISSIBLE**

| 324.43526 | Hunting deer without a firearm license |
| 324.43527 | Hunting deer without a bow & arrow license |
| 324.73102 | Recreational trespass |
| 324.52908 | Transporting Christmas trees without a manifest |

RI-1 (Rev. 03/11)
Michigan State Police

# MICR ARREST CHARGE CODES

## 01000 – Sovereignty

| FILE CLASS OFFENSE/ARREST CHARGES | ARR CHG |
|---|---|
| Treason | 0101 |
| Treason Misprision | 0102 |
| Espionage | 0103 |
| Sabotage | 0104 |
| Sedition | 0105 |
| Selective Service | 0106 |
| Sovereignty (Other) | 0199 |

## 02000 – Military

| FILE CLASS OFFENSE/ARREST CHARGES | ARR CHG |
|---|---|
| Desertion | 0201 |
| AWOL | 0297 |
| Military (Other) | 0299 |

## 03000 – Immigration

| FILE CLASS OFFENSE/ARREST CHARGES | ARR CHG |
|---|---|
| Illegal Entry | 0301 |
| False Citizenship | 0302 |
| Smuggling Aliens | 0303 |
| Immigration (Other) | 0399 |

## 09001 – Murder/Non-negligent Manslaughter (Voluntary)

| FILE CLASS OFFENSE/ARREST CHARGES | ARR CHG |
|---|---|
| Willful Killing: | |
| Family - Gun | 0901 |
| Other Weapon | 0902 |
| Non-family - Gun | 0903 |
| Other Weapon | 0904 |
| Public Official - Gun | 0905 |
| Other Weapon | 0906 |
| Police Officer - Gun | 0907 |
| Other Weapon | 0908 |
| Willful Killing - Gun | 0911 |
| Willful Killing - Other Weapon | 0912 |
| Human Trafficking Causing Death | |
| Homicide (Other) | 0999 |

## 09002 – Neg. Homicide/Manslaughter (Involuntary)

| FILE CLASS OFFENSE/ARREST CHARGES | ARR CHG |
|---|---|
| Weapon | 0910 |
| Deliver Controlled Substance Causing Death | 0996 |
| Assisted Suicide | 0997 |

## 09003 – Negligent Homicide Veh./Boat/Snowmobile

| FILE CLASS OFFENSE/ARREST CHARGES | ARR CHG |
|---|---|
| Negligent Homicide - Vehicle | 0909 |
| Negligent Homicide (Other) | 0998 |
| Felony Death by Drunk Driving: | |
| Snowmobile | 5466 |
| ORV | 5476 |
| Boat | 5486 |
| Vehicle | 8046 |
| Let Intoxicated Person Operate M/V Causing Death (Alcohol) | 8034 |
| Let Intoxicated Person Operate M/V Causing Death (Drugs) | 8035 |
| Felony Death While Under Controlled Substance | 8039 |
| Felony Death from Fleeing Vehicle | 8175 |
| Let Suspended Person Operate Causing Death | 8268 |

## 09004 – Justifiable Homicide

## 10001 – Kidnapping/Abduction

| FILE CLASS OFFENSE/ARREST CHARGES | ARR CHG |
|---|---|
| Kidnap Minor for Ransom | 1001 |
| Kidnap Adult for Ransom | 1002 |
| Kidnap Minor to Sexually Assault | 1003 |
| Kidnap Adult to Sexually Assault | 1004 |
| Kidnap Minor | 1005 |
| Kidnap Adult | 1006 |
| Kidnap Hostage for Escape | 1007 |
| Abduct - No Ransom or Assault | 1008 |
| Kidnap - Hijack Aircraft | 1009 |
| Human Trafficking | 1010 |
| Human Trafficking Causing Injury | 1011 |
| Kidnapping (Other) | 1099 |

## 10002 – Parental Kidnapping

| FILE CLASS OFFENSE/ARREST CHARGES | ARR CHG |
|---|---|
| Parental Kidnap MCL750.350A[1] | 1072 |

## 11001–11007 – Sexual Penetration / Sexual Contact Forcible

| FILE CLASS OFFENSE/ARREST CHARGES | ARR CHG |
|---|---|
| 11001 - Sexual Penetration — Penis/Vagina - CSC 1st Degree | 1171 |
| 11002 - Sexual Penetration — Penis/Vagina - CSC 3rd Degree | 1172 |
| 11003 - Sexual Penetration — Oral/Anal - CSC 1st Degree | 1173 |
| 11004 - Sexual Penetration — Oral/Anal - CSC 3rd Degree | 1174 |
| 11005 - Sexual Penetration — Object - CSC 1st Degree | 1175 |
| 11006 - Sexual Penetration — Object - CSC 3rd Degree | 1176 |
| 11007 - Sexual Contact Forcible — Forcible Contact - CSC 2nd Deg. | 1177 |
| Sex Offense Against Child - Fondle | 3601 |

## 11008 – Sexual Contact Forcible

| FILE CLASS OFFENSE/ARREST CHARGES | ARR CHG |
|---|---|
| Forcible Contact - CSC 4th Deg. | 1178 |

## 12000 – Robbery

| FILE CLASS OFFENSE/ARREST CHARGES | ARR CHG |
|---|---|
| Business - Gun | 1201 |
| Business - Other Weapon | 1202 |
| Business - Strong Arm | 1203 |
| Street - Gun | 1204 |
| Street - Other Weapon | 1205 |
| Street - Strong Arm | 1206 |
| Residence - Gun | 1207 |
| Residence - Other Weapon | 1208 |
| Residence - Strong Arm | 1209 |
| Forcible - Purse Snatching | 1210 |
| Banking Type Institution | 1211 |
| Motor Vehicle (Carjacking) | 1270 |
| Attempted Robbery - Unarmed | 1297 |
| Attempted Robbery - Armed | 1298 |
| Robbery (Other) | 1299 |

## 13001 – Nonaggravated Assault

| FILE CLASS OFFENSE/ARREST CHARGES | ARR CHG |
|---|---|
| A & B/Simple Assault | 1313 |

## 13002 – Agg./Felonious Assault

| FILE CLASS OFFENSE/ARREST CHARGES | ARR CHG |
|---|---|
| Family - Gun | 1301 |
| Family - Other Weapon | 1302 |
| Family - Strong Arm | 1303 |
| Non-family - Gun | 1304 |
| Non-family - Other Weapon | 1305 |
| Non-family - Strong Arm | 1306 |
| Public Official - Gun | 1307 |
| Public Official - Other Weapon | 1308 |
| Public Official - Strong Arm | 1309 |
| Police Officer - Gun | 1310 |
| Police Officer - Other Weapon | 1311 |
| Police Officer - Strong Arm | 1312 |
| Murder Attempt | 1371 |
| Mayhem | 1393 |
| Assault, Intent to Commit Felony | 1394 |
| Assault, Intent to Maim | 1395 |
| Assault Less Than Murder | 1396 |
| Assault with Intent to Murder | 1397 |
| Assault (Other) | 1399 |
| Fleeing Resulting in Assault | 8176 |

## 13003 – Intimidation/Stalking

| FILE CLASS OFFENSE/ARREST CHARGES | ARR CHG |
|---|---|
| Intimidation (Interfere w/911 Call) | 1316 |
| Tx. Used for Harassment, Threats | 1380 |
| Aggravated Stalking (Felony) | 1381 |
| Stalking (Misdemeanor) | 1382 |
| Stalking a Minor (Felony) | 1383 |
| Computer/Internet Used for Harassment, Threats | 1384 |
| Other Electronic Medium Used for Harassment, Threats | 1385 |
| Threat to Bomb | 5215 |
| Threat to Burn | 5216 |

## 14000 – Abortion

| FILE CLASS OFFENSE/ARREST CHARGES | ARR CHG |
|---|---|
| Abortion Act on Other | 1401 |
| Abortion Act on Self | 1402 |
| Submission to Abortional Act | 1403 |
| Abortifacient | 1404 |
| Selling, Manufacturing, etc. | |
| Abortion (Other) | 1499 |

## 20000 – Arson

| FILE CLASS OFFENSE/ARREST CHARGES | ARR CHG |
|---|---|
| Business - Endangered Life | 2001 |
| Residence - Endangered Life | 2002 |
| Business - Defraud Insurer | 2003 |
| Residence - Defraud Insurer | 2004 |
| Arson - Business | 2005 |
| Arson - Residence | 2006 |
| Setting Fire - Woods & Prairies | 2007 |
| Pub. Bldg. (Incl. Hotel/Motel) Endangered Life | 2008 |
| Arson - Public Building | 2009 |
| Burning of Real Property | 2072 |
| Burning of Personal Property | 2073 |
| Burning Insured Prop. (Own) | 2097 |
| Preparation to Burn | 2098 |
| Arson (Other) | 2099 |

## 21000 – Extortion

| FILE CLASS OFFENSE/ARREST CHARGES | ARR CHG |
|---|---|
| Threat to: Injure Person | 2101 |
| Damage Property | 2102 |
| Injure Reputation | 2103 |
| Accuse Person of Crime | 2104 |
| Threat of Informing of Violation | 2105 |
| Extortion (Other) | 2199 |

## 22001 – Burglary - Forced Entry

| FILE CLASS OFFENSE/ARREST CHARGES | ARR CHG |
|---|---|
| Burglary - Safe/Vault | 2201 |
| Forced Entry - Residence | 2202 |
| Forced Entry - Non-Residence | 2203 |
| Banking Type Institution | 2207 |
| Unoccupied Bldg. or Other Structure | 2275 |
| Burglary - (Other) | 2299 |

## 22002 – Burglary - Entry Without Force (Intent to Commit)

| FILE CLASS OFFENSE/ARREST CHARGES | ARR CHG |
|---|---|
| No Forced Entry - Residence | 2204 |
| No Forced Entry - Non-Residence | 2205 |

## 22003 – Burglary - Entry Without Authority, With or Without Force (No Intent)

| FILE CLASS OFFENSE/ARREST CHARGES | ARR CHG |
|---|---|
| Entering Without Permission | 2298 |

## 22004 – Poss. of Burglary Tools

| FILE CLASS OFFENSE/ARREST CHARGES | ARR CHG |
|---|---|
| Possession Burglary Tools | 2206 |

## 23001 – Larceny - Pocketpicking

| FILE CLASS OFFENSE/ARREST CHARGES | ARR CHG |
|---|---|
| Pocketpicking | 2301 |

## 23002 – Larceny - Purse Snatching

| FILE CLASS OFFENSE/ARREST CHARGES | ARR CHG |
|---|---|
| Purse Snatching - No Force | 2302 |

## 23003 – Larceny - Theft from Bldg.

| FILE CLASS OFFENSE/ARREST CHARGES | ARR CHG |
|---|---|
| From Bldg., (Library, Office, etc. - Used by Public) | 2308 |
| From Bank Type Institution | 2311 |

## 23004 – Larceny - Theft from Coin Operated Machine/Device

| FILE CLASS OFFENSE/ARREST CHARGES | ARR CHG |
|---|---|
| From Coin Machines (Includes Telephone Coin Box) | 2307 |

## 23005 – Larceny - Theft from Motor Vehicle

| FILE CLASS OFFENSE/ARREST CHARGES | ARR CHG |
|---|---|
| Personal Property from Vehicle | 2305 |

## 23006 – Larceny - Theft of Motor Vehicle Parts/Accessories

| FILE CLASS OFFENSE/ARREST CHARGES | ARR CHG |
|---|---|
| Parts and Accessories from Vehicle | 2304 |
| Strip Stolen Vehicle | 2407 |

## 23007 – Larceny - Other

| FILE CLASS OFFENSE/ARREST CHARGES | ARR CHG |
|---|---|
| From Shipment | 2306 |
| From Yards (Grounds surrounding a building) | 2309 |
| From Mails | 2310 |

R1-1 (Rev. 03/11)
Michigan State Police

# MICR ARREST CHARGE CODES

**Panel 1**

| FILE CLASS OFFENSE/ARREST CHARGES | ARR CHG |
|---|---|
| From Interstate Shipment | 2312 |
| Obstruct Corr. (Postal Violation) | 2313 |
| Theft of U.S. Govt. Property | 2314 |
| Larceny from U.S. Govt. Reserve | 2315 |
| Larceny Gas Self-Service Station | 2379 |
| Larceny (Other) | 2399 |
| Aircraft Theft (Taking/Using) | 2410 |
| **26001 - Fraud - False Pretense/ Swindle/Confidence Game** | |
| Confidence Game/Fortune Telling | 2601 |
| Swindle | 2602 |
| Mail Fraud | 2603 |
| **24001 - Motor Vehicle Theft** | |
| Theft and Sale | 2401 |
| Theft and Strip | 2402 |
| Theft - Use in Other Crime | 2403 |
| Vehicle Theft | 2404 |
| Theft by Bailee - Fail to Return | 2405 |
| Possess Stolen Vehicle | 2408 |
| Unauthorized Use (Incl. Joy Riding) | 2411 |
| Stolen (Other) | 2499 |
| **24002 - M/V as Stolen Property** | |
| Poss./Receive Stolen Vehicle/Parts | 2406 |
| Interstate Transport Stolen Vehicle | 2409 |
| Theft and Sale | 2472 |
| Theft and Strip (Incl. Chop Shop) | 2473 |
| Theft and Use | 2474 |
| Unauthorized Use (Incl. Joy Riding) | 2475 |
| Motor Veh. as Stolen Prop. (Other) | 2498 |
| **24003 - Motor Vehicle Fraud** | |
| Obt. Money/Goods - False Pretense | 2470 |
| Concealing Identity Motor Vehicle | 2471 |
| Acquire M/V During Denial | 2496 |
| Motor Vehicle Fraud (Other) | 2497 |
| **25000 - Forgery/Counterfeiting** | |
| Forgery of Checks | 2501 |
| Forgery of Other Object | 2502 |
| Counterfeiting of Any Object | 2503 |
| Pass Forged - Any Object | 2504 |
| Pass Counterfeited - Any Object | 2505 |
| Possess Forged - Any Object | 2506 |
| Poss. Counterfeited - Any Object | 2507 |
| Poss. Tools, Plates, Etc., for Forgery or Counterfeiting | 2508 |
| Transport Forged - Any Object | 2509 |
| Transport Counterfeit - Any Object | 2510 |
| Transport Tools, Plates, Etc. for Forgery or Counterfeiting | 2511 |

**Panel 2**

| FILE CLASS OFFENSE/ARREST CHARGES | ARR CHG |
|---|---|
| Forgery (Other) | 2589 |
| Counterfeiting (Other) | 2599 |
| **26002 - Fraud Credit Card/Automatic Teller Machine** | |
| Obtaining Money under False Pretenses | 2695 |
| Fraud (Other) | 2699 |
| Illegal Use of Credit Card | 2605 |
| **26003 - Fraud - Impersonation** | |
| Impersonation | 2604 |
| Identity Theft | 2609 |
| Pers Ident Info Obt/Poss/Trans W/I | 2610 |
| **26004 - Fraud - Welfare Fraud** | |
| Obtain Welfare | 2678 |
| **26005 - Fraud - Wire Fraud** | |
| Fraud by Wire | 2608 |
| **26006 - Fraud - Bad Checks** | |
| Non-Sufficient Funds Checks | 2606 |
| No-Account Check | 2676 |
| Uttering & Publishing Check | 2693 |
| **27000 - Embezzlement** | |
| Business Property | 2701 |
| Interstate Shipment | 2702 |

**Panel 3**

| FILE CLASS OFFENSE/ARREST CHARGES | ARR CHG |
|---|---|
| Banking Type Institution | 2703 |
| Pub. Property (Federal, State, City) | 2704 |
| Postal | 2705 |
| Misappropriate Funds | 2798 |
| Embezzlement (Other) | 2799 |
| **28000 - Stolen Property** | |
| Sale of Stolen Property | 2801 |
| Interstate Transportation of | 2802 |
| Receiving | 2803 |
| Possessing | 2804 |
| Concealing | 2805 |
| Stolen Property (Other) | 2899 |
| **29000 - Damage to Property** | |
| Business Property | 2901 |
| Private Property | 2902 |
| Public Property | 2903 |
| Business Property with Explosives | 2904 |
| Private Property with Explosives | 2905 |
| Public Property with Explosives | 2906 |
| Destruction of Tombs/Memorials | 2995 |
| Throwing Stone, etc., at Train or Motor Vehicle | 2996 |
| Computer Used in Commission of Crime | 2997 |
| Destroy, Injure Prop. of Police or Fire Department | 2998 |
| Damage to Property (Other) | 2999 |
| **30001 - Retail Fraud-Misrepresent** | |
| Misrepresentation 1st Degree | 3071 |
| Misrepresentation 2nd Degree | 3072 |
| Misrepresentation 3rd Degree | 3077 |
| **30002 - Retail Fraud - Theft** | |
| Retail Fraud - Theft 1st Degree | 3073 |
| Retail Fraud - Theft 2nd Degree | 3074 |
| Retail Fraud - Theft 3rd Degree | 3078 |
| Retail Fraud-Manufacture/Sell/ or Possession of Theft Detection Device | 3080 |
| **30003 - Retail Fraud - Refund/Exchange** | |
| Refund/Exchange 1st Degree | 3075 |
| Refund/Exchange 2nd Degree | 3076 |
| Refund/Exchange 3rd Degree | 3079 |

**Panel 4**

| FILE CLASS OFFENSE/ARREST CHARGES | ARR CHG |
|---|---|
| **35001 - Violation of Controlled Substance Act** | |
| Hallucinogen - Manufacture | 3501 |
| Hallucinogen - Distribute | 3502 |
| Hallucinogen - Sell | 3503 |
| Hallucinogen - Possess | 3504 |
| Hallucinogen (Other) | 3505 |
| Hallucinogen - Use | 3506 |
| Heroin - Sell/Manufacture | 3510 |
| Heroin - Smuggle | 3511 |
| Heroin - Possess | 3512 |
| Heroin (Other) | 3513 |
| Heroin - Use | 3514 |
| Opium or Derivative - Sell | 3520 |
| Opium or Derivative - Smuggle | 3521 |
| Opium or Derivative - Possess | 3522 |
| Opium or Derivative - (Other) | 3523 |
| Opium or Derivative - Use | 3524 |
| Cocaine - Sell | 3530 |
| Cocaine - Smuggle | 3531 |
| Cocaine - Possess | 3532 |
| Cocaine - Use | 3533 |
| Cocaine - Other | 3534 |
| Synthetic Narcotic - Sell | 3540 |
| Synthetic Narcotic - Smuggle | 3541 |
| Synthetic Narcotic - Possess | 3542 |
| Synthetic Narcotic (Other) | 3543 |
| Synthetic Narcotic - Use | 3544 |
| Synthetic Narcotic - Manufacture | 3545 |
| Methamphetamine - Deliver | 3546 |
| Methamphetamine - Possess | 3547 |
| Methamphetamine - Use | 3548 |
| Methamphetamine - Manufacture | 3549 |
| Ecstasy - Deliver | 3556 |
| Ecstasy - Possess | 3557 |
| Ecstasy - Use | 3558 |
| Ecstasy - Manufacture | 3559 |
| Marijuana - Sell | 3560 |
| Marijuana - Smuggle | 3561 |
| Marijuana - Possess | 3562 |
| Marijuana - Producing | 3563 |
| Marijuana (Other) | 3564 |
| Marijuana - Use | 3565 |
| Marijuana-Illegal Sale of Medical | 3566 |
| Amphetamine - Manufacture | 3570 |
| Amphetamine - Sell | 3571 |
| Amphetamine - Possess | 3572 |
| Amphetamine (Other) | 3573 |

**Panel 5**

| FILE CLASS OFFENSE/ARREST CHARGES | ARR CHG |
|---|---|
| Amphetamine - Use | 3574 |
| Barbiturate - Manufacture | 3580 |
| Barbiturate - Sell | 3581 |
| Barbiturate - Possess | 3582 |
| Barbiturate - Other | 3583 |
| Barbiturate - Use | 3584 |
| LSD - Manufacture | 3585 |
| LSD - Sell | 3586 |
| LSD - Possess | 3587 |
| LSD - Use | 3588 |
| LSD (Other) | 3589 |
| Crack - Sell | 3590 |
| Crack - Smuggle | 3591 |
| Crack - Possess | 3592 |
| Crack (Other) | 3593 |
| Crack - Use | 3594 |
| Drug, Illegal Use of | 3595 |
| Ephedrine/Pseudo > 12 grams poss | 3596 |
| Delivery Imitation Controlled Subs. | 3597 |
| Narc. Drugs, Fraud Procurement of | 3598 |
| Dangerous Drugs (Other) | 3599 |
| **35002 - Narcotic Equipment** | |
| Violations | 3550 |
| Operating/Maintaining Meth Lab | 3551 |
| Opr/Maint Meth Lab in Presense of Minor | 3552 |
| Firearm/Harmful Device | 3553 |
| Opr/Maint Meth Lab Near Specified Places | 3554 |
| Opr/Maint Meth Lab involving Hazardous Waste | 3555 |
| **36001 - Sexual Penetration - Nonforcible - Blood/Affinity** | |
| (CSC 1st/3rd degree) | 3691 |
| **36002 - Sexual Penetration Nonforcible - Other** | |
| (CSC 1st/3rd degree) | 3692 |
| **36003 - Peeping Tom** | |
| Peeping Tom | 3611 |

# MICR ARREST CHARGE CODES

RI-1 (Rev. 03/11)
Michigan State Police

## 36004 - Sex Offense - Other

| FILE CLASS OFFENSE/ARREST CHARGES | ARR CHG |
|---|---|
| Indecent Exposure | 3605 |
| Bestiality | 3606 |
| Seduction of Adult | 3608 |
| Gross Indecency | 3696 |
| Sex Offense (Other) | 3699 |

## 37000 - Obscenity

| FILE CLASS OFFENSE/ARREST CHARGES | ARR CHG |
|---|---|
| Obscene Material - Mfg./Publish | 3701 |
| Obscene Material - Sell | 3702 |
| Obscene Material - Mailing | 3703 |
| Obscene Material - Possess | 3704 |
| Obscene Material - Distribute | 3705 |
| Obscene Material - Transport | 3706 |
| Obscene Communication | 3707 |
| Obscenity (Other) | 3799 |

## 38001 - Family - Abuse/Neglect Nonviolent

| FILE CLASS OFFENSE/ARREST CHARGES | ARR CHG |
|---|---|
| Cruelty Toward Child/Nonviolent | 3802 |
| Cruelty Toward Spouse/Nonviolent | 3803 |
| Neglect Child | 3806 |
| Cruelty/Neglect (Other) | 3898 |

## 38002 - Family - Nonsupport

| FILE CLASS OFFENSE/ARREST CHARGES | ARR CHG |
|---|---|
| Neglect Family/Nonsupport Felony | 3801 |
| Non-Payment of Alimony | 3807 |
| Non-Support of Parents | 3808 |

## 38003 - Family - Other

| FILE CLASS OFFENSE/ARREST CHARGES | ARR CHG |
|---|---|
| Bigamy - Polygamy | 3804 |
| Contributing to Delinquency of Minor (Excluding Alcohol) | 3805 |
| Failing to Report Child Abuse | 3871 |
| Family Offense (Other) | 3899 |

## 39001 - Gambling - Betting/Wagering

| FILE CLASS OFFENSE/ARREST CHARGES | ARR CHG |
|---|---|
| Card Game - Playing | 3903 |
| Dice Game - Playing | 3906 |
| Lottery - Planning | 3917 |
| Gambling (Other) | 3999 |

## 39002 - Gambling - Operating/Promoting/Assisting

| FILE CLASS OFFENSE/ARREST CHARGES | ARR CHG |
|---|---|
| Bookmaking | 3901 |
| Card Game - Operating | 3902 |
| Card Game | 3904 |
| Dice Game - Operating | 3905 |
| Dice Game | 3907 |
| Lottery - Operating | 3915 |
| Lottery - Runner | 3916 |
| Lottery | 3918 |
| Transmit Wager Information | 3920 |
| Establish Gambling Places | 3921 |
| License/Rule Violations | 3970 |
| Gambling Activities Felony | 3971 |
| Gambling Activities Misdemeanor | 3972 |

## 39003 - Gambling - Equip. Violations

| FILE CLASS OFFENSE/ARREST CHARGES | ARR CHG |
|---|---|
| Gambling Device - Possess | 3908 |
| Gambling Device - Transport | 3909 |
| Gambling Device Not Registered | 3910 |
| Gambling Device | 3911 |
| Gambling Goods - Possess | 3912 |
| Gambling Goods - Transport | 3913 |
| Gambling Goods | 3914 |

## 39004 - Gambling - Sports Tampering

| FILE CLASS OFFENSE/ARREST CHARGES | ARR CHG |
|---|---|
| Sports Tampering | 3919 |

## 40001 - Commercialized Sex

| FILE CLASS OFFENSE/ARREST CHARGES | ARR CHG |
|---|---|
| Prostitution - Homosexual | 4003 |
| Prostitution | 4004 |

## 40002 - Commercialized Sex - Assist/Promoting Prostitution

| FILE CLASS OFFENSE/ARREST CHARGES | ARR CHG |
|---|---|
| Keeping House of Ill Fame | 4001 |
| Procure for Prostitute - Pimping | 4002 |
| Frequent House of Ill Fame | 4005 |
| Transport Female Interstate for Immoral Purpose | 4006 |
| Commercial Sex (Other) | 4099 |

## 41001 - Liquor License-Establishment

| FILE CLASS OFFENSE/ARREST CHARGES | ARR CHG |
|---|---|
| Violation of Liquor Control Laws | 4171 |

## 41002 - Liquor Violations - Other

| FILE CLASS OFFENSE/ARREST CHARGES | ARR CHG |
|---|---|
| Manufacture | 4101 |
| Sell | 4102 |
| Transport (Open Container, etc.) | 4103 |
| Poss. of Alcohol (Liquor in MV) | 4104 |
| Minor Misrepresenting Age | 4105 |
| Minor in Possession in MV | 4195 |
| Minor Poss/Cons/Purch; Attempts | 4196 |
| Minor Refusing PBT, Non-Driving | 4197 |
| Furnishing Alcohol to a Minor | 4198 |
| Liquor Violations (Other) | 4199 |

## 42000 - Drunkenness - Except OUIL

| FILE CLASS OFFENSE/ARREST CHARGES | ARR CHG |
|---|---|
| Drunkenness (All Criminal) | 4299 |

## 48000 - Obstructing Police

| FILE CLASS OFFENSE/ARREST CHARGES | ARR CHG |
|---|---|
| Resisting Officer | 4801 |
| Obstructing Criminal Investigation | 4802 |
| Making False Report | 4803 |
| Evidence Destroying | 4804 |
| Witness - Dissuading | 4805 |
| Witness - Deceiving | 4806 |
| Refusing to Assist Officer | 4807 |
| Compounding Crime | 4808 |
| Unauth. Communication/Prisoner | 4809 |
| Illegal Arrest | 4810 |
| Crossing Police Lines | 4811 |
| Failure to Report Crime | 4812 |
| Failing to Move On | 4813 |
| False Personation/Wearing Badge or Uniform of State Policeman | 4872 |
| False Personation of Police Officer | 4873 |
| Police Radio in Vehicle | 4874 |
| Police Radio Receiver in a MV | 4876 |
| Fleeing or Eluding (Felony) | 4877 |
| Obstructing Police and/or Fireman | 4898 |
| Obstructing Police (Other) | 4899 |

## 49000 - Escape/Flight

| FILE CLASS OFFENSE/ARREST CHARGES | ARR CHG |
|---|---|
| Escape - Prison | 4901 |
| Flight to Avoid Prosecution, etc. | |
| Absconding, Flee or Elude | 4902 |
| Aiding Prisoner Escape | 4903 |
| Harboring (Escapee or Fugitive) | 4904 |
| Escape - County Jail/Work Farm | 4971 |
| Escape Mental Institution - Crim. | 4975 |
| Breaking While En Route - Awaiting Court | 4976 |
| Escape - Youth Home, Youth Training Camp, etc. | 4991 |
| Fugitive | 4998 |
| Escape/Flight (Other) | 4999 |

## 50000 - Obstructing Justice

| FILE CLASS OFFENSE/ARREST CHARGES | ARR CHG |
|---|---|
| Bail - Secured Bond | 5001 |
| Bail - Personal Recognizance | 5002 |
| Perjury | 5003 |
| Subornation of Perjury | 5004 |
| Contempt of Court | 5005 |
| Obstructing Justice | 5006 |
| Obstructing Court Order | 5007 |
| Judicial Officer Misconduct | 5008 |
| Contempt of Congress | 5009 |
| Contempt of Legislature | 5010 |
| Parole Violation | 5011 |
| Probation Violation | 5012 |
| Conditional Release Violation | 5013 |
| Mandatory Release Violation | 5014 |
| Failure to Appear | 5015 |
| Violation of Preliminary Injunctive Order (Peace Bond) | |
| Failure to Register (Sex Offender) | 5070 |
| Failure to Comply with Reporting Duties (Sex Offender) | 5089 |
| Failure to Sign Registration (Sex Offender) | 5090 |
| Student Safety Zone - | 5091 |
| Work/Loitering Violation | 5092 |
| Obstruct (Other) | 5099 |

## 51000 - Bribery

| FILE CLASS OFFENSE/ARREST CHARGES | ARR CHG |
|---|---|
| Bribe - Giving | 5101 |
| Bribe - Offering | 5102 |
| Bribe - Receiving | 5103 |
| Bribe (Other) | 5104 |
| Conflict of Interest | 5105 |
| Gratuity - Giving | 5106 |
| Gratuity - Offering | 5107 |
| Gratuity - Receiving | 5108 |
| Gratuity (Other) | 5109 |
| Kickback - Giving | 5110 |
| Kickback - Offering | 5111 |
| Kickback - Receiving | 5112 |
| Kickback (Other) | 5113 |
| Bribery (Other) | 5199 |

## 52001 - Weapons Offense - Concealed

| FILE CLASS OFFENSE/ARREST CHARGES | ARR CHG |
|---|---|
| Altering Identification | 5201 |
| Carrying Concealed | 5202 |
| Carrying Prohibited | 5203 |
| Safety Inspection & Reg. Violation | 5210 |
| Possession of Weapon | 5212 |
| Selling & Purchase Violations | 5214 |
| Short Barreled Shotgun or Rifle | |
| Mfg., Sell, Offer Sale, Possess | 5273 |
| Possession of Firearm in Commission of Crime | 5275 |
| Carrying Pistol-Free Zone | 5287 |
| Concealed Pistol Permit Violations | 5288 |
| Firearm in Auto (CCW) | 5295 |
| Possession or Use of Firearm While Under Influence of Liquor/Drugs | 5297 |
| Weapons Concealed (Other) | 5289 |

## 52002 - Weapons Off - Explosives

| FILE CLASS OFFENSE/ARREST CHARGES | ARR CHG |
|---|---|
| Explosives (Bombs) - Teaching Use | 5204 |
| Explosives (Bombs) - Transporting | 5205 |
| Explosives (Bombs) - Using | 5206 |
| Incendiary Device - Possess | 5207 |
| Incendiary Device - Using | 5208 |
| Incendiary Device - Teaching Use | 5209 |
| Explosives - Mfg., Sale, Furnish | 5279 |
| Explosives (Bombs) Posses | 5281 |

RI-1 (Rev. 03/11)
Michigan State Police

# MICR ARREST CHARGE CODES

| FILE CLASS OFFENSE/ARREST CHARGES | ARR CHG |
|---|---|
| Fireworks - Possess, Sale, Use or Furnish | 5282 |
| Illegal Poss./Use of Blank Pistol | 5283 |
| Weapons Explosives (Other) | 5296 |
| **52003 - Weapons Offense - Other** | |
| Weapons, Firing (Include Careless, Reckless, Heedless Use) | 5213 |
| Weapons Offense (Other) | 5299 |
| **53001 - Disorderly Conduct** | |
| Disorderly Conduct | 5311 |
| Disturbing the Peace | 5312 |
| Affray, Jostling, Roughing Crowd | 5374 |
| Indecent, Immoral, Obscene or Vulgar Language | 5375 |
| Disorderly Conduct (Other) | 5393 |
| **53002 - Public Peace - Other** | |
| Anarchism | 5301 |
| Riot - Inciting | 5302 |
| Riot - Engaging In | 5303 |
| Riot - Interfere Fireman | 5304 |
| Riot - Interfere Officer | 5305 |
| Riot - (Other) | 5306 |
| Assembly - Unlawful | 5307 |
| False Fire Alarm | 5308 |
| Harassing Communications | 5309 |
| Telephone Used for Obscene Calls | 5372 |
| Public Peace (Other) | 5399 |
| **54001 - Hit & Run M/V Accident** | |
| Failed to Stop and Identify | 8011 |
| Failed to Give Assistance | 8012 |
| Accident, Failed to Report | 8013 |
| **54002 - OUI of Liquor or Drugs** | |
| Operating with BAC of .17% or more | 8027 |
| Operating with BAC of .08% or more | 8028 |
| Operating while in the Presence of Drugs (OWPD) | 8029 |
| Child Endangerment (Occupant Less Than 16) | 8030 |
| OUI of Drugs | 8031 |
| Permitted Persons UI Drugs Operate | 8032 |
| Ability Impaired by Drugs, Vol. | 8033 |

| FILE CLASS OFFENSE/ARREST CHARGES | ARR CHG |
|---|---|
| Let Intoxicated Person Operate M/V Causing Serious Injury (Alcohol) | 8036 |
| Let Intoxicated Person Operate M/V Causing Serious Injury (Drugs) | 8037 |
| OUI Alcohol | 8041 |
| Permitted Persons Under Influence of Alcohol to Operate | 8042 |
| Ability Impaired by Alcohol, Vol. | 8043 |
| Operating with B.A.C. of .10% or more Felony Long Term Incap. Injury | 8044 |
| Com. Drv. B.A.C. of .04%-.07% | 8047 |
| B.A.C. of Not Less Than 0.02% or more than 0.07% for Person Under 21 Years of Age | 8048 |
| OUIL-Dispose of Vehicle to Avoid Forfeiture | 8050 |
| OUI-Controlled Substance | 8053 |
| Off Road Vehicle | 5421 |
| Permitted Persons UI of Controlled Subs. to Operate Off Rd. Veh. | 5422 |
| Ability Impaired-Controlled Subs. Off Road Vehicle | 5423 |
| OUI-Intoxicating Liquor Off Road Vehicle | 5424 |
| Permitted Persons UI of Intoxicating Liquor to Operate Off Rd. Veh. | 5425 |
| Ability Impaired-Intoxicating Liquor Off Road Vehicle | 5426 |
| Operating with B.A.C. .10% or more Off Road Vehicle | 5427 |
| Operating UI Causing Serious Injury Off Road Vehicle | 5428 |
| OUI of Drugs - Snowmobile | 5451 |
| Permitted Persons UI Drugs Operate - Snowmobile | 5452 |
| Ability Impaired by Drugs, Voluntary - Snowmobile | 5453 |
| OUI of Alcohol - Snowmobile | 5461 |
| Permitted Persons UI Alcohol to Operate - Snowmobile | 5462 |
| Ability Impaired by Alcohol, Voluntary - Snowmobile | 5463 |
| "Per Se" - Violation of Operating with B.A.C. of .10% or More - Snowmobile | 5464 |
| Felony Long Term Incapacitating Injury - Snowmobile | 5467 |
| OUI of Drugs - Boat | 5471 |
| Permitted Persons UI of Drugs to Operate - Boat | 5472 |

| FILE CLASS OFFENSE/ARREST CHARGES | ARR CHG |
|---|---|
| Ability Impaired by Drugs, Voluntary - Boat | 5473 |
| OUI of Alcohol - Boat | 5481 |
| Permitted Persons UI of Alcohol to Operate - Boat | 5482 |
| Ability Impaired by Alcohol, Voluntary - Boat | 5483 |
| "Per Se" - Viol. of Operating with B.A.C. of .10% or More-Boat | 5484 |
| Felony Long Term Incapacitating Injury - Boat | 5487 |
| OUI-Controlled Substance Aircraft/Locomotive | 5491 |
| Permitted Persons UI Controlled Subs. Opr. Aircraft/Locomotive | 5492 |
| Ability Impaired Controlled Subs. Aircraft/Locomotive | 5493 |
| OUI-Intoxicating Liquor Aircraft/Locomotive | 5494 |
| Permitted Persons UI Intoxicating Liquor Opr. Aircraft/Locomotive | 5495 |
| Ability Impaired-Intoxicating Liquor Aircraft/Locomotive | 5496 |
| Unlawful Blood Alcohol Content Aircraft/Locomotive | 5497 |
| Operating W/I 8Hrs. of Consuming Intox. Liquor/Controlled Subs. | 5498 |
| **55000 - Health and Safety** | |
| Drugs - Adulterated | 5501 |
| Drugs - Misbranded | 5502 |
| Drugs - (Other) | 5503 |
| Food - Adulterated | 5510 |
| Food - Misbranded | 5511 |
| Food - (Other) | 5212 |
| Cosmetics - Adulterated | 5520 |
| Cosmetics - Misbranded | 5521 |
| Cosmetics - (Other) | 5522 |
| Large Carnivore Law Violations | 5559 |
| Dog Law Violations | 5560 |
| Animals at Large | 5561 |
| Viol. of Underground Storage Tank Regulatory Act | 5562 |
| Viol. of Above Ground Storage Tank Regulatory Act | 5563 |
| Sell/Give/Furnish Tobacco Products Persons Under 18 Years of Age | 5569 |

| FILE CLASS OFFENSE/ARREST CHARGES | ARR CHG |
|---|---|
| Persons Under 18 Years of Age in Possess/Use - Tobacco Products | 5570 |
| Aircraft Safety Violation | 5581 |
| Viol. of Boat & Navigation Laws | 5582 |
| Animals - Cruelty to | 5586 |
| Littering of Medical Waste | 5587 |
| Anhydrous Ammonia Possess/transport | 5588 |
| Anhydrous Ammonia Container - Unauthorized Tampering | 5589 |
| Inhalation of Chemical Agents | 5591 |
| Violation of Smokeless Tobacco Products Law | 5592 |
| Violation of Smoking Laws | 5593 |
| Agricultural Violation | 5598 |
| Health & Safety Violations (Other) | 5599 |
| **56000 - Civil Rights** | |
| Civil Rights - All Violations | 5699 |
| **57001 - Trespass - Other** | |
| Trespass - Other | 5707 |
| Trespass - Hunting & Fishing On Private Lands | 5767 |
| **57002 - Invasion of Privacy - Other** | |
| Divulge Eavesdrop Information | 5701 |
| Divulge Eavesdrop Order | 5702 |
| Divulge Message Contents | 5703 |
| Eavesdropping (Other) | 5704 |
| Eavesdrop Equipment | 5705 |
| Opening Sealed Communication | 5706 |
| Wiretap, Failure to Report | 5708 |
| Invade Privacy (Other) | 5799 |
| **58000 - Smuggling** | |
| Smuggle Contraband | 5801 |
| Smuggle Contraband into Prison County Jail | 5802 |
| Smuggle to Avoid Paying Duty | 5803 |
| Smuggling (Other) | 5899 |
| **59000 - Election Laws** | |
| Violation of Election Laws | 5999 |
| **60000 - Antitrust** | |
| Antitrust | 6099 |

| FILE CLASS OFFENSE/ARREST CHARGES | ARR CHG |
|---|---|
| **61000 - Tax/Revenue** | |
| Income Tax | 6101 |
| Sales Tax | 6102 |
| Liquor Tax | 6103 |
| Fuel Tax | 6104 |
| Cigarette Tax | 6173 |
| Tax/Revenue (Other) | 6199 |
| **62000 - Conservation** | |
| Out of Season, Over Limit, Etc.: Animals | 6201 |
| Fish | 6202 |
| Birds | 6203 |
| License - Stamp Violation | 6204 |
| Environment | 6205 |
| Uncased Gun in Vehicle (Conservation Violation) | 6272 |
| Hunting While Intoxicated | 6273 |
| Littering on Public or Private Property | 6274 |
| Snowmobile Violations (Except Trespass) | 6276 |
| Off Road Vehicle Violations | 6277 |
| Violation DNR Directors Order | 6280 |
| Violation DNR Conservation Order | 6281 |
| Viol. DNR Administrative Rule | 6282 |
| Viol. County Parks/Airport Rules/ Regulations | 6283 |
| Viol. Conservation Laws (Other) | 6299 |
| **63000 - Vagrancy** | |
| Curfew | 5313 |
| Loitering | 5314 |
| Vagrancy (Other) | 6399 |
| **70000 - Juvenile Runaway** | |
| Runaway | 7070 |
| **73000 - Miscellaneous Criminal** | |
| Miscellaneous Arrest | 7399 |
| **75000 - Solicitation (All Crimes Except Prostitution)** | |
| Solicitation | 7571 |
| **77000 - Conspiracy (All Crimes)** | |
| Conspiracy | 7771 |
| Conspiracy By Computer | 7772 |

# GLOSSARY

**14-Day Rule** A preliminary examination must be held within 14 days of an arraignment and may be adjourned for good cause only.

**180-Day Rule** Inmates of the Department of Corrections must be brought before the court for trial within 180 days. This allows a prisoner to serve his or her time concurrently if additional charges are brought against him or her. A good faith effort must be accomplished in bringing the inmate to trial within the time period.

**48-Hour Rule** Officers must secure a judicial determination of probable cause within 48 hours of a warrantless arrest in all but the most extraordinary situations.

**Absolute Immunity** Immunity given to judges, legislators, and prosecutors when they are performing their respective functions.

**Access** To instruct, communicate with, store data in, retrieve or intercept data from, or otherwise use the resources of a computer program, computer, computer system, or computer network.

**Accessory After the Fact** A person who knowingly helps a felon avoid discovery, arrest, trial, or punishment after the principal offense has occurred.

**Actus Rea** The guilty act or otherwise stated as a wrongful deed rendering the actor criminally liable, if combined with the *mens rea*.

**Adequate Care** The provision of sufficient food, water, shelter, sanitary conditions, exercise, and veterinary medical attention in order to maintain an animal in a state of good health.

**Adjudication** The trial phase of a juvenile criminal proceeding.

**Administration of Oath** The affiant for a search warrant must swear or affirm that the information contained in the affidavit is true to the best of his or her belief while holding up his or her right hand.

**Administrative Rules** Rules written and passed by executive branch agencies under statutory authority. These rules carry the force of law.

**Administrative Searches** Exception to the search warrant rule. A search pursuant to a statutory scheme to regulate a particular industry or business. The business must be a pervasively regulated industry and the search is to ensure compliance to the regulations.

**Admission** A partial admittance to crime involvement.

**Admission by Party-Opponent** A statement is not hearsay if the statement is offered against a party and is the party's own statement, in either an individual or a representative capacity. MRE 801(d)(2).

**Adulterated Food** Food that a person has placed pins, needles, razor blades, glass, or any other harmful substance in it.

**Affidavit for a Search Warrant** A written document prepared by a person called the affiant that contains facts by which the judge or magistrate may determine whether probable cause to search exists. The affiant (usually a police officer) must affirm under oath that the contents of the affidavit are true.

**Aggregate Amount** Any direct or indirect loss incurred by a victim or group of victims including, but not limited to, the value of any money, property or service lost, stolen, or rendered unrecoverable by the offense, or any actual expenditure incurred by the victim or group of victims to verify that a computer program, computer, computer system, or computer network was not altered, acquired, damaged, deleted, disrupted, or destroyed by the access. The direct or indirect losses incurred in separate incidents pursuant to a scheme or course of conduct within any 12-month period may be aggregated to determine the total value of the loss involved in the violation of this act.

**Aggravated Stalking** Stalking that also is in violation of a court order, where there is a previous stalking conviction, or where there was a credible threat against the victim or the victim's family.

**Aiding and Abetting** Intentionally assisting someone else in preparation to commit a crime or in committing a crime. Anyone who intentionally assists someone else in committing a crime is as guilty as the person who directly commits it and can be convicted of that crime as an aider and abettor.

**Alcoholic Liquor**    More than half of one percent of alcohol per volume.

**Analog**    An analog has a similar chemical structure to that of a schedule 1 or 2 controlled substance and has a narcotic, stimulant, depressant, or hallucinogenic effect on the nervous system.

**Animal**    Any vertebrate other than a human being.

**Animal Control Shelter**    A facility operated by a county, city, village, or township to impound and care for animals found in streets or otherwise at large contrary to any ordinance of the county, city, village, or township or state law.

**Animal Protection Shelter**    A facility operated by a person, humane society, society for the prevention of cruelty to animals, or any other nonprofit organization, for the care of homeless animals.

**Anticipatory Search Warrant**    A search warrant that is signed by a judge in anticipation of certain specific events occurring. If the events do not occur, the warrant is not valid.

**Antitheft Label**    A label containing the vehicle identification number affixed to a motor vehicle by the manufacturer in accordance with subtitle VI of Title 49 of the United States Code, 49 U.S.C. §§ 30101 to 33118.

**Any Bodily Alcohol Content (MIP)**    Either of the following: An alcohol content of 0.02 grams or more per 100 milliliters of blood, per 210 liters of breath, or per 67 milliliters of urine; or any presence of alcohol within a person's body resulting from the consumption of alcoholic liquor, other than consumption of alcoholic liquor as a part of a generally recognized religious service or ceremony.

**Apparent Authority**    When officers reasonably believed that the person who allowed them entry had common authority over the premises, the entry will be upheld even if the person lacked authority to grant such entry.

**Appears to Include a Child (child sexually abusive material)**    A depiction that appears to include, or conveys the impression that it includes, a person who is less than 18 years of age, and the depiction meets either of the following conditions: it was created using a depiction of any part of an actual person under the age of 18 or it was not created using a depiction of any part of an actual person under the age of 18, but all of the following apply to that depiction: the average individual, applying contemporary community standards, would find the depiction, taken as a whole, appeals to the prurient interest; the reasonable person would find the depiction, taken as a whole, lacks serious literary, artistic, political, or scientific value; and the depiction depicts or describes a listed sexual act in a patently offensive way.

**Arraignment**    The first appearance of the defendant before a judge or magistrate following his or her arrest. The defendant is formally advised of charges, an attorney may be appointed, and bond is set.

**Arraignment on the Information**    Occurs after bindover in a felony or circuit court misdemeanor.

**Arrest**    The taking, seizing, or detaining another person by either touching or putting hands on that person, or by any act that indicates an intention to take him or her into custody and subjects the person arrested to the actual control and will of the person making the arrest and must be so understood by the person arrested.

**Arrest Card**    A paper form or an electronic format prescribed by the department that facilitates the collection and compilation of criminal and juvenile arrest history record information and biometric data.

**Arson**    Willfully or maliciously, without just cause or excuse, starting a fire or doing anything that could result in the starting of a fire.

**Assault**    An attempt to commit a battery or an illegal act that caused victim to reasonably fear a battery. The defendant must, at the time of the assault, have the ability, appeared to have the ability, or thought he or she had the ability to commit a battery.

*Aggravated Assault* An assault and battery where physical injury occurs requiring immediate medical attention or that causes disfigurement or impairment.

*Assault with a Dangerous Weapon*    An assault where the suspect is armed with a dangerous weapon.

*Assault with the Intent to Do Great Bodily Harm Less Than Murder*    An assault with the intent to cause great bodily harm, but not the intent to kill. Actual injury is not necessary.

*Assault with the Intent to Maim* An assault with the intent to maim or disfigure that includes cutting out or maiming the tongue, putting out or destroying an eye, cutting or slitting or mutilating the nose or lips, or cutting off or disabling a limb, organ, or member.

*Assault with the Intent to Murder* An assault where the suspect intended to kill the victim without justification.

**Attorney General Opinions** Opinions issued by the Michigan Attorney General that answer a specific question posed by a member of the executive branch or the Legislature. Attorney General Opinions may be formal or informal. Informal opinions only provide legal guidance and are not binding. Formal opinions are published as a matter of public record and are binding on the executive branch of state government. Formal opinions are given deference by the courts, but they are not binding on the courts.

**Attempt** The defendant intended to commit a crime and took some action toward committing the offense but failed in completing it. An attempt goes beyond mere preparation to the point where the crime would have been completed if it had not been interrupted by outside circumstances.

**Audibly Impaired** The inability to hear air conduction thresholds at an average of 40 decibels or greater in the individual's better ear.

**Audiovisual Recording Function** The capability of a device to record or transmit a motion picture or any part of a motion picture by technological means.

**Authority**

*Actual Authority* A person who has access and control over a premise.

*Apparent Authority* If a person did not have the actual authority to give consent to search, the search will still be valid if the officer at the time of the entry reasonably believed that the person who is allowing him or her entry had common authority over the premises.

**Automated Sales Suppression Device** A software program carried on a memory stick or removable compact disc, accessed through an internet link, or accessed through any other means, that falsifies the electronic records of electronic cash registers and other point-of-sale systems, including, but not limited to, transaction data and transaction reports. See *zapper.*

**Automobile Exception** An exception to the search warrant rule where exigent circumstances automatically occur with a vehicle due to its mobility. If an officer possesses probable cause to believe that a vehicle contains contraband, the vehicle can be searched without a warrant. Also referred to as Probable Cause and Exigent Circumstances.

**Battery** A forceful, violent or offensive touching of the person or something closely connected with the victim.

**Best Evidence Rule** To prove the content of a writing, recording, or photograph, the original writing, recording, or photograph is required, except as otherwise provided by the rules or by the statute.

*Writings and Recordings* Consist of letters, words, or numbers, or their equivalent, set down by handwriting, typewriting, printing, photostating, photographing, magnetic impulse, mechanical or electronic recording, or other form of data compilation.

*Photographs* Include still photographs, X-ray films, videotapes, and motion pictures.

*Originals* The writing or recording itself or any counterpart intended to have the same effect by a person executing or issuing it. An "original" of a photograph includes the negative or any print therefrom. If data are stored in a computer or similar device, any printout or other output readable by sight, shown to reflect the data accurately, is an "original."

*Duplicates* A counterpart produced by the same impression as the original, or from the same matrix, or by means of photography, including enlargements and miniatures, or by mechanical or electronic re-recording, or by chemical reproduction, or by other equivalent techniques, which accurately reproduces the original.

**Beyond a Reasonable Doubt** A prosecutor's burden of proof in a criminal trial. See *reasonable doubt.*

**Bills of Attainder** Laws enacted naming individuals or an ascertainable group designed to punish them without a trial.

**Billy** A small bludgeon that may be carried in the pocket.

**Biometric Data** All of the following: fingerprint images recorded in a manner prescribed by the department; palm print images, if the arresting law enforcement agency has the electronic capability to record palm print images in a manner prescribed by the department; digital images recorded during the arrest or booking process, including a full-face capture, left and right profile, and scars, marks, and tattoos, if the arresting law enforcement agency has the electronic capability to record the images in a manner prescribed by the department; and all descriptive data associated with identifying marks, scars, amputations, and tattoos.

**Blackjack** A weapon consisting of a lead slug attached to a narrow strip, usually of leather.

**Blind** Having a visual acuity of 20/200 or less in the individual's better eye with correction, or having a limitation of the individual's field of vision such that the widest diameter of the visual field subtends an angular distance not greater than 20 degrees.

**Bludgeon** A short club, usually weighted at one end or bigger at one end than the other, and designed for use as a weapon.

**Body Armor** Clothing or a device designed or intended to protect an individual's body or a portion of an individual's body from injury caused by a firearm.

**Body Cavity** Includes the interior of the human body, stomach, rectal cavity, and vagina of females.

**Body Cavity Search** The physical intrusion into the body cavity to discover any object concealed therein.

**Bomb or Bombshell** A hollow container filled with gunpowder or other explosive or combustible material and designed to be set off by a fuse or other device.

**Bond Requirements** Under the Eighth Amendment, bail cannot be excessive. The judge sets bond by looking at such factors as the nature of the offense, community ties, prior record and flight risk. There is no bond for murder or treason.

**Border Search** An exception to the Fourth Amendment's requirement of probable cause or a warrant for routine searches conducted at the border because of the Government's interest in preventing the entry of unwanted persons and effects. Under this exception, searches of people and their property at the borders are per se reasonable, meaning that they typically do not require a warrant, probable cause, or even reasonable suspicion. Border searches may only be conducted by persons with lawful authority to do so.

**Breach of the Security of a Database or Security Breach** The unauthorized access and acquisition of data that compromises the security or confidentiality of personal information maintained by a person or agency as part of a database of personal information regarding multiple individuals.

**Breaking** Some force must have been used but there is no requirement that anything was actually broken. Any amount of force is sufficient, including opening a door that is already partially open. Examples include opening a closed door, raising a window, or removing a screen.

**Building** Any structure regardless of class or character and any building or structure that is within the curtilage of that building or structure or that is appurtenant to or connected to that building or structure.

**Burden of Persuasion** A party must persuade the trier of fact to accept his or her argument.

**Burden of Producing Evidence** A party must produce enough evidence so a reasonable person viewing the evidence in the light most favorable to that party could find in that party's favor.

**Burden of Proof** The evidentiary burden that must be overcome to allow a party to prevail on legal matter. See **beyond a reasonable doubt, clear and convincing evidence**, and **preponderance of the evidence**.

**Burglary Tool** Any tool or instrument or chemical, explosive, or other substance adapted and designed for breaking and entering. "Adapted and designed" means that the tools are not only capable of being used for a breaking and entering but are also designed or expressly planned to be used for this purpose.

**Burn** Setting fire to or doing any act that results in the starting of a fire, or aiding, counseling, inducing, persuading, or procuring another to do such an act.

**Caregiver of a Vulnerable Adult** An individual who directly cares for or has physical custody of a vulnerable adult.

**Carjacking** The taking of a motor vehicle from another person by force or violence, by threat of force or violence, or by putting the victim in fear. The vehicle was taken from the victim, a passenger, or other person with lawful possession.

**Chain of Custody** The one who offers real evidence must account for the custody of the evidence from the moment it reaches his or her custody until the moment it is offered into evidence.

**Challenge for Cause** The exclusion of a prospective juror based on an argument that the juror cannot be impartial because of some prejudice, bias, or interest.

**Character Evidence** Evidence of a person's character or a trait of character is not admissible for the purpose of proving action in conformity therewith on a particular occasion, except:

- *Character of Accused* Evidence of a pertinent trait of character offered by an accused, or by the prosecution to rebut the same; or if evidence of a trait of character of the alleged victim of the crime is offered by the accused and admitted as provided below, evidence of a trait of character for aggression of the accused offered by the prosecution.

- *Character of Alleged Victim of Homicide* When self-defense is an issue in a charge of homicide, evidence of a trait of character for aggression of the alleged victim of the crime offered by an accused, or evidence offered by the prosecution to rebut the same, or evidence of a character trait of peacefulness of the alleged victim offered by the prosecution in a charge of homicide to rebut evidence that the alleged victim was the first aggressor.

- *Character of Alleged Victim of Sexual Conduct Crime* In a prosecution for criminal sexual conduct, evidence of the alleged victim's past sexual conduct with the defendant and evidence of specific instances of sexual activity showing the source or origin of semen, pregnancy, or disease;

**Chemical Irritant** A solid, liquid, or gas that, through its chemical or physical properties alone or in combination with other substances, can be used to produce an irritant effect in humans, animals, or plants.

**Chemical Tests Rights** Rights given to a driver suspected of consuming alcoholic liquor or a controlled substance prior to the administration of a breath, blood, or urine chemical test.

**Child** A person younger than 18 years old who is not emancipated.

**Child Abandonment** The exposure of a child under the age of six, in any street, field, house, or other place, with intent to injure or wholly to abandon him or her.

**Child Abuse Suspect** Either a parent or guardian of a child, or a person who has care, custody, or authority over the child.

**Child Endangerment** When a person, whether licensed or not, operates a vehicle while intoxicated, visibly impaired, causing death, causing serious impairment of a body function, or with the presence of a controlled substance while another person who is younger than 16 years of age is occupying the vehicle.

**Child Kidnapping** Maliciously, forcibly, or fraudulently enticing away a child under 14 years of age with the intent to detain or conceal the child.

**Child Neglect** Harm or threatened harm to a child's health or welfare by a parent, legal guardian, or any other person responsible for the child's health or welfare that occurs through negligent treatment, including the failure to provide adequate food, clothing, shelter, or medical care, or placing a child at an unreasonable risk to the child's health or welfare by failure of the parent, legal guardian, or other person responsible for the child's health or welfare, to intervene to eliminate that risk when that person is able to do so and has, or should have, knowledge of the risk.

**Child Sexually Abusive Activity** Engaging with a child in sexual intercourse, erotic fondling, sadomasochistic abuse, masturbation, passive sexual involvement, sexual excitement, or erotic nudity or other sexual activity listed in MCL 750.145c.

**Child Sexually Abusive Material** Any depiction, whether made or produced by electronic, mechanical, or other means, including a developed or undeveloped photograph, picture, film, slide, video, electronic visual image, computer diskette, computer or computer-generated image, or picture, or sound recording which is of a child or appears to include a child engaging in a listed sexual act; a book, magazine, computer, computer storage device, or other visual or print or printable medium containing such a photograph, picture, film, slide, video, electronic visual image, computer, or computer-generated image, or picture, or sound recording; or any reproduction, copy, or print of such a photograph, picture, film, slide, video, electronic visual image, book, magazine, computer, or computer-generated image, or picture, other visual or print or printable medium, or sound recording.

**Child or Spousal Support**    Support for a child or spouse, paid or provided pursuant to state or federal law under a court order or judgment.

**Chop Shop**    Any area, building, storage lot, field, or other premises or place where one or more persons are engaged or have engaged in altering, dismantling, reassembling, or in any way concealing or disguising the identity of a stolen motor vehicle or of any major component part of a stolen motor vehicle or any area, building, storage lot, field, or other premises or place where there are three or more stolen motor vehicles present or where there are major component parts from three or more stolen motor vehicles present.

**Circuit Court**    Trial court responsible for civil suits in excess of $25,000, felony trials, serious misdemeanor trials, and issuing personal protection orders. These courts have supervisory control of district courts within their circuit.

**Civil Laws**    Laws concerned with private rights and remedies and designed to adjudicate differences between private persons.

**Clear and Convincing**    The burden of proof which requires the trier of fact to have less doubt and a firmer conviction about a decision than the usual civil standard of preponderance of the evidence. Party is usually relying upon a theory that is disfavored upon policy grounds (i.e., Mental Commitment Hearings).

**Coin Operated Device**    A device that provides some service after the coins are deposited.

**Commercial Film or Photographic Print Processor** A person or his or her employee who, for compensation, develops exposed photographic film into movie films, negatives, slides, or prints; makes prints from negatives or slides; or duplicates movie films or videotapes.

**Commercial Sexual Activity**    An act of sexual penetration or sexual contact for which anything of value is given or received by any person or the production, distribution, or promotion of child sexually abusive material.

**Competency**    Every person is competent to be a witness unless the court finds he or she does not have sufficient physical or mental capacity or sense of obligation to testify truthfully and understandably.

**Complaint**    A legal document consisting of essential facts constituting the offense charged.

**Computer**    Any connected, directly interoperable or interactive device, equipment, or facility that uses a computer program or other instructions to perform specific operations including logical, arithmetic, or memory functions with or on computer data or a computer program and that can store, retrieve, alter, or communicate the results of the operations to a person, computer program, computer, computer system, or computer network.

**Computer Network**    The interconnection of hardwire or wireless communication lines with a computer through remote terminals, or a complex consisting of two or more interconnected computers.

**Computer Program**    A series of internal or external instructions communicated in a form acceptable to a computer that directs the functioning of a computer, computer system, or computer network in a manner designed to provide or produce products or results from the computer, computer system, or computer network.

**Computer System**    A set of related, connected or unconnected, computer equipment, devices, software, or hardware.

**Confession**    The complete admittance to the involvement in a crime.

**Confidential Communication Privilege**    A married person or a person who has been married previously shall not be examined in a criminal prosecution as to any communication made between that person and his or her spouse or former spouse during the marriage without the consent of the person to be examined.

**Consent**    Authorization by a person with authority to conduct some action. Usually relates to the permission of a land or property owner to enter, remain on, search a premises or the permission of a private individual to engage in conduct with or search that individual.

**Consent-Once-Removed Doctrine**    Applies to the warrantless entry into a residence by backup officers summoned to assist an undercover officer with making an arrest when the undercover officer's initial entry into the residence was based on consent of someone with authority to consent. The doctrine is based on the theory that, because an undercover officer who establishes probable cause to arrest the suspect may in fact arrest the suspect then and there, the undercover officer should be entitled to call in the officer(s) with whom he is working to assist in the arrest.

**Consideration**  Any fee, cover charge, the storage of alcoholic liquor, the sale of food, ice, mixers, or other liquids used with alcoholic liquor drinks, or the furnishing of glassware or other containers for use in the consumption of alcoholic liquor in conjunction with the sale of food.

**Conspiracy**  Anyone who knowingly agrees with someone else to commit a crime is guilty of conspiracy.

**Constitutional Tort**  Any person who, acting under color of law subjects any other person to the deprivation of any rights, privileges, or immunities secured by the Constitution and laws, is liable to the party injured. Police officers are generally acting under color of state law.

**Container Approved by Law**  A container that was manufactured to satisfy the requirements for the storage and handling of anhydrous ammonia pursuant to the Michigan Administrative Code or its successor rule.

**Contemporary Community Standards**  The customary limits of candor and decency in this state at or near the time of the alleged violation of this section.

**Controlled Substance**

*Schedule 1*  substances have a high potential for abuse and has no accepted medical use.

*Schedule 2*  substances have a high potential for abuse, an accepted medical use, and abuse may lead to severe psychic or physical dependence.

*Schedule 3*  substances have potential for abuse, but less than schedules 1 and 2, has currently accepted medical use, and abuse may lead to moderate or low physical dependence or high psychological dependence.

*Schedule 4*  substances have low potential for abuse, current medical use, and abuse may lead to limited physical dependence or psychological dependence compared to schedule 3.

*Schedule 5*  substances have low potential for abuse, current medical use, and limited physical dependence or psychological dependence compared to schedule 4.

*Analog*  A substance with a similar chemical structure to that of a schedule 1 or 2 controlled substance and has a narcotic, stimulant, depressant, or hallucinogenic effect on the nervous system.

**Controlled Substance Offense**  A felony controlled substances violation—MCL 333.7401 to 333.7461.

**Conversion**  A type of larceny wherein property is voluntarily given to the defendant without an in then to transfer ownership or possessory rights and the defendant, by trick, fraud, pretense, or other wrongful act, interferes with the property rights of the owner.

**Convicted (SORA)**  A person who has a judgment of conviction or a probation order entered in any court having jurisdiction over criminal offenses; is assigned to youthful trainee status under MCL 762.11 to 762.15 unless a petition was granted under MCL 28.728 at any time allowing the individual to discontinue registration under this act; has an order of disposition entered under MCL 712A.18 if the individual was 14 years of age or older at the time of the offense, and the order of disposition is for the commission of an offense that would classify the individual as a tier III offender; or has an order of disposition or other adjudication in a juvenile matter in another state or country and the individual is 14 years of age or older at the time of the offense and the order of disposition or other adjudication is for the commission of an offense that would classify the individual as a tier III offender.

**Cooling Off Period**  A time that would enable a defendant to recover from the passion and provocation that inflamed him or her.

**Corporeal Lineups**  A police identification procedure by which the suspect in a crime is exhibited in person before the victim or witness to determine if he or she committed the offense.

**Corpus Delicti**  The "body of the crime" or substance of the crime. An evidentiary rule that requires the prosecutor to produce evidence that a crime has been committed before the prosecution can introduce the defendant's confession.

**Corrections Officer**  A prison or jail guard or other employee of a jail or a state or federal correctional facility, who performs duties involving the transportation, care, custody, or supervision of prisoners.

**Corrective Action**  Action taken by a licensee or a clerk, agent, or employee of a licensee designed to prevent a minor from further possessing or consuming alcoholic liquor on the licensed premises. Corrective action includes, but is not limited to, contacting a law enforcement agency and ejecting the minor and any other person suspected of aiding and abetting the minor.

**Counterfeit**    To make an unauthorized copy, imitation, or forgery of something with the intent to deceive or cheat someone by using the copy, imitation, or forgery as if it were real.

**Counterfeit Substance**    A controlled substance that bears the trademark, trade name, or other identifying marks of a manufacturer other than the person who in fact manufactured the substance.

**Course of Conduct**    A pattern of conduct composed of a series of two or more separate noncontinuous acts evidencing a continuity of purpose.

**Credible Threat**    A threat to kill another individual or inflict physical injury upon another individual that is made in any manner or context that causes the individual hearing or receiving the threat to reasonably fear for his or her safety or the safety of another individual.

**Credit Card**    Any instrument or device which is sold, issued, or otherwise distributed by a business organization or financial institution for the use of the person or organization identified on the instrument or device for obtaining goods, property, services, or anything of value on credit; or an instrument or device which is issued or otherwise distributed by an organization for the use of the person identified on the instrument or device for obtaining health care services or goods or reimbursement or payment for health care services or goods.

**Crime**    An act or omission forbidden by law that is not designated as a civil infraction, and that is punishable upon conviction by any one or more of the following: imprisonment; a fine other than a designated a civil fine; removal from office, disqualification to hold an office of trust, honor, or profit under the state; or other penal discipline.

**Criminal Laws**    Laws concerned with wrongs committed against society and not only against the victim.

**Cruel**    Brutal, inhuman, sadistic, or that which torments.

**Custody or Physical Control**    The forcible restriction of a person's movements or forcible confinement of the person so as to interfere with that person's liberty, without that person's consent or without lawful authority.

**Curtilage**    The land, yard, or buildings adjacent to a house, usually within an enclosure, that is protected by the Fourth Amendment just as the house is.

**Custody (under *Miranda*)**    The person is under arrest or the person's freedom has been deprived in any significant way.

**Custodial Detention**    An individual's being in a place of detention because a law enforcement official has told the individual that he or she is under arrest or because the individual, under the totality of the circumstances, reasonably could believe that he or she is under a law enforcement official's control and is not free to leave.

**Damage (arson)**    In addition to its ordinary meaning, includes, but is not limited to, charring, melting, scorching, burning, or breaking.

**Dangerous Animal**    A dog or other animal that bites or attacks a person, or a dog that bites or attacks and causes serious injury or death to another dog while the other dog is on the property or under the control of its owner. However, a dangerous animal does not include any of the following: an animal that bites or attacks a person who is knowingly trespassing on the property of the animal's owner; an animal that bites or attacks a person who provokes or torments the animal; an animal that is responding in a manner that an ordinary and reasonable person would conclude was designed to protect a person if that person is engaged in a lawful activity or is the subject of an assault; or livestock.

**Dangerous Stabbing Instruments**    A dangerous stabbing instrument is any object that is carried as a weapon for bodily assault or defense and that is likely to cause serious physical injury or death when used as a stabbing weapon.

**Dangerous Weapon**    Any object that is used in a way that is likely to cause serious physical injury or death. Some objects, such as guns or bombs, are dangerous because they are specifically designed to be dangerous. Other objects are designed for peaceful purposes but may be used as dangerous weapons. The way an object is used or intended to be used in an assault determines whether or not it is a dangerous weapon. If an object is used in a way that is likely to cause serious physical injury or death, it is a dangerous weapon.

**Data**    Computerized personal information.

**Dating Relationship**    Frequent, intimate associations primarily characterized by the expectation of affectional involvement. Does not include a casual relationship or an ordinary fraternization between two individuals in a business or social context.

**Deadly force**   Any force used by an officer that has a reasonable probability to cause death.

**Deaf**   The individual's hearing is totally impaired or the individual's hearing, with or without amplification, is so seriously impaired that the primary means of receiving spoken language is through other sensory input, including, but not limited to, lip reading, sign language, finger spelling, or reading.

**Debilitating Medical Condition (MMMA)**   One or more of the following: cancer, glaucoma, positive status for human immunodeficiency virus, acquired immune deficiency syndrome, hepatitis C, amyotrophic lateral sclerosis, Crohn's disease, agitation of Alzheimer's disease, nail patella, or the treatment of these conditions; A chronic or debilitating disease or medical condition or its treatment that produces one or more of the following: cachexia or wasting syndrome; severe and chronic pain; severe nausea; seizures, including but not limited to those characteristic of epilepsy; or severe and persistent muscle spasms, including but not limited to those characteristic of multiple sclerosis; Any other medical condition or its treatment approved by the department.

**Defense Attorney**   An attorney who safeguards guaranteed rights of the accused.

**Defrauding an Innkeeper**   To stay at a hotel, motel, inn, restaurant, or café as a guest and a suspect, with the intent to defraud, procured food, entertainment, or accommodation without paying and credit was not given by express agreement.

**Degrees of Affinity**   Relationship to an actor based on blood or marriage.

**Deinstitutionalization of Status Offenders**   A juvenile status offender cannot be placed in a secure institution, except those found in contempt of a court order and full due process protections are afforded.

**Delinquent**   A juvenile offender.

**Delivery of a Controlled Substance**   The transfer or attempt to transfer of a controlled substance to another person, where there is knowledge of the controlled substance and the intent to transfer said substance to another person.

**Deposition**   An interview under oath.

**Depository Institution**   A state or nationally chartered bank or a state or federally chartered savings and loan association, savings bank, or credit union.

**Device**   Includes, but is not limited to, an electronic, magnetic, electrochemical, biochemical, hydraulic, optical, or organic object that performs input, output, or storage functions by the manipulation of electronic, magnetic, or other impulses.

**Diligent Inquiry**   A diligent good faith effort to determine the age of a person, which includes at least an examination of an official Michigan operator's or chauffeur's license, an official Michigan personal identification card, or any other bona fide picture identification which establishes the identity and age of the person.

**Discovery**   The pretrial methods used to obtain facts and information about the case from the other party.

**Dispositional Phase**   Measures taken by the court after adjudication (similar to the sentencing phase in adult cases).

**Distribute or Promote Child Sexually Abusive Material**   Occurs when the suspect does one of the following: distributes, promotes, or finances the distribution or promotion of child sexually abusive material or activity; receives for the purpose of distributing or promoting child sexually abusive material; or conspires, attempts, or prepares to distribute, receive, finance, or promote child sexually abusive material or activity.

**District Court**   The court responsible for misdemeanor trials, small claims cases, civil suits under $25,000, and pretrial hearings for felonies and circuit court misdemeanors.

**DLAD Implied Consent Hearing**   If a person received a refusal for taking a chemical test, he or she has the right to an implied consent hearing with the Driver's License Appeal Division to determine if the refusal was properly taken.

**Dog Handler**   A peace officer who has successfully completed training in the handling of a police dog pursuant to a policy of the law enforcement agency that employs that peace officer.

**Domestic Relationship**   For purposes of the Domestic Violence Statute, a relationship that includes spouse or former spouse, resident or former resident of the same household, or persons who have had a child in common.

**Domestic Violence**   An assault or assault and battery that occurs within a domestic relationship.

**Double Jeopardy**   Double jeopardy is being tried twice for the same crime. Double jeopardy does not preclude trial by state and federal courts because they are separate sovereigns. In determining whether the same act constitutes a violation of two different crimes, the test to be applied is whether each crime requires proof of an additional fact that the other does not. Jeopardy attaches during different times in the judicial process. If the defendant is facing a jury trial, jeopardy attaches when the jury is impaneled and sworn. In a bench trial, jeopardy attaches when the first witness is sworn. If the defendant pleads guilty, jeopardy attaches when he or she is sentenced.

**Due Process**   The due process clauses prohibit the government from arbitrarily or unreasonably depriving a person life, liberty, or property. The essential purpose of due process is to ensure fundamental fairness. There are two types of due process: **procedural due process** and **substantive due process**.

**Duplicates**   Counterparts produced by the same impression as photocopy original, which accurately reproduces the original.

**Dwelling (for home invasion)**   A structure or shelter used permanently or temporarily as a place of abode, including an appurtenant structure attached to it.

**Dwelling House (under arson)**   Includes, but is not limited to, any building, structure, vehicle, watercraft, or trailer adapted for human habitation that was actually lived in or reasonably could have been lived in at the time of the fire or explosion and any building or structure that is within the curtilage of that dwelling or that is appurtenant to or connected to that dwelling.

**Dying Declaration**   In a prosecution for homicide or in a civil action or proceeding, a statement made by a declarant while believing that the declarant's death was imminent, concerning the cause or circumstances of what the declarant believed to be impending death.

**Eavesdrop or Eavesdropping**   To overhear, record, amplify or transmit any part of the private discourse of others without the permission of all persons engaged in the discourse. Neither this definition or any other provision of this act shall modify or affect any law or regulation concerning interception, divulgence or recording of messages transmitted by communications common carriers.

**Embezzlement**   The wrongful taking or conversion of money or property from a victim with whom the suspect had a relationship of trust.

**Electronic cash register**   A device that keeps a register or supporting documents through the means of an electronic device or computer system designed to record transaction data for the purpose of computing, compiling, or processing retail sales transaction data in whatever manner.

**Embezzlement**   A person who as the agent, servant, or employee of another person, governmental entity within this state, or other legal entity or who as the trustee, bailee, or custodian of the property of another person, governmental entity within this state, or other legal entity fraudulently disposes of or converts to his or her own use, or takes or secretes with the intent to convert to his or her own use without the consent of his or her principal, any money or other personal property of his or her principal that has come to that person's possession or that is under his or her charge or control by virtue of his or her being an agent, servant, employee, trustee, bailee, or custodian, is guilty of embezzlement.

**Embryo**   An unborn human from conception until the development of organs, approximately the eighth week of pregnancy. It use includes both viable and nonviable fetuses.

**Emergency**   A situation that leads an officer to reasonably believe a person is in need of aid.

**Emergency Exception**   Situations may allow officers to enter Fourth Amendment protected areas where they have reasonable (belief) suspicion that an emergency exists.

**Emergency Service Provider**   A uniformed employee or contractor of a fire department, hospital, or police station when that individual is inside the premises and on duty.

**Emotional Distress**   Significant mental suffering or distress that may, but does not necessarily, require medical or other professional treatment or counseling.

**Employee (SORA)**   An individual who is self-employed or works for any other entity as a full-time or part-time employee, contractual provider, or volunteer, regardless of whether he or she is financially compensated.

**Enclosed Locked Facility (MMMA)**   A closet, room, or other comparable, stationary, and fully enclosed area equipped with secured locks or other functioning security devices that permit access only by a registered primary caregiver or registered qualifying patient.

**Encrypted** Transformation of data through the use of an algorithmic process into a form in which there is a low probability of assigning meaning without use of a confidential process or key, or securing information by another method that renders the data elements unreadable or unusable.

**Entering** For breaking and entering charges, entry of any part of the suspect's body into the building is sufficient.

**Entering Without Breaking** When a suspect enters a building without breaking with the intent to commit a felony or a larceny.

**Enterprise** An individual, sole proprietorship, partnership, corporation, limited liability company, trust, union, association, governmental unit, or other legal entity or a group of persons associated in fact although not a legal entity. Enterprise includes illicit as well as licit enterprises.

**Entrapment** Occurs if (1) the police engage in impermissible conduct that would induce an otherwise law-abiding person to commit a crime in similar circumstances, or (2) the police engage in conduct so reprehensible that it cannot be tolerated by the court.

**Equal Protection** No person or class of persons shall be denied the same protection of the laws that is enjoyed by other persons or other classes in like circumstances in their lives, liberty, property, and in their pursuit of happiness.

**Erotic Fondling** Touching a person's clothed or unclothed genitals, pubic area, buttocks, or, if the person is female, breasts, or if the person is a child, the developing or undeveloped breast area, for the purpose of real or simulated overt sexual gratification or stimulation of one or more of the persons involved. Erotic fondling does not include physical contact, even if affectionate, that is not for the purpose of real or simulated overt sexual gratification or stimulation of one or more of the persons involved.

**Erotic Nudity** The lascivious exhibition of the genital, pubic, or rectal area of any person. As used in this subdivision, "lascivious" means wanton, lewd, and lustful and tending to produce voluptuous or lewd emotions.

**Escape** To leave without lawful authority or to fail to return to custody when required.

**Ethnic Intimidation** Occurs when a person causes or threatens to cause physical contact with a victim or damages, destroys or defaces or threatens damage, destruction, or defacement of property of the victim because of the race, color, religion, gender, or national origin of the victim, with the intent to intimidate or harass.

**Evidence** Any means by which an issue, fact, or the truth of the matter is proved or disproved.

*Circumstantial Evidence* A group of facts, that when linked together, give rise to a certain conclusion. Includes presumptions, inferences, habit, custom and many types of physical evidence. It is equally competent with direct evidence, and its relative weight is for the fact-finder to decide.

*Cumulative Evidence* Additional evidence tending to prove the same point.

*Demonstrative Evidence* Evidence used to illustrate something to the jury (i.e. photograph, sketches, maps, models of crime scene.)

*Direct Evidence* Evidence that, if believed, proves existence of fact in issue without inference or presumption. (i.e., witness identification, written statements by suspect).

*Material Evidence* Evidence having some logical connection with the facts of consequence or the issues.

*Probative Evidence* Evidence that tends to prove or disprove points in issue.

*Real Evidence* Tangible items (i.e., fingerprint, document, gun).

*Relevant Evidence* Evidence having any tendency to make the existence of any fact that is of consequence to the determination of the action more probable or less probable than it would be without the evidence.

*Secondary Evidence* Other forms of evidence may be allowed under the best evidence rule where it shows that the originals have been lost or destroyed.

*Testimonial Evidence* Evidence received from a witness. Witness testifies to what he or she directly saw or indirectly saw as to habit, custom, circumstantial evidence, etc.

**Excited Utterance** A statement relating to a starling event or condition made while the declarant was under the stress of excitement caused by the event or condition. (e.g., "My wife shot me!")

**Exclusion of Witnesses** At the request of a party, the court may order witnesses excluded so that they cannot hear the testimony of other witnesses, and it may make the order of its own motion. This rule does not authorize exclusion of a party who is a natural person, an officer or employee of a party which is not a natural person designated as its representative by its attorney, or a person whose presence is shown by a party to be essential to the presentation of the party"s cause.

**Exclusionary Rule**    When evidence has been obtained in violation of the accused's constitutional rights, the evidence will be excluded (also called suppressed) from court proceedings. The purpose of this rule is to deter illegal police conduct.

**Executive Branch**    The branch of government responsible for making treaties, appointing federal judges, and enforcing laws.

**Executive Orders**    Orders issued by the governor under authority granted by the Michigan Constitution. Executive Orders may (1) reorganize or rename departments or agencies within the executive branch; (2) reassign functions within the executive branch; (3) create or dissolve an executive body; or (4) proclaim or end a state of emergency. Executive Orders will eventually be codified as part of the MCL.

**Expert Opinion**    If the court determines that scientific, technical, or other specialized knowledge will assist the trier of fact to understand the evidence or to determine a fact in issue, a witness qualified as an expert by knowledge, skill, experience, training, or education may testify thereto in the form of an opinion or otherwise if the testimony is based on sufficient facts or data; the testimony is the product of reliable principles and methods; and the witness has applied the principles and methods reliably to the facts of the case. MRE 702.

**Ex Post Facto Laws**    Laws passed which are designed to punish conduct that occurred before the law was passed.

**Extortion**    The use of a threat to injure the victim, victim's property, victim's family (mother, father, husband, wife, or child) or falsely accusing the victim of a crime to obtain money or something of value from the victim or to compel the victim to act or refrain from acting in a certain manner. The threat must be stated or written down. By making the threat, the suspect intended either to get money or make the victim do something or refrain from doing something against his or her will. The threat may include a threat to expose any secret tending to subject a person to hatred, contempt, or ridicule.

**Fair Market Value**    The price the property would have sold for in the open market at that time and in that place if the following things were true: the owner wanted to sell but didn't have to, the buyer wanted to buy but didn't have to, the owner had a reasonable time to find a buyer, and the buyer knew what the property was worth and what it could be used for. Fair market value includes the reasonable and fair market value of repairing the damage or replacing the damaged property. The value will be considered at the time and in the place where the damage occurred.

**False Pretenses**    Includes, but is not limited to, a false, misleading, or fraudulent representation, writing, communication, statement, or message, communicated by any means to another person, that the maker of the representation, writing, communication, statement, or message knows or should have known is false or fraudulent.

**Federal Circuit Court of Appeals**    The courts to which cases are appealed after adjudication at the federal district court level.

**Federal District Courts**    The trial courts for the federal system.

**Federal Safety Certification Label**    A label affixed to a motor vehicle that certifies that the motor vehicle conforms to current safety standards at the time of production and displays the vehicle identification number.

**Felony**    An offense for which the offender may be punished by death or by imprisonment in state prison. "Felony" also means a violation of a penal law of this state for which the offender may be punished by death or by imprisonment for more than one year or an offense expressly designated by law to be a felony.

**Felony Murder**    Applies when a suspect commits murder while perpetrating or attempting to perpetrate arson, CSC first, second, or third degrees, child abuse first degree, major controlled substance offense, robbery, home invasion first or second degrees, larceny of any kind, extortion, kidnapping, or carjacking.

**Ferrous Metal**    A metal that contains significant quantities of iron or steel.

**Financial Harm**    Any adverse financial consequence, including criminal usury; extortion; and employment contracts that violate statutes regarding payment of wages and fringe benefits.

**Financial Institution**   One or more of the following, if located in or doing business in this state: an insured bank, as defined in section 3(h) of the Federal Deposit Insurance Act, 12 U.S.C. § 1813(h); a commercial bank or trust company, a private banker, an agency or branch of a foreign bank; a savings and loan institution; a thrift institution, a credit union; a broker or dealer registered with the Securities and Exchange Commission under the Securities Exchange Act of 1934, 15 U.S.C. § 78a-78nn; a broker or dealer in securities or commodities; an investment banker or investment company, a currency exchange; an insurer, redeemer, or cashier of traveler's checks, checks, or money orders; an operator of a credit card system; an insurance company; a dealer in precious metals, stones, or jewels; a pawnbroker; a loan, finance, or mortgage company; a travel agency; a licensed sender of money; or a telegraph company.

**Financial Transaction**   A purchase, sale, loan, pledge, gift, transfer, delivery, exchange, or other disposition of a monetary instrument or other property and, with respect to a financial institution, includes a deposit, withdrawal, transfer between accounts, exchange of currency, loan, extension of credit, purchase or sale of any stock, bond, certificate of deposit, or other monetary instrument, or any other payment, transfer, or delivery by, through, or to a financial institution, by whatever means effected.

**Financial Transaction Device**   An electronic funds card or ATM card, a credit card, a debit card, a point of sale card, or any other instrument, code number, PIN number, means of access to a credit or deposit account, a health insurance card, or an account, driver's license, or identification card that can be used either alone or with another device to obtain money, cash, credit, goods, services, or anything else of value, certify or guarantee that the device holder has available funds on deposit to honor a draft or check or to provide the device holder with access to an account in order to deposit, withdraw, or transfer funds to obtain information about a deposit account.

**Finding**   A determination by a judge or jury of a fact.

**Firearm**   A weapon from which a dangerous projectile may be propelled by an explosive or by gas or air. Firearm does not include a smooth bore rifle or handgun designed to shoot BBs not exceeding .177 caliber.

**First Purchaser**   The first buyer of a manufactured item that contains ferrous or nonferrous metal in a retail or business-to-business transaction. A person that purchases scrap metal, or other property described in section 10, in violation of this act, or an automotive recycler, pawnshop, scrap metal recycler, or scrap processor is not considered a first purchaser.

**Fleeing from Police**   Fleeing generally does not constitute a seizure for Fourth Amendment purposes. Fleeing from police may be a factor in allowing for an investigative detention.

**Foreign Protection Order (FPO)**   An injunction or other order issued by a court of another state, Indian tribe, or United States territory for the purpose of preventing a person's violent or threatening acts against, harassment of, contact with, communication with, or physical proximity to another person. Foreign protection order includes temporary and final orders issued by civil and criminal courts (other than a support or child custody order issued pursuant to state divorce and child custody laws, except to the extent that such an order is entitled to full faith and credit under other federal law), whether obtained by filing an independent action or by joining a claim to an action, if a civil order was issued in response to a complaint, petition, or motion filed by or on behalf of a person seeking protection.

**Force or Coercion**   Applies under the CSC law where the defendant used physical force, threats of force, surprise, or did something to make the victim reasonably afraid of present or future danger.

**Forced Labor or Services**   Labor or services that are obtained or maintained by or through causing or threatening to cause serious physical harm to another person; physically restraining or threatening to physically restrain another person; abusing or threatening to abuse the law or legal process; knowingly destroying, concealing, removing, confiscating, or possessing any actual or purported passport or other immigration document, or any other actual or purported government identification document, of another person; blackmail; or causing or threatening to cause financial harm to any person.

**Forgery**   Applies where a document is falsely made, altered, counterfeit or forged by the suspect who intended to injure or defraud another person.

**Former Testimony**   Testimony given as a witness at another hearing of the same or a different proceeding, if the party against whom the testimony is now offered, or, in a civil action or proceeding, a predecessor in interest, had an opportunity and similar motive to develop the testimony by direct, cross, or redirect examination. MRE 804(b)(1).

**Four Corners of the Affidavit**   The facts establishing probable cause must fall within the "four corners of the affidavit," that is, probable cause is established by facts within the affidavit.

**Fresh Pursuit**   An officer from another state to pursue felons into Michigan and make the arrest with the same arrest powers as those of Michigan peace officers. Once arrested, the person must be brought before the magistrate in the judicial district where the arrest was made pending extradition.

**Fruit of the Poisonous Tree**   Evidence obtained after illegal governmental action will be excluded. This includes not only materials subject to the exclusionary rule, but also subsequent confessions, admissions, identifications, and testimony obtained as a result of the primary taint. These "fruits" of the illegality will be excluded.

**Gambling**   When money or other valuable items are directly or indirectly taken, received, or accepted from a person with the agreement and understanding that they would be paid or delivered to another person contingent upon the result of any race, contest, game, or upon the happening of any uncertain event.

**Gang**   An ongoing organization, association, or group of five or more people, other than a nonprofit organization, that identifies itself by all of the following:

- A unifying mark, manner, protocol, or method of expressing membership, including a common name, sign or symbol, means of recognition, geographical or territorial sites, or boundary or location.
- An established leadership or command structure.
- Defined membership criteria.

**Gang Member or Member of a Gang**   A person who belongs to a gang.

**General Intent**   The intent to do the act that the law prohibits. It is not necessary for the prosecution to prove that the defendant intended the precise harm or the precise result, which occurred.

**General Warrants**   Warrants that do not limit the seizure only to those records connected to the criminal activity being investigated and which do not contain a particular description of things to be seized. Prohibited by the Fourth Amendment.

**Good Faith Exception**   An exception to the exclusionary rule where as long as the police acted in good faith and did not do anything illegal, the evidence should be admissible.

**Great Bodily Injury**   Serious impairment of a body function as that term is defined in section 58c of the Michigan Vehicle Code, 1949 PA 300, MCL 257.58l; or one or more of the following conditions: internal injury, poisoning, serious burns or scalding, severe cuts, or multiple puncture wounds.

**Governmental Unit**   A subdivision, agency, department, county, parish, municipality, or other unit of the government of the United States, this state, another state, or a foreign country.

**Habit**   A regular response to a repeated specific situation, a regular practice of meeting a particular kind of situation with a specific type of conduct, a set pattern or evidence of something that is done routinely or has been performed on countless occasions.

**Harass**   To engage in any conduct directed toward a guide, leader, hearing, or service dog that is likely to impede or interfere with the dog's performance of its duties or that places the blind, deaf, audibly impaired, or physically limited individual being served or assisted by the dog in danger of injury.

**Harassment**   Conduct directed toward a victim that includes, but is not limited to, repeated or continuing unconsented contact that would cause a reasonable individual to suffer emotional distress and that actually causes the victim to suffer emotional distress. Harassment does not include constitutionally protected activity or conduct that serves a legitimate purpose.

**Harmful Biological Substance**   A bacteria, virus or other microorganism or toxic substance derived from microorganism that can cause death, injury or disease in humans, animals or plants.

**Harmful Chemical Substance**   A solid, liquid, or gas that, alone or in combination with one or more other chemical substances, can cause death, injury, or disease in humans, animals, or plants.

**Harmful Radioactive Materials**   Material that is radioactive and can cause death, injury, or disease in humans, animals, or plants.

**Hazing**   An intentional, knowing, or reckless act by a person acting alone or acting with others that is directed against an individual and that the person knew or should have known endangers the physical health or safety of the individual, and that is done for the purpose of pledging, being initiated into, affiliating with, participating in, holding office in, or maintaining membership in any organization.

**Hazardous Waste** Waste or a combination of waste and other discarded material including solid, liquid, semisolid, or contained gaseous material that because of its quantity, quality, concentration, or physical, chemical, or infectious characteristics may cause or significantly contribute to an increase in mortality or an increase in serious irreversible illness or serious incapacitating but reversible illness, or may pose a substantial present or potential hazard to human health or the environment if improperly treated, stored, transported, disposed of, or otherwise managed. Hazardous waste does not include material that is solid or dissolved material in domestic sewage discharge, solid or dissolved material in an irrigation return flow discharge, industrial discharge that is a point source subject to permits under federal law, or is a source, special nuclear, or by-product material as defined under federal law.

**Hearsay** A statement, other than the one made by the declarant while testifying at the trial or hearing, offered in evidence to prove the truth of the matter asserted.

*Statement* Either the oral or written assertion of a person, or the nonverbal conduct of a person if it is intended by the person as an assertion.

*Declarant* A person who makes a statement.

**Heat of Passion** Actions that are the result of the temporary excitement by which the control of reason was disturbed, rather than of any wickedness of heart or cruelty or recklessness of disposition. The law, out of indulgence to the frailty of human nature, or rather, in recognition of the laws upon which human nature is constituted, very properly regards the offense as of a less heinous character than murder, and gives it the designation of manslaughter.

**Holding** A court's determination of a matter of law, a specific legal principle contained in an opinion, or a court's ruling concerning a specific question.

**Homicide** The killing of another human being.

**Honest Taking** An exception to larceny and theft laws wherein someone takes property because he honestly believes that he has the right to take or use it, even if the person who took it was mistaken.

**Hot Pursuit** Authorizes an officer to pursue a person suspected of committing a felony into a residence without a warrant where there are exigent circumstances.

**Ignition Interlocks** Devices attached to the ignition of a vehicle that will check a person's alcohol content before the vehicle can be started.

**Imitation Controlled Substance** A substance that is not a controlled substance or is not a drug for which a prescription is required under federal or state law, which by dosage unit appearance including color, shape, size, or markings, and/or by representations made, would lead a reasonable person to believe that the substance is a controlled substance.

**Immediately (SORA)** Within three business days.

**Immobilization** When a vehicle is held for a repeat offender violation under O.W.I. or DWLS violations.

**Impaired Driving** Due to the consumption of alcoholic liquor, a controlled substance, or other intoxicating substance, or a combination of alcoholic liquor, a controlled substance, or other intoxicating substance, the person's ability to operate the vehicle is visibly impaired.

**Impeachment** To attack the credibility of a witness.

**Implied Consent** A person who operates a vehicle upon a public highway or other place open to the general public or generally accessible to motor vehicles, including an area designated for the parking of vehicles, within this state is considered to have given consent to chemical tests of his or her blood, breath, or urine for the purpose of determining the amount of alcohol or presence of a controlled substance or any intoxicating substance or any combination in his or her blood or urine or the amount of alcohol in his or her breath if the person is arrested for specified offenses.

**Inchoate Offenses** Incomplete crimes or a step toward another crime where the step itself is punishable as a crime. See **attempt, conspiracy,** and **solicitation to commit a felony.**

**Independent Basis Test** Whether the in-court identification is due to the perceptions of the witness at the time of the offense or due to the improper suggestiveness of the lineup or show-up.

**Independent Test** A person who takes a chemical test administered at a peace officer's request shall be given a reasonable opportunity to have a person of his or her own choosing administer one of the chemical tests described in the statute within a reasonable time after his or her detention. The test results are admissible and shall be considered with other admissible evidence in determining the defendant's innocence or guilt. If the person charged is administered a chemical test by a person of his or her own choosing, the person charged is responsible for obtaining a chemical analysis of the test sample.

**Indictment**    A formal written accusation issued by a grand jury or similar entity charging one or more people with a crime.

**Indigent**    An individual who has been found by a court to be indigent within the last six months, who qualifies for and receives assistance from the department of human services food assistance program, or who demonstrates an annual income below the current federal poverty guidelines.

**Individual**    In the arson statute, means any person and includes, but is not limited to, a firefighter, a law enforcement officer, or other emergency responder, whether paid or volunteer, performing his or her duties in relation to a violation of this chapter or performing an investigation.

**Industrial or Commercial Customer**    A person that operates from a fixed location and is a seller of scrap metal to a scrap metal dealer under a written agreement that provides for regular or periodic sale, delivery, purchase, or receiving of scrap metal.

**Inevitable Discovery**    Any evidence obtained illegally may still be admissible if police were actively pursuing the evidence and the evidence would have been found anyway as a result of an ongoing investigation.

**Inference**    A conclusion reached by considering other facts and deducting a logical consequence from them.

**Information and Belief**    The belief something is true, but it is not based on firsthand knowledge.

**Injure**    To cause any physical injury to a dog that he or she knows or has reason to believe is a guide or leader dog for a blind individual, a hearing dog for a deaf or audibly impaired individual, or a service dog for a physically limited individual.

**Institution of Higher Education**    A public or private community college, college, or university or a public or private trade, vocational, or occupational school.

**Instrumentality**    An interest, real or personal property, or other thing of value, the use of which contributes directly and materially to the commission of an offense included in the definition of racketeering.

**Intentional Torts**    An act that is done with purpose. A typical example is where the officer strikes someone without justification.

**Interactive Computer Service**    An information service or system that enables computer access by multiple users to a computer server, including, but not limited to, a service or system that provides access to the Internet or to software services available on a server.

**Interim Bond**    If a person is arrested without a warrant for a misdemeanor or ordinance punishable by imprisonment for not more than one year or by a fine or both and the person arrested cannot be brought before a judge or magistrate immediately, the person may deposit an interim bond to guarantee the person's appearance. Bond may denied if, in the opinion of the arresting officer, the arrested person is under the influence of alcoholic liquor, a controlled substance or a combination of both; the person is wanted by police authorities to answer to another charge; the person is unable to establish or demonstrate his or her identity; it is otherwise unsafe to release him or her.

**Internet**    That term as defined in § 230 of Title II of the Communications Act of 1934, 47 U.S.C. § 230, and includes voice over Internet protocol services.

**Interrogation**    Questioning in a criminal investigation that may elicit a self-incriminating response from an individual and includes a law enforcement official's words or actions that the law enforcement official should know are reasonably likely to elicit a self-incriminating response from the individual.

**Interrogatories**    Written questions, submitted to a party who is to answer them as part of discovery under oath and signs a sworn statement that the answers are true. Interrogatories can only be required from a party of an action.

**Intervening Cause**    An event which occurs between the initial event in a sequence and the end result, thereby altering the natural course of events that might have connected a wrongful act to an injury.

**In the Course of Committing a Larceny of a Motor Vehicle**    Includes acts that occur in an attempt to commit the larceny, or during commission of the larceny, or in flight or attempted flight after the commission of the larceny, or in an attempt to retain possession of the motor vehicle.

**Intimate Part** The primary genital area, groin, inner thigh, buttock, or breast of a human being.

**Intoxicating Substance** Any substance, preparation, or a combination of substances and preparations other than alcohol or a controlled substance, that is either of the following:

- Recognized as a drug in the official United States pharmacopoeia, the official homeopathic pharmacopoeia of the United States, or the official national formulary.
- A substance, other than food, taken into a person's body, including, but not limited to, vapors or fumes, that is used in a manner or for a purpose for which it was not intended, and that may result in a condition of intoxication.

**Inventory Search** Police may make routine, warrantless searches of contents of any vehicle that lawfully comes into police custody as part of police care taking and as long as the search is in compliance with departmental policy.

**Investigatory Detention** A lawful detention where the officer has reasonable suspicion that a crime is afoot.

**Involuntary Manslaughter** Applies where a person acted in a grossly negligent manner or at the time of the act had the intent to hurt or injure another and these actions resulted in the death of another person.

**Jail** A facility that is operated by a local unit of government for the detention of persons charged with, or convicted of, criminal offenses or ordinance violations, or persons found guilty of civil or criminal contempt.

**Joint Access or Control** A person who possesses authority over premises or effects with one or more other persons has common authority to give consent. There must be a showing of mutual use of the property by persons generally having joint access or control so that each person has a right to permit inspection in his or her own right.

**Judicial Branch (interprets laws and treaties)** The branch of government that has jurisdiction in reviewing constitutional questions and treaties and interpreting the laws of the United States.

**Judicial Notice** An evidentiary shortcut where the court accepts certain facts without requiring formal proof. It is only permissible when the matter is not subject to reasonable dispute because the issue is generally known within the territorial jurisdiction of the court; or capable of accurate and ready determination by sources whose accuracy cannot reasonably be questioned (i.e., the City of Lansing is in Ingham County).

**Jurisdiction** Describes to power of a court to hear a certain subject matter or type of case.

**Juvenile History Record Information** Name; date of birth; personal descriptions including identifying marks, scars, amputations, and tattoos; aliases and prior names; social security number, driver's license number, and other identifying numbers; and information on juvenile offense arrests and adjudications or convictions.

**Kidnapping** Applies where a person forcibly confines or imprisons the victim against his or her will without legal authority and, during confinement, the suspect forcibly moved or caused the victim to be moved from one place to another for the purpose of kidnapping.

**Knock and Announce** Officers have the authority to break in or out of a building after giving notice of their authority and purpose and being refused admittance.

**Knock and Talk** A valid procedure, if done correctly, which involves going to the suspect house, engaging in conversation and attempting to gain consent to search. The mere fact that the officers initiated contact with a citizen does not implicate constitutional protections.

**Labeling Theory** In juvenile proceedings, the theory that if we label a juvenile as a criminal, then he or she will grow up to be a criminal. Some examples of the different terminology are:

- An offender is a delinquent, not a criminal.
- Officers will seek a petition, not request an arrest warrant.
- Juveniles are apprehended, not arrested.
- Juveniles must be forthwith turned over to their parents or the court, whereas an adult has to be brought to the court without unnecessary delay.
- The juvenile's guilt or innocence is determined in adjudication, not at a trial.
- After adjudication, the court will have a disposition, not a sentencing.

**Labor** Work of economic or financial value.

**Laboratory Equipment (controlled substances)** Any equipment, device, or container used or intended to be used in the process of manufacturing a controlled substance, counterfeit substance, or controlled substance analogue.

**Larceny** The suspect took someone else's property, without the owner's consent, with some movement of the property, intending to permanently deprive the owner of the property.

**Larceny by Conversion** Any person to whom any money, goods or other property, which may be the subject of larceny, shall have been delivered, who shall embezzle or fraudulently convert to his own use, or shall secrete with the intent to embezzle, or fraudulently use such goods, money or other property, or any part thereof, shall be deemed by so doing to have committed the crime of larceny and shall be punished as provided in the first section of this chapter.

**Larceny from the Person** Applies when the offense of larceny is committed by stealing from the person of another (pickpocket).

**Law Enforcement Identification** Any identification that contains the words "law enforcement" or similar words, including, but not limited to, "agent", "enforcement agent", "detective", "task force", "fugitive recovery agent", or any other combination of names that gives the impression that the bearer is in any way connected with the federal government, state government, or any political subdivision of a state government. However, law enforcement identification does not include "bail agent" or "bondsman" when used by a bail agent or bondsman operating in accordance with the law.

**Law Enforcement Official** Any of the following: a police officer of this state or a political subdivision of this state; a county sheriff or his or her deputy; a prosecuting attorney; a public safety officer of a college or university; a conservation officer of the department of natural resources and environment; an individual acting under the direction of a law enforcement official described above.

**Lay Opinion** A rational opinion based on the perception of a witness. The opinion is helpful for a clear understanding of the incident.

**Legislative Branch (lawmakers)** The bicameral branch of government responsible for making laws.

**Length of Detention** An investigative detention must be temporary and last no longer than is necessary to effectuate the purpose of the stop. In determining if the detention is too long, the court must examine whether police diligently pursued a means of investigation that was likely to confirm or dispel their suspicions quickly.

**Lesser Included Crimes** Crimes consisting of different degrees, where the fact finder may find the accused not guilty of the offense in the degree charged, but may find the accused person guilty of a lesser included offense, or of an attempt to commit that offense.

**Library (controlled substances)** A library that is established by the state; a county, city, township, village, school district, or other local unit of government or authority or combination of local units of government and authorities; a community college district; a college or university; or any private library open to the public.

**Listed Offense (SORA)** A tier I, tier II, or tier III offense. See Chapter 6, Registration of Sex Offenders, for a description of the tiers and offenses for each tier.

**Listed Sexual Act** Under the MCL 750.145c, the listed sexual acts include sexual intercourse, erotic fondling, sadomasochistic abuse, masturbation, passive sexual involvement, sexual excitement, or erotic nudity.

**Litter** Rubbish, refuse, waste material, garbage, offal, paper, glass, cans, bottles, trash, debris, or other foreign substances or a vehicle that is considered abandoned under MCL 257.252a.

**Livestock** Animals used for human food and fiber or animals used for service to human beings. Livestock includes, but is not limited to, cattle, swine, sheep, llamas, goats, bison, equine, poultry, and rabbits. Livestock does not include animals that are human companions, such as dogs and cats.

**Local Law Enforcement Agency** The police department of a municipality.

**Local Unit of Government** Any of the following: a city, village, township, or county; a local or intermediate school district; a public school academy; or a community college.

**Loiter (SORA)** To remain for a period of time and under circumstances that a reasonable person would determine is for the primary purpose of observing or contacting minors.

**Machine Guns**   Guns that fire more than one round with single pull of the trigger.

**Magistrate**   Magistrates assist the district court judge. They hear informal civil infraction hearings, issue search and arrest warrants, and set bail and accept bond.

**Major Felony**   A felony punishable by imprisonment for life, for life or any term of years, or for a statutory maximum of 20 years or more, or a violation of CSC 3rd degree.

**Major Felony Recording**   The interrogation recording required by statute or a duplicate of that recording.

**Make (child sexually abusive material)**   To bring into existence by copying, shaping, changing, or combining material, and specifically includes, but is not limited to, intentionally creating a reproduction, copy, or print of child sexually abusive material, in whole or part. Make does not include the creation of an identical reproduction or copy of child sexually abusive material within the same digital storage device or the same piece of digital storage media.

**Malicious Use of Phones**   Applies when a person maliciously uses any service provided by a communications common carrier with intent to terrorize, frighten, intimidate, threaten, harass, molest or annoy any other person, or to disturb the peace and quiet of any other person.

**Maliciously**   Any of the following done to a dog that he or she knows or has reason to believe is a guide or leader dog for a blind individual, a hearing dog for a deaf or audibly impaired individual, or a service dog for a physically limited individual:

- With intent to assault, beat, harass or injure a dog.
- With intent to impede or interfere with duties performed by the dog.
- With intent to disturb, endanger, or cause emotional distress to a blind, deaf, audibly impaired, or physically limited individual being served or assisted by a dog.
- With knowledge that the individual's conduct will, or is likely to harass or injure a dog.
- With knowledge that the individual's conduct will, or is likely to impede or interfere with duties performed by a dog.
- With knowledge that the individual's conduct will, or is likely to disturb, endanger, or cause emotional distress to a blind, deaf, audibly

impaired, or physically limited individual being served or assisted by a dog.

**Manufacture (controlled substance)**   The production, preparation, propagation, compounding, conversion, or processing of a controlled substance, directly or indirectly by extraction from substances of natural origin, or independently by means of chemical synthesis, or by a combination of extraction and chemical synthesis. It does not include repackaging, relabeling of a controlled substance or the performance of manufacturing activities performed by a preactitiononer or their agent in the performance of their professional practice or for research, training, or other activities if the substance is not offered for sale.

**Marihuana (MMMA)**   All parts of the plant Canabis sativa L., growing or not; the seeds thereof; the resin extracted from any part of the plant; and every compound, manufacture, salt, derivative, mixture, or preparation of the plant or its seeds or resin. It does not include the mature stalks of the plant, fiber produced from the stalks, oil or cake made from the seeds of the plant, any other compound, manufacture, salt, derivative, mixture, or preparation of the mature stalks, except the resin extracted therefrom, fiber, oil or cake, or the sterilized seed of the plant which is incapable of germination.

**Masturbation**   The real or simulated touching, rubbing, or otherwise stimulating of a person's own clothed or unclothed genitals, pubic area, buttocks, or, if the person is female, breasts, or if the person is a child, the developing or undeveloped breast area, either by manual manipulation or self-induced or with an artificial instrument, for the purpose of real or simulated overt sexual gratification or arousal of the person.

**Medical First Responder**   An individual who has met the educational requirements of a department approved medical first responder course and who is licensed to provide medical first response life support as part of a medical first response service or as a driver of an ambulance that provides basic life support services only. Medical first responder does not include a police officer solely because his or her police vehicle is equipped with an automated external defibrillator.

**Medical Records or Information**   Includes, but is not limited to, medical and mental health histories, reports, summaries, diagnoses and prognoses, treatment and medication information, notes, entries, and X-rays and other imaging records.

**Medical Use (MMMA)** The acquisition, possession, cultivation, manufacture, use, internal possession, delivery, transfer, or transportation of marihuana or paraphernalia relating to the administration of marihuana to treat or alleviate a registered qualifying patient's debilitating medical condition or symptoms associated with the debilitating medical condition.

**Mens Rea** Guilty mind.

**Mental Anguish** Under CSC law, mental anguish means extreme pain, extreme distress, or extreme suffering, either at the time of the incident or later as a result of it.

**Mentally Disabled** A person who has mental illness, is mentally retarded, or has a developmental disability.

**Mentally Incapable** When a person suffers from a mental disease or defect, which renders that person temporarily or permanently incapable of appraising the nature of his or her conduct.

**Mentally Incapacitated** When a person is temporarily incapable of appraising or controlling his or her conduct due to the influence of a narcotic, anesthetic, or other substance administered to that person without his or her consent, or due to any other act committed upon that person without his or her consent.

**Metallic Knuckles** Pieces of metal designed to be worn over the knuckles in order to protect them in striking a blow and to make the blow more effective.

**Minor** An individual younger than 18 years of age.

**Misdemeanor** A violation of a penal law of this state that is not a felony or a violation of an order, rule, or regulation of a state agency that is punishable by imprisonment or a fine that is not a civil fine.

**Misdemeanor Stalking** When a suspect has two or more willful, separate, and noncontinuous acts of unconsented contact with the victim. These contacts would cause a reasonable individual to feel terrorized, frightened, intimidated, threatened, harassed, and molested and cause the victim to feel terrorized, frightened, intimidated, threatened, harassed, and molested.

**Missing Senior or Vulnerable Adult** A resident of this state who is at least 60 years of age and is believed to be incapable of returning to his or her residence without assistance and is reported missing by a person familiar with that individual; or a **vulnerable adult**, as that term is defined, who is reported missing by a person familiar with that individual; or a person who is missing and suffering from senility or a physical or mental condition that subjects the person or others to personal and immediate danger.

**Mixture (controlled substance)** The combination of a controlled substance and a filler material such that a sample from anywhere in the mixture reasonably approximates in purity a sample taken elsewhere in the mixture and it is reasonably difficult to separate the drug from the filler material because of the mixing or blending of the two substances.

**Monetary Instrument** Coin or currency of the United States or another country, or group of countries, a traveler's check, personal check, bank check, money order, or investment security or negotiable instrument in bearer form or in any other form such that delivery is sufficient to pass title.

**Motion *in Limine*** A written motion to a judge requesting that the judge rule that certain evidence is admissible or inadmissible at trial.

**Motor Vehicle** All vehicles impelled on the public highways of this state by mechanical power, except traction engines, road rollers and such vehicles as run only upon rails or tracks.

**Moving Violation** An act or omission prohibited under Michigan law or a local ordinance substantially corresponding to this act that involves the operation of a motor vehicle, and for which a fine may be assessed.

**Muffler or Silencer** A device for muffling, silencing, or deadening the report of a firearm; a combination of parts intended for use in assembling or fabricating a muffler or silence; and a part intended only for use in assembling or fabricating a muffler or silencer.

**Municipality** A city, village, or township of this state.

**Named Product** Means either a product having a designated brand name, or a product having a street or common name with application sufficient to identify the product as a specific product within this state or within a local unit of government.

**Neglect** To fail to sufficiently and properly care for an animal to the extent that the animal's health is jeopardized.

**Negligence**

*Gross Negligence* More than carelessness. It means willfully disregarding the results to others that might reasonably follow from an act or failure to act.

*Ordinary Negligence* Means not taking reasonable care under the circumstances. A sensible person would have known that the actions could have caused injury.

*Slight Negligence* Doing something that is not usually dangerous.

**Negligent Homicide** A person was operating a motor vehicle in a negligent manner, which caused an accident that resulted in the death of another person.

**Neutral and Detached Magistrate** Search warrants may only be issued by a magistrate or judge who is neutral and detached. That is, the issuing person must be impartial, having no stake in the outcome of the case, any bias related to the case, or any role in the investigation of the case.

**No Account Check** Occurs when a person writes or delivers a check, draft, or money order that was drawn on a bank where the person did not have an account. The person must also have the intent to cheat or defraud someone.

**Non-Sufficient Funds (NSF)** Occurs when a person writes or delivers a check, draft, or money order that was drawn on a bank and at the time, the person knew there was not enough money or credit to pay the amount in full. The person must also have the intent to defraud or cheat someone.

**Nonferrous Metal** A metal that does not contain significant quantities of ferrous metal, but contains copper, brass, platinum group-based metals, aluminum, bronze, lead, zinc, nickel, or alloys of those metals.

**Notice to Appear** For minor offenses of 93-day misdemeanors or less, an appearance ticket may be issued in lieu of custodial arrest except in cases of domestic violence and PPO violations.

**Oath or Affirmations** The witness must declare that he or she will testify truthfully by oath or affirmation, administered in a form calculated to awaken his or her conscience and impress upon his or her mind with a duty to do so. MRE 603.

**Obstruct** In the resisting and obstructing context, obstruct includes the use or threatened use of physical interference or force or a knowing failure to comply with a lawful command.

**Official Proceeding** A proceeding heard before a legislative, judicial, administrative, or other governmental agency or official authorized to hear evidence under oath, including a referee, prosecuting attorney, hearing examiner, commissioner, notary, or other person taking testimony or deposition in that proceeding.

**Omission** Under the child abuse law, willfully failing to provide food, clothing, or shelter necessary for the welfare of the child or to abandon the child.

**Open Fields** Includes areas beyond the curtilage of the dwelling and are not protected by the Fourth Amendment.

**Open View** What a person knowingly exposes to the public, even in his or her own home, is not protected under the Fourth Amendment.

**Operate or Operating** Being in actual physical control of a vehicle regardless of whether or not the person is licensed under this act as an operator or chauffeur.

**Operating While Intoxicated (O.W.I.)** Means any of the following:

- The person is under the influence of alcoholic liquor, a controlled substance, or other intoxicating substance or a combination of alcoholic liquor, a controlled substance, or other intoxicating substance.
- The person has an alcohol content of 0.08 grams or more per 100 milliliters of blood, per 210 liters of breath, or per 67 milliliters of urine.
- The person has an alcohol content of 0.17 grams or more per 100 milliliters of blood, per 210 liters of breath, or per 67 milliliters of urine.

**Operator** A person, other than a chauffeur, who operates a motor vehicle upon a highway or street or operates an automated motor vehicle upon a highway or street.

**Opinion** A court's written statement explaining its decision in a case.

**Organization** A fraternity, sorority, association, corporation, order, society, corps, cooperative, club, service group, social group, athletic team, or similar group whose members are primarily students at an educational institution.

**Organized Retail Crime** The theft of retail merchandise from a retail merchant with the intent or purpose of reselling, distributing, or otherwise reentering the retail merchandise in commerce, including the transfer of the stolen retail merchandise to another retail merchant or to any other person personally, through the mail, or through any electronic medium, including the Internet, in exchange for anything of value.

**Owner**    A person who owns or harbors a dog or other animal.

**Pandering**    Applies to a person who entices a woman to become a prostitute.

**Parental Discipline**    Reasonable discipline by a parent, including physical force, that is not against the law.

**Parental Kidnapping**    Occurs when a parent or guardian takes and keeps a child for more than 24 hours with the intent to keep or conceal the child from another parent or legal guardian who had legal custody or visitation at the time.

**Passive Sexual Involvement**    An act, real or simulated, that exposes another person to or draws another person's attention to an act of sexual intercourse, erotic fondling, sadomasochistic abuse, masturbation, sexual excitement, or erotic nudity because of viewing any of these acts or because of the proximity of the act to that person, for the purpose of real or simulated overt sexual gratification or stimulation of one or more of the persons involved.

**Pat-Down**    Officers may pat the outer clothing of a person the officer has reasonable suspicion to believe may be armed and potentially dangerous. The purpose of the search is to look for weapons.

**Pattern of Racketeering Activity**    Not less than two incidents of racketeering to which all of the following characteristics apply:

- The incidents have the same or a substantially similar purpose, result, participant, victim, or method of commission, or are otherwise interrelated by distinguishing characteristics and are not isolated acts.
- The incidents amount to or pose a threat of continued criminal activity.
- At least one of the incidents occurred within this state on or after the effective date of the amendatory act that added this section, and the last of the incidents occurred within 10 years after the commission of any prior incident, excluding any period of imprisonment served by a person engaging in the racketeering activity.

**Peace Bonds**    A district or municipal judge may require a person to post a security to keep the peace.

**Peace Officer**    Any of the following:

- A sheriff or deputy sheriff of a county of this state.
- An officer of the police department of a city, village, or township of this state.
- A marshal of a city, village, or township of this state.
- A constable of any local unit of government of this state.
- An officer of the Michigan State Police.
- A conservation officer of this state.
- A security employee employed by the state under MCL 28.6c.
- A motor carrier officer appointed under MCL 28.6d.
- A police officer or public safety officer of a community college, college, or university within this state who is authorized by the governing board of that community college, college, or university to enforce state law and the rules and ordinances of that community college, college, or university.
- A park and recreation officer commissioned under MCL 324.1606.
- A state forest officer commissioned under MCL 324.83107.
- An investigator of the state department of attorney general.
- An agent of the state department of human services, office of inspector general.
- A sergeant at arms or assistant sergeant at arms commissioned as a police officer under MCL 4.382.

**Peremptory Challenges**    A limited challenge where a juror is excused from duty for reasons not stated.

**Perjury**    Occurs when a person knowingly makes a false statement that is material to the case after taking a recognized oath.

**Person**    An individual, sole proprietorship, partnership, cooperative, association, corporation, limited liability company, personal representative, receiver, trustee, assignee, or other legal or illegal entity.

**Person Familiar with the Missing Senior or Vulnerable Adult**    A missing senior's or vulnerable adult's guardian, custodian, or guardian ad litem or an individual who provides the missing senior or vulnerable adult with home health aid services, possesses a health care power of attorney for the missing senior or vulnerable adult, has proof that the missing senior or vulnerable adult has a medical condition, or otherwise has information regarding the missing senior or vulnerable adult.

**Person Requiring Treatment** A person who has mental illness, and as a result of that mental illness, can reasonably be expected within the near future to intentionally or unintentionally seriously physically injure himself, herself, or another individual, and who has engaged in an act or acts or made significant threats that are substantially supportive of the expectation; or who has mental illness, and who as a result of that mental illness is unable to attend to those of his or her basic physical needs such as food, clothing, or shelter that must be attended to in order for the individual to avoid serious harm in the near future, and who has demonstrated that inability by failing to attend to those basic physical needs.

**Personal Identifying Information** A name, number, or other information that is used for the purpose of identifying a specific person or providing access to a person's financial accounts, including, but not limited to, a person's name, address, telephone number, driver license or state personal identification card number, social security number, place of employment, employee identification number, employer or taxpayer identification number, government passport number, health insurance identification number, mother's maiden name, demand deposit account number, savings account number, financial transaction device account number or the person's account password, any other account password in combination with sufficient information to identify and access the account, automated or electronic signature, biometrics, stock or other security certificate or account number, credit card number, vital record, or medical records or information.

**Personal Information** The first name or first initial and last name linked to one or more of the following data elements of a resident of this state: social security number; driver license number or state personal identification card number; demand deposit or other financial account number; or credit card or debit card number, in combination with any required security code, access code, or password that would permit access to any of the resident's financial accounts.

**Personal Injury** Under the CSC law, personal injury includes bodily injury, disfigurement, mental anguish, chronic pain, pregnancy, abortion, disease or loss or impairment of a sexual or reproductive organ.

**Personal Protection Order (PPO)** An injunctive order issued by the circuit court restraining or enjoining individuals from certain conduct.

**Petition** A request for court action against a juvenile.

**Phantom-Ware** A hidden, preinstalled, or installed at a later time programming option embedded in the operating system of an electronic cash register or hardwired into the electronic cash register that can be used to create a virtual second till or may eliminate or manipulate transaction records that may or may not be preserved in digital formats to represent the true or manipulated record of transactions in the electronic cash register.

**Physical Harm** In abuse cases, any injury to a child's or vulnerable adult's physical condition.

**Physical Harm** In police animal cases, any injury to a dog's or horse's physical condition.

**Physical Injury (arson)** An injury that includes, but is not limited to, the loss of a limb or use of a limb; loss of a foot, hand, finger, or thumb or loss of use of a foot, hand, finger, or thumb; loss of an eye or ear or loss of use of an eye or ear; loss or substantial impairment of a bodily function; serious, visible disfigurement; a comatose state that lasts for more than three days; measurable brain or mental impairment; a skull fracture or other serious bone fracture; subdural hemorrhage or subdural hematoma; loss of an organ; heart attack; heat stroke; heat exhaustion; smoke inhalation; a burn including a chemical burn; or poisoning.

**Physically Helpless** Under the CSC law, physically helpless applies to a person who was unconscious, asleep, or for any other reason was physically unable to communicate an unwillingness to act.

**Physically Limited** Having limited ambulatory abilities and includes, but is not limited to, having a temporary or permanent impairment or condition that does one or more of the following: causes the individual to use a wheelchair or walk with difficulty or insecurity; affects sight or hearing to the extent that an individual is insecure or exposed to danger; causes faulty coordination; reduces mobility, flexibility, coordination, or perceptiveness.

**Pistol** A loaded or unloaded firearm, 26 inches or less in length, or by its construction or appearance conceals the fact that it is a firearm.

**Place of Detention** A police station, correctional facility, or prisoner holding facility or another governmental facility where an individual may be held in connection with a criminal charge that has been or may be filed against the individual.

**Plain Feel**    An object may be seized without a warrant during the course of a pat-down if the officer's sense of touch makes it immediately apparent that the object, though not threatening in nature, is contraband.

**Plain Smell (marihuana)**    The smell of marihuana alone by a person qualified to know the odor may establish probable cause to search a motor vehicle, pursuant to the motor vehicle exception to the warrant requirement.

**Plain View**    When police are lawfully in an area protected by the Fourth Amendment, and while in the protected area, they seize items that they have probable cause to believe are contraband or evidence. The fact that the items may be contraband or evidence must be readily apparent to the officer.

**Plea Bargaining**    The process where accused and prosecutor work out an agreement as to the disposition of a case. The primary types of plea bargaining are charge bargaining and sentence bargaining. The acceptance of a plea is a discretionary act by a judge.

*Charge Bargaining*    A type of plea bargaining where charges arising out of a criminal transaction may be dropped or reduced as part of the inducement of a plea. The judge's discretion in these plea agreements is limited to whether or not the plea is voluntary.

*Sentence Bargaining*    A type of plea bargaining where the prosecutor agrees to recommend a lower sentence in exchange for the defendant's guilty plea. The judge still has the discretion to apply a sentence anywhere between statutory minimum or maximum sentences regardless of the agreement.

**Pledge**    An individual who has been accepted by, is considering an offer of membership from, or is in the process of qualifying for membership in any organization.

**Pledging**    Any action or activity related to becoming a member of an organization.

**Police Dog**    A dog used by a law enforcement agency of this state or of a local unit of government of this state that is trained for law enforcement work and subject to the control of a dog handler.

**Police Horse**    A horse used by a law enforcement agency of this state or of a local unit of government of this state for law enforcement work.

**Posident Die Stamps**    Specially designed die stamps used by motor vehicle manufacturers to produce unique letters and numbers when stamping vehicle identification numbers upon vehicle identification plates, tags, and parts affixed to a motor vehicle.

**Possession**    Possession applies where a person knowingly possesses an object and either has physical control of the object or has the right to control the object.

**Preliminary Breath Test (PBT)**    A hand-held instrument utilized to determine if a person has alcohol in his or her system. Examples for use include minor in possessions and O.W.I. investigations.

**Preliminary Examination**    A hearing to determine if probable cause exists to believe a crime has been committed and to determine if probable cause exists that defendant committed the offense. A preliminary examination is held for felonies and circuit court misdemeanors.

**Premeditated**    A killing that was not the result of sudden impulse; rather, the defendant had a chance to think twice about the intent to kill.

**Premeditation**    An element for first-degree murder where the suspect deliberately killed another human being. It must be shown that the suspect had time for a "second thought" before the killing.

**Preparation to Burn**    A person who uses, arranges, places, devises, or distributes an inflammable, combustible, or explosive material, liquid, or substance or any device in or near a building, structure, other real property, or personal property with the intent to commit arson in any degree or who aids, counsels, induces, persuades, or procures another to do so is guilty of a crime.

**Preponderance of the Evidence**    Evidence sufficient to convince an impartial person to decide an issue one way rather than the other. This is often characterized as 51 percent. This is the burden of proof in civil trials and some evidentiary hearings.

**Present Memory Refreshed**    A witness may use any writing or object to refresh his or her memory when testifying. If the witness refreshes his or her memory, the adverse party is entitled to have the writing or object produced. If the witness refreshes his or her memory before testifying, the court at its discretion can determine if justice so requires that an adverse party is entitled to have the writing or object produced.

**Present Sense Impression**    A statement describing or explaining an event or condition made while the declarant was perceiving the event or condition, or immediately thereafter.

**Presentence Investigation**    An investigation by the probation department prior to sentencing. The probation department will review the defendant's criminal record, investigating officers' comments and other factors to make a recommendation to the judge for sentencing.

**Presumption**    A legal inference or assumption that a fact exists, based on the known or proven existence of some other fact or group of facts.

**Presumption of Innocence**    A person accused of a crime is presumed to be innocent. This means that you must start with the presumption that the defendant is innocent. This presumption continues throughout the trial and entitles the defendant to a verdict of not guilty unless you are satisfied beyond a reasonable doubt that he or she is guilty.

**Pretense**    Knowingly doing one or more of the following: make someone else believe something that is false; keep someone else from finding out important information about the property involved; sell, transfer, or mortgage property while hiding a claim or other legal obstacle against it; promise to do something or have something done knowing that it is not really going to be done.

**Pretext Stops**    Traffic stops for traffic violations when an officer has another underlying motive to pull the vehicle over. As long as the officer has probable cause that a violation has occurred, the stop will be reasonable under the Fourth Amendment.

**Pretrial Motions**    Motions presented to the judge in an attempt to obtain a ruling on a matter before trial begins; these motions usually seek to admit or suppress evidence. For example, during a Walker hearing, arguments are made to exclude confessions. Pretrial motions are also brought to exclude the admission of other types of evidence or to raise issues such as entrapment. The burden of proof in pretrial motions depends on the type of motion and who is bringing it. In a Walker hearing, the prosecutor has the burden, whereas in entrapment, the burden is on the defendant. The standard of proof is preponderance of the evidence.

**Primary Caregiver (MMMA)**    A person who is at least 21 years old and who has agreed to assist with a patient's medical use of marihuana and who has not been convicted of any felony within the past 10 years and has never been convicted of a felony involving illegal drugs or a felony that is an assaultive crime as defined in MCL 770.9a.

**Prior Convictions**    A conviction of a specified offense adjudicated before the current charges.

**Prior Statement of a Witness**    A statement which is not hearsay if the declarant testifies at the trial or hearing and is subject to cross-examination concerning the statement, and the statement is any of the following:

- Inconsistent with the declarant's testimony, and was given under oath subject to the penalty of perjury at a trial, hearing, or other proceeding, or in a deposition.
- Consistent with the declarant's testimony and is offered to rebut an express statement or to argue against the declarant of recent fabrication or improper influence or motive.
- One of identification of a person made after perceiving the person. MRE 801(d)(1).

**Prison**    A facility that houses prisoners committed to the jurisdiction of the department of corrections and includes the grounds, farm, shop, road camp, or place of employment operated by the facility or under control of the officers of the facility, the department of corrections, a police officer of this state, or any other person authorized by the Department of Corrections to have a prisoner under care, custody, or supervision, either in a facility or outside a facility, whether for the purpose of work, medical care, or any other reason.

**Private Place**    A place where one may reasonably expect to be safe from casual or hostile intrusion or surveillance but does not include a place to which the public or substantial group of the public has access.

**Privilege**    Certain confidential communications cannot be used against a person. (e.g., attorney/client).

**Probable Cause**    Facts and circumstances sufficient to cause a person of reasonable caution to suspect the person to be arrested is committing or has committed a crime, or that the place to be searched contains the evidence sought. It has been described as a "fair probability." Probable cause is also known as reasonable cause, sufficient cause, or reasonable grounds.

**Probable Cause and Exigent Circumstances**   Officers may search when they possess probable cause that items sought to be seized are in a specific location and at the time of the search there are exigent circumstances that require the officers to search without a warrant.

**Procedural Due Process**   Procedural due process examines the procedure required by the government when the government seeks to deprive people of life, liberty, or property. In general, the more important the person's interest that will be affected, the more process the government must afford. The basic requirements of procedural due process are notice and an opportunity to be heard by an impartial decision maker. Examples include the right to counsel at trial, right to a jury trial, the right of the accused to confront witnesses, and the right against self-incrimination.

**Proceeds**   Any real, personal, or intangible property obtained through the commission of an offense included in the definition of racketeering, including any appreciation in the value of the property.

**Proceeds of a Specified Criminal Offense**   Any monetary instrument or other real, personal, or intangible property obtained through the commission of a specified criminal offense, including any appreciation in the value of the monetary instrument or property.

**Process**   A summons, complaint, pleading, writ, warrant, injunction, notice, subpoena, lien, order, or other document issued or entered by or on behalf of a court or lawful tribunal or lawfully filed with or recorded by a governmental agency that is used as a means of exercising or acquiring jurisdiction over a person or property, to assert or give notice of a legal claim against a person or property, or to direct persons to take or refrain from an action.

**Process Server**   A person authorized under MCL 600.101 to 600.9947 or Supreme Court rule to serve process.

**Producing Child Sexually Abusive Material**   Occurs when the defendant does one of the following: persuades, induces, entices, coerces, causes, or knowingly allows a child to engage in activity to produce child sexually abusive material; arranges for, produces, makes, copies, reproduces or finances child sexually abusive material; or attempts, prepares, or conspires to arrange for, produce, make, copy, reproduce, or finance child sexually abusive material.

**Professional Investigator**   A person licensed under the professional investigator licensure act, MCL 338.821 to 338.851.

**Property**

*Personal Property*   Any moveable or intangible thing that may be owned and is not classified as real property.

*Real Property*   Land and anything growing on, attached to, or erected on it, excluding anything that may be severed without injury to the land (e.g., bar, barn, gas station, store, anything permanently attached to the building).

**Property (computer fraud)**   Includes, but is not limited to, intellectual property, computer data, instructions or programs in either machine or human readable form, financial instruments or information, medical information, restricted personal information, or any other tangible or intangible item of value.

**Prosecuting Agency**   The attorney general of this state, or his or her designee, or the prosecuting attorney of a county, or his or her designee.

**Prosecuting Attorney**   The chief law enforcement officer in a county, who authorizes complaints and represents state and county in all civil and criminal matters in county courts.

**Protective Custody**   A peace officer may take a person into custody who can reasonably be expected in the near future to intentionally or unintentionally injure him or herself or another and who has engaged in an act or made significant threats that are supportive of this expectation.

**Protective Order**   A personal protection order entered pursuant to law; conditions reasonably necessary for the protection of one or more named persons as part of an order for pretrial release; conditions reasonably necessary for the protection of one or more named persons as part of an order of probation; orders removing abusive persons from a juveniles home under the juvenile code; conditions intended for the protection of one or more named persons as part of a parole order; or, a **foreign protection order** as defined.

**Protective Sweeps**   Allows officers to search areas for persons that may harm the officers while they are attempting to do their lawful duties. The sweep, if justified by the circumstances, is nevertheless not a full search of the premises, but may extend only to a cursory inspection of those spaces where a person may be found. The sweep lasts no longer than is necessary to dispel the reasonable suspicion of danger and in any event no longer than it takes to complete the arrest and depart the premises.

**Provoke** To perform a willful act or omission that an ordinary and reasonable person would conclude is likely to precipitate the bite or attack by an ordinary dog or animal.

**Proximate Cause** An action or omission which in a natural and continuous sequence, unbroken by any new, independent cause, produces the injury, without which such injury would not have occurred.

**Prurient Interest** A shameful or morbid interest in nudity, sex, or excretion.

**Public Duty Doctrine** An immunity doctrine in tort that protects peace officers from negligence lawsuits arising from duties owed to the public in general that are performed incompetently, negligently, or inadequately unless a special relationship is established between the officer and the victim.

**Public Fixture** An item that contains ferrous or non-ferrous metal and is owned or under the exclusive control of a governmental unit. The term includes, but is not limited to, a street light pole or fixture, road or bridge guardrail, traffic sign, traffic light signal, or historical marker.

**Public or Private Property or Water** Includes, but is not limited to, any of the following: the right-of-way of a road or highway, a body of water or watercourse, or the shore or beach of a body of water or watercourse, including the ice above the water; a park, playground, building, refuge, or conservation or recreation area; residential or farm properties or timberlands.

**Public Records and Reports** Records, reports, statements, or data compilations, in any form, of public offices or agencies setting forth activities of the agency or matters observed pursuant to a duty imposed by law. This does not include criminal matters observed by police officers and other law enforcement personnel. MRE 803(8)(B).

**Public Utility** A utility that provides steam, gas, heat, electricity, water, cable television, telecommunications services, or pipeline services, whether privately, municipally, or cooperatively owned.

**Publishing** Publishing means to declare, by words or actions, that a forged document is genuine.

**Purchase Transaction (scrap metal)** A purchase of scrap metal, or the purchase of property described in the statute if the knowing purchase or offer to purchase that property is not prohibited by a scrap metal dealer.

**Qualified Immunity** Immunity given to governmental officials for violating constitutional rights when they act in good faith and reasonably believe their actions are constitutional.

**Qualifying Patient or Patient (MMMA)** A person who has been diagnosed by a physician as having a debilitating medical condition.

**Racketeering** Committing, attempting to commit, conspiring to commit, or aiding or abetting, soliciting, coercing, or intimidating a person to commit an offense for financial gain, involving any of the following: tobacco tax felonies; hazardous waste felonies; controlled substances felonies; welfare fraud felonies; Medicaid fraud felonies; gaming felonies; securities fraud; display or dissemination of obscene matter to minors; animal fighting; arson felonies; bank bonds, bills, notes, and property; breaking and entering or home invasion; bribery; jury tampering; child sexually abusive activity or material; Internet or computer crimes; credit cards or financial transaction devices; felony embezzlement; explosive and bomb felonies; extortion; false pretenses felonies; firearms or dangerous weapons felonies; forgery and counterfeiting felonies; securities fraud; food stamp fraud; gambling; murder; horse racing; kidnapping; larceny felonies; money laundering; perjury and subornation of perjury; prostitution; human trafficking; robbery; receiving and concealing felonies; terrorism; obscenity; felony identity theft; liquor control felonies; an offense committed within this state or another state that constitutes racketeering activity as defined in 18 U.S.C. § 1961(1); an offense committed within this state or another state in violation of a law of the United States that is substantially similar to a violation listed above; an offense committed in another state in violation of a statute of that state that is substantially similar to a violation listed above.

**Rape Shield Statute** Evidence of specific instances of the victim's sexual conduct, opinion evidence of the victim's sexual conduct, and reputation evidence of the victim's sexual conduct shall not be admitted in CSC cases unless and only to the extent that the judge finds that the following proposed evidence is material to a fact at issue in the case and that its inflammatory or prejudicial nature does not outweigh its probative value: evidence of the victim's past sexual conduct with the actor or evidence of specific instances of sexual activity showing the source or origin of semen, pregnancy, or disease.

**Reasonable Cause**    *See* **probable cause.**

**Reasonable Doubt**    A fair, honest doubt growing out of the evidence or lack of evidence. It is not merely an imaginary or possible doubt, but a doubt based on reason and common sense. A reasonable doubt is just a doubt that is reasonable, after a careful and considered examination of the facts and circumstances of this case.

**Reasonable Expectation of Privacy**    Privacy rights that society and the courts are prepared to recognize as reasonable.

**Reasonable Suspicion**    An objective basis, supported by specific and articulable facts, for suspecting a person of committing a crime. This is a standard most commonly applied in the context of searches such as *Terry* stops and pat-downs.

**Reckless Act or Reckless Failure to Act**    Conduct that demonstrates a deliberate disregard of the likelihood that the natural tendency of the act or failure to act is to cause physical harm, serious physical harm, or serious mental harm.

**Record**    Information that is inscribed on a tangible medium or that is stored in an electronic or other medium and is retrievable in perceivable form.

**Records of Regularly Conducted Activity**    A memorandum, report, record, or data compilation, in any form, of acts, transactions, occurrences, events, conditions, opinions, or diagnoses, made at or near the time by, or from information transmitted by, a person with knowledge, if kept in the course of a regularly conducted business activity, and if it was the regular practice of that business activity to make the memorandum, report, record, or data compilation, all as shown by the testimony of the custodian or other qualified witness, or by certification that complies with a rule promulgated by the supreme court or a statute permitting certification, unless the source of information or the method or circumstances of preparation indicate lack of trustworthiness. MRE 803(6).

**Records or Documentary Materials**    A book, paper, document, writing, drawing, graph, chart, photograph, phonorecord, magnetic tape, computer program or printout, any other data compilation from which information can be obtained or translated into usable form, or any other functionally similar tangible item.

**Recorded Recollection**    A memorandum or record concerning a matter about which a witness once had knowledge, but now has insufficient recollection to enable the witness to testify fully and accurately, shown to have been made or adopted by the witness when the matter was fresh in the witness' memory and to reflect that knowledge correctly. If admitted, the memorandum or record may be read into evidence, but may not itself be received as an exhibit unless offered by an adverse party.

**Recreational Trespass**    Entry or remaining upon the land of another to engage in recreational activities such as hunting, fishing, or trapping, without the consent of the landowner where the land is fenced or enclosed or marked in a conspicuous manner against entry. Farmland or a wooded area connected to farmland does not have to be fenced, enclosed, or posted for the tress pass to occur. Exceptions: A fisherman may enter property within the clearly defined banks of a river without consent of the landowner to avoid hazards or obstructions and an unarmed person may enter land, unless prohibited in writing, for a reasonable time to retrieve a hunting dog.

**Registering Authority (SORA)**    The local law enforcement agency or sheriff's office having jurisdiction over the individual's residence, place of employment, or institution of higher learning, or the nearest department post designated to receive or enter sex offender registration information within a registration jurisdiction.

**Registration Jurisdiction (SORA)**    Each of the 50 states, the District of Columbia, the Commonwealth of Puerto Rico, Guam, the Northern Mariana Islands, the United States Virgin Islands, American Samoa, and the Indian tribes within the United States that elect to function as a registration jurisdiction.

**Registry Identification Card (MMMA)**    A document issued by the department that identifies a person as a registered qualifying patient or registered primary caregiver.

**Res Gestae**    Includes circumstances, facts, and declarations which surround the commission of a crime. The evidence should be contemporaneous with the crime and serve to illustrate its character.

**Res Gestae Witness**    An eyewitness to a criminal event whose testimony will aid in developing a full disclosure of all the facts. Also includes all witnesses having contact with the defendant reasonably contemporaneous with the crime, whose testimony tends to show the state of mind in which the criminal act was done.

**Residence (SORA)**    As used in this act, for registration and voting purposes means that place at which a person habitually sleeps, keeps his or her personal effects, and has a regular place of lodging. If a person has more than one residence, or if a wife has a residence separate from that of the husband, that place at which the person resides the greater part of the time shall be his or her official residence for the purposes of this act. If a person is homeless or otherwise lacks a fixed or temporary residence, residence means the village, city, or township where the person spends a majority of his or her time. This section shall not be construed to affect existing judicial interpretation of the term residence for purposes other than the purposes of this act.

**Response Activity Costs (controlled substances)**    All costs incurred in taking or conducting a response activity, including enforcement costs.

**Restrain**    To restrict a person's movements or to confine the person so as to interfere with that person's liberty without that person's consent or without legal authority. The restraint does not have to exist for any particular length of time and may be related or incidental to the commission of other criminal acts.

**Retail Fraud**    A larceny of property by theft, price switching, or through a refund scam. The property must be offered for sale and the incident must occur inside a store or in the immediate area around the store while it is open to the public.

**Retaliate**    Means committing or attempting to commit a crime against any person or threatening to kill or injure any person or threatening to cause property damage.

**Rifles**    A firearm, designed or redesigned, made or remade, and intended to be fired from the shoulder, which uses the energy of an explosive in a fixed metallic cartridge to fire a single projectile through a rifled bore for each single pull of the trigger.

**Riots**    Five or more persons working together who are engaged in violent conduct and intentionally or recklessly creating a serious risk of causing public terror or alarm.

**Robbery**

*Armed Robbery*    Larceny where the victim is assaulted by a suspect who is armed with a dangerous weapon or an object used or fashioned in a manner to lead the person who was assaulted to reasonably believe it was a dangerous weapon, or where suspect indicates that he has a weapon.

*Unarmed Robbery*    Occurs when a person who is unarmed forcibly takes property from another. The property must have been moved and the suspect had the intent to permanently deprive the victim of the property.

**Rosette Rivet**    A special rivet designed to prevent removal or tampering with a vehicle identification number plate affixed by the manufacturer to a motor vehicle and that, when used to affix a vehicle identification number plate, forms five or six petals at the rivet head.

**Ruling**    The outcome of a court's decision on a specific point or a case as a whole.

**Sadomasochistic Abuse**    Abuse that is either flagellation or torture, real or simulated, for the purpose of real or simulated sexual stimulation or gratification, by or upon a person or the condition, real or simulated, of being fettered, bound, or otherwise physically restrained for sexual stimulation or gratification of a person.

**Sand Club or Sandbag**    A narrow bag filled with sand and used as a bludgeon.

**Sanitary Conditions**    Space free from health hazards including excessive animal waste, overcrowding of animals, or other conditions that endanger the animal's health. This definition does not include any condition resulting from a customary and reasonable practice pursuant to farming or animal husbandry.

**Scale Operator**    The employee of a scrap metal dealer who operates or attends a scale that is used to weigh the scrap metal in a purchase transaction.

**School (SORA)**    A public, private, denominational, or parochial school offering developmental kindergarten, kindergarten, or any grade from one through 12. School does not include a home school.

**School (Weapon Free School Zone)**    School property and a vehicle used by a school to transport students to or from school property.

**School Bus** Every motor vehicle, except station wagons, with a manufacturers' rated seating capacity of 16 or more passengers, including the driver, owned by a public, private, or governmental agency and operated for the transportation of children to or from school, or privately owned and operated for compensation for the transportation of children to or from school.

**School Property (controlled substance)** A building, playing field, or property used for school purposes to impart instruction to children in grades kindergarten through 12, when provided by a public, private, denominational, or parochial school, except those buildings used primarily for adult education or college extension courses.

**School Property (SORA)** A building, facility, structure, or real property owned, leased, or otherwise controlled by a school, other than a building, facility, structure, or real property that is no longer in use on a permanent or continuous basis, that is either is used to impart educational instruction or used by students not more than 19 years of age for sports or other recreational activities.

**Scope of Search** The scope of a search under a consent search turns on whether it is objectively reasonable for the officer to believe that the scope of the consent permits the officer to open a particular closed container.

**Scrap Metal** Ferrous or nonferrous metal, or items that contain ferrous or nonferrous metal, that are sold or offered for sale for the value of the ferrous or nonferrous metal they contain rather than their original intended use; ferrous or nonferrous metal removed from or obtained by cutting, demolishing, or disassembling a building, structure, or manufactured item; or other metal that cannot be used for its original intended purpose but can be processed for reuse in a mill, foundry, die caster, or other manufacturing facility.

**Scrap Metal Dealer** A person or governmental unit that buys scrap metal and is not a first purchaser. The term includes, but is not limited to, a person, whether or not licensed under state law or local ordinance, that operates a business as a scrap metal recycler, scrap processor, second hand and junk dealer, or other person that purchases any amount of scrap metal on a regular, sporadic, or one time basis.

**Scrap Metal Recycler** A person that purchases ferrous or nonferrous metal that is intended for recycling or reuse, whether regarded as a scrap processor, core buyer, or other similar business operation.

**Scrap Processor** A person, utilizing machinery and equipment and operating from a fixed location, whose principal business is the processing and manufacturing of iron, steel, nonferrous metals, paper, plastic, or glass, into prepared grades of products suitable for consumption by recycling mills, foundries, and other scrap processors.

**Seizure of a Person** Occurs whenever, because of a police show of authority or force, a reasonable person would believe that he or she is not free to leave, and submits, or custody of the individual is achieved through the application of physical force.

**Seller (scrap metal)** A person that either regularly, sporadically, or on a one time basis receives consideration from any other person from the purchase by a scrap metal dealer of scrap metal offered by that seller.

**Student Safety Zone (SORA)** The area that lies 1,000 feet or less from school property.

**Scope of Discovery** Parties in civil actions are able to obtain discovery regarding any matter, not privileged, that is relevant to the subject matter involved in the pending action.

**Search and Rescue Dog** A dog that is trained for, being trained for, or engaged in a search and rescue operation.

**Search and Rescue Operation** An effort conducted at the direction of an agency of this state or of a political subdivision of this state to locate or rescue a lost, injured, or deceased individual.

**Search Incident to Arrest** Officers may, incident to a lawful custodial arrest, search for weapons and evidence that is within the reach of the person being arrested. The search must occur contemporaneously with the arrest.

**Search Warrant Rule** A search warrant is required to conduct a search unless the search falls under one of the specifically stated exceptions.

**Security Officer** An individual lawfully employed to physically protect another individual or to physically protect the property of another person.

**Sentencing Requirements** Some sentences are set by statute—for example, first-degree murder, which is mandatory life in prison. Others are left more to the discretion of the judge who must sentence within guidelines.

**Sequestration of Witness** Occurs where a witness is isolated from the trial proceedings prior to testifying.

**Serious Impairment of a Body Function** Includes, but is not limited to, one or more of the following: the loss of a limb or use of a limb; the loss of a hand, foot, finger, or thumb or use of a hand, foot, finger, or thumb; the loss of an eye or ear or use of an eye or ear; the loss or substantial impairment of a bodily function; a serious visible disfigurement; a comatose state that lasts for more than three days; any measurable brain damage or mental impairment; a skull fracture or other serious bone fracture; or a subdural hemorrhage or subdural hematoma.

**Serious Injury** Permanent, serious disfigurement, serious impairment of health, or serious impairment of a bodily function of a person.

**Serious Mental Harm to a Child** "In child abuse cases, any injury to a mental condition that results in visible signs of impairment in a child's judgment, behavior, ability to recognize reality, or ability to cope with ordinary demands of life.

**Serious Mental Harm to a Vulnerable Adult** In vulnerable adult abuse cases, when there is substantial alteration of mental functioning that is manifested in a visibly demonstrable manner.

**Serious Misdemeanor** That term as defined in MCL 780.811to include the following:

- Assault and battery. MCL 750.81.
- Assault, infliction of serious injury. MCL 750.81a.
- Breaking and entering, or illegal entry. MCL 750.115.
- Child abuse in the fourth degree. MCL 750.136b(6).
- Contributing to the neglect or delinquency of a minor. MCL 750.145.
- Using the Internet or a computer to make a prohibited communication. MCL 750.145d.
- Intentionally aiming a firearm without malice. MCL 750.233.
- Discharging a firearm intentionally aimed at a person. MCL 750.234.
- Discharge of an intentionally aimed firearm resulting in injury. MCL 750.235.

- Indecent exposure. MCL 750.335a.
- Stalking. MCL 750.411h.
- Injuring a worker in a work zone. MCL 257.601b.
- Leaving the scene of a personal injury accident. MCL 257.617a.
- O.W.I. and impaired driving, if the violation involves an accident resulting in injury or death to another person or damage to another's property. MCL 257.625 & .625a.
- Operating a vessel while under the influence of or impaired by alcoholic liquor or a controlled substance, or with an unlawful blood alcohol content, if the violation involves an accident resulting in damage to another individual's property or physical injury or death to any individual. MCL 324.80176.
- Selling or furnishing alcoholic liquor to an individual less than 21 years of age if the violation results in physical injury or death to any individual. MCL 436.1701.
- A local ordinance substantially corresponding to the above.

**Serious Physical Harm** In police animal cases, any injury to a dog's or horse's physical condition or welfare that is not necessarily permanent, but that constitutes substantial body disfigurement, or that seriously impairs the function of a body organ or limb.

**Serious Physical Harm to a Child** In child abuse cases, any physical injury to a child that seriously impairs the child's health or physical well-being, including, but not limited to, brain damage, a skull or bone fracture, subdural hemorrhage or hematoma, dislocation, sprain, internal injury, poisoning, burn or scald, or severe cut.

**Serious Physical Harm to a Vulnerable Adult** An injury that threatens the life of a vulnerable adult, causes substantial bodily disfigurement, or seriously impairs the functioning or well-being of the vulnerable adult.

**Services (computer fraud)** Includes, but is not limited to, computer time, data processing, storage functions, computer memory, or the unauthorized use of a computer program, computer, computer system, or computer network, or communication facilities connected or related to a computer, computer system, or computer network.

**Severe Mental Pain or Suffering** A mental injury that results in a substantial alteration of mental functioning that is manifested in a visibly demonstrable manner caused by or resulting from any of the following: the intentional infliction or threatened infliction of great bodily injury, the administration or application, or threatened administration or application, of mind-altering substances or other procedures calculated to disrupt the senses or the personality, the threat of imminent death, the threat that another person will imminently be subjected to death, great bodily injury, or the administration or application of mind-altering substances or other procedures calculated to disrupt the senses or personality.

**Sex Offender Registration Act (SORA)**    Collection of statutes that require the registration of persons convicted of sex offenses and establishes the manner of administration and execution of registration.

**Sexual Assault Medical Forensic Examination**    An examination that includes the collection of a medical history, a general medical examination, including, but not limited to, the use of laboratory services and the dispensing of prescribed pharmaceutical items, and one or more of the following:

- A detailed oral examination.
- A detailed anal examination.
- A detailed genital examination.
- Administration of a sexual assault evidence kit and related medical procedures and laboratory and pharmacological services.

**Sexual Contact**    Includes the intentional touching of the victim's or actor's intimate parts or the intentional touching of the clothing covering the immediate area of the victim's or actor's intimate parts, if that intentional touching can reasonably be construed as being for the purpose of sexual arousal or gratification, done for a sexual purpose, or in a sexual manner for revenge, to inflict humiliation, or out of anger.

**Sexual Excitement**    The condition, real or simulated, of human male or female genitals in a state of real or simulated overt sexual stimulation or arousal.

**Sexual Intercourse**    Intercourse, real or simulated, whether genital-genital, oral-genital, anal-genital, or oral-anal, whether between persons of the same or opposite sex or between a human and an animal, or with an artificial genital.

**Sexual Penetration**    Includes sexual intercourse, cunnilingus, fellatio, anal intercourse or any other intrusion, however slight, of any part of a person's body or of any object into the genital or anal opening of another person's body, but emission of semen is not required.

**Sexually Delinquent Person**    Any person whose sexual behavior is characterized by repetitive or compulsive acts which indicate a disregard of consequences or the recognized rights of others, or by the use of force upon another person in attempting sex relations of either a heterosexual or homosexual nature, or by the commission of sexual aggressions against children under the age of 16.

**Shelter**    Adequate protection from the elements and weather conditions suitable for the age, species, and physical condition of the animal so as to maintain the animal in a state of good health.

**Short-Barreled Rifle**    A rifle with one or more barrels less than 16 inches, or an overall length less than 26 inches.

**Short-Barreled Shotgun**    A shotgun with one or more barrels less than 18 inches, or an overall length less than 26 inches.

**Shotgun**    A firearm, designed or redesigned, made or remade, and intended to be fired from the shoulder, which uses the energy of an explosive in a fixed shotgun shell to fire through a smooth bore either ball shot or a single projectile for each single pull of the trigger.

**Show-Ups**    One-on-one confrontations done either physically or by photograph between a witness and a person meeting the description of a perpetrator of a crime. The show-up must occur promptly after the crime.

**Sight and Sound Separation**    There must be total sight and sound separation between juveniles and adults held in the same facility.

**Signed**    The person did either of the following to authenticate or adopt the record: executed or adopted a tangible symbol; attached to or logically associated with the record an electronic symbol, sound, or process.

**Six-Hour Rule**    Federal and state guidelines permit locking juveniles in adult facilities for a maximum of six hours, for processing purposes only. This applies only to those juveniles who are charged with a crime. The sight and sound rule still applies.

**Skimming Device**    Any combination of devices or methods that are designed or adapted to be placed on the physical property of another person and to obtain the personal information or personal identifying information of another, or any other information that allows access to a person's financial accounts, from a financial transaction device without the permission of the owner of the financial transaction device.

**Sodomy**    Occurs when a person commits an abominable and detestable crime against nature with another person or an animal.

**Solicitation to Commit a Felony**    A person, through words or actions, offered, promised or gave money, services, or anything of value (or forgave or promised to forgive a debt or obligation owed) to another person. The person intended that what he or she said or did would cause the felony to be committed.

**Special Relationship**    A relationship that arises when circumstances are such that an officer owes a duty to a specific person. A special relationship existed if: the police officer made assurances of protection or assumed, by his or her actions, the protection of the individual; the police officer knew that without his or her action, harm could come to the victim; the police officer was in direct contact with the victim; and the victim relied on the officer's assurances of protection.

**Specific Intent**    For specific intent, the prosecution must prove not only that the defendant did certain acts, but that he or she did the acts with the intent to cause a particular result. For example, larceny requires the prosecutor to prove that the defendant had the specific intent to permanently deprive the owner of the property.

**Spousal Privilege**    In criminal prosecution, a husband shall not be examined as a witness for or against his wife without his consent, or a wife for or against her husband without her consent, except in the above causes of action

**Staleness**    Probable cause must exist when a search warrant is sought and executed. If officers wait too long to execute a search warrant, the probable cause may become stale.

**Stalking**    A willful course of conduct involving repeated or continuing harassment of another individual that would cause a reasonable person to feel terrorized, frightened, intimidated, threatened, harassed, or molested, and that actually causes the victim to feel terrorized, frightened, intimidated, threatened, harassed, or molested.

**Standing**    In order to challenge a search, a person must assert that he personally had a reasonable expectation of privacy in the area searched.

**State Correctional Facility**    A facility or institution that houses a prisoner population under the jurisdiction of the Department of Corrections. State correctional facility does not include a community corrections center or a community residential home.

**State of Good Health**    Freedom from disease and illness, and in a condition of proper body weight and temperature for the age and species of the animal, unless the animal is undergoing appropriate treatment.

**Statement Against Interest**    A statement which was at the time of its making so far contrary to the declarant's pecuniary or proprietary interest, or so far tended to subject the declarant to civil or criminal liability, or to render invalid a claim by the declarant against another, that a reasonable person in the declarant's position would not have made the statement unless believing it to be true. A statement tending to expose the declarant to criminal liability and offered to exculpate the accused is not admissible unless corroborating circumstances clearly indicate the trustworthiness of the statement.

**Statements Made for Medical Treatment or Diagnosis**    Statements made for purposes of medical treatment or medical diagnosis in connection with treatment and describing medical history, or past or present symptoms, pain, or sensations, or the inception or general character of the cause or external source thereof insofar as reasonably necessary to such diagnosis and treatment.

**Status Offender**    A status offender is a person who commits an act that is a violation because of the person's special status, such as the person's age (i.e., runaways, truants, MIP).

**Statute**    Laws enacted by the Legislature and governor or directly by the people. Statutes in Michigan are codified in the Michigan Compiled Laws.

**Stop and Frisk**    Officers may stop a person when they have reasonable suspicion to believe that a crime is afoot and may frisk the person for weapons when they have reasonable suspicion to believe the person is armed and potentially dangerous.

**Strangulation or Suffocation**    Intentionally impeding normal breathing or circulation of the blood by applying pressure on the throat or neck or by blocking the nose or mouth of another person.

**Strip Searches**    Searches that include the removal of clothing exposing underclothing, breasts, buttocks, or genitalia of another person. These searches are limited to certain situations and have specific requirements.

**Student (SORA)**  An individual enrolled on a full- or part-time basis in a public or private educational institution, including, but not limited to, a secondary school, trade school, professional institution, or institution of higher education.

**Stun Gun**  A portable device or weapon from which an electric current, impulse, wave, or beam may be directed, which current, impulse, wave, or beam is designed to incapacitate temporarily, injure, or kill.

**Subpoena**  A writ or order commanding a person to appear before a court or other tribunal, subject to a penalty for failing to appear.

**Substantive Due Process**  Substantive due process protects individual liberty and property interests from arbitrary government actions regardless of the fairness of any implementing procedures. The right to substantive due process is violated when legislation is unreasonable and clearly arbitrary, having no substantial relationship to the health, safety, morals, and general welfare of the public.

**Substituted Proceeds**  Any real, personal, or intangible property obtained or any gain realized by the sale or exchange of proceeds.

**Summons**  A writing used to notify a person of an action that was commenced against him or her.

**Surveil**  To subject an individual to surveillance.

**Surveillance**  To secretly observe the activities of another person for the purpose of spying upon and invading the privacy of the person observed.

**Tabulation**  A list of the items seized during the execution of a search warrant.

**Tabulation and Receipt**  All property taken from a residence during the execution of a search warrant must be tabulated. The tabulation must be done in the presence of at least one other person. The officer must leave a copy of the tabulation at the place searched and another copy must be presented to the court.

**Tacit Admission**  An acknowledgment of guilt inferred from silence.

**Tender Years Rule**  A statement describing an incident that included a sexual act performed with or on the declarant by the defendant or an accomplice is admissible to the extent that it corroborates testimony given by the declarant during the same proceeding, provided the declarant was under the age of ten when the statement was made; the statement is shown to have been spontaneous and without indication of manufacture; either the declarant made the statement immediately after the incident or any delay is excusable as having been caused by fear or other equally effective circumstance; and the statement is introduced through the testimony of someone other than the declarant.

**Tethering**  The restraint and confinement of a dog by use of a chain, rope, or similar device.

***Terry* (investigatory) Stops**  Officers may detain persons on reasonable suspicion that a crime may be occurring. The stop must be no longer than is necessary to extinguish their suspicions or build up to probable cause.

**Theatrical Facility**  A facility being used to exhibit a motion picture to the public, but does not include an individual's residence or a retail establishment.

**Then Existing Mental, Emotional, or Physical Condition**  A statement of the declarant's then existing state of mind, emotion, sensation, or physical condition (such as intent, plan, motive, design, mental feeling, pain, and bodily health), but not including a statement of memory or belief to prove the fact remembered or believed unless it relates to the execution, revocation, identification, or terms of declarant's will.

**Threat for Extortion**  A threat that does not have to be said in certain words, but it can be made in general or vague terms without exactly stating what kind of injury is being threatened. It can be made by suggestion, but a threat must be definite enough to be understood by a person of ordinary intelligence as a threat of injury.

**Totality of the Circumstances**  The test for determining if a statement is voluntary by looking at such things as age, education, intelligence, criminal experience, lack of advice of constitutional rights, unnecessary delay, injuries, intoxication/drugs, ill health, deprivation of food, sleep, or medical attention, physical abuse, and threats of abuse.

**Torment**  An act or omission that causes unjustifiable pain, suffering, and distress to an animal, or causes mental and emotional anguish in the animal as evidenced by its altered behavior, for a purpose such as sadistic pleasure, coercion, or punishment that an ordinary and reasonable person would conclude is likely to precipitate the bite or attack.

**Tort**　A civil wrong against another person.

**Tracking Device**　Any electronic device that is designed or intended to be used to track the location of a motor vehicle regardless of whether that information is recorded.

**Transaction Data**　Information regarding items purchased by a customer, the price for each item, a taxability determination for each item, a segregated tax amount for each of the taxed items, the amount of cash or credit tendered, the net amount returned to the customer in change, the date and time of the purchase, the name, address, and identification number of the vendor, and the receipt or invoice number of the transaction.

**Transaction Report**　A report that includes, but need not be limited to, the sales, taxes collected, media totals, and discount voids at an electronic cash register that is printed on cash register tape at the end of a day or shift, or a report documenting every action at an electronic cash register that is stored electronically.

**Transferred Intent**　A legal doctrine wherein defendant is held responsible for injuries and acts upon a third party when he intended to do an act to a particular person, but injures a third party instead. Intent from the intended act is transferred to the accidental or incidental injury of the third party and the defendant is held liable as if the injury to the third party were his intended result.

**Transient Merchant**　Any person, firm, association, or corporation engaging temporarily in a retail sale of goods, wares, or merchandise, in any place in this state and who, for the purpose of conducting business, occupies any lot, building, room or structure of any kind.

**Trespass**　Entry or continued presence upon the lands or premises of another without lawful authority after having been forbidden to do so by the owner or occupant or the agent of the owner or occupant.

**Trial (juvenile offenders)**　The fact-finding adjudication of an authorized petition to determine if the minor comes within the jurisdiction of the court.

**Unauthorized Use of an Automobile (joyriding)**　Any person who takes or uses without authority any motor vehicle without intent to steal the same, or who is a party to such unauthorized taking or using.

**Unavailable Under the Hearsay Rule**　Occurs under the hearsay rule where the declarant refuses to testify, lacks sufficient memory to testify, or cannot be located after due diligence. This also includes if the declarant is dead, has a physical or mental illness or infirmity, or when the statement is exempt under a privilege (i.e., attorney/client, right against self-incrimination, etc.).

**Unavailability as a Witness (under the hearsay rule)**　Includes situations in which the declarant: is exempt from testifying by a court's ruling that the statement is privileged; refuses to testify despite an order of the court to do so; has a lack of memory of his or her statement; is unable to be present or to testify because of death or then existing physical or mental illness or infirmity, the proponent of the statement is unable to produce the declarant's attendance and testimony at trial by reasonable means and has shown due diligence.

**Unconsented Contact**　Any contact with another individual that is initiated or continued without that individual's consent or in disregard of that individual's expressed desire that the contact be avoided or discontinued.

**Under the Influence**　Because of drinking alcohol or consuming a controlled substance or other intoxicating substance, the defendant's ability to operate a motor vehicle in a normal manner was substantially lessened.

**United States District Courts**　The trial courts for the federal court system. The district courts hear both civil and criminal matters. There are 94 federal judicial district courts, including at least one district in each state, the District of Columbia and Puerto Rico.

**United States Court of Appeals**　Federal appeals courts. U.S. Courts of Appeals have appellate jurisdiction over U.S. district and administrative courts within their jurisdiction. Their decisions create binding precedent on lower federal courts within their circuit. The Sixth Circuit Court of Appeals has jurisdiction over appeals arising out of Michigan, Ohio, Kentucky, and Tennessee.

**United States Supreme Court**　The highest court in the United States. The U.S. Supreme Court has discretionary appellate jurisdiction over all federal courts as well as state court decisions involving constitutional or federal law questions. The Supreme Court has limited original jurisdiction in cases involving diplomats or disputes between two or more states.

**Unlawful Bodily Alcohol Content (UBAC)** 0.08 grams or more of alcohol per 100 milliliters of blood, 210 liters of breath, or 67 milliliters of urine.

**Unlawful Entry** When a suspect enters a building without first getting permission to enter from someone who had authority to give permission. This is essentially breaking and entering without the "intent" element and includes unauthorized entries where the suspect intends to commit a misdemeanor but not a felony or a larceny.

**Unlawfully Driving Away an Automobile (UDAA)** When a suspect willfully and without authority, takes possession of and drives or takes away any motor vehicle belonging to another.

**Usable Marihuana (MMMA)** The dried leaves and flowers of the marihuana plant, and any mixture or preparation thereof, but does not include the seeds, stalks, and roots of the plant.

**Utter and Publish** To offer something as if it is real, whether or not anyone accepts it as real.

**Uttering** To put something into circulation.

**Vehicle** Every device in, upon, or by which any person or property is or may be transported or drawn upon a highway, except devices exclusively moved by human power or used exclusively upon stationary rails or tracks.

**Venue** The geographic areas a court may preside over.

**Vessel** Every description of watercraft, other than a seaplane, used or capable of being used as a means of transportation on water irrespective of the method of operation or propulsion.

**Victim** Any of the following: an individual who suffers direct or threatened physical, financial, or emotional harm as a result of the commission of a crime, serious misdemeanor, or juvenile offense; or, sole proprietorships, partnerships, corporations, associations, governmental agencies, or any other legal entity that has suffered direct physical or financial harm as a result of a crime, serious misdemeanour, or juvenile offense.

**Victim's Rights** Certain rights mandated by statute that law enforcement must provide to victims of certain crimes.

**Violent Felony** An offense against a person in violation of the following: felonious assault; assault with intent to commit murder; assault with intent to commit great bodily harm less than murder; assault with intent to maim; assault with intent to commit felony; assault with intent to rob; assault with intent to rob while armed; first-degree murder; second-degree murder; manslaughter; kidnapping; prisoner taking hostage; enticing a child under 14; mayhem; CSC 1st degree; CSC 2nd degree; CSC 3rd degree; CSC 4th degree; assault with intent to commit CSC; armed robbery; carjacking; or unarmed robbery.

**Visiting Qualifying Patient (MMMA)** A patient who is not a resident of this state or who has been a resident of this state for less than 30 days.

***Voir Dire* Examination** The questioning of prospective jurors to determine their suitability to sit as jurors.

**Voluntary Manslaughter** When the defendant acted, his or her thinking was disturbed by emotional excitement to the point that a reasonable person might have acted on impulse, without thinking twice, from passion instead of judgment. The emotional excitement must have been something that would cause a reasonable person to act rashly or on impulse; and, the killing itself must result from this emotional excitement. The defendant must have acted before a reasonable time had passed to calm down and return to reason.

**Vulnerable Adult** An individual age 18 or over who, because of age, developmental disability, mental illness, or physical disability requires supervision or personal care or lacks the personal and social skills required to live independently; or a person who is placed in an adult foster care family home or an adult foster care small group home pursuant to statute, or is in a condition in which an adult is unable to protect himself or herself from abuse, neglect, or exploitation because of a mental or physical impairment or because of advanced age.

**Vulnerable Targets** Places described under the laws dealing with explosives such as daycare centers, healthcare facilities, a building open to the general public, a church or other place of religious worship, or a school, K–12 or a college or university.

**Warrant for Arrest** Document issued by a judge if the information contained in the complaint establishes probable cause to substantiate the offense charged.

**Water** Potable water that is suitable for the age and species of animal that is made regularly available unless otherwise directed by a licensed veterinarian.

**Warrantless Misdemeanors** Under MCL 764.21, officers may not enter a residence to effectuate an arrest for a warrantless misdemeanor arrest.

**Weapon Free School Zone** School property and a vehicle used by a school to transport students to or from school property.

> *School* School property and a vehicle used by a school to transport students to or from school property.

> *School Property* A building, playing field, or property used for school purposes to impart instruction to children or used for functions and events sponsored by a school, except a building used primarily for adult education or college extension courses.

**Webpage** A location that has a uniform resource locator or URL with respect to the World Wide Web or another location that can be accessed on the Internet.

**Wingspan of Control** Applies to where an officer can search while making a lawful custodial arrest.

The officer may search the area within reach of the person being arrested.

**Writ of *Certiorari*** An order by the United States Supreme Court to a lower court to deliver its record in a case so that the higher court may review it. If the court agrees to review the case, it grants *certiorari* and issues a writ of *certiorari*. If the United States Supreme Court decides to not review the case, it denies *certiorari*.

**Written Certification (MMMA)** A document signed by a physician, stating all of the following: The patient's debilitating medical condition; the physician has completed a full assessment of the patient's medical history and current medical condition, including a relevant, in-person, medical evaluation; In the physician's professional opinion, the patient is likely to receive therapeutic or palliative benefit from the medical use of marihuana to treat or alleviate the patient's debilitating medical condition or symptoms associated with the debilitating medical condition.

**Zapper** A software program carried on a memory stick or removable compact disc, accessed through an Internet link, or accessed through any other means, that falsifies the electronic records of electronic cash registers and other point-of-sale systems, including, but not limited to, transaction data and transaction reports.

# INDEX